ANNALS OF COMMUNISM

Each volume in the series Annals of Communism will publish selected and previously inaccessible documents from former Soviet state and party archives in a narrative that develops a particular topic in the history of Soviet and international communism. Separate English and Russian editions will be prepared. Russian and Western scholars work together to prepare the documents for each volume. Documents are chosen not for their support of any single interpretation but for their particular historical importance or their general value in deepening understanding and facilitating discussion. The volumes are designed to be useful to students, scholars, and interested general readers.

Katyn

A Crime Without Punishment

Edited by

Anna M. Cienciala, United States of America
Natalia S. Lebedeva, Russian Federation
Wojciech Materski, Poland

Documents translated by Marian Schwartz with
Anna M. Cienciala and Maia A. Kipp

Yale University Press
New Haven & London

This volume has been prepared with the cooperation of the Federal Archival Agency of Russia (ROSARKHIV) and the Head Office of State Archives in Poland in the framework of an agreement concluded among them and Yale University Press.

Designed by James J. Johnson and set in Sabon Roman type by The Composing Room of Michigan, Inc. Printed in the United States of America by Vail-Ballou Press, Binghamton, New York.

Library of Congress Cataloging-in-Publication Data

Katyn : a crime without punishment / edited by Anna M. Cienciala, Natalia S. Lebedeva, and Wojciech Materski ; documents translated by Marian Schwartz with Anna M. Cienciala and Maia A. Kipp.
    p. cm. — (Annals of Communism)
    Translated from Polish and Russian; documents selected from previously published volumes of Katyn documents.
    Includes bibliographical references and index.
    ISBN 978-0-300-10851-4 (alk. paper)
    1. Katyn Massacre, Katyń, Russia, 1940—Sources.   I. Cienciala, Anna M.
II. Lebedeva, N. S. (Natal'ia Sergeevna).   III. Materski, Wojciech.
    D804.S65K359 2007
    940.54′05′094727—dc22   2007005082

A catalogue record for this book is available from the British Library.

The paper in this book meets the guidelines for permanence and durability of the Committee on Production Guidelines for Book Longevity of the Council on Library Resources.

10 9 8 7 6 5 4 3 2 1

Yale University Press gratefully acknowledges the financial support given for this publication by the John M. Olin Foundation, the Lynde and Harry Bradley Foundation, the Historical Research Foundation, Roger Milliken, the Rosentiel Foundation, Lloyd H. Smith, Keith Young, Jeremiah Milbank, and the David Woods Kemper Memorial Foundation.

Yale University Press wishes to acknowledge the contribution of the editorial boards of the Russian and Polish volumes of Katyn documents in cooperation with whom we are publishing this volume.

There comes a time when certain events find their own unavoidable place in history, which belongs only to them. This is the case here.

ALEKSANDR N. YAKOVLEV, preface to *Katyn: Plenniki Neobiavlennoi Voiny*

Be faithful to the truth and to its transmission, for truth endures; truth will not go away. Truth will not pass or change.

POPE JOHN PAUL II

Contents

Illustrations follow page 120

Preface

This American edition of the Katyn documents contains English translations of selected documents published in the two Russian and four Polish volumes coedited by Dr. Natalia S. Lebedeva of the Institut Vseobschei Istorii RAN [Institute of General History, Russian Academy of Sciences], Moscow, and Professor Wojciech Materski, director of the Instytut Studiów Politycznych PAN [ISPPAN—Institute of Political Studies of the Polish Academy of Sciences], Warsaw, and their assistants. Natalia Lebedeva was one of the first Russian historians to find the documents in hitherto closed Russian archives. In 1994 she published the first extensively documented book on Katyn, *Katyn: Prestuplenie Protiv Chelovechestva* [Katyn: A Crime Against Humanity] (Moscow, 1994); Polish edition, *Katyń: Zbrodnia Przeciw Ludzkości* and *Suplement* (Warsaw, 1998), as well as several books and many articles. Wojciech Materski is a well-known historian of Polish-Soviet relations in the interwar and World War II periods. He has written twenty-three books, including one on interwar Polish-Soviet relations, *Na Widecie: II Rzeczpospolita wobec Sowietów, 1918–1943* [The Outpost: The Second Republic Facing the Soviets, 1918–1943] (Warsaw, 2005), as well as many articles and chapters in books.

The three parts in this American Katyn volume are roughly equivalent to the divisions in the already published Russian and Polish volumes. I wrote new introductions to each part and am fully responsible for the interpretations and opinions expressed in them, which do not always reflect those of the coeditors. These introductions are aimed at English-language readers interested in the Katyn crime but not familiar with the history of Polish-Soviet/Russian relations and Katyn's place in it. The endnotes, which I prepared, give information provided in the Russian and Polish volumes supplemented with information from additional English-language publications as well as other Russian and Polish works, especially those that have appeared since 2001, when the second Russian and third Polish volumes were published. The fourth Polish volume appeared in April 2007. New information has also become available over the years, up to and including the first reports in early August 2006 on finding Polish military insignia and personal items near the village of Bykovnia [Polish: Bykownia], now on the northeastern outskirts of Kiev, Ukraine, which is the burial site of tens of thousands of Ukrainian victims of the Stalinist Terror.

I am indebted to several people for their help. First, I would like to thank Dr. Lebedeva and Professor Materski for their answers to my many questions over the years. A joint session with Natalia Lebedeva—made possible by Yale University Press at its offices in New Haven in December 2000—was particularly useful, as were several conversations and numerous e-mail exchanges with Wojciech Materski, who also graciously permitted me to read photocopies of edited Polish documents during an earlier visit to Warsaw funded by Yale University Press. I also thank both of them for their comments and corrections to the proofs. I am grateful to Professor Inessa Yazhborovskaia, a Russian political scientist, for sending me a copy of the book on the Katyn "syndrome" in Soviet-Polish and Russian-Polish relations that she edited with the assistance of a former Russian prosecutor in the Russian Katyn investigation and a Russian historian of Poland. The book, edited and written by I. S. Yazhborovskaia, A. Yu. Yablokov, and V. S. Parsadanova, is titled *Katynskii Sindrom v Sovetsko-Polskikh i Rossiisko-Polskikh Otnosheniakh* [The Katyn Syndrome in Polish-Soviet and Polish-Russian Relations] (Moscow, 2001).

I owe a great debt of gratitude to Professor Emeritus Janusz K. Zawodny, the author of the first scholarly study of Katyn, *Death in the Forest: The Story of the Katyn Massacre* (Notre Dame, Ind., 1962). It is still of great value as a survey and analysis, based on the extensive personal testimonies and documentary sources available at the time. I would also like to thank him for giving and lending me several important recent Polish publications on Katyn, mostly unavailable in American libraries.

I would like to thank Dr. Maciej M. Siekierski, curator, East European Collections, Hoover Institution on War, Revolution and Peace,

Stanford, California, for lending me his personal copy of an invaluable collection of data and information, *Facts and Documents Concerning Polish Prisoners of War Captured by the U.S.S.R. during the 1939 Campaign* (London, 1946), as well as selecting and reproducing some German photographs of the Katyn exhumations of 1943. On the basis of this selection, Dr. Vadim Staklo, project manager for the Annals of Communism series of Yale University Press, had new photographs made according to the press's printing requirements, for which I thank him.

I would like to express special thanks to Mr. Wacław Godziemba-Maliszewski, the preeminent analyst of German wartime aerial photographs of Katyn, Kharkov, and Mednoe, for supplying photographs of the same with annotations. I would also like to thank him for providing the excellent maps of these regions and supplying the accompanying annotations (maps 5–7). Finally, I wish to thank him for helping to make a final selection of the German photographs printed in this book, as well as for sharing a great deal of valuable information gained from many years of studying Katyn and for giving and lending me some rare Polish works on Katyn.

My sincere thanks go to the Polish Katyn expert Mr. Tadeusz Pieńkowski of Warsaw for sending me copies of his valuable articles on Katyn and especially for his help in securing photographs of exhumation work at Kharkov and Mednoe from the Katyn Museum, Warsaw. I also wish to thank him for identifying persons in the photographs, for providing Dr. Janina Gellert's photographs of the Polish War Cemetery at Katyn in 2004—for which I thank her—and for sending me the photograph of the memorial tablet for two Polish officers, the older one of whom was his father, artillery captain Ludwik Pieńkowski, from the Polish War Cemetery in Kharkov. I also wish to thank Colonel Zdzisław Sawicki, who had many photographs made for me in June 2001, when he was director of the Katyn Museum, Warsaw. For technical reasons, only one of these—the composite photograph of some Polish officers shot at Katyn—was selected for inclusion in this volume. I would like to thank Dr. Hab. Janusz Cisek, the director of the Muzeum Wojska Polskiego [Museum of the Polish Army], Warsaw, for permission to have the Katyn Museum photographs reproduced in this American volume.

My thanks also go to Dr. Iwona Korga of the Józef Piłsudski Institute for the Study of Modern Polish History, New York, for photocopies of two items in the institute's Katyn Collection: (1) a March 1948 issue of *Nowy Świat* [New World], a Polish New York newspaper with articles on Katyn and (2) lists of names of Polish prisoners of war identified at Katyn in 1943 that were compiled by regional Polish Red Cross agencies in Poland in 1944.

I would like to thank Dr. Simon Schochet of New York for sending me copies of his articles on the Jewish officers in the Polish Army, who were prisoners and victims in the USSR, for providing the photograph of the Chief Rabbi of the Polish Army, Dr. Baruch Steinberg, taken in Kraków in 1935, and for supplying the relevant information. Steinberg's name appears on an NKVD list, dated 9 April 1940, of prisoners to be sent from Kozelsk camp to Smolensk Oblast. It is assumed that he perished at Katyn.

I am grateful to Professor Emerita Maia A. Kipp of the Departments of Slavic Studies and Theater and Film, University of Kansas, for help in translating some complex Russian phrases and terminology. I also wish to thank her husband, Dr. Jacob Kipp, a specialist on Russian/Soviet military history, a professor at the Command and General Staff College (CGSC), Leavenworth, Kansas, and an adjunct professor of history at the University of Kansas, for information on some high-level Soviet military commanders. My thanks also go to Dr. Bruce Menning, a historian of the Russian and Soviet armies, a professor at CGSC, and an adjunct professor of history at the University of Kansas, for translating some Russian military ranks, for giving me copies of his conference papers on the Soviet armed forces in 1938–1939 and a volume of Russian documents on Polish-Soviet military relations during World War II, and for lending me volumes of documents on Soviet state security in 1938–1941.

I would like to thank Pam LeRow and Paula Courtney of the College of Liberal Arts and Sciences Word Processing Center, University of Kansas, for their help in the initial stages of this work.

I owe a great debt of gratitude to my former graduate student Judith Olsak-Glass, without whose major input this book could not have been completed. While working with me over four years, she made many helpful comments and suggestions; tirelessly inserted my many additions and changes in several versions of the manuscript; caught spelling and grammar mistakes in both English and Polish; caught errors of content and source reference; checked and standardized references; made a combined, computerized graphic of the camp and execution site sketch maps in the first two Polish volumes of documents on Katyn; helped to select and prepare the photographs; and helped greatly with proofreading and with the index. I would also like to thank her husband, Dr. Robert (Bob) Glass, for taking the time to read parts of the manuscript and for offering insightful comments and suggestions. I am, of course, responsible for any errors and omissions.

I would like to thank Jonathan Brent, editorial director, Yale University Press, and Dr. Vadim Staklo for initiating and supporting this project over many years. My special thanks go to my manuscript editor, Mary Pasti, for her detailed comments and suggestions and for her painstaking attention to detail, which averted many pitfalls and errors. She also is responsible for many clarifications in the endnotes.

Last but not least, I wish to thank my friend Romana Boniecka for creating the environment that made my work possible, even though she did not always share my views or choice of research topics.

Anna M. Cienciala

Note on the Documents

President Mikhail Gorbachev's policy of *glasnost,* or open discussion of past and present problems, which took off in 1987–1988, led to public discussion of the Stalinist period in the USSR. This, in turn, opened hitherto closed state archives to Russian historians who found documents concerning the Polish prisoners of war held in the three NKVD special camps of Kozelsk, Ostashkov, and Starobelsk in 1939–1940. Most of the prisoners were massacred by the NKVD at Katyn, Kalinin [Tver], and Kharkov [Kharkiv] in April–May 1940. The imminent publication of articles by these historians, plus pressure on the Polish government by a Polish public who desired the truth and the Polish government's pressure on the Soviet government, led Moscow to admit Soviet responsibility for the crime on 13 April 1990, after a cover-up that lasted half a century (1940–1990). The Soviet, then Russian, investigation of the Katyn crime began in 1991, and on 14 October 1992, Boris Yeltsin, president of the Russian Federation, made public the contents of the special "Packet no. 1" in the Presidential Archives, which included the key Politburo decision of 5 March 1940 to shoot the Polish prisoners of war, along with documents on the Soviet cover-up. At the same time, copies of these documents were transmitted to Polish President Lech Wałęsa in Warsaw.

Meanwhile, in pursuance of an agreement signed on 27 April 1992 by representatives of the Head Office of State Archives in Poland and the Federal Archival Agency of Russia, a protocol was signed in February 1993 establishing the principles for the publication of the Katyn documents. They were to appear in two parallel versions: the Russian volumes with texts in the original version, and the Polish volumes in

Polish translation. Both versions were to have the same editorial board. Furthermore, in June 1992 the Polish Ministry of Defense established a Military Archival Commission whose members were given access to Russian archives; they photocopied about 200,000 documents pertaining to the Polish prisoners of war in the three special camps, and deposited the copies in the Central Military Archives, Warsaw.

The chief responsible editor on the Russian side is Dr. Natalia S. Lebedeva of the General History Institute, Russian Academy of Sciences, Moscow; the chief responsible editor on the Polish side is Professor Wojciech Materski, director of the Institute of Political Studies, Polish Academy of Sciences, Warsaw; both are coeditors of the present American volume. Professor Materski also translated and edited the Russian Katyn documents given by President Boris Yeltsin of the Russian Federation to President Lech Wałęsa of Poland in mid-October 1992. They were first published in Poland under the title *Katyń: Dokumenty Ludobójstwa* [Katyn: Documents of Genocide] (Warsaw, 1992). The English edition was published as *Katyn: Documents of Genocide* (Warsaw, 1993).

The first Polish volume of the joint publication was titled *Katyń: Dokumenty Zbrodni* [Katyn: Documents of a Crime], volume 1: *Jeńcy Nie Wypowiedzianej Wojny, Sierpień 1939–Marzec 1940* [Prisoners of an Undeclared War, August 1939–March 1940] (Warsaw, 1995). The parallel Russian volume, titled *Katyn: Plenniki Neobiavlennoi Voiny* [Katyn: Prisoners of an Undeclared War] (Moscow, 1997), appeared two years later in the series *Rossiia, XX Vek: Dokumenty* [Russia, the Twentieth Century: Documents]. The documents published in these two volumes are almost exactly the same. The Russian volume also has a supplement, *Rasstrel* [Death by Shooting], with facsimiles of key documents on the extermination. The second Polish volume, titled *Katyń: Dokumenty Zbrodni*, volume 2: *Zagłada, Marzec–Czerwiec 1940* [Extermination, March–June 1940], appeared in Warsaw in 1998, and the third, titled *Katyń: Dokumenty Zbrodni*, volume 3: *Losy Ocalałych, Lipiec 1940–Marzec 1943* [The Fate of the Survivors, July 1940–March 1943], appeared in 2001. The last Polish volume, *Katyń: Dokumenty Zbrodni*, volume 4: *Echa Katynia, Kwiecień 1943–Marzec 2005* [Echoes of Katyn, April 1943–March 2005] (Warsaw, 2006), contains many important supplementary materials (most previously published), including the full text of the Burdenko Commission report, as well as diplomatic correspondence; the key documents, however, are the same as in the second Russian volume (see below). This Polish volume was not released until April 2007, too late to be fully referenced in the American edition, but matching documents are noted in the List of Documents with Sources. All the Polish and Russian volumes had the same editors. Lack of funding on the Russian side resulted in the publication of only one additional Russian volume, edited by the same chief editors who worked on the first Polish and Russian volumes and the later Polish volumes; it is titled *Katyn: Mart 1940 g.–Sentiabr 2000 g. Rasstrel, Sudby Zhivykh, Ekho Katyni: Dokumenty* [Katyn: March 1940–September 2000. Execution by Shooting, the Fate of the Survivors, the Echoes of Katyn: Documents] and also contains facsimiles of documents on extermination. It appeared in Moscow in late 2001, thanks to the enormous work of Russian historians and archivists, the publisher Ves Mir, and the financial support of the Polish Rada Ochrony Pamięci Walk i Męczeństwa [Council for the Protection of the Memory of Combat and Martyrdom].

Most of the Russian documents in Part I of the current volume come from the Narodny Komissariat Vnutrennykh Del [NKVD, or Narkomvnudel—People's Commissariat of Internal Affairs], specifically the NKVD Upravlenie po Delam Voennoplennykh [UPV—Administration for Prisoner-of-War Affairs], whose papers are now housed in the Rossiiskii Gosudarstvenny Voenny Arkhiv [RGVA—Russian State Military Archive]. Except for a few documents of Polish origin, most of the documents in Parts II and III come from the relevant NKVD organizations, Soviet government and party bodies, and the government of the Russian Federation. The number of documents selected for the present volume is small compared with the number of Russian and Polish documents already published, but they should provide a representative selection of the whole.

The Federal Archival Agency of Russia gave permission to Yale University Press to publish the Russian documents in English. Dr. Daria Nałęcz, director of the Head Office of State Archives in Poland in 1996–2006, gave her permission to include the letter of 15 October 1992 (in Anna M. Cienciala's translation) by Polish President Lech Wałęsa to Russian President Boris Yeltsin, as well as to cite another letter by Wałęsa to Yeltsin written earlier that year, for which Anna Cienciala thanks her.

The Russian documents were very competently translated by Marian Schwartz, with some additional translations by Maia Kipp and Anna M. Cienciala. Anna Cienciala's translations also include excerpts from the Polish-language report on a preliminary visit to Katyn in April 1943 by Kazimierz Skarżyński, secretary general of the Polish Red Cross (PRC) in German-occupied Poland, as well as the report, which he edited, of the PRC Technical Commission on the exhumations in Katyn, April–June 1943. Anna Cienciala would like to thank his daughter, Maria Skarżyńska of Calgary, Canada, for permission to include the translated excerpts in this American volume and for identifying her father in the photograph of three men praying at the edge of a Katyn burial pit.

Each document is preceded by a brief introduction regarding its contents. A list of documents appears together with source information at the end of the book. In most cases when existing English translations of documents are used, they have been modified either to provide a more precise translation or to conform to standard English style.

There are two sets of notes. Footnotes indicate significant original corrections and marginal comments on the documents that are essential to understanding them. Endnotes give source references and additional information.

In references the abbreviation used for the Russian volumes is *KD,* volume number, slash, document number—for example, *KD2/201.* For the Polish volumes it is *KDZ,* volume number, slash, document number—for example, *KDZ1/187.*

The dating given in this volume differs in style from that used in the original documents, which was in Roman numerals. It is rendered here in Arabic numerals with the sequence of day, month, year.

Titles of organizations, books, journals, and newspapers are given in the original language, followed by a translation. Titles of books and periodicals are capitalized in customary English style. Citations are given in full at first mention in the endnotes for each part and abbreviated thereafter. Polish names appear in the documents in Polish spelling without the original Russian transliteration; but patronymics, when they appear, are retained from the Russian documents for identification purposes. (Russian transliteration of Polish names was sometimes faulty, and in some cases several Poles shared the same family name.)

The list of abbreviations and acronyms gives the full names of archives and organizations mentioned more than once in the text and notes.

Russian military ranks are literal translations from the Russian, except for the NKVD rank of junior lieutenant, which is rendered as "1st lieutenant," and the rank of senior lieutenant, which is rendered as "lieutenant."

Names of countries are given in the English forms customarily used at the time if these are available—for example, the Soviet socialist republic was Belorussia, not Byelorussia or Byelorus, and the inhabitants were Belorussians. The contemporary name is Belarus, and the inhabitants are Belarusians.

Place-names are given in the form used in the documents at the time, with contemporary names and names in other languages provided for clarity. Most localities in former eastern Poland, now in Belarus and Ukraine, have three names, Polish, Russian, and Belorussian or Ukrainian. Recognized anglicized forms of place-names are used if available—for example, Kiev, Moscow, Warsaw. In other cases, English transliterations from the Russian are used—for example, Katyn, Kharkov, Kozelsk, Ostashkov, and Starobelsk.

It should be noted that the numbers of prisoners in the NKVD documents sometimes do not add up. They are given in the documents as they appear in the documents.

Anna M. Cienciala

Notes on Russian Transliteration and Polish Pronunciation

Russian Transliteration

Strict Library of Congress transliterations are used for bibliographic information. But to make pronunciation easier for the nonspecialist reader, some spellings are simplified in the text and documents.

In Final Position

ii	=	y	e.g., Podvodsky
iia	=	ia	e.g., istoria
oi	=	oy	e.g., Tolstoy
nyi	=	ny	e.g., Nagorny

In Initial Position

E	=	Y	e.g., Yeltsin
Ia	=	Ya	e.g., Yakovlev
Iu	=	Yu	e.g., Yuri

In Internal Position   e.g., Dostoevsky, Krupskaia, Miliukov

Hard and Soft Signs

All soft and hard signs are dropped, and ë is generally transliterated as *yo*, unless it follows *sh, ch, schch,* when it is presented as *e*—e.g., Semyon, Pyotr, Solovyov, Gorbachev, Kruchenykh.

Although the soft sign is dropped, there is special treatment of the soft sign in the sequence C'ev, as in Grigoriev, Vasilievich, Vasielievna, Zinoviev; but: Solovyov, Vorobyov.

Polish Pronunciation

In pronouncing Polish personal names and place-names, the following English equivalents may be a useful guide.

Vowels

ą	*on* in "gong"
ę	*en* in "Bengali"
ó	*oo* in "booth"
y	*i* in "bit" or "lip"

Consonants

c	*tz* in "blitz," or *ts* in "cats," except in combinations such as *ci, cz*
ch	*h* as in "hat"
Ć, ć, ci	*ch* in "cheek" or "cheese," but softer
cz	*ch* in "church"
dz	*j* in "jam"
j	*y* in "yellow"
g	*g* in "guest"
Ł, ł,	*w* in "water" or "wet"
ń	initial *n* in "onion"
Ś, ś	*sh* in "shut," but softer
sz	*sh* in "shake" or "shelf" but harder
rz, Ż, ż	*zh* in "Zhukov" or s in "pleasure"
w	*v* in "vowel" or "vine"
Ź, ź	in final *g* in "garage" but softer

Abbreviations and Acronyms

A name in brackets is the larger administrative unit under which the smaller one is subsumed. Full citations of the book titles abbreviated here are given in the notes.

AGC	Armee Gruppe Mitte	(German) Army Group Center
AK	Armia Krajowa	Home Army (Polish underground)
AKhU	Administrativno-Khoziastvennoe Upravlenie	Administrative-House-keeping Board [NKVD]
APRF	Arkhiv Prezidenta Rossiiskoi Federatsii	Archive of the President of the Russian Federation
ASSR		Autonomous Soviet Socialist Republic
AVPRF	Arkhiv Vneshnei Politiki Rossiiskoi Federatsii	Foreign Policy Archive of the Russian Federation
BSSR	Belorusskaia Sovetskaia Sotsialisticheskaia Respublika	Belorussian Soviet Socialist Republic
CAW	Centralne Archiwum Wojskowe	Central Military Archive, Warsaw
CC		Central Committee (of the Communist Party)
Com.		Comrade
CPSU		Communist Party of the Soviet Union

c-r	kontrrevoliutsionny	counterrevolutionary
d.	delo	archival file
DGFP		*Documents on German Foreign Policy*
DPSR		*Documents on Polish-Soviet Relations*
DVP	Dokumenty Vneshnei Politiki	*Documents on Foreign Policy*
f.	fond	archival collection
GARF	Gosudarstvenny Arkhiv Rossiiskoi Federatsii	State Archive of the Russian Federation
GB	Gosudarstvennaia Bezopasnost	State Security
GEU	Glavnoe Ekonomicheskoe Upravlenie	Main Economic Administration [NKVD]
GKO	Gosudarstvenny Komitet Oborony	State Defense Committee
Gosbank	Gosudarstvenny Bank	State Bank
GRU	Glavnoe Razveditelnoe Upravlenie RKKA/Krasnoi Armii	Main Military Intelligence Administration of the RKKA/Red Army (short name for GRU: Razvedka)
GTU	Glavnoe Transportnoe Upravlenie	Main Transport Administration [NKVD]
GUGB	Glavnoe Upravlenie Gosudarstvennoi Bezopasnosti	Main Administration for State Security
GUKV	Glavnoe Upravlenie Konvoinykh Voisk	Main Administration of Convoy Troops [NKVD]
GULAG	Glavnoe Upravlenie Lagerei	Main Administration of (Labor) Camps [NKVD]
IMC		International Medical Commission
IMT		International Military Tribunal
IPN	Instytut Pamięci Narodowej—Komisja Ścigania	Institute of National Remembrance—Commission for

	Zbrodni Przeciwko Narodowi Polskiemu	Prosecuting Crimes against the Polish Nation
IRC		International Red Cross
KD1	*Katyn: Plenniki Neobiavlennoi Voiny*	*Katyn: Prisoners of an Undeclared War* (Russian edition, vol. 1)
KD2	*Katyn: Mart 1940 g.– Sentiabr 2000 g.*	*Katyn: March 1940– September 2000* (Russian edition, vol. 2)
KDG	*Katyn: Documents of Genocide*	English edition of *KDL* (Warsaw, 1993)
KDL	*Katyń: Dokumenty Ludobójstwa*	*Katyn: Documents of Genocide*
KDZ1	*Katyń: Dokumenty Zbrodni*, vol. 1: *Jeńcy Nie Wypowiedzianej Wojny, Sierpień 1939–Marzec 1940*	*Katyn: Documents of a Crime*, vol. 1: *Prisoners of an Undeclared War, August 1939–March 1940* (Polish edition)
KDZ2	*Katyń: Dokumenty Zbrodni*, vol. 2: *Zagłada, Marzec– Czerwiec 1940*	*Katyn: Documents of a Crime*, vol. 2: *Extermination, March–June 1940* (Polish edition)
KDZ3	*Katyń: Dokumenty Zbrodni*, vol. 3: *Losy Ocalałych, Lipiec 1940– Marzec 1943*	*Katyn: Documents of a Crime*, vol. 3: *The Fate of the Survivors, July 1940–March 1943* (Polish edition)
KDZ4	*Katyń: Dokumenty Zbrodni*, vol. 4: *Echa Katynia, Kwiecień 1943– Marzec 2005*	*Katyn: Documents of a Crime*, vol. 4: *Echoes of Katyn, April 1943– March 2005* (Polish edition)
KGB	Komitet Gosudarstvennoi Bezopasnosti	Committee for State Security
KMF		Katyn Memorial Fund
KOP	Korpus Okhrany Pogranichia [Korpus Ochrony Pogranicza]	Polish Frontier Protection Corps

KP(b)U	Kommunisticheskaia Partiia (Bolshevikov) Ukrainy	Communist Party (Bolshevik) of Ukraine
KPP	Komunistyczna Partia Polski	Polish Communist Party
KSSR	Kazakhskaia Sovetskaia Sotsialisticheskaia Respublika	Kazakh Soviet Socialist Republic
l.	list	archival page or card
MID	Ministerstvo Inostrannykh Del	Ministry of Foreign Affairs
Narkomchermet	Narodny Komissariat Chernoi Metallurgii	People's Commissariat of Ferrous Metallurgy
Narkomfin	Narodny Komissariat Finansov	People's Commissariat of Finance
Narkomles	Narodny Komissariat Lesov	People's Commissariat of Forests
Narkomtorg	Narodny Komissariat Torgovli	People's Commissariat of Trade
Narkomvnudel		*See* NKVD
NKChM		*See* Narkomchermet
NKF		*See* Narkomfin
NKGB	Narodny Komissariat Gosudarstvennoi Bezopasnosti	People's Commissariat of State Security
NKID	Narodny Komissariat Inostrannykh Del	People's Commissariat of Foreign Affairs
NKO	Narodny Komissariat Oborony	People's Commissariat of Defense
NKPS	Narodny Komissariat Putei Soobshcheniia	People's Commissariat of Communications
NKVD	Narodny Komissariat Vnutrennikh Del	People's Commissariat of Internal Affairs
OITK	Otdel Ispravitelno-Trudovykh Kolonii	Department of Correctional Labor Colonies (for young criminals) [NKVD]
OO	Osoboe Otdelenie	Special Section (in camp)
OO	Osoby Otdel	Special Department [NKVD, Moscow]
op.	opis	inventory within a *fond*
OSO	Osoboe Soveshchanie	Special Board [NKVD]

OUN	Orhanizatsiia Ukrainskykh Natsionalistiv	Organization of Ukrainian Nationalists
p.	papka	archival folder
PIS	Prawo i Sprawiedliwość	Law and Justice (party)
port.	portfel	archival file
POV	Polskaia Voennaia Organizatsiia	Russian name for P.O.W.
POW		prisoner of war
P.O.W.	Polska Organizacja Wojskowa	Polish Military Organi-zation
PPR	Polska Partia Robotnicza	Polish Workers' Party (communist)
PPS	Polska Partia Socjalistyczna	Polish Socialist Party
PRC		Polish Red Cross
PZPR	Polska Zjednoczona Partia Robotnicza	United Polish Workers' Party
R	*Rasstrel* [supplement to *KD1*, with facsimiles of documents on extermination]	*Execution by Shooting*
RGASPI	Rossiiskii Gosudarstvenny Arkhiv Sotsialno-Politicheskoi Istorii	Russian State Archive of Social and Political History
RGO	Rada Główna Opiekuńcza	Main Welfare Council
RGVA	Rossiiskii Gosudarstvenny Voenny Arkhiv	Russian State Military Archive
RKKA	Raboche-Krestianskaia Krasnaia Armiia	Worker-Peasant Red Army
RSFSR	Rossiiskaia Sovetskaia Federativnaia Sotsialis-ticheskaia Respublika	Russian Soviet Federated Socialist Republic
RTsKhIDNI	Rossiiskii Tsentr Khranenia i Izuchenia Dokumentov Noveishei Istorii	Russian Center for the Preservation and Study of Documents of Recent History
SDFP		*Soviet Documents on Foreign Policy* (ed. Degras)
Sevzheldorlag	Severny Zheleznodorozhny Lager	Northern Railway camp

SLD	Sojusz Lewicy Demo-kratycznej	Democratic Left Alliance (party)
SNK	Sovet Narodnykh Komissarov	Council of People's Commissars
SOE	sotsialno-opasny element	socially dangerous element
Sovinformburo	Sovetskoe Informationnoe Buro	Soviet Information Office
Sovmin	Sovet Ministrov	Council of Ministers
Sovnarkom		*See* SNK
Spetsotdel	Spetsialny Otdel	Special Department [NKVD]
SSR	Sovetskaia Sotsialisti-cheskaia Respublika	Soviet Socialist Republic
SSSR	Soiuz Sovetskikh Sotsialisticheskikh Respublik	USSR—Union of Soviet Socialist Republics
TASS	Telegrafnoe Agentsvo Sovetskogo Soiuza	Telegraphic Agency of the Soviet Union
TsA FSB RF	Tsentralny Arkhiv Federalnoi Sluzhby Bezopastnosti Ros-siiskoi Federatsii	Central Archive of the Federal Security Service of the Russian Federa-tion
TsFPO	Tsentralny Finansovo-Planovy Otdel	Central Financial Planning Department
TsK	Tsentralny Komitet	Central Committee (of the Communist Party)
TsKhIDK	Tsentr Khranenia Istoriko-Dokumental-nykh Kollektsii	Russian Center for Preserving Historical-Documentary Collections
UITK	Upravlenie Ispravitelno-Trudovykh Kolonii	OITK Administration
UkSSR	Ukrainskaia Sovetskaia Sotsialisticheskaia Respublika	Ukrainian Soviet Socialist Republic
UNKVD	Upravlenie Narodnogo Komissariata Vnutrennikh Del	NKVD Administration
UPV	Upravlenie po Delam Voennoplennykh	Administration for Prisoner-of-War Affairs [NKVD]
UPVI	Upravlenie po Delam Voennoplennykh i Internirovannykh	Administration for Prisoner-of-War and Internee Affairs [NKVD]

URO	Uchetno-Raspredelitelnoe Otdelenie Lagiera	[UPV] Reception, Records, and Barracks Assignment Section (POW camp)
URO	Uchetno-Registratsionny Otdel	Records Registration Department [UPV, NKVD, Moscow]
VKP(b)	Vsesoiuznaia Kommunisticheskaia Partiia (Bolshevikov)	All-Union Communist Party (Bolshevik)
VOA		Voice of America
VTs SPS	Vsesoiuzny Tsentralny Soviet Professionalnykh Soiuzov	All-Union Central Council of Trade Unions
WIN	Wolność i Niepodległość	Freedom and Independence
ZPP	Związek Patriotów Polskich	Union of Polish Patriots [USSR]

Katyn

PART I

Prisoners of an Undeclared War,
23 August 1939–5 March 1940

Today the word "Katyn" stands for one of the most heinous yet least known of the Stalinist crimes: the massacre in spring 1940 of some 14,500 Polish officers and policemen taken prisoner by the Red Army during the September 1939 invasion of eastern Poland. The prisoners were held for several months in three special NKVD prisoner-of-war camps at Kozelsk, Ostashkov, and Starobelsk. They corresponded with their families and friends from late November–early December 1939 until mid-March 1940, when all trace of them disappeared. The 7,300 Polish prisoners held in NKVD jails in the western regions of the Ukrainian Soviet Socialist Republic (now the Ukrainian Republic) and the Belorussian Soviet Socialist Republic (now the Republic of Belarus) likewise disappeared. After the German attack on the USSR, a Polish-Soviet agreement was signed, and in 1941–1942, Soviet authorities allowed a Polish army to be formed on Soviet soil. Army and police officers were badly needed, so Polish military and civilian authorities in the Soviet Union, as well as the Polish government-in-exile in London, made numerous inquiries about the missing prisoners. Soviet authorities replied either that all prisoners had been released or that nothing was known about them.

In mid-April 1943 the German government announced the discovery of the remains of several thousand Polish officers from Kozelsk camp buried in Katyn Forest, near Smolensk. Joseph Stalin broke off relations with the Polish government after it rejected his demand to blame the Germans and requested the International Red Cross to investigate the massacre. In spring–summer 1943, German, Polish, and other forensic experts examined the exhumed bodies and concluded

that the crime had been committed on the orders of the Soviet authorities who now accused the Germans.

For the next forty-seven years successive Soviet governments claimed
that the Germans were guilty of the Katyn massacre. They engaged in
a series of cover-ups, the most elaborate of which were the fabricated
report of the Soviet Commission of Inquiry into the Katyn Massacre
(the Burdenko Commission) in January 1944 and the fabricated Soviet
case for German guilt at the International War Crimes Tribunal held at
Nuremberg in 1945–1946. Although the Soviet charge was disproved,
German guilt was proclaimed by all Soviet and other communist governments for almost half a century.

The historiography of this mass murder shows that the topic is an
extremely sensitive one. It is clear that the responsibility for the crime
lies with Stalin and his close collaborators and not with the Russian
people. They, like the murdered Poles, were the victims of Stalinism,
but the Poles were a special case. They were not Soviet citizens, and
most were prisoners of war taken by the Red Army in September 1939.
All were murdered in the spring of 1940. After a silence of fifty years,
many Russian documents exposing the truth were revealed and published, so the Katyn massacre is now the most amply documented Stalinist crime.

The roots of the Katyn massacre lie in the Nazi-Soviet Non-Aggression Pact of 23 August 1939, which led to the German-Soviet partition
of Poland. Katyn must also be viewed, however, in the broad context of
past Polish-Russian relations—the past was very much in the minds of
Poles and Russians in 1939, though mainly in the shape of mutually
negative stereotypes. There was more continuity than change in this
history, for Russia had played a dominant role in Polish political life in
one way or another since the early 1700s, when Russian tsars began to
dominate Polish politics. Catherine the Great annexed most of Poland
in the partitions of 1772, 1793, and 1795; those lands were ruled by
Russia until 1915, when German and Austro-Hungarian Armies
pushed out the Russians in the course of World War I. Most Russians
considered this domination natural, but most Poles opposed it, sometimes with arms in hand. For much of their common history since
1772, most Poles viewed Russia as the foremost enemy of Polish independence, whereas most Russians viewed the Poles as a threat to the
security of the empire, and later the USSR.

Russian-Polish Relations to 1918

The key area of Russian-Polish conflict in early modern times, and
again in the twentieth century, was in the "Borderlands" between the
two countries, that is, today's Ukraine and Belarus (Belorussia). These
territories belonged originally to Kievan Rus, the medieval state of the
Eastern Slavs, but after its destruction by the Tatars in 1240, Lithuania
expanded into the area. Both the Polish and the Lithuanian states were
threatened by the Duchy of Muscovy, as well as by the military might
of the Teutonic Knights of East Prussia. In response, the personal/dy-
nastic union of Poland and Lithuania was arranged in 1385, when
Lithuanian Grand Duke Władysław Jagiełło [Lithuanian: Jogailo] accepted the Catholic religion for his people—many of whom belonged,
like the Russians, to Orthodox or Eastern Christianity—as the condition for his marriage to Jadwiga, queen of Poland. At this point, a
power struggle began over the Borderlands and the southern Baltic
coast, between Poland-Lithuania on the one hand and the Duchy of
Moscow, later the Russian Empire, on the other.

In 1569 the dynastic union was replaced by a federation, the Polish-
Lithuanian Commonwealth.[1] (See the shaded areas in map 1.) The
Commonwealth was victorious in the late sixteenth-century wars with
Moscow over Livonia, today's northern Latvia and southern Estonia.
In the early seventeenth century a Polish army temporarily occupied
Moscow, which reinforced the hostile stereotypes established in earlier
Polish-Russian contacts. A negative image of the Polish occupation of
Moscow, and of Poles in general, became firmly lodged in the Russian
collective memory thanks mainly to a literary work and an opera. The
first was a historical novel written by Mikhail N. Zagoskin, *Yuri
Miloslavsky, ili Russkoe v 1612 godu: Istoricheskii Roman* [Yuri
Miloslavsky, or The Russians in 1612: A Historical Novel], first published in 1820, which depicted the Poles as brutal and cruel to the
Muscovites. This was so, but their behavior did not differ from soldiers' behavior elsewhere at the time. The book was very popular; it
went through eleven printings, with the last appearing in 1991. The
second was Mikhail Glinka's opera *A Life for the Tsar* (1836), later
known as *Ivan Susanin*, which also gave a poor image of the Poles in
1612, although it included attractive Polish dances. The memory of
the Polish occupation of Moscow still lives in Russia today. On 24 December 2004 the Russian Duma abolished the communist holiday cel-

ebrating the Bolshevik Revolution of 1917 on 7 November and replaced it with the Day of Unity, celebrated on 4 November as "The
Liberation of Moscow from the Polish Interventionists" in 1612.[2]

In the mid-seventeenth century, the Polish-Lithuanian Commonwealth became involved in a series of disastrous wars with Russia and
Sweden. Called the Deluge by Polish historians, the wars exhausted
the Commonwealth and led to its decline. The Russian Empire expanded. Russia, Austria, and Prussia partitioned the Commonwealth
in 1772. Poland reformed its government in 1791, but it was partitioned again in 1793. A revolt in 1794 led the Commonwealth to suffer a third partition in 1795, after which it disappeared from the map
of Europe (see map 2).[3] After the Napoleonic Wars, the largest part of
ethnic Poland became the Kingdom of Poland within the Russian Empire (1815–1830). From that time forward, most educated Russians
came to consider the Borderlands and Russian Poland as rightfully
part of Russia, whereas most educated Poles saw both as rightfully
part of Poland and identified the loss of the Borderlands with the loss
of Polish independence. At that time, the peasants who constituted
most of the population in the old Commonwealth had no voice in de-
ciding their own fate.

Polish rights and freedoms, granted by Tsar Alexander I, were reduced after his death, and a revolt erupted in November 1830, at the
time of the European revolutions. In fact, the nineteenth century witnessed six Polish uprisings against the partitioning powers, those
against Russia in 1830–1831 and 1863–1864 being the longest and
strongest. Both were crushed by Russian military might and were followed by severe repression, including the penal deportation to Siberia
of thousands of Polish insurgents, as well as the resettlement there of
hundreds of Polish gentry families deported from what are today Belarus and Ukraine. A policy of intensive Russification was implemented in Russian Poland after 1864.

For the next two decades, Polish intellectuals condemned uprisings
as the way to regain independence and advocated a "positivist" approach, that is, working for the education and economic development
of the Polish people within the legal limits established by the ruling
powers.[4] The Positivists, however, began to lose out to the new generation, raised after the uprising of 1863–1864, whose leaders renewed
the struggle for independence in the early 1890s. When Russia was
torn by revolution in 1905–1907, the same was true of Russian

Poland, where many industrial workers joined the independence movement led by the Polska Partia Socjalistyczna [PPS—Polish Socialist Party]. The Russian government made some concessions to Polish demands, but they were far from satisfying national aspirations. In 1914, Russian Poland still suffered under a system of repressive rule, as compared with Galicia (Austrian Poland), which enjoyed de facto self-government within the Austro-Hungarian Empire after 1868. Prussian Poland enjoyed stability and prosperity but suffered from harsh Germanization policies after 1880. Meanwhile, the negative Russian image of the Poles was reinforced by several authors in Russian political writings, and in literature by the great Russian writer Fyodor Dostoevsky. Conflicting Polish and Russian claims to the Borderlands further radicalized Russian perceptions of the Poles.[5] Indeed, Russian attacks on the Polish core would take a new, class form in Soviet policy toward independent Poland.

The Rebirth of Poland, 1918–1920

In the last years of the nineteenth century two leaders emerged who were to dominate the politics of interwar Poland, Józef Piłsudski (1867–1935) and Roman Dmowski (1864–1939). Piłsudski read books on socialism with a circle of friends in Wilno [Lithuanian, Vilnius; Russian, Vilna] but was arrested in 1886 in connection with a failed attempt to assassinate Tsar Alexander III in which his elder brother Bronisław, a student at the University of St. Petersburg, was implicated. The conspirators were betrayed before they could act. Józef Piłsudski, though innocent, was arrested because of his brother's involvement and spent five years in Siberian exile (1887–1892). There he read more on socialism, which attracted him not as an ideology but because it opposed Russian imperial rule and stressed the need to improve the terrible conditions of industrial workers. Thus, writing in 1903, he combined socialism and independence, stating: "A Socialist in Poland must aim at the country's independence, and independence is the defining condition of the victory of Socialism in Poland."[6] By this time, he was a prominent leader of the PPS, established in Paris in 1892 and in Warsaw the following year. Its goal was an independent, socialist Poland. Piłsudski saw Russia as the foremost enemy of Polish independence. He exerted a dominant influence on the Polish Officer Corps, formed in 1918 and active until 1945.

Roman Dmowski obtained a science degree from the Russian university in Warsaw in 1892. As a student, he was very active in the secret student organization Związek Młodzieży Polskiej [Zet—Union of Polish Youth], which strove to preserve Polish national identity and worked to teach peasants to be Polish patriots. He transformed the émigré Liga Polska [Polish League] into the Catholic, socially conservative Liga Narodowa [National League], which later became the ethnocentric Narodowa Demokracja [National Democracy]. Like the Socialists, the National Democrats also worked for Polish independence, but they opposed socialism; the two movements often clashed in Russian Poland during the Revolution of 1905–1907.

The two future statesmen, one a Socialist, one a National Democrat, also differed fundamentally in their perceptions of Russia. Piłsudski always saw Russia as Poland's foremost enemy, whereas Dmowski viewed Germany as such. He switched in 1906 from the immediate goal of gaining Polish independence to cooperation with the imperial Russian government within the new constitutional system established that year. His aim was to gain Polish self-government within the empire as the first step toward the union of all Polish territories and then independence. Thus, in the international line-up preceding the outbreak of World War I, the National Democrats planned to trade their support of Russia for the latter's agreement to the unification of Polish lands in an autonomous Poland under Russian sovereignty. The imperial government and Russian public opinion, however, opposed this goal, seeing it as the first step toward dismantling the empire. In any case, Russian military defeats in the First World War led Dmowski to transfer his activities to the West, with headquarters in Paris. After the Russian Revolution of March 1917, he and his Komitet Narodowy Polski [KNP—Polish National Committee] began to raise a Polish army in France with the blessing of the Russian Provisional Government (March–November 1917), which recognized Poland's right to independence, though in close alliance with Russia. After the Bolshevik revolution of 7 November 1917, the KNP worked openly for Polish independence.[7]

In the early part of World War I, Piłsudski raised and led the Polish Legions in the Austro-Hungarian Army, and his Legionnaires fought several battles with the Russians. In November 1916 the German and Austro-Hungarian emperors promised to establish an independent Poland, and Berlin, aiming to raise a Polish army, allowed a Polish administration in German-occupied Poland. Piłsudski cooperated with it for a while but became increasingly doubtful that the Central Powers

(Germany and Austria-Hungary plus the Ottoman Empire and Bulgaria) would tolerate the existence of a truly independent Polish state. Furthermore, the Russian Revolution of March 1917 led him to conclude that there was no point in fighting any longer on the side of Berlin and Vienna. In summer 1917 the Germans arrested Piłsudski for refusing to swear brotherhood in arms with the German and Austrian forces and imprisoned him in Germany. The new Social Democratic government in Berlin, however, believed that he was less anti-German than other Polish leaders, so they released him on 9 November 1918 and arranged for his return to Warsaw. When Piłsudski arrived there the next day, he was welcomed as a national hero. He became head of state as well as commander in chief of the Polish armed forces, cleared Warsaw of its German garrison, and declared Polish independence on 11 November 1918. It was not, however, until after the famous pianist Ignacy Jan Paderewski became prime minister and foreign minister of a new Polish government on 16 January 1919 that Poland gained official recognition abroad.

Paderewski and Dmowski became Poland's chief representatives at the Paris Peace Conference (12 January–28 June 1919). In February, Dmowski and his supporters in the Polish delegation were joined by Piłsudski delegates. They all strove for a large Poland in the belief that a small Polish state could not survive, placed as it was between its traditional enemies, Germany and Russia, but they differed over Poland's eastern boundaries. Piłsudski aimed at a federation with Lithuania and Belorussia and an alliance with an independent Ukraine (but East Galicia was to go to Poland), whereas Dmowski wanted Poland to include the western fringes of today's Belarus and all of today's western Ukraine (then East Galicia and Volhynia), where the Polish landowning gentry wielded significant economic and cultural influence. Poland's eastern border, however, could not be settled at the Paris Peace Conference because of the ongoing Russian Civil War (1918–1922) and the Polish-Soviet War (1919–1920). In the west, the Polish-German border established by the Versailles Treaty was in overall accord with ethnically Polish territory, most of which was taken by the Poles from the Germans in the Wielkopolska [Great Poland] Uprising of 1918–1919. Paderewski and Dmowski signed the Versailles Treaty for Poland on 28 June 1919.[8]

Although the Russian Provisional Government of 1917 recognized the Polish right to independence, as did the Bolshevik government, which abolished all treaties signed by tsarist Russia, mutual hostility continued between Poles and Russians. Indeed, the governments of So-

viet Russia and Poland viewed each other as enemies. Piłsudski continued to see Russia, White (anticommunist) or Red (communist), as the
greatest threat to Polish independence. He wished to weaken Russia
and strengthen Poland by establishing a Polish-Lithuanian-Belorus-
sian federation allied with an independent Ukraine.[9] At the same time,
the leader of the new Soviet state, Lenin (Vladimir I. Ulianov, 1870–
1924), viewed Poland as a puppet of the Western Powers (Britain,
France, and the United States) who supported the Whites in the Russian Civil War, even though Piłsudski rejected British and French pleas
to do so. In any case, Lenin and his close collaborators in the Bolshevik
leadership aimed to set up Soviet republics in Russia's former western
provinces as members of a Soviet federal state. They saw Poland as a
bridge to Germany, the most highly industrialized European country,
without whose help (as a communist state) the economically back-
ward Soviet state could not survive.

Local Polish-Soviet clashes in Lithuania and Belorussia in early
1919 became a full-scale war in late April 1920. At that time, Piłsudski
moved to forestall a Soviet attack by concluding an alliance and military convention with the Ukrainian leader Semyon Petliura, after
which Polish armies marched together with Petliura's Ukrainian divisions into Soviet-ruled Ukraine. They reached Kiev in early May
1920, and there Piłsudski and Petliura proclaimed an independent
Ukraine.[10] They found little local support, however, and the Red
Army forced them to retreat to the very gates of Warsaw.

The Western Powers, fearing the establishment of a German communist state, wanted to prevent a Soviet incursion into Germany. On
11 July 1920, after deliberations at an Allied conference in Spa, Belgium, on what to do about the Red Army's advance into Poland, the
British government (but not the French) proposed to Moscow a Polish-
Soviet armistice line, known as the Curzon Line, named after the
British foreign secretary of the time, Lord George Nathaniel Curzon.
The details are important because during World War II Stalin demanded that it serve as the basis for the postwar Soviet-Polish frontier,
although he extended Ukrainian territory a little west of it.

The Curzon Line was based on a provisional demarcation line between Polish and Russian administrations proposed during the Paris
Peace Conference of 1919. Most of this line was not new, for it ap-
proximated the eastern border of Congress Poland (1815–1830), well
known to Western statesmen of 1919 from their school atlases, which

designated the lands east of Poland as Russian, though they were inhabited by Ukrainians, Poles, Belorussians, and Jews. It also happened to coincide with the eastern limits of predominantly ethnic Polish territory. The southern segment of the Curzon Line, however, was to follow one of the two lines proposed at the Paris Peace Conference of 1919 for a possible division of East Galicia (today part of western Ukraine): variant *A* of the two lines proposed in June 1919 left most of East Galicia, including Lwów [Russian, Lvov; Ukrainian, Lviv] and the oil fields, outside Poland, while variant *B* left them in Poland. East Galicia had been part of the Polish-Lithuanian Commonwealth and then of the Habsburg Empire, later the Austro-Hungarian Empire, whose lands outside of Austria proper were put at the disposal of the powers victorious in World War I.

In 1918 the population was about 60 percent Ukrainian, 30 percent Polish, and 10 percent Jewish, but the cities and some other areas had Polish majorities with significant Jewish minorities, and the small towns were Jewish. East Galicia was claimed and fought over in 1918–1919 by Poles and Ukrainians, who wanted it as part of a large Ukrainian state. The war ended with a Polish victory, which left long-lasting and bitter memories on both sides. East Galicia, gaining which had been an imperial Russian war aim, was also claimed as Russian by émigré Russian statesmen in Paris and by the Soviet government. The British government, though officially supporting Ukrainian self determination, wanted to keep East Galicia out of Polish hands to preserve it as a bargaining counter with Soviet Russia, so it proposed autonomy or a League of Nations mandate with a high commissioner. (This was similar to the arrangement the British managed to obtain for Danzig [Gdańsk], which was made a Free City.) At the end of 1919, the Supreme Council of the League of Nations agreed on East Galician autonomy with a twenty-five-year mandate for Poland, but it was "suspended" on the plea of the French government. Indeed, the French were interested in the East Galician oilfields and saw Poland as a barrier to Bolshevism, so they supported the Polish claim to East Galicia. (The Poles had been allowed to take over the region in order to stem the Bolshevik tide advancing from the east.)

On 10 July 1920, when the Red Army neared Warsaw during the Polish-Soviet War, the Polish government delegation at Spa, Belgium, accepted an armistice with the Soviets along the current Polish-Soviet front line, which left Lwów and the neighboring oil fields on the Polish side. The line was changed, however, in the Foreign Office, London, to line *A* of 1919, leaving both on the Soviet side, presumably to make the offer more acceptable to the Soviets. France and Britain declared they would come to Poland's aid if the Red Army entered ethnically Polish territory, that is, land west of the Curzon Line, even though Paris had not supported line *A*. The Soviet government, however, rejected the Curzon Line (line *A*), proposing direct Polish-Soviet negotiations instead, in which they put forward demands incompatible with Polish independence. As Lenin admitted at a party conference in September 1920—after the Polish victory over the Red Army—the Soviet leadership rejected the Curzon proposal because they believed the Western Powers would not fight. Therefore, they decided to carry the revolution not only into ethnic Poland but also further west to Germany and perhaps to Italy as well. Lenin also said they believed that Poland's defeat would mean the collapse of the Versailles Treaty, the foundation of the whole international system.[11] As Soviet-Polish negotiations began, the Red Army continued its advance into ethnically Polish lands, but much to everyone's surprise, Piłsudski led the Poles to victory in the Battle of the Vistula (August 1920).[12] It is worth noting that many of the Polish officers taken prisoner by the Red Army in September 1939 had fought against it in 1920. Indeed, the war was very much a part of popular memory in both Poland and the USSR in 1939, though presented in very different images by each country's media.

The Polish victory secured the independence of not only Poland but also the Baltic States (Estonia, Latvia, and Lithuania) and perhaps other Central European states as well. Peace came with the Treaty of Riga (18 March 1921), which left what is today western Belarus and western Ukraine in Poland. The British government opposed these Polish gains, but the Western Powers grudgingly recognized Poland's sovereignty in March 1923, conditional on the grant of autonomy to East Galicia (not implemented) and no assumption of Western responsibility for the settlement. As for the Russians, most viewed these territorial losses as an outrage because the lands had belonged to Russia from the time of the partitions of Poland to World War I. They also looked on the Ukrainians and Belorussians as their junior Slavic brothers. Last but not least, they viewed the losses as a grave diminution of Soviet security. That is why the defeat of 1920 rankled so deeply with the Soviet leadership, especially Joseph Stalin, who was attached as a commissar to Semyon Budenny's cavalry marching on Polish Lwów in summer

1920. Indeed, the brilliant Bolshevik commander Mikhail Tukhachev-sky blamed Stalin for the Red Army's disaster, ostensibly because Stalin did not press Budenny to follow orders and move north in time to prevent it. More than likely, however, Budenny would have arrived too late to prevent Soviet defeat. Indeed, Polish military cryptographers had broken Red Army radio codes so that Piłsudski knew the location of Soviet units in August 1920. Furthermore, Polish military radio-telegraphers sometimes blocked Tukhachevsky's orders to his troops by reading Bible excerpts on the same wavelength as that used by the Soviet commander.[13]

The Red Army's defeat by the Poles in 1920 made Soviet leaders view Poland throughout the interwar period as the most immediate threat to the USSR. For the Poles, victory over the Soviets ensured independence, although it also created overconfidence in the Polish Army, especially the cavalry, which had performed brilliantly in what is now viewed as the last cavalry war in Europe.[14] The Poles saw the Polish-Soviet frontier established by the Treaty of Riga (18 March 1921) as the recovery of old Polish lands, especially the two preponderantly Polish-speaking cities that were then centers of Polish culture, Wilno and Lwów. At the same time, they saw the eastern territories as critical to Polish national security against the Soviet Union, viewed as a "Red" version of the old Russian Empire. Thus, in a mirror image of the Soviet view of Poland, for most of the interwar period the Poles saw the USSR as the greatest threat to their country. The Polish Officer Corps, like the majority of Poles, believed that no territorial concessions could be made to either Germany or the USSR without compromising Poland's independence.

Soviet-Polish Relations, 1921–1939

After the Treaty of Riga, Soviet-Polish relations were cool until the early 1930s. Indeed, in 1924–1934 the "Poland-Romania" series of Soviet military plans envisaged war between the USSR on the one hand and a coalition of Central European states led by Poland and Romania and backed by the Western Powers on the other. This was the Soviet reaction to the Polish-Romanian defensive alliance and secret military convention signed in 1921.[15] In the same period, German-Soviet relations were very good, including not only trade but also secret military cooperation, which was a direct threat to Poland.[16] Both Germany and the USSR refused to accept their territorial losses to Poland. Although Germany signed the Versailles Treaty, no German government officially recognized the Polish-German frontier, and Soviet propaganda attacked Poland. Still, Moscow and Warsaw moved closer in 1931–1932, when the Great Depression apparently made Stalin fear a possible German attack on the USSR, supported by France and Britain, through a vanquished Poland. Therefore, a Soviet-Polish Non-Aggression Pact was signed in Moscow on 25 July 1932.[17] Indeed, Poland also feared Germany. After Adolf Hitler came to power in 1933 and continued to rant against the Versailles Treaty, Piłsudski feared Western support for a possible revision of the Polish-German frontier at Poland's expense. Hitler, for his part, decided to improve relations with Poland, and a Polish-German Declaration of Non-Aggression was signed on 26 January 1934.[18]

Despite the extension of the Polish-Soviet pact for ten years on 5 May 1934, the Soviet leadership suspected a secret Polish alignment with Nazi Germany against the USSR, a view fueled by reports of the Razvedka [GRU—Main Military Intelligence Administration of the RKKA/Red Army] and still widely held in Russia today. In light of these Soviet assumptions, it is not surprising that the "Poland-Germany" series of Soviet war plans drawn up in 1935–1939 envisaged an attack on the USSR by a Polish-German coalition, which was the worst-case scenario for Soviet military planners. Soviet distrust of Poles also led to the arrest of some 140,000 ethnically Polish Soviet citizens during the Stalin Terror of 1935–1938. Charged with spying for Poland, many were shot or died in labor camps.[19]

The Polish government, however, held to the French alliance and had no intention of joining Nazi Germany in an attack on the Soviet Union, for this would have meant German armies entering Poland.[20] Both Piłsudski and Foreign Minister Józef Beck refused to discuss German proposals for a joint attack on the USSR and Polish expansion into Soviet Ukraine. They aimed at maintaining a balance between Germany and the USSR—that is, good relations with both but alliance with neither.[21] Clearly, however, the Soviet leadership believed that if Poland had to choose between her two great neighbors, the choice would be Nazi Germany. Therefore, the extension of the Soviet-Polish Non-Aggression Pact in 1934 did nothing to assuage Soviet suspicions. Indeed, they were strengthened by the Polish rejection of the "Eastern Locarno" treaty proposed by France the same year, whereby the USSR would be responsible for the security of France's Eastern European allies.[22]

Four years later, during the Czechoslovak crisis of 1938, Soviet diplomacy supported Prague, while the Polish foreign minister waited to see if the Western Powers would fight for Czechoslovakia. Beck's policy was aptly described in a June 1938 report by the U.S. ambassador in Warsaw, Anthony J. Drexel Biddle. On the basis of his talks with Beck and high-ranking Polish officials, Biddle reported that if the Western Powers fought, Poland would be on their side, for it would never align with Germany; but if they did not fight, Poland would look after its own interests. Finally, whatever happened, Poland would never go into Soviet Ukraine. Biddle's report confirms Beck's account of his statement on Polish foreign policy to the Polish Council of Ministers in summer 1938, as well as statements by other Poles recorded by British officials later that year.[23] Contrary to the widely accepted view that the Polish government rejected Soviet proposals for the passage of Red Army troops through Polish territory to help Czechoslovakia in September 1938, no official Soviet proposal to this end has been found in either Polish or Russian archives. Furthermore, no Soviet military plan to carry out such an action has come to light, so the Red Army mobilization on the western frontier may have been a demonstration of support for Czechoslovakia rather than a prelude to military action.[24]

Through the ups and downs of interwar Polish-Soviet relations, Soviet resentment of the Polish-Soviet border established by the Treaty of Riga was a constant, though muted issue. The political line followed by Soviet historians, as well as Polish historians in communist Poland (1945–1989), was that Polish cession of western Ukraine and western Belorussia to the USSR would have led to a Soviet-Polish alliance safeguarding Polish independence in 1939, and such an alliance would have been the right policy for Poland to follow in World War II. Both the prewar Polish government and the wartime government-in-exile were condemned for being unrealistic in rejecting this option. Similar views are held by many Western historians today.[25] All interwar (and later wartime) Polish governments, however, as well as the vast majority of Poles, adamantly rejected such a policy. In any case, even if a Polish government could have ceded the eastern territories to the Soviet Union in 1939 and remained in power, it seems most unlikely that Stalin would have risked war with Hitler over Poland. Distrust of

France and Britain and the aim of keeping the USSR out of a European
war were the dominant features of Soviet foreign policy at the time. As
for the Poles, they expected the principal attack on their country to
come from the USSR. This was due not only to distrust of Moscow
but also to the nature of the Franco-Polish Alliance (19 February
1921). The secret military convention attached to the alliance stipulated active French military support in a Polish-German war but not
in a Polish-Soviet war, when only French military supplies were envisaged.[26] Until the turn of 1938–1939, Polish war plans mandated defensive action by the bulk of the country's armed forces in the east, but
this was read in Moscow to mean aggressive Polish designs on Soviet
territory.

The German-Soviet Non-Aggression Pact
and the German-Polish War, 1939

The German-Soviet Non-Aggression Pact was signed in Stalin's presence at the Kremlin on 23 August 1939 by the German Foreign Minister Joachim von Ribbentrop and the Soviet Commissar for Foreign Affairs Vyacheslav Molotov (doc. 1). Historians still disagree about the
timing of Stalin's policy decision and his motives. Did he really aim at
an alliance with France and Britain and decide in Hitler's favor only
when they failed to secure Polish and Romanian agreement to the passage of Soviet troops in case of war with Germany, or was he aiming at
an agreement with Hitler all along? Available documentation seems to
indicate that both pragmatism and ideology led Stalin in the second direction. On the one hand, why should he risk a war with Germany in
which the Western Powers might not help the USSR, whereas a German war with France and Britain would exhaust both sides, thus
strengthening communist movements and eventually bringing Soviet
domination over a devastated Europe? On the other hand, a Soviet alliance with the Western Powers could prevent a war between them and
Germany, which might lead to a Western-supported German attack on
the USSR. Thus, Stalin could see an agreement with Berlin as being in
the Soviet interest, while the expected Polish refusal to allow the passage of Soviet troops in case of war with Germany could serve as its
justification. The secret German-Soviet talks on trade and spheres of
interest in Eastern Europe, held in Berlin in the summer of 1939, can

be viewed as preparing the way for the German-Soviet Non-Aggression Pact of 23 August 1939.[27]

The core of the German-Soviet Non-Aggression Pact was the Secret Supplementary Protocol, negotiated in the Kremlin during the night of 23–24 August, when Ribbentrop consulted Hitler on some of Stalin's territorial demands by telephone via the German Embassy in Moscow. The protocol specified Soviet and German spheres of influence in the Baltic States and drew a line dividing Poland in half between the two powers. This line followed the Vistula and San Rivers (the Pisa River was added in a supplementary agreement signed on 28 August). Because the Vistula runs through Warsaw, the eastern part of the Polish capital was left on the Soviet side (see map 3). Germany also recognized predominant Soviet interest in Bessarabia (now Moldova), then part of Romania but previously part of the Russian Empire (doc. 2). The contents of the Secret Protocol were leaked to Washington, Paris, and London, but the Poles were informed neither by their French and British allies nor by the United States.[28] It is true, however, that rumors of a German-Soviet agreement had circulated since the spring of 1939. In particular, Walter Krivitsky, a high-ranking Soviet intelligence agent who had defected to the West in 1937, warned the British Foreign Office repeatedly two years later that Stalin would conclude a pact with Hitler, but his warnings were treated as "twaddle" and "rigamarole."[29] The Secret Protocol was condemned fifty years later by a freely elected Supreme Soviet on 25 December 1989. But the point of view prevalent in Russian official circles today is that the German-Soviet Non-Aggression Pact was in many respects similar to the Munich agreement of 1938.[30]

Once Hitler had secured the pact with Moscow, he made it clear that peace depended on full Polish acceptance of his demands: the return of the Free City of Danzig to Germany and a German corridor through the Polish Corridor (Polish Pomerania), thus giving Germany direct land access to Danzig and East Prussia. Danzig, Poland's second seaport after Gdynia, was predominantly German, but the Polish Corridor, where Gdynia was located, was predominantly Polish even according to the Prussian census of 1910. These demands, already rejected by Poland in late March 1939, were unacceptable to both the Polish government and the Polish people because they were seen as making Poland economically and, thus, politically a satellite of Germany. Józef Lipski, the Polish ambassador in Berlin, saw German Foreign Minister Ribbentrop on 31 August 1939 and told him that the Polish government was considering British suggestions for a Polish-German agreement (actually these were German terms communicated by the British to the Poles). When it became clear that Lipski did not have the authority to accept the German demands, Ribbentrop ended the interview. The sixteen "proposals" broadcast by German state radio on the evening of 31 August 1939 were formulated to appeal to Western public opinion. Aside from the immediate return of Danzig to Germany, there was to be an internationally supervised plebiscite in the Polish Corridor (with the vote limited to people living there before 1918); free transit for the side that lost; and a commission of inquiry to investigate minority problems. The terms were made public by German state radio at 9 p.m. on 31 August, along with the claim that Poland had rejected them. This was the signal for the German attack on Poland, which began in the early hours of 1 September 1939.

Five German armies (1,500,000 men) invaded Poland from the west, north, and south. As they battered the Poles on land and sea and from the air, the French and British governments showed interest in Italian dictator Benito Mussolini's proposal for a Great Power conference. On 1 September they demanded the withdrawal of German forces from Polish territory but also stated that if Germany complied, they would be ready to support German-Polish negotiations. (They hoped that Poland would agree to Hitler's terms in return for international guarantees of its new frontiers and independence.)[31] The Führer sent no answer by the deadline, so France and Britain found themselves at war with Germany on 3 September 1939.

The Polish Army was no match for the German war machine, then the most modern and powerful in the world. Their only hope was a French offensive against Germany, due fifteen days after a German attack on Poland (to allow for French mobilization), as specified in the Franco-Polish protocol to the Military Convention of 1921, signed in Paris on 19 May 1939. The French offensive, however, did not take place. This was not because the Poles had collapsed after fifteen days—fighting was still going on—but because the British and French General Staffs had agreed beforehand to fight a defensive war if Germany attacked Poland. They did not inform their ally: the French military wanted the Poles to fight as long as possible in order to gain time for France.[32] Thus, there was a "phony war" in the west as German armies advanced quickly into central Poland. The largest and longest battle took place on the Bzura River in central Poland, 7–16 September, while General Kazimierz Sosnkowski defeated a German division in southeastern Poland, and Warsaw withstood a three-week German siege from land and air. By 27 September the city was running out of food and water and surrendered on the orders of the former Polish commander in chief, Marshal Edward Śmigły-Rydz. The last Polish unit fighting the Germans disbanded on 6 October.[33] The outmatched Poles had fought the Germans for five weeks, or almost as long as the French, supported by the British, fought them in France in 1940. Whatever chance the Polish forces retained to regroup in the southeastern part of the country was lost when the Red Army invaded eastern Poland on 17 September.

The Soviet Invasion of Poland, 17 September 1939

As the Germans advanced into Polish territory, they pressed the Soviet government to enter their part of Poland but Stalin took his time, perhaps owing to war in the Far East. Fighting had been going on since May 1939 between the Red Army and part of the Japanese Kwantung Army near the frontier between Manchukuo (Japanese-controlled Manchuria) and Soviet Mongolia. Richard Sorge, the Soviet spy in Tokyo with access to high-level Japanese officials, had reported in June that Japan would not be ready for war before 1941, and the Japanese High Command was trying to rein in the Kwantung Army, which had acted against the express wishes of the Japanese government, but this was probably not enough to convince Stalin. In any case, Komandarm [General] (later Marshal) Georgy K. Zhukov launched an offensive against the Japanese on 20 August. He drove them back by 22 August, defeating them by the end of the month, and a Soviet-Japanese armistice was signed on 15 September.[34] Perhaps the Far Eastern war delayed the Red Army's incursion into eastern Poland, but Stalin also may have waited to see whether the French would launch an offensive against Germany. Whatever was uppermost in his mind, mobilization in the Belorussian and Ukrainian military regions bordering Poland began on 7 September. Attack orders were signed on 9 September, but the date was changed to 14 September, and two days later, action was set for the dawn of 17 September.[35]

When Stalin decided the time had come for the Red Army to invade eastern Poland, he wanted to issue a declaration that the USSR was coming to save the Ukrainians and Belorussians from the Germans. On 17 September at 2 a.m. he and Molotov met with the German ambassador in Moscow, Friedrich Werner von der Schulenburg. Molotov and Stalin told Schulenburg that the Red Army would enter Poland at 6 a.m. The three agreed on the text of the Soviet note to be handed to the Polish ambassador; Stalin also accepted Schulenburg's objections to his proposed public declaration and agreed to alter the text to make it acceptable to the Germans.[36] The Soviet note stated that Warsaw was no longer the Polish capital and that the government showed no sign of life. Since the Polish state and government no longer existed, Polish-Soviet agreements had "ceased to operate," and this situation could be a threat to the USSR. Furthermore, the Soviet government could not leave its Ukrainian and Belorussian kin unprotected, so the Red Army would come in to protect them. Finally, the Soviet government would give the Polish people "the opportunity to live a peaceful life" (doc. 4). The wording was designed to justify Soviet aggression against Poland in the eyes of communists as well as influence general public opinion at home and abroad. Indeed, many Western communists expressed support for Poland when it was attacked by Germany, and were appalled by the Soviet attack that began on 17 September. Critical remarks by citizens were also reported in the USSR.[37]

The Stalin-Molotov conversation with Ambassador Schulenburg took place at almost the same time as another diplomatic encounter. The Polish ambassador in Moscow, Wacław Grzybowski, was summoned by Soviet Deputy Commissar for Foreign Affairs Vladimir Potemkin to his office in the early hours of 17 September. There Potemkin read him the Soviet note. Grzybowski rejected the references to Warsaw and the Polish government. He stated that Polish armies were still fighting and refused to accept the note, but he finally consented to communicate its contents to his government. Copies of the Soviet note were sent to all foreign embassies and legations in Moscow, informing them that the USSR would conduct a policy of neutrality in its relations with each country. Molotov read the contents of the note on Soviet radio that day as well. Furthermore, a Soviet-German communiqué was issued on 18 September stating that Germany and the USSR would restore order and peace in Poland, a peace disturbed by the (alleged) collapse of the Polish government. They would also help the Poles reorganize their economic life.[38]

Meanwhile, the Polish government, the commander in chief, and the

General Staff had left Warsaw on 6 September to escape the impending German encirclement of the city. They retreated east, then southeast to the border with Romania. On 17 September the government and diplomatic corps were stationed at Kuty, on the Cheremosh [Czeremosz] River, which separated the Romanian province of Bukovina from Poland, with the General Staff stationed at nearby Kolomija [Kołomyja]. The Polish authorities received the news of the Soviet entry into eastern Poland at 6 a.m. that day and were at first uncertain as to whether the Russians were coming to aid the Poles or attack them. When the contents of the Soviet note to Grzybowski arrived at Kuty (via the Polish Embassy in Bucharest) soon thereafter, it dispelled any lingering illusions. The Polish government issued a strong protest against the Soviet invasion, which violated the Polish-Soviet Non-Aggression Pact, as well as against Soviet allegations regarding itself and the Polish Army.[39] With the Red Army advancing swiftly toward their location, the Polish authorities decided to cross into Romania with the aim of proceeding thence to France, where they were assured of hospitality and intended to raise a new Polish army to fight the Germans. The Romanian government, however, acting under strong German pressure, interned the top Polish civil and military authorities, although it soon allowed General Władysław Sikorski, some officials, and thousands of Polish military to leave for France (via Yugoslavia and Italy).[40] Hungary also released many Polish soldiers. A new Polish government was formed in Paris on 30 September with Sikorski as premier and, soon thereafter, also commander in chief of the Polish armed forces.

The USSR did not declare war on Poland, and neither the old nor the new Polish government declared war on the USSR. (The new Polish government however, considered itself to be at war with the Soviet Union.) Indeed, before crossing into Romania on the night of 17–18 September, Marshal Śmigły-Rydz issued an order to Polish troops not to fight the Soviets unless the latter attacked or tried to disarm them. He ordered Warsaw and the nearby fortress of Modlin to defend themselves against the Germans, but also ordered towns approached by the Soviets to negotiate with them to secure their garrisons' exit to Romania or Hungary (doc. 6). (His order for Warsaw to surrender came ten days later.) Some 35,000 Polish military made their way from Romania and Hungary to France, but many others were prevented from crossing into Romania and Hungary by Soviet troops. The War Council of the Ukrainian Front issued orders on 19 September to close a segment of the Polish frontier running along the Zbruch [Zbrucz] River and west of it to prevent Polish soldiers and officers from crossing into Romania.[41] Among those taken prisoner while attempting to reach Hungary was General Władysław Anders, who was released only after the German attack on the USSR on 22 June 1941. There was no secret about the plan to raise a Polish army in France, so it is very likely that the Soviet government knew of it even before the new Polish government was established there. In November 1939, Commissar Lev Mekhlis, head of the Red Army's Political Administration, told a group of Soviet writers that captive Polish officers should not be released because they would provide leadership for Polish "legions" being formed in the west. He said the Poles could raise an army of 100,000 in France.[42]

The Soviet forces entering Poland in September 1939 numbered around 500,000, although by the end of the campaign the number stood at about 1,500,000. Most of the regular Polish troops normally stationed in eastern Poland were sent west to fight the Germans, so most of the resistance was offered by several thousand soldiers of the Korpus Ochrony Pogranicza [KOP—Polish Frontier Protection Corps], supplemented by a few army groups from central Poland formed with units retreating ahead of the Germans. Soviet armed superiority was overwhelming. The armies of the Ukrainian and Belorussian Fronts, commanded by Komandarm Semyon Timoshenko and Komandarm Vasily Kuznetsov, included elite armored and air force units whose task was less to crush Polish resistance than to prevent a possible massive German incursion into the agreed-on Soviet share of Poland. Indeed, before the Red Army moved in, some German troops drove east of the demarcation line and even besieged Lwów, which was in the Soviet zone. The Polish commander, General Władysław Langner, a Piłsudski Legionnaire in World War I and veteran of the Polish-Soviet War, decided to surrender to the Soviets rather than the Germans, who retreated as the Red Army drew near the city. In the surrender agreement, even though Timoshenko's representatives agreed that the Polish military should go free, they were arrested and imprisoned in Starobelsk, near Kharkov [Ukrainian, Kharkiv], Ukraine. Once there, the officers protested that their captivity violated the surrender terms (docs. 20, 21).

Meanwhile, although some Polish units fought the Red Army, especially in defense of Grodno (now in Belarus), many surrendered without a fight. Some did so in the belief that the Soviets were coming to fight the Germans; others, who received the 17 September order of Marshal Śmigły-Rydz (doc. 6), interpreted it to mean surrender. Some Polish officers were stopped and shot on the spot by officers of the Narodny Komissariat Vnutreknnykh Del [NKVD or Narkomvnudel—People's Commissariat of Internal Affairs]. This was the case with General Józef Olszyna-Wilczyński, prewar commander of the 3rd Military District, with headquarters in Grodno, and commander of the Grodno Operational Group in September 1939. Ironically, he had opposed fighting the Soviets, had ordered his units to retreat to Lithuania, and was on his way there when he was shot. Despite his orders, the Poles of Grodno crushed an internal attempt to take over the town and defended it for three days; some 300 Polish defenders were shot after the Soviets took the town. The Wilno Poles also put up a brief fight before being overwhelmed by Soviet troops.[43]

At this time, many Polish officers and noncommissioned officers (NCOs), police, and civilians were shot in several localities without any semblance of a trial. In 2002 the remains of eighteen high-ranking KOP officers were found in a mass grave in Melnyky, near Shatsk, Ukraine. It is true that Red Army Military Councils in western Ukraine and western Belorussia were empowered to ratify death sentences for "*kontrrevoliutsionny*" [c-r—counterrevolutionary] crimes committed by civilians and former Polish Army personnel (doc. 15), but no trial record for the Melnyky victims has surfaced thus far. In fact, it is not known how many Poles were killed in eastern Poland in September 1939; one estimate cites 1,000–2,500 civilians and 200–300 military.[44] Most of the civilians were not victims of the Red Army or the NKVD but of roving Belorussian and Ukrainian bands that attacked both ethnic Poles and Jews.

Soviet Policy in Eastern Poland, 1939–1941

The ideological justification for the Soviet attack on Poland was proclaimed in the Order to the Troops issued by the Military Council of the Belorussian Front. The order stated that the Red Army was coming to the aid of "brother Belorussians and Ukrainians" to rescue them from "the threat of ruin and massacre by their enemies" (doc. 3). Indeed, the majority of the population in these regions was made up of

Belorussians and Ukrainians. In 1939, out of a total eastern population of some 13,199,000, there were, according to Polish estimates, 5,274,000 ethnic Poles; 4,529,000 Ukrainians; 1,945,000 Belorussians; 1,109,000 Jews; and 342,000 others.[45] Poles formed majorities in the larger cities, especially Lwów and Wilno, which also had significant Jewish populations, while Jews predominated in the small market towns (shtetls).

Polish rule over national minorities was generally heavy-handed, although implementation depended largely on the provincial governors. Various degrees of discrimination and repression were applied, particularly in southeastern Poland, where the extreme nationalist Orhanizatsiia Ukrainskykh Natsionalistiv [OUN—Organization of Ukrainian Nationalists] and its military arm, the Ukrainskaia Voennaia Organizatsiia [UVO—Ukrainian Military Organization], carried out terrorist acts against Polish officials, including assassinations. A series of UVO attacks against Poles and Polish property in the fall of 1930 led to Polish troops being quartered in the troubled areas and to widespread destruction of Ukrainian property. At the same time, however, minorities had extensive cultural and press freedom, as demonstrated by the large number of Ukrainian, Belorussian, and Jewish newspapers, periodicals, and publications.[46]

In general, minority populations in most Eastern European states— except for Jews—had ties with neighboring countries where they formed majorities, so they were viewed with suspicion and subjected to assimilation policies. This perception accounted for most of the repression suffered by minorities in each country during the interwar period, including democratic Czechoslovakia, where the Poles of Zaolzie (a territory just west of the Olza River) were subjected to various assimilation policies. The generally hard lot of most of Poland's Ukrainians, Belorussians, and Jews was still much better than that of their ethnic kin across the eastern border. Stalin's forced collectivization of agriculture in the early 1930s cost millions of lives, mostly Ukrainian. Soviet Jews enjoyed limited civil rights, but were not free to practice their religion and lost their communal institutions.[47]

In September 1939 many Belorussians, Ukrainians, and Jews welcomed the Red Army when it invaded eastern Poland, though not for the same reasons. The western Ukrainians, most of whom lived in East Galicia and belonged to the Uniate, or Ukrainian Church, wanted their own state, which would include Volhynia, where most Ukrainians belonged to the Polish Autonomous Orthodox Church. The western Belorussian peasants, many of whom belonged to the Catholic Church, did not have a strong sense of national identity but wanted the Polish gentry's land, as did the Ukrainian peasants. The vast majority of the Jewish population professed the Jewish Orthodox faith, while many young Jews were either Zionists or communists, and all were greatly relieved to escape German occupation.[48] The end of Polish rule was welcomed by many Belorussians, Ukrainians, and Jews, but Soviet rule hardly amounted to political or economic liberation. The Ukrainians were soon disabused of their hopes for independence, as were educated Belorussians, and the Jews suffered the confiscation of their property as well as the dissolution of their communal organizations.

Contrary to widespread Polish opinion at the time and later, only some of the Jews, mostly young people, actively collaborated with the new communist authorities. Many of them worked in the militia and helped to track down and arrest Poles targeted by Soviet authorities. Although these collaborators were not numerous, they were visible, unlike Polish agents and informers, so Polish resentment came to include all Jews, thus radicalizing traditional anti-Semitism.[49] As for the peasants, their dissatisfaction became evident in early 1940. The popular land reform carried out through the confiscation and distribution of Polish estates was soon followed by the imposition of product delivery quotas, confiscation of kulak property (kulaks were peasants owning at least a horse and a cow), and forced collectivization, imposed in April 1940. For all these reasons, even the generally passive Belorussian peasants offered resistance to Soviet rule, and some even recalled former Polish rule with nostalgia.[50]

The Soviets arrested Polish, Belorussian, Ukrainian, and Jewish political leaders, as well as specific categories of people of all nationalities viewed as anti-Soviet. Some were shot on the spot, but most were imprisoned or deported.[51] Soviet authorities viewed Polish Army officers, police, administrators, officeholders, judges and other legal personnel, politicians, educators, and clergy as counterrevolutionary; by virtue of their professions, they were automatically classified as opponents of communism. These people were sought out on the basis of NKVD lists or denunciations. A property owner was viewed as a class enemy and classified as a *sotsialno opasny element* [SOE—socially dangerous element]. Poles were the owners of medium to large estates as well as some manufacturing firms, so many were arrested and jailed.

The Polish landowning class—already decimated during the Russian Revolutions of 1917 and the Civil War of 1918–1922—was wiped out. The families of officers and "counterrevolutionary" elements made up most of the deportees from eastern Poland to labor camps and "special settlements" in Soviet Central Asia and Siberia. Jews made up about one-third of all deported Polish citizens.[52] Thousands of Ukrainians, mostly politicians and clergy, as well as some Belorussians, shared the same fate. Soviet citizens knew little or nothing of the complex ethnic, political, economic, and social structure of eastern Poland. It is not surprising, then, that the image of Ukrainians and Belorussians persecuted by Polish "lords" was widespread in the USSR and that the notion of "liberation" from the "Polish yoke" was popular. This stereotypical view was strengthened by the vilification of Poles in a propaganda campaign of articles and poems justifying the Soviet attack on Poland.[53]

The Secret Protocol to the German-Soviet Non-Aggression Pact of 23 August 1939 left open the possibility of a rump Polish state, and Stalin may have considered it. This is suggested by an internal political directive of 16 September, issued by the War Council of the Belorussian Front, stating that a soviet, or assembly, elected in a preponderantly Polish district could vote for the district to join the USSR as a Soviet republic.[54] Another indication is recorded by General Anders, who had been a cavalry staff officer in the Russian Army in 1914–1917. He was asked, while held a prisoner in Lwów, if he would join a Polish government under Soviet control and, later, if he would serve as a high officer in the Red Army. Anders rejected both proposals, thereby incurring brutal treatment.[55] Furthermore, the Soviets supported a small group of Polish communists and sympathizers led by the left-wing Polish writer Wanda Wasilewska.[56] Whatever Stalin's thoughts may have been, he told the German ambassador in Moscow on 25 September that he was opposed to leaving a rump Polish state because it might lead to friction between Germany and the USSR. At the same time, he proposed to exchange some of his preponderantly Polish territory for predominant Soviet influence in Lithuania.[57]

On 28 September 1939, Ribbentrop and Molotov signed the German-Soviet Treaty on Friendship and the Border between the USSR and Germany (doc. 12). The treaty significantly modified the German-Soviet demarcation line agreed to in the Secret Protocol of 23 August. Stalin gave up part of his ethnically Polish territory (Lublin Province and part of Warsaw Province) in exchange for predominant Soviet influence in Lithuania, except for Memel [Klaipeda], which stayed with Germany, while Vilnius became the capital of Lithuania (doc. 13a; see map 3). The treaty had three secret protocols, one of which specified the signatories' agreement to cooperate in suppressing Polish agitation affecting each other's territory (doc. 13b), which meant cooperation against Polish resistance movements. Another secret protocol specified the mutual exchange of persons formerly resident in the territories of the signatories, which referred to Germans living in Soviet Poland and Ukrainians and Belorussians living in German Poland. A few days later, the Politburo approved the proposal by Lavrenty Beria, head of the NKVD, to return some 33,000 Polish rank-and-file soldiers, residents of German Poland, to the Germans (doc. 18). This led to an exchange of prisoners of war between the two powers.

The German-Soviet treaty of 28 September was followed by intensive political preparations and propaganda for Soviet-style elections to the National Assemblies in Western Ukraine and Western Belorussia, held on 22 October 1939. (Western Ukraine and Western Belorussia were the official Soviet names for the former Polish territories until early November 1939.) The assemblies then "requested" union with the respective Soviet republics, requests granted by the Supreme Soviet on 1–2 November 1939. Nikita Khrushchev, then 1st Secretary of Ukraine, played a starring role in preparing and carrying out the elections, as well as the subsequent Sovietization of western Ukraine.[58]

Polish Prisoners of War in the USSR, 1939–1940

The Polish officers taken prisoner were shocked in their first encounters with the Red Army when they were treated as "enemies of the people" and sometimes deliberately humiliated by army political officers, who viewed them as *Pans,* or nobles, just as Soviet propaganda had presented them in 1920.[59] In fact, in 1939 only 3 percent of Polish officers were of aristocratic origin, and more than two-fifths came from farmer or worker families.[60] Most came from the intelligentsia, members of which were generally impoverished gentry, whose sons traditionally went into the military or civil service. Red Army *politruks,* or political instructors, sometimes tried to set Polish officers against their own authorities. In at least one case, a Soviet officer called on captive Polish officers to publicly condemn their generals and their government, which they refused to do.[61] This was a more sophisticated variant of the appeal contained in Soviet leaflets air-dropped on Polish troops, telling them to beat up their officers and generals and come over to the Soviet side.[62]

Polish historians believe that 230,000–240,000 members of the Polish military were prisoners of war, including some 10,000 officers. The officers, however, were probably more numerous, since many concealed their rank and some escaped from provisional prisoner-of-war camps in Western Ukraine.[63] The Red Army was simply overwhelmed by the huge number of prisoners on its hands (doc. 11). In response, the Politburo decided in early October to approve the existing procedure: that privates of Ukrainian and Belorussian nationality be released to return home, although some 25,000 of them, as well as some Poles, were to work on the Novograd Volynsky–Lvov [Nowogród Wołyński–Lwów] highway (doc. 14). Later, several thousand prisoners were sent to work in Soviet mines (doc. 19). Officers were separated from the rank and file after first being held together with them in the transit-distribution camps. The captive Polish officers did not represent a typical officer corps. According to an NKVD report of 28 February 1940, out of a total of 8,442 officers held at that time in the special camps, 2,336 were regulars, 5,456 were reservists, and 650 were retired.[64] Many of the reservists had higher-education degrees and some were prominent in their professions.

The Politburo decided on 18 September that NKVD Convoy Troops were to take charge of the prisoners from the Red Army (doc. 7). In fact, the army was not equipped to run prisoner-of-war camps, whereas the NKVD had long and extensive experience in running the huge network of Soviet labor camps known as the GULAG [Glavnoe Upravlenie Lagerei—Main Administration of (Forced Labor) Camps], as well as experience conducting interrogations.[65] On the following day, 19 September, Beria issued orders establishing the Upravlenie po Delam Voennoplennykh [UPV—Administration for Prisoner-of-War Affairs] and setting up camps for the Polish prisoners of war. Seven of these camps were to serve at first as transit-distribution centers, but three were to become special prisoner-of-war camps—Kozelsk, Ostashkov, and Starobelsk—and four were to become labor camps (doc. 9; see map 4).[66] The UPV was subordinated to Beria, as was the division commander, Deputy Commissar of Internal Affairs Ivan Maslennikov, who was responsible for NKVD border, convoy, and interior troops. It was, however, the 1st Deputy Commissar of Gosudarstven-naia Bezopasnost [GB—State Security] Vsevolod Merkulov, one of Beria's closest collaborators and a personal friend, who kept a close eye on Polish prisoner-of-war affairs.[67]

Beria immediately gave orders to organize the collection of data/evidence on specific categories of "anti-Soviet" prisoners. The whole Polish officer contingent was subjected to detailed investigation. They were to be "infiltrated" by agents and informers recruited from among the prisoners. Prisoners of war belonging to specific categories were to be "arrested" in the camps on the basis of material provided by agents and informers. In a decree of 8 October 1939, Beria listed the anti-Soviet groups to be uncovered and penetrated, "chiefly among former members of Polish c-r political parties, officers, and military officials" (doc. 16). These were the same categories of people as those listed for arrest in Beria's directive of 15 September 1939, just before the Red Army marched into eastern Poland.[68]

On 2 October the Politburo approved the proposals submitted by Beria and Mekhlis, head of the Red Army Political Administration, to place higher-ranking Polish officers and officials in Starobelsk; the police, intelligence agents, and prison guards in Ostashkov; and privates from the German part of Poland in Kozelsk and Putivl (doc. 14). It was soon obvious, however, that Starobelsk could not hold all the officers and officials, so several thousand were sent to Kozelsk, which became an officer camp after the departure of the privates in late October. Privates coming from German Poland were to be held until negotiations took place with the Germans and a decision was made whether to return them to their homeland. In the same decision of 2 October, the Politburo agreed to release 800 Czechs captured while serving in the Polish Army, after each signed a statement that he would not fight against the USSR. Unlike the Czechs, who were traditionally pro-Russian, remembered Soviet diplomatic support for their country in the Munich Crisis, and had not lost any territory to the Soviet Union, the vast majority of captured Polish officers viewed the USSR as no better than Nazi Germany. Some, however, told the politruks they would like to see Russia as Poland's ally against Germany.[69]

As it turned out, not only regular officers but also reserve officers, retired officers, some noncommissioned officers, policemen, and members of paramilitary youth organizations were detained in the prisoner-of-war camps. When Nikolai Smirnov, commander of the Putivl distribution camp, inquired about the release of some reserve officers, UPV head Pyotr Soprunenko instructed him on 23 October 1939 that professors, journalists, physicians, artists, and other specialists detained in the camp were to remain there together with intelligence agents, gendarmes, police, prominent military officials, those active in anti-Soviet political parties, landowners, and princes. Soprunenko wrote that these persons were not subject to release even if they were residents of Western Belorussia, Western Ukraine, or Polish territory ceded to Germany (doc. 22). The same instruction was sent on 27 October to Pavel Borisovets, commander of Ostashkov camp. When Polish physicians and pharmacists referred to the Geneva Convention in their plea for release and Aleksandr Berezhkov, commander of Starobelsk camp, asked for instructions, he was told that it was not the Geneva Convention but the NKVD UPV that should guide him in his work.[70]

Some Polish officers not taken prisoner in September 1939 escaped to Lithuania and were interned there.[71] On 9 November the Sovnarkom [SNK—Council of People's Commissars] approved the voluntary entry into the USSR of former Polish military personnel interned in Lithuania. The privates were to be sent home, but the officers, military officials, and police were to be sent to two camps where they would be subject to "selection." This was to be treated as top secret (doc. 27), perhaps to prevent other Polish officers interned in Lithuania from going into hiding. (Most of those who remained interned in the Baltic States were transferred to prisoner-of-war camps in the USSR after the Soviet military occupation of those countries and the "elections" in 1940.) On 3 December 1939 the Politburo also approved the arrest of all registered officers of the former Polish Army, that is, those registered in former eastern Poland. The arrests were carried out a few days later (docs. 31, 33, 34). To ensure that all captive Polish officers were placed in the camps, Aleksandr Zverev, head of the NKVD Upravlenie Ispravitelno-Trudovykh Kolonii [UITK—Administration of Correctional Labor Colonies], was instructed on 15 December to send "recuperated" officers to Kozelsk camp and police and gendarme officers to Ostashkov camp. Privates who were residents of German Poland were to be sent to Brest-Litovsk [Brześć-Litewski] for delivery to the Germans, and residents of western Belorussia and western Ukraine were to be sent home (doc. 35). According to one estimate, about 10 percent of all Polish Army officer prisoners were Jewish.[72] Some of them, residents of German Poland, petitioned the Soviet authorities not to be sent home. However, most of these petitions were rejected (doc. 23).

Three Special NKVD Camps

The prisoners of war were brought to the camps partly by forced marches and partly by rail. Like most prisoners in the USSR, they traveled in crowded cattle cars with minimal food and drink. They could not wash, so they suffered from lice and bed bugs. When they arrived at the camps, the housing, kitchen, and other facilities proved inadequate for the large numbers involved.[73] By early November most of the privates had been released, so conditions improved. The higher-ranking officers were placed in Starobelsk; the overflow was transferred to Kozelsk; and the police and gendarmes were sent to Ostashkov.

Kozelsk camp lay near the Zhizdra River about 250 kilometers by rail southeast of Smolensk, 5 kilometers from the town of Kozelsk, and 7 kilometers from its railway station (see map 4). The camp site was an old dilapidated monastery known as the Optyn Hermitage, which included the *skit* (secluded part of a monastery) and a few barracks. Although the prisoners did not know it, they were imprisoned in a monastery complex famous in nineteenth-century Russia, the Kozelsk Vvedenskaia Optina Pustyn. It included a cathedral—the main building in which the prisoners were lodged—and the skit, where Gogol, Dostoevsky, and Tolstoy had written some of their works and where the Polish officers were interrogated. In 1939–1940 the church and monastery buildings were dilapidated and the whole complex was known as the Dom Otdykha Imenii Maxima Gorkogo [The Maxim Gorky Rest Home].[74] On 3 October 1939 the camp held 8,843 Polish military, including 117 officers, but by early November it held mostly officers. On 1 April 1940 the NKVD counted 4,599 prisoners, mostly officers, including four generals and an admiral.[75] There were 200 airmen in the camp, including a woman pilot, Janina Lewandowska, shot down in a reconnaissance plane in September 1939, who seems to have been the only female prisoner of war in the three special camps. According to information gathered by the wartime Polish government in London from officer survivors who left the USSR in 1942, reserve officers formed about half of the prisoners in Kozelsk camp. Among them were twenty-one docents (associate professors) and lecturers; more than 300 military and civilian physicians; and several hundred judges, prosecutors, attorneys, and other law officials. Several officers had engineering degrees, and several hundred were primary and middle school teachers.[76]

Ostashkov camp lay 165–170 kilometers west of Kalinin (Tver). It used the church buildings of the former Nil Hermitage, named after the saintly monk Nil (d. 1554), on Stolbny Island in Lake Seliger, which lies 10 kilometers from the town of Ostashkov.[77] On 28 September 1939, the camp held 8,731 prisoners; 12,235 arrived between that date and 29 October, and a total of 15,991 passed through the camp. Of these, 9,413 privates and noncommissioned officers resident in German Poland were released to the Germans; others were transferred to the Narkomchermet [NKChM—Narodny Komissariat Chernoi Metallurgii—People's Commissariat of Ferrous Metallurgy] to work in the mines. Ostashkov camp was designated for police and gendarmes but also held some army officers, Polish military settlers, law personnel, and others taken prisoner in former eastern Poland. Of the 6,364 prisoners in the camp on 16 March 1940, police officers numbered 288. These men, together with a few priests, landowners, and law personnel, had varying degrees of higher education. They were joined by more military settlers after Soprunenko, on 29 October 1939, instructed the commanders of all prisoner-of-war camps to send them to Ostashkov (doc. 24).[78] However, in late February 1940, the nonmilitary prisoners in the three camps were sent to NKVD prisons in the Kalinen/Tver, Smolensk, and Voroshilovgrad (Luhansk) regions (doc. 42).

Starobelsk camp was located about 210 kilometers southeast of Kharkov. As in the two other camps, the site was occupied by religious buildings, in this case an old monastery with two churches and barracks. This might have been the old Starobelskii-Skorbiashchenskii convent near Kharkov.[79] Unlike the other camps, Starobelsk also took over some buildings in the town itself. The number of prisoners brought here between 28 September and 16 November 1939 was 11,262. On 14 October the camp held 7,045 men, including 4,813 privates and noncommissioned officers, 2,232 officers, and 155 civil servants and gendarmes. The privates were soon released, however, while other non-officer prisoners were transferred to prisons in late February 1940. Starobelsk held the greatest number of high-ranking officers, including eight generals. It is estimated that of the 3,893 prisoners present on 1 April 1940, the reserve officers included many with civilian professions, including several hundred university professors and lecturers; about 400 physicians; several hundred engineers, lawyers, and other law personnel; middle and primary school teachers; poets and journalists; social welfare workers; and some politicians.[80]

Details of Polish prisoner-of-war life in the three special camps can be found in reports by NKVD UPV inspectors, camp commanders, and commissars. In early October inspectors found a disastrous situation in Kozelsk, which was unprepared for large numbers of prisoners. The monastery buildings and barracks had no windows. They had been equipped with two-tier instead of three-tier bunks, so many prisoners had to sleep on the floor, and some had to take turns sleeping. There was not enough water; the bathhouse and laundries were out of order; and the kitchen could provide only one hot meal a day. There was no straw for mattresses, no dishes, changes of underwear, or warm clothes. The situation was somewhat better, though still far from satisfactory, in late November, when Soprunenko and Commissar Semyon Nekhoroshev visited the camp (doc. 30). The memoirs of Kozelsk survivor Stanisław Swianiewicz, a professor at the Stefan Batory University, Wilno, and diaries found on the bodies exhumed at Katyn confirm the bad living conditions, inadequate food, and poor medical facilities at Kozelsk.

Similar conditions were noted in a 3 October inspection report on Starobelsk, which stated that the camp was not prepared to receive prisoners: there were inadequate supplies of materials, vegetables, and other food, and the living quarters were inadequately furnished. By late November, however, much had been done to improve the situation (doc. 32).[81] These reports are confirmed and fleshed out by more extensive information on Starobelsk in the memoirs of the artist Józef Czapski and his fellow prisoner Bronisław Młynarski.[82]

Little is known about conditions in Ostashkov because the two accounts known thus far were written by prisoners transferred to German captivity in October 1939.[83] These accounts also speak of crowded housing and generally inadequate amounts of poor food. The prisoners did a great deal of work to improve housing in return for extra food. They also built a dike to connect the island with the mainland (doc. 83). On a poignant note, Ostashkov prisoners discovered an inscription on the foundations of the landing gateway at Stolbny Island: "Kowalski, 1863." They saw it as a symbol of the continuing martyrdom of the Polish nation.[84]

Polish memoirs mention constant hunger because the prisoners of war never had enough to eat. The standard daily fare was two servings of very thin soup, often with bits of rotten fish, rarely meat, and two small rations of soggy black bread. No vegetables and little if any sugar were provided—facts also mentioned in NKVD reports—and the tobacco ration was inadequate for smokers. The prisoners sold valuables—those not lost to thieves or confiscation—to acquire rubles with which to buy food and other goods. When these private sales were forbidden, they sold their valuables to the Glaviuvelirtorg [Main Jewelry Trade Administration], but were not allowed to receive more than 50 rubles at a time which they could spend in one month, although according to Beria's regulations, they could possess up to 150 rubles per month. In any case, the "shops" that intermittently came to the camps always sold out immediately—partly because they had few goods to begin with and partly because the camp's NKVD officers bought goods for themselves at the shop's back door, as was the case in Starobelsk and probably the other two camps as well.[85] The shortages were alleviated for some prisoners by parcels from home. These were sent to prisoners of war in all three camps between the end of November or early December 1939 and mid-March 1940, when correspondence with families was allowed. The camp personnel helped themselves to part of the parcel contents, but the recipients shared what they had with less fortunate colleagues.

Housing was always crowded. Medical service, generally performed by Polish doctors, was hampered by an almost total lack of medications. Officers had to do some heavy physical work, such as gathering wood for the kitchen and hauling water. They complained that such work was exhausting, not only for the old and sick prisoners but also for the healthy ones who worked on starvation rations. The prisoners also had to construct tiers of bunks, barracks, and other buildings. Prisoner labor reduced upkeep costs to the Soviet state (food, lodging, etc.) as pointed out in the final report of the Ostashkov camp commander, Pavel Borisovets (doc. 83).

The prisoners were subjected to many restrictions, the most onerous of which at first was lack of contact with relatives. They worried about the fate of their families, for they could not correspond with them, a right they allegedly possessed even according to Beria's regulations on the treatment of prisoners of war.[86] They complained and demanded permission to correspond with their families (doc. 20). In late November–early December 1939 they were finally granted the right to write one letter or postcard per month and to receive mail. This correspondence gave them and their relatives much comfort until it was canceled in mid-March 1940. By that time, of course, their existence and postal addresses were known not only to their families and to the German authorities but also to the Polish government-in-exile, which functioned in France from late September until mid-June 1940. After the French defeat by the Germans, it relocated to London.

Other restrictions pertained to religious practices and cultural-educational activities. At first, religious services were held openly. A survivor of Starobelsk noted: "Prisoners of the Mosaic [Jewish], Protestant, and Orthodox faiths participated en masse in Catholic services . . . and joined in the fraternal singing of religious hymns."[87] However, religious services were prohibited almost immediately, as were public prayer and hanging crosses on walls (doc. 32). Later, services were held secretly in dark corners of the former church buildings, where most of the prisoners in each camp were housed. In Kozelsk, a few minutes' silence was proclaimed by an anonymous speaker each evening, when the prisoners could pray.[88] Forty-five members of the military clergy— Catholic, Protestant, and Jewish—including the chief rabbi of the Polish Army, Major Baruch Steinberg, were prisoners in the camps. Most of the clergy held in Starobelsk and Kozelsk were removed over Christmas, 1939, and taken to Moscow. They were sent back to the camps later, though not always the same ones. Out of the forty-five clergymen held in the three camps, only two survived; in July 1940 they were joined by five others, presumably interned earlier in Lithuania.[89]

The officers in Kozelsk and Starobelsk immediately organized discussion groups and lectures by specialists on various subjects. When this type of activity was forbidden, it continued in secret. Another forbidden activity was playing cards, prohibited in the USSR at this time as a "capitalist" game. The Starobelsk prisoners also defied the authorities on 11 November 1939 with a special celebration of Polish Independence Day. Prisoners housed in the large church celebrated the holiday with recitals of patriotic poems by the Polish national poet Adam Mickiewicz (1798–1855) and some contemporary poets.[90] The moving spirits in organizing cultural activities in Starobelsk, judged "c-r" (counterrevolutionary) by the NKVD, were Captain Mieczysław Ewert, Captain Ludwik Domoń (misspelled in NKVD reports as Domel), and Lieutenant Stanisław Kwolek. In a 3 December 1939 report by

Starobelsk camp commander Berezhkov and camp commissar Mikhail Kirshin, all three were charged with "c-r" activity under the cover of cultural work. They were also charged with inspiring resistance to camp regulations and telling fellow prisoners to always speak Polish when some, to please their captors, took to speaking Russian. Domoń was involved in another illegal activity, that of organizing a monetary fund from which prisoners could borrow cash to be returned after the war (doc. 32). Kwolek committed the crime of making and displaying a large, wooden cross.[91] He was taken out of the camp immediately after 11 November, together with Captains Józef Rytel and Mieczysław Ewert, and all three were placed in NKVD Prison no. 5 in Kharkov. They escaped the executions of spring 1940 but were charged a few months later with anti-Soviet activity and sentenced to eight years in the GULAG. Domoń, Rytel, and Ewert survived to join the Polish Army in the USSR in 1941–1942. Kwolek, however, who suffered from tuberculosis, was deprived of medical care in prison after March 1940 and also in the labor camp he was sent to in Komi Autonomous Soviet Socialist Republic [ASSR], where he died in April 1941. In May 1989 all three were declared innocent of anti-Soviet activity.[92]

NKVD political workers devoted a great deal of time and effort to the political "reeducation" of the Polish prisoners of war. They were shown Soviet films, a long list of which is given in the NKVD report on Starobelsk camp dated 3 December 1939 (doc. 32). They could read Russian as well as Polish communist newspapers published in western Ukraine and western Belorussia. They were subjected to a constant loudspeaker barrage of news and propaganda, as well as Soviet songs—in particular, one which described the USSR as "the only land of true freedom." The official goal of NKVD "mass political work" was rehabilitation, which meant conversion to communism, but the real objective was the recruitment of prisoners as informers or agents.

It is clear, however, that political education had little effect on the prisoners. The officers listened to the political talks but often heckled the politruks; they went to see the films but protested against those defaming Poland (doc. 39). They used newspapers mostly for cigarette and toilet paper, uses also common in Soviet life outside the camps. NKVD reports mention the patriotism of the officers, most of whom believed that Poland would rise again in its previous shape (doc. 30). In Kozelsk there was even a mini-underground press. Two handwritten newspapers circulated for a while before their editors were discov-

ered and punished. After this, news was generally presented orally after lights out by specially designated persons whose identity was never
discovered.[93] In Ostashkov prisoners organized a small musical group
that played Polish folk music on handmade instruments. They also
sang patriotic songs, some whose verses have survived. These spoke of
the prisoners' longing and pain and of the enemies who came by
stealth like criminals to tear at their country, of going into captivity
without complaint, mourned by mothers and wives and in the prayers
and tears of children. The last verse said: "When we are needed, if fate
so decrees, we will not think of wounds and graves, and for Thee,
beloved country, we will give our lives."[94]

NKVD Interrogations and Investigations

During the whole period between their capture in September 1939
and the "clearing out of the camps" in spring 1940, the prisoners were
constantly subjected to interrogations, mostly at night. They were
questioned about their prewar activities, their political views, their
families and friends. Most of the NKVD interrogators were ignorant
of the world outside the USSR. For example, Reserve Captain Józef
Czapski—an artist who had spent eight years in Paris—wrote that his
Starobelsk interrogators were convinced that he had been sent there by
the Polish foreign minister as a spy to draw a plan of the city. They
could not believe that a city map could be bought for a few cents at the
newsstands on every street corner in Paris.[95] More sophisticated interrogators proposed "cooperation" to selected prisoners if they would
either report on their colleagues in the camp or perform intelligence
work on the other side of the "cordon" (the German-Soviet demarcation border in Poland) or elsewhere. Colonel (later General) Zygmunt
Berling, who declared his willingness to cooperate, wrote in his memoirs that he angered his interrogator by rejecting a proposal to report
on colleagues either in the camp or in Vilnius, if sent there.[96] Despite
his refusal, Berling was chosen to survive along with a group of about
sixty Starobelsk prisoners of war who reacted positively to NKVD
proposals, or declared readiness to serve in the Red Army, or stated
that they preferred to stay in the USSR rather than go home, the
choices offered to them.

The most intensive interrogations took place from late November
1939 to the end of January 1940. At this time, special NKVD officers

were sent from Moscow to the three camps. They were given powers overriding those of the camp commanders and commissars (doc. 26). These men were more educated and sophisticated than the camp interrogators, which was especially true of NKVD Major Vasily Zarubin who had spent several years at Soviet diplomatic posts in Western Europe.[97] He employed his cultural prowess and courtesy to extract more information from the Polish officers in Kozelsk camp than the "Special Section" had managed to do earlier.[98]

Why did the NKVD conduct this special intelligence operation in the three camps at this time? Perhaps a decision was made in Moscow to carry out a more efficient operation than the one implemented by the camp intelligence personnel in order to select prisoners who might be useful to the Soviet government and sentence the rest. Perhaps the operation was directly connected with the outbreak of the Soviet-Finnish War (30 November 1939) and Soviet fear of Western intervention. Perhaps the goal was to have reliable prisoner data on hand in case of negotiations with the Polish government for their release. Whatever the case may be, no documents have been found from late 1939–early 1940 stating what was to be done with the prisoners. Very little has been found on the special investigations, and most of them deal with Ostashkov. Sometime in November 1939, Soprunenko proposed using the policemen prisoners of war to replace prisoner-of-war residents of Western Ukraine and Western Belorussia working at Construction Site no. 1 (the Novograd Volynsky–Lvov highway) and in the Narkomchermet mining operations who wanted to go home (doc. 29).

This proposal was not taken up, but Soprunenko's suggestion may have inspired Beria to send a special investigation brigade headed by Lieutenant Stepan Belolipetsky to Ostashkov on 4 December 1939. At the end of December, Beria ordered the brigade to prepare all the Ostashkov cases for presentation to the NKVD Osoboe Soveshchanie [OSO—NKVD Special Board] by the end of January 1940, and Soprunenko himself was ordered to proceed to Ostashkov with ten NKVD officers to oversee the operation. Beria specified that cases of "operational" [intelligence] interest were to be selected separately in order to expose the prisoners' contacts both in the USSR and abroad and that former Polish intelligence service agents were to be probed for knowledge about persons sent at a previous time to the USSR. The prisoners of operational interest belonged, in fact, mostly to the same categories as those listed in Beria's directive of 8 October (doc. 16), to which he referred in his directive of 31 December (doc. 37). Beria ordered similar operations for Kozelsk and Starobelsk, but without mentioning the OSO.

Soprunenko and Belolipetsky reported to Beria on 1 February 1940 that the investigation in Ostashkov was finished and the cases were being transferred to the OSO (doc. 40). The only documented case that has survived, out of thousands of cases for both police and army prisoners, is that of policeman Szczepan Olejnik, dated 6 January 1940. He was born in 1911 in the village of Tarnovka [Tarnówka], Volhynia [Wołyń], and served in the town of Borschev [Borszczów], today in western Ukraine. Olejnik was indicted on the basis of Article 58, Paragraph 13, of the Criminal Code of the Russian Soviet Republic (the paragraph is the same in the code of the Soviet Union), which specified as a crime any active struggle against the working class or the revolutionary movement, either under the tsarist regime, which collapsed in March 1917, or during the Civil War of 1918–1922 (doc. 38). Of course, the accused was too young to have committed such a crime in those years, so it is clear that Article 58, Paragraph 13, of the Criminal Code was stretched to cover any alleged anti-Soviet activity after 1917. Nor is there any mention of evidence or witnesses, so it seems that Olejnik was convicted simply because, as a Polish policeman, he must have "struggled against the revolutionary movement" or "the working class." If this is correct, it is possible that those prisoners in the three special camps whose cases were actually completed before Stalin decided to have all of them shot, were convicted on the basis of Article 58, Paragraph 13, of the Soviet Criminal Code. The same would apply to the other prisoners transferred from the three camps to NKVD jails in western Ukraine and western Belorussia, as well as those already held in these jails. Olejnik was shot with the other Ostashkov policemen in Kalinin (Tver).

The special investigations of the Polish prisoners of war in the three special camps and of the casework in Ostashkov may have been connected with "clearing out" the camps, originally perhaps to hold expected Finnish prisoners of war from the Soviet-Finnish War (30 November 1939–12 March 1940). The constant counting of the Polish officer prisoners, however, along with their classification by rank, prewar residence, and nationality (docs. 28, 36, 43, 44), may have been related to other plans. Their fate does not appear to have been sealed either during the investigation period or even somewhat later. On 20 February 1940, Soprunenko sent Beria the UPV proposals regarding the army officers. He suggested that about 300 sick men in the Kozelsk and Starobelsk officer contingents, as well as invalids and men over sixty, be sent home. He proposed the same for some 400–500 reserve officers, residents of the western regions of Soviet Ukraine and Soviet Belorussia, who were farmers, engineers, technicians, physicians, and teachers. At the same time, however, he requested permission to draw up cases against officers of the KOP, law personnel, landowners, activists of the Polska Organizacja Wojskowa [P.O.W.—Polish Military Organization], the Sokół [Hawk—a Polish sports-education organization], and intelligence and information officers, about 400 men in all. He proposed that these cases be examined by the OSO. Finally, Soprunenko suggested that the investigation of the above categories of prisoners take place in the Belorussian and Ukrainian Commissariats of Internal Affairs, or, if this was not feasible, he proposed concentrating all the prisoners in the specified categories in Ostashkov camp and conducting the investigation there (doc. 41).

Soprunenko's proposals indicate that at this time, even the head of UPV thought it possible to release old and sick officers, as well as certain categories of reserve officers whose civilian professions could make them useful to the USSR. There is no documented Beria reply, but it is clear that he rejected this part of Soprunenko's report; the other part may have inspired the commissar to issue a directive that certain categories of prisoners, targeted from the beginning, be taken out of the camps and transferred to detention elsewhere. Thus, on 22 February 1940, Deputy Commissar of State Security Merkulov ordered that all former prison guards, intelligence agents, provocateurs, military settlers, law personnel, landowners, merchants, and large property holders held in the three special camps be transferred to prisons and the control of *oblast* [administrative region] NKVD organs. All the materials collected on them were to be transferred to the appropriate investigative units of the NKVD administration (doc. 42). Beria's more detailed directive to this end stipulated that the transfer be carried out in "absolute secrecy." Unlike the Soprunenko-Nekhoroshev proposal, Beria's directive did not mention the OSO.

In any case, it seems that army officers and police were to be subjected to special treatment at this time. Thus, a few days later, on 26 February, Soprunenko informed Berezhkov at Starobelsk camp that Commissar Nekhoroshev's instructions for a second round of filling out prisoners' personal data (presumably on special cards) had been approved by Beria. Berezhkov was therefore to continue the work of filling out the detailed information on all the prisoners, especially the supplementary questions in the personal questionnaire.[99] On 27 February, Ivan Makliarsky, head of the UPV Uchetno-Registratsionny Otdel NKVD SSSR [URO—Records Registration Department, UPV NKVD USSR], sent a similar instruction to Vasily Korolev, Kozelsk camp commander, who was also told to provide four photographs of each officer and higher-level civil servant. The supplementary questions were probably related to those sent out in early January 1940.[100] This may or may not have been connected with the prisoners' impending doom. However that may be, on 5 March 1940, the Politburo decided that they were to be shot (doc. 47). For a discussion of this decision, see the introduction to Part II.

The text of the Non-Aggression Pact between Germany and the USSR had been agreed on before German Foreign Minister Joachim von Ribbentrop arrived in Moscow on 23 August 1939. Both German and Russian documents use the term "treaty," but in historical literature it is called a "pact."

· 1 ·

Non-Aggression Pact between Germany and the Soviet Union
23 August 1939, Moscow

Treaty of Non-Aggression between Germany and the Soviet Union

The Government of the USSR and the Government of Germany
Guided by the desire to strengthen the cause of peace between the USSR and Germany, and proceeding from the basic provisions of the neutrality pact concluded between the USSR and Germany in April 1926,[101] we have reached the following accord:

Article I
Both Contracting Parties obligate themselves to refrain from any violence, any aggressive action, or any attack on each other either separately or in conjunction with other powers.

Article II
In the event that one of the Contracting Parties becomes the object of military actions on the part of a third power, the other Contracting Party shall not in any way support that power.

Article III
The Governments of both Contracting Parties shall remain in contact with one another in the future for [the purpose of] consultation, in order to inform each other on issues affecting their common interests.

Article IV
Neither of the Contracting Parties shall participate in any grouping of powers that is aimed directly or indirectly at the other party.

Article V
In the event that disputes or conflicts arise between the Contracting Parties on issues of one kind or another, both parties shall resolve these disputes or conflicts exclusively in a peaceful way through the friendly exchange of opinions or, if necessary, by creating a commission to settle the conflict.

Article VI
This treaty is concluded for a period of ten years,[102] and unless one of the Contracting Parties denounces it one year before its expiration, the treaty shall be considered as automatically extended for the next five years.

Article VII
This treaty is subject to ratification within the shortest possible time. The exchange of ratification documents must take place in Berlin. The treaty shall go into force immediately upon its signature.[103]

Done in two originals, in the German and Russian languages, in Moscow, on 23 August 1939.

<table>
<tr><td>On the Authority
of the USSR Government
V. Molotov</td><td>For the Government
of Germany
I[J]. Ribbentrop</td></tr>
</table>

The outlines of the territorial agreement were sketched out in secret German-Soviet talks in Berlin in July-August 1939. The provisions of the Secret Supplementary Protocol were negotiated in the Kremlin by Molotov and Ribbentrop with the help of their legal experts on the night of 23–24 August 1939.

· 2 ·

Secret Supplementary Protocol to the Non-Aggression Pact
between Germany and the Soviet Union
23 August 1939, Moscow

Secret Supplementary Protocol to the Treaty of Non-Aggression
between Germany and the Soviet Union

Upon signing the Non-Aggression Treaty between Germany and the
Union of Soviet Socialist Republics,[104] the undersigned plenipotentiaries
of both parties discussed in strict confidentiality the issue of delimiting
their respective spheres of interest in Eastern Europe. This discussion led
to the following result:

1. In the event of a territorial and political restructuring of the regions
belonging to the Baltic States (Finland, Estonia, Latvia, Lithuania), the
northern border of Lithuania shall simultaneously be the border between
the spheres of interest of Germany and the USSR. In this regard, Lithuania's interests with respect to the Vilna [Wilno, Vilnius] region shall be recognized by both parties.

2. In the event of a territorial and political restructuring of the regions
that are part of the Polish state, the border between the spheres of interest
of Germany and the USSR shall approximately follow the line of the
Narew, Wisla [Wisła], and San Rivers.[105]

The question of whether it is desirable in their mutual interests to preserve an independent Polish state, and, if so, what the borders of this state
would be, can be definitively clarified only in the course of further political developments.

In any case, both governments will resolve this question by amicable
mutual agreement.[106]

3. Regarding southeastern Europe, the Soviet side emphasizes the
USSR's interest in Bessarabia. The German side declares its complete political disinterest in these regions.

4. This protocol will be kept in strict secrecy by both parties.

> Moscow, 23 August 1939
> On the Authority   For the Government
> of the USSR Government   of Germany
> V. Molotov   I[J]. Ribbentrop

The German attack on Poland began at dawn, 1 September 1939.
Polish armies retreated before an overwhelming foe but fought battles

in central and southeastern Poland while Warsaw suffered a devastating siege by German artillery and dive bombers, 7–27 September. Historians give different reasons for Stalin's resistance to German pressure to send Soviet forces into eastern Poland, but it was probably due to a combination of factors: uncertainty as to what military action would be taken by Warsaw's Western allies; a desire to conclude peace with Japan; military supply problems in the western USSR; and a desire to wait until the fall of the Polish capital was imminent. In any case, although the military orders for the Ukrainian and Belorussian fronts were first dated 9 September, the date was changed to 14 September and the final orders for battle readiness were set for the end of the day on the 16th for the Ukrainian and the dawn of the 17th for the Belorussian front. The order below set forth the political orientation for the Red Army troops involved.

· 3 ·

Order no. 005 of the Military Council of the Belorussian Front to the Troops
on the Goals of the Red Army's Entry into Western Belorussia
16 September 1939, Smolensk

Secret
Order no. 005 of the Military Council of the Belorussian Front
16 September 1939, Smolensk

Comrade Red Army Soldiers, Commanders, and Political Workers!

The Polish landowners and capitalists have enslaved the working people of Western Belorussia and Western Ukraine.[107]

Through the use of White terror, field courts-martial, and punitive expeditions, they are suppressing the revolutionary movement, imposing national oppression and exploitation, and sowing ruin and devastation.[108]

The Great Socialist Revolution gave the Polish people the right to secede.[109] Polish landowners and capitalists, having crushed the revolutionary movement of workers and peasants, seized Western Belorussia and Western Ukraine, deprived these peoples of their Soviet homeland, and shackled them in the chains of bondage and oppression.[110]

The rulers of the lords' Poland have now thrown our Belorussian and Ukrainian brothers into the meat grinder of a second imperialist war.[111]

National oppression and the enslavement of laborers led Poland to military defeat.

The oppressed peoples of Poland are facing the threat of total ruin and extermination by their enemies.

In Western Ukraine and Belorussia a revolutionary movement is spreading. Demonstrations and uprisings by the Belorussian and Ukrainian peasantry in Poland have begun. The working class and peasantry of Poland are uniting their forces in order to wring the necks of their bloody oppressors.[112]

Comrade fighters, commanders, and political workers of the Belorussian Front, our revolutionary duty and obligation is to render immediate assistance and support to our brother Belorussians and Ukrainians in order to rescue them from the threat of ruin and massacre by their enemies.

In fulfilling this historic task, we have no intention of violating the non-aggression pact between the USSR and Germany.[113] We cannot allow the enemies of the Belorussian and Ukrainian peoples to harness them to a new yoke of exploitation and ruin, or to subject them to massacre and mockery.

We come not as conquerors but as liberators of our brother Belorussians and Ukrainians and the workers of Poland.[114]

I ORDER:

1. Units of the Belorussian Front shall act decisively to aid the workers of Western Belorussia and Western Ukraine, moving all along the front in a decisive offensive.

2. In a lightning, crushing blow, rout the lordly-bourgeois Polish troops and liberate the workers, peasants, and laborers of Western Belorussia.

Under the slogans "For our happy Soviet homeland" and "For our great Stalin," let us fulfill our military oath and our duty to our homeland.

The order shall be read out loud in all companies, batteries, squadrons, escadrilles, and garrisons, starting at 1600 hours, 16 September 1939.

> Troop Commander of the Belorussian Front
> Army Commander 2nd Rank Kovalev
>
> Members of the Military Council of the Belorussian Front:
> Corps Commissar Susaikov
> Divisional Commissar Smokachev
> Divisional Commander Gusev
> Ponomarenko

On 14 September, Molotov had informed the German ambassador in Moscow, Friedrich Werner von der Schulenburg, that Soviet military action could begin earlier than expected. On the same day, Ribbentrop sent Schulenburg a memorandum stating that Warsaw would fall in the next few days. At 2 a.m. on 17 September, Stalin, Molotov, and Schulenburg agreed on the text of the note to be handed to the Polish ambassador. Immediately thereafter, Soviet Deputy Commissar for Foreign Affairs Vladimir Potemkin roused Polish Ambassador Wacław Grzybowski and requested him to come to his office. He tried to hand the note to Grzybowski and, when the latter refused to accept it, had it delivered to the Polish Embassy while the ambassador was still in his office. Grzybowski did, however, agree to notify the Polish government of the contents of the note. The Soviet note was sent to all the heads of foreign diplomatic missions in Moscow, with the statement that the Soviet government would conduct a policy of neutrality toward their countries.

· 4 ·

Soviet Government Note Handed to the Polish Ambassador
in the USSR, Wacław Grzybowski
17 September 1939, Moscow

Mr. Ambassador!

The Polish-German War has revealed the internal bankruptcy of the Polish state. In ten days of hostilities, Poland has lost all its industrial regions and cultural centers. Warsaw no longer exists as the capital of Poland.[115] The Polish government has collapsed and shows no signs of life. This means that the Polish state and its government have, in fact, ceased to exist.[116] Therefore, the agreements concluded between the USSR and Poland have ceased to operate.[117] Left to its own devices and bereft of leadership, Poland has become a fertile field for all kinds of accidents and surprises, which could pose a threat to the USSR. Therefore, the Soviet government, which has been neutral until now, can no longer maintain a neutral attitude toward these facts.

Nor can the Soviet government remain indifferent to the fact that its kindred Ukrainian and Belorussian peoples, living on Polish territory, are abandoned to their fate and left unprotected.[118]

In view of this state of affairs, the Soviet government has directed the High Command of the Red Army to order troops to cross the frontier and to take under their protection the lives and property of the population of Western Ukraine and Western Belorussia.

At the same time, the Soviet government intends to take all measures to liberate the Polish people from the disastrous war into which they have been dragged by their unwise leaders and to give them the opportunity to live a peaceful life.

Please accept, Mr. Ambassador, assurances of my sincere respect,

People's Commissar for Foreign Affairs of the USSR
V. Molotov

· 5 ·

From the Official Diary of Soviet Deputy People's Commissar of Foreign Affairs
Potemkin on a Conversation with Polish Ambassador Grzybowski
17 September 1939, Moscow

Secret
Extract no. 2
From the Diary of V. P. Potemkin
No. 5483
Meeting with Polish Ambassador Grzybowski,
17 September 1939
3:15 a.m.

To the ambassador, woken up by us at 2 a.m., who arrived at the Commissariat for Foreign Affairs at 3 a.m. visibly frightened, I read Comrade Molotov's note to the Polish government.[119]

The ambassador, pronouncing the words with difficulty due to his agitation, declared to me that he could not accept the note handed to him. He rejects the evaluation of the Polish military and political situation contained in the note. The ambassador considers that the Polish-German War is just beginning and that one cannot speak of the collapse of the Polish state. The main forces of the Polish Army are untouched and are preparing to mount a decisive counterattack against the German armies. In these circumstances, the Red Army's crossing of the Polish frontier constitutes a completely unprovoked attack on the [Polish] Republic. The ambassador refuses to inform [his] government of the Soviet note, which [he says] tries to justify this attack by unfounded statements that Poland has been allegedly smashed by the Germans and that the Polish government no longer exists.[120]

I countered Grzybowski [by saying] that he could not refuse to accept the note handed to him. This document, coming from the government of the USSR, contains declarations of the utmost importance, about which the ambassador is obliged to immediately inform his government. The ambassador would be burdened with a very heavy responsibility to his own country if he rejected carrying out this, his most important obligation. The question of Poland's fate is being decided. The ambassador does not have the right to hide from his own country the declarations contained in the note of the Soviet government, addressed to the Polish Republic.

Grzybowski clearly did not know how to counter the above arguments. He attempted to argue that our note should be handed to the Polish government through our embassy. I replied that we no longer had an embassy in Poland. All its personnel are already in the USSR, except perhaps for a small number of purely technical workers.[121]

Then Grzybowski stated that he did not have any regular telegraphic contact with Poland. Two days ago, it was suggested that he contact [his] government through Bucharest. Now the ambassador is not certain whether he can utilize even this path.[122]

I asked the ambassador about the location of the Polish foreign minister [Józef Beck]. Having received the reply that he was most probably in Kremenets [Krzemieniec], I proposed to the ambassador that if he so wished, I could ensure the immediate transmission of his telegraphic reports through our lines [of communication].[123]

Grzybowski again repeated that he cannot accept the note, for it would not be in keeping with the dignity of the Polish government.

I told the ambassador that the note had been already read to him, so he knew its contents. If the ambassador did not want to take the note with him, it would be delivered to him at the embassy.

At this moment, having decided to send the note to the embassy and have it delivered in return for a receipt before the ambassador went back there, I asked Grzybowski to wait a few minutes for me, explaining that I intended to inform Com. [Comrade] Molotov by telephone of his statements.

After leaving [the room], I gave the order to use my car to send the note to the embassy, where a member of my secretariat was to deliver it and take a receipt.

Having informed Com. Molotov by telephone of the stand taken by the ambassador, I returned to Grzybowski and resumed the conversation. The ambassador again tried to prove that Poland was not at all crushed by Germany, all the more so because England and France were already demonstrating their real aid for it.[124] Referring to our entry into Polish territory, the ambassador cried that if it took place, it would mean the fourth partition of Poland and its annihilation.

I pointed out to the ambassador that our note heralded the liberation of the Polish people from war and our help for them to begin a peaceful life. Grzybowski could not calm down, arguing that we were helping the Germans to annihilate Poland. In this situation, the ambassador did not understand the practical sense of our informing the Polish government about the order for Soviet armies to cross into Polish territory.

I observed to the ambassador that when the Polish government received our note, it would perhaps not only understand the motives for our decision but also agree on the pointlessness of any counteraction to our entry [into Poland]. In this way, it might perhaps be possible to prevent armed clashes and unnecessary loss of life.[125]

Since I constantly returned to warning the ambassador of the responsibility he might bear to his own country in refusing to transmit our note to [his] government, Grzybowski finally began to give way. He declared to me that he would inform his government of the contents of our note. He even turned to me with the request to give him all possible help in [securing] the fastest way of sending telegraphic information to Poland. [But] regarding the note as a document, the ambassador [said] that, as before, he could not accept it.

I repeated to Grzybowski that the note would be delivered to him at the embassy.

After the ambassador left, I was informed that the note had been transported to the embassy and delivered there in return for a receipt while the ambassador was still with me.[126]

V. Potemkin

Extract sent to: J. Stalin, V. Molotov, and the Deputy Commissars of Foreign Affairs V. G. Dekanozov and S. A. Lozovsky.

The Polish commander in chief, Marshal Edward Śmigły-Rydz,[127] issued this order to the Polish armed forces just before crossing into Romania with the government to avoid capture by Soviet troops. Both the government and Śmigły-Rydz planned to proceed to Allied France and reconstruct the Polish Army there. Owing to German pressure on the Romanian government, most of the high officials and officers were interned in Romania, but on 30 September 1939 a new government was formed in France headed by General Władysław Sikorski as premier. He raised a new Polish army from some 35,000 soldiers who had traveled from Romania and Hungary to France and from Polish immigrant workers living in France. In November he became commander in chief of Polish armed forces.

· 6 ·

Order of the Commander in Chief of the Polish Army, Marshal
Edward Śmigły-Rydz, Regarding the Entry of Soviet Forces into Poland
17 September 1939, Kuty[128]

The Soviets have come in. I order a general retreat into Romania and Hungary by the shortest routes. Do not fight the Soviets except in case of their [attack] or attempts to disarm our units. The assignment for Warsaw and [Modlin] is unchanged: they are to defend themselves against the Germans.[129] [The towns] approached by the Soviets should negotiate with them to allow the garrisons to leave for Romania or Hungary.[130]

> Commander in Chief
> Marshal of Poland
> E. Śmigły-Rydz

Contrary to custom, the military did not look after prisoners of war. The NKVD took charge of the Polish prisoners of war as of 18 September 1939.

· 7 ·

Politburo Decision on Placing POW Reception Points under NKVD Protection (Excerpt)
18 September 1939, Moscow[131]

Top Secret
From the special file
To Comrades Beria and Safonov
No. P 7/150
18 September 1939
Excerpt from Minutes no. 7 of the TsK [Central Committee] Politburo
Meeting of 193[9]
Decision of 18 September 1939
150—Item of the KO [Komitet Oborony—Defense Committee]
On the transfer of USSR NKVD Convoy Troops to a wartime footing

Ratify the following decision of the KO:
1. To put the NKVD Convoy Troops in the Belorussian, Kiev, and Leningrad Special Military Districts on a wartime footing as of 20 September 1939.

2. To take under the protection of the NKVD Convoy Troops all POW reception points located in the Belorussian and Kiev Special Military Districts, also the camps and reception points for POWs in Kozelsk (BSSR) [Belorussian SSR, or Soviet Socialist Republic] and Putivl (UkSSR) [Ukrainian Soviet Socialist Republic].

Secretary, Central Committee

The NKVD institution established to be in charge of the Polish prisoners of war was the Upravlenie po Delam Voennoplennykh [UPV—Administration for Prisoner-of-War Affairs].

· 8 ·

Lavrenty P. Beria's Order no. 0308 on the Organization of the UPV
and POW Camps under the NKVD USSR
19 September 1939, Moscow

Secret
Order of the USSR People's Commissar of Internal Affairs
19 September 1939
No. 0308
Moscow

1. On the basis of the Regulations on Prisoners of War,[132] organize a Prisoner-of-War Administration under the NKVD USSR.
2. Approve the appended staff for the Prisoner-of-War Administration.[133]
3. Appoint Com. Major P. K. Soprunenko to be head of the Prisoner-of-War Administration and Regimental Commissar Com. Nekhoroshev to be commissar of the administration.
   Appoint as deputies to the head of the administration:
   1) GB [State Security] Lieutenant Com. I. I. Khokhlov
   2) Com. Major I. M. Polukhin for security
4. Organize the following eight camps to hold POWs:
   1) Ostashkov camp—use the buildings of the former NKVD children's colony on Stolobnoe [Stolbny] Island (in Lake Seliger), Kalinin Oblast [Administrative Region], for 7,000 persons, to be increased to 10,000 by 1 October.
   2) Yukhnov camp—use the buildings of the Pavlishchev Woods Sanatorium, Babynino Station, Western Railway, for 5,000 men, to be increased to 10,000 men by 1 October.

3) Kozelsk camp—use the buildings of the Gorky Rest Home at Kozelsk Station, Dzerzhinsky Railway, for 7,000 men, to be increased to 10,000 men by 1 October.

4) Putivl camp—use the buildings of the former Sofronevsk Monastery and peat works at Tetkino Station, Moscow-Kiev Railway, for 7,000 persons, to be increased to 10,000 by 25 October.

5) Kozelshchansk camp—use the buildings of the former Kozelshchansk Monastery at Kozelshchina Station, Southern Railway, for 5,000 persons, to be increased to 10,000 by 1 October.

6) Starobelsk camp—use the buildings of the former Starobelsk Monastery at Starobelsk Station, Moscow-Donbass [Donets coal basin] Railway, for 5,000 persons, to be increased to 8,000 by 1 October.

7) Yuzha camp—use the buildings of the former NKVD children's labor colony at Vyazniki Station, Northern Railway, for 3,000 persons, to be increased to 6,000 by 5 October.

8) Oranki camp—use the buildings of the former Oranki Monastery, at Znamenka Station, Moscow-Kazan Railway, for 2,000 persons, to be increased to 4,000 by 1 October.

5. Approve the appended standard staff contingent for POW camps ~~and the instruction on POW camps' operation and daily routine.~~ *[134]

6. Approve as commanders and commissars of the camps:

1) Ostashkov—
   Major Com. P. F. Borisovets as commander
   Senior Political Instructor I. V. [A.] Yurasov as commissar

2) Yukhnov—
   Major Com. F. I. Kadyshev as commander
   Battalion Commissar E. Sh. Gilchonok as commissar

3) Kozelsk—
   Major Com. V. N. Korolev as commander
   Senior Political Instructor M. M. Alekseev as commissar

4) Putivl—
   Major Com. N. N. Smirnov as commander
   Battalion Commissar S. P. Vasiagin as commissar

5) Kozelshchansk—
   GB 1st Lieutenant Com. V. L. Sokolov as commander
   Captain Com. F. S. Akulenko as commissar

6) Starobelsk—
   GB Captain Com. Berezhkov as commander
   Battalion Commissar Com. M. M. Kirshin as commissar

* Crossed out in Beria's hand.

7) Yuzha—
  GB 2nd Lieutenant Com. A. F. Kii as commander
  GB 1st Lieutenant Com. G. V. Korotkov as commissar
8) Oranki—
  GB 1st Lieutenant [I.] Sorokin as commander
  GB Lieutenant V. D. Kuznetsov as commissar

7. Assign Cheka operational servicing of POWs in the camps to the NKVD USSR Special Department and its local organs.[135]

Coms. Kobulov (responsible), Belianov, Soprunenko, and Kornienko shall, within two days' time, draw up the essential instructions to the NKVD District Special Departments and submit them to me for approval.[136]

8. Ratify the salary rates for the commanders and commissars of the camps: Ostashkov, Yukhnov, Kozelsk, Putivl, Kozelshchansk, and Starobelsk at 2,400 rubles; Yuzha and Oranki, at 2,000 rubles.[137]

Establish salary rates for workers in the administration and POW camps at the level of current wages in the GULAG [administration] and GULAG camps.[138]

9. Assign to the NKVD GULAG the [task of] drawing up requisitions and [ensuring] the timely utilization of funds for the provision of food, materials, and medical supplies.

Assign personal responsibility for provisioning the POW camps to my deputy divisional commander, Com. Chernyshov.

10. Assign the financing of the UPV and the POW camps to the USSR NKVD Tsentralny Finansovo Planovy Otdel [TsFPO—Central Financial Planning Department].

Assign personal responsibility for the financing of the UPV and the prisoner-of-war camps to USSR NKVD TsFPO Divisional Quartermaster Com. Berenzon.

11. My deputy, Divisional Commander Com. Maslennikov, shall provide for the organization of security at the reception points, the convoying of POWs during their transport from reception points to camps according to the orders of the head of the UPV, and the organization of security for the POW camps, for which he shall allocate the necessary number of convoy force subunits, according to the attached list of distribution.*

12. The head of the Kalinin Oblast UNKVD [NKVD Administration], Colonel Com. Tokarev; the head of the Smolensk Oblast UNKVD, GB Captain Com. Kuprianov; the head of the Chernigov Oblast UNKVD, GB Captain Com. Dmitriev; the head of the Poltava Oblast UNKVD, GB Captain Com. Bukhtiarov; the head of the Voroshilovgrad Oblast UNKVD, GB

---

* List not found in file.

Captain Com. Cherevatenko; the head of the Ivanovo Oblast UNKVD, GB Captain Com. Blinov; and the head of the Gorky Oblast UNKVD, GB Major Com. Fediukov, in conjunction with the heads and commissars of the camps, shall:

1) ensure in accordance with the mobilization plan of the Otdel Ispravitelno-Trudovykh Kolonii [OITK—Department of Correctional Labor Colonies] the development of the POW camps organized in accordance with point 7 of this order;[139]

2) following the typical staff contingent for camps ratified by this order, complete their personal contingent in accordance with the existing mobilization plan of the NKVD OITK;

3) for the purpose of rendering assistance in starting up the POW camps, delegate for a period of ten days:

To Kalinin Oblast, the deputy head of the GULAG Department, Com. Poliakov

To Smolensk Oblast, the deputy head of the GULAG, Brigade Commissar Com. Vasiliev

To Ivanovo Oblast, the head of the USSR NKVD OITK, GB 1st Lieutenant Com. Yatskevich

To Gorky Oblast, the deputy head of GULAG inspection, GB Lieutenant Com. Lobudev

My deputy, GB Commissar 3rd Rank Com. Kruglov shall, within two days' time, complete the personnel assignments for the USSR NKVD UPV.

USSR People's Commissar of Internal Affairs
GB Commissar 1st Rank L. Beria

GB Captain Pyotr Soprunenko headed the NKVD UPV, which had specified duties.

· 9 ·

Statute of the NKVD UPV[140]
Not before 19 September 1939, Moscow

I approve
People's Commissar of Internal Affairs, GB Commissar 1st Rank
(L. Beria), September 1939
Statute on [Establishing] the Administration
for Prisoner-of-War Affairs under the NKVD, USSR

I. General Regulations

1. The UPV forms a part of the USSR People's Commissariat of Internal Affairs as an independent administration.

The head of the UPV is subordinated to the People's Commissar of Internal Affairs.

The direct leadership of the UPV is carried out by Deputy People's Commissar of Internal Affairs, Divisional Commander Com. Chernyshov.

2. The head of the UPV heads the administration and directs its activities in accordance with the decisions of the USSR government on POWs, current orders of the USSR People's Commissar of Internal Affairs, and this statute.

3. The USSR NKVD UPV directly controls the organization of the camps: placement, reception, registration, maintenance, and the utilization of POWs for work. It draws up regulations on reception points and POW camps and issues instructions and directives on camp maintenance and internal regulations in the camps.

4. The head of the USSR NKVD UPV is responsible for the conditions at reception points and camps. He implements the day-to-day control of all the work of the administration and its organs in the territory.

II. Tasks of the Administration

The UPV is assigned the following tasks:

1) organization of POW reception points, distribution camps, and permanent camps in coordination with the RKKA [Worker-Peasant Red Army] General Staff.

2) reception of POWs from the RKKA field command.

3) timely evacuation of POWs from reception points to camps.

4) establishment of internal order at reception points and camps as well as the rules and system for maintaining custody of the POWs.

5) working out norms for providing POWs with housing space, clothing, food, and other essential items and organizing the procedure for supplying these items.

6) working out norms for a monetary allowance for POWs while they are in the camps.[141]

7) establishing limits for sums of money permitted to POWs while they are in the camps.

8) establishing the norms for and the assortment of foods allowed to be sent to POWs.

9) organizing the labor utilization of POWs in the industry and agriculture of the USSR according to the "Regulations on Prisoners of War."[142]

10) directing the political and cultural-educational work among POWs and developing the appropriate instructions.

11) issuing regulations on the procedure for the imposition and implementation of disciplinary punishment in accordance with the disciplinary and sentry regulations of the RKKA.

> Head of the USSR NKVD UPV
> (Soprunenko)

The Osoboe Otdelenie [OO—Special Section], responsible for intelligence work in each POW camp, was mandated to keep detailed records, to search for members of Polish prewar political parties, and to establish files for any such members as well as for all the officers. Document 10 shows the detailed recordkeeping mandated to the "Special Sections" in the POW camps; the search for members of Polish prewar political parties and other organizations; and the establishment of files for the above as well as for all the officers.

· 10 ·

USSR NKVD Instruction to the Osoboe Otdelenia [Special Sections]
of POW Camps on Recording Operational Data on the Prisoners
19 September 1939, Moscow

Top Secret
Instruction to Special Sections of Prisoner-of-War Camps of NKVD
USSR on Recording Operational Data on Prisoners of War

Records and Registration
To create a unified system of operational records on prisoners of war, the following procedure has been established:
1. For each prisoner of war, upon his arrival at the camp, the camp's Uchetno-Raspredelitelnoe Otdelenie Lagiera [URO—Reception, Records, and Barracks Assignment Section] immediately fills out and submits to the camp's OO [Special Section] a personal questionnaire and photograph (Enclosure no. 1) (Form no. 2).* [143]
2. For each prisoner of war, the [camp] OO fills out from the questionnaires two alphabetical cards [144] (Enclosure no. 3) and opens a record file [145] (Enclosure no. 4).
3. The record file for the prisoner of war is to be entered into the regis-

---

* None of the enclosures mentioned in this document were included with it.

tration ledger (Enclosure no. 8), whose ordinal numeral is to be the number of the record file.

The personal questionnaire is to be inserted in the record file.

4. The number of the record file is to be entered on the alphabetical cards, after which one card is to be inserted into the files of the [camp] OO and the second copy is to be sent to the corresponding 1st Spetsotdel [Special Department] of the NKVD-UNKVD in whose territory the camp is located.

On the cover of the record file a note shall be made as to when and where the index cards were sent and the outgoing number.

The work on records in each camp shall be conducted personally by a worker especially assigned to this task (in large camps, an operational records group).

On the Procedure for Opening Agent and Investigation Files
on Prisoners of War Present in the Camps

5. Files are to be established for POWs conducting anti-Soviet work, suspected of espionage activity, and those belonging to the PPS [Polish Socialist Party], "Piłsudski-ites," National Democrats, Social Democrats, anarchists, and other c-r parties and organizations,[146] as well as the entire officer contingent, and these files are to be registered in a separate ledger (Enclosure no. 6).

For each document-form created, [such as] an intelligence file or investigative file, one copy of the form (Enclosure, Form no. 1) is to be filled out and sent to the 1st Spetsotdel of the USSR NKVD in order [for the information] on anti-Soviet elements be reflected in the records.

6. Arrest formalities are to be implemented in conformity with USSR NKVD Order no. 00931 of 11 August 1939[147] and in accordance with the special recommendations of the USSR NKVD.

[Agent] Recruitment Formalities

7. The formalities connected with the recruitment of POWs in the camps are to be effected in accordance with USSR NKVD Order no. 00858 of 28 June 1939.[148]

Transmitting Prisoner-of-War Record Files

8. In case of the departure of POWs for other camps, their records and files, as well as the personal files of agents (informants) are to be sent by the [camp] OO to the NKVD organ [regional administration] at the place of departure of the POWs, and the appropriate notations are to be made [there] on the cards and in the ledgers.

9. For POWs released from the camps, files are to be sent to the appro-

priate 1st Spetsotdel of the NKVD (UNKVD), and notations are to be made in the card files.

Control over the organization of operational records for POWs in camps is assigned to the heads of the Special Departments of the NKVD military districts on whose territory the camps are located.

10. On the first of each month, the OO carrying out the operational servicing of the camp [shall] submit an operational report to the [regional] USSR NKVD Spetsotdel and a copy to the 1st Spetsotdel of the USSR NKVD concerning the following items:

a) the number of prisoners of war held in the camp and, of these, the officer contingent, gendarmes, and workers in state security departments;

b) the number of files established, the identifications made by agents, the number of recruited agents and informants, the number arrested (showing what they were arrested for and what they admit to).[149]

11. Responsibility for supplying all the essential record materials is assigned to the head of the appropriate NKVD UNKVD on whose territory the camp is located.

12. Upon the liquidation of the OOs in NKVD prisoner-of-war camps, all utilized agent-operations and records materials shall be transmitted with a protocol for safekeeping to the 1st Spetsotdel of the regional NKVD (UNKVD).

> Head of the 1st Special Department of the USSR NKVD
> GB Captain (Petrov)
>
> Deputy Head of the Special Department of the USSR NKVD
> GB Major (Belianov)

The problems in the Stanislavov [Stanisławów] region were common to all former Polish territories occupied by the Red Army.

· 11 ·

Report of the USSR Deputy People's Commissar of Defense, Army Commander
1st Rank Grigory Kulik, on the Actions of Red Army Units and Formations
in Western Ukraine and the Political and Economic Situation in the Region
21 September 1939, Stanislavov [Stanisławów]

Top Secret
[For] Moscow. To Comrades Stalin, Molotov, and Voroshilov

1. When the Red Army went on the offensive, the Polish Army was so demoralized that it offered almost no resistance, with the exception of mi-

nor isolated instances of resistance by border forces,[150] the Osadniki [military settlers],[151] and retreating units under the leadership of the high command.

2. A great many rank-and-file soldiers and officers were captured. Some of the captured prisoners could be sent by rail from Stanislavov to Gusiatin [Husiatyń]. However, a large number of prisoners managed to disperse to their homes because the Dirt-Road Sector [military road service unit] was not ready [to move the prisoners];[152] there was nothing to feed them with; and in general we proved unprepared to receive such a large number of captives. It is mainly the officers who are being selected [to be held]. Political work is being done among the prisoners. I think that a government instruction on allowing Belorussians and Ukrainians to go home, after they have been registered, is essential since there is nothing to feed them and convoys require large numbers of men.

3. The movement of units during the first two days (17–18 September) was made very difficult by heavy rains so the roads were muddy and clogged with trucks. Conditions proved especially difficult for the left wing of the motorized corps of Com. [Ivan V.] Tiulenev's group, who on 17 September had to cross the Zbruch [Zbrucz] River after a heavy downpour and on 18 September had to force the crossing of the Dnestr [Dniestr] River under constant rain. However, through joint efforts and by individuals pushing through traffic jams, a rate of advance was achieved of 50–60 kilometers for every twenty-four-hour period. The rate of advance ordered by the command of the Ukrainian Front was not sustained because of the rain. The infantry had been put in motor vehicles, but the civilian drivers proved unprepared to operate motor vehicles, and the commanders are incapable of maintaining order or eliminating the traffic jams that formed during the advance.

4. The overwhelming mass of the population greeted the Red Army with enthusiasm. However, in the large towns, especially Stanislavov, the intelligentsia and merchants greeted it with restraint.[153]

5. In the town of Zaleshchiki [Zaleszczyki] near the Romanian border, a bank holding some securities and paper money that had not been removed was seized. Also seized there was a bus with money that was attempting to cross into Romania.[154] The command organized a guard for the bank and the transfer of the valuables to Stanislavov because this town [Zaleshchiki] is located right on the Romanian border, and the garrison remaining there is weak.

6. Our men assigned to organize local authorities in the territory, after its capture by the RKKA, are not keeping up with the tempo of [army] movement, and often, in larger towns and cities, authorities are organized one to two days after the arrival of the troops, which undermines our authority and dampens the population's enthusiasm.[155] Instructions are

needed from the TsK of the KP(b)U [Communist Party (Bolshevik) of Ukraine] regarding a faster rate of progress for these people and the organization of local authorities. In the major towns, our comrades who have been assigned to them need to be reinforced by the [state] apparatus.

7. The rail network and the bridges remained undamaged due to our swift movement, with the exception of damage to a few small bridges. An apparatus is needed from the NKPS [People's Commissariat of Communications] to organize transport for the purpose of supplying the Red Army with food and for provisioning the towns. In particular, we must accelerate shipping to the towns goods in very short supply: sugar, salt, matches, tea, kerosene.[156]

8. Because of the rapid rate of our advance, the region is not under our control. The Polish Army has thrown away its weapons and scattered to the villages. In Com. Tiulenev's area of operations, it is necessary to send an additional strong NKVD operational group because along the Romanian and Hungarian borders scattered bands will undoubtedly be operating and carrying out provocative diversionary actions against the Red Army and demoralizing the local population. If the cleanup of this area is not accelerated, partisan actions could begin. A great many bourgeois and landowner refugees have gathered in Stanislavov, where they are cut off from the Romanian border. [They wanted to flee to Romania.] It is essential to organize a cleanup of this town from the influx of this gang as quickly as possible.

9. We must also resolve the question of our ruble; zlotys here have a higher value than our rubles. In future, our industrial products must obviously be sold in line with local prices.

10. We must resolve the issue of the local militia and its wages.

11. In the landowners' estates, grain has been left unthreshed in ricks and a large number of livestock have been left behind as well. On these estates there are also sugar refineries and alcohol distilleries, whose workers have run away. There have been attempts to loot the landowners' estates.[157] On this issue, too, urgent instructions are needed. I personally think that the landowners' grain can be used to feed the towns and the Red Army.

12. Local schools have been conducting lessons in Polish, and the Ukrainian language has been taught only partially. On this issue there are no instructions as to how the schools should continue to operate.[158]

13. Publishing newspapers and supplying them to the population is an acute problem. The people have for their use only the oral agitation of [Soviet] political workers, commanders, and soldiers. Above all, we need to provide for the publication of Ukrainian newspapers, [but] for this we need personnel.

14. Before it fled, the Polish government paid the higher officials their salaries seven months in advance, but the workers have not received their salaries for four months. What are we to do about this matter? Evidently workers will have to be paid their salaries; [we will] square accounts with each one on the spot.

15. More literature must be sent in Ukrainian, Belorussian, and Hebrew.[159]

16. In connection with the great national oppression inflicted by the Poles on the Ukrainians, their cup of suffering is overflowing, and in isolated instances there have been fights between Ukrainians and Poles, and there are even threats to slaughter the Poles.[160] The government must immediately issue an address to the population because this could turn into a major political factor.

> Kulik
> Transmitted by Major Shtemenko
> Received by Duty Officer Major Postnikov

[Handwritten:] 1st Section. For the file. N. Vatutin. 24 September 1939. Directives file. Sent to Army and RKKA General Staff.

On 27–28 September 1939, German-Soviet negotiations took place in Moscow, resulting in the conclusion of a treaty. This established a new border between the two powers on former Polish territory, thus excluding the possible establishment of a rump Polish state. Ribbentrop came to Moscow to sign the treaty with Molotov.

· 12 ·

German-Soviet Treaty on Friendship and the Border
between the USSR and Germany
28 September 1939, Moscow

The Government of the USSR and the German Government consider it exclusively their task, after the collapse of the former Polish state, to restore peace and order in this territory and secure for the peoples living there a peaceful existence suited to their national characteristics. With this goal in mind, they have come to an agreement on the following.

Article I
The Government of the USSR and the German Government hereby establish as the border between their mutual state interests on the territory of

the former Polish state the line that has been drawn on the map attached herewith and that will be described in greater detail in a supplementary protocol.[161]

Article II
Both parties recognize the border between their mutual state interests, established in Article I, as final and will reject any interference by third powers in this decision.

Article III
The necessary state restructuring on the territory to the west of the line specified in Article I shall be carried out by the German Government [and] on the territory to the east of this line by the Government of the USSR.

Article IV
The Government of the USSR and the German Government consider the above-mentioned restructuring to be a sound foundation for the further development of friendly relations between their peoples.

Article V
This treaty is subject to ratification. The exchange of ratification documents should take place as soon as possible in Berlin.[162]
    The treaty comes into effect immediately upon signing.
    Drawn up in two originals, in the German and Russian languages.

By authorization   For the Government
of the Government of the USSR   of Germany
V. Molotov   I[J]. Ribbentrop
Moscow, 28 September 1939

    In a Secret Supplementary Protocol to the Treaty of 28 September 1939, Stalin ceded to Germany part of the Polish territory awarded to the USSR by the Secret Protocol of 23 August 1939 in return for German recognition of predominant Soviet interest in most of Lithuania (see map 3).
    Subsequently, on 10 October 1939 the USSR and Lithuania signed a mutual assistance pact allowing Soviet troops to be stationed on Lithuanian territory and ceding Vilnius and its region to Lithuania. The USSR signed similar pacts with Latvia and Estonia.

· 13a ·

Secret Supplementary Protocol to the German-Soviet Treaty on Friendship
and the Border between the USSR and Germany [Identifying
Spheres of Interest and Affirming Agreements]
28 September 1939, Moscow

———————————

The undersigned plenipotentiaries declare the agreement of the German
Government and the Government of the USSR to the following:

The Secret Supplementary Protocol, signed on 23 August 1939,[163] shall
be amended in part 1 in such a way that the territories of the Lithuanian
state are included in the sphere of interests of the USSR, while, on the
other hand, the Lublin *voevodship* [province] and parts of the Warsaw
voevodship are included in the sphere of influence of Germany (see map to
the Treaty on Friendship and Borders between the USSR and Germany
signed today). As soon as the Government of the USSR takes special measures on Lithuanian territories to protect its interests, the [present] Ger-
man-Lithuanian border shall be, for the purpose of establishing a natural
and simple boundary, rectified in such a way that the Lithuanian territory
lying to the southwest of the line shown on the map falls to Germany.[164]

Further, it is established that the economic agreements now in force between Germany and Lithuania shall not be affected by measures taken by
the Soviet Union as indicated above.

As Plenipotentiary of the   For the Government of Germany
Government of the USSR
V. Molotov   I[J]. Ribbentrop
28 September 1939   28 September 1939

· 13b ·

Secret Supplementary Protocol to the German-Soviet Treaty on
Friendship and the Border between the USSR and Germany
[Establishing Cooperation against Polish Resistance]
28 September 1939, Moscow

———————————

In concluding the Soviet-German Border and Friendship Treaty, the undersigned plenipotentiaries stated their agreement to the following:

Neither party will allow on its territory any Polish agitation that affects
the territory of the other country. Both shall liquidate such agitation on

their territories in embryo and shall inform each other about expedient measures to accomplish this.[165]

By authorization of the
Government of the USSR
V. Molotov
Moscow, 28 September 1939

For the Government
of Germany
I[J]. Ribbentrop
28 September 1939[166]

A Politburo decision of 3 October 1939 on prisoners of war established a special camp for Polish higher officers and higher state officials and another special camp for intelligence and counterintelligence officials, gendarmes, jail guards, and police.

· 14 ·

Excerpt from a Politburo Protocol: Decision on Prisoners of War
[2–3] October 1939, Moscow

Top Secret
From a special folder
TsK VKP(b) [Central Committee, All-Union
Communist Party (Bolshevik)]
No. P7/260
To Comrades Beria, Voroshilov, Mekhlis and Molotov—everything
To Pomaznev—7 and 9
To Khokhlov—9
Decision of 2 October 1939

260.—On Prisoners of War[167]
(Politburo, 1 October 1939, Minutes no. 7, point 252, subpoint 32)
Approve the following proposals of Comrades Beria and Mekhlis:[168]

1. Prisoners of war, soldiers of Ukrainian, Belorussian, and other nationalities whose homeland is in the territory of Western Ukraine and Western Belorussia shall be released to go home.

2. For the construction of the Novograd Volynsky–Korets–Lvov [Nowogród Wołyński–Korzec–Lwów] road, leave 25,000 POWs up to the end of December (end of the first phase of construction).[169]

3. Place into a separate group prisoner-of-war soldiers whose homeland is in the German part of Poland and hold them in camps until negotiations [take place] with the Germans and a decision is made on sending them back to their homeland.

4. Organize a separate camp for prisoner-of-war officers. Hold officers from the rank of lieutenant colonel to general inclusive, as well as prominent state and military officials, separate from the rest of the officer cadre.

5. Hold intelligence agents, counterintelligence agents, gendarmes, prison guards, and police in a separate camp.

6. Release the approximately 800 captured Czechs after obtaining from each of them a signed statement saying that they will not fight against the USSR.[170]

7. Require the Ekonomsovet [Council for Economic Affairs] to allocate to the UPV twenty portable film projectors and five field printing presses to serve the POWs.

8. Establish for prisoner-of-war officers a somewhat better food ration than for soldiers.

9. Require Tsentrosoiuz [Central Union of Consumer Societies] to organize kiosks in the camps for selling food and manufactured goods.

10. All POWs, both officers and soldiers, are required to surrender all valuables, as well as money over and above the norm established by the UPV, to the camp administration for safekeeping in exchange for a receipt.

11. Distribute POWs to the following camps:

a) place generals, lieutenant colonels, prominent military and state officials, and all other officers in the south (in Starobelsk);

b) place intelligence agents, counterintelligence agents, gendarmes, police, and prison guards in Ostashkov camp, Kalinin Oblast;

c) hold captured soldiers whose homeland is in the German part of Poland in Kozelsk camp,[171] Smolensk Oblast, and Putivl camp, Sumy Oblast.

TsK Secretary

An estimated 1,000–2,500 Polish civilians were killed in former eastern Poland in September 1939. Some of them, as well as 200–300 Polish military, were sentenced by Military Tribunals.

· 15 ·

Politburo Decision on Ratifying Military Tribunal Sentences
in Western Ukraine and Western Belorussia
3 October 1939, Moscow

Top Secret
Special folder
From 3 October 1939
270.—On the Procedure to Ratify the Sentences of Military Tribunals
in Western Ukraine and Western Belorussia

Entrust the Military Councils of the Ukrainian and Belorussian Fronts
with the right to ratify the sentences of tribunals for the maximum punishment for counterrevolutionary [c-r] crimes by civilians of Western
Ukraine and Western Belorussia and military personnel of the former Polish Army.[172]

Secretary of the VKP(b) TsK
I[J]. Stalin
Extracts sent to:
Coms. Kalinen, Voroshilov, Ulrikh, Mekhlis, Beria, Goliakov, Pankratev

Beria's directive on Operational-Cheka [Intelligence] Work among
the POWs lists Polish and non-Polish organizations and parties regarded as especially hostile to the USSR. The objectives were to ferret
out members for special investigation and perhaps arrest them; to recruit agents and confidants from among the POWs; to find intelligence
officers; and to report on prisoners' moods.

· 16 ·

Beria's Directive on Operational-Cheka Work among POWs in NKVD Camps
8 October 1939, Moscow

Top Secret

The OOs [Special Sections] of Ostashkov, Yukhnov, Kozelsk, Putivl,
Kozelshchansk, Starobelsk, Yuzha, and Oranki USSR NKVD camps, created in accordance with USSR NKVD Order no. 0308 of 19 September

1939,[173] are assigned the following tasks for Operational-Cheka work among POWs:

§1

The creation of an agency-informational network to uncover c-r groupings among the POWs and to shed light on their moods.

In so doing, bear in mind the necessity of creating two categories of agencies:

1. [Secret] agencies that, while outwardly maintaining the position of continuing the fight for the "restoration" of Poland, must infiltrate all anti-Soviet groups that form among the POWs, chiefly among former members of Polish c-r political parties, officers, and military officials.

2. [Secret] agencies with the task of shedding light on the political moods of the POWs—those belonging to the same [military] unit and those from the same area of residence.

In creating a network of [secret] agencies, make extensive use of the registration of POWs arriving in the camps, in the process of which operational workers from the OOs should do everything possible to familiarize themselves with the POWs being registered and select from among them those who are suitable candidates for recruitment.

§2

Assign to the agencies the task of uncovering and penetrating the following contingents:

a) individuals who served in the intelligence, police, and security organs of former Poland—branch agencies, intelligence posts, state security departments in the voevodships [provinces], police stations, intelligence sections attached to military units, intelligence sections attached to "Dovudstvo Okrengovo Korpusnove" [District Corps Commands][174]—prison employees, and those serving in KOP [Polish Frontier Protection Corps]

b) [secret] agencies of the organs listed above (informants, intelligence agents)

c) participants in fascist military and nationalistic organizations of former Poland (POV [P.O.W.—Polish Military Organization], PPS [Polish Socialist Party], Osadniki [Polish Military Settlers], Streltsy [Strzelcy—Riflemen's Association], Legion Mladykh [Legion Młodych—Legion of Youth], Biskupa Kubina [Bishop Teodor Kubina's Organization], Soiuz Unterofitserov [Noncommissioned Officers' Union], Soiuz Ofitserov [Officers' Union], Soiuz Advokatov [Attorneys' Union], Komitet Zashchity Krestov [Komitet Obrony Krzyżów—Committee for the Defense of Crosses], Belorussky Natsionalny Komitet [Belorussian National Committee], and Sionisty [Zionists])[175]

d) employees of law courts and the prosecutor's office

e) [secret] agencies of other foreign intelligence services

f) participants in foreign White émigré terrorist organizations (ROVS [Rossiiskii Obshchevoiskovoi Soiuz—Russian All-Military Union], BRP [Bratstvo Russkoi Pravdy—Brotherhood of Russian Truth], NTSNP [Natsionalny Trudvoi Soiuz Novogo Pokolenia—National Labor Union of the New Generation], Zeleny Dub [Green Oak], Savinkovtsy [Savinkovites], Soiuz Russkoi Molodzezhi [Union of Russian Youth], Soiuz Byvshykh Voennikh [Union of Former Military Men], Soiuz Povstantsev Volyni [Union of Volyn Insurgents], Komitet Pomoshchi Russkim Emigrantam [Aid Committee for Russian Émigrés], UNDO [Ukrainskoe Natsionalno-Demokraticheskoe Obiedinenie—Ukrainian National-Democratic Union], OUN [Orhanizatsiia Ukrainskykh Natsionalistiv—Organization of Ukrainian Nationalists], Komissia dlia Rossii [Commission for Russia])

g) provocateurs from the former tsarist secret police, and persons who served in the police and prison institutions of pre-revolutionary Russia

h) provocateurs from the secret police in the fraternal communist parties of Poland, Western Ukraine, and Belorussia[176]

i) kulak and anti-Soviet elements who fled to the former Poland from the USSR

Assign to the agency the additional task of uncovering and preventing both group and individual escapes of POWs from the camps.

§3

Immediately enter the entire exposed c-r element into the operational data, open agency files on them, and secure the uncovering both of organized c-r formations among POWs inside the camp and of the foreign ties of those who are being investigated.

§4

Make arrests of POWs on the basis of materials obtained by the agency, with the sanction of the head of the Special Department and the military prosecutor of the corresponding military district [*okrug*].

§5

Investigation into the affairs of c-r groups and individuals—spies, saboteurs, terrorists, and conspirators—is, as a rule, to be conducted by the Special Departments of the corresponding military districts.[177]

The camp Special Sections shall conduct investigations only into cases of violations of camp regulations, as well as instances requiring immediate investigation (an attempt to escape from the camp, hooliganism, theft, etc.), and will subsequently transfer documents to the district military prosecutor.

Investigation into prisoner-of-war matters shall be conducted in strict compliance with existing criminal and procedural regulations.

§6
The Special Departments of military districts [are to] conduct investigations to reveal the anti-Soviet connections of arrested POWs and individuals who could be used for drops across the cordon [border with German Poland].

The recruitment of agents to be dropped across the border is to be made only with the advance sanction of the head of the USSR NKVD Special Department, and the drop across the border [can be made] only with the sanction of the USSR People's Commissar of Internal Affairs [Beria].[178]

§7
For the purpose of the timely exposure and prevention of the possible utilization by POWs of individuals among the camp service personnel for criminal purposes (transmission of messages and letters, bribery for the purpose of escape), the camp Special Sections shall, alongside the political instruction and political work carried out by the camp administration and political apparatus, ensure agency security for the supervisory and convoy staff of the camp and the populated areas surrounding the camp.

§8
The heads of the camp Special Sections [are to] inform the camp commander on the basis of all the materials in their possession about the moods of the POWs, instances of violations of camp regulations, and crimes uncovered (including c-r crimes), and coordinate arrests of the POWs with him.

§9
The heads of the camp Special Sections [are to] subordinate themselves in their Cheka operations to the heads of the Special Departments of the corresponding military districts, the people's commissars of internal affairs of union and autonomous republics, and the heads of the NKVD administrations for their territory.

USSR People's Commissar of Internal Affairs
(L. Beria)

Verified as accurate:
Deputy Head of the USSR NKVD Special Department
GB Major Belianov

NKVD UPV Information on the Number of POWs Subject to Release
and Those Remaining in the Camps as of 8 October 1939[179]

8 October 1939, Moscow

Prisoners of War by Category

Ordinal No.	Camp Name	Generals, Officers, Officials (for Starobelsk)	Intelligence Agents, Counterintelligence Agents, Gendarmerie, Prison Guards, Police (for Ostashkov)	Soldiers Subject to Release *	Czechs Subject to Release [180]	Soldiers Remaining in Camps	Women Participants in the War	Refugees (Men/Women)	Total
1.	Oranki	129	31	2,277	—	4,612	1	7	7,057
2.	Starobelsk	559	125	1,809	—	4,789	—	69/1	7,352
3.	Griazovets	47	215	2,593	—	229	—	15	3,099
4.	Vologda	66	45	2,406	—	945	2	2	3,466
5.	Putivl	1,462	490	1,219	—	3,149	—	1,056	7,376
6.	Kozelschansk	1,206	1,331	1,573	—	2,080	1	—	6,191
7.	Kozelsk	177	347	5,470	—	2,820	—	231	9,045
8.	Yukhnov	508	569	5,030	—	1,801	—	187	8,095

9. Ostashkov	184	92	6,928	—	1,913	14	—	9,131
10. Yuzha	801	353	3521	—	6,810	—	149	11,634
Total All camps	5,139	3,598	32,826	—	29,148	18	1,717	72,446
Total At UkSSR and BSSR reception points	2,171	478	11,825	—	3,698	—	9	18,181
Total All camps and reception points	7,310	4,076	44,651	—	32,846	18	1,726	90,627

Sent to Construction Site no. 1–23,681[181]

Head of the USSR NKVD UPV

Major Soprunenko†

---

* The Polish edition has an extra set of figures in this column—soldiers subject to release—not printed in the Russian edition; see *KDZ1*, p. 156.

† The Polish edition also shows the signature of the UPV head, Nekhoroshev; see *KDZ1*, p. 156.

· 18 ·

Beria's Memorandum to Molotov on Sending Home Polish Soldier POWs,
Residents of Western Belorussia and Western Ukraine, and Delivering to the
German Authorities POWs Who Are Residents of German Poland[182]
11 October 1939, Moscow*

No. 4584/B
Top Secret

SNK USSR
To Comrade Molotov.

In accordance with the decision of the VKP(b) TsK and the SNK USSR on POWs,[183] the USSR NKVD has completed the work of selecting POWs who are residents of Western Ukraine and Western Belorussia, and their dispatch to their homeland began on 10 October. Their departure will be finalized on 18 October.

After the dispatch of these POWs, out of the rank-and-file contingent in the camps about 33,000 soldier prisoners of war will remain who are residents of territories of former Poland now part of Germany, primarily Poles.

The USSR NKVD considers it expedient to ratify the following proposals of Com. Beria: *that all soldier POWs who are residents of the German portion of the former Poland,* numbering about 33,000 people, *be handed over in the near future to German authorities,* for which purpose negotiations should begin with the government of Germany.†

The transfer of POWs shall be carried out directly on the border at these points:

a) Terespol—sending echelons via Zhitkovichi [Żytkowice], Luninets [Łuniniec], and Pinsk [Pińsk], and

b) Dorogusk [Dorohusk]—sending echelons via Olevsk [Olewsk], Sarny, and Kovel [Kowel].

---

* Handwritten across the top part of the first page: "*Za* [For] Molotov, K. Voroshilov, Stalin."

Above the words "To Com. Molotov" are the following names written one beneath the other, probably in the hand of Stalin's secretary: "Com. Mikoyan, Com. [Andrei] Andreev, Com. Kaganovich, Com. Zhdanov, Com. Kalinin."

In the margin of the first page: "O. P. [Special file]. NKVD matter."

On the lower portion of the second page: "Extracts to Beria, Molotov, and L. M. Kaganovich." Below that: "Protocol 8/61 of 13 October 1939."

Stamp of the VKP(b) TsK Secretariat in the upper left-hand corner of the first page; under it: "11 October 1939 No. 4584/5."

† The italicized phrases were underlined in red pencil by Stalin.

~~Both these routes have been chosen in consultation with the NKPS in order to avoid the overburdened Bobruisk and Lvov railway junctions.~~

c) ~~*Coordinated with the NKPS*~~ *dispatch the echelons in the period between 23 October and 3 November.**

The USSR NKVD requests your recommendations.[184]

USSR People's Commissar of Internal Affairs
L. Beria

Some of the rank-and-file POWs were sent to work in the mines run by the Narkomchermet [NKChM—Commissariat of Ferrous Metallurgy]. The specifications for feeding, clothing, and ensuring services for the prisoners were not observed in practice, which led to much discontent and even refusal to work.

· 19 ·

Agreement between the NKVD UPV and the Narkomchermet on Utilizing POWs
14 October 1939, Moscow[185]

Secret
Protocol of the Agreement between the USSR NKVD UPV
and the USSR NKChM on the Labor Placement
of 10,000–11,000 Prisoners of War

§1
The specified number of POWs shall be distributed to the following points:

1. In the "Glavneruda" system—in the Yelenovka Ore Administration, Yelenovka Station, Southern Donetsk Railway—*900 people*

In the Karakub Ore Administration, Kuteinikovo Station, Southern Donetsk Railway—*900 people*

A camp shall be created out of two camp sections with the center in Karakuba and a camp section in Yelenovka.

2. In the "Glavruda" system—in the "Dzerzhinskruda Trust" in the Krivoy Rog iron ore basin, Mudrenaia Station, Stalin Railway, with em-

---

* Crossed out by Stalin in red pencil. The first struck-out sentence refers to point 2b (originally c) of the minutes of the Politburo meeting that ratified Beria's proposals as a Politburo decision on 13 October. Stalin's secretary probably drew up the decision of the Politburo based on the text of Beria's memorandum; see *KD1/52*. For other changes in the original text, see *KD1/52*, notes on p. 144; *KDZ1/52*, notes on pp. 160, 162.

ployment in Pervomaiskaia, "Kommunard," and "Ilich" mines—*1,700 people*

To the Karnavatka Station, Stalin Railway, for work in the Kirov and Yuzhna mines—*700 people*

For the "Oktiabrruda Trust," Vecherny Kut Station, Stalin Railway, with employment in the "Komintern," "Frunze," "Krasny Gorniak," and "Bolshevik" mines—*1,600 people*

The "Leninruda Trust," Kalachevskaia Station, Stalin Railway, with employment in the "Kaganovich," "Shilman," "Roza," and "Krasny Gorniak" mines—*1,700 people*

The "Nikopol-Marganets Trust," Marganets Station, Stalin Railway—*750 people*

Zaporozhstal—*2,000 people*

1. Prisoners of war are utilized to work at the decision of Narkomchermet.[186]

2. Prisoners of war are transported at the expense of Narkomchermet.

§2

1. Narkomchermet shall supply the entire contingent of POWs with the necessary special clothing of appropriate quality in accordance with VTsSPS [All-Union Central Council of Trade Unions] standards and at its own expense.

2. In the event of carrying out hazardous jobs, Narkomchermet, at its own expense, shall provide the POWs with the necessary additional special clothing and special food in accordance with the standards established for free hired workers.

3. It is the duty of Narkomchermet to organize the feeding of the POWs, the first month of feeding being gratuitous according to the norms enclosed,* and, subsequently, for payment on the usual terms.[187]

4. The entire contingent of POWs shall be employed primarily in piecework and paid beginning with the second month in accordance with current norms, rates, and assessments, on an equal footing with free hired workers of the given enterprise.

5. It is the duty of Narkomchermet to provide all the essential conditions regarding safety techniques.

In the event of injury, both criminal and financial responsibility shall be borne by the enterprises of Narkomchermet.

6. Narkomchermet must provide gratuitously, at its own expense, the appropriate equipment and heated buildings and the necessary quantity of bedding for the housing of the entire contingent of POWs, as well as for their guard.

*Missing from the file.

7. Narkomchermet shall provide at its own expense and through its own efforts regular health checkups for POWs (at least once every ten days).[188]

8. Narkomchermet shall, every month, cover all the expenses connected with the guard and apparatus [bureaucracy] of the camp, according to the actual cost.

> USSR Deputy People's Commissar of Internal Affairs
> Divisional Commander (Chernyshov)
>
> USSR People's Commissar of Ferrous Metallurgy
> (Merkulov)

The prisoners were not allowed to write or receive letters, which was against International Red Cross (IRC) regulations on the treatment of POWs and even those established by Beria himself. The prisoners demanded the right to correspond with their families, as shown by the petition below. They were finally allowed limited correspondence rights in late November–early December 1939.

· 20 ·

Petition by Lieutenant Colonel T. Petrażycki to Starobelsk Camp Commander
Aleksandr Berezhkov Regarding POW Correspondence with Families
15 October 1939, Starobelsk

To the Citizen Commander of the Prisoner-of-War Camp at Starobelsk

I request permission to enter into contact with the USSR Red Cross or the UkSSR Red Cross [for] the purpose of implementing the resolution of the International Treaty of the Red Cross, in particular [for] the purpose of jointly organizing correspondence between POWs and their families.[189]

> Member of the Central Administration of the Polish Red Cross
> Petrażycki Tadeusz
> Retired Colonel, Lawyer

General Franciszek Sikorski's letter provides information on the terms of General Władysław Langner's surrender of Lwów to Army Commander Semyon Timoshenko, as well as the violation of those terms and the problems and requests of the officers imprisoned in Starobelsk.

· 21 ·

Letter from Polish General Franciszek Sikorski to Army Commander
Semyon K. Timoshenko on the Illegal Holding of Polish Lvov
[Lwów, Lviv] Defenders in a Camp[190]
20 October 1939,* Starobelsk

The Commander of the Troops for the Defense of Lvov, Brigadier General
Sikorski
To the Commander of the Ukrainian Front, Army Commander 1st Rank
Timoshenko

I have the honor of informing you that General Langner, before his departure for Moscow, conveyed to me the content of his conversation with
you.[191] Hence I know that you fully understood the essence of our decision—that is, that we, despite possessing written proposals from the German command with conditions of capitulation most advantageous to us,
did not yield either to their attacks or to their threats of a final assault by
four divisions accompanied by heavy bombardment of the city.

It was perfectly clear to you that we, beyond the shadow of a doubt, entered decisively into negotiations with representatives of the state in
which, in contrast to Germany, the principles of justice toward nations
and individuals are binding, although we did not have as yet any concrete
offers from the Red [Army] command.[192]

You could convince yourself that we fulfilled to the utmost our soldierly
duty to fight the German aggressor and that at that time, and in the appropriate manner, we executed the order of the Polish Supreme Command
not to consider the Red Army a belligerent party.[193]

You demonstrated your just assessment by confirming the agreement
concluded regarding our capitulation.[194]

In connection with this, I consider it my duty to present to you our real
present-day situation.

I am in Starobelsk, where all the officers were sent who, according to
the order of the Polish Supreme Command, surrendered their weapons to
the Red Army not only in Lvov but also in the remaining portions of the
territory to which your power extended as the commander of the Ukrainian Front.

I am well aware that at the present time you face many important problems and therefore our problem is one of many for you. For this reason I
do not want to submit any claims regarding various shortcomings that
have occurred.

---

* Date of registration in the Secretariat of the USSR Deputy People's Commissar of Internal
Affairs.

Nevertheless, I take the liberty of directing your attention to the following points:

1. The delay in releasing us has put all of us and our families in an extremely difficult position, although Soviet authorities are going to great lengths to alleviate our living conditions.

2. Moving our place of registration and [future] release more than 1,000 kilometers to the east has complicated the issue of our return to our places of permanent residence and has completely excluded the possibility of direct contact with our families.

3. Our sojourn in Starobelsk and the restrictions on our personal freedom, even in this place, are an extremely difficult experience for us.

In connection with the above, and since we have not been released as yet, although General Langner made a special trip to Moscow regarding this matter,[195] I ask you to take all possible measures to speed our release.[196]

In conclusion, I wish to assure you that I am addressing you directly because the capitulation agreement was concluded through your authorized representatives.

F. Sikorski
Brigadier General [signature in Polish]

The Soviet leadership decided that the NKVD was to detain certain categories of prisoners in its POW camps.

· 22 ·

NKVD UPV Instruction to the Head of Putivl Camp on Detaining POWs
with Various Specializations and Backgrounds
23 October 1939, Moscow

No. 2066468
Top Secret
To No. 79 of 20 October 1939

To the Commander of the Putivl NKVD Prisoner-of-War Camp
Com. Major Smirnov

As a supplement to No. 14028, we clarify that professors, journalists, physicians, artists, and other specialists being detained in the Putivl camp, who served in the Polish Army as officers, as well as intelligence agents, counterintelligence agents, gendarmes, police, provocateurs, prominent military and state officials, secret agents of the police and the counterintelligence, active figures in anti-Soviet political parties and organizations, landowners, and princes—both residents of the territories of Western Ukraine and Western Belorussia and residents of territory now part of Germany—that are discovered among the specialists are subject to detainment in the camp.[197]

The remaining specialists who are residents of the territories of Western Ukraine and Western Belorussia are subject to dispatch to their homeland in the usual manner, and those who are residents of territory that has gone to Germany must be sent off together with the rank and file and NCOs who are subject to being handed over to German authorities.[198]

In the event of the categorical refusal of any of the specialists to go to the territory now part of Germany, they should be reported to the UPV, together with detailed information on these specialists and the reasons for their refusal.

> Head of the USSR NKVD UPV
> Major (Soprunenko)
>
> Head of the 2nd Section of the Administration
> GB Lieutenant (Makliarsky)

Some Polish POWs, former residents of territory that had gone to Germany—especially Jews—did not want to return there, but their objections were generally overruled.

· 23 ·

NKVD UPV Report to Beria on the Refusal of Some POWs
to Travel to German Poland
28 October 1939, Moscow

No. 2066678*
Top Secret

To the USSR People's Commissar of Internal Affairs
GB Commissar 1st Rank
Comrade L. P. Beria

According to reports from the commanders of camps and reception points, there have been instances of POWs refusing to proceed to territory gone to Germany.

---

* Handwritten note in the top left-hand margin, in red pencil: "Comrade Soprunenko. I am returning your note. You already have your instructions. Chernyshov."

Among those refusing are many Jews.

Reasons for refusal:

1. Fear of persecution by German authorities for past revolutionary activity.

2. According to those refusing, their affiliation with the Communist Party.

3. Many resided on territory that is now part of Germany, but their relatives are in Western Ukraine and Belorussia, and they ask to be allowed to stay at their relatives' places of residence.

I request your instructions.[199]

> Head of the USSR NKVD UPV
> Major Soprunenko

> Head of the Political Section of the USSR NKVD UPV
> Regimental Commissar Nekhoroshev

Polish military settlers from former eastern Poland, called up to serve in the Polish Army and taken prisoner in September 1939, or taken from their homes, were considered a "dangerous social element" and thus not subject to release.[200]

· 24 ·

Pyotr Soprunenko's Instructions to the Commanders of the POW Camps
on Sending [Military] Settlers to Ostashkov Camp
29 October 1939, Moscow

Top Secret
Note [for] transmission by direct wire

No [military] settlers discovered among the soldiers and junior officers shall be subject to dispatch home [to] Western Belorussia and Western Ukraine. They should be dispatched [to] Ostashkov camp.

Report the number discovered and dispatched. Soprunenko. No. 2066728.

Polish physicians and pharmacists requested release in accordance with the Geneva Convention on the treatment of POWs; their petition was rejected.

· 25 ·

Petition from POW Physicians and Pharmacists to Marshal Kliment Ye. Voroshilov
Regarding Their Illegal Detention
30 October 1939, Starobelsk

To the Commander in Chief of USSR Forces
Citizen Marshal Voroshilov

The physicians and pharmacists of the Polish Army who are concentrated in the prisoner-of-war camp at Starobelsk, Voroshilovgrad Oblast, numbering 130 men (104 physicians and 26 pharmacists), take the liberty of stating to you, Citizen Marshal, the following:

All the physicians and pharmacists were captured by Soviet troops while they were carrying out their physician duties, either in hospitals or in military units. On the basis of the international Geneva Convention regulating the rights of physicians and pharmacists during military operations,[201] we request that you, Citizen Marshal, either facilitate sending us to one of the neutral states (United States of North America, Sweden) or send us to our places of permanent residence.[202]

> Starobelsk
> 30 October 1939[203]
> [Followed by 112 signatures in Polish]

GB Major Vasily Zarubin made a very favorable impression on the officer prisoners in Kozelsk camp. He was courteous, spoke three Western languages, and lent them books in those languages. Few suspected that his task was to direct investigative work and recruit agents. Later, in spring 1940, he was actively involved in "clearing out" the camp (extermination).

· 26 ·

NKVD UPV Telegram to Vasily Korolev on Sending the UPV Inspector GB Major
Vasily Zarubin to Kozelsk Camp[204]
31 October 1939, Moscow

Telegram
Kozelsk, Smolensk [Oblast]
NKVD Camp
To Korolev
On 31 October, the UPV inspector GB Major Zarubin left [for] your
camp in order to assist in the camp's operations. Send a car for him. All of
Zarubin's instructions are to be carried out.

Soprunenko. Nekhoroshev. No. 2066803.

In September 1939, several thousand Polish military and police
crossed into Lithuania and Latvia to escape Soviet captivity. Some
were transferred to Russia in late 1939 and interned there. Secrecy surrounded all mention of the officers, military officials, and police.

· 27 ·

SNK Resolution on the Admission to the USSR of Polish Military Personnel
Interned in Lithuania[205]
9 November 1939, Moscow

Top Secret
Special Folder
Resolution no. 1851–484ss of the USSR Council of People's Commissars
9 November 1939, Moscow, the Kremlin
On Admitting Military Personnel of the Former Polish Army
Interned in Lithuania into the USSR

The USSR Council of People's Commissars resolves:
1. To receive from the Lithuanian government POWs of [the] former
Polish Army interned in Lithuania [who are] residents of Western Ukraine
and Belorussia [and who] express a desire to return to their homeland.
2. To send the rank and file and junior officers of the army of the former
Poland received [from Lithuania] to their places of residence. Officers,
military officials, and police are to be received and sent for detention: offi-

cers to the Yukhnov [POW camp], officials and police to the Yuzha prisoner-of-war camp, where they will be subject to selection.[206]

This point, concerning officers and police officials, is to be treated as top secret.

3. To have the internees cross the border at four checkpoints located in Gudogantsy [Gudogańce] and Martsinkantse [Marcinkańce] at a rate of 250 men per day at each point.

4. To assign the entire receiving operation for internees to the USSR Narkomvnudel [NKVD].

5. To send to Lithuania to select and receive the internees a government commission consisting of Brigadier Commander Com. G. A. Petrov (chairman) [with the following] members: Captain Com. M. M. Udachin, Captain Com. V. A. Solovyov, Captain Com. G. Ya. Zlochevsky, GB Captain Com. S. A. Roditelev, GB Lieutenant Com. I. G. Variash, GB 1st Lieutenant Com. B. I. Kutyn, and GB 1st Lieutenant Com. A. A. Pchelkin.

6. USSR Narkomfin [People's Commissariat of Finance] shall allocate funds at the request of USSR Narkomvnudel for the payment of additional expenses incurred in the reception of internees, with confirmation of these expenses by the USSR Sovnarkom [SNK].

7. The NKPS, in accordance with the requests of Narkomvnudel, is to provide for the rail transport of internees of the former Polish Army received in our territory.[207]

> Chairman of the USSR SNK
> V. Molotov
>
> Chief of the USSR SNK Chancellery
> M. Khlomov*

On 19 November, the UPV reported the number of POWs released and the number held in NKVD camps. (Some numbers in the report were underlined in pencil.)

---

* The facsimile of the original page 2 has a handwritten list of officials to whom copies were sent: "1—original copy; 2—Com. Stalin, I. V.; 3—NKID [People's Commissariat of Foreign Affairs] Com. Molotov, V. M.; 4—NKVD Com. Beria, L. P.; 5—NKO [People's Commissariat of Defense] Com. Voroshilov, K. Y.; [illegible word], 1543; 6—NKID Com. Potemkin; 7—Com. Chernukha. Extracts NKFin [People's Commissariat of Finance], p[oint] 6; NKPS, p. 7"; see *KDZ1*, p. 246.

· 28 ·

NKVD UPV Report on the Number of POWs Sent Away and Held in the Camps
19 November 1939, Moscow

Top Secret
Report on Prisoners of War Received, Dispatched,
and Remaining in NKVD Camps

Total POWs received	125,000 people
Sent to Western Belorussia and Western Ukraine	*42,400 people**
Handed over to the German authorities	*43,000 people*
Detained in camps:	
a) officer contingent	8,500 people
b) police and gendarmes	6,500 people
Total officers, police, and gendarmes detained in Starobelsk, Kozelsk, and Ostashkov camps	*15,000 people*[208]
Rank and file and junior officers detained in camps for Narkomchermet operations	10,400 people
Rank and file and junior officers detained in Rovno camp	14,200 people
Total soldiers and NCOs detained in Narkomchermet and Rovno camps	*24,600 people*
Total detained in all NKVD prisoner-of-war camps	*39,600 people*[209]

Head of the USSR NKVD UPV
Major P. Soprunenko

After the accession of Western Ukraine and Western Belorussia to the USSR (1–2 November 1939), Soprunenko, head of the NKVD UPV, formulated two proposals: (1) to change the status of POWs being used as forced labor by the NKVD and the People's Commissariat of Ferrous Metallurgy and (2) to use police POWs as forced labor, as well as possibly some of the officer contingent. His proposals were not approved by Beria.

* Italic entries are underlined in the document.

· 29 ·

To the USSR People's Commissar of Internal Affairs
GB Commissar 1st Rank
Comrade L. P. Beria

A large part of the prisoner-of-war soldiers of the former Polish Army coming from the territories of Western Ukraine and Western Belorussia have been released to [their] homelands. The release of soldiers to the [Polish] territory [now] belonging to Germany, in an exchange procedure with the latter, is coming to a close.[210]

At present, there are a good number of prisoner-of-war soldiers employed in productive jobs: 18,000 at Construction Site no. 1[211] and 10,396 in USSR Narkomchermet mining operations.[212]

The rank-and-file soldiers of the former Polish Army held in our camps, especially from the territories of Western Ukraine and Western Belorussia, have openly expressed their desire for, and pleaded to be released to their homes as soon as possible in order to take up active participation with their entire people in the organization and construction of a new and happy life.

Now, after the decision of the 5th Extraordinary Session of the USSR Supreme Soviet on the union of Western Ukraine and Western Belorussia with the USSR, they are citizens of the USSR, and their detention as POWs contradicts the session's decision.[213] The moods of the POWs up to the present day express more and more strongly their desire to return to their homelands as soon as possible. In an organized fashion they are requesting to be released (two letters addressed to Comrade Stalin from Construction Site no. 1) and are running away unlawfully in small numbers (1,000 men [from] Construction Site no. 1), and there are instances of escapes from other camps.

In this situation, their further detention as POWs could give rise to false interpretations among them and, through them, among the workers of Western Ukraine and Western Belorussia, providing our enemies with ammunition for anti-Soviet agitation. This could happen also because it was announced to 1,470 men as they were leaving Putivl camp that they were going home, whereas they were in fact sent to Krivoy Rog.

---

* This report was apparently sent soon after the end of the 5th Extraordinary Session of the Supreme Soviet on 2 November 1939, when it agreed to the incorporation of Western Belorussia and Western Ukraine into the respective Soviet republics.

Based on the above, we consider it possible to submit for your consideration the following proposals:

1. In connection with the decision of the 5th Extraordinary Session of the USSR Supreme Soviet, change the status of the POWs working at Narkomchermet ore extraction sites to that of freely hired workers; [but] first conduct among them preliminary propaganda—explanatory work to secure them as a workforce in the mines with the same rights as all USSR workers.

2. Release all POWs from Construction Site no. 1 and replace them with the police in our camps, who number 4,977, of whom the 3,000 [originating] from the territories of Western Ukraine and Western Belorussia are idle. Sooner or later they will have to be trained to work. Assign a reinforced guard to them.

3. Differentiate among the officer contingents detained in our camps, a total of 8,980 men, 4,500 of whom are from the territories of Western Ukraine and Western Belorussia, in order to decide where to utilize those in each category.[214]

Head of the USSR NKVD UPV
Major (Soprunenko)

Commissar of the USSR NKVD UPV
Regimental Commissar (Nekhoroshev)

Several detailed NKVD reports were written at this time on conditions in the camps, on prisoner moods, on "political work," and on films (see also doc. 32). These aspects of camp life are also described in the memoirs and diaries found at Katyn when exhumations were carried out there in spring 1943. The diaries show that in the first few weeks the food, clothing, and housing sometimes were even worse than presented in this NKVD report, and medical supplies were totally inadequate.

· 30 ·

NKVD UPV Report to Vasily Chernyshov on Conditions in Kozelsk Camp
Not before 1 December 1939, Moscow

Top Secret
To USSR Deputy People's Commissar of Internal Affairs
Divisional Commander Com. Chernyshov
Report on the Situation in Kozelsk NKVD Prisoner-of-War
Camp as of 1 December 1939

As a result of the inspection of the condition of the camp carried out by workers of the USSR NKVD UPV, the following has been established:

Since 1 November of this year, a prisoner-of-war officer contingent has arrived at Kozelsk camp numbering 4,727 people,[215] consisting of:

1. Admirals	1	man
2. Generals	4	men
3. Colonels	24	"
4. Lieutenant colonels	79	"
5. Majors	258	"
6. Captains	654	"
7. Naval captains	17	"
8. Other officers	3,420	"
9. Military clergy	7	"
10. Landowners	3	"
11. Princes	1	"216
12. High state officials	43	"
13. Rank and file, subject to being sent away	85	"

Initially, the camp was not fully prepared to receive a prisoner-of-war officer contingent, having refitted the buildings with two-tiered instead of the [former] three-tiered bunks. In addition, the POWs arrived in large batches.

At the present time, the POWs are housed satisfactorily.

Housekeeping Provisions for Camp Operations
The camp has been experiencing interruptions in the food supply; in particular, recently there has been a total lack of vegetables (cabbage, carrots, onions) and there are no prospects for obtaining them in the *rayon* [district]. There are enough potatoes for a few days, [but] the delivery orders are not filled satisfactorily, and the district leadership explains this by saying that Moscow has priority for potato shipments.

The camp is lacking certain material supplies; there are not enough blankets, sheets, or pillowcases. Many POWs are wearing summer clothes and worn-out, torn footwear. Considering the winter season, quilted jackets, quilted trousers, and footwear are needed.

The buildings occupied by the POWs are perfectly suitable for housing in the winter, but some blocks are still overcrowded, so it has been proposed to make capital repairs to two buildings in which it will be possible to place up to 350 men, so making it possible to reduce the congestion.

One of the initial deficiencies in provisioning the POWs was the delayed supply of bedding; in particular, there was not enough straw for stuffing mattresses.

The camp is provided with fuel, primarily peat. Before the onset of frost, there were interruptions in the fuel supply because of poor access to the peat works. The camp is supplied only intermittently with firewood because of the delayed execution of the orders [given] by Viazemlag [Viazma camp].

The basic economic problem in the camp is the poor condition of the water pump station; the motor and pump are completely out of order, [and] as a result, the normal water supply is breaking down. Measures have been taken by the UPV to replace the water pump station immediately. The electric power station is in almost the same condition and will also be replaced with a new one.

The camp's provisioning apparatus still functions incompletely; there is a lack of proper decisiveness, of responsibility for the work being carried out to accomplish the assigned tasks, and the camp's housekeeping apparatus requires assistance on a daily basis. There are many organizational flaws in the camp that frequently involve a lack of personal responsibility, carelessness, and letting things slide. This refers primarily to the housekeeping apparatus; there is a lack of proper control over the implementation [of their work] by the camp command and, hence, a lack of timely assistance.

Prisoner-of-War Records
At this moment the registration records on the prisoner-of-war officer contingent have been completed. The photographing continues. The staff of the Records Section has changed frequently as the result of a poor choice of personnel.

Sanitary Conditions in the Camp
Until recently, the cleaning of the buildings housing the POWs was not done on a regular basis.

Cleaning of the camp grounds has started only recently. There are not enough lavatories in the camp; there is only one enclosed winter lavatory, and now construction has begun on two more such lavatories. Lavatories are not disinfected on a regular basis.

Sanitary oversight for the camp is inadequate; the buildings occupied by the kitchens are not kept clean enough; one of them is too small, and measures have been taken to expand it. At present, permanent sanitary oversight has been established over the kitchens.

The existing bathhouse at the camp, which has a capacity of up to 200–250 men per day, cannot serve the entire contingent of the camp in the course of fifteen days. The camp laundry is fully equipped, but its operations are still not producing the appropriate effect for lack of a normal water supply and a good drying room.

The Medical Section and field hospital are located in buildings that are wholly appropriate from the medical standpoint. Lately the Medical Section has been fully staffed with physicians, some of them POWs.

On average there are from thirty-five to forty very sick men in sick bay, most of them ill with flu, pulmonary disease, or rheumatism. The camp has been supplied with sufficient quantities of medications. There have been no epidemics or group infections. Lice infestations have been reduced to 2–3 percent.[217]

Political and Moral Condition of the Prisoners of War

The officer contingent of the POWs noticed on arriving in the camp that they were concentrated in one area and that their detention would evidently be lengthier [than expected], so they began to make increased demands regarding their living conditions—for example, money payments in the form of [military] "pay," shoe brushes, shoe polish, etc.

Some officers manifest patriotic feelings and openly state that "Poland will exist again in its previous shape."

Several officers, when they were together with the soldiers, cut off their stars so now, when only officers are detained in the camp, they have restored respect for rank, and some of them have sewn their marks of distinction, their "little stars," back on their epaulettes.[218]

For the most part, the officer contingent is religious, and there was an instance when they attempted to hold public prayer in one of the blocks, but when the camp's political workers appeared, this was prevented, and it was immediately made clear that henceforth the guilty would be held responsible for similar attempts to hold public prayers, and the hanging of icons or crosses in the buildings was also prohibited.

Among the officer contingent, card playing has been noted, and up to fifteen packs of cards have been confiscated.[219]

The POWs pay attention to the political talks that are held, except for some individuals who ignore them or try to ask casuistic questions in order to confuse or disrupt the presentation. Such individuals are placed under observation, in cooperation with the [camp] Special Section, and are checked up on with the goal of isolating them.

The POWs show an increased need to buy sugar, tobacco, and candies. The availability of Soviet money among POWs is connected with the opening of a purchase point for jewelry by the Glaviuvelirtorg [Main Jewelry Trade Administration].

On this basis, there are unhealthy attitudes—for instance, "Why sell valuables if you can't buy anything with the money you get, anyway?"

The existing shop of the Kozelsk Potrebsoiuz [Consumer Union] really does not have the goods specified, and measures taken through the Smolensk Obltorg [Regional Trade Administration] have not yielded a positive resolution of the issue. The shop has been empty up to the present time.

No instances of theft have been recorded among the officer contingent. There have been no escapes or attempted escapes by individuals or groups.

On 28 November 1939, there was an incident when prisoner-of-war soldiers from two blocks refused to eat. The commission created [to investigate this] established that the food was edible in all respects, after which this food (soup) was accepted by the POWs. The reason for their refusal was provocation by hostile individuals.

On 2 December 1939, at Kozelsk camp, the prisoner-of-war Ensign Bazyli Zacharski, son of Antony, who was born in 1898, a lathe operator until 1914 and serving continuously in the Polish Army since 1919, committed suicide (hanged himself).[220] Zacharski's corpse was discovered in the (unoccupied) storeroom of Barracks no. 48 by prisoner of war Ożóg.[221] Zacharski left no notes. From questioning, it is clear that Zacharski badly missed his family, which remained in Grodno.

An investigation is being conducted into the case of Zacharski's suicide.[222]

Political Work among the Prisoners of War
Political work among the POWs is being conducted by workers of the [camp] Political Section through talks, newspaper reading, explanations of current political issues, and answers to questions.

Mass cultural work among the POWs is being carried out by showing films, three or four showings every other day, which is enough for the entire contingent.

A string orchestra has been created in the camp club, and choral singing is being organized by teaching the songs of the Soviet Union.

Radio networks have been established in each block, and there is a loudspeaker near the club.

The POWs are supplied with fiction and socio-economic literature, newspapers, and magazines through the existing library. Glass [display] cases have been made for the central newspapers; the club and the territory of the camp are decorated with slogans and posters.

Organizational Measures

In order to strengthen the work of the camp's provisioning apparatus, the camp commander's housekeeping assistant has been replaced by a sturdier comrade.

All measures have been taken to have the water tower pump replaced with a new one. An order has been given for a new motor to be sent.

With respect to political work, attention has been called to the education of the freely hired camp staff and their need of training in order to increase vigilance and the struggle against immoral acts.[223]

The Party organization is focused on rendering assistance to the camp's provisioning apparatus.

Workers previously delegated from the [UPV] administration have done significant work to bring the housekeeping apparatus up to the desired level. A series of irregularities was eliminated—for example, with respect to fuel, straw, vegetables, sanitary conditions, construction, record taking, and photograph taking. Also, assistance has been given in political and mass party work.

> Head of the USSR NKVD UPV
> Major (Soprunenko)
>
> Commissar of the USSR NKVD UPV
> Regimental Commissar (Nekhoroshev)

The Politburo decision of 3 December 1939 to arrest all regular Polish officers registered in the western regions of Belorussia and Ukraine added to the number already held in the camps.

· 31 ·

Politburo Decision to Arrest All Registered Regular Officers
of the Former Polish Army
3 December 1939, Moscow

Top Secret
Special Folder
From 3 December 1939
151.—NKVD Matter

Ratify the NKVD proposal to arrest all registered regular officers of the former Polish Army.[224]
Excerpt sent to:
Comrade Beria

VKP(b) TsK Secretary
I[J.] Stalin
[Facsimile signature of J. Stalin stamped with a round red seal, with the legend "All-Union Communist Party of Bolsheviks" and, in the inner circle, the letters "CC."]

Starobelsk camp held most of the high-ranking military officers, and it is clear that special propaganda efforts were made to find agents and informers among them. However, the vast majority proved as immune to these efforts as were the officers in Kozelsk camp.

· 32 ·

Report from the Commander of Starobelsk Camp to Semyon Nekhoroshev
on the Political and Moral Conditions in the Camp in November 1939
3 December 1939, Starobelsk

No. 5–37
Top Secret
To the Head of the Political Department of the USSR NKVD UPV
Regimental Commissar Com. Nekhoroshev
Political Report on the Political and Moral Conditions
in the Starobelsk NKVD Camp for November 1939[225]

I report that the political-educational work among the POWs was carried out on the basis of your directives.

All political-educational work was done in the form of readings, talks, political information sessions, and answers to questions from POWs; by providing the POWs with newspapers and books and showing films; by extensive use of radio; and by strict daily oversight over providing for the POWs all the necessary supplies according to established norms.

The following work was done in November:

Mass political work was done for 3,907 POWs.

All mass political work among the POWs was organized according to plan, in the fulfillment of which the Party and Komsomol [Communist Youth League] organizations took the lead.

The measures foreseen in the plan of party-political work among the POWs were carried out for the most part in full.

A. *Talks were given on the [following] topics:*

a) The reasons for the victory of the October Socialist Revolution in the USSR and its international significance

b) The twenty-second anniversary of the Great October Socialist Revolution

c) The beginning of the new imperialist war and the foreign policy of the Soviet Union

d) What the victory of socialism has given the workers of the USSR

e) The material and cultural welfare of the workers of the USSR

f) What tsarist Russia was and what the USSR has become

g) A discussion was held with the POWs about the film *Lenin v Oktiabre* [Lenin in October]

B. *Readings were held and explanations conducted of material read in newspapers:*

1. On the foreign policy of the Soviet Union (report by Com. Molotov of 31 October 1939).[226]

2. The report by Com. Molotov at the ceremonial plenum devoted to the twenty-second anniversary of the Great October Socialist Revolution, 6 November 1939.[227]

3. An English magazine on the reasons for Poland's defeat (*Pravda* [Truth], 18 November 1939).

4. Materials from the 5th Session of the Supreme Soviet of the USSR.[228]

5. Twice a week a political information [session] is held on the topic "What's New in the USSR and Abroad."

6. The reading of newspapers out loud has been organized in the blocks.

C. *Organizational-instructional measures carried out among the POWs:*

1. Talks were given in all the blocks on the topic "Internal Regulations in the Camp."

2. Conversations took place with block commandants and [POW] elders group[229] on the topic "Internal Regulations in the Blocks."

3. Explanatory work has been done among the POWs about permission to write letters.[230]

a) a conversation took place with the heads of the r——ns [rayons—districts].

b) a conversation took place with the block commandants and group elders.

4. An organized procedure for answering questions was established, and a journal for questions was hung in each block. Each prisoner of war personally receives a reply to a written question from an instructor of the Political Section in two days.

D. *The following films have been shown to the POWs:*
  1. *Chelovek s Ruzhem* [Man with a Rifle]
  2. *Gorny Marsh* [Mountain March]
  3. *Povest o Zavoevannom Schaste* [Tale of Happiness Hard Won]
  4. *Lenin v Oktiabre* [Lenin in October]
  5. *Sluchai na Polustanke* [Incident at the Stop]
  6. *Noch v Sentiabre* [A Night in September]
  7. *Lenin v 1918 g.* [Lenin in 1918]
  8. *Morskoi Post* [The Sea Post]
  9. *Pyotr Pervy* [Peter the First, Part 1]
  10. *Pyotr Pervy* [Peter the First, Part 2]
  11. *Marseleza* [The Marseillaise]
  12. *Vragi* [Enemies]
  13. *Bogatyri Rodiny* [Heroes of the Homeland]

As many as 30,000 POWs have attended the film shows. The POWs liked each picture and are interested in what the next film will be. Two movie showings were organized at the municipal cinema for the former brigadier generals and colonels, who were also pleased and thanked [the organizers] for the attention [shown them].

E. *Glass cases for photocopies of newspapers on the [following] topics have been installed in the camp:*
  1. The Difficult Past of Our Homeland
  2. The USSR—Land of Victorious Socialism
  3. The Third Stalinist Five-Year Plan

The camp buildings were decorated with slogans and posters for the twenty-second anniversary of the October [Revolution]. Preparations are now under way for the [propaganda] setting on the day that workers' deputies are elected to local councils.

F. *Library operations:*

The library has 3,443 different books. It receives 805 different newspapers and 173 magazines. The library systematically serves 1,280 readers. The reading room is used by 200 readers per day.

G. Radio service organized for POWs:

Forty-two radio [reception] points have been established to serve the POWs; thirty-two are provided with speakers, two of which are loud-speakers.

The POWs have radio service daily from 05:00 in the morning until 24:00 at night.

Large groups of 200–500 POWs have listened to the following:

a) Com. Molotov's report at the 5th Session of the USSR Supreme Soviet[231]

b) Reports by members of the Plenipotentiary Commission of Western Ukraine and Western Belorussia

c) Com. Molotov's report at the ceremonial plenum of the Moscow Council on 6 November 1939

d) Com. Molotov's radio speech of 29 November 1939[232]

Daily, in the morning, afternoon, and evening, the POWs listen to the radio broadcast of the latest news from Moscow.

H. Cultural inventory:

The following cultural property has been acquired and issued to the POWs for their use:

Harmonicas	3
Chess sets	20
Checkers sets	25
Domino sets	14

Preparations are under way for a chess tournament in each barrack, after which an all-camp chess tournament will be held.

The lack of housing for a club has been a major impediment to conducting political-educational work among the POWs.

All the talks, readings, and information sessions are held by the political apparatus in each block; films are shown in the yard. These circumstances make the normal conduct of work very difficult and do not allow us to involve the entire mass of POWs in the systematic work of the political apparatus.

The workers of the Political Section, along with implementing the plan for mass agitation work, have directly supervised operations to dispatch, receive, and lodge POWs, also to organize the blocks' food supply and hygiene service, and have assisted in the work of the camp's URO. The construction of two new barracks was serviced by an instructor especially assigned for this, Comrade Kaganer.

The following measures are planned in December for the conduct of political-educational work among the POWs:

I. All workers in the Political Section have been assigned barracks in which to conduct talks, political information sessions, readings, talks, and other forms of mass work among the POWs.

In the month of December it is planned to explain the following topics to the POWs in the form of talks, lectures, and papers:

a) the radio speech of the chairman of the USSR government, Com. Molotov, of 29 November 1939.

b) on the Stalin Socialist Constitution.[233]

On social structure:

c) the USSR—a mighty industrial power.

d) the USSR—land of the most outstanding socialist agriculture in the world.

e) the USSR—the most democratic country in the world. The state structure of the Soviet Union and the electoral system.

f) the inviolable alliance between workers and peasants—the foundation of the Soviet system.

g) the fraternal alliance of the peoples of the USSR—the implementation of the Leninist-Stalinist nationalities policy. The USSR—the great family of Soviet peoples.

h) the life and career of I. V. Stalin.

i) the new intelligentsia of the Soviet people.

II. Organize collective listening to the radio, utilizing the local radio relay center:

1. Com. Stalin's report on the Constitution at the 8th [Extraordinary] USSR Congress of Soviets [24 November 1936].

2. Com. Molotov's speech at the 8th USSR Congress of Soviets.

3. Com. Stalin's speech on the preelectoral assembly.

III. Equip the club building and develop club work.

1. By 15 December, obtain a building vacated [for this purpose] and equip the club [as follows]:

a) a viewing hall for 400 persons

b) a library

c) a reading room

d) a game room—for chess, checkers, and dominos

e) a room for study group work

2. Set up the mobile movie projectors received for film service for the POWs (we request that the [UPV] administration send a transformer to convert the electric current from 220v to 110v and a Pathenor electric dynamo generator).

3. To give lectures to the POWs on these topics:

a) The New Intelligentsia of the Soviet People

b) The Friendship and Fraternity of the Peoples of the USSR

4. Organize circles for:
   a) artists
   b) music
   c) chess and checkers
5. Hold a camp-wide chess tournament
6. Install the following photo exhibit cases:
   a) The Life and Work of Sergei Mironovich Kirov[234]
   b) The Life and Work of Joseph Vissarionovich Stalin
   c) The First Elections under the Stalin Constitution
7. Organize the showing of the following films:
   1. *Veliky Grazhdanin* [The Great Citizen]
   2. *Parad Molodosti* [The Parade of Youth]
   3. *Beleet Parus Odinoky* [The Lone White Sail]
   4. *Vysokaia Nagrada* [A High Reward]
   5. *Trinadtsat* [Thirteen]
   6. *Traktoristy* [Tractor Drivers]
   7. *Noch v Sentiabre* [A Night in September]
   8. *Komsomolsk*[235]
   9. *Chelovek s Ruzhiem* [A Man with a Rifle]
   10. *Baltitsy* [The Baltic Sailors]
   11. *Druzhia* [Friends]
   12. *V Liudiakh* [Among People]
   13. *Karmeliuk*
   14. *Chest* [Honor] and others
8. Expand the radio network in the camp by providing eleven points with loudspeakers (there will be forty-three radio points in all), and provide radio service in the club building by installing five loudspeakers.
9. Give talks on and explain the film *A Man with a Rifle*.

The Political-Moral Condition of the Prisoners of War
In the past month, the political apparatus has discovered the following instances of c-r operations among the POWs:

1. Com. Kaganer, an instructor in the Political Section, has established that prisoner of war Mieczysław Ewert, a former captain in the Polish Army, organized a group out of the officer contingent—Major Ludwig Domoń, Stanisław Kwolek,[236] and others—with the aim of conducting c-r work under the guise of "cultural enlightenment work" (lectures on hygiene, foreign language study, [lectures] on technology in capitalist states, etc.), but in fact during these "talks" on the above issues, c-r activity was conducted against the internal regulations of the camp and the camp administration [using such slogans as] "Speak only Polish," "Don't go to your camp jobs," "The worse it is in the camp, the better for us—this way

we will compromise the camp administration and the camp procedures before the international commission that is going to come soon," etc.[237]

The above-mentioned incident was immediately reported to the Special Section, and as a result of the search conducted, a list was uncovered of the individuals participating in this group, as was the group's plan of activity. The group's organizers, consisting of three men—Ewert, Domoń, and Kwolek—have been removed from the camp.

2. Com. Mikhailenko, an instructor in the Political Section, during a tour of the blocks, discovered that in one of the blocks prisoner of war Major L. J. Domoń had been reading at length to a group of POWs the register of loans issued in zlotys through the mutual aid fund organized among the officer contingent. The register listed eighty names, seventy-eight of which had a signature for the receipt of 100 zlotys a piece and a "declaration" promising to return the money upon return from captivity. Upon clarification of this fact, it was established that the fund had been organized on the principle of [collecting] "voluntary" dues from individuals possessing large sums of zlotys. The fund operated under the leadership of Ludwig Domoń (a major in the former Polish Army), who has been removed from the camp.

The fund's administration consisted of five men and a review commission of three men. The fund's administration, according to incomplete information, has issued loans exceeding 10,000 zlotys.

At present, both the former and the latter group have been disbanded, and the c-r activity under the guise of the "mutual aid fund" and the "cultural commission" has ceased.

The political apparatus for the blocks, as well as the groups and blocks among the POWs, has conducted the appropriate work to prevent the creation of groups and circles and has also strengthened oversight in order to prevent any organized work among the POWs under any pretense whatsoever.

3. There was an attempt to organize prayer services on camp territory on the Polish national holiday. Through the efforts of the party apparatus, this attempt was prevented, but in one of the blocks a prayer service was held nonetheless and lasted fifteen minutes, after which the prayer service was stopped. There have been attempts to hang crosses and icons in the buildings, and such practices have been categorically forbidden.*

4. Regarding events in the international situation, individual officers say: "The USSR has become the land of Red imperialism." These a[nti]-S[oviet] actions were halted immediately.

---

* Handwritten note in red pencil, in the margins alongside point 3: "Religious rites should have been allowed. Prohibition—a mistake."

There have been no instances of suicide. The prisoner-of-war physician who in October attempted to slit his throat with a razor has recovered and is in the camp.

There have been no epidemic illnesses.

No group or individual escapes have been reported.

There have been no instances of refusal to eat either by a group or by isolated individuals.

With the arrival of the POWs from Shepetovka [Szepietówka],[238] there was an incident of boot theft from one prisoner of war and the resale of goods purchased at the local kiosk. The political apparatus took appropriate measures, and no more such incidents have been reported.

There has been no drunkenness.

There have been no accidents, breakdowns, or fires.

The Housekeeping Condition of the Camp
The following measures were carried out in November:

1. Two barracks were built for 1,040 men.
2. One artesian well was dug and equipped.
3. Work began on installing a sewer system inside the camp.
4. A kitchen was built for 3,000 men and put into use.
5. The building used for the medical unit and the infirmary was renovated. The medical unit was moved to new quarters.
6. Wooden sidewalks were built and installed in the camp yard.
7. A dining hall for camp workers was equipped and put into use.
8. Accommodation was prepared for the laundry.
9. A plan was drawn up for the construction of a dining hall and a kitchen for 1,200 men. For construction work, it is absolutely necessary to speed up the unloading of nails (5 metric tons) and roofing paper.

Medical Services for the Prisoners of War
The following activities were carried out in the month of November:

1. Prisoners of war were taken to the municipal bathhouse on the average of three times each.

In connection with the arrival of the new contingent from Shepetovka, who had not changed clothes in a long time, there was a delousing of POWs. The operating and medical departments took urgent measures to eliminate this abnormality, and at present lice infestation among the POWs who arrived has been eliminated.

2. There has been systematic cleaning and disinfection of the yard and all places of contamination.

3. The housing has been cleaned and disinfected—3,117 cubic meters.

4. Sewage has been carried out of the camp yard on 614 horsecarts.

5. Injections have been given:
  a) for typhoid fever
    primary   2,432 men
    secondary   1,897 men
    tertiary   1,123 men
  b) smallpox shot   2,345 men
6. Clinic visits   4,945 men
  a) first time   1,786 men
  b) repeat   3,026 men

By type of illness:
  a) surgical   875 men
  b) respiratory tract ailments 438 men
  c) gastrointestinal ailments   425 men
  d) skin ailments   646 "
  e) eye ailments   448 "
  f) dental ailments   538 "
  g) flu and angina   144 "
  h) venereal diseases   65 "
  i) change dressing   446 "
  j) ailments of the ear, throat, and nose 232 "
  k) miscellaneous ailments 611 "

No acute gastric ailments were reported during visits to the outpatient clinic.

7. The camp infirmary provided service for 557 cot-days, [listed here] by type of illness:
  a) respiratory tract ailments 185 men
  b) surgical ailments   31 "
  c) flu and angina   81 "
  d) gastrointestinal ailments 101 "
  e) heart   3 "
  f) miscellaneous   134 "

8. Five men were in the interregional hospital for treatment.

The nature of their illnesses: pneumonia, ileitis, and gastritis. In all, for the month of November there were in the venereal disease clinic for treatment for:
  1. Syphilis   one man
  2. Gonorrhea   one man
9. There was no mortality among the POWs in the month of November.

URO Work
As of 1 December, the following had been accomplished:

1. Personal questionnaires filled out   3,800 copies
2. Personal files created and registered   3,500 items
3. Form no. 2 cards sent to the USSR
   NKVD Administration   3,500 items
4. Remaining:
   a) unfilled personal questionnaires   107 items
   b) Form no. 2 cards to be prepared
   and sent to the administration   407 items
   c) by 3 December, lists of POWs from among the former leadership cadre (generals, colonels, lieutenant colonels, landowners, and other officials) will be completed and sent to the [NKVD] Administration
5. The card file both for those present [in camp] and for those who have left is 100 percent complete.

6. In the registration book 2,000 men from the present contingent have been recorded. A registration book was not established for the departed contingent.

All the URO work will be completed by 8 December of this year. The photographic work is proceeding unsatisfactorily. The chief obstacle to this is the shortage of materials (plates and paper)—the photo materials sent from Moscow turned out to be useless.

The Work of the Finance Section
The financing of the camp during the month of November was greatly delayed, which slowed down the normal pace of work. The receipt of money into the camp's account actually began on 21 November; before that it was necessary to provide food for the POWs and other goods by using the credit of trade organizations without permission.

As of 29 November, there were unpaid accounts totaling 350,000 rubles. After the head of the Finance Section, Com. Kobelev, left for Voroshilovgrad [renamed Luhansk in 1958] on 25 November, and after two telegrams addressed to the Administration (Com. Berenzon), the camp's account received 300,000 rubles, which did not cover payment of the debt of 350,000 rubles. After a second telegram addressed to the Administration (Com. Berenzon) and the Voroshilovgrad Oblast NKVD, 200,000 rubles were paid into the camp's account on 2 December.

In accordance with the camp financing plan, there are allocations of 1,300,000 [rubles] for November and December; of this, 700,000 has been received, and we request that the remaining 600,000 be sent no later than 12 December 1939. We request that measures be taken for the timely and continuous financing of the camp during the month of December.

Head of the NKVD camp
GB Captain Berezhkov

Commissar of the NKVD camp
Battalion Commissar Kirshin

The new NKVD reception-distribution centers, ordered by Beria on
10 December 1939, were to hold Polish Army officers who were to be
arrested in the UkSSR the same day (doc. 34).[239]

· 33 ·

NKVD Commissar's Order no. 0408 to Organize New Reception
and Distribution Centers in the UkSSR
10 December 1939, Moscow

Secret
Order of the USSR People's Commissar of Internal Affairs for 1939
No. 0408
10 December 1939
Moscow
Content: On the Organization of NKVD Reception
and Distribution Centers in the New Oblasts of the UkSSR

In connection with the organization of new oblasts in the UkSSR, I OR-
DER:
 1. Organize in Lvov, Tarnopol, Lutsk [Łuck], Rovno, Dragobych [Dro-
hobycz], and Stanislavov NKVD reception-distribution centers with a
transitional stationing capacity of fifty men apiece, with their maintenance paid out of local resources.
 2. In connection with this, add a supplement to [the instruction for] the
displacement of reception-distribution centers and NKVD labor colonies
for minors, as announced in USSR NKVD Order no. 0155 of 29 December 1937.[240]

 USSR Deputy People's Commissar of Internal Affairs
 Divisional Commissar Chernyshov

The arrest of all Polish officers registered in the oblasts of western
Ukraine was carried out according to the Politburo decision of 3 December 1939 (doc. 31), which ratified Beria's order to this effect issued
two days earlier.

· 34 ·

Ivan Serov's Report to Beria on the Arrest of Polish Regular Officers
in the Oblasts of Western Ukraine[241]
14 December 1939, Kiev

To the People's Commissar of Internal Affairs, USSR
GB Commissar 1st Rank Com. Beria
   I hereby report the results of the operation carried out on 10 December
1939 to arrest regular officers of the former Polish Army in the oblasts of
western Ukraine:

Tarnopol Oblast
143 men have been arrested. 51 of these are reserve officers. The arrested
include 5 colonels, 3 lieutenant colonels, 14 majors, 65 captains, and 56
lieutenants.
   Up to 10 December 1939, 153 men were arrested as participants in various c-r organizations.

Stanislavov Oblast
50 have been arrested. 7 of these are reserve officers. The arrested include
1 general, 2 colonels, 8 majors, 12 captains, and 27 lieutenants.
   Up to 10 December 1939, 140 men were arrested as participants in various c-r organizations.

Lutsk Oblast
151 men were arrested on 10 December 1939. 35 of these are reserve officers. The arrested include 26 captains, 2 majors, 32 lieutenants, and 91
2nd lieutenants.
   Up to 10 December 1939, 65 men were arrested.

Lvov Oblast
226 men were arrested on 10 December 1939. The arrested include 5 generals, 23 colonels, 42 majors, 28 lieutenant colonels, 61 captains, 22 lieutenants, and 46 2nd lieutenants.
   Up to 10 December 1939, 129 men were arrested.

   570 men were arrested on 10 December 1939 in the oblasts of western
Ukraine.
   Up to 10 December 1939, 487 men were arrested as participants in var-
ious c-r organizations.
   A total of 1,057 former officers of the Polish Army were arrested.

In addition, 3,878 officers, taken prisoner during the operation in western Ukraine, are being detained in the Starobelsk camps.[242]

UkSSR People's Commissar of Internal Affairs
GB Commissar 3rd Rank Serov

Soprunenko's instruction ordered the separation of officers and policemen from rank-and-file POWs. Remaining rank-and-file soldiers and NCOs were to be sent home, and information was requested on wounded German military personnel.

· 35 ·

Soprunenko's Instruction Sent by Direct Line to the Head of the UkSSR NKVD
Administration of Correctional Labor Colonies, Aleksandr Zverev,
on Dispatching Recuperated POW Officers to Various Destinations
15 December 1939, Moscow*

Top Secret
Kiev NKVD UITK to Zverev
Note [for] Transmission [by Direct Line]

Dispatch recuperated prisoner-of-war officers of the former Polish Army under convoy [to] Kozelsk camp, Kozelsk Station, Dzerzhinsky Railway. If among these officers there are officers of the police or gendarmerie, they should be sent [to] Ostashkov camp, Ostashkov Station, Kalinin Railway.[243]

You may dispatch the officers [in] a *vagonzak* [railway car], which you are to request [from] the Kiev brigade of convoy troops.

Send the rank-and-file soldiers and NCOs of the former Polish Army [from] the territory of Poland now part of Germany under convoy [to] Brest-Litovsk [Brześć-Litewski], [to] the Fourth Army transfer point for handing them over to the German authorities. Send home the prisoner-of-war privates and junior officers of the former Polish Army who are residents of western Ukraine and western Belorussia. Inform me of these departures. At the same time, immediately send by telegraph the surnames and detailed basic data on all soldiers and officers of the German Army be-

---

* Handwritten notes on the document: "To Comrade Khudiakova—Verify from replies whether everything has been done. Goberman. 3 January [1940]." And, "To Comrade Khudiakova—For those waiting. Makliarsky. 15 December." "Those waiting" may refer to the Germans in Soviet hospitals.

ing held [in] hospitals, indicating the circumstances and dates of capture.[244]

Soprunenko [no.] 2068534

Soprunenko probably wrote his 29 December 1939 report on Beria's instruction, preparatory to the special investigations that Beria ordered in Ostashkov camp (doc. 37), as well as in the two officer camps. Officers were subject neither to repatriation to western Belorussia or western Ukraine nor to exchange with the Germans.

· 36 ·

Soprunenko's Report on the Number of Polish POW Officers, Police,
and Gendarmes, Inhabitants of Western Ukraine, Western Belorussia,
and German Poland, Being Held in the NKVD POW Camps
29 December 1939, Moscow

Top Secret
Summary

1. Total officer contingent detained in the camps   8,488 people[245]
   Of these:
   a) residents of the territory included in Germany   5,800 people
   b) residents of western Belorussia
      and western Ukraine   2,688 people

2. Total police and gendarmes detained in the camps   6,176 people
   Of these:
   a) residents of the territory included in Germany   3,600 people
   b) residents of western Belorussia
      and western Ukraine   2,576 people

Head of the USSR NKVD UPV
Major (Soprunenko)

Beria's instruction to Soprunenko of 31 December 1939 on his departure to Ostashkov camp heralded a new round of intensive interrogations of Polish POWs in the three special camps. The goal was to extract intelligence information and prepare cases for submission to the Osoboe Soveshchanie [OSO—NKVD Special Board].

· 37 ·

Beria's Instruction to Soprunenko as Head of the USSR NKVD
Investigatory Brigade for Ostashkov Camp[246]
31 December 1939, Moscow

No. 5866/b
Top Secret

To the Head of the USSR NKVD UPV
Com. Major Soprunenko
Copy: To the Head of the UNKVD, Kalinin Oblast
Colonel Com. Tokarev

I command you to leave for the town of Ostashkov and conduct the following operation:

1. Familiarize yourself with the work status of the group of USSR NKVD investigators preparing cases against prisoner-of-war policemen from the former Poland for a report to the NKVD Special Board.[247]

Take the necessary measures to restructure the work of the investigation group in such a way that the drawing up of investigation cases against all the imprisoned prisoner-of-war police can be completed during the month of January.[248]

2. Separate out from the entire mass of prisoner-of-war police the document files of individuals that are of operational interest, and make a thorough investigation of these cases in order to expose all their contacts both inside the USSR and abroad, as well as [their knowledge of] agents of the former Polish intelligence that have been planted at one time or another in the USSR.[249]

3. The following comrades are being sent with you to carry out this operation:

1. N. F. Bykov—investigator, GB lieutenant;
2. A. M. Marisov—investigator, GB lieutenant;
3. N. K. Kleshchev—investigator, GB 2nd lieutenant;
4. V. I. Senkin—investigator, GB lieutenant;
5. V. A. Maklakov—investigator, GB 2nd lieutenant;
6. M. S. Galafeeev—investigator, GB sergeant;
7. N. A. Kiselev—investigator, GB lieutenant;
8. P. N. Volchenkov—junior investigator, GB sergeant;
9. A. Z. Fedonin—investigator, GB lieutenant;
10. V. P. Shishkin—investigator, GB 2nd lieutenant;

who must put themselves at the disposal of the head of the Ostashkov camp investigative group, GB Lieutenant Com. Belolipetsky.

4. Simultaneously, you should, together with those under your command—Senior Operational Plenipotentiary Officer of the 2nd Department of GEU [Main Economic Administration], GB Lieutenant Com.
Kholichev, and Senior Operational Plenipotentiary Officer of the 2nd Department of the GEU, GB Lieutenant Com. Logunkov—familiarize your-
selves with the status of the agent-informant work being conducted by the
OO [Special Section] of Ostashkov camp according to USSR NKVD Directive no. 4/56190 of 8 October 1939.[250]

Ascertain the degree to which the agency and information work among
prisoner-of-war policemen is secure, and render practical assistance on the
spot to set up work with the agency information network.

In so doing, pay attention to the value of the existing informants' work
and the degree of its reliability in providing a comprehensive picture of the
moods of all categories of POWs.

5. Verify the work of the camp's OO in exposing the outside connections of POWs, the nature of these connections, and the presence of the
agency both among the service personnel and in the environment outside
the camp.

6. Organize the work of the camp's evidence-recording apparatus, [and]
instruct the workers precisely on the data on prisoner-of-war policemen,
ensuring the high quality of the data, the receipt of precise and clear answers from POWs to the questions on the [personal] questionnaire,[251]
and the exposure in the course of interrogation of all the connections of
the POWs, both in the USSR and abroad.

7. Ascertain the status of camp security and of discipline among the
POWs, and take any necessary measures to exclude the possibility of escapes by POWs from the camp and their violation of camp order [regula-
tions].

Bring all malicious violators of the camp regulations to account; arrest
those caught attempting to escape, and bring them to trial.

Report on the results of the work done by you.[252]

> USSR People's Commissar of Internal Affairs
> GB Commissar 1st Rank
> L. Beria

Policeman Szczepan Olejnik's indictment is in the only personal file
found thus far for any of the 6,361 prisoners held in Ostashkov as of
16 March 1940. This file survived because it was accidentally sent
from Ostashkov to Griazovets camp, where it was forwarded to the
UPV. Olejnik was indicted under Article 58, Paragraph 13, of the Soviet Criminal Code pertaining to c-r activity in the Russian Empire

(which collapsed in March 1917) or during the Russian Civil War (1918–1922). Born in 1911, he was too young to participate in such activity in either period but was condemned nonetheless. He was murdered with the other Ostashkov prisoners in the spring of 1940.

· 38 ·

Conclusion of the Indictment in the Case of POW Szczepan Olejnik[253]
6 January 1940, Ostashkov

I approve
Head of the Special Section
Ostashkov NKVD Camp
GB [2nd] Lieutenant Korytov
Conclusion of Indictment
In Investigation Case no. 649
Indicting Olejnik, Stefan, son of Stefan (Polish: Szczepan)
under Art. 58, Par. 13, of the RSFSR
Criminal Code

6 January 1940

On the 29th day of December 1939, I, Section Head of the Special Department of the NKVD of the 7th Army, GB 2nd Lieutenant Milovidov, having examined Investigation Case no. 649 indicting the prisoner of war of the former Polish state Olejnik, Szczepan, born in 1911, a native of [the village of] Tarnovka [Tarnówka], Volhynian [Wołyń] Gubernia [Province], a Pole by nationality, for the crime stipulated in Art. 58, Par. 13, of the [Criminal Code of the] RSFSR,[254] and having found that Olejnik, being in the former Polish state from 1936 to 1939, served in the police in Borshchevo [Borszczów], where he conducted an active struggle against the revolutionary movement, have resolved:

to send Investigation Case no. 649 indicting prisoner of war S. S. Olejnik to the NKVD Special Board for examination.

Director, Special Section of the NKVD GUGB [Main Administration for State Security], Special Department, 7th Army, 2nd Lieutenant
(Milovidov)

Agreed: Senior Investigator of the Investigations Department of the USSR NKVD GUGB
(Belolipetsky)

Information: The accused Olejnik is being held in Ostashkov
NKVD camp, Kalinin Oblast.
Correct: (Signature)*

Polish prisoners continued to demand their rights. The colonels' petition from Starobelsk illustrates their living conditions and lists their
requests.

· 39 ·

Petition to Soviet Authorities from a Group of Polish POW Colonels to Define
Their Status and Observe International Standards for the Treatment of POWs[255]
7 January 1940, Starobelsk

Copy
Town of Starobelsk
Colonels' Group
Starobelsk
32 Kirov Street
7 January 1940
I. General Matters

We request that you clarify for us the relationship of the USSR government toward us, specifically:

1. Are we considered prisoners of war?

If so, we ask to be treated according to the rules accepted by all governments regarding POWs, and above all:

a) give us the possibility of freely contacting the embassy accredited to
the USSR government that has taken upon itself the protection of the interests of Polish citizens and, consequently, of POWs as well;[256]

b) make contact with the Red Cross in order to give us the possibility of
corresponding with our families who are outside the frontiers of the
USSR;[257]

c) publish a list of POWs so that our families can learn where we are;

d) release those in the reserves who were not mobilized and those who
are retired;

e) grant us an appropriate monetary allowance, as is due to us, for our
immediate personal needs because, for example, our clothing and foot-

---

* The Russian version has "illegible signature"; the Polish version has a handwritten note:
"Korytov."

wear are becoming useless, but we do not possess the necessary material means [money to replace them].

2. If we have been arrested?

If so, we ask that you inform us of the crimes for which we have been deprived of our freedom and present us with formal charges.

3. If we are detained (interned):

We request that you explain to us what actions of ours provoked this restriction of our freedom, especially since we were detained on Polish territory.

II. We request that you explain why the old and the infirm, who had nothing to do with the recent war, are being detained in the camp, and we ask that they be released to go home.

III. The issue of correspondence with our families has not yet been settled.

Normal human feelings demand that you enable us finally to contact our families and that they, in turn, can learn of our fate.

We request that you issue [the following] instructions:

Apply no restrictions to the correspondence [of those] conducting searches for their families.

Each person is to have the right to write a letter or postcard at least once a week, rather than once a month.[258]

Inform the sender if a letter is to be held back.

Give us the right to receive packages from our families with food, underwear, and other things that we need.

Give us writing paper and envelopes.

We request that you clarify whether our letters have gone to German-occupied territory and, if not, [that you] give us the opportunity to write them through the Red Cross.

IV. Medical assistance is inadequate.

In practice, it is limited to supplying [us] only with the simplest medications. Many officers are still awaiting treatment for their eyes, teeth, etc; in particular, we are painfully aware of the impossibility of providing appropriate diets for the sick.

In the event of illness of a more serious nature, there have been difficulties with sending the patient immediately to the hospital.

The cramped and damp quarters on the ground floor are having a disastrous effect on the health of the officers, especially since the food ration is barely sufficient for people who are not engaged in physical work, whereas we are all being made to perform heavy labor in the daily preparation of food.[259]

V. On our visits to the cinema, we request that we not be shown films or episodes that might insult our national feelings or the honor of our homeland.

We request also, especially, that lower-ranking officials address us in an appropriate manner. Although we are POWs, we nonetheless remain soldiers and retain our military ranks.

VI. At the time when Polish zlotys were in circulation, we were not given an opportunity to exchange our money for rubles or to send it to our families, and in this manner we and our families have been deprived of all means [of subsistence]. In addition, it should be said that the existence of our families was supported by our labor, and here in the camp, despite our being deprived of monetary funds, we are required to pay in rubles for the satisfaction of our most essential needs (shoe repair, purchase of fats [beef or pork drippings or bacon fats], etc.).

We request:

[That you] exchange our zlotys for rubles and keep us steadily supplied with money in the form of an advance on the money due to us for our participation in the war.

[That you] allow us to send from the camp, and our families to send to the camp, zlotys as well as rubles and other currency.

VII. Finally, we ask that you grant the following [requests]:

Allow us to organize in groups for foreign-language lessons, and make it possible for us to purchase the necessary notebooks and aids, which we could order from Lvov.

Order a regular and frequent supply of books for reading (fiction, scientific, and military-historical) in various languages.

Allow us to take walks outside the camp in appropriate weather at least three times a week.

Allow us to meet with relatives and comrades who are in the main camp and on Volodarskaia Street.[260]

Give us a list of those [held] in Starobelsk camp so that we can search for relatives.

Return the things and money taken from us.

Provide us with equipment for sports and indoor games.

Give me and the man in charge of our housekeeping the opportunity to speak at least once a week with you or the camp's deputy housekeeping director.[261]

[Copy] Verified as correct: Administration Secretary
Militia 2nd Lieutenant (Bashlykov)

By 1 February most of the POW cases in Ostashkov camp had been processed, with the remainder to be completed in a week's time. Investigations were also taking place in the Kozelsk and Starobelsk camps, but without instructions to prepare cases for the OSO.

· 40 ·

Cipher Telegram from Soprunenko and Stepan Belolipetsky to Beria
on the Conclusion of the Investigation and Transfer of POW Cases
from Ostashkov Camp to the OSO[262]
1 February 1940, Ostashkov

Top Secret
No. 4888
USSR NKVD
Received 1 February 1940
From Ostashkov

To People's Commissar of Internal Affairs Com. Beria
The investigation [of] the former Polish police detained [at] Ostashkov camp is complete; 6,050 cases have been drawn up.[263] I have begun sending cases [to] the OSO. We will finish sending them on the 8th of February. The measures essential for the investigation have been completed.

Soprunenko
Belolipetsky
Subject to return. NKVD USSR.[264]

In February 1940, the UPV was preparing to "clear out" the POW camps. Soprunenko's suggestions to Beria indicate that he did not envisage the extermination of all the prisoners in the Kozelsk and Starobelsk camps, but suggested that cases be drawn up against those belonging to certain categories.

· 41 ·

NKVD UPV Proposals to Beria on Clearing Out Starobelsk and Kozelsk Camps[265]
20 February 1940, Moscow

Top Secret

To USSR People's Commissar of Internal Affairs
GB Commissar 1st Rank Comrade L. P. Beria*

In order to clear Starobelsk and Kozelsk camps, I request your decision on carrying out the following measures:

1. From the officer contingent, release to their homes all those [who are] seriously ill, total invalids, tuberculosis patients, and older men sixty years old and above, who number about 300 men.

2. From among the reserve officers and residents of the western oblasts of the UkSSR and BSSR, release to their homes the farmers, physicians, engineers and technicians, [and] teachers for whom there are no compromising materials. According to preliminary data, 400–500 men may be released from this category.[266]

3. I request your permission to draw up cases against the officers of KOP, workers in law courts and prosecutors' offices, landowners, activists in the POV [P.O.W.] and Streltsy [Strzelcy] parties,[267] officers of the 2nd Department of the former Polish General Staff,[268] [and] information officers (about 400 men) for examination by the OSO.

It would be desirable to conduct the investigation of these categories in the People's Commissariats of Internal Affairs of the BSSR and UkSSR or, if this is impossible, to concentrate all those specified at Ostashkov camp, where the investigation could be conducted.

Head of the USSR NKVD UPV
Major P. Soprunenko

Commissar of the USSR NKVD UPV
Regimental Commissar Nekhoroshev

The categories of prisoners listed below were moved out of the camps to NKVD prisons. They, too, would be subject to the death penalty under the Politburo decision of 5 March 1940 (doc. 47).

---

* Handwritten across the page from left to right in blue pencil: "Comrade Merkulov. Discuss this with me. L. Beria. 20 February 1940. Com. Soprunenko. V. Merkulov. 21 February."

· 42 ·

USSR Deputy People's Commissar of Internal Affairs Vsevolod Merkulov's
Directive on Transferring to Prisons Certain Categories of Prisoners
Detained in Starobelsk, Kozelsk, and Ostashkov Camps
22 February 1940, Moscow

No. 641/b
Top Secret

To the Head of the UPV, Major Com. Soprunenko
To UkSSR NKVD GB Commissar 3rd Rank Com. Serov
To the Head of the Voroshilovgrad UNKVD,
    GB Captain Com. Cherevatenko
To the Head Smolensk Oblast UNKVD, GB Captain Com. Panfilov
To the Head of the Kalinin Oblast UNKVD, Colonel Com. Tokarev

According to the instruction of People's Commissar of Internal Affairs
Comrade Beria, I direct that all former prison guards, intelligence agents,
provocateurs, [military] settlers, judicial employees, landowners, merchants, and large property holders detained in Starobelsk, Kozelsk, and
Ostashkov NKVD camps are to be moved to prisons, transferring them to
the control of NKVD organs.[269]

All existing materials available on them are to be transferred to the investigative units of the UNKVD for the conduct of the investigation.

Additional instructions will be given on the procedure for further action
in these cases.[270]

Report on the number of arrested [prisoners] transferred.

USSR Deputy People's Commissar of Internal Affairs
GB Commissar 3rd Rank
V. Merkulov

At the end of February 1940, the NKVD UPV reported on the nationality of the officers in the three special camps.

· 43 ·

NKVD UPV Report on the Nationality of Polish POW Officers
Held in Starobelsk and Kozelsk Camps
28 February 1940, Moscow

Top Secret
Report on the National Composition of the Prisoner-of-War Officers
from the Former Polish Army Detained in NKVD Camps

Starobelsk camp
Total officers detained in the camp   3,908 people[271]
Of these:
  a) Poles   3,828 people
  b) Jews   71   ″
  c) Ukrainians   4   ″
  d) Germans   1   ″
  e) Hungarians   1   ″
  f) Lithuanians   1   ″
  g) Latvians   1   ″
  h) Bulgarians   1

Kozelsk camp
Total officers detained in the camp   4,486 people[272]
Of these:
  a) Poles   4,347 people
  b) Jews   89   ″
  c) Belorussians   23   ″
  d) Germans   11   ″
  e) Lithuanians   8   ″
  f) Ukrainians   6   ″
  g) Czechs   1   ″
  h) Georgians   1   ″[273]

Total officers held in Starobelsk and Kozelsk camps   8,394 people[274]
Of these:
  a) Poles   8,175 people
  b) Jews   160   ″[275]
  c) Belorussians   23   ″
  d) Germans   12   ″
  e) Ukrainians   10   ″
  f) Lithuanians   9   ″

g) Hungarians   I   "
h) Latvians   I   "
i) Bulgarians   I   "
j) Czechs   I   "
k) Georgians   I   "

Head of the USSR NKVD UPV
Major (Soprunenko)

At this time, the NKVD UPV was ordered to provide reports on the number of police and gendarmes held in the camps. The vast majority of these prisoners were held in Ostashkov camp.

· 44 ·

Soprunenko's Report on the Number of Polish Police and Gendarmes
Held in NKVD POW Camps
2 March 1940, Moscow

Secret
Report on Police and Gendarmes Detained in NKVD
Prisoner-of-War Camps

The following are detained in the camps:
a) officers of the police and gendarmerie   282 people
b) junior officers of the police and gendarmerie   780   "
c) rank-and-file police and gendarmes   5,008   "
d) prison guards   114   "
e) intelligence agents and provocateurs   8   "
Total   6,192 people[276]

Head of the USSR NKVD UPV
Major P. Soprunenko

The date of this deportation decision, 2 March 1940, may be connected with Stalin's decision to shoot the prisoners held in the three special camps, Kozelsk, Ostashkov, and Starobelsk (point 2). According to Natalia Lebedeva the decision was probably made at the Stalin-Beria meeting on 28 February, and Beria's letter/resolution to Stalin to shoot the Polish prisoners of war was formulated on 3 March 1940 (see doc. 47).

· 45 ·

Excerpt from Protocol no. 13, Decisions of the Politburo: Decision
on Guarding the State Borders of the UkSSR and BSSR
2 March 1940, Moscow

---

2 March 1940[277]
Top Secret
Special folder
114. On Guarding the State Borders in the Western Oblasts
of the UkSSR and BSSR
Approve the following proposals
by Comrades Beria and Khrushchev:[278]

1. Require the Councils of People's Commissars of the UkSSR and BSSR within two months' time:

a) to deport residents from an 800-meter border zone, with the exception of the towns of Peremyshl [Przemyśl], Zaleshchiki [Zaleszczyki], Lisko, Ugnuv [Uhnów], Sokal, Ustilug [Uściług], Druia [Druja], Druskeniki [Druskienniki], and Novogrud [Nowogród Wotyński]

b) the removal from the 800-meter zone of the residents of the towns, enumerated in point "a," to be carried out on the basis of the materials [held by] the NKVDs of the UkSSR and the BSSR

c) to clear the 800-meter border zone of all structures belonging to the deported residents

2. Direct the USSR NKVD to [do the following]:

a) by 15 April of this year, deport to the rayons [districts] of the Kazakh SSR for a term of ten years all the families of the repressed and those who are now in prisoner-of-war camps, former officers of the Polish Army, police, prison guards, gendarmes, intelligence agents, former landowners, manufacturers, and prominent officials in the former Polish state apparatus, numbering 22,000–25,000 families.[279]

b) arrest the most malicious members of the families subject to deportation with respect to whom the NKVD organs possess materials about their anti-Soviet work in the past or present, with subsequent preparation of their cases for examination by the OSO.[280]

c) deport all prostitutes who were registered with the organs of the former Polish police and now continue to work in prostitution.

d) within twenty days' time, to work out and submit for approval to the USSR Council of People's Commissars a procedure for the deportation of the families specified in point "a."

3. Establish that the real estate, trade, and industrial enterprises of the

deported families enumerated in point 2 are subject to confiscation and that the latter have the right either to sell or to take with them to their place of deportation all the remaining property, not exceeding 100 kilograms for each family member.

4. Transfer all housing and commercial buildings standing empty after the deportation to the disposition of the local Soviet organs. The UkSSR and BSSR Councils of People's Commissars are to ensure their preservation, and that they are properly utilized, first of all, for the settlement of RKKA servicemen, party and Soviet workers, and those sent to work in the western oblasts of Ukraine and Belorussia.

5. Forbid individuals (refugees) who have arrived on the territory of the western oblasts of Ukraine and Belorussia since the start of military actions in Poland (September 1939), and who have expressed the desire to remain on the territory of the Soviet Union, to reside in the 100-kilometer border zone for a term of five years. When issuing passports, issue to this category of citizens passports with the appropriate notations.[281]

6. Instruct the USSR NKVD that refugees who have expressed the desire to leave the Soviet Union for territory now occupied by the Germans, and who have not been accepted by the German government [that] in accordance with the current agreement, [they shall] be sent within one month's time from the western oblasts of Ukraine and Belorussia to the northern districts of the Soviet Union to be utilized in logging and other operations.[282]

7. Within twenty days' time, the USSR NKVD shall work out and submit for approval by the USSR Council of People's Commissars the procedure for the eviction and deportation of the refugees specified in points 5 and 6.

8. Within twenty days' time, the USSR NKVD shall submit to the USSR Council of Ministers estimates of the essential expenses involved in carrying out the proposed measures.

Copies sent to: Com. Beria; CC Ukrainian Communist Party (b); CC Belorussian Communist Party (b); Com. Khlomov

> Secretary of the CC CPSU(b)
> J. Stalin
> [Here, a facsimile signature, "I. V. Stalin," embossed with a round, red seal and the legend "All-Union Communist Party of Bolsheviks," with "CC" in the inner circle of the seal.]

In early March 1940 the head of the Special Section in Ostashkov camp, Grigory Korytov, participated in a conference called by Soprunenko at the 1st Special Department of the NKVD, Moscow. The conferees discussed how to arrange the transport of Ostashkov prisoners to labor camps after their sentencing by the OSO [Special Board]; they assumed that the destination was Kamchatka. Toward the end of Korytov's report, where he mentions that 600 of the 6,005 cases had been examined by the NKVD OSO thus far, resulting in sentences of three, five, or eight years in Kamchatka, he writes: "Further examination has been suspended by the People's Commissar [Beria] for the time being." (A meeting with the commanders of the Kozelsk and Starobelsk camps was held in Moscow on 15 March.)

· 46 ·

Report by Grigory Korytov to the Head of the Special Department
of Kalinin Oblast UNKVD, Vasily Pavlov, on the Discussion in the NKVD
1st Special Department about "Clearing Out" the Ostashkov POW Camp[283]
No later than 4 March 1940, Ostashkov[284]

Com. Pavlov!
I was called to Moscow, as I have already informed you, by a telegram from the head of the UPV, Com. Soprunenko. Upon my arrival, Com. Soprunenko stated that he had summoned me at the request of the head of the 1st Special Department concerning the question of organizing the dispatch of POWs after decisions have been issued by the OSO.

The conference took place at the 1st Special Department and lasted over the course of two days.

Attending the conference besides the leadership of the 1st Special Department were the head of Convoy Troops, a GULAG representative, a representative of the UPV, and several others.

The principal issues were:
1. Preparation in the camp for the dispatch of those convicted.
2. Where to announce the decision of the OSO.
3. Where to hand over those convicted to the convoy: in the camp or at the train station.
4. Operational servicing en route.
5. Housekeeping service [provisions].

At the beginning of the conference, I was asked to express the view of the [Ostashkov] Special Section on how we would view the organization of the dispatch.

Considering the mood of the POWs and their number, and especially bearing in mind that this entire contingent represents an active c-r force, I expressed my thoughts as follows:

1. Prepare the dispatch in the same way as we prepared earlier to send them to Germany and to the districts of our territory, i.e., observing the territorial principle, which can give the convicted [prisoners] reason to think that they are being prepared for dispatch home.[285]

2. In order to avoid various types of excesses and disturbances, in no instance announce the decision of the OSO here [at Ostashkov], but announce it [after the POWs' arrival] in the camp where they will be held. If during the journey questions come from the POWs as to where they are being taken, the convoy can tell them only: "To work in another camp."

3. Deliver the convicted men to the convoy as before, here in the camp.

4. With regard to operational servicing en route, I asked the conference to free the [Ostashkov] Special Section from this responsibility, considering the small number of staff in the camp's Special Section, the lack of staff in the *okrug* [military district] Special Department, and the fact that each batch of convicted men should be traveling to its destination for at least a month and that there will be four such batches in all.[286]

Consequently, we would need 8 or more men for the operations contingent. Operational servicing should be assigned to another operations department.

All this was debated for a long time, and I had to defend my point of view and justify it thoroughly. Finally, everyone agreed with this, and in this spirit the organizational plan for the [POW] dispatch was written and handed over for approval to Deputy People's Commissar Merkulov.

The head of the Convoy Troops took the operational servicing upon himself.

How soon will we be clearing out the camps[?]

Of the 6,005 cases we have submitted [to OSO], 600 have been examined so far, with sentences of three or five or eight years (Kamchatka).[287] Further examination has been suspended by the People's Commissar [Beria] for the time being.

But it is rumored that in March we must basically clear out the camps and prepare to receive the Finns.[288]

There is an instruction from the People's Commissar to put certain categories of POWs in local prisons. On this account, the head of the Kalinin Oblast [NKVD] Administration has a directive dated 29 February 1940, no. 25/1869, with which I ask that you familiarize yourself.[289]

> Head of the Special Section of Ostashkov Prisoner-of-War Camp
> GB 2nd Lieutenant (Korytov)

The Politburo resolution of 5 March 1940 is the key evidence proving the Soviet leadership's responsibility for the massacre in spring 1940 of 14,465 Polish prisoners of war held in the three special camps as well as 7,300 prisoners held in NKVD jails in Belorussia and Ukraine (see Part II). Soviet responsibility was concealed and vigorously denied for half a century until it was admitted in the Soviet press on 13 April 1990 (doc. 117) when Russian President Mikhail Gorbachev also handed the NKVD spring 1940 camp departure lists to President Wojciech Jaruzelski of Poland. However, it was not until 14 October 1992 that, because of a political decision by Russian President Boris Yeltsin, the Politburo resolution was published in the Moscow press. On the same day, it was also delivered to President Lech Wałęsa in Warsaw, together with documents on the Soviet cover-up of the crime (doc. 119).

· 47 ·

Beria Memorandum to Joseph Stalin Proposing the Execution
of the Polish Officers, Gendarmes, Police, Military Settlers, and Others
in the Three Special POW Camps, Along with Those Held in the Prisons
of the Western Regions of Ukraine and Belorussia, Accepted by the Politburo
5 March 1940, Moscow[290]

No. 794/B
Top Secret

Central Committee of the All Union Communist Party (b)
To Comrade Stalin

In the USSR NKVD prisoner-of-war camps and prisons of the western regions of Ukraine and Belorussia, there are at present a large number of former officers of the Polish Army, former workers in the Polish police and intelligence organs, members of Polish nationalist c-r parties, participants in exposed c-r insurgent organizations, refugees, and others. They are all sworn enemies of Soviet power, filled with hatred for the Soviet system of government.

Prisoner-of-war officers and police in the camps are attempting to continue their c-r work and are conducting anti-Soviet agitation. Each one of them is just waiting to be released in order to be able to enter actively into the battle against Soviet power.

The NKVD organs in the western oblasts of Ukraine and Belorussia have exposed several c-r insurgent organizations. In all these c-r organizations, an active guiding role is played by former officers of the former Polish Army and former police and gendarmes.[291]

Among the detained refugees and those who have violated the state border, a significant number of individuals who are participants in c-r espionage and insurgent organizations have also been uncovered.[292]

The prisoner-of-war camps are holding a total (not counting the soldiers and the NCOs) of 14,736 former officers, officials, landowners, police, gendarmes, prison guards, [military] settlers, and intelligence agents,
who are more than 97 percent Polish by nationality.
Among them are:

generals, colonels, and lieutenant colonels	295
majors and captains	2,080
lieutenants, 2nd lieutenants, and ensigns	6,049
police officers, junior officers, border guards, and gendarmerie	1,030
rank-and-file police, gendarmes, prison guards, and intelligence agents	5,138
officials, landowners, priests, and [military] settlers	144

In the prisons of the western oblasts of Ukraine and Belorussia a total of
18,632 arrested people (including 10,685 Poles)[293] are being held, including:

former officers	1,207
former police, intelligence agents, and gendarmes	5,141
spies and saboteurs	347
former landowners, factory owners, and officials	465
members of various c-r and insurgent organizations and of various c-r elements	5,345
refugees	6,127

Based on the fact that they are all hardened, irremediable enemies of Soviet power, the NKVD USSR believes it is essential:
I. *To direct the NKVD USSR to:**

1) examine the cases of the 14,700 former Polish officers, officials,
landowners, police, intelligence agents, gendarmes, [military] settlers, and
prison guards who are now in the prisoner-of-war camps

2) and also examine the cases of those who have been arrested and are
in the prisons of the western oblasts of Ukraine and Belorussia, numbering
11,000, members of various c-r espionage and sabotage organizations,
former landowners, manufacturers, former Polish officers, officials, and

---

* The phrase in italics was underlined by hand. Parts I–III of Beria's memorandum were
used in the decision of the Politburo of the Central Committee as formulated in points I–III,
which were evidently drawn up by Stalin's secretary; see *KD1/217*; *KDZ1/217*.

refugees, [and] using the special procedure, apply to them the supreme punishment, [execution by] shooting.

II. Examine [these] cases without calling in the arrested men and without presenting [them with] the charges, the decision about the end of the investigation, or the document of indictment, according to the following procedure:

a) [examine the cases] against individuals in the prisoner-of-war camps on the basis of information presented by the USSR NKVD UPV

b) [examine the cases] against individuals who have been arrested on the basis of information from files presented by the UkSSR NKVD and the BSSR NKVD

III. Assign the examination of cases and the carrying out of decisions to a *troika* [threesome] consisting of Comrades ~~Beria,~~* Merkulov, Kobulov,† and Bashtakov (Head of 1st Special Department NKVD USSR).[294]

USSR People's Commissar of Internal Affairs
L. Beria‡

---

* Crossed out by hand in blue pencil.
† "Kobulov" was added by hand after "Merkulov"; both were written above the line in blue pencil, evidently by Stalin.
‡ On the document, written across the text: "*Za*" [For] with the signatures "I. V. Stalin, K. Voroshilov, A. Mikoyan" in blue pencil and "V. Molotov" in regular pencil (page 1).

In the margin, evidently written by Stalin's secretary: Kalinin—*za*, Kaganovich—*za*" (page 1).

Before point 1: the symbol Z, signifying the beginning of the decision (page 3).

In the margin: "Special folder. USSR NKVD question" (page 3).

Below Beria's signature on the document, on the left side of page: "Vm Beria. [Implement Beria]." Below that by hand: "Protocol 13/144." Below that: "5 March 1940" (page 4 of the facsimile in *KDZ1*/216, p. 475; *KD1*/216, p. 388).

View of Katyn Forest from the Dnieper [Dnepr] River with the NKVD dacha visible through the trees. Spring–summer 1943.

The NKVD dacha, called Dnjepr-Schlösschen [Little Castle on the Dnieper] by the Germans. It stood 300 meters from the execution site in Katyn Forest. Spring–summer 1943.

Oblique view of disinterred corpses at Katyn photographed from a low-flying German airplane, April 1943.

The bound hands of a murdered officer showing that the rope bit deep into his flesh. Katyn, 1943.

A German officer with Allied officers brought in from prisoner-of-war camps in Germany, standing over an opened burial pit. Katyn, 1943.

A German officer speaking to a group of European journalists at the edge of a burial pit. Katyn, 1943.

Cleaned-up shoulder straps showing the remains to be those of a major from the Józef Piłsudski Cavalry Regiment. Katyn, 1943.

Members of the International Medical Commission at Katyn in 1943: Dr. Ferenc Orsos of Budapest University examining the remains of a Polish prisoner of war, observed by Dr. A. Saxen of Helsinki University.

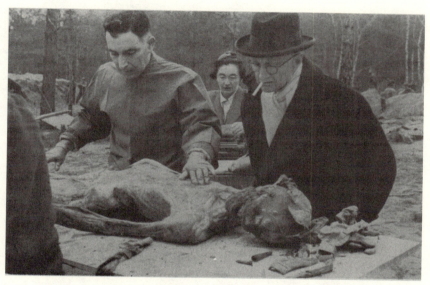

Members of the International Medical Commission at Katyn in 1943: Professor Vincenzo Mario Palmieri of Naples University (*left*) with Professor François Naville of Geneva University.

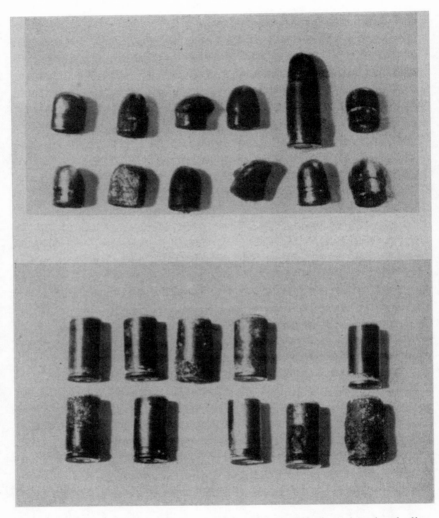

Top, Several deformed bullets and one original bullet found in the skulls of murdered Polish officers at Katyn. *Bottom*, Several partly corroded shell casings found in the Katyn burial pits.

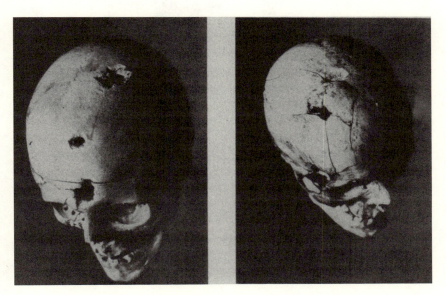

Two exhumed skulls from a Katyn burial pit. The left one has three exit holes. The right one has two exit holes and a bullet still lodged in it from a third shot. The large size of the anterior exit hole is caused by the victim's having been shot from behind, in the occipital region at the base of the skull.

Three men praying at the edge of a Katyn burial pit, 16 April 1943. *Left to right,* Prelate Stanisław Jasiński (sent by the Polish Metropolitan Archbishop of Kraków, Adam Stefan Sapieha); Kazimierz Skarżyński, secretary of the Polish Red Cross Executive Board, Warsaw; and Dr. Jerzy Wodzinowski of the Polish Red Cross, Warsaw.

Certificate in the name of General Mieczysław Smorawiński for the Silver Cross of the Virtuti Militari, the Polish decoration for valor, dated Warsaw, 1 May 1933. The general was murdered at Katyn.

French Vichy officers accompanied by a German officer at Katyn, spring 1943. The man second from the right, in the braided cap of an air force general, is Count Ferdinand de Brinon (1892–1947), then French ambassador to Berlin, who was visiting French volunteers fighting alongside the Germans in Russia. In the background are the graves of Generals Mieczysław Smorawiński and Bronisław Bohatyrewicz [Bohaterewicz].

Photographs of some Polish officers murdered at Kharkov.

Major Baruch Steinberg, Chief Rabbi of the Polish Army, with Polish
Army officers, presumably Jewish, at the Postępowa [Progressive] Syna-
gogue, Kraków, on 5 September 1935. Steinberg was among the forty-
five chaplains in the Polish armed forces taken prisoner by the Red Army
in September 1939 and known to have been murdered by the NKVD in
spring 1940. He was held in Starobelsk camp, taken to Moscow in December 1939, sent to Kozelsk camp, and shot at Katyn. In the photo he is
holding what looks like a memorial tablet. Jewish Polish Army veterans
of the War of Independence met in Kraków on 5 September 1935 to offer
a collective prayer for Marshal Józef Piłsudski, who died in May.

Main entrance of the Polish War Cemetery at Katyn, 29 October 2004.
The Katyn victims are memorialized on tablets in the walls bordering the
path to the cemetery.

Tablets at the Polish War Cemetery at Katyn with the symbols of the four
religions of the prewar Polish Army: Roman Catholicism, Judaism, Polish Orthodoxy, and Islam. 29 October 2004.

Exhumation work at a Kharkov grave pit, summer 1991. A Soviet officer, probably from the Main Military Prosecutor's Office, stands at the left at the edge of the pit, holding an open file.

Soldiers from a detached company of the Kharkov [Kharkiv] Mechanized Division of the Soviet Army assigned to wash the exhumed bones of Polish prisoners of war from Starobelsk camp. Kharkov, summer 1991. (The Soviet Union ceased to exist on 31 December 1991.)

Sorted skulls and bones. Kharkov, summer 1991.

Members of the Polish exhumation team at Kharkov in summer 1991.
Left to right, Professor Roman Mądro from the Institute of Forensic
Medicine, Medical Academy, Lublin; Prelate Zdzisław Peszkowski,
Kozelsk survivor and chaplain to the Katyn Families in Poland; Stefan
Śnieżko, Polish deputy prosecutor general and chief of the exhumation
team. The rods in the exhumed skulls show bullet trajectories, indicating
the professional skill of the executioners.

Memorial tablet at the Polish War Cemetery, Kharkov, 2000. The name on the upper part of the tablet is that of 2nd Lieutenant in Communications, Reserve, Antoni Pieńkowski (1912–1940); the name on the lower part is that of Artillery Captain Ludwik Pieńkowski (1895–1940), father of Tadeusz Pieńkowski, a Polish Katyn expert.

Soldiers of the Guards Company, Kantemir Armored Division, Soviet
Army, assigned to exhume the remains of Ostashkov prisoners from a
burial pit at Mednoe, summer 1991.

Extracting remains at Mednoe with the aid of a backhoe, summer 1991.

The Polish deputy prosecutor general Stefan Śnieżko (*center*) with members of the Polish exhumation team, standing in a grave pit at Mednoe beside a victim's remains on a stretcher, summer 1991.

Members of the Polish exhumation team at Mednoe in summer 1991 paying homage to the murdered Ostashkov prisoners by lighting a small candle (foreground). *Left to right*, Prelate Zdzisław Peszkowski; Jędrzej Tucholski, a Katyn expert; Zbigniew Mielecki, a prosecutor from the Polish Ministry of Justice who gave legal assistance to the Soviet investigators of the Katyn massacres; an unidentified team member; Roman Mądro, a medical doctor; another team member, mostly hidden; Colonel Zdzisław Sawicki, an expert on military insignia and uniforms; and another team member.

PART II

Extermination, March–June 1940

The Politburo decision of 5 March 1940 to shoot the Polish prisoners of war—those in the three special camps, Ostashkov,
Starobelsk, and Kozelsk, as well as those in the jails of western
Belorussia and western Ukraine (docs. 47, 53)—set the NKVD killing
machine in motion. In April, NCOs still at liberty in the western USSR
and officers in Soviet hospitals were also swept up in the dragnet (docs.
58, 68). The prisoners' families also suffered. A month earlier, orders
had gone out to camp commanders to compile lists of the prisoners
and their families (doc. 49), and record forms were drawn up for each
prisoner family and for each prisoner (docs. 50, 51). Orders were also
sent to the NKVD authorities in Kazakhstan to prepare for the "resettlement" of prisoner families there (doc. 52). The deportation was approved by the Soviet Council of Ministers on 2 March, but the detailed
NKVD instruction was not approved until 10 April, more than a
month later (docs. 64a, 64b). Its approval led to the second great wave
of deportations of Polish citizens from western Ukraine and western
Belorussia. On 13 April 1940 as many as 25,000 families were deported; as in the February wave, which carried off the families of military settlers, these were again mostly women and children. The deportees were "resettled" on collective and state farms in Kazakhstan.
There they were forced to do heavy physical work. Wives and children
appealed even to Stalin himself for the release of their husbands and fathers (doc. 80), but to no avail. Many died from malnutrition and disease, especially the very young and the old.[1]

The Executions

The executions of the prisoners held in the three special camps began in early April and continued until late May 1940, with the Ostashkov prisoners coming last. The final death transport left Kozelsk on 12 May; however, it was sent not to Katyn (Gnezdovo Station) but to Babynino Station for Yukhnov camp (also known as Pavlishchev Bor), so the lives of these prisoners were spared (docs. 84, 85). The last batch of Starobelsk prisoners left for Kharkov on 10 May, and like their predecessors, most were likely shot in the Kharkov NKVD jail two days later. The last death transport left Ostashkov for Kalinin (Tver) on 19 May, and most of the prisoners were probably shot in the NKVD jail there on 21–22 May.[2] NKVD reports on prisoner moods show their belief that they were being sent home. The camp authorities spread such rumors and did everything they could to confirm the prisoners in this belief in order to avoid resistance. This explains why most of the prisoners were anxious to leave and went willingly (doc. 67).

The extermination mechanism is well documented. NKVD procedures involved checking and rechecking prisoners (doc. 63), compiling and sending to camp commanders lists of those to be sent out of the camps to be shot (doc. 62), and reporting on the number sent to their death (doc. 65). The documents show that Beria's deputy, Merkulov, was informed about the execution of each batch of Ostashkov prisoners in the Kalinin NKVD prison. Similar reports must have been sent to him on the execution of the Starobelsk and Kozelsk prisoners as well, but they either have been destroyed or are still classified. Solomon Milshtein, head of the Glavnoe Transportnoe Upravlenie [GTU—NKVD Main Transport Administration], reported to Merkulov on the railway prison cars used to transport prisoners to the execution sites; for example, on 5 April he reported on the movement of railway cars which had transported prisoners from Kozelsk to Smolensk the day before (doc. 61).

The departure lists sent to the camp commanders were sometimes changed. Some prisoners were selected to live either before or at the date set for sending them from the camps. Cases for shooting were processed by the 1st Special Department in Moscow for prisoners held in the Russian Soviet Republic and by the 1st Special Departments of the Belorussian and Ukrainian Soviet Republics for prisoners held there. Selected to live were those chosen by Soviet intelligence services;

those requested by the German Embassy in Moscow; ethnic Germans and Latvians who had no compromising materials against them; informants; persons who might be important sources of intelligence; and, finally, those not included in the categories listed in the Politburo decision of 5 March 1940. All these people were put "under control" and carefully verified. The Troika then made its decisions, recorded in special protocols, but apparently these have not survived. It is not known why the last prisoner echelon to leave Kozelsk on 12 May was not sent to Gnezdovo, the station for Katyn, but to Babynino, the station for Yukhnov camp, so that these prisoners survived. If all of these prisoners were not individually put "under control," their survival might have been connected with the German attack on Holland, Belgium, and France, which began on 10 May. This attack seems to have caught Stalin by surprise, for there is no evidence of Razvedka [Soviet military intelligence] warnings.[3] Indeed, German Ambassador Schulenburg did not inform Molotov of the invasion until the day it began, 10 May, and the commissar for foreign affairs remarked that Germany's allies might now find themselves "in a difficult situation."[4]

Ostashkov

The most abundant documentation on transports and executions concerns the police and gendarmes who made up the vast majority of prisoners of war at Ostashkov; therefore, an account of their fate precedes the others. Unlike the military officers in Starobelsk and Kozelsk, many policemen worked for extra food by improving and adding to the camp buildings, thus costing the Soviet government very little for their upkeep (doc. 83). They were given a fine send-off. According to a survivor, "In order to give a more festive air to the departure, the camp authorities organized a band to play as the convoys left. This produced an excellent effect on the prisoners."[5] In April–May 1940 the prisoners were transported by rail to Kalinin (Tver), escorted by the NKVD 236th Convoy Regiment. There are several reports on this "action"—for example, the report on more than 5,000 prisoners who were dispatched to their death between 6 and 29 April 1940 (doc. 72) and the report of 14 May 1940 on lists received, prisoners dispatched, and those remaining in the camp (doc. 76). NKVD figures frequently fluctuated because some names were duplicated, some dead prisoners were included in the lists of those to be dispatched, some of those on the dispatch lists were spared, and some prisoners were added after the lists were made. According to NKVD UPV figures, the total number of prisoners sent to Kalinin was 6,287 (doc. 84), but verification by Polish researchers half a century later yielded a higher number: 6,314.[6] The arrival of each batch of Ostashkov prisoners was noted on a "receipt," and most of these "receipts" were signed by Gosudarstvennaia Bezopasnost [GB—State Security] Lieutenant Timofei Kachin (doc. 59), whereas reports on executions carried out, called "implementations," were sent directly to Beria's deputy, Merkulov. Most of these "implementation" reports were signed by the head of the NKVD for Kalinin Oblast [Administrative Region], Dmitry Tokarev (docs. 60, 82).

NKVD documents do not show how the Ostashkov prisoners were killed, but an eyewitness was found half a century after the event who deposed testimony on this particular mass murder. In March 1991 the aged Tokarev (b. 1902) gave many details on the fate of the Ostashkov prisoners during his interrogation by Lieutenant Colonel Anatoly Yablokov, a military prosecutor in the Soviet Main Military Prosecutor's Office, who was in charge of the Soviet Katyn investigation from 1991 to 1994. Tokarev claimed that he was not personally involved in the killing because a special group of NKVD men came from Moscow to do the "work." He stated that those in charge of the operation were GB Major V. M. Blokhin, head of the Komendatura [Command] of the AKhU [Administrative-Housekeeping Board of the NKVD]; Kombrig [Brigade Commander] M. S. Krivenko, head of NKVD Convoy Troops; and Senior GB Major N. I. Sinegubov, head of Intelligence for the NKVD Main Transport Administration and its deputy chief.

According to Tokarev, about thirty NKVD men, mostly drivers and some prison guards, took part in shooting the prisoners, always at night, after which they would retire to their special quarters and drink a lot of vodka. Blokhin was the chief executioner. His special uniform consisted of a leather cap, an apron, and gloves reaching above the elbows. The prisoners were divided into batches of 250 because more could not be shot easily in one night. They were led from their cells in the Kalinin NKVD jail to the cellar, and once there, to the Krasny Ugolok [Red Corner] room—used by prison personnel for recreation and political education—where each man's personal data was checked.

When the information was confirmed, the prisoner was handcuffed and led to a cell outfitted with soundproof material. Then, as Tokarev put it, "Two men held [the prisoner's] arms and the third shot him in the base of the skull. They led him into the cell and shot him in the base of the skull. That's all." The executioners used the German Walther pistol—more reliable than the Soviet Nagan—and Geko ammunition. (Large quantities of each had been imported from Germany in the late 1920s and early 1930s.) Tokarev said he did not participate in the killing, but remembered a young boy who had been a telephone operator in the Polish border guard for only six months. When Tokarev asked him in Polish how old he was, the boy smiled and replied, "Eighteen."

Some of the Ostashkov prisoners may have been shot in another way that was used and then abandoned. Prosecutor Yablokov told Tokarev that he had heard from Leonov (unidentified) that the Poles were taken from Kalinin jail to the village of Mednoe, about 30 kilometers from Kalinin, and shot on the edge of a great pit into which the bodies were thrown. Yablokov also stated he had heard that this shooting was done by the workers of the NKVD Kalinin command, headed by Andrei Rubanov. Tokarev's answer to this statement is indecipherable because there was a break in the recording, but he did say soon thereafter that he had heard in Smolensk of "a more stupid procedure. There they began to shoot [the prisoners] at the burial site." (Indeed, during the spring 1943 exhumations at Katyn, one grave was found—no. 5—where prisoners' arms were tied behind their backs with their coats secured over their heads, indicating resistance; see Part III.) It is possible that some Ostashkov prisoners were also shot at the edge of the burial pits in Mednoe, because Polish exhumation experts found one burial pit at Mednoe where, unlike in the other pits, the remains were buried in a disorderly fashion, suggesting execution at the pit's edge. Also, in the 1990s, Polish exhumation work was confined by the Russian authorities to the Mednoe-Yamok village area, whereas the analysis of aerial photographs points to other possible burial areas nearby. According to Tokarev, however, all the prisoners were shot in the Kalinin jail according to the procedure he described. He recalled that after the execution of each batch of prisoners, the bodies were loaded onto trucks and driven to Mednoe, near the area where NKVD officers had their dachas (countryhouses). The dead were buried in large pits dug beforehand by a mechanical backhoe. Everything was done at night, and the burial site was secret, but each head of the NKVD Kalinin Oblast informed his successor of the location.

Tokarev recalled the case of a prisoner spared at the last moment, a Polish officer who was the nephew of Mikhail Romm, the Soviet film director. His namesake, Michał Romm, a 2nd lieutenant in the Polish Army Health Service, was to be shot that night, but Tokarev was ordered by telephone from Moscow to cross him off the list. Indeed, an order was sent on 27 April 1940 by GB Captain Gertsovsky to the deputy head of the NKVD UPV, Lieutenant Khokhlov, not to send prisoner Stanisław Swianiewicz from Kozelsk to Smolensk, or Michał Romm from Ostashkov to Kalinin. Both were rescued at the last moment. (Romm became a Soviet citizen and film director like his uncle; for Swianiewicz see below.) Tokarev's claim, that three of the executioners went mad and committed suicide, is incorrect. One died an alcoholic; another died of natural causes; and Blokhin was repeatedly decorated and promoted—he managed to reach retirement age—but died in disgrace in 1955.[7]

Starobelsk

The Starobelsk prisoners traveled to Kharkov by rail, most likely in prison cars. Although detailed convoy reports are available for the Ostashkov prisoners, only a reconstruction of the train schedules for 5 April–4 May 1940, the first month of executions, is known; it was made on the basis of reports sent to Merkulov by Milshtein, head of the NKVD GTU. This reconstruction gives the dates, the departure stations (Voroshilovgrad and Valooiki), the arrival station (Kharkov), the number of railway cars—a total of sixty for this period of extermination—and the individual car numbers, but not the number of prisoners transported on each date nor the total for the month.[8] According to NKVD UPV data, by late May 1940, the number of men sent from Starobelsk to Kharkov was 3,896 (doc. 84), although a high-level official's note of 3 March 1959 lists 3,820 (doc. 110). Later verification by Polish researchers yielded a lower number, 3,739.[9]

Only one eyewitness deposition is available on the deaths of Starobelsk officers. Mitrofan Syromiatnikov (b. 1908), UNKVD militia lieutenant working in the inner NKVD prison at Kharkov in 1940–1941, was interrogated by a Soviet prosecutor, then by Russian and

Polish prosecutors, in five sessions between June 1990 and March 1992. At the first interrogation, he claimed only to have worked at digging burial pits and transporting the bodies of the victims to their burial place in what is now the sixth sector of the wooded park in Kharkov (on the territory of an NKVD sanatorium), about 2 kilometers (really about 500 meters, near the Belgorod highway) from the village of Piatikhatki. Syromiatnikov said that he worked only ten days in May, after which he was sick in the hospital. He stated that he and other workers did not know who was arrested nor the charges against those held in the jail; the guards were told only that these people were enemies of the Soviet nation. Syromiatnikov told the prosecutors that the Polish officers were brought by truck from the railway station to the inner jail, where they were held before being shot, but he did not know who did the shooting.[10]

In the second session, he was more forthcoming. He said he had heard that Polish Army officers and gendarmes were brought in from a POW camp where they had staged a revolt. His job was to receive the Poles and place them in prison cells. After a day or two, they were led in groups to the cellar, in which activity he also took part. In the cellar sat the prosecutor and the jail commander, Timofei Kupry, as well as other workers of the prison command. The prisoners were then taken to a separate windowless room, where they were executed. At this interrogation, Syromiatnikov said he did not know who did the shooting, but that the weapon was a Nagan, produced in the USSR. Syromiatnikov saw one of the prison command workers loading the gun. This man had about five Nagans on the table beside him; he was taking out the spent shell casings and loading new shells into the Nagans. The corpses of the dead Poles were loaded onto trucks and taken to the pits in the wooded zone of the park in Kharkov. Syromiatnikov said that he did this loading and rode on the truck several times. The bodies were placed in large pits, after which some white powder was scattered over them; he heard that it was to speed up decomposition. As the pits were filled up, they were covered with earth. Later the bodies of executed Soviet citizens were also buried there. All the activities connected with the shooting of the Poles were "controlled" (supervised) by NKVD representatives from Moscow. Syromiatnikov also recalled that when Soviet forces were evacuating Kharkov at the beginning of the war (with Germany in late June 1941), the wooden fencing around the graves was burned down and Kupry personally blew up the cellar room where the executions took place. When asked who the NKVD leaders in the Kharkov district were at the time, Syromiatnikov named them. He elaborated on these accounts during the third interrogation session.[11]

Syromiatnikov gave the most information at the fourth session, on 30 July 1991, when he was grilled by the senior Russian military prosecutor in the case, Lieutenant Colonel Aleksandr Tretecky, and Polish Deputy Prosecutor General Stefan Śnieżko. At this time—as the first exhumations were taking place—Syromiatnikov admitted that he had helped, along with other prison staff, to dig a pit (in the wooded park zone) large enough for a truck to drive into, and that digging this pit took six prison workers ten days. This was done on Commander Kupry's orders before the Polish prisoners arrived. As regards the prison itself, he said that the inner jail had two floors with various sizes of cells, holding a total of 250 prisoners. Just before the arrival of the Poles, two or three persons arrived from Moscow; these were "twosomes" and "threesomes" who wore civilian clothes. He claimed that even the Soviet prosecutor Roman Rudenko came and read the sentences (presumably to high Kharkov NKVD officials). Kupry said these persons had come to "control" the workers, so everyone was to look sharp. The Poles arrived in echelons of 200 at the Southern Railway Station, but were brought to the prison in batches of 100 men each, although on two occasions there were 200 men.

One of the interrogators reminded Syromiatnikov that earlier he had said that the first prisoners to arrive were kept for a time in the prison before being shot, but later he had said that prisoners were in the prison only a few hours before execution. The interrogator asked if the procedure had been speeded up. Syromiatnikov agreed. He also recalled that when the Poles arrived, Kupry detailed a guard with a suitcase to collect Soviet money and give the prisoners receipts. The prisoners had to leave their suitcases but could have these brought to their cells to take out what they needed. (It is impossible to verify whether this actually happened.) They had canned food, including cans of Polish *smalec* [bacon fat or pork drippings], which, declared Syromiatnikov, was "exceptionally good." (The prisoners had received food packages from home.) On arrival, the prisoners were undressed and searched, and their belts were taken away. Later the prisoners' belongings were sorted out and put in the prison warehouse.

The prisoners were led unwittingly to their death, said Syromiatnikov. They undressed so that they wore only shirts and trousers, and had to give up their caps as well. They did not wear rubber boots or *valenki* [Russian felt boots], but shoes with high heels (officers' top boots). The jail guards escorted each prisoner, hands bound, along a corridor in the cellar. One of the guards, perhaps Syromiatnikov, would open a door to the [death] room and ask, "May I?" and hear the response "Come in." The prosecutor, who sat behind a table with Commander Kupry, asked the prisoner his family name, patronymic, date of birth. Then he said [it is not clear whether to the prisoner or to the guard], "You may go." "There was a clack," said Syromiatnikov, "and that was the end." Syromiatnikov said he did not see the shooting, only heard it. "Kupry only shouted 'Alyo' [the Russian street gang word for "hello"], and then two of us were to jump in and take [the body] to a separate cell." The bodies were placed on trucks, which drove up to a camouflaged entrance, and the heads were wrapped in the prisoners' coats to prevent bloodstains on the truck platform. The bodies were buried in the park in pits dug beforehand and placed in three or four rows on top of each other. Syromiatnikov admitted that Kupry did the shooting. He denied receiving an 800-ruble reward from Beria (doc. 90), claiming that Kupry listed the NKVD workers' names for rewards but kept the money for himself instead.[12] (Syromiatnikov repeated this claim in the fifth interrogation of 6 March 1992, when he did not provide any new information.) In the second interrogation, he also asserted that the executions had been supervised by members of the NKVD Administrative-Housekeeping Board sent from Moscow (just as in Ostashkov), but he gave no names. He did mention the NKVD chief for Kharkov Oblast, Major (P. S.) Safonov; his deputy, Captain (P. P.) Tikhonov; the commander of the Smolensk Oblast UN-KVD, 1st Lieutenant (T. F.) Kupry, and others. Syromiatnikov's testimony provided much information on the fate of the Starobelsk officers, but did not account for all the deaths. Exhumations conducted in the Kharkov wooded park area in the 1990s indicated that some of the victims were shot at the burial site itself.[13]

Kozelsk

No eyewitness testimony has surfaced so far on the deaths of the Kozelsk camp prisoners whose corpses were exhumed at Katyn in spring

1943. It is known that the camp authorities arranged for a farewell reception for the fourth group to leave, which included Generals Bronisław Bohatyrewicz, Henryk Minkiewicz-Odrowąż, and Mieczysław Smorawiński, and that their colleagues formed a guard of honor for them as they left.[14] Most of the Kozelsk prisoners are known to have traveled in railway prison cars from Kozelsk through Smolensk to Gnezdovo Station, located about 6.5 kilometers from the town of Katyn (see map 5). They were then taken to a location known in Russian as Koze Gory [Goat Hills], which lies on the outskirts of Katyn Forest.

What did the prisoners see on arrival in Gnezdovo and later? Professor Stanisław Swianiewicz—spared at the last moment because NKVD Intelligence wanted him for interrogation—was removed from the train at Gnezdovo Station by an NKVD colonel on 29 April, just as his comrades were disembarking. Swianiewicz wrote in his memoirs that he saw a passenger bus, its windows whitened with cement, make several trips. Lying on the top bunk of his prison car compartment, he observed the scene through a slit in the carriage wall. He had no watch but estimated that the bus took about thirty prisoners each time and returned after half an hour to pick up the next batch.[15]

What happened next can be learned from the diary of Major Adam Solski, whose body was exhumed at Katyn in spring 1943. He wrote the last two entries on 9 April 1940. The method of transportation used that day for the trip from the train to the execution area was the *chyorny voron* ["black crow"], the standard Soviet prison car, and not the bus described by Swianiewicz, who was at Gnezdovo Station at the end of the month. Solski wrote:

> 9.04 [9 April]. A few minutes before five in the morning—wake-up call in the prison railway cars and preparations to leave. We are to go somewhere by car. And what then?
> 9.04. Five a.m. The day began in a special way at dawn. Departure in a prison car in cells (awful!). We were driven to some place in a wood; something like a summer resort. Here, a detailed search took place. They took my watch, showing 6:30. They asked about my wedding ring. . . . They took rubles, main belt, penknife.[16]

Most historians of Katyn accept as true the depositions made by local Russians to the German and other investigative commissions at Katyn in spring 1943. These Russians stated that the prisoners traveled in a bus or prison van a couple of kilometers along the Smolensk-Vitebsk road and arrived at or near the main building of the NKVD summer resort, a building called Schlösschen [Little Castle] by the Germans. Their accounts fit those in Solski's diary and another diary entry similar to Solski's that was made a few days later by an officer whose name cannot be deciphered. Under the date of 17 April, the author wrote, in a barely legible hand: "5 hrs. 5 [?] km past Smolensk, there is a summer resort [?] 127 [?] people." This sounds like the NKVD dacha, but an analysis of aerial photographs indicates that some of the 4,410 Kozelsk victims could have been shot in one or more of the structures located in the *lesopolosa* [edge of the forest] area near the Gnezdovo Station. Furthermore, there may have been summer cottages or villas for the use of Soviet officials in the Gnezdovo-Katyn area. If so, one of them could have served as an execution site.[17]

Although no eyewitness seems to have survived to tell the terrible tale, the exhumations conducted under German supervision at Katyn in April–June 1943 by the Polish Red Cross (PRC) Technical Commission found that most of the victims' hands were at their sides. Only about 20 percent had their hands bound behind their backs, and only a few, who apparently put up strong resistance, had their mouths filled with sawdust and coats or sacks thrown over their heads. Their hands were bound with a rope looped around their necks so they would suffocate if they pulled at the rope. In spring 1943 these corpses were found mainly in a water-logged pit (doc. 105b), now known as grave no. 5. Until recently, the prevalent view was that all the prisoners must have been shot standing or kneeling on open ground, or perhaps even standing or kneeling over the burial pits, and that some may even have been shot while lying face down on their dead and dying comrades. Very few shell casings, however, were found in the burial pits or in the area nearby, which indicates that most of the victims were executed elsewhere. Indeed, in most burial pits the bodies were stacked neatly head to toe in rows, one on top of the other, while in others they were thrown in at random. When examined in spring 1943, the largest pit, in the shape of an *L,* held twelve rows of bodies stacked on top of one another.

It is noteworthy that the two diaries quoted above speak of a summer resort, which could have been the NKVD rest area, whose country house was located very near the banks of the Dnieper River and also near Katyn Forest, which lies close to the Smolensk-Vitebsk highway. The information was confirmed later by Ivan Krivozertsev—one of the Russian peasants who testified before the German Inquiry Commission, the International Commission of Forensic Medicine Experts (known as the International Medical Commission—IMC), and the PRC Technical Commission in spring 1943. He fled ahead of the Red Army to the western zone of occupation in Germany and made another deposition on 31 May 1945 at a refugee camp in Verden, a town southwest of Bremen. He said he thought the prisoners had been brought to the dacha, where they were "written down [on lists]" and then either shot one by one right there or taken to the execution site in the nearby wood. He did not hear any shots and doubted whether anyone else did.[18]

As for the method of killing the prisoners, Tokarev made a significant comment in the deposition cited earlier. He said, "They told me in Smolensk about a stupider procedure. There they began by shooting at the burial site"—clearly a reference to Katyn. It is possible, then, that at the outset some prisoners were shot at Katyn near or at the graves, but they resisted, so the NKVD reverted to the standard method of killing the prisoners individually, taking the victims by surprise in the same manner as those in the jail cellars at Kalinin/Tver and Kharkov. This would explain why the majority of the bodies laying in the pits at Katyn had their hands unbound. But if this was so, where would they have been shot? Some proponents of this theory suggest that it may have been in the cellar of a villa—burned down later—that stood on the nearby Dnieper River bank or in a special room in the NKVD dacha—also burned down—because the two diaries cited above indicate that the prisoners were brought to the "summer resort" from Gnezdovo Station either in a bus or in a "black crow." Afterward, the bodies could have been taken by another "black crow" to the burial pits in nearby Katyn Forest. No documents, however, support the hypothesis. In particular, German records do not mention any evidence of executions in the NKVD dacha, and an inspection in spring 1943 of the nearby garage—which still exists—failed to turn up any spent cartridges there. Furthermore, in the 1990s Russian authorities refused permission for Polish archaeological-exhumation digs at the site of the former dacha or elsewhere in the vicinity, except in a restricted area. The theory could nevertheless explain the apparent lack of resistance by all but a few out of the more than 4,000 physically fit men buried in Katyn Forest, and this leaves open the possibility that they might have been killed in a similar way elsewhere in the Gnezdovo-Katyn area, such as the edge-of-the-forest area northeast of Gnezdovo Station.[19]

There is, however, indirect testimony on how at least some of the Kozelsk officers might have been murdered. The former Russian Federal Security officer Oleg Z. Zakirov, who worked on the rehabilitation of KGB men in the Smolensk Oblast, provided some data in his own Katyn investigation of the early 1990s. On the basis of his conversations with NKVD/KGB veterans, Zakirov named some of the participants in the executions. The men involved in the Katyn massacre included N. A. Gvozdovsky, I. I. Gribov, and S. M. Mokrzhitsky. From a conversation with GB Major N. N. Smirnov, who had heard this from Mokrzhitsky, Zakirov learned that groups of Poles were brought to a barrack in a specially fenced place where a roll call was organized. They were then seated close together on a bench, with their backs against the barrack wall, to have a smoke. Meanwhile, Mokrzhitsky and other workers of the command got up on special stools inside the barrack, a plank in the wall was raised, and a shooter stood behind each prisoner. The shooters, synchronizing their action, pressed their triggers, aiming downward, and shot the prisoners in the back of the head. The corpses were dragged to pits behind the shrubbery. Similar NKVD methods of shooting prisoners are noted by other authors. However, in the early 1990s during exhumations at Katyn, as well as at Kharkov and Mednoe, Polish forensic medicine experts concluded that the bullet trajectories always went upward from the lower occipital area to exit through the forehead.[20]

Other indirect evidence on the Katyn massacre was given by members of the local population, who told the Germans, members of the IMC, and the PRC Technical Commission in spring 1943 that they saw the trains arrive at Gnezdovo Station; but only one man said he heard shots from the Katyn Forest area. The names of those interrogated by German officials are listed in the official German report. They included Ivan Andreev, Parfemon Kiselev (he was the only one to hear shots), and Ivan Krivozertsev.[21] When the war ended, Krivozertsev—whose May 1945 deposition was cited above—fled from Germany to Italy and arrived at the headquarters of the Polish 2nd Corps in Ancona. Here, at just about the time the Katyn case was brought before the International Military Tribunal (IMT) at Nuremberg in 1946, he told his story at length to, among others, an émigré Polish journalist, Józef Mackiewicz, the well-known editor of the prewar Polish newspaper in Wilno, *Słowo* [Word], and, in 1939–1941, of a German-controlled Polish paper there. With the approval of Polish underground leaders in Wilno, he visited Katyn in May 1943, when he first met Krivozertsev. Three years later, in Ancona, Krivozertsev told him of seeing a convoy of trucks coming from Smolensk along the road toward Koze Gory in early March 1943; they carried prisoners with picks and spades, and local people said they were going to dig pits. Krivozertsev said that he also saw a convoy of vehicles on 14 March; it was preceded by a passenger car, then a "black crow," followed by a third car. He was told that the passengers were Poles, and he said he saw more such transports moving along the road daily through the month of April. A locksmith from nearby Krasny Bor Station, Semyon Andreev, told him he heard from railway workers that in Smolensk the transports were broken up into smaller groups of two or three railway cars each and sent to Gnezdovo, where they were parked on a dead-end track north of the station. Prison cars drove up several times to each train, and the prisoners were loaded into them. Krivozertsev also heard that the executioners, who numbered over fifty, were volunteers from the Minsk NKVD.[22]

Krivozertsev stuck with the Poles. He sailed from Italy to Britain with the soldiers of the Polish 2nd Corps who had come out of the USSR with General Anders to Iran and the Middle East in 1942 and who later fought the Germans in Italy (see Part III). Krivozertsev lived with them in their camps in Britain. His last known residence was in the county of Somerset, where he died a mysterious death in 1947. Mackiewicz, after many attempts, finally learned that Krivozertsev's body had been found in an orchard on 30 October 1947 and that, according to the police report, he had hanged himself.[23] It is at least likely, however, that he was murdered by NKVD agents because he talked openly about what he had seen and heard at Katyn.

As for Semyon Andreev, who also gave testimony to the Germans and to the IMC at Katyn, and whom Krivozertsev had characterized to Mackiewicz as a deeply religious man who could not be forced to lie, his name surfaced in 1967 in a book on the GULAG written by the Soviet dissident Anatoly Marchenko and published in English translation two years later. Marchenko mentioned meeting a forest ranger named Andreev in Vladimir jail in the mid-1960s. Andreev allegedly told him he had been incarcerated there for twenty years because he had "accidentally witnessed the slaughter of the Polish officers in Katyn Forest." Marchenko's account seemed to be confirmed in January 1980, when a Polish émigré paper in London published an interview with Świato-sław Karawański (Sviatoslav Karavansky), a Ukrainian independence activist, imprisoned for his political activity and then sentenced to an additional ten years for collecting information on Katyn. He told of seeing Andreev in the Vladimir jail in 1967. Karavansky wrote that Andreev had told him he was imprisoned there with his wife and was pressured from time to time to revoke his statements to the IMC, which he refused to do. Karavansky made a note of Andreev's statement and hid it, but it was discovered and he was sentenced to ten years for this "crime."[24]

Andreev's file, containing his case records, which became accessible in the Russian Federal Security Archive, Smolensk Oblast in the early 1990s, tells a different story. According to these records, Andreev was sentenced to prison for twenty-five years on the basis of Article 58, point 1a, of the Soviet Criminal Code (Treason to the Fatherland). The file does not mention the fact that he was a Katyn witness and was held in Vladimir jail—where all Katyn witnesses were imprisoned—from 11 December 1955 to 7 March 1956. On 27 February 1956 the Central Case Review Commission cancelled the former sentence and set him free. It appears that Andreev, who did not mention Katyn in his complaints nor when making the claims of innocence contained in his file, signed a declaration that he would not speak about the shooting of Polish prisoners of war at Katyn, and this presumably led to his release. His later whereabouts are unknown. It is worth noting that most of the locals who gave testimony to the Germans and the IMC reversed themselves under NKVD pressure when they "testified" before the Soviet State (Burdenko) Commission in January 1944. Most died suddenly in circumstances that are unclear.[25]

To return to where the Kozelsk prisoners may have been murdered, some could have met their deaths not at Katyn but in the NKVD jail in Smolensk. An alleged eyewitness testified to these executions half a century later. Pyotr Klimov, a former worker in the Smolensk NKVD, described the execution procedure in a letter to the Soviet (later Russian) Commission for the Rehabilitation of the Victims of Political Repression. He wrote:

> In a tiny cellar room, there was a sewer manhole. They brought in the victim, opened the manhole, laid the head on the edge and shot him either in the back of the head or in the forehead. . . . They did the shooting almost every day in the evening and took [the bodies] to Koze Gory, returning around 2 a.m. at night. . . . Besides the driver, there were two–three men and the commander. . . . Those who did the shooting, that I can remember, were the following: Gribov, [I. I.]; Stelmakh, I.; Gvozdovsky, [N. A.]; Reinson, Karl.[26]

The first three names cited by Klimov figure in Beria's list of rewards for NKVD workers "for the successful carrying out of special tasks" (doc. 90). It is known that some of the prisoners got off the train at Smolensk, but no documentary confirmation of Klimov's account has been found thus far.

Poles Held in NKVD Prisons

While much is known about the fate of the prisoners of war in the three special camps, the same does not apply to those held in the NKVD prisons of the western regions of Ukraine and Belorussia who were transferred to NKVD prisons in Kiev, Kharkov, Kherson, and Minsk following Beria's order of 22 March 1940 (doc. 53). According to Beria's resolution, approved by the Politburo on 5 March, these prisoners were also to be shot. Beria stated that out of a total of 18,632 persons arrested and held in the NKVD prisons, 10,685 were Poles (doc. 47). However, in a document of March 1959, the number of those shot in the prisons was given as 7,305 (doc. 110). The lists of victims shot in Ukraine have been found; the total number is 3,435, more than 2,000 of whom have been identified. Their burial sites are unknown, but since Beria ordered them to be moved to NKVD jails in Kiev, Kharkov, and Kherson, presumably they were buried in or near each of these cities.[27] The lists must have included at least some of the prisoners whom Merkulov ordered on 22 February 1940 to be taken out of the three camps and transported to NKVD prisons (doc. 42). Most, however, seem to have been arrested and jailed in western Ukraine (East Galicia), which was part of interwar Poland. There is still no trace of the prisoners taken from NKVD prisons in western Belorussia, who were shipped to Minsk according to Beria's directive of 22 March 1940 and presumably shot in the NKVD prison there. The government of the Republic of Belarus has not released any relevant documents or permitted any archeological investigation of presumed Polish burial sites.

The Debate on the Politburo's Decision

In late October 1940, Beria ordered that rewards be given to the NKVD men who had participated in the executions (doc. 90). Thirty-nine received a month's extra pay, including Blokhin, who shot many

of the Ostashkov prisoners at Kalinin/Tver, and Kupry, who participated in the shooting of Starobelsk prisoners in Kharkov. Eighty-one
workers received 800 rubles each, including Syromiatnikov—although
he claimed that Kupry had pocketed the money. Ironically, about the
same time that Beria decreed these rewards, he and Merkulov were interrogating two groups of surviving Polish officers in Moscow—to
find those willing to draw up plans for and lead a Polish division in the
Red Army (doc. 91). It is clear that Stalin now viewed Germany as a
potential threat, but he did not think so in spring 1940. This brings us
to questions about Stalin's motives and the timing of the Politburo decision of 5 March 1940—questions that are at the heart of the continuing debate over the Politburo's decision to exterminate the Polish
prisoners of war.

The debate over when and why Stalin decided to have the prisoners
shot has continued ever since the Germans announced the discovery of
the Katyn graves in April 1943. As for the timing of the decision, the
eminent Russian expert on Katyn, Professor Natalia Lebedeva, believes that between 22–26 February Beria discussed with Stalin the 22
February directive on removing special categories of prisoners from
the three camps to prisons (doc. 42). Furthermore, she regards Beria's
request for lists of prisoners in the special camps and Soprunenko's
subsequent reports of 2 and 3 March (e.g., doc. 44) as preparatory
steps for the NKVD commissar's proposal to Stalin that the prisoners
be shot.[28] Indeed, Beria was to detail the number and ranks of the
Poles in his "resolution" addressed to Stalin and the Politburo on 5
March 1940 (doc. 47). In Lebedeva's opinion, the decision was made
no earlier than 2–3 March 1940. Further, she connects it to the Politburo decision of 2 March 1940 on "guarding the state borders of the
UkSSR and BSSR" (the Ukrainian and Belorussian Soviet Socialist Republics). This particular decision mandated the deportation of people
from certain western frontier regions. It also stated that the families of
the prisoners held in the three special camps would be deported to
Kazakhstan on 15 April 1940, listing the number of families as between 22,000 and 25,000 (docs. 45, 64a, 64b). She suggests that the
proposal to strengthen security in the immediate proximity of the
western frontier of the Soviet Union, originally made by Nikita Khrushchev, first secretary in Ukraine, and cowritten by Beria, may have inspired Stalin to shoot the army officers and police who were the heads
of these families.

In support of this view, Lebedeva points to the established NKVD practice of deporting the families of prisoners condemned to death in order to conceal the murder of their relatives.[29] It is true that this was an NKVD procedure, although the deportation of "undesirable" persons and populations from border areas was also an established practice. For example, during the Stalin Terror of 1935–1938, the entire populations of ethnically Polish villages were deported from the western border regions of Soviet Belorussia and Soviet Ukraine to Kazakhstan.[30] Likewise, on 10 February 1940, Polish military settlers and their families were deported from the Wilno [Vilnius] region as well as from western Belorussia and Volhynia, an action not connected with the prisoners in the special camps but taken to clear border territories of "socially dangerous elements" (SOE, Russian abbreviation).[31] On 2 March, Beria also ordered the deportation of refugees from German Poland, condemned for the crime of illegally crossing the frontier— that is, attempting to enter or leave the western regions of the Ukrainian and Belorussian Republics without official permission. Such persons were also held in the camps, most of them in Ostashkov, but they were ordered to be transferred to prisons in late February 1940 and were executed in spring 1940. It is clear they had been categorized as "counterrevolutionaries" or spies because most of the run-of-the-mill refugees from German-occupied Poland, arrested on this charge in the western regions of the USSR, were not condemned to death by shooting; instead, Beria ordered them deported to the northeastern group of NKVD labor camps in the Vladivostok region.[32] In sum, it seems that the families of the Polish prisoners of war held in the three special camps would have been deported at some time anyway, as "socially dangerous elements," but in this case the date of the decision on their deportation may well have been connected with the imminent Politburo decision of 5 March 1940.

Beria's order that the prisoner-of-war families be deported in April 1940 led to a second wave of deportations from the western USSR, which swept up 66,000 people. These were followed by the third and fourth waves in 1941 that were unconnected with the prisoners of war.[33] Previous estimates of the total number of Polish citizens deported in 1940–1941 vary from the 1,000,000–1,200,000 figure cited by the wartime Polish government in London to a later estimate of 1,450,000 deportees given by an émigré Polish scholar. These figures probably included Polish citizens conscripted into the Red Army as well as those arrested and placed in Soviet jails and those who signed up voluntarily for work in the USSR. The number of deported Polish citizens as recorded by the NKVD is, however, 309,000 to 327,000. This number is probably too low because in 1941–1942 Soviet authorities prohibited the conscription of Ukrainians, Belorussians, and Jews from eastern Poland into the Polish Army then being raised in the USSR on the grounds that they were not Polish but Soviet citizens. Furthermore, in early 1943, even ethnic Poles living in the USSR who happened to be in the former eastern Poland in November 1939 were pressured to accept Soviet citizenship.[34]

Whether or not the order of 2 March 1940 to deport the POW families was connected with Stalin's decision to have the prisoners shot, it seems that Beria made the proposal to him around this time. Stalin may have made the initial suggestion, however, and, as always, he made the final decision. The fateful decision may well have been made while a conference was being held in Moscow to discuss "clearing out" the Ostashkov camp. This conference apparently took place in late February or early March 1940 in the NKVD 1st Special Department. A report written by the head of the Special Section in Ostashkov camp, Grigory Korytov, to Vasily Pavlov, head of the NKVD Special Department for the Kalinin/Tver region, thought to be dated no later than 4 March, documents the fact that such a conference took place there and the topics of discussion. Korytov wrote that the conference members discussed what methods to use in dispatching prisoners from Ostashkov to the (new) camps to which they would be transferred, where they would be informed of what their sentences were, and how they would be attended to on the way. The death penalty was not mentioned. On the contrary, Korytov wrote that of the 6,005 cases submitted from Ostashkov to the NKVD Special Board, 600 had been examined, and those prisoners had been given sentences of three to eight years in Kamchatka, in Russia's Far East. He noted, however, that "further examination of these cases was suspended by the Narkom [People's Commissar Beria]. Finally, Korytov wrote, "But it is rumored that in March we must basically clear out the camps and prepare to receive the Finns" (doc. 46). He also mentioned Beria's instruction, forwarded by Merkulov, that several categories of prisoners be transferred to prisons (doc. 42).

It is clear that the conference members assumed that the Ostashkov prisoners would be sentenced to several years' hard labor in Kamchatka, but that "further examination was suspended"—possibly because Stalin decided to shoot all the prisoners in the three special camps even as the debate on those in Ostashkov was under way. Indeed, on 5 March 1940 the Politburo approved Beria's resolution to this effect. The resolution, contained in his letter to Stalin of 5 March (the date is written in by hand, so the original date may have been earlier), began with the justification for executing the prisoners held in the NKVD POW camps and the NKVD prisons in the western regions of Ukraine and Belorussia. Beria wrote that they were former workers of Polish intelligence "organs," members of Polish "counterrevolutionary" parties and uncovered "c-r" insurgent organizations, and refugees. There were also people who had tried to "violate the state frontier" (to enter or depart illegally from the USSR). "They are all sworn enemies of Soviet rule, filled with hatred for the Soviet system," he said. He claimed that the officers and police in the (special) camps were trying to continue their c-r work and were conducting "anti-Soviet agitation," just waiting for their release in order to continue the struggle against Soviet authority. As further justification, he stated that the NKVD had exposed several "c-r organizations" in the western regions of Ukraine and Belorussia, and in all of them, former officers of the former Polish Army and former police and gendarmes played "an active guiding role." Furthermore, the refugees from German Poland and those who had "violated the state border" also included, he said, members of "c-r" espionage and insurgent organizations.

Beria gave the number of prisoners in the camps as 14,736, listed them by rank, and designated 97 percent as Polish. Those held in NKVD prisons in the western regions of Ukraine and Belorussia totaled 18,632, he stated, of whom 10,685 were Poles.[35] He concluded: "Based on the fact that they are all hardened, irremediable enemies of Soviet power, the NKVD USSR believes it is essential" to "examine the cases of those who have been arrested and are in the prisons . . . [and] using the special procedure, apply to them the supreme punishment, [execution by] shooting."

At the end of the resolution, the "special procedure" was defined as the "examination" of cases and the "carrying out of decisions" by a troika consisting of Beria (his name was changed by hand to read "Kobulov," evidently by Stalin), Merkulov, and [Leonid F.] Bashtakov. On the resolution itself, written across the first page, are the signatures, in blue pencil, of I. V. Stalin, K. Voroshilov, and A. Mikoyan and, in ordinary pencil, of V. Molotov. In the margins, evidently written in by Stalin's secretary, Aleksandr Poskrebyshev, are the votes in favor of two absent Politburo members, Kalinin and Kaganovich (doc. 47). The resolution was also summarized in an extract from Protocol no. 13 of the 1940 Politburo sessions.[36]

High-level conferences followed in Moscow with camp commanders, NKVD regional commanders, and commanders of NKVD Convoy Troops. On 13 March the commanders of Kozelsk, Ostashkov, and Starobelsk camps were called to the capital, together with the heads of their Special Sections, for a conference that evidently took place on 15 March 1940. They were instructed also to send lists of prisoners whose families resided in German Poland.[37] There is no documentary record of this conference, but it is likely that the camp commanders were given instructions on how to prepare for dispatching the POWs for extermination.

The lack of documents on Stalin's motive for the decision to shoot the prisoners leaves the question unresolved to this day. One theory that can be dismissed out of hand is that Stalin ordered them shot because he feared they would stage an uprising that would undercut the secret protocols he had agreed on with Hitler.[38] In a pioneer study of Katyn, published in 1962—and thus without access to the Russian documents that were unavailable until the early 1990s—Janusz K. Zawodny listed four possible motives for the Politburo decision to murder the prisoners, three of which are shared by most Katyn historians today: (1) Soviet officials viewed them as enemies of the Soviet Union; (2) their extermination would eliminate a significant part of the Polish elite, to be replaced by "Soviet-groomed" leaders; (3) the NKVD believed that "the prisoners could not be induced to adopt pro-Soviet attitudes." Here Zawodny presciently concluded that "later, at the highest level of policy making, an order was given to 'liquidate' the prisoners. Such an order was given, in all probability, by Stalin through Beria (the chief of the N.K.V.D.) or by Stalin himself." Zawodny's last listed motive was (4) Beria misinterpreted an order by Stalin to "liquidate" the camps as meaning the liquidation of the prisoners. Zawodny noted that at one time this motive was circulated by word of mouth but could not be substantiated.[39] The most common view, held by Polish and Russian historians of the Katyn massacre—who also agree with the other motives listed by Zawodny—is that Stalin wanted to destroy the prisoners because they constituted an elite, the potential leaders of a future, independent Poland. Norman Davies, the leading Western historian of Poland, adds the class factor—"From the Soviet point of view, they were the cream of the class enemy"—although he cautions that class was not the only criterion for eliminating Stalin's enemies, as evidenced by the murder of independent-minded Polish communists.[40]

Whereas it is clear that Soviet officials viewed the prisoners as enemies of the Soviet system who could not be induced to support it, neither the elite theory nor the class theory can provide a satisfactory explanation for the massacres in Katyn, Kharkov, and Kalinin/Tver. Indeed, according to NKVD records, out of the 14,552 prisoners of war from the three special camps shot in spring 1940 (doc. 110), about 5,000 from Ostashkov were rank-and-file policemen who clearly did not belong to the Polish elite. (See police and gendarme rank and file in Appendix, table 2B.) It is true that among the army officers, there were prominent Polish intellectuals, as well as many doctors, architects, and representatives of other professions, but others were middle-school teachers and office workers. Thus, it can be said that most of the prisoners were political enemies rather than class enemies. Also, Stalin exempted some 400 prisoners, including Polish officers willing to serve his interests, such as Colonel (later General) Berling and his group.

In discussing the question of Stalin's motives, the views of three historians of Katyn who have worked with the documents accessible since 1990 merit special consideration. Lebedeva believes the Polish officers were exterminated because Soviet efforts to "reeducate" them had failed, for they were clearly determined to continue the fight to restore their country's independence. She writes that according to the logic of Stalin and his closest collaborators, it was necessary to destroy those bearers of a different way of thinking, those potential warriors for Polish freedom. She adds that another factor contributing to Stalin's hatred of the Polish officers was the bitter memory of the crushing defeat the Red Army, and he personally, suffered in Poland in 1920.[41] Berling, however, had fought the Russians in 1920, and this did not prevent Stalin from promoting him to general and giving him the command of the Kościuszko Division, the embryo of a communist-led Polish army, established in spring 1943 (see Part III).

Wojciech Materski, an eminent Polish historian of Katyn, generally agrees with Lebedeva's view of Stalin's motive but adds his own thoughts on the matter. He thinks the decision to execute the prisoners ripened during the special investigations, especially of the police and gendarmes, but of the army officers as well. Since the investigation process was completed in the three special camps by 1 February 1940, however, he asks why the Politburo did not decide to exterminate the POWs until a month later. He agrees with Lebedeva that the decision to "clear out" the camps was originally connected with the expected influx of Finnish prisoners, but notes that there were fewer than 1,000 Finns, so one camp (Griazovets) was sufficient for them; he thinks space was needed for prisoners expected from the Baltic States. Materski agrees with Lebedeva that Beria and Stalin must have discussed the matter before 5 March, and he views the unanimous Politburo vote that day as indicative of prior approval by Stalin.

In discussing other theories, Materski states that while there was co-operation between the Gestapo and the NKVD, there is no documentary evidence for the view that the extermination of the Polish prisoners of war in the USSR in spring 1940 was connected with the German "A-B Aktion"—the shooting of several thousand prominent Poles—carried out at about the same time in German Poland. Likewise, he notes the lack of evidence to confirm another theory: that Stalin wanted to show the Germans he would not use the imprisoned Poles to create an army to attack them in case they were unsuccessful on the Western Front. He also dismisses the view that Stalin's decision was due to his resentment of the Polish victory over the Red Army in August–September 1920. Finally, he rejects the theory that Stalin's decision was connected with the known agreement of General Sikorski, premier of the Polish government-in-exile and commander in chief of the Polish armed forces, to include a Polish brigade in the projected Anglo-French expedition to aid the Finns in fighting the Russians in the Soviet-Finnish War, November 1939–March 1940. He notes that none of these hypotheses is confirmed by either Russian or German documents.[42]

Another eminent Russian historian of Katyn, Inessa Yazhborovskaia (Jażborowska), chief author of a study of Soviet policy on Katyn, believes there was never any question of releasing the Polish prisoners of war, whose deaths were only a matter of time. In her opinion, the Soviet leadership never considered freeing "class enemies," who were subject to liquidation in the USSR. She believes that intelligence gathering in the prisoner-of-war camps was carried out to recruit spies and collect the data necessary for the deportation of the prisoners' families.[43] There is some evidence, however, that indicates the possibility of prisoner release in exchange for important concessions by the Polish government, but before considering this matter, the question of timing needs to be disposed of.

Contrary to Materski's opinion, the timing of Stalin's decision may well have been connected with the Allies' plan of sending a Polish brigade to Finland as part of the projected Anglo-French expeditionary force to help the Finns fight the Red Army. This much-delayed Allied project was finally canceled by the Finnish government's decision to seek peace with the USSR. Finnish Foreign Minister Väinö Tanner told the French minister in Helsinki on 28 February 1940 that the Finns would have to accept the Soviet peace terms rejected earlier in view of the inadequate aid offered by France and Britain. This news was probably in the hands of the Swedish government two or three days later, and was officially communicated to the Soviet government by the Swedish minister in Moscow on 6 March 1940.[44] Stalin, however, may have learned of the Finnish decision as soon as it was made or in the next few days, that is, 1–4 March, through Soviet intelligence in Helsinki.[45] If this assumption is correct, the news of a forthcoming peace with Finland could have triggered Stalin's decision to shoot the Polish prisoners. There is no direct evidence of such a connection, but there are strong indications that Stalin had kept the prisoners alive as a bargaining counter in possible negotiations with the Polish government in London on the postwar Soviet-Polish frontier. In Anna Cienciala's opinion, this theory provides the best answer to the question of why Stalin did not decide to murder the Polish prisoners until early March 1940—when the Finns were ready to surrender and the Polish government, far from indicating readiness to discuss postwar frontiers, had even agreed to send a brigade with the proposed but abandoned Allied Expeditionary Force to Finland.

Lebedeva and Yazhborovskaia have, of course, ample ground to stress that Stalin would have exterminated the prisoners anyway as enemies of the Soviet Union. It seems at first sight that the survival of these patriotic Poles was incompatible with Stalin's long-term goal: the establishment of a Polish government and army controlled by the USSR. Such a government would have had to accept a postwar Soviet-Polish frontier that incorporated most of prewar eastern Poland in the Soviet Union and agree to a foreign policy friendly to the USSR. However, Stalin was a pragmatic statesman willing to use any means to achieve his goals. Thus, he showed an interest in recruiting Poles for such a government and army, even those known to be hostile to the Soviet Union. This would explain the Soviet attempt to recruit General Anders into the government of a Polish Soviet republic in September 1939, although Stalin soon abandoned this idea in favor of exchanging some of his Polish lands for dominant Soviet influence in Lithuania. From September 1939 to March 1940, while supporting Wanda Wasilewska's group of Polish communists and socialists in Lviv, he may well have envisaged using the POWs as leverage to secure Sikorski's recognition of the Soviet annexation of most of eastern Poland and his agreement to adopt a policy friendly to Moscow.

Indeed, unofficial Soviet proposals in the form of "theses" were reported by Polish intelligence agents from Bucharest, Romania, in late October 1939. These theses assumed the Polish government's recognition of Soviet sovereignty over Western Ukraine and Western Belorussia. In return, the Soviet government would support the creation of an ethnic Poland, with eventual frontier "rectifications" in its favor. Polish agreement to these conditions would, it was said, greatly facilitate Soviet rapprochement with the Allies. The USSR would not try to incorporate (ethnic) Poland, but the latter would have to pursue a friendly policy toward its eastern neighbor. Finally, such an agreement would lead to a complete change of Soviet policy toward Germany.[46] All these theses—except those on Soviet rapprochement with the Allies, no longer needed after the German attack on the USSR on 22 June 1941—would reappear in one form or another after the breakdown of Polish-Soviet relations in late April 1943 (see Part III).

It is more than likely that there was a connection between these Soviet policy objectives and what was happening with the prisoners of war in the three special camps. As noted earlier, the prisoners' correspondence with their families from late November–early December 1939 to mid-March 1940 made their detention and locations in the USSR known not only to their relatives and the Germans, but also to the Polish government-in-exile, then based in France. The beginning of this correspondence was preceded by an indirect Soviet sounding of the Polish government in mid-November 1939. Stefan Litauer, a Polish journalist working for the Polish government, who later turned out to be a Soviet agent, claimed in a book published just after the war that he had had a long conversation with General Sikorski in London on 16 November 1939, during the latter's visit to the British capital. Litauer alleges that Sikorski drew up a memorandum on Polish cooperation with the USSR that envisaged raising a Polish army of 250,000 men from the prisoners of war held there. The memorandum was allegedly given to British Foreign Secretary Lord Halifax, but it did not lead to any results "because the time was not right." In fact, Litauer confused Sikorski's supposed November 1939 memorandum with a memorandum he himself drew up for the general in mid-June 1940, which appears to have been another Soviet sounding of Sikorski when France was falling to the Germans. It is possible, however, that in November 1939, Sikorski showed interest in some form of cooperation with the USSR. Whatever the general may have said to Litauer—and it is known that Sikorski privately envisaged a postwar Poland minus part of its eastern territories but retaining Lwów and Wilno—Litauer reported to the British Foreign Office on 25 November that Sikorski saw the restoration of Poland's prewar frontiers as "very problematic." Sikorski reportedly said that if it proved impossible to recover the territories lost to Russia, Poland might be compensated with military control over East Prussia.[47]

Thus, the permission granted the Polish prisoners in late November–early December 1939 to correspond with their families might well have resulted from Litauer's report on his conversation with Sikorski, a report that no doubt also reached the Soviet Embassy in London even before he made it to the British Foreign Office. This, in turn, might have led Stalin to assume that Sikorski could be persuaded to recognize the Soviet acquisition of eastern Poland and pursue a friendly policy toward the USSR in return for the release of the prisoners of war and perhaps the promise of permission to raise a Polish army there when the time came. This hypothesis finds partial confirmation in a statement made in October 1990 by Soprunenko, head of the UPV from 1939 to 1944. Fifty years later, he told a Soviet prosecutor investigating the Katyn massacre that the captured Polish officers were kept in the camps because the NKVD counted on an agreement with the Polish government in London.[48] It is not clear whether Soprunenko was referring here to the prisoners kept in the camps until 1940, when they were shot, or to the surviving prisoners, plus those brought in from Lithuania and Latvia, who were held in Griazovets camp from the summer of 1940 to August 1941, and allowed to correspond with their families in October 1940. Whatever the case may be, if Stalin wanted a frontier agreement with the Polish government in 1939–1940, he would have had good grounds for keeping the prisoner-of-war officers and police alive and allowing them to correspond with their families. The prisoners might have become even more important to Stalin after the Soviet attack on Finland on 30 November 1939, which led to the formulation of Allied plans to send an expeditionary corps, including a Polish brigade, to help the Finns. If such plans had materialized, Stalin could have threatened Sikorski with killing the Polish prisoners in case the general sent the brigade from France to Finland. Of course, this hypothesis must remain one until the time—if ever—that a Russian government sees fit to reveal the appropriate documentation.

Whatever Stalin's plans regarding the Polish prisoners might have been, his decision in early March 1940 to have them shot must have been made when he concluded that they were of no further use to him. On hearing of the Finnish government's readiness to negotiate peace with the USSR, either Beria or Stalin could have argued that most of the Polish prisoners of war were not only anti-Soviet but also loyal to General Sikorski, who gave no sign of recognizing the Soviet acquisition of eastern Poland and had even planned to send a Polish brigade to fight the Red Army in Finland. The conclusion to this line of thought might have been that the Polish prisoners had no further value as bargaining chips for Moscow and should be exterminated.

Whatever sparked Stalin's decision to shoot the prisoners, the vast majority were patriotic Poles, which automatically made them counterrevolutionary and anti-Soviet, as Beria claimed they were. These qualifications were more than enough to have them shot, just as some two million Soviet citizens were shot between the late 1920s, when Stalin achieved total power in the USSR, and March 1953, when he died. The key difference is that these Poles were not Soviet citizens but prisoners of war. The decision to shoot them violated not only generally accepted moral standards, as was also the case with Soviet citizens, but also international standards, as embodied in the Geneva Conventions on the treatment of prisoners of war.

It is also clear that in early March 1940, when peace with Finland was in the offing, the Soviet leadership did not consider a German-Soviet war as likely in the near future. This view of the situation, combined with the loyalty of most of the Polish prisoners to Sikorski, may well have sealed the fate of all but some 400 selected to survive. The Soviet leaders changed their minds about Polish prisoners of war after the fall of France in 1940, for they did not shoot the Polish officers brought into NKVD camps in the USSR from Lithuania and Latvia in the summer of that year. Indeed, in October 1940, with Germany dominating most of Europe and Britain fighting for its life, Stalin evidently began to envisage the possibility of a German attack on the USSR. In any event, as mentioned earlier, Beria and Merkulov sought out among the surviving Polish officers those who would be willing to organize and lead a Polish division in the Red Army (doc. 91). A few were ready to serve, but there were far from enough to staff a division. Berling writes that when he presented a list of officers and NCOs for the projected Polish division to Beria and Merkulov in early January 1941, Beria inquired whether the list contained only the names of officers held in the Kozelsk and Starobelsk camps. When the answer was affirmative, Beria replied, "Nothing will come of this. These people are not in the USSR." To this Merkulov added, "We made a big mistake with them." Berling assumed that the Polish officers had left the USSR for other countries.[49] Little did he suspect that they had been murdered.

The Politburo resolution of 5 March 1940 (doc. 47) to shoot the Polish POWs set off the NKVD killing machine. Soprunenko's instruction to Korolev, commander of Kozelsk camp, regarding prisoners categorized as secret agents and provocateurs and Merkulov's instructions regarding their transport, show the attention paid to this type of prisoner, as well as the close supervision of every detail. Merkulov was then Beria's first deputy as commissar of internal affairs.

· 48 ·

Soprunenko's Instruction to Korolev at Kozelsk Camp
on Transferring POWs to the Smolensk Oblast UNKVD
7 March 1940, Moscow

No. 25/2473
Series K
Top Secret

Commander Kozelsk Camp
Captain Com[rade]. Korolev
Copy: Chief, UNKVD Smolensk Oblast
  Captain of GB [State Security] Com. Kuprianov
As a result of thorough verification of camp and Special Section evidence data, the following POWs held in your camp, can be assigned to the

group of secret agents and provocateurs—Sachnowski (case no. 291), Starszyński (case no. 4379), Russek (case no. 3214), Radziszewski (case no. 674), Piotrowicz (case no. 694), Mielnik (case no. 873), Morawski (case no. 1583), Graniczny (case no. 160), Kretowicz (case no. 788), Sarnecki (case no. 971), Oniszczenko (case no. 1216), Sobiessski [Sobieski] (case no. 1827).[50]

On the basis of Directive no. 641/b of 22 February 1940, of Deputy Narkom of Internal Affairs USSR, GB Commissar 3rd Rank Com. Merkulov, the above-named POWs are to be sent by special *vagonzak* [prison railway car] to be at the disposal of the NKVD Smolensk Oblast.[51]

The transfer is to be carried out in accordance with our Instruction no. 25/1869 of 23 February 1940.[52]

Report on implementation.*

> Head of USSR NKVD UPV
> Major Soprunenko
>
> Commissar, USSR NKVD UPV
> Regimental Commissar Nekhoroshev

Lists of Polish POWs held in the three special camps and of their families with their addresses (doc. 64a) were to be made in connection with deporting the families.

· 49 ·

Beria's Directive to Soprunenko on Compiling Lists of Polish POWs
and Family Members
7 March 1940, Moscow

No. 886/b

To the Head of the USSR NKVD UPV
Com. Soprunenko
  I order:
  1. Organize the compilation of precise lists of those former Polish officers, police, gendarmes, prison guards, overt and covert police agents, for-

---

* Two handwritten notes across the text: "Com. Khudiakova. To Kozelsk camp files. Mak[liarsky]. Please verify whether these persons are in our file data. Makliarsky."
  Typewritten instruction in the left margin, middle of the page: "Carry out the transfer in case there is a vagonzak at Kozelsk Station; if not, do not send [prisoners] without my order."
  Handwritten note in the bottom left corner: "Received. V. Kor[olev] 7 March 1940."

Extermination

mer landowners, manufacturers, and prominent officials of the former Polish state apparatus now being held in the prisoner-of-war camps.[53]

2. In the compilation of the lists, be guided by the following:

a) The lists must specify the composition of the family of each prisoner of war and their [family's] exact address. Members of the family are considered to be the wife and children, as well as parents, brothers, and sisters if they reside with the family of the prisoner of war.[54]

b) Lists must be compiled for each town and district of the western oblasts of Ukraine and Belorussia, separately for each town or district, and sent to the NKVDs of the UkSSR and BSSR, to Com. [Ivan A.] Serov and Com. [Lavrenty F.] Tsanava.

c) The lists of POWs whose families, according to the information in your records, reside in the territory of the former Poland, now in Germany, must also be compiled in alphabetical order and sent to the NKVDs of the UkSSR and BSSR.[55]

d) All lists must be compiled on the basis of materials from the prisoner-of-war record files already kept in the camps. The questioning of POWs is permitted for the purpose of clarifying existing record files only in individual cases.

3. The work of compiling the lists must be completed within five days' time.[56]

Report implementation.

> People's Commissar of Internal Affairs USSR
> GB Commissar 1st Rank
> (L. Beria)

This form for gathering information on the prisoners' families was to be filled out according to region and then sent to the NKVD in western Ukraine and western Belorussia for carrying out the deportations. UPV officers were sent to the camps to help draw up lists of prisoners and their families.

· 50 ·

Record Form Used for the Families of Prisoners of War
7 March 1940, Moscow

_____

List

of members of families of prisoners of war held in
_____ camp, living in the town of
_____ in the oblast of
_____, UkSSR or BSSR.[57]

Serial number	Family name, first name, patronymic, year and place of birth, last rank or function of prisoner, his property or social status	Family composition (give family name, first name, patronymic, degree of kinship, age, nationality)	Family address

Function and signature of [person] compiling the list:

_____

ATTENTION: Lists of family members residing on the territory of the former Poland now included in Germany are to be made on the same model.[58]

ATTESTATION
One copy of the directive and one of the model list is enclosed for the personal use of the delegated comrades.

Secretary of the USSR NKVD UPV
Junior Lieutenant of Militia Bashlykov[59]
7 March 1940

It is clear that the Troika—Merkulov, Kobulov, and Bashtakov—was to pass sentences on the prisoners on the basis of information supplied by the UPV. This information was contained in the model form, drawn up by Kobulov. The third section of the form, for the sentence, was to be filled in.[60]

· 51 ·

Record Form for a Polish Prisoner of War
16 March 1940, Moscow*

Top Secret
INFORMATION

From personal file no. _____
for prisoner of war (<u>last name, name, patronymic</u>)

Family name, name, patronymic	Personal data	Last function and rank in former Polish army or in police, intelligence, and prison organizations	Sentence
	Give year, place of birth, property, family, social status, where prisoner is held, when taken prisoner		

(Date)_____ 1940

Head of NKVD UPV
GB Captain (Soprunenko)

Beria's directive of 20 March 1940 led to the deportation of 66,000 people, mainly women and children from former eastern Poland, to Kazakhstan in Soviet Central Asia. Some died on the way, and many died in their places of resettlement.

---

* Handwritten note in upper right-hand corner of page: "Received from Com. Kobulov. P. Soprunenko. 16 March 1940."

· 52 ·

Beria's Directive to the Commissar of Internal Affairs, Kazakh SSR, GB Senior
Major Semyon Burdakov, on the Resettlement in Kazakhstan of Polish POW
Families to Be Deported from the Western Oblasts of Ukraine and Belorussia[61]
20 March 1940, Moscow

No. 1042/b

To the People's Commissar of Internal Affairs of the Kazakh SSR
GB Senior Major Com. Burdakov

Twenty-five thousand families of repressed former officers of the Polish
Army, police, prison guards, gendarmes, intelligence agents, former landowners, manufacturers, and prominent officials of the former Polish state
apparatus being held in prisoner-of-war camps are subject to deportation
from the western oblasts of the Ukrainian SSR and Belorussian SSR to the
northern oblasts of the Kazakh SSR for a term of ten years.

The indicative number of these family members is approximately
75,000–100,000 people.[62]

In addition, 2,000–3,000 prostitutes are subject to deportation from
the western oblasts of the UkSSR and BSSR to the same oblasts of the
Kazakh SSR.[63]

You must work out specific measures for settling the deportees in Kustanai, Akmolinsk, Aktiubinsk, Northern Kazakhstan, Pavlodar, and Semipalatinsk Oblasts, figuring on placing 15,000–20,000 people in each
oblast, based on the number of districts and populated points in each
oblast.

In order to ensure complete order, excluding any possible excesses or escapes by the deportees, both along the route of their journey and in the
places of settlement, you should:

1. Establish operational groups to direct the operation in the Kustanai,
Akmolinsk, Aktiubinsk, Northern Kazakhstan, Pavlodar, and Semipalatinsk NKVD Oblast Administrations and the corresponding district sections.

2. Have the leaders of the operational groups ensure an organized reception of the [disembarking] deportees by the heads of the echelons [train
formations] and their further transfer to their places of settlement.

3. Establish records for all the deportees in compliance with USSR
NKVD Order no. 001223—[19]39.[64]

4. Set up agent-operational servicing of the deportees, ensuring the
timely exposure of their hostile work and the prevention of escape attempts.

5. Issue passports to all deportees, specifying in section 10 that the passport is valid only within the boundaries of the rayon of residence specified for the deportee.[65]

In the event that deportees express the desire to move in order to find work in other districts of the above-mentioned oblasts of the KSSR, the heads of the corresponding NKVD organs, with the consent of the heads of the oblast NKVD administrations, may give permission for this.

[You are to] present to the USSR NKVD by 5 April 1940 a plan for settling the deportees that specifies the final [destination] railway stations where the echelons are to be unloaded for further dispatch of the deportees to their places of settlement and the surnames of the leaders of the operational groups responsible for their settlement.

> People's Commissar of Internal Affairs USSR
> (L. Beria)

Beria's Directive no. 00350 did not refer to the Politburo decision of 5 March 1940 (doc. 47) or to Beria's personal supervision of its implementation—Merkulov, Maslennikov, and Chernyshov were ordered to report to him on its course—but it clearly concerned the Polish POWs as well as all other Poles held in NKVD prisons in the western regions of the Soviet Belorussian and Ukrainian Republics. They were to be transferred to NKVD prisons in Minsk, Kiev, Kharkov, and Kherson to be shot there.

· 53 ·

Beria's Order no. 00350 on "Clearing Out" the NKVD Prisons
in the Western UkSSR and BSSR
22 March 1940, Moscow

Top Secret
No. 00350
Order of the People's Commissar of Internal Affairs USSR for 1940
Contents: On Clearing Out the NKVD Administration Prisons of
Western UkSSR and BSSR
22 March 1940, Moscow

In order to clear out the NKVD Administration prisons in the western oblasts of the UkSSR and BSSR,
I ORDER:

1. For the NKVD of the Ukrainian SSR:

1) Transfer 3,000 arrested persons from the prisons of the western oblasts of the Ukrainian SSR to the prisons of the central oblasts of the UkSSR. Of these:

From Lvov prison	900 people
from Rovno prison	500 "
from Volynsk prison	500 "
from Tarnopol prison	500 "
from Drogobych prison	200 "
from Stanislavov prison	400 "

2) Relocate the arrested persons in the Kiev, Kharkov, and Kherson prisons.[66]

3) Send the head of the Main Prison Administration of the USSR NKVD, GB Major Com. [Pavel N.] Zuev, to render assistance to the UkSSR NKVD in organizing the transportation of these arrested persons.

4) UkSSR People's Commissar of Internal Affairs, GB Commissar 3rd Rank Com. Serov, and the head of the Main Prison Administration of the USSR NKVD, GB Major Com. Zuev, are to complete the operation of transporting the 3,000 arrested persons from the prisons of the western oblasts of the UkSSR to the prisons of the central oblasts of the UkSSR within ten days' time.

5) Bearing in mind the possibility of escapes by the arrested persons and attempted attacks on the convoy by counterrevolutionary (c-r) elements in order to free the arrested [persons], entrust Coms. Serov, Zuev, and the commander of the 13th Division of the NKVD Convoy Troops, Colonel Com. A. I. Zavialov, with the responsibility of ensuring the strictest order among and guarding of the arrested persons, during both their reception [from the prisons] and their being loaded [onto the trains] and all along the route of the echelons [carrying] the arrested persons.

6) USSR Deputy People's Commissar of Internal Affairs, Divisional Commander Com. Chernyshov, shall within ten days' time remove from their NKVD places of imprisonment in the Ukrainian SSR and send to USSR NKVD correctional labor camps 8,000 convicted prisoners, including 3,000 from the Kiev, Kharkov, and Kherson prisons.[67]

2. For the NKVD of the Belorussian SSR:

1) Transfer 3,000 arrested persons from the prisons of the western oblasts of the Belorussian SSR to Minsk prison, of these:

from Brest prison	1,500 persons
from Vileika prison[68]	550 "

| from Pinsk prison | 500 | " |
| from Baranovichi prison | 450 | "69 |

2) Send the section head of the Main Prison Administration of the USSR NKVD, GB Captain Com. [Aleksandr] Chechev, to render assistance to the BSSR NKVD in organizing the transfer of these arrested persons.

3) BSSR People's Commissar of Internal Affairs, GB Commissar 3rd Rank Com. Tsanava, and the head of the Department of the Main Prison Administration of the USSR NKVD, GB Captain Com. Chechev, shall complete the operation of transporting the arrested persons from the prisons of the western oblasts of the BSSR to Minsk prison within ten days' time.

4) Entrust Coms. Tsanava, Chechev, and the commander of the 15th Brigade of the NKVD Convoy Troops, Colonel Com. P. S. Popov, with the responsibility of ensuring the strictest order among and guarding of the arrested persons, both during reception and loading and all along the route of the echelons with the arrested persons.

3. USSR Deputy People's Commissar of Internal Affairs, Divisional Commander Com. Chernyshov, shall ensure the delivery on time of the necessary number of echelons for the above-specified transports of arrested persons, both for transporting the arrested [people] from the western oblasts of the UkSSR and BSSR and for shipping out 8,000 prisoners from the UkSSR to correctional labor camps.[70]

4. USSR Deputy People's Commissar of Internal Affairs, Corps Commander Com. Maslennikov, and the head of the Main Administration of Convoy Troops, Brigade Commander Com. V. N. Sharapov, are to allocate the necessary number of convoy [soldiers] and organize the careful guarding of the convoyed arrested persons, not allowing even one to escape.

Coms. Maslennikov and Chernyshov shall report to me along the way on the progress in implementing the present order.

> USSR People's Commissar of Internal Affairs
> GB Commissar 1st Rank
> L. Beria[71]

The rank order for sending information on the officers in this instruction turned out to be generally the same as the order in the death transports.

· 54 ·

Soprunenko's Instruction to [Aleksandr G.] Berezhkov, Starobelsk Camp,
on Sending Information about Polish POWs to the USSR NKVD UPV
30 March 1940, Moscow

No. 49534/8474
Top Secret

Starobelsk. NKVD Camp. To Berezhkov.

I direct the sending of information first on the highest-ranking, then on the senior and middle-level officer cadres, and last on physicians, teachers, agronomists, and other civilians who have no compromising materials about them.[72]

P. Soprunenko

The first lists of victims to be dispatched to their death were dated 1 April 1940. Sixty-seven lists were signed for Ostashkov prisoners between April and 19 May, most of them for ninety to a hundred people each.

· 55 ·

Soprunenko's Directive to Borisovets on Sending Forty-Nine Polish POWs
from Ostashkov Camp to the Commander of the Kalinin Oblast UNKVD[73]
1 April 1940, Moscow

Top Secret
For Addressee Only

To the Head of the Ostashkov Prisoner-of-War Camp
Major Com. Borisovets, Ostashkov

Upon receipt of this, immediately send to the city of Kalinin, into the charge of the commander of the Kalinin Oblast UNKVD, the POWs listed below who are being held at Ostashkov camp.

[The numbers after names refer to ranks, if known.]*

---

* According to *KDZ2/51*: (1) official of the Polish Police (PP); (2) PP functionary; (3) PP constable; (4) PP senior constable; (5) PP senior inspector; (6) PP 1st constable; (7) prison official; (8) prison guard; (9) PP superintendent; (10) colonel, senior chaplain.

1. Ekiert, Józef (1), son of Ludwik   b. 1883
2. Studnicz, Jan (2), son of Antoni   b. 1890
3. Golema, Ludwik, son of Piotr   b. 1890
4. Rysik, Stanisław, son of Tomasz   b. 1910
5. Wróblewicz, Szczepan (3), son of Jan   b. 1891
6. Dec, Franciszek (4), son of Józef   b. 1897
7. Włodarczyk, Jan, son of Antoni   b. 1890
8. Różański, Marian, son of Adam   b. 1901
9. Łonczek (or Łączek) Adam, son of Wojciech   b. 1890
10. Jędrzejczyk, Antoni (3), son of Maciej   b. 1891
11. Bajwoluk, Paweł (5), son of Franciszek   b. 1901
12. Bieda, Stanisław (4), son of Jan   b. 1897
13. Dąbrowski, Marian (4), son of Józef   b. 1893
14. Bińkowski, Józef, son of Adam   b. 1890
15. Włoszczal, Piotr, son of Wojciech   b. 1895
16. Kucharek, Stanisław, son of Józef   b. 1907
17. Kaszub, Franciszek(4), son of Józef   b. 1899
18. Jędrejek, Czesław (3), son of Michał   b. 1912
19. Łażewski, Jan (6), son of Stanisław   b. 1896
20. Figlewicz, Stefan (4), son of Wojciech   b. 1892
21. Matyja, Władysław (2), son of Franciszek   b. 1891
22. Lechowski, Bronisław, son of Ignacy   b. 1896
23. Janosko, Antoni, son of Kacper   b. 1905
24. Danilczuk, Marcin, son of Marcin   b. 1900
25. Kostrzewski, Zygmunt, son of Jacenty   b. 1899
26. Maciejewski, Ignacy (6), son of Ludwik   b. 1898
27. Wieczorek, Stanisław, son of Józef   b. 1910
28. Kozłowski, Jerzy (7), son of Bronisław   b. 1904
29. Pełka, Bogumił (4), son of Józef   b. 1899
30. Dworzyński, Jan, son of Jan   b. 1909
31. Kozioł, Józef (5), son of Franciszek   b. 1900
32. Stankiewicz, Michał (8), son of Andrzej   b. 1900
33. Piaszczyk, Ludwik (2), son of Józef   b. 1912
34. Miller, Alfred, son of Fryderyk   b. 1884
35. Latosiński, Feliks, son of Antoni   b. 1892
36. Szalka, Antoni (6), son of Idzi   b. 1899
37. Sikora Jan, son of Jan   b. 1892
38. Zarzycki, Stanisław, son of Wawrzyniec   b. 1901
39. Krakowiak, Stanisław (4), son of Wojciech   b. 1900
40. Suski, Stefan, son of Józef   b. 1903
41. Lewicki, Władysław (4), son of Andrzej   b. 1892
42. Lubawa, Kazimierz, son of Michał   b. 1887
43. Sitko, Władysław (3), son of Józef   b. 1913
44. Wesołowski, Władysław, son of Zygmunt   b. 1888
45. Wiczyński, Kazimierz (2), son of Piotr   b. 1889
46. Raspończyk, Wacław, son of Adam   b. 1908

47. Biechoński, Jerzy (9), son of Adam   b. 1892
48. Wojtyniak, Czesław (10), son of Walenty   b. 1889
49. Rysiowski, Władysław, son of Piotr   b. 1896

   Head of the NKVD USSR UPV
   GB Captain
   P. Soprunenko

The delivery of lists for dispatching prisoners to their deaths was a highly secret operation.

· 56 ·

Soprunenko's Directive to the Heads of Ostashkov, Starobelsk, and Kozelsk Camps on Receiving Lists of Polish POWs from the NKVD UPV
4 April 1940, Moscow

———————————

49540/8903
Top Secret

Ostashkov, Kalinin Oblast NKVD Camp, to Borisovets
Starobelsk, Voroshilovgrad Oblast NKVD Camp, to Berezhkov
Kozelsk, NKVD Camp Smolensk Oblast NKVD Camp, to Korolev
 In order to receive the lists from the UPV, immediately send to Moscow the responsible staff member whom you have assigned to make regular trips for this specified purpose.[74]

   Soprunenko

The aim of Soprunenko's instruction of 4 April 1940 was to save the informants and intelligence agents among the prisoners. According to Natalia Lebedeva, out of 395 survivors of the three camps, about 100 were probably agents.[75]

· 57 ·

Soprunenko's Instruction to the Heads of Ostashkov, Starobelsk,
and Kozelsk Camps on Sending Agent Record Files to the NKVD UPV
4 April 1940, Moscow

No. 4954/8919
Top Secret

Kozelsk NKVD Camp to Zarubin, Korolev.
Starobelsk NKVD Camp to Mironov, Berezhkov.
Ostashkov NKVD Camp to Kholichev, Borisovets.

If the lists of POWs subject to dispatch from the camp include your agents, do not send the latter anywhere until [you receive] special instructions.

Select camp record files on agents that have not already been sent to the UPV and send these together with any agent materials you have on them by courier in top secret procedure to me personally.

Basis: Instruction from Deputy People's Commissar Com. Merkulov

P. Soprunenko

Beria's directive of 4 April 1940 indicates the goal of exterminating not only the officers and police held in the camps but also the NCOs from western Ukraine and western Belorussia, who had been released to their homes and given internal passports as Soviet citizens.

· 58 ·

Beria's Directive to UkSSR and BSSR People's Commissars
of Internal Affairs Serov and Tsanava to Arrest NCOs of the
Former Polish Army in Western Ukraine and Western Belorussia
4 April 1940, Moscow

N1173/b

To the UkSSR People's Commissar of Internal Affairs
GB Commissar 3rd Rank Com. Serov
To the BSSR People's Commissar of Internal Affairs
GB Commissar 3rd Rank Com. Tsanava

Regarding the cases of counterrevolutionary organizations of Polish nationalists that have been liquidated in the western oblasts of the UkSSR and BSSR, it has been established that the noncommissioned cadres of the former Polish Army (corporals, platoon leaders, sergeants, etc.) play the most active and, in many instances, the leading role in these organizations.[76]

In connection with this, I hereby propose:

1. To arrest all the individuals from among the noncommissioned officers of the former Polish Army who are conducting c-r work.

2. To include in operational data the noncommissioned officer cadres of the Polish Army: corporals, platoon leaders, senior sergeants, sergeants, ensigns, and officer cadets, utilizing for this the passportization [issuing of passports] being carried out in the western oblasts of the UkSSR and BSSR and the registration of those subject to military service.[77]

3. In the process of exposing the noncommissioned officer cadres of the former Polish Army, provide secret surveillance of the dubious and suspicious elements [among them].

4. Inform the USSR NKVD on the results of the data collected.

People's Commissar of Internal Affairs USSR
GB Commissar 1st Rank
(L. Beria)

Lieutenant Kachin's report of 5 April 1940 is the first of a whole series of "receipts," that is, reports on the arrival of Ostashkov POWs at Kalinin/Tver.

· 59 ·

Receipt

Received from the convoy, prisoners numbering three hundred and forty-three people (343).[78]

> Received. T. Kachin
> 5 April 1940

This is the first of many reports by the UNKVD head of Kalinin Oblast, Dmitry Tokarev, on the "implementation," that is, the murder of the Polish police and gendarme POWs from Ostashkov camp. He gave a harrowing description of these executions half a century later to officials of the Soviet Main Military Prosecutor's Office and the Polish Ministry of Justice.

· 60 ·

Report from Dmitry Tokarev, UNKVD, Kalinin Oblast, to Merkulov
on the Implementation of the First Order
5 April 1940, Kalinin

No. 13974
Top Secret

To Deputy People's Commissar of Internal Affairs Com. Merkulov
First order implemented no. 343.[79]

> Tokarev

The head of the NKVD Glavnoe Transportnoe Upravlenie [GTU—Main Transport Administration], Solomon Milshtein, sent Merkulov reports, sometimes twice a day, on every transport of Kozelsk POWs on the Moscow-Kiev or Dzherzhinsky Railway Lines to Smolensk.

· 61 ·

Solomon Milshtein's Report to Merkulov on the Rail Transport
of Polish POWs from Kozelsk to Smolensk on 4 April 1940
5 April 1940, Moscow*

Top Secret

To the Deputy People's Commissar of Internal Affairs USSR
GB Commissar 3rd Rank
Com. Merkulov

Report on the Movement of Prison Cars in Railway Transport
on 4 April 1940[80]

On 4 April of this year, at Kozelsk Station, Dzherzhinsky Railway Line,
four train cars were loaded [with prisoners], instead of the three train cars
according to the plan.

At 20:30, train cars no. 3006 and no. 663 were delivered, by train no.
1173, to the Moscow-Kiev Railway Line and, at 22:10, sent to Smolensk
from Sukhinichi Station with train no. 1145.

At 24:00, train cars no. 684 and no. 650 were delivered, by train no.
1169, to the Moscow-Kiev Railway Line. They will be sent from Sukhinichi Station to Smolensk on 5 April at 12:00.

At the request of the representative of the Main Administration of Convoy Troops, Colonel Stepanov, on 5 April of this year four train cars are to
be loaded.

On 5 April of this year, at 00:45, two train cars, nos. 720 and 708, were
sent with train no. 88 from Smolensk to Kozelsk, as per the plan. No train
cars were sent out with freight trains on 4 April. Requests to couple three
train cars at Smolensk Station as per the plan were not received from the
representative of the Main Administration of Convoy Troops.

Head, GTU NKVD USSR
GB Commissar 3rd Rank
Milshtein

Soprunenko's instruction to Korolev of 6 April 1940 was, in fact, a
death list, one of at least two sent to Kozelsk that day, and is typical of
several surviving lists. These prisoners (except General Jerzy Wołko-

---

* Handwritten notes on document: "Com. Soprunenko, 5. April 40. M[erkulov]." And,
"Stepanov is sending requests for the departure of prison cars. P. Soprunenko. 5 April 1940."

wicki, the only Kozelsk general to be spared) were to be sent to Smolensk, but their remains were found at Katyn. Most prisoners were sent through Smolensk to Gnezdovo Railway Station (see map 5). However, some may have been shot in the NKVD prison or elsewhere in Smolensk, even though their bodies were buried at Katyn.

· 62 ·

Soprunenko's Instruction to Korolev on Sending Eighty-Nine Polish POWs from Kozelsk Camp to the Head of the Smolensk Oblast UNKVD[81]
6 April 1940, Moscow

USSR NKVD no. 015/2
Top Secret
For Addressee Only

To the Head of Kozelsk Prisoner-of-War Camp
GB Senior Lieutenant Com. Korolev
Kozelsk, Smolensk Oblast
Upon receipt of this [instruction], immediately send to Smolensk to the charge of the head of the Smolensk Oblast UNKVD the POWs listed below who are being held in Kozelsk camp:[82]
[Names are given in Polish. The numbers after names refer to ranks, if known.]*

	Record No.
1. Goździewski, Stanisław (1), son of Stanisław, b. 1886	1187
2. Dziurzyński, Kazimierz (2), son of Jan, b. 1891	1147
3. Dobrowolski, Kazimierz (3), son of Zygmunt, b. 1889	1163
4. Certowicz, Jan (1), son of Wojciech, b. 1889	2768
5. Pietrzak, Franciszek (4), son of Jakub, b. 1897	3481
6. Smorawiński, Mieczysław (5), son of Jan, b. 1893	1140
7. Bohatyrewicz, Bronisław (6), son of Kazimierz, b. 1870	1139
8. Wołkowicki, Jerzy (6), son of Faddiei [Tadeusz], b. 1883	436
9. Czarnek, Zbigniew (1), son of Władysław, b. 1887	1193
10. Byczkowski, Mikołaj (1), son of. Wincenty, b. 1887	1165

* According to *KDZ2/69*: (1) lieutenant colonel, retired; (2) lieutenant colonel, active; (3) lieutenant, reserves; (4) captain, active; (5) brigadier general, active; (6) brigadier general, retired; (7) captain, reserves; (8) major, active; (9) major, retired; (10) lieutenant colonel, active; (11) lieutenant commodore, retired; (12) major, reserves; (13) captain, retired; (14) chaplain, major; (15) lieutenant colonel, reserves; (16) lieutenant commodore; (17) colonel, reserves; (18) division general, retired.

11. Raczkowski, Jan (7), son of Józef, b. 1893   3338
12. Koman, Zygmunt, son of Józef, b. 1882   783
13. Florczak, Tadeusz (13), son of Michał, b. 1895   2653
14. Pyszko, Jan (9), son of Paweł, b. 1881   3362
15. Piotrowski, Jan, son of Jakub, b. 1897   4156
16. Kasprzykiewicz, Wilhelm (10), son of Antoni, b. 1896   2327
17. Gotkiewicz, Leon (10), son of Edward, b. 1885   1191
18. Machowski, Franciszek (10), son of Wincenty, b. 1893   509
19. Trojan, Stanisław (8), son of Kacper, b. 1894   2063
20. Szyfter, Paweł (7), son of Paweł, b. 1893   2620
21. Kwaskowski, Bronisław (8), son of Piotr, b. 1899   4850
22. Staszkiewicz, Włodzimierz (11), son of Marian, b. 1891   3011
23. Czubiński, Stanisław (8), son of Franciszek, b. 1893   4322
24. Stolarz, Stefan (10), son of Tomasz, b. 1889   1196
25. Stępkowicz, Władysław (10), son of Teofil, b. 1893   2480
26. Kutyba, Józef (10), son of Jan, b. 1899   1175
27. Bauerfeind, Gustaw (12), son of Gustaw, b. 1886   3330
28. Drewski, Karol (13), son of Stanisław, b. 1894   2904
29. Opieliński, Edmund (4), son of Ludwik, b. 1896   1815
30. Orłowski, Walerian (8), son of Walerian, b. 1893   4295
31. Chojecki, Edmund (8), son of Józef, b. 1892   2603
32. Kronenberg, Artur (9), son of Walenty, b. 1887   2207
33. Sapiejewski, Jan (8), son of Jan, b. 1892   3541
34. Sarnowicz, Kazimierz (4), son of Władysław, b. 1891   4171
35. Iwaszkiewicz, Wacław (10), son of Jan, b. 1894   135
36. Czajka, Józef (12), son of Wincenty, b. 1885   4187
37. Lewakowski, Jerzy (10), son of Aleksander, b. 1891   2006
38. Lesiński, Piotr (4), son of Piotr, b. 1899   354
39. Ziółkowski, Jan (14), son of Jan, b. 1889   1801
40. Rzecki, Jan (4), son of Tadeusz, b. 1895   4093
41. Solski, Adam (8), son of Marian, b. 1895   2159
42. Zwierkowski, Łukasz (8), son of Stanisław, b. 1893   3038
43. Zajączkiewicz, Józef (9), son of Gabriel, b. 1881   3420
44. Gołkowski, Kazimierz (10), son of Wilhelm, b. 1892   1167
45. Janicki, Jan (4), son of Franciszek, b. 1897   2017
46. Wójtowicz, Marian (15), son of Stanisław, b. 1892   3191
47. Hajzik, Antoni (8), son of Jan, b. 1895   2939
48. Matzner, Bolesław (2), son of Klemens, b. 1889   1158
49. Kulesza, Władysław (2), son of Hieronim, b. 1888   1791
50. Reichenberg, Gwido Arnold (8), son of Walerian, b. 1892   4387
51. Janik, Jan (8), son of Michał, b. 1895   4176
52. Baranowski, Adolf (1), son of Jan, b. 1883   1199
53. Sadowski, Aleksander (16), son of Antoni, b. 1887   1170
54. Stefanowski, Antoni (17), son of Adam, b. 1885   2125
55. Sielewicz, Julian (10), son of Franciszek, b. 1892   139
56. Pileski, Julian (9), son of Bolesław, b. 1883   3112
57. Bartaszyński, Kazimierz, son of Władysław, b. 1888   2263

58. Błażewski, Bolesław (2), son of Hipolit, b. 1890   1202
59. Horak, Stefan (7), son of Franciszek, b. 1892   1018
60. Jackowski, Kazimierz (12), son of Aleksander, b. 1886   1968
61. Szypowski, Antoni (9), son of Antoni, b. 1885   4196
62. Pałczyński, Wincenty (8), son of Jan, b. 1898   3763
63. Jamiołkowski, Konstanty (10), son of Rudolf, b. 1895   3451
64. Światołdycz-Kisiel, Wilhelm Julian (9), son of Ludwik, b. 1885   1636
65. Borozdin, Konstanty (8), son of Jan, b. 1897   3262
66. Mikiewicz, Wojciech (12), son of Kazimierz, b. 1892   3124
67. Potrzobowski, Karol (12), son of Karol, b. 1885   3442
68. Minkiewicz, Henryk (18), son of Kazimierz, b. 1880   1141
69. Choma, Edward (14), son of Michał, b. 1889   4911
70. Zaremba, Mieczysław (8), son of Damian, b. 1894   3239
71. Studnicki, Bronisław (8), son of Julian, b. 1899   3737
72. Sadowski, Jan (8), son of Wojciech, b. 1890   1923
73. Wanat, Józef (10), son of Wojciech, b. 1894   1873
74. Adamski, Stanisław (8), son of Antoni, b. 1897   4274
75. Młynarczyk, Franciszek (8), son of Jan, b. 1894   4007
76. Bauer, Jan (12), son of Jakub, b. 1884   2801
77. Staniszewski, Jerzy (10), son of Władysław, b. 1896   1168
78. Popławski, Antoni (8), son of Antoni, b. 1892   2436
79. Perkowski, Hipolit (4), son of Franciszek, b. 1896   409
80. Ząbkowski, Jarosław (4), son of Adam, b. 1897   933
81. Łęgowski, Józef (8), son of Julian, b. 1896   4354
82. Załuska, Jan (2), son of Aleksander, b. 1889   1151
83. Paczesny, Antoni (10), son of Ignacy, b. 1886   1189
84. Świderski, Kazimierz (10), son of Jan, b. 1893   2334
85. Jarząbkowski, Marian (4), son of Józef, b. 1900   3308
86. Wania, Edward (10), son of Jan, b. 1897   279
87. Owczarski, Józef (10), son of Marcin, b. 1893   517
88. Lisowski, Henryk (10), son of Władysław, b. 1894   1178
89. Kajetanowicz, Antoni (10), son of Rafał, b. 1888   2037
Total Eighty-Nine People

    Chief, NKVD Administration for Prisoner-of-War Affairs
    Captain of State Security
    (Soprunenko)

The note at the beginning of the document, "Status as of 8 April This Year," is misleading. Instead, the lists provide the number and various ranks and categories of Polish POWs in the three special camps and the Narkomchermet camps as of 1 April.

· 63 ·

Report by USSR NKVD UPV on the Number of Polish POWs Held
in NKVD and Narkomchermet Camps According to Rank or Profession
Not earlier than 8 April 1940, Moscow

Top Secret
Register of the Numbers of Prisoners of War in NKVD Camps

Status as of 8 April This Year
1. *Starobelsk Camp*

Total held in the camp		3,894 people
Of these:	a) Generals	8 ″
	b) Colonels	55 ″
	c) Lieutenant colonels	126 ″
	d) Majors	316 ″
	e) Captains	843 ″
	f) Other officers	2,527 ″
	g) Priests	9 ″
	h) Landowners	2 ″
	i) Prominent government officials	5 ″
	j) Police	1 ″
	k) Son of a colonel	1 ″
	l) Valet of Mościcki[83]	1 ″

Comment: The policeman and the colonel's son have been left in the camp
for operational consideration.

2. *Kozelsk Camp*

Total held in the camp		4,599 people
Of these:	a) Admiral	1 ″
	b) Generals	4 ″
	c) Colonels	26 ″
	d) Lieutenant colonels	72 ″
	e) Majors	232 ″
	f) Captains	647 ″
	g) Naval captains	12 ″
	h) Naval captains 1st rank	2 ″
	i) Naval captains 2nd rank	3 ″
	j) Other officers	3,480 ″[84]
	k) Priests	8 ″
	l) Landowners	9 ″
	m) High government officials	61 ″

n) Soldiers and noncommissioned officers
   (to be sent to Construction Site no. 1)[85]   5   "
o) Others (being verified for a decision on
   their further referral)   37   "

3. *Ostashkov Camp*
Total held in the camp   6,364 people
Of these: a) Army officers   48   "
              b) Police and gendarmerie officers   240   "
              c) NCOs of the police and gendarmerie   775   "
              d) Rank-and-file police and gendarmerie   4,924 "
              e) Prison guards   189   "
              f) Intelligence agents and provocateurs   9   "
              g) Priests   5   "
              h) [Military] settlers   35   "
              i) Merchants   4   "
              j) Transferred from former Polish prisons 4   "
              k) Judiciary workers   5   "
              l) Soldiers and NCOs   72   "
              m) Others (being verified for a decision
                 on their further referral)   54   "

Total Prisoners of War Held in NKVD Camps   14,857 people[86]
Of these: a) Admirals   1   "
              b) Generals   12   "
              c) Colonels   81   "
              d) Lieutenant colonels   198   "
              e) Majors   548   "
              f) Captains   1,490 "
              g) Naval captains   12   "
              h) Naval captains 1st rank   2   "
              i) Naval captains 2nd rank   3   "
              j) Other officers   6,055 "
              k) Priests   22   "
              l) Landowners   11   "
              m) High government officials   66   "
              n) Police and gendarmerie officers   240   "
              o) NCOs of the police and gendarmerie   775   "
              p) Rank-and-file police and gendarmerie   4,925 "
              q) Prison guards   189   "
              r) Intelligence agents and provocateurs   9   "
              s) [Military] settlers   35   "

t) Merchants and major property holders	4	"
u) Transferred from former Polish prisons	4	"
v) Judiciary workers	5	"
w) Son of a colonel	1	"
x) Soldiers and NCOs (being sent to Construction Site no. 1)	77	"
y) Others (being verified for a decision on their further referral)	92	"

Camps for Prisoners of War Employed by Narkomchermet

1. *Karakuba Camp*[87]

Total held in the camp	820 people	
Of these: a) NCOs and rank and file	816	"
b) Police and gendarmerie	4	"

2. *Yelenovka Camp*

Total held in the camp	1,070 people	
Of these: a) Officers (left by the head of the Stalin Oblast UNKVD)	1	"
b) NCOs and rank and file	1,068	"
c) Refugees	1	"

3. *Zaporozhye Camp*

Total held in the camp	1,544 people	
Of these: a) NCOs and rank and file	1,516	"
b) Refugees	28	"

4. *Oktiabrruda Camp*[88]

Total held in the camp	2,662 people	
Of these: a) NCOs and rank and file	2,662	"

5. *Dzherzhinskruda Camp*

Total held in the camp	2,925 people	
Of these: a) Officers	2	"
b) Police and gendarmerie	55	"
c) NCOs and rank and file	2,834	"
d) Refugees	34	"

[6.] *Nikopol Camp*

Total held in the camp	1,146 people	
Of these: a) NCOs and rank and file	1,103	"
b) Refugees	43	"

Total Prisoners of War Held in Narkomchermet
   Camps and Operations: 10,167 people
Of these: a) NCOs and rank and file   9,999   *"*
           b) Newly discovered officers   3   *"*
           c) Police and gendarmerie (newly exposed)   59   *"*
           d) Refugees   106   *"*

[7.] *Rovno Camp*
Total held in the camp   12,702 people
Of these: (a) Officers   4   *"*
           (b) Police and gendarmerie   11   *"*
           (c) NCOs and rank and file   12,593   *"*
           (d) Others (being verified for decision on
                  their further destination)   94   *"*

Total Held in Prisoner-of-War Camps   37,726 people

    Head of USSR NKVD UPV
    GB Captain
    (Soprunenko)

On 10 April 1940 the Sovnarkom [SNK—Council of People's Commissars] approved Beria's instruction on deporting the POW families from western Ukraine and western Belorussia; it had approved the deportation on 2 March 1940 (doc. 45). (For detailed instructions on the deportation, see doc. 64b.)

· 64a ·

SNK Resolution Confirming the Deportation from Western UkSSR and BSSR
of Individuals as Specified in the SNK Decision of 2 March 1940[89]
10 April 1940, Moscow

No. 1180/b
Top Secret
10 April 1940
Moscow, the Kremlin*
Resolution of the Council of People's Commissars USSR no. 497–177 ss.
On Confirming the NKVD USSR Instruction "Regarding the
Deportation from the Western Oblasts of the UkSSR and BSSR of the
Persons Indicated in the SNK USSR Resolution of 2 March 1940,
No. 289–127 ss."[90]

The USSR Council of People's Commissars hereby resolves:

1. To approve the instruction submitted by the USSR NKVD for deportations from the western oblasts of the UkSSR and BSSR:

a) of the families of former officers of the Polish Army, police, prison guards, gendarmes, intelligence agents, former landowners, manufacturers, officials of the former Polish state apparatus, and participants in c-r insurgent organizations being held in prisoner-of-war camps and prisons;

b) of refugees from the territory of former Poland now in Germany who have expressed the desire to leave the borders of the Soviet Union for the territory now occupied by the Germans, but have not been accepted by the German government;[91]

c) of prostitutes previously registered with the organs of the former Polish police who continue to engage in prostitution.

2. To instruct the Sovnarkom of the Kazakh SSR to take the necessary measures to relocate the families enumerated in point 1-a, numbering 22,000–25,000 families in the northern oblasts of the Kazakh SSR, and to secure their living conditions and labor utilization.[92]

3. To obligate the NKPS [People's Commissariat of Communications] to provide for the conveyance of deported persons, eighty-one echelons of fifty-five train cars each, to the railway stations of the western oblasts of

---

* In Molotov's hand in the top left corner: "*Za*" [For] and signature in blue pencil—"V. Molotov"—followed by "*Za*" after each of the following signatures in indelible pencil: "N. Voznesensky, A. Vyshinsky, Bulganin, A. Mikoyan, Kaganovich."

In the top right corner someone crossed out "Top Secret" and wrote: "Secret."

Handwritten comment in ink on the reverse of the first page: "Gave for distribution immediately after signature of Com. Khlomov. 11 April 1940, 0 hr. 55 min. P. Ivanov."

Handwritten in the lower corner of the second page: "P. Ivanov. 10 April 1940."

the UkSSR and BSSR within the periods of time specified in the request of the USSR NKVD.

4. The USSR people's commissar of health (Com. Miterev) shall provide the echelons of deportees along the route of their journey with medical personnel and the necessary medications and equipment as per the requests of the USSR NKVD.

5. To require the USSR Narkomtorg [People's Commissariat of Trade] to organize the feeding of the deportees along the route of their journey at points to be determined by the USSR NKVD.

6. To require the USSR Narkomles [People's Commissariat of Forests] (Com. Antselovich) and Narkomchermet [People's Commissariat of Ferrous Metallurgy] (Com. Samokhvalov) to carefully prepare the reception, placement, housing, and labor utilization of the deported families of refugees specified in point 1-b, being sent to work in the enterprises of USSR Narkomles and Narkomchermet.

7. To require the [local] executive committees where the refugees are being deported to render the USSR NKVD, USSR Narkomles, and Narkomchermet the necessary assistance in transporting and placing the deported families of refugees.

8. The USSR Narkomfin [People's Commissariat of Finances] (Com. Zverev) shall make provision, based on the USSR NKVD estimate for 1940, for an additional allocation in the amount of 30,250,000 rubles for expenses involved in deporting the individuals specified in point 1 of the present resolution.

> Chairman of the USSR SNK
> (V. Molotov)
>
> Head of the Chancellery USSR SNK
> (M. Khlomov)

The deportation of the prisoners' families began on 13 April 1940. The detailed instructions on providing medical care and food for the transport of the deportees were observed more in the breach than in practice. Many died on the way from malnutrition and disease, especially the old and the very young. According to the memoirs of survivors, corpses were tossed out of the railway cars. When the deportees arrived at their destinations—state and collective farms in Soviet Central Asia—they faced primitive housing and living conditions, backbreaking labor, and wages insufficient to buy the food they needed. Inability to meet—or fake—the work "norms" led to disease and death for many of the resettled Poles.

· 64b ·

Instruction on the Deportation of Specified Persons
from the Western Oblasts of UkSSR and BSSR
10 April 1940, Moscow

[Enclosure with doc. 64a]
Approved by the Decision of the SNK, USSR,
of 10 April 1940, No. 497–177 ss.
Instruction on the Deportation from the Western Oblasts of the
UkSSR and BSSR of the Individuals Specified in the USSR SNK
Resolution of 2 March 1940, No. 289–127 ss.[93]

1. The deportation of the families of the former officers of the Polish Army, police, prison guards, gendarmes, intelligence agents, former landowners, manufacturers, officials of the former Polish state apparatus, and participants in c-r insurgent organizations being held in the prisoner-of-war camps and prisons of the western oblasts of the UkSSR and BSSR shall be implemented simultaneously throughout the UkSSR and BSSR on a day to be designated by the USSR NKVD.[94]

The deportation of refugees who have expressed the desire to leave for the territory of the former Poland now occupied by the Germans and who have not been accepted by the German government, and of prostitutes, shall also be implemented simultaneously on the days designated by the USSR NKVD.[95]

2. In [the course of] deporting the families specified in point 1 of this instruction, the real estate and commercial and industrial enterprises of those being deported are to be confiscated and handed over to the local organs of power. The deportees have the right to sell or take all their remaining property with them to their place of resettlement up to an amount not exceeding 100 kilograms of weight per family member.

Comment: The deportees may take personal valuables (rings, watches, earrings, bracelets, cigarette cases, etc.) as well as Soviet currency (unlimited amount) with them.

3. The dispatch of the deportees to their place of resettlement shall be carried out in echelons of fifty-five railcars each, equipped for human transport (including one passenger car for the guard, one equipped medical isolation car, and a shop car). Each car shall accommodate thirty adults and children and their belongings. For bulky items, four freight cars shall be assigned to each echelon.

4. For each echelon, the USSR NKVD shall appoint an echelon head and the appropriate security.

5. The USSR People's Commissariat of Health shall provide the echelons with medical staff based on the rate of one physician, one medical assistant, and two nurses per echelon, with the appropriate medications.

6. The train cars required for the transport of the deportees shall be provided by the NKVD as per the plan previously agreed upon by the USSR NKVD and NKPS.

Five days before the provision of the train cars, the USSR NKVD shall present the NKPS with a notification for the echelons, specifying exactly the day the echelons are to be brought in, the loading stations, and the stations of destination.

7. Along the journey by rail, the deportees shall receive free hot food and 600 grams of bread per person once every twenty-four hours. The preparation and serving of food on the way shall be carried out at the request of the echelon heads by the unions of railway restaurants and buffets of the USSR Narkomtorg.[96]

Payment for expenses incurred in feeding the deportees along the route shall be made by the echelon heads.

8. The deportees shall be sent [as follows]:

a) the families of POWs being held in the USSR NKVD camps and prisons of the western oblasts of the UkSSR and BSSR—to the Aktiubinsk, Kustanai, Northern Kazakhstan, Pavlodar, Semipalatinsk, and Akmolinsk Oblasts of the Kazakh SSR for a period of ten years;

b) refugees who have expressed their agreement to leave for Germany [German Poland] and have not been accepted by the German government—to the northern regions of the USSR for resettlement in special settlements and utilization in logging operations and other work;

c) prostitutes—to districts in the Kazakh and Uzbek SSRs (with the exception of border districts).

9. The transport of the families of the refugees specified in point 8b of this instruction from the stations of disembarkation to their place of settlement shall be organized by the USSR NKVD utilizing the vehicular transport of the enterprises belonging to the people's commissariats receiving the deported refugees.

When absolutely necessary, the *krai* [territorial] and oblast [regional] executive committees of the Councils of Workers' Deputies are required to put at the disposal of the USSR NKVD additional vehicular transport by involving local organizations and collective farms in this matter.

10. In places where the refugees are resettled, USSR NKVD commandants' offices shall be created and shall function in compliance with the "Regulation on Special Settlements and the Labor System for [Military] Settlers, Deported from the Western Oblasts of the UkSSR and the BSSR,"

approved in the USSR SNK resolution of 29 December 1939, No. 2122–617 ss.[97]

> USSR People's Commissar of Internal Affairs
> (L. Beria)

The dispatch of the prisoners of war to their deaths began in early April 1940 (doc. 59). This 11 April 1940 report from Kozelsk shows that 1,643 officers were murdered in nine days. Camp commanders had to report to UPV the number of prisoners dispatched in every transport.[98]

· 65 ·

Korolev's Report to Soprunenko on the Number of Polish POWs
Dispatched from Kozelsk Camp
11 April 1940, Kozelsk

————————

Top Secret

To the Head of the NKVD UPV
GB Captain Soprunenko
I hereby report: on 11 April, 394 people were dispatched in accordance with the lists sent.
In all, since 3 April, 1,643 people have been dispatched.[99]

> Camp Commander
> GB Senior Lieutenant
> V. Korolev

Beria clearly wanted to capture all Polish Army officers and police, hence the instruction to seek out any such prisoners who might be concealing themselves in labor camps. (Names are given in Polish spelling.)

· 66 ·

Ivan Khokhlov's Instruction to Zaporozhye Camp Commander L. P. Lebedev
to Seek Out Policemen and Officers among Polish POWs
14 April 1940, Moscow

No. 25/3784
Top Secret
Series K
For Addressee Only

To the Commander of Zaporozhye NKVD Camp
GB Lieutenant Com. Lebedev
According to information from the Zaporozhye Oblast UNKVD (No.
1366541/14 of 28 March 1940), there are in your camp a number of
POWs who are concealing their past service in the police or the fact that
they belong to officer categories.

Included among these are the following POWs: Edward Modzielak,
Mieczysław Stolarek, and Krzysztof Sławiński (who served in the police);
Koczyński, Rysak, and Czerwiecki (lieutenants), Rankowski (a captain),
and several other names that are not cited [here].

You are required:

1. To establish immediately who, according to agency information, is
reckoned to have served as policemen and officers.

2. To call in all indicated persons personally and carefully interrogate
them in order to establish their real employment status up to the moment
they were taken prisoner.

3. Immediately inform us about all the police and officers established as
such on the basis of this questioning, attaching copies of the questionnaires in order to receive instructions for their dispatch to the special
camps.

4. I warn you that this operation must be carried out extremely carefully
and within three days' time.

5. Do not delegate the implementing of this instruction to the apparatus.[100]

Deputy Head of the NKVD UPV
GB Lieutenant
(Khokhlov)[101]

This report, written by two UPV officers on 22 April 1940—based
on previous reports from each of the three camps—shows the moods
of the prisoners as they were being dispatched unwittingly to their

deaths. The rumors that they would be sent home were spread by NKVD camp personnel to avoid POW resistance. Other means to this end included anti-typhoid inoculations, routinely given to all prisoners transferred or released, and allowing the prisoners to give a festive send-off to senior officers. (Names are given in Polish spelling.)

· 67 ·

Political Report of the USSR NKVD UPV to Merkulov on the Mood
of Polish POWs Dispatched from the Three Special Camps
22 April 1940, Moscow

No. 25/3429
Top Secret

To the USSR Deputy People's Commissar of Internal Affairs
GB Commissar 3rd Rank
Comrade Merkulov

Political Report

I. [A total of] 794 POWs were sent out from Starobelsk camp between 10 and 14 April; since 5 April of this year, altogether 1,717 people have left, including:

Generals	8 people	
Lieutenant colonels	36	″
Colonels	61	″
Majors	106	″
Captains	436	″
Other officers	1,170*	″

The remaining POWs are being held now exclusively in the camp zone, which has made it possible to concentrate the internal security personnel contingent and improve security.[102] There have been no escapes or attempted escapes.

No negative moods have been noted other than those highlighted in the political report of 14 April of this year, No. 25/3301.[103]

Applications are arriving in large numbers from POWs requesting to be left in the USSR and not to be sent to the territory of Germany or a neutral

---

* Merkulov underlined the number in red pencil and drew perpendicular strokes in the margin. (The correct total is 1,817.)

country. The applications are being submitted mostly by POWs with special training—physicians, engineers, teachers.

The content of the applications is of the following nature:

[Prisoner no.] 1. "I ask not to be handed over to any German or neutral power but to be given the opportunity to remain and work in the Soviet Union. I have the following grounds for making this request:

1) Until now, I was apolitical, but recently I have gotten to know better and become strongly drawn to the ideology of the socialist country [USSR]. I do not doubt that I personally will be able to fulfill honorably the duty of a Soviet citizen.

2) By specialty and education I am an engineer in the textile industry, and I do not doubt that my knowledge and experience will be very useful to the country of the Soviets.

3) I am a Jew and was, until now, subjected to national oppression, which allows me to appreciate fully the policy of national freedom of the Soviet Union." (Jerzy Altman.)

[Prisoner no.] 2. "I ask with all my heart, in view of the liquidation of the camp, to be left in the USSR. I am a tailor's son . . . and do not want to go to Germany or any other country." (Abram Siemiontek.)

[Prisoner no.] 3. A physician—a reserve lieutenant, Jakub Tenenbaum, writes: "When the camp is cleared out, I ask to be left in the USSR. Do not send me to any other country. I am a doctor, a medical worker, and [while] living in a capitalist country I saw all the injustice of that system, I saw the terrible life of poor people, and therefore I have always felt sympathy for the communist movement. I dreamed of living in the conditions of a free socialist state in which there is no national oppression, which I, as a Jew, have always felt."[104]

Other statements are analogous. [Members of] the regular officer contingent of Polish nationality have not been writing applications to remain in the USSR.

II. In connection with the dispatch of POWs from Kozelsk camp that began on 3 April 1940, most of the officers are calm and satisfied that they have lived to see their release from "slavish captivity." [They say,] "Wherever they take us is where we'll go, just so we don't stay here in the camp."

On the first day of the dispatch, among POWs in territory no. 2 [the Skit], there was some distress provoked by the fact that on the first day ten officers were taken from there, including five from the regular contingent and four [military] settlers. [Therefore] it was thought that they were being sent not home but "somewhere," to some other place, and only on the second day, 4 April, when officers of various categories were dispatched, did the mood change.

Conjectures have been expressed that they are being taken to the west, where four distribution centers have been created: Brest, Podvolochisk [Podwołoczyska], Busk, and Kobrin [Kobryń], where combined [German-Soviet] commissions have been created that will question each one as to where he would like to go—to a neutral country or to stay in the USSR—and after the questioning each will be asked to sign a declaration. In connection with this, the generals have issued an order that the officer POWs are not to sign any declarations.

The greater part of the officer POWs who come from the German side [German Poland] have expressed their unwillingness to go to the territory of Poland occupied by Germany, but [say they] must leave for neutral countries from where they can reach France, volunteer for the French Army, and fight the Germans. Once Germany has been defeated, [they will] attack the USSR and restore Poland from the Oder River to the Dnieper River.

Some officer POWs dream of reaching Romania, making their way to General Weygand's army, and making war on the Soviet Union.[105]

Some of the POWs whose families reside in German territory express the conviction that they are going to Germany and that there can be no question of leaving for neutral countries, for at the "distribution centers" they will be forced to sign a declaration of loyalty to the German government. Those people who refuse to sign a declaration will be sent to a camp deep in the Soviet Union.

Individual POWs whose families reside in the territory of Ukraine and Belorussia (the western oblasts) are panicking, and among them one observes a fear of going home. They explain the reason for their fear of returning to their homeland this way:

"Here we are sitting calmly in the camp under the care of the NKVD and the camp authorities, and as [we are] POWs, no one will touch us. At home we will cease to be POWs, and as citizens of the USSR, we will be subject to the laws of the Soviet Union; there they can arrest us and jail us and judge us, since almost every one of us has committed some sin regarding the Soviet authorities."

Instances of anti-Soviet manifestations have been noted. They express the opinion that "the USSR is ill at ease, since it is threatened by danger from its allies, and even though the Soviet Union is big, it stands on 'feet of clay'—one shove and it falls down."

Prisoner-of-war Officer Birnbaum, a journalist in the past, goes from block to block giving lectures on anti-Soviet themes.

Generally people have a passive attitude toward organized talks [by political instructors], and they very often state: "Why do you keep stuffing us with your talks? We're in a 'suitcase mood' now, and here you are with your talks. Our minds are focused on when they're going to take us away and where."

[But some] individuals, for instance, Tabaczyński and the Różańskis, father and son, make provocative statements, for example: "You don't have anything; everything's going for armaments. You knifed us in the back. But Poland will rise again and we're going to pay you back. You're going to be our prisoners yet."

Prisoner-of-war Lieutenant Birnbaum, in the lectures he gives in the blocks, has tried to prove that a blow is being readied on the Turkish border against the USSR by General Weygand's troops, whose assignment is to seize the oil regions in the Caucasus and thereby deprive the Soviet Union of fuel, which will lead to the disruption of industry and the [production of] mechanized units for the Red Army."[106]

Measures have been taken to stop the spread of anti-Soviet slander among the POWs.

Individual officers are spreading rumors that the POWs, regardless of where their families are located, are being sent to Germany, and in connection with this [they] are making threats against those who have manifested a loyal attitude toward the Soviet Union. The latter, wishing to merit trust, are beginning to show themselves to be sharply anti-Soviet. For example, prisoner of war Nowik, because he suggested adding firewood to the stove in Russian, was attacked by prisoner of war Tabaczyński, who not only insulted him but also threatened that "when we're released from captivity we'll settle the score with him." Tabaczyński was put in the guardhouse for twenty days. Attempting to avenge Tabaczyński, POWs Różańskis (father and son) wanted to beat up Nowik. The Różańskis were put in the guardhouse.

A negligible number of the POWs still do not believe they are being sent home, based on the fact that everyone being dispatched is carefully searched by the convoy and transported in prison cars. The POWs are trying to soften up the service personnel [so they will] explain where they are being sent.

It has been established that information about the transport in prison cars leaked into the camp from the cinema technicians Levashov and Gorshkov. The service personnel have been warned sternly in connection with this.

Some POWs say they are being sent to Smolensk. But they are not sure of this and are trying to explain that if they are taken off in Smolensk, then it will only be for feeding.

The source of this information has not been precisely established, but there has been an instance when the convoy head from the 226th Convoy Regiment, Political Instructor D. I. Fedorov, upon returning from his service trip, told certain camp associates that the POWs are being taken off [the train] in Smolensk, where they are received very rigorously and with every strictness.[107] In connection with which, this question is being passed around among individual camp workers.

The talkativeness of Political Instructor D. I. Fedorov was reported to Colonel Comrade Stepanov and the battalion command.*

It has been established that the higher ranks of the former Polish Army who are in the camp, gave the officers leaving in the first parties instructions to write inscriptions in the cars they are going to travel in indicating their final stations so that those who follow can know where they are being taken.

On 7 April, upon the return of the first cars, an inscription was discovered in Polish: "Second party Smolensk 6 April 1940."

In addition, all the walls of these cars had been written over previously, evidently in the transporting of prisoners, with the crudest of anti-Soviet inscriptions, under which many of the POWs had written inscriptions in Polish expressing their satisfaction with the content of these inscriptions.

An order was given to wash them all off and to check the cars in the future.

For the purpose of the greatest possible isolation of POWs from service personnel, the latter have been reduced to a minimum in the camp zone, and access to the camp has been restricted for the rest.

The overwhelming majority of officer POWs are certain they are going home. In connection with which a mood has been noticed to get going as quickly as possible, and they are turning to the camp administration [with requests] to be included in the next transport for departure.

On 7 April, the prisoner-of-war generals Minkiewicz and Smorawiński tried to use their authority to influence the remaining POWs to demand departure for neutral countries. These generals issued an instruction that none of the officer POWs sign any declarations at the distribution centers obligating them to go to the territory of Germany or to remain in the USSR. Those who sign such declarations will be considered deserters from the Polish Army.

This instruction from the generals was distributed by some of the officers through the blocks, but it is notable that it has had no effect. Thus, on 7 April, during the dispatch of the higher ranks, many remaining officers expressed satisfaction that they were not going with them, [thus] avoiding "landing in some problem [situation] with them."

In connection with a certain break in the dispatch [of prisoners], due to the holdup of the lists,[108] the mood among the POWs has fallen [into de-

---

* Merkulov's handwritten note in the left margin: "Remove Political Instructor Fedorov from convoying."

pression]. Suppositions began to be spread by the POWs themselves that "on the basis of complications due to military actions in the west (the events in Norway), Germany has refused to accept prisoners of war."

On 13 April prisoner of war Pienłowski expressed the opinion that "they're not going to be sending anyone out of the camp at all any more. They sent some, it's looser in the camp, and that's where it ended, and we're going to keep on sitting here."

All these conversations have had an extremely dispiriting effect on the mass of the POWs. Many are going to the camp administration and asking whether more will be sent away. Receiving an affirmative answer, they have left satisfied and conveyed this to the [other] POWs.

Among individual POWs, all the talk about the dispatching being stopped has made them start thinking about trying to escape (Colonel Fronik and 2nd Lieutenants Zieleński/Zieliński and Jastrzębski).*

III. In connection with the dispatch from Ostashkov camp, the mood among the majority of POWs is better, especially among the rank-and-file police, who are sure they are going home. Some individuals doubt this, and POWs from the territory of Germany say they have no desire to return to Germany.

Those being sent out from the camp have, upon leaving, tossed out matchboxes with notes in which they write that "during the inspection they search for weapons, personal items and valuables are not taken away, they hear all grievances, treat us politely; from the search you cannot tell where they are sending us."

The dispatch is proceeding in a calm, organized fashion.[109]

> Commissar of the USSR NKVD UPV
> Regimental Commissar
> Nekhoroshev

> Deputy Head of the Political Section
> Senior Political Instructor
> Vorobyev

In late April the UPV was making sure that even sick POWs would not be overlooked.

---

* Merkulov drew perpendicular strokes in red pencil in the margin and wrote: "Keep an eye on them."

· 68 ·

Khokhlov's Instruction to Camp Heads on Sending the Record Files
for Hospitalized Polish POWs to the USSR NKVD UPV
22 April 1940, Moscow

No. 49560/10497
Top Secret
To Addressees Only

To the Heads of the Ostashkov, Kozelsk, and Starobelsk Camps
Com. Borisovets, Com. Korolev, Com. Berezhkov
Regarding all POWs being held in camp infirmaries and municipal hospitals for whom record files with personal data have not been sent [to UPV] so far, immediately send their data files with information on which hospital they are staying in and their state of health.[110] In the absence of photo cards in the records and lacking the possibility of photographing these POWs, send the files without the photo cards.

Khokhlov

Most prisoners sent to Yukhnov camp, situated due north of Kozelsk, were exempted from the death lists for various reasons: interest by Soviet intelligence, official requests from Germany or Italy, and the perception of their potential usefulness to the USSR.

· 69 ·

NKVD UPV Directive to the Heads of Ostashkov, Kozelsk,
and Starobelsk Camps on Sending Certain Prisoners to Yukhnov Camp
22 April 1940, Moscow

No. 25/3434
Top Secret
Series K
To Addressees Only

To the Heads of the Ostashkov, Kozelsk, and Starobelsk Camps
Com. Borisovets, Com. Korolev, Com. Berezhkov
In accordance with the order of Deputy Commissar of Internal Affairs USSR, GB Commissar 3rd Rank Com. Merkulov, immediately send the POWs held in your camp, numbering [number not given], according to the list enclosed to Yukhnov camp, Babynino Station on the Western Railway Line.[111]

On departure, provide each prisoner with the necessary food.

For each prisoner sent, establish a new evidence file and hand over these sealed files to the convoy for [delivery to] the head of the Yukhnov camp.

At the same time, make an *etap* [transport stage] list, a copy of which immediately send to us.

The departure destination (Yukhnov camp) is subject to strict secrecy. No one in the camp apparatus, except for yourself and the head of URO [Reception, Records, and Barracks Assignment Section], should know where the prisoners named are to be sent.

We have put in the request for the convoy and the railway cars through the NKVD Main Administration of Convoy Troops.

> Deputy Head of the NKVD UPV
> (Khokhlov)
>
> Head of the 2nd Department of UPV
> GB Lieutenant
> (Makliarsky)

The removal of a prisoner's file from "control" and submitting it for "examination" meant that their cases would be reviewed.

· 70 ·

Arkady Gertsovsky's Instruction to Khokhlov on Submitting
Certain POW Files for Examination
25 April 1940, Moscow

No. 9/30–49–30
Instruction for the Deputy Head of the NKVD UPV,
GB Lieutenant Com. Khokhlov

I hereby request that you remove from records' control and submit for examination the files for the POWs detained in the USSR NKVD camps from the attached list.

Enclosure—list for twelve people [names are given in Polish spelling]

> Deputy Head of the USSR NKVD, 1st Special Department
> GB Captain Gertsovsky

List of Prisoners of War Located in USSR NKVD Camps
Whose Files Are Subject to Examination[112]

1. Walicki, Witold, son of Aleksander	Starobelsk camp
2. Czernicki, Ksawery, son of Edward	Kozelsk camp
3. Bross, Juliusz, son of Edward	Ostashkov camp
4. Grabowski, Włodzimierz, son of Józef	" "*
5. Nowakowski, Witold, son of Edmund	" "*
6. Sikorski, Bronisław, son of Stanisław	" "
7. Prokop, Franciszek, son of Mateusz	" "
8. Swoboda, Jan, son of Edward	" "
9. Teodorowicz, Aleksy, son of Aleksander	" "113
10. Janisz, Aleksander, son of Jan	" "
11. Janasik, Franciszek, son of Józef	" "
12. Sałaciński, Zygmunt, son of Tomasz	" "

Deputy Head of the 1st Special Department of the USSR NKVD
GB Captain
Gertsovsky
25 April 1940

In a few cases prisoners were saved from death at the last possible moment. The best known is Stanisław Swianiewicz, a professor at the prewar Stefan Batory University, Wilno [Vilnius].

· 71 ·

Gertsovsky to Khokhlov on Sending Polish POW S. Swianiewicz,
Held in Kozelsk Camp, into the Charge of the USSR NKVD[114]
28 April 1940, Moscow†

No. 03692

To the Deputy Head of the USSR NKVD UPV
GB Lieutenant Com. Khokhlov
On the instruction of USSR People's Commissar of Internal Affairs Com. Beria, I request you to issue an instruction on the transit by stages to Moscow, to the interior prison of the USSR NKVD, to the charge of

---

* Handwritten note on page 1: "Reply given: about Grabowski and Nowakowski No. 25/3499. 25 April. Goberman."
† Handwritten notes on document: "Com. Makliarsky. Give instruction. 28 April 40. Khokhlov." And, "Carried out. Information sent. M[akliarsky]. 28 April 1940."

the 2nd Department of Glavnoe Upravlenie Gosudarstvennoi Bezopasnosti [GUGB—Main Administration for State Security], of prisoner of war Stanisław Swianiewicz, born [in] 1899 (file no. 4287), who is being held in Kozelsk camp.[115]

Please inform me of the day of dispatch.

> Deputy Head of the 1st Special Department of the USSR NKVD
> GB Captain
> A. Gertsovsky

The records of the NKVD 236th Convoy Regiment show how many Ostashkov prisoners were transported daily to the NKVD prison at Kalinin/Tver between 6 and 29 April: a total of 5,291 prisoners. According to the deposition of the NKVD Kalinin Oblast chief Dmitry Tokarev, the victims in each batch of about 250 people were shot one by one in the cellar of the prison, generally within twenty-four hours of arrival. They were buried secretly about 20 kilometers from Kalinin, near the village of Mednoe, where NKVD officers had their country cottages. It is possible, however, that some were shot at the edge of a burial pit (see the introduction to Part II).

· 72 ·

Summary Report on the Dispatch of Polish POWs from Ostashkov Camp
between 6 and 29 April
After 29 April 1940, Moscow

———————

Summary Report on the Dispatch of Polish Prisoners of War
from Ostashkov Camp between 6 and 29 April 1940

Ostashkov

				[Echelon No.]
6 April	Sent	494	people	(No. 22)
8 April	Sent	349	"	(No. 25)
9 April	Sent	233	"	(No. 28)
10 April	Sent	290	"	(No. 28)
12 April	Sent	300	"	(No. 30)
13 April	"	300	"	(No. 30)[116]
14 April	"	299	"	(No. 32)
16 April	"	346		(No. 34)
17 April	"	350	"	(No. 36)

18 April	"	345	"	(No. 39)
[no date]	"	136	"	(No. 41)
21 April	"	296	"	(No. 43)
22 April	"	292	"	(No. 45)
23 April	"	195	"	(No. 47)
24 April	"	294	"	(No. 50)
25 April	"	290	"	(No. 53)
26 April	"	294	"	(No. 65)
27 April	"	188	"	(No. 66)

5,291[117]

By 3 May, the UPV together with the 1st Special Department NKVD and with the personal help of Merkulov, had processed the cases of 14,908 prisoners and sent out dispatch lists—death sentences—for 13,682. Since it was impossible for the Troika—Merkulov, Kobulov, and Bashtakov—to process thousands of cases between 5 March and early May 1940, it is likely that they simply signed or stamped the "Kobulov Forms" (doc. 51) with the death warrant already filled in. A similar method had been used with case summaries of Soviet Poles arrested during the Stalin purges of 1936–1938.[118] However, in 1940 the NKVD had an interest in sparing some of the Polish prisoners of war. Therefore, 395 were sent to Yukhnov camp; they were selected to live (see docs. 84, 85.)

· 73 ·

Soprunenko's Report on the Cases against Polish POWs
in Ostashkov, Starobelsk, and Kozelsk Camps
3 May 1940, Moscow

Top Secret
Report on the Progress of Cases

1. Lists have been sent to the camps for   13,682 people
    Of these: a) To Kozelsk camp   4,252 people
               b) To Starobelsk camp   3,750 "
               c) To Ostashkov camp   5,680 "

2. Remaining in the 1st Special Department are cases on   154 people
   Of these: a) For Kozelsk camp   —*
              b) For Starobelsk camp   —
              c) For Ostashkov camp   —
3. Awaiting special orders are cases on   609 people
   Of these: a) For Kozelsk camp   144 people
              b) For Starobelsk camp   26   "
              c) For Ostashkov camp   439   "
4. For correction in the camps are cases on   29 people
   Of these: a) For Ostashkov camp   15 people
              b) For Starobelsk camp   14   "
              c) For Kozelsk camp   —
5. Sent to Yukhnov camp   200 people
6. Ongoing cases   49 people
7. Cases prepared for reports   185 people

Total cases processed   14,908 people[119]

       Head of the USSR NKVD UPV
       GB Captain (Soprunenko)

On 4 May, Soprunenko had instructed the heads of the three camps to telegraph the number of POWs held in their camps as of 3 May.[120]

· 74 ·

Soprunenko's Report on POWs Left in Camps
Not earlier than 5 May 1940, Moscow

Top Secret
Report on the Number of Prisoners of War in NKVD Camps

According to the Status as of 5 May 1940
1. Starobelsk camp—the camp holds   88 people
2. Kozelsk camp—the camp holds   270 people
3. Ostashkov camp—the camp holds   707 people
Total held in these camps   1,065 people

       Head of the USSR NKVD UPV
       GB Captain (Soprunenko)

* A dash (—) indicates where figures are missing in the document.

In May 1940, it was decided to transfer prisoners doing forced labor in the Krivoy Rog mining camps to the Sevzheldorlag [Northern Railway camp], at Kotlas Railway Station, to build a railway line from North Pechora to Vorkuta. As with all instructions regarding feeding, clothing, and caring for the health of prisoners and deportees during their transport to a new location, this one, too, was more likely to have been observed in the breach than in practice.

· 75 ·

Deputy People's Commissar for Internal Affairs Chernyshov's Directive
to G. I. Antonov on Transporting Polish POWs from the
Krivoy Rog Basin to the Northern Railway Camp[121]
10 May 1940, Moscow

Top Secret
Note for Transmission by Direct Line
Krivoy Rog NKVD Camp
To Antonov

Except for the 2,000 people being sent to NKVD Construction Site no. 1,[122] send all the remaining POWs located in the camps of Dzherzhinskruda, Oktiabrruda, Leninruda, and Nikopol-Marganets to Kotlas Station, address NKVD Northern Railway camp.

NKVD UPV deputy head Khokhlov is leaving to direct the dispatch.

Appoint to each echelon an echelon head, a political instructor, a housekeeping chief. Complete the number of housekeeping personnel with verified POWs [trusties].

Supply the echelon with the necessary housekeeping inventory [as well as] with field kitchens for the organization of feeding [the transportees] with hot food on the journey and provide a fifteen-day supply of foodstuffs.

Provide hot food [on] the journey [according] to the rates for POWs of the rank-and-file contingent.

Depending [on] what there is in the camp, provide each prisoner of war with bedding, a pair of underwear, boots. After providing them [with the above], send all the material provisions remaining in the camp, bedding, housekeeping inventory, as well as foodstuffs, with the echelon.

Compile a detailed protocol for the entire inventory sent, the foodstuffs, and the material provisions, and deliver [them] to the head of the echelon [in exchange] for a receipt.

Before dispatching [the prisoners], conduct a thorough hygiene operation, sending the bedding through the disinfecting chamber.

Conduct a medical survey of the people to be transported to establish the possibility of their traveling with the transport according to their state of health.

Do not include patients with fevers or acute illnesses [in] the transport.

If the number in the echelon is a thousand or more, equip it with a medical isolation car.

Appoint medical personnel to accompany the echelon to the designated destination, calculating one medic for up to 500 people, two medics for 500 to 1,000 people, and one physician and two medics for over 1,000.

The health service of the sender camp shall issue a health transit card [with] data on the state of health of those being sent and the absence of epidemic illnesses [in] the camp.

Hand over to the head of the echelon all registration files for the POWs being sent according to the [file] list, having inserted in them a model 3 card, including those with photo cards.

Compile the echelon lists strictly according to instruction. After the dispatch [of the prisoners], report separately how many rank and file and noncommissioned officers there are.

Immediately provide information [as to] the station to which the train cars should be sent and as to the station where the echelons are to be formed. No. 27/3976.

Chernyshov

This report gives the number of lists of names received in the camp and the number of prisoners sent out from Kozelsk camp to their deaths on each date between 3 April and 11 May and those spared who were to be sent elsewhere, showing a total of 4,602 sent. The last transport, dispatched on 12 May, was redirected to Yukhnov (Babynino Station), which saved the prisoners' lives. The only other transport of Kozelsk prisoners sent there during this period of time was dispatched on 26 April.

· 76 ·

Korolev's Report on the Number of Orders for Polish POW Death Transports
and the Number of Prisoners Dispatched from Kozelsk Camp to Smolensk,
Moscow, and Yukhnov According to USSR NKVD UPV Lists[123]
14 May 1940, Kozelsk

Top Secret
Information

Day.Month	List Numbers		Number	Day.Month	Number	Remarks*
	Received:				Sent:	
3.4	No number		692	3.4	74	
	1–2 April			4.4	323	
				5.4	282	
6.4	014,	– 015/1	580	7.4	91	
	015/2,	– 017/1,		8.4	267	
	017/2,	– 1/17/3		9.4	212	
10.4	022/1,	– 025/2,	597	11.4	394	
	022/3,	– 025/1,		12.4	194	
	025/2,	– 025/3				
15.4	029/1,	– 029/2,	891	15.4	148	
	029/3,	– 029/4,		16.4	439	
	029/5,	– 032/1,		1.4	295	
	032/2,	– 032/3,				
	032/4					
18.4	035/1,	– 035/2,	785	19.4	304	
	035/3,	– 035/4,		20.4	342	
	036/1,	– 036/2,		21.4	155	
	036/3,	– 036/4				
21.4	040/1,	– 040/2,	300			
	040/3			22.4	304	
25.4	25/3434		107	26.4	107	Yukhnov
28.4	052/1,	– 052/2,				
	052/3,	– 052/4	407	28.4	411	
7.5	054/3		54	10.5	70	
10.5	059/1		113	11.5	98	
10.5	053/III		1	11.5	1	To Moscow
11.5	25/3854,	– 25/3856	193	12.5	91	Yukhnov

* All departures, unless otherwise indicated, were to Smolensk, or to Gnezdovo through Smolensk,
for execution.

Total received [number of names on lists]	4,620	Total [prisoners] sent [out]	4,602
[Number] of these [for]:		[Number] of these [sent to]:	
a) Yukhnov	200	Yukhnov	198
b) Moscow	1	Moscow	1
c) [Total] according to the lists	4,419	[Total] according to the lists	4,403[124]

Camp Commander
GB Lieutenant V. Korolev

Errors were often made in the dispatch lists sent to the camps, as this report shows.

· 77 ·

Borisovets's Report on the Dispatch of Polish POWs Sent to Kalinin
Oblast UNKVD and the Number Remaining in the Camp
17 May 1940, Ostashkov

Top Secret
Report of the Ostashkov Distribution Camp to the USSR NKVD
[Administration] for Prisoner-of-War Affairs

1. An order was given to send 6,263 people to the Kalinin Oblast UNKVD.

Sent by stages to the UNKVD were 6,229.[125] Held back for various reasons were 35 people.

a) Order mistakenly given by the center [for] 4 people.
b) Also for 2 men, which is being clarified.
c) Order given twice by mistake for (1) person [Czechowicz].
d) Previously sent to other cities (2) people.
e) Detained on instruction from the center—9 people.
f) Deceased who had been subject to dispatch—16 people.

2. Order for dispatch to Yukhnov camp—99 people; 98 dispatched.

One detained, having been sent previously to the Kalinin Oblast UNKVD.

3. Remaining in the camp—73 people.

Commander of Ostashkov Camp
Major Borisovets
[Enclosure][126]

A report to Soprunenko shows the number of people destined for execution according to the lists received at Starobelsk camp and the number dispatched between 5 April and 12 May 1940. Before extermination began, the camp held 3,896 prisoners (see Appendix, table 2D, 16 March). The figure of 3,810 victims (see table below) is higher than the verified Polish figure of 3,739, but an even higher figure is possible. According to witness testimony (Syromiatnikov), the prisoners were executed in the cellar of the NKVD inner prison in Kharkov, but exhumations in the 1990s indicate that some were shot at the burial site. The cover letter itemizes errors in the dispatch lists.

· 78 ·

Berezhkov's Letter to Soprunenko on the Number of Lists Received
and the Number of Polish POWs Dispatched from Starobelsk Camp
between 5 April and 12 May 1940, with Reports Attached
18 May 1940, Starobelsk

No. 36/106
Top Secret

To the Head of the USSR NKVD Administration for Prisoner-of-War Affairs
GB Captain Com. Soprunenko
Moscow

Presenting herewith information on the number of lists received for the dispatch of POWs and on the number of POWs dispatched from the camp between 5 April and 12 May 1940, I report that I have received lists for 3,891 people and sent 3,885 people accordingly, and that without lists (on the basis of your cipher communication of 12 May 1940) 3 people were sent to the 2nd Department of the USSR NKVD in Moscow, for a total of 3,888 people dispatched.[127]

The lists sent [to me] included Edward Marzec and Edward Bokser, whom we had excluded according to the report on their health status, because they had left for the hospital in Kharkov for treatment.

In the list of 3 April 1940, under No. 75, and on the list of 27 April 1940, No. 053/2, under No. 56, the same individual was listed twice—Krzyżanowski, Edward, son of Stanisław.

In addition, the lists included Mardas-Żylinski, Tadeusz, son of Michał;

Barbiulek, Michał, son of Jakub; and Jekatov, Leon, son of Eugeniusz, who are definitely not present in Starobelsk camp.[128]

Commander of Starobelsk NKVD Camp
GB Captain Berezhkov

[Enclosures]

Information on the Number of Lists Received between 3 April and 10 May 1940 from the USSR NKVD Administration for Prisoner-of-War Affairs on Prisoners of War to Be Sent Out from Starobelsk Camp

Serial No.	List Nos.	From (day.month.year)	For How Many People	Remark
1.	no number	3.4.40	98	
2.	06/2	"	100	
3.	06/3	"	100	
4.	no number	"	83	
5.	no number	"	152	
6.	06/4	"	97	
7.	011/1	4.4.40	99	
8.	011/2	"	99	
9.	011/3	"	95	
10.	018/1	7.4.40	100	
11.	018/2	"	100	
12.	018/3	"	97	
13.	013/1	"	101	
14.	021/1	9.4.40	100	
15.	021/2	9.4.40	100	
16.	021/3	9.4.40	98	
17.	024/1	10.4.40	100	
18.	024/2	"	99	
19.	028/1	13.4.40	100	
20.	028/2	"	100	
21.	028/3	"	99	
22.	021/1*	14.4.40	100	
23.	031/2	"	100	
24.	031/3	14.4.40	99	
25.	034/1	16.4.40	100	
26.	034/2	16.4.40	100	
27.	034/3	"	100	
28.	034/4	"	106	
29.	039/1	20.4.40	100	

* Should be 031/1.

Serial No.	List Nos.	From (day.month.year)	For How Many People	Remark
30.	039/2	"	100	
31.	039/3	"	98	
32.	046/1	22.4.40	100	
33.	046/2	"	100	
34.	046/3	"	100	
35.	046/4	"	93	
36.	25/3434	"	64	
37.	053/1	27.4.40	100	
38.	053/2	"	137	
39.	054/4	5.5.40	27	
40.	059/2	9.5.40	34	
41.	25/3837	10.5.40	16	
		Total	3,891	

Commander of Starobelsk Camp
GB Captain Berezhkov

Information on the Number of Prisoners of War Sent
from Starobelsk Camp between 5 April and 12 May 1940

Serial No.	When Sent [day.month.year]	Where Sent	Number Sent
1.	1.4.40 [should be 5.4.40]	Kharkov UNKVD	195
2.	6.4.40	"	200
3.	7.4.40	"	195
4.	8.4.40	"	170
5.	9.4.40	"	163
6.	10.4.40	"	200
7.	11.4.40	"	170
8.	12.4.40	"	164
9.	13.4.40	"	130
10.	14.4.40	"	130
11.	15.4.40	"	107
12.	16.4.40	"	260
13.	17.4.40	"	260
14.	18.4.40	"	75
15.	19.4.40	"	200
16.	20.4.40	"	130

Serial No.	When Sent [day.month.year]	Where Sent	Number Sent
17.	21.4.40	"	65
18.	22.4.40	"	257
19.	23.4.40	"	50
20.	24.4.40	"	260
21.	25.4.40	"	131
22.	25.4.40	Yukhnov camp[129]	63
23.	2.5.40	Kharkov UNKVD	235
24.	8.5.40	"	25
25.	10.5.40	"	33
26.	12.5.40	"	2
27.	12.5.40	Yukhnov camp	15
28.	12.5.40	USSR NKVD 2nd Department, Moscow	3
		Total:	3,888
		[added later by	−78
		hand]	3,810

Commander of Starobelsk NKVD Camp
GB Captain Berezhkov

More prisoners were dispatched from all three camps by about 19 May. Those selected for survival were sent to Yukhnov camp (Pavlishchev Bor sanatorium grounds, Babynino Station), although some were killed later.

· 79 ·

UPV Information on the Implementation of Orders to Send Polish POWs from the Special Camps into the Charge of the UNKVD of the Corresponding Oblasts Not earlier than 19 May 1940, Moscow

Information

Ostashkov Camp
1. Orders given for dispatch to UNKVD   *6,263 people

* " + " added by hand.

2. Dispatched to the UNKVD — 6,236* ″130
3. Instructions not implemented for — 27 ″
Of these:
Included by mistake — 6 people
Duplicate instructions for — 1 person
Died — 16 people
Sent previously to the UNKVD
(Kalinin and Chernigov) — 2 ″
Held back on the basis of an NKID
[People's Commissariat of Foreign
Affairs] letter — 2 ″
4. Subject to dispatch to Yukhnov camp — 99 ″
Of these:
Sent — 98† ″
Sent mistakenly from this category to
the UNKVD — 1 person

Kozelsk Camp
1. Orders given for dispatch to UNKVD — 4,419 ″131
2. Sent — 4,403 ″‡
3. Instructions not implemented for — 16 ″
Of these:
By directive of GUGB 5th Department — 2 ″
Mistakenly included — 2 ″
Duplicate instructions written for the
same person — 4 ″
Sent previously to Smolensk Oblast UNKVD — 3 ″
Sent to the charge of the GUGB
NKVD 2nd Department — 1 person
Died — 1 ″
In Smolensk Psychiatric Hospital — 2 people
Held back on the basis of an NKID letter — 1 person
4. Subject to dispatch to Yukhnov camp — 199 ″
Of these:
Sent — 198 people§
Left behind from this category due
to illness — 1 per[son]

---

* "+ 51" added by hand.
† "+ 12" added by hand.
‡ "+ 1" added by hand.
§ "+ 4" added by hand.

Starobelsk Camp
1. Orders given for dispatch to the UNKVD   3,811 people*[132]

Soviet leaders received many letters from the deported wives and children of POWs held in the three camps, who appealed for the release of their husbands and fathers. This letter reached the Central Committee of the Communist Party, USSR.[133]

· 80 ·

Petition from the Children of Polish POWs to Stalin to Release Their Fathers
from Ostashkov Camp (punctuated as in the original text)
20 May 1940, Rozovka, Zaporozhye Oblast[†]

20 May 1940
Rozovka

Beloved Father Stalin
    We little children [come] with a great plea to the Great Father Stalin [and] from a burning heart ask [him] to return to us our fathers who are working in Ostashkov. We were sent from western Belorussia to Siberia and we were not allowed to take anything with us. It's hard for us to live now, all children have mothers who are not well and can't work. No one thinks of us, how we are living and there's no work—they won't give [us] any. For this [reason] we little children are dying of hunger and we humbly ask Father Stalin not to forget about us. We will always be good working people in the Soviet Union only it's hard for us to live without our fathers. Goodbye father,

> [Polish spellings: last name, first name.]
> Denyszyn, Iwan[134]
> Jędrzejczyk, Zbigniew[135]
> Zawadzki, Figej[136]
> Kowalewska, Barbara[137]
> (signatures in pencil)

---

* "+11" added by hand.
† Stamps on the document: "Received in TsK VKP(b), 27 May 1940." And, "Secretariat NKVD USSR, 5 June 1940."

NKVD troops were rewarded for completing special tasks—in this case, convoy troops for "clearing out" Kozelsk camp and convoying the prisoners to their place of execution.

· 81 ·

Command Order to the 136th Detached Convoy Battalion on the Successful Execution of the Assignment to "Clear Out" Kozelsk Camp[138]
21 May 1940, Smolensk

Order to the 136th Detached Convoy Battalion of the Convoy Troops of the NKVD USSR
21 May 1940
No. 119/a
Smolensk
CONTENTS: On the Rewards for Carrying Out
an Operational Assignment

Between 23 March and 13 May 1940, the 2nd Company and the 1st Platoon of the 1st Company completed one of the important assignments set by the Main Administration of Convoy Troops and the Brigade Command [in] clearing out the Kozelsk NKVD prisoner-of-war camp. Despite all the strain and complexity of the operation, both in the convoying as well as in the guarding of the camp itself, the set assignment to clear out the camp without permitting a single escape by POWs or [any] service violation was carried out. The representative of the USSR NKVD Main Administration of Convoy Troops, Colonel Com. Stepanov, evaluated the work done as good. An especially model example in the implementation of the assignment both in the guarding as well as in the convoying [work] for this period was set by the following comrades: Unit Commander of the 2nd Company Com. Tatarenko, [who] exceptionally precisely, competently, and ably executed the important and responsible role assigned to him in this operation as head of the operational group.

Unit Commander of the 2nd Company Com. Korablev excellently performed his duty as convoy commander. Platoon Commander of the 1st Company 2nd Lieutenant Com. Bezmozgy, despite the fact that he was fulfilling for the first time the duties of a convoy head, handled his assignment excellently. In addition, the entire personnel contingent of the troops, commanded by 2nd Lieutenant Com. Bezmozgy, participated in carrying out the work assigned to them and performed it excellently without a single violation of the law. Platoon Commander of the 2nd Company 2nd Lieutenant Com. Koptev, being the convoy head, excellently carried out the assignment set him—for [all of] which I declare thanks to all the comrades listed above and reward [them as follows]: Com. Tatarenko, 70 rubles; Com. Korablev, 50 rubles; Com. Bezmozgy, 70 rubles; Com. Koptev, 70 rubles.

Red Army soldiers of the 2nd Company, Coms. Pavlenko, Gavrilov, Dubrov, Prokofiev, Panov, V. L. Zakharov, M. F. Sharin, [and] Red Army soldiers of the 1st Company, Coms. Antropov, Khramtsov, Ponomarev, Shchukin [and] Kuchumov, have excellently performed their duties, for which I declare thanks and reward [them as follows]: Com. Pavlenko [with] 60 rubles; Coms. Zakharov, Sharin, Antropov, Khramtsov, Ponomarev, Kuchumov, and Shchukin with ten days' home leave each. I thank Coms. Gavrilov, Dubrov, and Prokofiev and reward them with 25 rubles each.

Battalion Dispatcher Com. Goriachko performed his work exceptionally precisely, seriously, and competently, for which I thank him.

Battalion Commander, Major Mezhov

Battalion Military Commissar, Senior Political Instructor Snytko
For Battalion Chief-of-Staff, Lieutenant Uglov

One of the last executions of POWs from the Ostashkov camp took place on 22 May 1940. On that day, camp commanders, except for Ostashkov, received orders from the UPV to collect all prisoner data cards and send them to Moscow. Ostashkov prisoners were still being executed that day, so their cards were sent in later.[139]

· 82 ·

Tokarev's Report to Merkulov on Sixty-Four Executions Carried Out
22 May 1940, Kalinin

No. 19690
Top Secret
Deputy People's Commissar of Internal Affairs Com. Merkulov
22 May, 64 implemented. 22 May, Tokarev

From 3 October 1939 to late May 1940, Ostashkov camp was used to hold policemen, gendarmes, prison workers, and military settlers, but prisoners in the last two categories were moved to prisons in late

February 1940. The camp commander's report on the prisoners' stay in the camp includes information on prisoner files, a record of the Ostashkov prisoners sent to their deaths in Kalinin/Tver, and an accounting of how the prisoners' labor reduced the expense of their upkeep.

· 83 ·

Borisovets's Report to Soprunenko on the Sojourn
of Polish POWs in Ostashkov Camp
25 May 1940, Ostashkov

No. 383/ss
Top Secret
To the Head of the USSR NKVD UPV
GB Captain
Com. Soprunenko
Report on Ostashkov Prisoner-of-War Camp

A. Daily Regime and Security

In Ostashkov camp, there was a special contingent of White [anticommunist] Polish POWs[140]—police, gendarmes, prison guards, intelligence agents, counterintelligence agents, provocateurs, etc.—which required high-quality security.

The internal security [staff], assembled on the basis of the list [of conscripts] in the mobilization plan, was unable to carry out such major assignments. Reinforcement was required with a younger contingent and an appropriate party layer, which was done by the camp [party members were added from the camp personnel]. The internal security staff (forty-four people) was complete.

External security—a company of the 235th Detached Battalion of the 11th Brigade of USSR NKVD Convoy Troops, numbering 112 people—served [as security] along the [camp] perimeter. In April this year, it was replaced by the 12th Company of the 236th Convoy Regiment, which proceeded to carry out the service incomparably better.

In order to strengthen security around Stolbny Island on Seliger Lake, a prohibited zone was established that is 250 meters wide. The Ostashkov District Executive Committee issued a resolution on the prohibited zone and informed the surrounding population.

The technical measures to strengthen security were [the following]:

1) The installation of a high-quality barbed wire fence around the camp in two circles of twelve rows each and crosswise (two rows crosswise) for a length of 1,855 meters.

2) The building of a new fence 2.5 meters high and 580 meters long—in addition to the existing enclosure.

3) The installation of electrical lighting around the camp (eight search-lights put in).

4) The installation of telephone communications with internal and external guard posts.

5) Finally, bases of assistance among the local population were created.

All these measures had their proper effect on security. With this reinforcement the dangerous element of counterrevolution from the West could be securely guarded.[141]

True, this winter there was one instance of escape, but timely discovery made it possible to organize a pursuit and detain him.

It is typical, too, that the fact of the escape was discovered by internal security, the block commander, and not the operational section [Intelligence].

The quality of the internal security service team and of the 236th Convoy Regiment unit can be evaluated as satisfactory.

B. The Contingent [Prisoners]
1. *The total contingent supplied*   15,991 people:
   a) Rank-and-file army contingent   9,413 people
   b) Special contingent and officers   6,578   "
2. *Total sent by stages*   15,991 people:
   a) To Germany   2,313   "
   b) To Latvia   7   "
   c) Released to their homes   7,094   "
   d) Sent by stages to NKVD organs   13   "
   e) Sent to other camps   235   "
   f) Sent to Kalinin Oblast UNKVD   6,288   "142
   g) Died in the camp   41   "
   h) In Kalinin Psychiatric Hospital   1   "

                                         Total: 15,991 people

3. *Prisoner-of-war records*
   a) Registration files opened for POWs   7,430
   b) Questionnaires completed for rank and file   8,150
      (received according to the lists without
      completing questionnaires   1,263)
   c) Photographed   6,240
   d) Fingerprinted   6,407

4. *Complaints and petitions*

On various issues the POWs submitted 1,365 complaints, which were examined by the camp command. The majority of the complaints concerned the confiscation of belongings in places of preventive confinement without issuing a receipt. Many belongings have been returned at the camp's request. Some of the statements requested that the [petitioners] be released home as quickly as possible, and about fifty requests were addressed to higher offices to the names of Comrades Stalin, Molotov, and Kalinin.

5. *Disturbances*

There have been no disturbances during the time of the camp's existence. Incidentally, the camp held a contingent of the most criminal counterrevolutionaries.[143] True, there were attempts on the part of [Polish] counterintelligence to organize external observation; they set up sentry posts for the purpose of studying the camp's work methods and service, but this was uncovered in good time and the camp command took the necessary measures (isolation, arrests, and other regulation measures).

C. Camp Maintenance and Expenses

All expenses to maintain the POWs at Ostashkov camp for their eight-month stay (including the staff) come to 5,070,041 rubles and 56 kopecks.

The value of property remaining in the camp is expressed in the sum of 1,619,540 rubles, not counting the housing area restored from destroyed stone buildings by the manual labor of the POWs—2,489 cubic meters; the newly constructed wooden housing—1,651 cubic meters; the service [staff] quarters—2,444 cubic meters; and the 270 meters of dikes, 30-meter bridge, and others.

All these jobs are worth 350,000–400,000 [rubles].

The stay of the POWs in the camp expressed in man-days is [worth] 1,241,880 [rubles].

In this way, the maintenance of one prisoner of war per day cost the state (not counting the work done by the prisoners themselves) 2 rubles 78.2 kopecks.

If we count the value of property made by the hands of the POWs, then their upkeep per day drops to 2 rubles 58 kopecks.

D. Operational and Political Provision

Up until January [1940], I, as the camp commander, did not have operational [intelligence] service. The materials presented to me were third-rate or not full-value data. How the prisoners lived, what interested them, what shortcomings there were in the units performing the security (internal and external)—I did not possess these data. All this work, both with the prisoners and with my staff, had to be done [as though we were] groping in the dark.

For the same reason, until December 1939, the political security [work] was clearly insufficient. If to this we add the fact that the political apparatus did not have any experience in the work and was, for the most part, in a mood to be demobilized, then clearly all this hindered the [camp] commissar in developing political work to its full extent, so he had to carry it out in [separate] segments.

After November 1939, there were certain advances in general security, as the party organization stated numerous times at its meetings, but the full range of work was not achieved until early 1940.

E. Conclusions
1. The introduction by the camp of heads of blocks (from among the watchmen) for guarding the prisoners in their quarters justified itself and yielded good results for reconnoitering the contingent.

2. The organization of work procedures reduced the cost to the state of maintaining the prisoners and hindered them from forming groups, organizing disturbances, etc., which in the opinion of the command should be taken into consideration in future camps.

3. Shortcomings:
a) For a long period discipline in the camp was weak because 90 percent of the camp personnel had not undergone any kind of military training before being conscripted to [work at] the camp.

b) The absence of detailed regulations for the camp led to multiple authorities, when the deputy, the assistant, and the head of the Special Section also considered themselves camp commanders, replaced the head of the camp himself as the sole authority, and issued a great many contradictory instructions that undermined the authority of the commander.

c) The weak service preparation of the internal security unit command made it necessary at the beginning to overload it with service and training—and this created dissatisfaction.

d) The weak [preparation] of the URO workers at first slowed the work. The Special Section, by using the URO [workers] in creating its own registration data, lowered the quality of the URO registration itself.

e) The Housekeeping Department lacks an apparatus capable of keeping its accounts, as a result of which its work was poorly planned, although it carried out a lot of work.[144]

4. Ostashkov camp managed to perform its work, and the camp command asks that individual workers be given special rewards.
Enclosure: List[145]

Camp Commander Major Borisovets
Commissar Senior Political Instructor Yurasov

Given the number of POWs sent to their deaths and the number sent to Yukhnov camp, according to UPV lists, it is clear that only about 3 percent of those held in the three camps survived.

· 84 ·

UPV Report on the Number of Polish POWs Dispatched from the Special Camps
into the Charge of Three Oblast UNKVDs and to Yukhnov Camp
Before 25 May 1940, Moscow

Top Secret
Information on the Dispatch of Prisoners of War

I. Ostashkov Camp
Sent: 1) To Kalinin Oblast UNKVD   6,287 people
      2) To Yukhnov camp   112   "[146]
        Total: 6,399   "

II. Kozelsk Camp
Sent: 1) To Smolensk Oblast UNKVD   4,404 people
      2) To Yukhnov camp   205   "
        Total: 4,609   "

III. Starobelsk Camp
Sent: 1) To Kharkov Oblast UNKVD   3,896 people
      2) To Yukhnov camp   78   "
        Total: 3,974   "

Total Sent: 1) To UNKVDs   14,587   "[147]
         2) To Yukhnov camp   395   "[148]

Head of the USSR NKVD UPV
GB Captain (Soprunenko)

Head of the 2nd Department of the USSR NKVD UPV
GB Lieutenant [signature] (Makliarsky)

PART III

Katyn and Its Echoes, 1940 to the Present

The search for the missing officers began long before the Katyn revelations of spring 1943. The selected survivors from the three special camps were transferred first to Yukhnov camp near Smolensk and then to Griazovets camp near Vologda (docs. 84–86; see map 4). It is clear that some of those who found themselves in Griazovets were chosen for their pro-Soviet attitudes; some were requested by the German and Italian governments; others, requested by NKVD Intelligence, were most likely informers or agents; and the rest seem to have been chosen with a view to their potential usefulness to the USSR. Whatever the NKVD criteria of choice, the majority of the survivors turned out to be just as patriotic as their murdered comrades in arms, and they gave the camp authorities a hard time. They intimidated fellow prisoners taking Marxist instruction and protested the prohibition on corresponding with their families—even threatening a hunger strike (doc. 89). They were granted this right in October 1940, when the Soviet leadership began to look askance at Germany. They received letters from the relatives of their missing comrades asking about their comrades' whereabouts and assumed they were being held in other camps. In summer 1941, as the Germans advanced into the USSR, the original Griazovets prisoners were joined by several hundred Polish officers—mostly second lieutenants formerly interned in Lithuania and Latvia who had been transferred to Kozelsk 2 (so numbered because new prisoners were held there after the massacre of spring 1940) and Yukhnov camps in July–August 1940—as well as by some French, British, and Belgian military escapees from German camps.[1]

It has been known for some time that all the prisoners in Kozelsk 2 were interrogated and that most of the police were condemned to hard labor in the Murmansk region. About 4,000 rank-and-file soldiers and NCOs were also sent there from Yukhnov camp. The dispatch of officers to Ponoi was delayed and then canceled because of the approaching war. It was assumed that all the military officers from Kozelsk 2 were sent on to Griazovets. But a Polish researcher recently discovered copies of NKVD documents in the Central Military Archive, Warsaw, identifying 111 officers and police held in Kozelsk 2, who were sent elsewhere. Thirty-nine were identified as members of the Polish Intelligence and as politically active in "former Poland"; of these, 38 disappeared without a trace after being taken to the Lubianka prison, Moscow. The charges against them are unknown, but one document may illustrate what they were. According to a "Testimonial of Rehabilitation" for one of these officers, issued by the Supreme Court of the Belarus Republic on 1 January 1995, Major Józef Olędzki was condemned by the Military Tribunal of the Special Western Military District on 27 March 1941, on the basis of Paragraph 68, point "a," and Paragraph 78 of the Criminal Code of the Belorussian Socialist Soviet Republic to the highest punishment, death by shooting. His "crime" was that he had joined the Polish Army as a volunteer in the Polish-Soviet War and thus participated as an officer in fighting the Red Army. This verdict was quashed in 1995, and the officer was rehabilitated for lack of evidence of criminal activity. In a similar case, Leon Kozłowski (Polish premier, 1934–1935) was arrested in Lviv and was condemned to death in early July 1941 on charges of having served in the anti-Soviet P.O.W., participating in the Polish-Soviet War of 1919–1920, and persecuting communists while in office in the 1930s. His sentence was then changed to ten years in the GULAG. He was fortunate, however, because he was released after the signing of the Sikorski-Maisky Pact of 30 July 1941. Many years later, his nephew Maciej Kozłowski obtained his uncle's file from the Russian Security Service, together with a copy of the verdict signed by V. V. Ulrikh.[2]

Plans for a Polish Division in the Red Army, October 1940–July 1941

In fall 1940 a small group of pro-Soviet officers led by Colonel (later General) Zygmunt Berling were selected by Beria and Merkulov to draw up plans for a Polish division in the Red Army (doc. 91). Ironically, this selection took place in late October 1940, about the same time as Beria's decree rewarding the NKVD workers who had participated, directly or indirectly, in shooting the Polish POWs in the three camps (doc. 90). Berling and other members of his planning group counted on including many colleagues from the camps in the officer cadre of the proposed Polish division. As Berling tells it, in early January 1941, when he and Colonel Eustachy Gorczyński presented a list of some 500 officers for this division to Beria and Merkulov, Beria asked if the list included those held in the Kozelsk and Starobelsk camps. When the answer was affirmative, Beria said they were not in the USSR, so Berling concluded they had left the country. According to another member of the group, Colonel Narcyz Łopianowski, Beria told Gorczyński and Colonel Leon Tyszyński in October 1940, "We gave them to the Germans."[3] This seems to have been the first time that a high-level Soviet official offered an explanation involving the Germans. Other reports have Beria or Merkulov saying, "We made a big mistake."[4] Nevertheless, Berling and his group continued to work on plans for the division, and on 4 June 1941 the Sovet Narodnykh Komissarov, or Sovnarkom [SNK—Council of People's Commissars], ratified the decision of the commissar of people's defense, Marshal Semyon Timoshenko, that a Polish rifle division was to be established in the Red Army by 1 July 1941 (doc. 93). This project was shelved with the outbreak of the German-Soviet War and the subsequent reestablishment of Polish-Soviet relations, but was taken up again after their breakdown in late April 1943.

The Polish Army in the USSR and Polish-Soviet Relations, from Reestablishment to Breakdown, 30 July 1941–25 April 1943

On 22 June 1941, three German armies, North, South, and Center, invaded the Soviet Union in "Operation Barbarossa." On 30 July 1941, General Władysław Sikorski, head of the Polish government-in-exile and commander in chief of the Polish armed forces, signed an agreement in London with Soviet Ambassador Ivan Maisky reestablishing Polish-Soviet relations. The border issue was patched over for the time being by a compromise formula worked out by Sikorski and supported by British Foreign Secretary Anthony Eden. It read: "The Government of the Union of Soviet Republics recognizes that the Soviet-German treaties of 1939 relative to territorial changes in Poland have lost their validity" (doc. 94).[5] The lack of express Soviet recognition of the prewar frontier led to the resignation of three ministers from the Polish government, but Sikorski went ahead because of his firm belief in the need for good relations with Moscow and, in particular, his goal of raising a Polish army from the prisoners in the USSR. According to the agreement, all Polish citizens held in the USSR were to be "amnestied"—a face saver for Moscow—and a Polish army was to be raised there. General Władysław Anders was accepted by the Soviet leadership as the commander of this army and was set free. He left the Lubianka prison on 4 August 1941 in Beria's limousine after twenty months of imprisonment, seven of them in isolation.[6] A military agreement was signed in Moscow on 14 August 1941. It did not specify the number of Polish divisions, and this became a bone of contention between the two sides (doc. 95).

As soldiers and officers began arriving at Polish army centers in Buzuluk, Tatishchev, and Totskoe near Kuibyshev (Samara)—where most Soviet government agencies and all diplomatic missions were evacuated from Moscow in October 1941—Polish military authorities noticed that most of the officers from the Kozelsk and Starobelsk camps were missing, as were the policemen and gendarmes from Ostashkov. Their names were known, for survivors of the three camps compiled lists of the missing men from memory. Anders made inquiries and appointed Captain Józef Czapski—a Russian-speaking artist called up as a reserve officer in 1939, captured, and held in Starobelsk, then Griazovets—to question various high-ranking Soviet officers about the missing Poles. He learned nothing. Professor Stanisław Kot, Polish ambassador to the USSR, also inquired about the officers in conversations with Deputy Commissar for Foreign Affairs Andrei Vyshinsky, Commissar Vyacheslav Molotov, and Stalin himself, but to no avail. The Soviet respondents always claimed that all the prisoners had been released.[7]

In late November 1941, Sikorski flew from Britain to the USSR by way of Cairo and Tehran. Accompanied by Anders and Kot, he had a long conversation with Stalin and Molotov in the latter's office in the Sovnarkom building on the evening of 3 December. Earlier that day, the NKVD in Moscow received a UPV report on the number of Polish prisoners of war captured in 1939; the number released to their homes in western Ukraine and western Belorussia; the number handed over to the Germans; the number sent to the disposition of NKVD regional administrations (that is, murdered); and finally, the number sent to join the Polish Army or otherwise dispersed or dispensed with (doc. 96). Stalin had all these numbers in hand when he met with Sikorski, Kot, and Anders that evening. When Sikorski asked for the release of all Polish POWs, Stalin said that all had been released and suggested that some might have fled to Manchuria (then under Japanese rule). Anders complained that his men did not receive enough food and other supplies, so most of the conversation concerned the question of whether the Polish troops should be moved to Iran, where supplies were plentiful. This was an issue on which Stalin was very sensitive owing to British and American pressure to send the Polish troops there. But when Sikorski said that he wanted the troops to stay in the USSR, Stalin agreed to increase food supplies and move the army to the Tashkent (now Toshkent) region in southwestern Uzbekistan. This region had a much warmer climate and lay within reach of the Iranian border, so the British could send supplies there from Iran (doc. 97). Three weeks after this conversation, on 25 December 1941, the Soviet State Defense Committee (GKO) approved an increase in the number of Polish divisions from one to three, with food supplies for 96,000 persons.[8]

Stalin increased the number of Polish divisions and, consequently, the food supplies apparently because he expected Sikorski to return to Moscow and agree to a slightly modified version of the German-Soviet demarcation line of 28 September 1939 (doc. 12; see map 2). According to Anders, who translated and took notes on the Stalin-Sikorski conversation at the Kremlin banquet of 4 December, Stalin said, "We should settle our common frontier between ourselves, and before the peace conference, as soon as the Polish Army enters into action. We should stop talking on this subject. Don't worry, we will not harm you." Sikorski said the 1939 frontier could not be touched, and asked to return to the problem, to which Stalin replied, "Please, you will be welcome."[9] After the banquet, the two leaders signed a Declaration of Friendship and Mutual Assistance.[10]

What Stalin meant by not harming Poland is evident from the proposals he made to British Foreign Secretary Anthony Eden in the discussions on a Soviet-British alliance held in Moscow a few days later. Stalin proposed that the Polish-Soviet frontier follow the Curzon Line of 1920, but with small modifications in Poland's favor and compensation with German territory in the west. He told Eden that "Poland should be given all the lands up to the Oder [River] and let the rest be

Prussia, or to be more exact, not Prussia but the State of Berlin."[11] Furthermore, a confidential protocol stated that the USSR was willing to allow Lvov to return to Poland if Belostok and Vilna (all place-names in the document are given in the Russian form) were transferred to the USSR; or Belostok and Vilna could go to Poland, leaving Lvov to the USSR. In either case, Poland was to get the western part of East Prussia, but this time there was no mention of the Oder River as a boundary. The Soviet leader also demanded the part of East Prussia with Königsberg [postwar name, Kaliningrad] for the USSR, as well as the Baltic States and territory from Finland and Romania.[12] In fact, Stalin conditioned the Soviet signing of the Anglo-Soviet alliance on British recognition of the Soviet western frontier of June 1941, but Eden—who privately agreed—did not have the power to grant it. The Soviet leader also proposed a division of Europe into spheres of British and Soviet influence, a proposal the British could not accept either.[13]

Sikorski—who had no knowledge of these proposals—had planned to return to Moscow after reviewing Polish troops but decided not to. He had influenza, but this may not have been the key reason; perhaps he feared being presented with an Eden-Stalin agreement at Poland's expense. Whatever the case may be, after returning to London he informed Winston Churchill of his conversation with Stalin—and warned of Soviet plans to expand westward.[14] In giving this warning, he must have had in mind his recent conversation with the British ambassador to the USSR, Sir Stafford Cripps, who told him of the proposals Stalin had made to Eden in Moscow. Cripps advised acceptance, but Sikorski found them totally unacceptable. However, as Stefan Litauer had reported to the Foreign Office in November 1939, Sikorski privately envisaged giving up some of Poland's former eastern territories to the USSR. Indeed, he told Eden on 3 March 1942 that "if Poland were to acquire East Prussia, it might well be that Poland could make concessions to the Soviet government in regard to Poland's eastern frontiers. But no concession could be made about either Vilna or Lwów." Sikorski added that during their conversations in Moscow, "Stalin had seemed to have moderate ideas about this frontier, particularly as regards Lwów."[15]

Soviet-Polish relations deteriorated in early 1942. Soviet communiqués began referring to towns in former eastern Poland as Soviet towns. The Polish government, for its part, not only protested this terminology but also stated its views on the future of the Baltic States and

Eastern Europe. The Soviet ambassador to the exile governments in London, Aleksandr Bogomolov, delivered a note of protest on 23 January 1942 against statements made by Polish Foreign Minister Edward Raczyński in an interview published in the London *Sunday Times*. Raczyński had outlined federal plans for postwar Eastern Europe, mentioned guarantees for the independence of Eastern European and Baltic States, and included Lithuania in the projected Polish-Czechoslovak federation. The Soviet government claimed that the people of the Baltic States had voted freely in 1940 to become Soviet republics, so Bogomolov protested Raczyński's statements. He said they could produce an unfavorable impression on Soviet public opinion and could not contribute to the development of friendly relations between the USSR and Poland. Sikorski saw this as unacceptable pressure. He told Bogomolov sharply that they were not living in the times of Catherine the Great and that Bogomolov was not a Count (Nikolai) Repnin or an (Otto M.) Stackelberg (Russian ambassadors in Warsaw before and during the late eighteenth-century partitions of Poland).[16] It was in this political context that Soviet military authorities began to pressure General Anders in early February 1942 to send a Polish division to the front. Anders declared that, given the exhaustion of his men, the army could not be ready to fight for at least six months. He also insisted that the army go to the front as a unit, which accorded with Sikorski's policy. This stance, combined with the political standoff, led to reductions of food supplies by the Soviet side, all the more painful because the soldiers shared their meager rations with military families and orphans.

Soviet pressure on Anders increased in March 1942, probably because Sikorski gave no sign of recognizing the Soviet western frontier of 1939–1941, while at the same time the British were pressing Moscow to send the Polish troops to Iran. Thus, on 18 March 1942 a conversation took place in the Kremlin between Anders and Stalin that led to the latter's agreement to supply food rations for 44,000 soldiers in the Polish Army and to Anders's request to evacuate those above that number to Iran (doc. 98). This led to the first stage of the evacuation, which took place between the end of March and early April 1942 (doc. 99).

Later, upon Anders's return from London, where he consulted with the Polish government, he decided, contrary to Sikorski's wishes, to evacuate the rest of the army and the civilians attached to it. He did so in the belief that otherwise most of them would die of disease and starvation in the USSR. Indeed, large numbers were dying every day, especially from typhoid fever. Furthermore, in June 1942, Churchill pressed Molotov—then in London—to transfer the rest of the army to Iran. At this time, Molotov also met with Sikorski and rejected Sikorski's requests for continued recruitment for the Polish Army and the evacuation of 50,000 children to Iran.[17] Finally, Stalin knew that the Polish Army in the USSR was strongly anti-Soviet, and he probably planned to use the thousands of Poles of military age still in the Soviet Union to form a new, communist-led Polish army when the time came (as he indeed did in spring 1943). Thus, in early July 1942 he agreed to the evacuation of the rest of the army to Iran. Anders telegraphed Stalin on 31 July 1942, thanking him and appealing to him to allow new conscription in the USSR to supplement the Polish Army.[18] The second stage of the evacuation was carried out in August–September 1942 (doc. 100), establishing a Polish Army of about 76,000 in Iran. Later it moved to Iraq and Palestine, became the 2nd Polish Army Corps, and fought in Italy. (On 18 May 1944, it took Monte Cassino, opening the Allied way to Rome.) However, there was no further recruitment in the USSR, and the Soviet government did not agree to the evacuation of more Polish citizens, even children.

Soviet-Polish relations continued to deteriorate in late 1942 and early 1943.[19] It is true that Stalin gave up his demand for British recognition of the (June 1941) Soviet western frontier in the Anglo-Soviet Treaty on mutual aid, so it was signed in London on 26 May 1942 without mentioning frontiers. The British government had offered to recognize Soviet demands in an exchange of letters, but Stalin decided not to press the issue, most likely because he knew of President Franklin Delano Roosevelt's opposition to making agreements on territorial changes in wartime. In any case, on 24 May he instructed Molotov to stop insisting on British recognition of the June 1941 western frontier of the USSR. As he put it, "The question of our frontiers, or to be exact, of guarantees for the security of our frontiers at one or another section of our country, will be decided by force."[20]

In the meantime, Stalin was grooming Polish communist leaders who could take power in Poland after the war, with or without the London Poles. Indeed, some Polish communists had already received training in the Comintern [Communist International] school in 1940–1941, and the first leadership group was dropped by parachute just outside Warsaw at the end of December 1941. They brought with them a political manifesto worked out with the head of the Comintern, Georgy M. Dimitrov.[21] In early January 1942 these leaders formed the Polska Partia Robotnicza [PPR—Polish Workers' Party] with a military arm, the Gwardia Ludowa [GL—People's Guard], later the Armia Ludowa [AL—People's Army], but their role in Polish resistance to the Germans was minor in comparison with that of the anticommunist Armia Krajowa [AK—Polish Home Army], which was loyal to the Polish government in London.

In early 1943, Stalin increased his pressure on the Polish government. In mid-January the Soviet government announced that all persons residing in the Soviet-occupied territories of Poland on 1–2 November 1939—when these lands became part of the USSR—were Soviet citizens.[22] In April 1943 the Polish Embassy in the USSR estimated on the basis of its delegates' reports and other sources that 271,325 deported Polish citizens lived in various parts of the country and that 39.3 percent of them were Jewish. Beria's count, in his note to Stalin of 15 January 1943, was 215,081 Polish citizens, of whom 92,224 were ethnic Poles, 102,153 were Polish Jews, 14,202 were Ukrainians, and 6,502 were Belorussians.[23] Whichever numbers were correct, these people were pressured to accept Soviet citizenship and faced imprisonment if they refused, as was the case with the Polish writer and poet Aleksander Wat.[24] But these were only the preliminary steps in Stalin's Polish strategy, in which a pro-Soviet Polish communist, Wanda Wasilewska—who headed a group of Polish left-wingers and communists in Lviv [Lvov, Lwów] from 1939 to 1941—was to play an important part.

Wasilewska recounts in her memoirs that in late January 1943—just before the German capitulation at Stalingrad, where she and her husband, the Ukrainian writer Oleksandr Korneichuk were traveling to witness and report the event—Stalin summoned both of them to Moscow. He told Korneichuk that he expected a breakdown in Soviet-Polish relations and that Wasilewska could be of great help if she so wished. She met with Stalin and they agreed that a new Polish political center should be established in the USSR—which she had proposed earlier—and that a new Polish newspaper was to appear by 1 March. The new center was to be called Związek Patriotów Polskich w ZSSR [ZPP—Union of Polish Patriots in the USSR], and the newspaper would be named *Wolna Polska* [Free Poland]. Both names were suggested by

Stalin, and Wasilewska became chair of the union's executive board.[25] Thus, it is clear that in the first days of February 1943, if not earlier, Stalin was planning to break off relations with the Polish government in London and establish a rival Polish center in the USSR. This was two months before the Katyn massacre became public knowledge and almost three months before Stalin severed relations with the Polish government in London.

The Katyn Graves and the Breakdown of Polish-Soviet Relations, Spring 1943

The Germans occupied the Smolensk region in July 1941. The Army Group Center (AGC) 537th Signals Regiment made its headquarters in a building located in the former NKVD recreation area at Koze Gory [Goat Hills]. These hills are on the eastern border of the Katyn Forest, near the two Katyn villages and the railway station of Gnezdovo, which is 20 kilometers northwest of Smolensk (see map 5). In summer 1942 a few Polish workers employed by the German labor organization Todt learned from local Russians that Polish officers had been shot in the Katyn Forest. They did some digging, found Polish military insignia and bones, and erected some crosses. This did not attract German attention at the time, but Lieutenant (later Colonel) Friedrich Ahrens, commander of the AGC 537th Signals Regiment, allegedly noticed wolf tracks in Katyn Forest in early 1943 and was informed that human bones had been found there. He interrogated local Russians, who told of the shooting of Polish officers. Ahrens ordered digging, which led to the discovery of a mass grave. A report was sent to the AGC Command in early January 1943 (some accounts say February), where it was read by Colonel Rudolph-Christoph von Gersdorff, an intelligence officer on the AGC General Staff. He claims in his memoirs that the massacre site came to be known as Katyn because he chose that name to differentiate it from Gnezdovo, with its prehistoric kurgans (burial mounds).[26] The AGC Command waited until 29 March—presumably because the ground was frozen—before ordering the graves to be opened, the number of victims to be estimated, and the circumstances of their deaths to be established.

The Germans soon decided to exploit the propaganda value of the Katyn graves, at first to secure the support of Poles in German Poland against the Soviets and then to split the Allies. On 7 April the German

governor of Warsaw, the Nazi lawyer Ludwig Fischer, told the Polish
writer Ferdynand Goetel of the discovery of mass graves of Polish officers at Katyn and said that a delegation, including Goetel, would be
sent to view the site.[27] Two days later, the German propaganda minister, Joseph Goebbels, noted in his diary that he had given permission to
send neutral journalists to Katyn from Berlin, as well as permission to
send Polish journalists from occupied Poland.[28] On 10 April, a Polish
delegation flew to Smolensk and visited Katyn the next day. It included
Poles from all walks of life, including workers. A prominent member
from Kraków was Dr. Edmund Seyfried, director of the Rada Główna
Opiekuńcza [RGO—Main Welfare Council], who went as a private
person and wrote a detailed report. Except for the pro-German journalist Emil Skiwski, the Poles refused to make statements serving German propaganda aims. They secretly reported what they had seen to
the AK Command in Warsaw, which radioed the news to the Polish
government in London.[29]

   The first public mention of the Katyn graves was made by the German news agency Trans-Ocean on 11 April 1943; it broadcast the report made by German military authorities in Smolensk confirming the
discovery of a mass grave in the Smolensk region with the corpses of
some 3,000 Polish officers killed by the GPU (it used the acronym for
a previous incarnation of the NKVD) in February and March 1940.
Identification of some of the victims was possible through personal papers found on the bodies, and one of those identified was General
Mieczysław Smorawiński. This broadcast was countered on the following day by the pro-Soviet Polish-language Kościuszko radio station in
Moscow, which called it German propaganda and termed its conclusions "monstrous."[30] However, it was the Berlin radio communiqué of
13 April that was reported in world media. This communiqué went into
more detail, named the area Kosogory, and gave the estimated total
number of victims as 10,000, which tallied with the Polish government's estimate of officers taken prisoner in 1939 (doc. 101).[31] Two
days later, on 15 April, the Sovinformburo [Soviet Information Office]
issued a reply. It blasted "Goebbels's slanderers" for the allegation that
the Soviets had shot the Polish prisoners and pointed to archaeological
excavations in Gnezdovo. The Sovinformburo claimed that the Germans had shot the Poles along with Soviet people in summer 1941, after the withdrawal of Soviet troops from the Smolensk area (doc. 102).

   The Polish government faced a shocked and outraged Polish public in German Poland, in the West, and, most importantly, in the Polish Army formed in the USSR, then stationed in Iraq. On the day of the Soviet communiqué, General Anders cabled the Polish defense minister, General Marian Kukiel, in London, detailing the search for the missing officers while he was in the USSR, stating that there was great dismay in the army, and demanding that the government secure an official Soviet explanation of the Katyn graves.[32] The Polish government was under great pressure to take a stand.

General Sikorski met with some members of the Polish cabinet at 11 a.m. on 15 April to discuss the issue. It was decided to send a note to the Soviet Embassy demanding an explanation, to request the International Red Cross (IRC) to investigate the crime, and to publish a statement by the national defense minister, who was responsible for questions regarding prisoners of war.[33] Sikorski and Foreign Minister Edward Raczyński met with Prime Minister Churchill at 10 Downing Street for lunch at noon the same day. The conversation concerned Polish-Soviet relations, especially the Polish government's request for British support to save Polish citizens and sustain Polish relief organizations in the USSR. When Katyn came up, Churchill said he could believe in Soviet guilt, but warned the Poles against raising the issue publicly. Sikorski said that his government was forced to do so. He also pressed for the evacuation of Polish citizens from the USSR and informed Churchill about secret Soviet plans to form a Polish communist army there. Churchill promised to help, but said that at the end of the war it might be necessary to seek a compromise solution in Polish-Soviet relations, which might be on the lines of territorial compensation for Poland. Sikorski rejected this suggestion. Churchill repeated his warning on the Katyn issue, but Sikorski said that the Polish government would be forced to take a clear and decided stand on the matter.[34] On 16 April, the Polish defense minister, General Marian Kukiel, issued a long communiqué giving the known number of missing Polish officers held in the three camps (8,300) and stating that the camps had been broken up in April 1940, that groups of officers had been removed every few days until mid-May, and that only about 400 had been moved in June of that year to Griazovets in the Vologda region. He also enumerated Polish efforts to obtain information on the missing officers from the Soviet government and mentioned Stalin's assurances to Sikorski on 3 December 1941 that all Polish prisoners had been freed. Kukiel went on to state: "Neither the Polish Government nor the Polish Embassy in Kuibyshev has ever received an answer as to the whereabouts of the missing officers and other prisoners who had been deported from the three camps mentioned above." He said that Poles were accustomed to the lies of German propaganda and understood its goal, but in view of the detailed information about the graves near Smolensk, it was necessary for an investigation to be conducted by a competent international body like the IRC. The Polish government had approached the latter about sending a delegation to the site.[35]

On 17 April, the Polish government issued a formal statement to the effect that it had asked the IRC to send a delegation to investigate the graves, but at the same time, it denied the Germans any right to use the issue for their own defense and listed German crimes in Poland (doc. 103). Goebbels now saw an opportunity to divide the Allies. He wrote in his diary that as soon as he heard of this statement, he secured Hitler's sanction for the German Red Cross to ask the IRC for an investigation of the Katyn graves.[36] In fact, the first German request was sent by wire on 15 April, but it was not made officially until two days later. A liaison officer at the Polish Embassy in Bern reported that the official Polish request was submitted to the IRC on 17 April at 4:30 p.m., half an hour after the German delegate submitted his request.[37]

The almost simultaneous filing of official requests by the Polish and German governments with the IRC in Geneva gave Stalin the pretext to break off relations with the Polish government, as he had planned to do earlier. Furthermore, according to a Polish source, a Polish communist was parachuted from a Soviet plane into German Poland on 19 March 1943 with information from Comintern Secretary General Georgy Dimitrov that a breakdown in Polish-Soviet relations was to be expected.[38] A Soviet press campaign against the Polish government began on 19 April with an article in *Pravda* titled "Hitler's Polish Collaborators," which accused the Germans of murdering the Polish officers at Katyn and the Polish government in London of collaborating with the Germans.[39] Two days later, Stalin wrote Churchill and Roosevelt that the Polish government was colluding with Hitler, so he had decided to "interrupt" relations with it.[40] Both statesmen appealed to him not to do so, and on 24 April, British Foreign Secretary Eden informed Sikorski of Stalin's conditions for not breaking off relations with the Polish government. According to Eden, Stalin demanded that the Polish government withdraw its request to the IRC and blame the

Germans for the Katyn massacre. As Sikorski wrote in his report of the conversation, when he asked Eden about the position of the British government, Eden replied: "First of all, the British government did not believe the Germans, and secondly, it could not estrange such a powerful ally. The British Premier would issue a declaration on these lines and I was asked to agree to these two requests of Stalin, as it was imperative for the sake of the common cause." Eden also said that only if Sikorski agreed could the British government intervene on behalf of Polish nationals in Russia. Sikorski said he would not press the request to the IRC, but he could not state that the Germans had murdered the Polish officers, because he had evidence of Soviet guilt.[41] Indeed, given the fact that the Germans had already published convincing reports and photographs in Poland and that there was much criticism in the Polish Army of Sikorski's policy of good relations with the USSR, the general could not have blamed the Germans without risking a revolt in the Polish armed forces and forfeiting his government's authority among Poles everywhere, except, of course, among the small minority—mostly communists—who chose to believe the Soviet claims.

Despite the pleas of Churchill and Roosevelt, Stalin proceeded to break off relations with the Polish government. The Soviet note officially communicated on 25 April by Molotov to Polish Ambassador Tadeusz Romer in Moscow recapitulated the essence of Stalin's messages to Churchill and Roosevelt, plus the charge that the Polish government was slandering the USSR in order to obtain territorial concessions at the expense of Soviet Ukraine and Belorussia—a reference to the Polish government's official stand on the eastern frontier of 1921–1939 (doc. 104).

There is an eyewitness account of how the Soviet note was presented to Romer. The Polish ambassador's assistant, Aleksander Mniszek, who accompanied him that day, recorded that Molotov's Secretariat had telephoned Romer at his Moscow hotel on 25 April at 11:30 p.m. to say that Molotov wished to see him, giving him the choice of midnight or a quarter-hour after midnight. Romer chose the first option and met with Molotov in his office. Mniszek writes that they arrived at midnight and waited for fifteen minutes; they assumed that the text of the note might not be ready, for they noticed officials coming and going from Molotov's office. The meeting on 26 April continued until 00:40 a.m. The Soviet commissar for foreign affairs quickly read the note to Romer in Russian, and the translator laboriously rendered it into French. Romer protested the accusations and conclusions regarding the Polish government as expressed in the Soviet note—which were the same as those in Stalin's letters to Churchill and Roosevelt—and refused to accept it, so Molotov placed it on the desk in front of the ambassador. At the end of the conversation, when Romer asked about leaving the USSR with the embassy staff, Molotov said that the Soviet government would do everything to facilitate their departure. The Soviet note was delivered later to Romer's hotel in a sealed envelope, but he returned it. He also sent a note to Molotov rejecting the Soviet accusations. At the same time, he made a public statement to the effect that both countries remained in the same camp to fight Germany to the finish, and appealed to the Soviet government to secure the future of Polish deportees in the USSR. He left the country unhindered with all the embassy staff and arrived in Tehran in mid-May 1943.[42]

Stalin now stepped up his campaign to undermine the Polish government in London. On 27 April, Georgy Dimitrov wrote Paweł Finder, head of the Polish Worker's Party in German Poland. He gave the Soviet government's reasons for breaking off relations with the Polish government, including the charge that the Polish government was pressuring the USSR into making territorial concessions at the cost of Soviet Ukraine, Belorussia, and Lithuania. Dimitrov wrote that the PPR was to launch a propaganda campaign against the London Poles. The next day Wasilewska made a radio speech in which she declared that the Sikorski government did not represent the Polish nation. She appealed to Poles in the USSR to cooperate with the Soviet Union and its allies in the war against Germany and thus earn their return to an independent Poland. On 30 April the Polish government declared that in view of the IRC statement on the difficulties in complying with the request to investigate the Katyn graves—that is, the lack of Soviet agreement—the Polish government regarded its appeal to the IRC as having lapsed.[43] This did not satisfy Moscow.

Although Stalin rejected the pleas of Churchill and Roosevelt to renew relations with the Polish government, he took care to publicize his benevolent attitude toward Poland. On 3 May (a Polish national holiday), he received a written question from Ralph Parker, Moscow correspondent for the *Times* of London, asking whether the Soviet Union wanted a strong, independent Poland after the defeat of Nazi Germany and how he envisaged postwar Polish-Soviet relations. The next day Stalin gave an affirmative answer to the first question; he answered the second by saying these relations should be friendly and neighborly and could include, if the Polish nation so wished, an alliance against Germany as the main enemy of both the USSR and Poland.[44] On 6 May, Deputy Commissar for Foreign Affairs Andrei Vyshinsky made a long statement to British and American correspondents in Moscow on Polish-Soviet relations. He presented the Soviet point of view and announced the formation of Polish army units in the USSR.[45] Three days later the Soviet State Defense Committee agreed to the formation of the Kościuszko Division.[46] It was led by General Berling, promoted in rank by Stalin. Georgy S. Zhukov, who had served as the NKVD and Red Army liaison officer with General Anders in 1941–1942, was also involved with the new Polish military units led by General Berling, this time as the Sovnarkom plenipotentiary to foreign military forces being formed in the USSR.

A week later another event was widely reported in the world press. On 15 May 1943—one day after the beginning of the Roosevelt-Churchill conference in Washington, D.C., at which they were expected to decide whether to open a second front in Europe that year—the Soviet press wrote about the dissolution of the Comintern. (In fact, the decision to dissolve it was made on 11 May, and the official announcement came on 22 May.) This was welcomed by the Western Powers as a sign that the Soviets were renouncing the aim of world revolution and, by the same token, the aim of imposing communism on the Poles. It was not known at the time that the Comintern departments had been transferred to the Department of International Information in the Central Committee of the Communist Party of the Soviet Union (CPSU). The *Biuletyn Informacyjny* [Information Bulletin], the official AK underground newspaper, did caution, however, on 3 June 1943 that, pending the appearance of evidence to the contrary, the dissolution of the Comintern should be viewed as no more than a "political maneuver."[47]

In the meantime, exhumations were proceeding under German supervision in Katyn Forest. They continued until early June 1943, when warm weather set in. Also, the Soviet Air Force was bombing Smolensk and the surrounding area. As mentioned earlier, some Polish intellectuals had visited the burial site in early April. After their return, the German authorities in Warsaw exerted great pressure on the Polish Red Cross (PRC) to send delegates there. On the basis of the writer Goetel's report on his visit to the PRC Executive Board, the latter decided that its secretary general, Kazimierz Skarżyński, and a small technical commission should visit Katyn to see whether the German allegations were true. They were joined by several other persons from Kraków; flew to Smolensk on 14 April; arrived there the next day; briefly visited Katyn on 16 April; and returned to Warsaw, leaving three PRC members behind to work on the exhumations. On his return, Skarżyński reported to the PRC Executive Board and to the Polish underground commissioner for civilian warfare in Warsaw (doc. 105a). The PRC board's decision—based on Skarżyński's report—was to send a larger technical commission of nine members—later expanded to twelve—to work on the exhumations at Katyn.

The report of the PRC Technical Commission gives an account of how its members worked and what they found at Katyn in April–June 1943. There was no doubt in their minds that the correlation between the names of officers known to be missing and the victims identified at Katyn, as well as newspapers and diaries dating from spring 1940 found on the corpses, pointed conclusively to Soviet guilt. They shared the view, expressed by the German Inquiry Commission and the International Medical Commission (IMC), that the massacre had taken place in spring 1940. They concluded that the officers had been shot at the edge of the burial pits and some even in the pits, where they were forced to lie on their dead and dying comrades before they were shot (doc. 105b). This view of the executions in Katyn Forest went almost unchallenged until 2001, when three authors—two Poles and a Polish-Canadian—argued that since most of the Kozelsk victims were found in the burial pits with their hands unbound, they must have been killed in the same way as the Ostashkov prisoners in Kalinin [Tver] and the Starobelsk prisoners in Kharkov, that is, one by one in an enclosed space. As for the some 20 percent whose hands were bound, the authors believed that these officers realized they were about to be murdered—perhaps when led to the edge of a pit—and tried to resist.[48] This must remain just a plausible theory because no eyewitness accounts or NKVD documents giving details of the executions have surfaced to this day.

The Katyn Documents Saga

The story of what happened to the documents and other items found on the bodies at Katyn is a fascinating tale in itself. The German authorities wanted to examine them on site but, persuaded by a PRC member that this was impossible for lack of proper facilities, decided to send them to the Chemical Section of the former Polish State Institute of Forensic Medicine on 7 Kopernik Street in Kraków, now under German control. After the Katyn Forest exhumations ended in early June 1943, nine or ten plywood chests arrived at this institute, where a small team of forensic experts and Polish workers, headed by Dr. Jan Zygmunt Robel, managed to examine 285 out of 3,000 numbered envelopes containing items found on the corpses. (Some of the envelopes were numbered by the Germans before the arrival of the PRC Technical Commission and then by the latter. In both cases, each body was reburied with a metal tag bearing the same number as the envelope.) Robel and his team examined the contents of the envelopes under the supervision of the German director of the Institute of Forensic Medicine, Dr. Werner Beck, who held the German Army rank of major. The German propaganda office in Kraków pressed the Polish staff to proceed quickly because it wanted to establish the identification of the bodies within two months, but the experts—supported by Beck, who hated the propaganda people—resisted this pressure. In fact, as Robel and his staff separately deposed in Kraków to the regional deputy prosecutor Dr. Roman Martini in summer 1945, it took several hours to separate out the contents of an envelope, which formed a solid lump stuck together with fatty body wax, all of which was contaminated with soil. This lump, containing such items as correspondence, photographs, drawings, identity cards, inoculation certificates, documents on military decorations, scraps of Soviet newspapers, banknotes, billfolds, medallions, handmade cigarette holders and cigarette cases, combs and brushes, and, most important, diaries, had to be placed in a special chemical bath, de-fatted and cleaned. Only then could the documents be read.

This was slow work, so before the evacuation of these materials from Kraków in August 1944 ahead of the advancing Red Army, Dr. Robel and his staff managed to examine and describe the contents of only 285 envelopes. A detailed protocol was written on each, giving its number, the family name of the murdered officer, and all the items it contained, including texts that had been read. All the protocols were signed by Robel and his staff, who typed several carbon copies of each. These protocols, describing the materials acquired from the 285 envelopes, represented only a part of the recovered items, but they al-

224 *Katyn and Its Echoes*

lowed the later identification of 2,333 Katyn victims out of the total number of 4,143 exhumed. (About 1,000 were identified on site.) Furthermore, Dr. Robel and his staff secretly typed several carbon copies of the twenty-two legible diaries found on the bodies, fifteen of which were delivered by special courier that summer to the Polish government in London.[49]

In July 1944, Beck told Robel that the Katyn documents had to be moved to the main building of the Institute of Forensic Medicine in Kraków because the German police expected an attempt by the AK to seize them. There was indeed such a plan, but it failed because the documents were moved and strict German security measures were in place. As the Red Army continued its advance westward, the German authorities decided to destroy the Katyn relics and documents. According to Beck's testimony, given in Frankfurt am Main to members of the U.S. congressional committee on Katyn in June 1952, he received orders to destroy the documents so they would not fall into Russian hands, but decided to disobey them. He said he agreed with the pleas of Adam Ronikier, head of the RGO, and Dr. Pronaskou [Professor Zbigniew Pronaszko], director of the Akademia Sztuk Pięknych [Academy of Fine Arts] in Kraków, to do all he could to prevent the destruction of the material evidence of the crime. So he arranged for the evacuation of the items, now repacked in fourteen chests, to Breslau [Wrocław], where they were taken in August 1944 and stored in the Anatomical Institute of the university there. Beck said that work on the documents continued under the supervision of the German forensic medicine expert, Professor Gerhard Buhtz of Breslau University, who had supervised the exhumations at Katyn, and that Robel himself visited several times from Kraków. As the Russians drew near, Beck decided to evacuate the chests to Dresden, but upon arrival there, he could not procure a storage place from the police. Instead, they gave him a truck, which he used to transport them to the railway station at Radebeul, a suburb of Dresden, where they were placed in a storage building. Beck said he had wanted to deliver the chests to the IRC, which had a branch in Prague. In the first days of May 1945 he had traveled to Prague but could not find the IRC because of the war, so he went to Pilsen [Czech, Plzeň], then occupied by U.S. troops, and obtained permission to travel to Dresden. The Russians were already there, however, so he went to the U.S. occupation zone in Bavaria. In his deposition, Beck claimed that the chests were burned at Radebeul

Station on his orders, that this was done by the railway shipping agent there, and that he received confirmation of this fact. He also stated that the Russian secret police knew about the storage place for the chests in Radebeul, as well as the evacuation route. They searched his parents' house in Dresden and the houses of friends where he had stayed. His mother was jailed for six months when the police tried to get his address from her, and the railway shipping agent who burned the chests was deported to the USSR. The Katyn author Janusz Zawodny, however, writes that former Polish Premier Stanisław Mikołajczyk told him in 1957 that one of the chests left by Beck at Radebeul Station survived, and he was certain that it was in American hands. Mikołajczyk also told Zawodny that a small chest containing the original diaries had disappeared in Kraków.[50]

No chest of Katyn documents has surfaced thus far in the United States, but a well-preserved, sealed packet with typed copies of the diaries was found in March 1991 by construction workers renovating the Institute of Forensic Medicine, on Westerplatte Street (postwar name), Kraków, where it had been moved in summer 1944. The packet was hidden in the attic so as not to fall into the hands of the Soviets or the new communist government of Poland. It had been carefully packed and placed there by Stanisław Grygiel, a worker at the institute, who did not disclose the hiding place to anyone.[51] Some of the Katyn documents—perhaps salvaged from the fire at the PRC office in Warsaw during the Warsaw Uprising of 1944—also turned up in Kraków in 1991; they had been hidden by Robel's high school friend Professor Franciszek Bielak.[52] Finally, some of the Katyn items, still in the original envelopes, were hidden by a staff member of the Kraków City Archives, Dr. Henryk Münch, a former AK soldier, who also hid in these archives documents of the underground organization Wolność i Niepodległość [WIN—Freedom and Independence], to which he belonged. He was arrested by Polish Security Police, who pressured the archive director, Professor Marian Friedberg, to find and deliver all other documents of interest to them. Friedberg knew of the hidden Katyn items and spent many hours combing the archives until he found them by their smell. They were hidden behind a large cupboard and packed in waxed paper. Friedberg took them home, where his wife repacked them, preserving the original envelope numbers, after which he entrusted them to the care of the Metropolitan Curia in Kraków—more specifically, to Archbishop Adam Stefan Sapieha. The Polish Security Police seized the packet in November 1953 and took it to Warsaw, where it was stored first in the Ministry of Public Security and then in the Ministry of Internal Affairs. It stayed there for almost half a century and was neither destroyed nor reported to Moscow. Polish authorities—probably General Czesław Kiszczak, then minister of internal affairs—returned it to the Metropolitan Curia in Kraków on 3 April 1990, ten days before the government of President Mikhail Gorbachev admitted Soviet guilt for Katyn. The contents of the envelopes, along with papers and other memorabilia of thirty-one Katyn victims, were exhibited in Kraków in spring 2000.[53]

The Burdenko Commission and Its Report of 24 January 1944

The Red Army liberated the Smolensk region from the Germans on 25 September 1943. Three weeks earlier, the chief surgeon of the Red Army, the brain specialist and academician Nikolai Burdenko, a member of the Special State Commission for Investigating the Crimes of the German Fascist Aggressors, had written a letter to Molotov. He said that his comparison of the German method of shooting 200 Soviet citizens at Orel, approximately 370 kilometers southeast of Smolensk—whose bodies were found among the 1,000 corpses buried there—with the method used at Katyn, a shot at the base of the skull, had convinced him the Germans had murdered the Polish officers, and offered his expert services. On 22 September the chief of the Propaganda Department of the Central Committee, Georgy Aleksandrov, wrote to Aleksandr Shcherbakov, head of the Main Political Administration of the Red Army, proposing the establishment of a special commission, made up of members of the Special State Commission and intelligence services, and sending them to the Katyn site. This was the basis for the later special Soviet commission for investigating the Katyn massacre, designed to counter the German "provocation" (that is, charging the Soviets with the Katyn crime) by carrying out an investigation of its own at Katyn. In a letter to Molotov of 27 September, Burdenko wrote that on the previous day he had received from Professor I. P. Trainin the commissar's instruction regarding an investigation in Smolensk Oblast, especially of the Katyn tragedy. In view of the need to exhume the corpses and examine the wounds, Burdenko proposed adding Efim Yuzefovich Smirnov, deputy head of the 1st Special Department of the

NKVD and a member of the Smolensk Oblast Committee, and his competent subordinates. This would allow the compilation of relevant documents to supplement Burdenko's own collection, and Burdenko hoped that everything would be organized by 29 September. Molotov noted that he did not speak with Trainin.[54]

It is now known that a large group of NKVD operational workers arrived in Katyn shortly after the Red Army liberated the area, and a report was prepared on the results of the preliminary investigation of the "so-called Katyn Question." This report, dated 10–11 January 1944, was signed by 1st Deputy Commissar for Internal Affairs Vsevolod Merkulov—who had supervised the extermination of the Polish officers and police in spring 1940—and Deputy Commissar for Internal Affairs Sergei Kruglov, who was also the supervisor of NKVD cadre affairs, including the staff of the UPV and the POW camps. They concluded, of course, that the Germans had committed the crime. The details of this NKVD preparatory work became known in 1990, when the investigators of the Russian Federation Main Military Prosecutor's Office learned that the operational workers sent from Moscow had prepared forged documents with dates later than May 1940 and placed them in the clothes of selected victims. The operational workers had also detained many persons who had worked for the Germans in Smolensk and in the villages near Katyn, and prepared selected "witnesses." According to a Soviet decree of 19 April 1943, these people were liable to the death penalty for the crime of "cooperating with the enemy," so when interrogated by NKVD officers, they agreed to say whatever they were told. Between 5 October 1943 and 10 January 1944, NKVD investigators interrogated ninety-five persons and "verified" (that is, formulated) seventeen statements later made before the special state commission.[55]

The Special State Commission for Ascertaining and Investigating the Circumstances of the Shooting of the Polish Prisoners of War by the German Fascist Invaders in the Katyn Forest was officially established on 13 January 1944. It was chaired by Burdenko, so it is commonly referred to as the Burdenko Commission. Its members included such nationally known figures as the writer Alexei Tolstoy, also a member of the Special State Commission for Ascertaining and Investigating the Crimes Committed by the German Fascist Invaders and Their Associates, and Nikolai, Metropolitan of Kiev and Galicia. The commission was enlarged the next day by adding Vladimir Makarov, head of the special commission that Tolstoy was a member of, as its secretary and five experts in forensic medicine, who later signed the report. It is clear that by 13 January—the first session—at least Burdenko had read the Merkulov-Kruglov report, for he cited it, while others asked Kruglov questions. It is also clear that the commission had to support the Merkulov-Kruglov conclusions. It is not known how many of its members knew or suspected the truth at the time, but Burdenko may have done so. Shortly before his death in 1946, he reportedly admitted to a family friend—Boris Olshansky—that as a doctor, he knew the graves were four years old, which would have dated them to 1940. He also said he believed the NKVD comrades had made a "great blunder." Burdenko's daughter-in-law allegedly confirmed this statement to Yuri Zoria, son of the Soviet deputy prosecutor at the Nuremberg Trials, who died a mysterious death at Nuremberg in May 1946.[56]

The Burdenko Commission report on the Katyn graves focused on rejecting the conclusions and evidence cited in the 1943 report of the IMC. The IMC consisted of experts in forensic medicine from countries allied with or occupied by German forces and one neutral country (Switzerland) who visited Katyn under German auspices on 28–30 April 1943. Their report appeared in the chief Nazi paper, the *Völkischer Beobachter* [People's Observer] in Berlin, on 4 May 1943, and in a German documentary collection published shortly thereafter. The IMC members cited local Russians who told of the shooting in Katyn Forest and concluded on the basis of examining a few exhumed corpses that the victims had been shot in spring 1940, thus placing the blame squarely on the Russians.[57] The Burdenko Commission report argued against the medical evidence and conclusions of the IMC; it claimed that the Polish prisoners of war had fallen into German hands and were executed by the Germans at Katyn between July and September 1941. The report named three German officers of the 537th Construction Battalion who allegedly carried out the massacre: Lieutenants Ahrens, Rekst, and Hodt (the names were misspelled). The German authorities were also accused of manipulating the evidence and intimidating Russian witnesses at Katyn in spring 1943 (the NKVD did both in 1943–1944) and of murdering the Russian prisoners of war who had worked on digging in the grave pits and extracting the corpses, but evidence for such murder is lacking. The English version of the Burdenko Commission report was published in the *Voks Bulletin,* no. 1 (Moscow, 1944), and in a special supplement to the *Soviet War Weekly* (London) 3 February 1944.[58] An extract of the report was presented as evidence in 1946 by the Soviet prosecution at the Nuremberg Trials of Nazi war criminals (doc. 106). Henceforth, the Katyn report of the Burdenko Commission was always presented and cited in Soviet media, encyclopedias, history books, and notes to foreign governments until the official admission of Soviet guilt on 13 April 1990.

The Katyn Question at the Nuremberg Trials, 1946

In late summer 1945 the victorious Allies agreed to set up the International Military Tribunal to try enemy war criminals, worked out a legal basis, and decided the tribunal should sit in the relatively undamaged German city of Nuremberg, then in the American zone of occupation. According to Article 6 of the IMT Charter, the tribunal was "established for the trial and punishment of the major war criminals of the Axis countries." It was to "have the power to try and punish persons who, acting in the interests of the European Axis countries, whether as individuals or as members of organizations," committed crimes against peace. These crimes were listed as the planning, preparation, initiation, or waging of a war of aggression. The tribunal was also empowered to try "violations of the laws or customs of war." These included the murder, ill-treatment, or deportation to slave labor of civilians; the murder or ill-treatment of prisoners of war or seamen; the killing of hostages; and plunder, as well as wanton destruction and devastation, unjustified by military necessity. The leaders and organizers of such acts were held responsible for them. Finally, the IMT was empowered to try "crimes against humanity." These were listed as assassination, extermination, enslavement, deportation, ill-treatment of prisoners of war, and any other inhuman action committed against civilians before or after the war, as well as persecution on political, racial, or religious grounds.[59]

The Soviet government named Roman Rudenko, public prosecutor for the Ukrainian Soviet Republic, as chief Soviet prosecutor for the USSR.[60] A special state commission was established in Moscow in September 1945 to prepare materials for the Soviet prosecutor at

Nuremberg. The importance attached to this issue by the Soviet leadership is shown by the fact that it was supervised by Molotov, and its materials were sent for approval to Stalin, Molotov, and Beria; Deputy Chairmen of the Soviet Council of Ministers Georgy Malenkov and Anastas Mikoyan; Politburo member Andrei Zhdanov; and Deputy Commissar for Foreign Affairs Vladimir Dekanozov.[61]

At the outset of the trials, a decision favored Moscow. The tribunal accepted the American-British proposal not to allow attacks by the defense on the Allied powers. Each delegation was to prepare a list of matters not to be discussed at the trial. The Soviet "blacklist," prepared in late November 1945, included the German-Soviet Non-Aggression Pact of 23 August 1939 (docs. 1, 2), the Baltic States, the German-Soviet population exchange agreements, the Balkans, Soviet-Polish relations, and Soviet foreign policy. However, this list was not presented to the Allied Prosecutors' Committee until after the chief American prosecutor, Supreme Court Justice Robert H. Jackson, noted on 8 March 1946 that the French and Soviet lists had not been received, and intimated that the defense could attack the policies of France and the USSR.

The Soviet charges against the German Nazi leaders included the murder of the Polish officers at Katyn. This charge was added against the advice of Jackson and British Attorney General Sir Hartley Shaw-cross. In the English text of the indictment, dated 6 October 1945, the number of victims was specified as 925—the number of exhumed bodies reported by the Burdenko Commission—but in the Russian text dated three days later, it was 11,000. The Soviet side interpreted Article 21 of the IMT Charter to mean that the report of the Burdenko Commission—an extract of which was submitted on 14 February 1946 as USSR Document-054 (doc. 106)—would suffice as proof. Article 21 of the charter read: "The Tribunal shall not require proof of facts of common knowledge but shall take judicial notice thereof. It shall also take judicial notice of official governmental documents and reports of the United Nations, including the acts and documents of the committees set up by the various countries for the investigation of war crimes, and the records and findings of military and other tribunals of any of the United Nations."[62]

Since Hermann Goering, the former commander of the German Air Force, was accused of all the war crimes, his defender, Dr. Otto Stahmer, saw an opportunity to relieve him of responsibility for at least one—the Katyn massacre. On 3 March 1946, he asked to call as witnesses for the defense the German officers listed in the Soviet accusation. Indeed, at the tribunal session of 14 February, Soviet deputy prosecutor General Yuri Pokrovsky had read an extract from the report of the Burdenko Commission, according to which the Katyn massacre had been committed by the 537th Sappers (should be: Signals) Regiment of the Wehrmacht; it named the commanding officers, Ahrens, Rekst, and Hodt, as the murderers (doc. 106).

On 11 March, the Soviet delegation presented its blacklist of topics not to be raised in the trials; it was almost the same as the one drawn up but not presented the previous November. That day, Rudenko insisted on the Soviet interpretation of Article 21 of the charter and opposed calling the German witnesses requested by Stahmer. The tribunal members met in closed session on 12 March to consider Rudenko's claim that USSR Document-054 should be accepted as sufficient proof of the Soviet charge that the Germans had murdered the Polish officers at Katyn, without calling witnesses. During an internal debate among the U.S. IMT members, some strong protests were made against the Soviet stand, especially by former U.S. Attorney General Francis Biddle. He called Rudenko's petition "slanderous," said that its author should be cited for contempt, and even suggested sending him to prison immediately. Finally, the tribunal cut a deal with its Soviet member, Judge Yona Nikitchenko: to deny Rudenko's petition with no reason given. Nikitchenko dissented but did not raise Article 21 again.[63] Such was the background of the instructions sent to Rudenko on 15 March to insist on the Soviet interpretation of this article. If this failed, he was to request the attachment of the whole Burdenko report to the Soviet accusation and demand the right to present Soviet witnesses (doc. 107).

When the tribunal agreed to the admission of witnesses by both sides of the Katyn massacre case, the Special State Nuremberg Commission in Moscow issued instructions, on 21 March, to select and prepare witnesses for the Soviet side. Two months later the commission nominated three witnesses. Later still, in June, it selected eight witnesses, but the tribunal decided to limit the witnesses to three for each side.[64] Thus it was that on 1–2 July 1946 three witnesses were heard for the defense: Colonel (formerly Lieutenant) Friedrich Ahrens, the commanding officer of the Army Group Center 537th Signals Regiment; Lieutenant Reinhard von Eichborn, who had been attached to the regiment in August 1939 but had been transferred to the AGC Communications Department in August 1940 and arrived with it in Smolensk in late September 1941; and Major General Eugen Oberhäuser, head of AGC communications. Likewise, three witnesses were heard for the prosecution: the former deputy mayor of Smolensk, Boris Bazilevsky, a professor of astronomy; the Bulgarian forensic medicine expert Professor Anton Marko Markov, who had testified in support of Soviet guilt in 1943 but now testified in support of German guilt; and Victor Prozorovsky, a Soviet professor of forensic medicine and a member of the Burdenko Commission. Stahmer's examination of the German witnesses cleared them of responsibility for the Katyn massacre, and the Katyn case was not listed in the IMT final verdicts.[65] Still, Hermann Goering and other top Nazi leaders were pronounced guilty of all the crimes with which they were charged under Article 6 (war crimes and crimes against humanity), and until mid-April 1990, all Soviet governments and official publications claimed that the Soviet Union had won its case on Katyn at Nuremberg.

The London Poles made several attempts to present their information to the IMT but failed. The PRC Technical Commission report was given to the British government in London in March 1946, when it was also delivered by former PRC Secretary General Skarżyński to the British diplomat Robert Hankey at the British Embassy in Warsaw. The British government did not take any steps in this matter, even though Sir Owen O'Malley, ambassador to the Polish government-in-exile, had made a convincing case of Soviet guilt three years earlier in his letter of 24 May 1943 to Foreign Secretary Sir Anthony Eden and wrote a devastating critique of the Burdenko Commission report in February 1944.[66] Undersecretary of State Sir Alexander Cadogan wondered in May 1943 whether, if Russian guilt were established, Britain could expect the Poles to live amicably side by side with the Russians. He was also disturbed by the thought "that we may eventually, by agreement and in collaboration with the Russians, proceed to the trial and perhaps execution of Axis 'war criminals' while condoning this atrocity. I confess I shall find that extremely difficult to swallow."[67] Both he and other British officials were to swallow it when the time came.

Three years later, in April 1946, the British government had at its disposal not only the PRC report of June 1943 but also a dossier compiled for the Polish government-in-exile in London titled *Facts and*

Documents Concerning Polish Prisoners of War Captured by the U.S.S.R. in the 1939 Campaign.[68] On 17 May, Goering's defending counsel, Dr. Stahmer, wrote General Władysław Anders asking for Polish documents on Katyn, but Anders decided he could not cooperate in defending Goering. On 9 July 1946, his aide sent a copy of Stahmer's letter together with Anders's offer to provide a considerable number of documents on Katyn to the IMT—but only at its express written and official request—to Colonel J. L. Tappin, U.S. Army Liaison Section, American Forces Headquarters. There was no reply.[69]

Two questions involving Poland surfaced at Nuremberg. One was the case of the Secret Protocol attached to the German-Soviet Pact of 23 August 1939, which claimed the life of the Soviet lawyer Nikolai Zoria. The other was the Katyn case, which may have been connected in some way with the death of a Polish lawyer, Roman Martini. In the summer and fall of 1944, N. Zoria, a military lawyer with the rank of general, served as legal counselor to Nikolai Bulganin, Soviet deputy minister of defense and special envoy to the communist-dominated Polish Committee of National Liberation in Lublin. Zoria asked to be relieved of his duties there in January 1945 and was appointed assistant to Soviet Prosecutor General Konstantin Gorshenin in May that year. In this capacity, he received a delegation of Polish lawyers led by the Polish minister of justice. After this visit the Polish deputy prosecutor for the Kraków region, Dr. Roman Martini of Kraków, was given the task of interrogating witnesses, writers, and literary critics about the Katyn massacre. In July 1945, he interrogated Skarżyński about his visit to Katyn. He also interrogated Dr. Robel and his co-workers about their work on the Katyn envelopes. All members of Polish delegations to Katyn were accused of collaboration with the Germans. Skarżyński and Goetel managed to escape, but others, including Dr. Edmund Seyfried, director of the RGO, received prison sentences.[70] Martini was murdered in his Kraków apartment on 12 March 1946. As rumor had it, this was because he was convinced of Soviet guilt by an NKVD document he found in the Gestapo archives in Minsk, Belarus, and wrote a report blaming the USSR, naming several NKVD offices involved. Some, however, pinned the murder on the NKVD, while others saw it as revenge for Martini's seduction of a young girl.[71] According to the Katyn author Zawodny, the murderers were reported to be "two hot-headed, youthful communists—a girl of seventeen, Jolanta Słapianka, and a man of twenty, Stanisław Wróblewski," but he doubted this was true. According to another source, Słapianka and her alleged fiancé, Wróblewski, committed the murder, after which they were both tried and sentenced. In fact, Wróblewski escaped from jail and joined a partisan unit fighting against the communist regime. He was caught, charged with actions aiming to overthrow the "democratic" system of the Polish state, and executed in 1947.[72] Thus, Wróblewski's political profile points to yet another possibility—that Martini was murdered on the orders of a Polish underground organization as a "collaborator" with the communist regime.

Whatever the truth about Martini's death, his alleged report was certainly a fake. It appeared in an article published in the Swedish paper *Dagens Nyheter* [Daily News] on 13 February 1948. The anonymous author claimed that Martini dug up some of the Katyn graves himself, although it is clear that he could not have done so without Soviet permission, and it is most unlikely that permission would have been given. Worse still, in citing Martini's alleged report, the author gave the names of Jewish NKVD officers allegedly involved in the massacre—names cited in a German propaganda leaflet of 1943, hence obviously false.[73] In conclusion, it is known that Martini interrogated many people on what they knew about Katyn, but while his death still needs clarification, it is clear that he did not write a report on the Katyn massacre pointing to Soviet guilt.

The case of Nikolai Zoria's death is more clear-cut. At the end of December 1945, he flew to Nuremberg to serve as the assistant to Rudenko at the IMT. Zoria had orders to prevent former German Foreign Minister Joachim von Ribbentrop from speaking about the Secret Protocol to the German-Soviet Non-Aggression Pact of 23 August 1939. Although the tribunal refused to allow the reading of the text by Rudolf Hess's defender, Alfred Seidl, because he would not divulge his source, former German Deputy Foreign Minister Ernst von Weizsäcker revealed the contents when cross-examined by Seidl on 21 May 1946. The text appeared the next day in the *St. Louis Post-Dispatch*— and Zoria was found dead in his room at Nuremberg.[74] That afternoon, his son Yuri was called to the Prosecutor General's Office in Moscow and told that his father had shot himself. A year later, when young Zoria entered the Soviet Naval School, he was given an official statement that his father had died by accident due to the "careless handling of arms."[75] Zoria Junior's quest to find the truth about his father's death led him to work together with Natalia Lebedeva on a new

Russian edition of the documents of the Nuremberg Trials and then to research on the Katyn massacre.

The Congressional (Madden) Committee Investigation of the Katyn Forest Massacre, 1951–1952

Like the British government, the Roosevelt administration also suppressed media coverage of Katyn in 1943–1945 in the interest of Allied unity, so the issue was unfamiliar to the American public. Interest in Katyn revived among Polish-Americans with a series of articles and Polish documents that appeared in the leading Polish-American newspaper of the time, *Nowy Świat* [New World], in March 1948. But they were written in Polish, so they had no impact on public opinion generally.[76] These articles, combined with the Cold War climate (the Soviet Berlin Blockade and Western airlift from spring 1948 through June 1949), led the Polish-American Congress (PAC, founded in May 1944) to push for an investigation of the Katyn massacre. On 13 April 1949, PAC President Charles Rozmarek sent a telegram to the U.S. ambassador to the United Nations, the Republican lawyer and politician Warren Austin, requesting him to raise the Katyn issue and "demand an immediate and impartial investigation of one of the world's most heinous crimes." This venture failed.[77]

The topic was next taken up by the journalist Julius Epstein, who published a series of articles in the *New York Herald Tribune* in July 1949. Epstein had worked in the Office of War Information during the war and became interested in Katyn at that time, but did not write about it owing to the government's policy of suppressing media discussion of the topic. Now he called for the establishment of an American Committee of Investigation of the Katyn Murders,[78] and at the request of Congressman George A. Dondero (D-Mich.), the first Epstein article was reprinted in the *Congressional Record*.[79] Soon thereafter, Congressman Ray J. Madden (D-Ind.) addressed a PAC group meeting on 18 September 1949 at Gary, Indiana, that unanimously passed a resolution calling for an investigation of the Katyn massacre. The resolution demanded that the Soviet government accept an investigation by the International Red Cross, whose findings would be submitted to an international tribunal. On 29 September, Madden submitted the PAC resolution for consideration by the House of Representatives but found that most of his fellow congressmen had not heard of the Katyn massacre. Meanwhile, when Epstein approached the State Department with a proposal to write a program on Katyn for the Voice of America (VOA), he was told that the department was not interested. When Epstein pressed for an explanation, the head of the VOA Polish Desk told him that Katyn "would create too much hatred against Stalin among the Poles and that the [desk chief] hadn't gotten the green light from Washington to use anything . . . about Katyn."[80]

Epstein then had the idea of establishing a private committee of distinguished Americans and turned to Arthur Bliss Lane, a former U.S. ambassador to Poland who had resigned over the rigged elections "won" by the Polish communists in January 1947. Lane welcomed the idea and, together with Epstein, established the American Committee for the Investigation of the Katyn Massacre. Lane became its president, with Epstein as executive secretary; the committee members included the former director of the Office of Strategic Services (OSS), William Donovan, and his former agent in Switzerland, Allan Dulles; the well-known journalists Claire Boothe Luce and Dorothy Thompson; and PAC President Charles Rozmarek. The committee, announced at the Waldorf Astoria Hotel, New York, on 21 November 1949, was cold-shouldered by the administration. The State Department sent a representative but refused to broadcast the proceedings. The Internal Revenue Service was also uncooperative, refusing to grant the committee tax-exempt status on the grounds that "it had no educational value."[81]

The Lane Committee paved the way for more action on Katyn. The time was propitious. The communist victory over Chiang Kai-shek in China in October 1949 spurred suspicions that like Poland at Yalta, China had been "sold down the river" with the aid of communists within the U.S. government. Indeed, Senator Joseph McCarthy (R-Wis.) made this charge repeatedly in his Senate hearings. After the Korean War broke out in June 1950, U.S. war crimes investigators soon documented cases of American prisoners killed by a shot at the base of the skull. This was too reminiscent of the Katyn executions to escape the notice of American supporters of a Katyn investigation.[82] Congressman Timothy P. Sheehan (R-Ill.), who had promised to work for a Katyn investigation in order to win the Polish-American vote in his district, introduced House Resolution 282 on 26 June 1951. It called for the establishment of a select committee of thirteen representatives of the House, appointed by the Speaker, to conduct a full investigation of the Katyn massacre. His resolution became stuck for a while in the Rules Committee, but moved forward thanks to thousands of letters sent by Polish-Americans. On 18 September 1951, Congressman Madden, supported by the House majority leader, John McCormack, reintroduced the Sheehan resolution as House Resolution 390; it called for a Katyn investigation to be carried out by a committee of seven House members. This time, the resolution passed unanimously. House Speaker Sam Rayburn appointed a bipartisan committee with members from districts with significant Polish-American populations.[83]

The Madden Committee was unique in the annals of Congress but fit well into the contemporary American political scene. The Republicans launched strong attacks on the Democrats for "selling out" Eastern Europe, as well as China, to the communists. This atmosphere allowed Senator McCarthy to call for the repudiation of the Yalta agreements of February 1945 and to press his witch hunt for communists within the U.S. government. Rozmarek supported McCarthy's call because of his great personal resentment of President Franklin Delano Roosevelt. The president had secured Rozmarek's support, and thus the votes of most Polish Americans in the elections of November 1944, with a promise he did not keep. He had promised to work for an independent Poland or justice for Poland—one or the other.[84] However, Roosevelt and Churchill went on to sign the Yalta agreements, which, as it turned out, placed Poland and most of Eastern Europe under Soviet domination.[85]

The Madden Committee hearings, designed to gather evidence for a trial before an international tribunal, began on 4 February 1952. Letters of invitation had been sent on 18 September 1951 to the governments of the USSR, Poland, the Federal Republic of Germany (FRG), and the exiled Polish government in London. The FRG and the London Poles accepted with alacrity, but this was not the case with Moscow and Warsaw. On 25 February 1952 the State Department sent the resolution, together with a letter by Madden, to the Soviet Embassy in Washington, D.C. Madden requested the Soviet government to provide information about the Katyn massacre. The Soviet Embassy replied on 29 February in a note to the State Department. It returned Madden's letter and the resolution, describing it as contrary to the norms of international behavior and insulting to the Soviet Union. The note also stated that the Katyn question had been investigated by a special (Soviet) government commission—that is, the Burdenko Commission—which concluded that the massacre was the work of Nazi criminals. It went on to say that this report had been published in the press on 26 January 1944, and the U.S. government had not expressed any reservations during the eight years since that time, so the aim of raising this question now could only be to slander the USSR and rehabilitate the Nazi criminals.[86] The embassy also enclosed the text of the special commission's conclusions of 26 January 1944 (doc. 106). The Soviet response was broader, too. A press campaign was unleashed in the USSR and the communist states of Eastern Europe; the findings of the Burdenko Commission were published again, and the Madden Committee was attacked for allegedly repeating Nazi lies. While the committee held its hearings, Soviet propaganda—surely not coincidentally—accused the United States of committing war crimes in Korea, especially massacring Chinese and North Korean prisoners of war.[87]

The Madden Committee interviewed many witnesses in both the United States and Europe. Its interim report, submitted to Congress on 2 July 1952, stated that the evidence conclusively proved the massacre of Polish officers at Katyn had been carried out by the NKVD, and not later than spring 1940. The committee members also stated their belief that the massacre "was a calculated plot to eliminate all Polish leaders who subsequently would have opposed the Soviet's plans for communizing Poland."[88] The committee then proceeded to investigate why the Katyn massacre was never adequately revealed to the American people and the rest of the world and why it was not adjudicated at the Nuremberg Trials. Prominent U.S. officials subpoenaed to appear before the committee included W. Averell Harriman, the former U.S. ambassador in Moscow; Justice Robert Jackson, chief American prosecutor at the Nuremberg Trials; Admiral William H. Standley, Harriman's predecessor in Moscow; and former Undersecretary of State Sumner Welles. All denied knowledge of any attempt by the State Department to suppress information incriminating the USSR. However, they also stressed the need for Soviet military cooperation in the war against Germany and the goal of Soviet entry into the United Nations as key factors in U.S. wartime policy on the Katyn issue. Still, when, the committee presented its conclusions on 22 December 1952 (doc. 109), it emphasized the deliberate withholding of information by the U.S. government, pointing in particular to the case of Colonel John H. Van Vliet, who had been brought to Katyn by the Germans as part of a group of Allied prisoners of war. His report to General Clayton Bissell, then head of Army Intelligence, disappeared, and no one could shed any light on the matter. Two other Americans whose reports on Katyn were suppressed were Colonel Henry Szymanski, U.S. liaison officer with the Polish Army 2nd Corps (led by General Anders), and George Earle, Roosevelt's special emissary in the Balkans and Turkey. It should also be noted that in 1943–1945 the U.S. government censored media reports on Katyn.[89]

The Madden Committee failed to achieve its main goal, a trial of the Katyn case by the United Nations or some other international tribunal. The new Republican administration delivered the committee's final report to the United Nations on 10 February 1953, and the U.S. ambassador to the United Nations, Henry Cabot Lodge, Jr., sent two sets of the published hearings to U.N. Secretary General Trygve Lie. The U.S. government, however, had more important concerns. Peace negotiations with North Korea were stalled at Panmunjon (Panmunjeom) and President Dwight D. Eisenhower, who had campaigned on the promise of ending the war, needed Soviet cooperation to achieve this goal.[90] In any case, the Madden Committee was unpopular in Democratic circles not only because it seemed to align itself with McCarthy, but also because many prominent members of the Roosevelt and Truman administrations were charged with suppressing information on Katyn. The same circles also had a generally negative attitude toward the exiled Polish government in London, which was pushing for a trial of the Katyn case. For all these reasons, the hearings received wide publicity in Polish-American but not in mainstream American media. Their primary importance now is as a mine of information on Polish prisoners of war in the USSR and on the Katyn massacre. On 13 April 2003, the sixtieth anniversary of the German announcement on the Katyn graves, the documents collected by the Madden Committee were delivered to the Rada Ochrony Pamięci Walk i Męczeństwa [Council for the Protection of the Memory of Combat and Martyrdom] by Allen Paul, the author of a valuable work on the massacres of spring 1940.[91]

The Soviet Destruction of Evidence and the Monuments to Katyn, 1952–1976

Nikita Khrushchev did not list Katyn among the Stalinist crimes that he excoriated in his famous speech at the Twentieth Party Congress in February 1956. His son, Sergei Khrushchev, writes that he first heard

of Katyn sometime in 1956 but did not believe the story until Ivan
Serov, NKVD head in Ukraine from 1939 to 1941, confirmed it. As
Sergei recalls, when asked about Katyn, Serov "reacted angrily, I
would even say painfully, to the question. He started to make caustic
remarks about the Belorussian Chekists [that is, the NKVD], who, in his
opinion, had been unforgivably careless. [Serov said] 'They couldn't
cope with such a small matter'—in a fit of anger he let the cat out of
the bag. 'There was a lot more in the Ukraine when I was there. But not
a thing was said about it, nobody found even a trace.'"[92]

There were rumors in Poland that Khrushchev had proposed admitting Soviet guilt for Katyn to Polish communist leader Władysław Gomułka, who was elected First Secretary by the Central Committee of
the Polska Zjednoczona Partia Robotnicza [PZPR—United Polish
Workers' Party] in October 1956. Though undocumented, these rumors cannot be dismissed out of hand. Soviet Central Committee official Pyotr Kostikov told a Polish journalist and personal friend of hearing from "a highly reliable source"—after the most important facts
about the Katyn massacre became known—that the Soviet leader
made such a proposal to Gomułka during his official visit to Moscow
(no date, but most likely in late 1956). Khrushchev, who had been
drinking, allegedly suggested that he would state at a "peace meeting"
in a Moscow factory where both leaders were to speak, that Katyn was
an evil deed of Stalin's. He allegedly proposed that Gomułka support
this statement by saying that the Polish nation condemned Stalin's action and that common misfortune strengthened their friendship. Khrushchev said this would put an end to the whole terrible affair once and
for all. Gomułka, however, allegedly declined the offer, saying that
Khrushchev did not realize what the Polish reaction to this would be: a
chain reaction. He also asked if Khrushchev had any documents and
said there would be other questions—for example, were all the Polish
officers buried at Katyn, and if not, where? Therefore, the matter had
to be considered seriously and not just mentioned at a meeting.[93] In
fact, Gomułka ordered the Polish media to be silent on Katyn, a silence
maintained until 1989.

Meanwhile, important evidence of the crime was eliminated in Moscow, following a decision made in 1959 to destroy the personal files
of the Polish prisoners who had been murdered in spring 1940. In a
note for Khrushchev dated 9 March 1959, Aleksandr Shelepin, then
head of the KGB, gave the total number of Polish victims shot in spring

1940, including those shot in prisons, as 21,857 and stated, "All the 21,857 files have been kept in a sealed facility." He commented that these files were of no "operational value" and that it was doubtful whether they were of any interest to "our Polish friends"—a reference to the ruling Polish party, the PZPR. Because of his view of the files, as well as the conclusions of the Burdenko Commission, Shelepin pro-posed that all the files of those shot in 1940 be destroyed. Nevertheless, to answer any potential questions, he suggested preserving the protocols of the NKVD Troika that had sentenced the prisoners, along with the files concerning the implementation of the sentences (doc. 110).[94]

It is likely that not only the personal files were destroyed at this time but also those Shelepin had proposed keeping. According to the ac-count of an unnamed NKVD veteran, Khrushchev ordered both kinds of files to be destroyed.[95] Polish historians doubt this was done, be-cause there is no record of the destruction, whereas a vast number of documents have been found in the Russian archives relating to the Pol-ish prisoners of war held in the USSR in 1939–1940. Whatever the case may be, no personal files (with the exception of the file for the po-liceman Stefan [Szczepan] S. Olejnik; doc. 38) and no documents on the Troika decisions on the prisoners of war from the three special camps, or their implementation, are accessible to this day.

Whatever the fate of the NKVD files on these prisoners, the Soviet version of Katyn became enshrined not only in Soviet history books and encyclopedias but also in monuments. A monument to the Polish victims was erected at Katyn in the late 1940s, to be replaced by a new one in the early 1960s. The first one, probably erected in 1945, read: "Here are buried the prisoner officers of the Polish Army murdered in terrible torments by the German-Fascist occupiers in the fall of 1941." Another inscription, noted some thirty years later, read: "Here rest the remains of Polish officers, prisoners of war bestially martyred by the German-Fascist occupiers in the fall of 1941."[96] The Soviet govern-ment also erected a memorial to people murdered by the Germans in a Belorussian village near Minsk named Khatyn, which misled some for-eign tourists, politicians, and journalists. For instance, two American journalists writing about President Richard Nixon's state visit to the USSR in May 1972 stated, "He visited Katyn, where 149 Russians had been forced into a barn and burned alive by Nazi troops on 22 March 1943."[97]

Anglo-American media were silent on Katyn until the publication of Zawodny's book, *Death in the Forest,* in the United States in 1962. Neither this excellent study nor the publication of *The Crime of Katyn* (a translation of *Zbrodnia Katyńska*) in London in 1965 led to much discussion or action in the West. The situation changed, however, in January 1971 with the reprint of Zawodny's book in England. This led to reviews in the *Times* of London, which published correspondence on the topic in January–February, followed by correspondence in the *Daily Telegraph* in March–April. Next, the American journalist Louis FitzGibbon published a book titled *Katyn: A Crime without Parallel,* and then it was announced that a film would be shown on a British Broadcasting Corporation (BBC) television program. All this activity worried the Soviet government. On 15 April 1971, the Politburo approved the instructions for the Soviet ambassador in London. He was to point out that the IMT at Nuremberg had judged the chief German war criminals guilty of conducting a policy of extermination against the Polish nation—in particular, of shooting the Polish prisoners of war in Katyn Forest. He was to express the Soviet expectation that the British Foreign Office would prevent the spread of "slanderous materials" on Katyn, whose authors wished to worsen British-Soviet relations. The protest was to no avail, for the film, titled *The Issue to Be Avoided,* was shown on BBC TV Channel 2 on 19 April 1971.[98]

At this time, some British Conservatives used Katyn as a weapon in attacking the Labour government of the day as too friendly to the USSR. Others, however, seized the opportunity to seek justice for the murdered Poles. On 21 April, a Conservative member of Parliament, Airey Neave—an admirer of the Polish contribution to the defeat of Nazi Germany in World War II—proposed a resolution in the House of Commons that the British government request the United Nations to appoint a committee to examine the Katyn case. Although this resolution was signed by 224 members of Parliament, it did not impact the government's policy toward the USSR. On 17 July 1971 there was a debate in the House of Lords, initiated by another admirer of the Poles, Lord St. Oswald, whose wife was Polish. Lord Robin Hankey, who had received a copy of the PRC Technical Commission report of 1943 from Skarżyński in March 1946, stated, however, that the key issue still unresolved was the dating of the documents on the corpses, so "there is a residual, legitimate doubt."[99] Indeed, until the Soviet admission of guilt in April 1990, the attitude of successive British governments was that the "lack of conclusive evidence" prevented out-right condemnation of the USSR. That attitude notwithstanding, the dominant consideration was the desire for good relations with Moscow and Warsaw, and the same was true for the United States. In July 1971, when PAC Chairman Alojzy Mazewski requested the U.S. ambassador to the United Nations, George Herbert Walker Bush, to propose a U.N. investigation of Katyn, no action followed.

In January 1972, the opening of the British Foreign Office archives for 1943–1944 led to the establishment of the Katyn Memorial Fund (KMF), which was the first to publish Ambassador Owen O'Malley's letters to Foreign Secretary Anthony Eden on Katyn. The prospective site for the monument was the long-unused cemetery of St. Luke's (Anglican) Church, Chelsea, offered to the KMF by the town council of the Borough of Kensington-Chelsea, located near the center of London.[100] The proposal to build a monument provoked another Soviet protest in September that year, this time to the British ambassador in Moscow. Soviet Deputy Minister for Foreign Affairs Andrei Kozyrev made the protest to British Ambassador Sir John Killick, but the latter replied that "this was not a matter within the direct responsibility of HMG [Her Majesty's Government]." However, the head of the East European and Soviet Department in the Foreign and Commonwealth Office noted that the Katyn memorial project was sponsored, among others, by a number of bitterly anti-Soviet Poles who viewed building it as a political act. Believing that the Foreign and Commonwealth Office must, above all, attend to British relations with Poland and the USSR, he advised "that everything possible be done to ensure that any Katyn memorial that may be put up is (a) inconspicuously sited and (b) not provocative in any respect, particularly in its inscription."[101]

Nevertheless, in October 1972 it appeared that the Katyn memorial would be placed in the cemetery of St. Luke's Church, Chelsea. Furthermore, the intended inscription mentioned 1940 as the date of the Katyn massacre and read: "The conscience of the world cries out for a testimony of the truth." Deputy Undersecretary of State Sir Thomas Brimelow thought the date incriminated the Russians and would have adverse political consequences, but he did not object to the inscription if there were no date.[102] In Moscow, Foreign Minister Andrei Gromyko proposed countering the "anti-Soviet campaign" in Britain, and on 2 March 1973 instructions were sent to the Soviet ambassador in London to make an official protest to the British government about the

Katyn memorial project (doc. 111). Some local opposition was also re-ported in Chelsea, and since St. Luke's was an Anglican church, the Diocesan Consistory Court of the Church of England became in-volved. In summer 1974, the court heard the proponents and oppo-nents of locating the memorial in St. Luke's Cemetery. The lawyer for the Church of England proposed a compromise formula on the date—it was to be 1941, which may indicate British government intervention in favor of the Soviet stand. The KMF rejected the formula, so on 15 January 1975 the consistory court issued a negative verdict. The KMF appealed the verdict but lost.[103]

The Soviet government won this battle, but the KMF triumphed in the end. In late 1975 the Borough of Kensington-Chelsea council of-fered a new site for the memorial on land it owned in the Kensington Church Cemetery, Gunnersbury Avenue, Hounslow, Middlesex, on the outskirts of Greater London. In the face of this development, the Politburo decided on 5 April 1976 to abstain from official declarations but to work closely with its "Polish friends" (the PZPR leadership) re-garding the Katyn question and to use unofficial channels to persuade people in Western government circles that such actions and "forg-eries" (reference to the 1940 date of the massacre) were seen as pro-vocative by the Soviet government, and aimed to worsen international relations (doc. 112).

Despite Soviet pressure on the Kensington-Chelsea Borough Council to refuse permission for the memorial, and the unsympathetic attitude of the Labour government of the day, the Katyn obelisk was finally un-veiled on 18 September 1976 at a well-attended ceremony in the Ken-sington Church Cemetery.[104] Although the anniversary of the Soviet in-vasion of former eastern Poland was 17 September, the unveiling took place on the 18th because it was a Sunday and more people could at-tend. The War Office forbade attendance by British military personnel in uniform; still, a few retired British officers attended in full uniform with decorations. The British government declined to send an official representative, justifying this by the lack of "conclusive evidence" of Soviet guilt; its attitude was heavily criticized in the press. Nonethe-less, Margaret Thatcher, the leader of the Conservative Party, sent a representative, and a prominent participant in the ceremony was the ninety-four-year-old Lord Emmanuel Shinwell, a Labour peer. He hewed to the official line in saying that he was not sure who had com-mitted the crime, Germans or Russians. However, he also regretted that the government had not sent a representative, and asked, "What are they afraid of? The big bad wolf?"[105]

Public Pressure in Poland and the Crumbling of the Soviet Cover-Up, 1980–1990

After the unveiling of the Katyn monument in London, Katyn disappeared for many years from Western media headlines, but it was not forgotten in Poland. A symbolic Katyn grave in the military section of Old Powązki Cemetery, Warsaw, was always decorated with fresh flowers, and a cross was built there by activists of the Komitet Katyński [Katyn Committee] on 31 July 1981, that is, during the Solidarity period (30 August 1980–13 December 1981). The cross was taken down by the authorities, as was the cross put up there in December 1981, but the Katyn Committee persisted in organizing ceremonies and speeches on key anniversaries: the discovery of the Katyn massacre on 13 April 1943, the Soviet invasion of eastern Poland on 17 September 1939, and the prewar Independence Day, 11 November. Four leaders of the underground Konfederacja Polski Niepodległej [KPN—Confederation of Independent Poland], which organized the Katyn commemorations, were tried in October 1982 by a military court on charges of slandering the USSR and advocating an "anti-national policy." They were sentenced to prison for three to seven years, but the sentences were quashed after the collapse of communism in Poland in summer 1989.[106]

In 1988 the media liberalization that accompanied President Mikhail Gorbachev's *glasnost* [open discussion] policy and the ensuing public discussion of Stalinist crimes in the USSR also led to the relaxation of censorship in Poland, resulting in growing pressure for the truth on Katyn. This time, the pressure enjoyed official toleration, for Polish Premier General Wojciech Jaruzelski and his advisers believed that Soviet admission of the truth about Katyn, and the filling in of other "blank spots" in the history of Polish-Soviet relations, would lead to broader public acceptance of close relations with the USSR, while also making the government more popular at home. Indeed, Jaruzelski asserts that he had proposed the resolution of the Katyn problem to Gorbachev on the latter's first state visit to Poland in April 1985, but Gorbachev said that while he understood the need, he had just taken up his duties and needed time to study the matter. In spring 1987, during

Jaruzelski's visit to Moscow, and on his initiative, the two leaders agreed to set up the Joint Commission of Soviet-Polish Party Historians to study historical blank spots in mutual relations. It was duly established in May 1987.[107]

The Polish historians set themselves the goal of finding the truth about Katyn, the Molotov-Ribbentrop pact, and other painful issues in mutual relations by obtaining access to Soviet archives. These archives, however, remained closed, and the Soviet historians on the joint commission could not give up their support for the Burdenko Commission report (doc. 106) without the permission of the Politburo. Most of the Politburo members, however, opposed changing the party line, and Gorbachev had to take this into account. Anatoly Chernaev, Gorbachev's foreign policy adviser since 1986, wrote that in summer 1987, when Gorbachev received a series of letters "inspired by Poland" (presumably the Polish government) from England and the Scandinavian countries, "we [the group of advisers headed by Chernaev] wrote a memo summarizing the letters for Gorbachev. They blamed the USSR for the execution of the Polish officers, demanded that the guilty be punished, and asked that the Poles be given permission to visit the burial grounds." The advisers mentioned the Soviet special state (Burdenko) commission report and the failure of Soviet prosecutors at Nuremberg to get the tribunal to name the Katyn massacre in the final verdict. They wrote: "But now that joint research concerning historical 'blank spots' is under way, we will not be able to talk ourselves out of this issue. We should make everything clear, at least for ourselves. The Central Committee staff reports that some evidence even survived in the Smolensk archives. Obviously, then, there must be something in the KGB and Central Committee archives. Could we have Comrades Chebrikov, Lukianov, and Boldin work on this?" Gorbachev did not reply, so presumably there was no support for this proposal, or it was not even considered.[108]

The most the Politburo would do in May 1988 was decide that a memorial to the Polish officers should be built at Katyn as part of the next five-year plan, with the participation of the Polish side if it so wished, but that it should be built together with a memorial to Soviet prisoners of war allegedly murdered there by the Germans. The Politburo also agreed to simplify the procedure for visits to the site by relatives of the victims.[109] Indeed, on 25 May 1988, *Pravda* gave an account of—and two days later Radio Moscow's English-language program *World Service* reported on—a ceremony for unveiling the Katyn memorial in the village of Katyn near Smolensk. The memorial inscription read: "To the Polish officers shot by the fascists in 1941." The ceremony was attended by a delegation from the Polish province of Częstochowa, whose governor, General Grzegorz Lipowski, laid a wreath and stated that the officers had been murdered by the Germans.[110]

The Polish political situation changed dramatically in early 1989. There was increased pressure by Polish public opinion for the admission of the truth about Katyn, and the Polish leadership was negotiating on political and economic issues with the opposition, the Solidarity movement. Roundtable Talks began in early February between the party and government leaders on the one hand and the Solidarity leadership and its advisers on the other; these talks ended in a series of agreements signed in early April, including the setting of elections for 4 June 1989. Meanwhile, the Joint Commission of Soviet-Polish Party Historians was marking time. At the suggestion of a member of the Soviet group, Professor Oleg Rzheshevsky, who wanted to delay discussion of the Katyn question, the Polish historians analyzed the Burdenko report, and in May they unexpectedly delivered to their Soviet colleagues a devastating critique that deprived it of any credibility. The Soviet historians, however, had no mandate to reveal new documents to buttress the Burdenko Commission findings, which they were still bound to support.[111]

The political situation in Poland was the backdrop for the 22 March 1989 note to the Central Committee of the CPSU signed by Eduard Shevardnadze, then Soviet foreign minister; Valentin Falin, director of the International Department of the CC CPSU; and Vladimir Kriuchkov, chairman of the KGB (doc. 113). This is the first documented suggestion by high-level Soviet officials that the government admit the crime was committed by the NKVD. They had in mind the pressure of Polish public opinion for the truth about Katyn. Furthermore, they knew that reformers in the Polish Party and, in particular, General Jaruzelski, believed that Soviet admission of the truth was the only way to build sincere and trusting relations between the two countries. Accordingly, the Katyn report of the PRC Technical Commission (doc. 105b) was published in the Polish weekly *Odrodzenie* [Rebirth] on 16 February 1989 and was the main feature in the most outspoken weekly *Polityka* two days later. These publications were echoed in the Soviet

capital when Moscow radio cited the PRC report on 20 February and
stated that the evidence pointed to a massacre date in early 1940 and
to the NKVD. The next day, Jerzy Urban, the Polish government
spokesman, referred to the Polish press and the Moscow radio comments. He went further on 7 March, when he told a press conference
that Polish historians on the Joint Commission of Soviet-Polish Party
Historians believed that the NKVD was the perpetrator of the Katyn
massacre. The British Embassy in Warsaw noted: "Through Urban,
the Polish authorities have for the first time placed the blame for Katyn
directly on the Russians."[112]

In this situation, the Politburo decided on 31 March 1989 to instruct the Prosecutor General's Office, the Committee for State Security (KGB), the Ministry of Foreign Affairs (MID), and the Central
Committee Departments of State Law, International Affairs, and Ideological Affairs to come up with a proposal on the future Soviet line on
the Katyn question, and to do so within a month (doc. 114). Three
weeks later, a note signed by several officials stated that the extermination in 1939 (*sic*) of about 12,000 (*sic*) Polish officers gave grounds for
the conclusion that only some part of that number were killed at
Katyn. The fate of the rest was unknown, although Polish and Western
publications mentioned Bologoe in Kalinin Oblast and Dergachi in
Kharkov Oblast. The note suggested an investigation by the Prosecutor General's Office in cooperation with the KGB (doc. 115). The KGB
dragged its feet, but events in Poland put increasing pressure on the Soviet government to take action.

The elections of 4 June 1989 to the Sejm [lower house of the Polish
Parliament, pronounced Seym], in which the PZPR lost overwhelmingly to Solidarity candidates, marked the beginning of the collapse of
communism in that country, but this was not clear at the time. In a political compromise, the non-PZPR majority in the Sejm elected General Wojciech Jaruzelski as president in July—though with just one
vote more than the number required—and the first mostly noncommunist government was formed by Premier Tadeusz Mazowiecki, a
Solidarity leader, in early September 1989.

The Polish media now increased their pressure for the truth about
Katyn. The Polish Party historians' devastating critique of the Burdenko Commission report of 1944, handed to their Soviet colleagues
in May 1988, was summarized in the 19 August 1989 issue of *Polityka*. Here, Polish historians related the known history of the Katyn

crime, concluded that the Burdenko Commission findings were undoubtedly false, and claimed that the NKVD bore full responsibility
for the extermination of the Kozelsk prisoners at Katyn, as well as the
extermination of the prisoners of Starobelsk and Ostashkov, even
though their burial sites could not be established without access to
Russian documents.[113] On 30 September the secretary of state in the
Polish Foreign Ministry, Bolesław Kulski, stated in the Sejm that it was
necessary to uncover the full truth about Katyn. The Polish government had asked the Soviet government several times for the archival
documents, he said, and once the full truth was revealed, the Polish
government could seek compensation for victims' families and follow
the trail of those responsible for the crime. On 12 October the Polish
press reported that the Polish prosecutor general had requested his
Soviet opposite number to conduct an investigation. On 23 November, Premier Mazowiecki, then on a visit to Moscow, asked President
Gorbachev for an honest appraisal of past Soviet crimes, and Gorbachev was reported as saying that "he was more than ready to cooperate."[114]

In the meantime, the Soviet Foreign Ministry approved the request
of Dr. Zbigniew Brzezinski, former national security adviser to President Jimmy Carter, to visit Katyn when he visited the USSR in late October. The U.S. ambassador to the USSR, Jack F. Matlock, Jr., accompanied him when they visited the site on 1 November 1989, when
several busloads of Poles, relatives of the victims, arrived to honor the
deceased on the Catholic All Souls' Day. Matlock noted a modification
to the inscription on the Katyn monument, which stated that the Polish officers had been murdered by the Gestapo in 1941. Matlock
wrote, "Someone had covered 'Gestapo' and '1941' with hand-let-
tered signs reading 'NKVD' and '1940.' The Soviet custodians had not
removed the corrections from the monument." Brzezinski, who was
interviewed by a Russian television crew, called on the Soviet government to admit the crime, saying this could form the basis for Soviet-
Polish reconciliation. Matlock, asked for his opinion, echoed Brzezinski. These interviews, together with the opinions of some Polish
visitors and the changed inscription on the monument, were broadcast
on Soviet TV Channel 1 that evening.[115]

Opposition from the KGB head, Vladimir Kriuchkov, and the head
of the Main Administration of Soviet Archives, Fyodor Vaganov, hindered progress in the Katyn investigation, but another factor now

came into play. Gorbachev's policy of glasnost led to the opening of
some state archives to three Russian historians in 1989, and they
found hitherto unknown documents on the Polish prisoners of war.
On 23 February 1990, Valentin Falin wrote a note for Gorbachev stating that the historians Yuri Zoria, Valentina Parsadanova, and Natalia
Lebedeva had found archival materials on the Polish prisoners of war
held in the three special camps. The prisoners had disappeared in
April–May 1940, and a comparison of the lists of names of persons
sent out of the camps at that time with the lists compiled by the Germans in spring 1943 showed "numerous coincidences that appear to
prove the relationship between the two." Falin noted that these historians would publish their articles in June–July. Therefore, he suggested
that as the fiftieth anniversary of the Katyn massacre was drawing
near, and the new Polish president, General Jaruzelski, was to visit
Moscow at the time, the old denial could no longer be maintained.
Falin believed the least damage would result from informing Jaruzelski
that the investigation of archival materials allowed the conclusion that
the extermination of the Polish officers at Katyn "was the work of the
NKVD and personally of Beria and Merkulov" (doc. 116). Falin's proposal was rejected, and the Politburo decided in late February that the
three historians would not be allowed to publish their findings.

Indeed, the historians listed in Falin's note for Gorbachev of 22 February 1990 had a significant impact on the unraveling of the Katyn
cover-up. Lebedeva writes of first learning that the 136th NKVD Convoy Battalion escorted the Kozelsk prisoners to their deaths at Katyn
from a letter by Alexei Lukin, a former commander of the battalion,
which guarded Kozelsk camp in 1939–1940 and convoyed the prisoners to their death sites in spring 1940. The letter, forwarded from the
Ministry of Internal Affairs to *Literaturnaia Gazeta* [The Literary
Newspaper], was brought to her attention by the journalist Vladimir
Abarinov in late July 1988. Lukin denied that the battalion had had
any part in the executions. Lebedeva asked for and received permission from her superior in the Institute of General History, Soviet Academy of Sciences, Professor Oleg A. Rzheshevsky, to do research on the
battalion in the Central Archive of the Red Army. There she found the
battalion order book with departure dates from Kozelsk to Smolensk
and Gnezdovo in April–May 1940, dates that tallied with the execution dates of the Kozelsk prisoners. She also found documents from the
Main Administration of the NKVD Convoy Troops, and learned that

directives for them came from the UPV (Administration for Prisoner-of-War Affairs), whose documents were in the Central Special Archive. She asked Professor Vladimir Volkov, head of the Academy's Institute of Slavic and Balkan Studies, for authorization to work in that archive, but it was given instead to Valentina Parsadanova, a member of that institute who specialized in the history of Polish-Soviet relations. Lebedeva also told Yuri Zoria about the UPV collection in the Central Special Archive, and Zoria, too, obtained access to it.[116]

Zoria, who had become involved in research on Katyn because of his quest to learn the truth about his father's death at Nuremberg, struggled to gain access to the UPV documents. Here he received help from Aleksandr Nikolaevich Yakovlev, who was not only in charge of international relations in the Central Committee, but also chaired the Presidential Commission for the Rehabilitation of Victims of Political Repression and was then a close ally of Gorbachev. In summer 1989, Zoria also had Falin's support to photocopy Katyn documents for the Ministry of Foreign Affairs and the CC CPSU. He was given access to the Central Special Archive and wrote a detailed report with a short accompanying note, which he sent to Yakovlev. Yakovlev decided to send the photocopies to Valery Boldin, head of the Central Committee's General Department, not by courier as Boldin requested, but through Gorbachev's Kantselaria [Chancellery] in order to make them "bureaucratic property," protected with red stamps and numbers. Yakovlev phoned Gorbachev and told him about the documents. It was Yakovlev's impression that Gorbachev phoned Jaruzelski, then president of Poland, to inform him of this news, and Jaruzelski later confirmed this personally to Yakovlev. Parsadanova also found documents on Katyn in the Central Special Archive. Lebedeva obtained access there a little later and also worked in the Central Archive of the Red Army.[117]

The Truth Revealed, 1990–1992

Two key factors finally impelled the Politburo to admit the truth about Katyn. One was Jaruzelski's ultimatum—which he says was sent officially in the first months of 1990—that he would not proceed with his planned presidential visit to Moscow in mid-April 1990 unless the Soviet government admitted the truth about Katyn. He received the reply that documents of the convoy troops had been found, so he decided that the visit should go forward as planned.[118] This tallies with Yakovlev's statement that Gorbachev informed Jaruzelski about the documents being found. Jaruzelski must have known that an admission of the truth would be made in Moscow.

The other key factor was the publication in *Moskovskie Novosti* [Moscow News], on 25 March 1990, of an interview with Lebedeva, together with some of the documents she had found, titled "The Katyn Tragedy." This interview—published without government permission—seems to have given the decisive push to the Politburo to reverse its earlier decision not to allow the publication of articles and documents on Katyn. Perhaps its members were also influenced by what occurred at this time in Ukraine: on 22 March the Kharkov Prosecutor's Office, on its own initiative, opened a criminal investigation of the mass graves of Soviet and Polish victims discovered in the city's wooded park. Whatever the case may be, Lebedeva writes that her interview and the documents she sent to the newspaper through her colleague at the Institute of General History, Sergei Stankevich—who also happened to be a member of the Moscow City Council—had the effect of a bomb explosion. Fortunately, she left that day for London on a planned research trip. On her return, she learned that the Central Committee of the CPSU was furious with her. Falin had called Aleksandr Chubaryan, the director of her institute, and threatened that she would not be allowed access to any archive, or permitted to go abroad, or allowed to publish even one line.[119] He wanted Chubaryan to phone her in England and forbid her to give any interviews, but Chubaryan said that if he did that, she would give interviews to everybody, but if he did not, she would not give any. Furthermore, she learned that the author of the interview with her, Gennadi Zhavoronkov, and the chief editor of *Moskovskie Novosti*, Yegor Yakovlev, almost lost their jobs. The day after her return, however, the whole situation changed.

On 13 April 1990, the fiftieth anniversary of the official German radio communiqué on the Katyn graves, President Jaruzelski was in Moscow on a state visit. That day, at a reception in the Polish Embassy, Gorbachev handed Jaruzelski the NKVD dispatch lists for the prisoners who were executed in spring 1940.[120] On the same day, the Soviet news agency TASS stated that all but 394 of the approximately 15,000 prisoners from the Kozelsk, Ostashkov, and Starobelsk camps had been handed over to the NKVD Administrations in Smolensk, Voroshilovgrad (now Luhansk), and Kalinin (now Tver) Oblasts and did not appear again in NKVD records. Beria and Merkulov were named as personally responsible for the crime in Katyn Forest, described as one of the most heinous Stalinist crimes, for which the Soviet side expressed its deep regrets. The communiqué also said that copies of the documents that had been found had been given to the Polish side and that the search for archival materials continued (doc. 117).

Indeed, many documents were still missing—in particular, the decision to shoot the Polish prisoners. In early November 1990, Gorbachev ordered the Office of the Soviet Prosecutor General to speed up the investigation into the fate of Polish officers held in the three special camps. He also requested that archival materials be found proving that the Soviet Union had suffered losses in bilateral relations with Poland (doc. 118), probably to counter possible compensation claims by the victims' families. Whatever Gorbachev intended, Soviet Prosecutor General Nikolai Trubin reported to him in May 1991 that in the course of the Katyn investigation, lists of prisoners sent to the NKVD Administrations in Smolensk, Kharkov, and Kalinin had been found after a search in the archives. (It seems that these were the lists handed by Gorbachev to Jaruzelski on 13 April 1990.) Furthermore, NKVD workers involved in the crime who were still living had been identified and questioned, including the head of the UPV, Soprunenko; the head of the NKVD Kalinin/Tver region, Tokarev; and certain investigators who had interrogated Polish prisoners, as well as Soviet citizens. Finally, eyewitnesses were found in various parts of the country who made depositions regarding the tragic fate of the Polish military. Trubin wrote that evidence gathered thus far allowed the conclusion that the Polish prisoners of war could have been shot in the NKVD administrative regions of Smolensk, Kharkov, and Kalinin in April–May 1940 on the basis of a decision by the Osoboe Soveshchanie [OSO—NKVD Special Board] and that they were buried in Katyn Forest, in the Mednoe district, 32 kilometers from Tver, and in the sixth quadrant of the wooded park in Kharkov. Nevertheless, the investigation files of the executed prisoners and the protocols of the NKVD Special Board had not been found, although it was clear from witness depositions that there was a decision of the Central Committee signed by Stalin on the "liquidation" of the prisoners held in the Kozelsk, Ostashkov, and Starobelsk camps by the oblast NKVD Administrations. Trubin asked Gorbachev to instruct the Central Committee's General Department to look through its documents and send Katyn-related copies to his office.

He concluded by saying that his office had agreed to the Polish request for exhumations to be conducted with the participation of Polish experts at the burial sites. Indeed, exhumations began in summer 1991.[121]

It was in late December 1991 that the "smoking gun" document on Katyn was first seen by Aleksandr Yakovlev, who had been looking for it for some time. As he tells it, he was present on 23 December 1991, when Gorbachev handed over power to Boris Yeltsin in the Kremlin. Along with other very important papers, Gorbachev handed Yeltsin an envelope containing some documents, saying it was necessary to take counsel on how to act on them. He said, "I'm afraid they can lead to international complications. However, it is up to you to decide." Yeltsin read the documents and agreed that the matter would have to be seriously considered. Yakovlev was shocked—these were secret documents on Katyn, evidence of the crimes of the Stalinist regime. He was all the more shocked because Gorbachev spoke with striking calmness, as if Yakovlev had not asked him repeatedly to instruct the Presidential Archive to look for them. He looked at Gorbachev but did not see any sign of embarrassment. Yakovlev went into more detail in an interview he granted to the *Washington Post* correspondent Michael Dobbs in July 1993. He then said that Gorbachev had asked him to witness the handing over of top secret documents to Yeltsin. In one of the sealed envelopes they found the original Russian text of the Secret Protocol to the German-Soviet Non-Aggression Pact of 23 August 1939 (the existence of a verified copy had been revealed to the public, and condemned, on 25 December 1989), and in another envelope they found the Politburo decision of 5 March 1940 to shoot the Polish prisoners of war. Yakovlev had been asking for these documents for some time, but was told they could not be found.[122]

Gorbachev claims in his memoirs that his calm demeanor was due to the fact that these documents were not new to him on the eve of his meeting with Yeltsin in December 1991. The director of his staff, Grigory Revenko, had brought him a file "from a special archive" containing Beria's memorandum of 5 March 1940 on shooting the Polish prisoners. Gorbachev wrote, "It took my breath away to read this hellish paper."[123] It is clear, however, that he had seen it before. Valery Boldin—who joined in the failed attempt to overthrow Gorbachev in August 1991 that brought Yeltsin to power—wrote in his memoirs that in March 1989, Gorbachev asked him to find documents on Katyn. Boldin brought him two sealed envelopes. Gorbachev opened them, looked quickly at the documents, resealed the envelopes, and said, "One concerns the real circumstances of the shooting of the Poles at Katyn; the other contains the conclusions of the commission which studied the matter after the liberation of the Smolensk region, still during the war." He told Boldin not to show them to anyone without his knowledge, saying, "This is a hanging matter."[124] Gorbachev wrote that he saw two files shown to him by Boldin on the eve of his visit to Poland (summer 1989) and described them as "a random set of documents" meant to confirm the Burdenko Commission conclusions. According to the historian Dmitri Volkogonov, the file record shows that Boldin opened the file with the decision to shoot the Polish prisoners on 18 April 1989, so he probably also reported the contents to Gorbachev at that time.[125] This was a little less than a month after the Shevardnadze, Falin, and Kriuchkov memorandum to the Central Committee advising admission of what really happened at Katyn (doc. 113).

Whenever Gorbachev was told, we know that Yeltsin learned of the 5 March 1940 Politburo document at the end of December 1991. He proceeded slowly. At the time, he appointed Volkogonov as chairman of the Russian Supreme Soviet Commission for the transfer of Communist Party and KGB documents to the public domain. (The other members were Rudolf Pikhoia, the chief state archivist, and Professor A. Korotkov, director of the State Archives.) As Volkogonov tells it, toward the end of 1992, members of the commission found the original Russian texts of the secret German-Soviet agreements concluded in 1939–1941. There was a 10 July 1987 note by A. Moshkov, the section head (presumably head of Section 6 of the Central Committee's General Department) who had reported the find to Valery Boldin, who ordered him "to keep this at hand in the section for the time being." The records on the Katyn envelope showing that it had been opened by Boldin in April 1989 also show that Yuri Andropov, a secretary of the CC CPSU and member of the Politburo—who succeeded Leonid Brezhnev as party leader in November 1982—read the file on 15 April 1981. It seems clear that all Soviet Party leaders after Stalin reviewed the contents of the files, which were kept, along with other top secret documents, in sealed packets in Section 6 of the Central Committee's General Department.[126] While Volkogonov and his colleagues were reading the documents in the "special files," Polish historians were demanding access to Russian archives. On 13 January 1992, President Lech Wałęsa wrote Yeltsin requesting the return of certain Polish state documents taken by the NKVD in September 1939—in particular, documents relating to the Polish Army officers who were held in Kozelsk, Starobelsk, and Ostashkov.[127] The documents were not returned to Poland, but Polish historians obtained access to Russian archives a few months later.

Ultimately, internal Russian politics led to the public disclosure of the Politburo decision of 5 March 1940 and other hitherto secret documents concerning Katyn. When President Yeltsin faced strong opposition from the Russian Communist Party, he issued a decree de-legalizing it. Communist deputies in the Duma (Parliament) protested that the decree was unconstitutional, and the issue was placed before the Constitutional Court. Yeltsin then decided that one of the many documents to be presented as evidence of the criminal nature of the Communist Party was the Politburo decision of 5 March 1940 to shoot the Polish prisoners of war. On 14 October 1992, chief Russian archivist Pikhoia presented it, in Yeltsin's name, to President Wałęsa in Warsaw, together with other hitherto secret Katyn documents from the special archives. On the same day, the Beria resolution approved by the Politburo on 5 March 1940 appeared in a news report by ITAR-TASS. The report summarized the Politburo decision to shoot the Polish prisoners of war. It included a map showing the location of Katyn Forest, pictures of Pikhoia pointing to the execution order and of German officers standing over a mass grave at Katyn in 1943. It also included comments by the presidential spokesman, Vyacheslav Kostikov, attacking Gorbachev for concealing the document. Celestine Bohlen, the American journalist reporting this event wrote: "Coming during a politically charged inquest into the legality of the banned Soviet Communist Party now being held before Russia's Constitutional Court, the release of the Katyn documents today became a weapon in the Yeltsin government's campaign to discredit the Party, and its last leader, Mr. Gorbachev." Gorbachev, for his part, denied seeing the document before handing it over to Yeltsin on December 1991, and expressed surprise that Yeltsin had not shown it to Wałęsa during the latter's visit to Moscow in May 1992. He suggested that Yeltsin had kept it secret for future use at a politically advantageous moment.[128]

Ignoring the Russian political context, Wałęsa sent an emotional letter of thanks to Yeltsin on 15 October. Among other things, he wrote that he hoped "this page of dramatic history [would] never be repeated" (doc. 119). But Polish historians and public opinion pressed for more information, so on 28 October, Wałęsa wrote Yeltsin that he was sending to Moscow "a personal presidential mission" headed by Marian Wojciechowski, a historian and director of the Polish State Archives.

Wałęsa asked Yeltsin to help the mission gain access to all the Russian archives, including the Presidential Archive and the archives of the KGB. Copies of documents specified in the enclosures were to be given to the Poles.[129] Indeed, the Polish Military Archival Commission gained access to a large number of archival documents relating to Polish prisoners of war held in the USSR in 1939–1941; photocopies were made and deposited in the Central Military Archives in Warsaw.

The Katyn Question in Polish-Soviet Relations since 1992

The publication of the infamous Politburo decision of 5 March 1940 and the handing over of many other Russian documents were great steps toward dealing with the truth about Polish prisoners of war who ended up in Soviet hands during Word War II. However, Polish and Russian historians working in Russian archives could not find documentation on the Troika protocols (death sentences) and their implementation, nor documents showing where the prisoners jailed in Belarus and Ukraine had been shot and buried in spring 1940. German President Roman Herzog apologized to the Polish nation in August 1994 for German crimes committed in Poland during World War II, and there was talk in Poland about the need for an official Russian apology for the Katyn massacre. There was also talk of compensation for the victims' families.

President Yeltsin addressed all these questions in his letter to President Wałęsa of 22 May 1995. He wrote that he understood the significance of the fifty-fifth anniversary of the Katyn tragedy for Poles, but protested the Polish media's "escalation of demands presented to the Russian side, from making an apology to organizing a trial and the payment of compensation." He noted that the attitude of democratic Russia toward Katyn was well known and that about 9,000 victims of various nationalities were buried alongside Polish officers at Katyn. Russians thought that a memorial should be built there to all the innocent victims of totalitarianism and Nazism within the framework of which there should be a dignified memorial to the Polish officers. The Russian government would proclaim a competition for the best project; it had also instructed the authorities in Smolensk and Tver/Kalinin to place memorial signs in places designated for Polish cemeteries. Yeltsin informed Wałęsa that the documents he requested (on the Troika sentences and their implementation) were not in the Russian

archives. The investigation of the Katyn crime was proceeding, however, and the Main Military Prosecutor's Office had received about
two hundred document files and thirty-five volumes of documents on
the Burdenko Commission. The materials regarding the deaths of Polish officers in 1940 in the prisons of western Ukraine and western Belorussia had been sent to the prosecutor generals of these now independent states. Finally, Yeltsin wrote, "I am fully convinced that the steps
taken jointly by us will promote the finalization of the Katyn case in all
its aspects and, by the same token, the further successful development
of relations between our two peoples" (doc. 120).

Indeed, a Polish-Russian agreement signed in 1994—in which the
Polish government undertook to maintain Russian war graves in Poland
as well as the memorials to Polish victims in Russia—and a Polish
agreement with Ukraine led to the laying of cornerstones for Polish
military cemeteries, established alongside Russian and Ukrainian cemeteries, in Katyn, Mednoe, and Kharkov in summer 1995. The three cemeteries were officially opened in 2000: on 27 June in Kharkov, with the
participation of Polish President Aleksander Kwaśniewski and Ukrainian President Leonid Kuchma; on July 28 in Katyn, with the participation
of Polish Premier Jerzy Buzek and Russian Deputy Premier Viktor B.
Khristenko; and on September 2 in Mednoe, with the participation of
Polish Premier Buzek and Russian Minister of Internal Affairs Vladimir
B. Rushailo. In a speech at the unveiling of the Polish memorial in the
Katyn Cemetery complex, Buzek mentioned the long-lasting lie about
Katyn, the need to punish the guilty and pursue the Katyn crime investigation to the very end and thus to settle accounts with the past. He then
said, "In this place I pay homage to all the people murdered and tortured
to death at Katyn, as well as in the whole territory of the Soviet Union.
Our pain is equal to yours" (doc. 121). Khristenko spoke of honoring the
victims of "totalitarian repression" and said that the nations of the Soviet Union were the first victims of the "inhuman Stalinist machine,"
which took the lives of millions of Soviet citizens (doc. 122). Kwaśniewski sent a message to the participants at the ceremonial opening of the
cemetery at Mednoe, where Buzek and Rushailo made speeches.[130]

Obstacles to Reconciliation

The opening of the Polish and Russian cemeteries at Kharkov, Katyn,
and Mednoe did not put an end to the Katyn question. Although much

is known today about the fate of the Polish prisoners of war held in the three special NKVD camps in the USSR in 1939–1940, many questions still remain unanswered. Documentation is lacking on Stalin's motive and timing for the decision of 5 March 1940 to have the prisoners shot (doc. 47). No eyewitness accounts have surfaced on the executions at Katyn itself. The executions and burial sites of those held in the NKVD prisons of western Ukraine and shot in other parts of Ukraine are unknown, as are the names and execution and burial sites of the victims who were held and shot in western Belorussia. The Russian Memorial society announced in mid-June 2006 that it was cataloguing 800 Stalinist execution sites and that Polish remains had been found in almost all of them. It is known that Polish military insignia and fragments of uniforms have been found over the years at Bykovnia [Polish: Bykownia], on the northeastern outskirts of Kiev, which is the burial ground of an estimated 100,000 Ukrainian victims of the Stalinist Terror. A team of Polish archeologists and forensic medicine experts began work there in summer 2006. Their first reports indicated that Poles on the Ukrainian Katyn list are likely buried there. However, identification will be very difficult, if not impossible, due to the Soviet practice of using backhoes or bulldozers to move or remove criminal evidence on burial sites.[131]

Meanwhile, the Soviet—later Russian—Katyn investigation, begun by the Main Military Prosecutor's Office in 1990, dragged on for years. In September 2004 this office unofficially made it known that it had discontinued the investigation and that no one would be charged with the crime. Finally, on 11 March 2005, the head of the office, Aleksandr Savenkov, announced that the investigation was closed and no one would be condemned because all members of the wartime Politburo were dead. He concluded there was no evidence that genocide had been committed against the Polish nation. This statement caused outrage in Poland. In February 2006 the Russian military prosecutor general rejected a request for rehabilitation, submitted years ago by the widow of an officer shot at Katyn, on the grounds that documentation was lacking to show that the officer had been sentenced to death for political reasons. Thus, Savenkov ignored the publication of the Politburo decision of 5 March 1940 and the well known fact that the prisoner-of-war files had been ordered destroyed in 1959 so they could not be produced as documents for rehabilitation. The Polish reaction was to support the opening of a Polish Katyn investigation.[132]

To understand Russian decisions and rationales in connection with Katyn, it is necessary to take a brief look at the course of the Russian Katyn investigation. On 13 June 1994, after three years of intensive work, Anatoly Yablokov, then the Russian military prosecutor in charge of the Katyn case, filed a motion for a procedural decision on criminal case no. 159, Katyn, as a case under Russian criminal law. He proposed that Stalin and his close collaborators in the Politburo be judged guilty of the Katyn crime on the basis of Articles 6a and 6b of the Charter of the International Military Tribunal at Nuremberg, that is, guilty of crimes against peace and humanity, war crimes, and the crime of genocide aimed at Polish citizens. Furthermore, he suggested that the members of the Special Soviet Commission headed by Burdenko, as well as those who gave falsified testimony to the IMT and those who concealed the Katyn crime later, were guilty under certain articles of the Soviet Russian Criminal Code in its 1926 version (abuse of power). Finally, he argued that those who had carried out illegal orders (murder) were subject to the death penalty according to the Criminal Code of the Russian Federal Republic, and that the crime itself was not subject to the statute of limitations. He stated that since the Katyn crime could not receive adequate legal evaluation within the framework of the existing Russian law, which did not recognize the crime of genocide or crimes against humanity, the question of providing the necessary legislation could be decided only by the highest legal organ of the state, by which he meant the Duma. Here it should be noted that Yablokov's motion followed the suggestions of the Report of the Russian Commission of Experts on the Katyn Case of 2 August 1993. The commission included Inessa Yazhborovskaia, Valentina Parsadanova, and Yuri Zoria.[133]

Yablokov's motion was rejected by the Main Military Prosecutor's Office, but the investigation continued, mainly because of Polish Deputy Prosecutor General Stefan Śnieżko, who argued that the Prosecutors' Offices of Belarus and Ukraine should be asked to search their archives for Katyn documents. Hopes were raised by President Yeltsin's visit to Warsaw in August 1993, when he laid a wreath at the Katyn memorial and asked for forgiveness, but this was seen as a personal gesture. Yazhborovoskaia and Parsadanova continued to press for a verdict based on the criteria proposed by the Russian Commission of Experts and by Prosecutor Yablokov.[134] Katyn, however, soon became an unpopular issue in Russia, so even Yeltsin was unwilling to risk losing support over it. As mentioned earlier, in his letter to President Wałęsa of 22 May 1995, Yeltsin objected to unofficial Polish demands for a Russian apology and compensation for victims' families (doc. 120). His appointment of Vladimir Putin as his successor on 31 December 1999 seemed to augur a new beginning, but this failed to materialize. Neither the change in Russian leadership nor the opening of Polish war cemeteries at Katyn, Kharkov, and Mednoe in summer 2000 produced any progress toward meeting the demands of the Polish Katyn Families Association for a Russian admission of genocide, an apology, and compensation. Hopes were raised again in connection with President Putin's visit to Warsaw in mid-January 2002. He rejected a comparison of Stalinist repressions with Nazi German genocide, but mentioned the possibility of broadening the Russian law concerning rehabilitation of Russian victims of political repression to make it applicable to Polish citizens as well.[135] A joint Polish-Russian group was formed to study "difficult questions." As mentioned, the Russian Main Military Prosecutor's Office declared its Katyn investigation closed in March 2005.

The key obstacles to a Russian verdict along the lines proposed by Yablokov and the Russian Commission of Experts, and also to satisfying the demands of the Katyn Families Association in Poland, are legal and psychological. The concept of genocide was absent from Russian criminal legislation until it became enshrined in Article 357 of the new criminal code that came into force in January 1997. Article 357 also qualified as criminal the cruel treatment of prisoners of war or civilians, while Article 358 condemned deportations of civilian populations. Another article, 353, condemned as criminal the planning, preparation, unleashing, or conduct of aggressive war. These articles brought the new Russian criminal code in line with international law. Article 10 of the new code, however, stated that punishment for these crimes did not apply to crimes committed before the code entered into force. Thus, Article 10 of the new code made it legally impossible for the Russian authorities to prosecute the criminals responsible for the massacres at Katyn, Kalinin, and Kharkov in 1940. At the same time, the new code followed Russian legal tradition in not allowing the prosecution and judgment of criminals no longer living. Thus, both the new Russian code and Russian legal tradition are contrary to Article 6 of the IMT Charter, as well as Article 2 of the 1968 international convention on the inapplicability of the statute of limitations to war crimes and crimes against humanity.[136]

The Russian legal stance is incompatible with the Polish legal stance. The Polish government, Polish historians, and, of course, the Katyn Families Association view the Katyn massacres as genocide. The latter is defined in Article II of the Genocide Convention of 1948 as "actions directed towards the full or partial destruction of a national, ethnic, racial, or religious group" (see the introduction to Part II). The Polish prisoners of war clearly constituted a national group. However, the justification given in Beria's resolution to shoot them, adopted by the Politburo on 5 March 1940, was that they were "counterrevolutionaries," "spies," and "implacable, irremediable enemies of Soviet power" (doc. 47). Since any action or intent of action directed against the Soviet state was "counterrevolutionary," the Poles were criminals according to various paragraphs of Article 58 of the Soviet Criminal Code (doc. 38), even though the Soviet criminal code was not invoked by Beria and even though the sentencing of the Polish prisoners of war by the Troika did not conform with Soviet legal procedures of the time. Thus it can be argued that the massacres constituted murder on political rather than ethnic or national grounds.

The psychological obstacle to a Russian condemnation of the decision makers and implementers of the Politburo decision of 5 March 1940, as well as the falsifiers of the Katyn case that followed, may well be rooted in the difficulty most Russians find in facing the terrible truth about the Stalin years.[137] Indeed, people of all nationalities find it difficult to acknowledge the dark pages of their history, and this is especially difficult for Russians because the "Great Fatherland War" is a glorious memory, and most view Stalin as a great war leader who made the USSR a world power. This ranks Stalin alongside Peter the Great, Catherine the Great, and especially Alexander I, who defeated Napoleon. Russians also remember that millions of Soviet soldiers and citizens died in World War II and that the Red Army liberated Eastern Europe from German occupation or domination. The fact that this liberation also meant the imposition of communism and Soviet control over most of the region generally goes unmentioned. It is not surprising that for most Russians these glorious memories overshadow Stalin's crimes, including the murder in one way or another of at least twenty million Soviet citizens, along with many citizens of other countries, particularly those bordering the USSR in 1939–1940.

Indeed, some Russians even claim that the Burdenko Commission report (doc. 106) is the final word on Katyn. They see charges of Russian guilt as mean, anti-Russian lies and claim that the published documents are fakes. Public demonstrations sometimes take place in support of this view.[138] While most Russians who are knowledgeable about Katyn do not go this far, some question Soviet guilt for Katyn by pointing out discrepancies between the names of the Katyn victims published by the Germans and those on the NKVD lists that Gorbachev gave to Jaruzelski in April 1990. But Aleksei Pamiatnykh of the Russian Memorial society has shown that the discrepancies are due to spelling or transliteration errors and has reconciled all but some thirty names on both lists. Other Russians accuse the Poles of having carried out a massacre of Soviet prisoners of war captured in the Polish-Soviet War of 1919–1920 and view this as the Polish equivalent of Katyn.[139] A recent example of this view was expressed by the Russian historian Mikhail Meltiukhov, who claims that 60,000 Russian prisoners of war perished in Polish prisoner-of-war camps in 1920. He argues that just as the Russian leadership accepted responsibility for the massacre of Polish officers in the USSR (doc. 117), so the Polish leadership should accept responsibility for the deaths of Soviet prisoners of war in Poland twenty years earlier.[140] This argument seems reasonable, but one must consider the number and circumstances of these deaths. According to Polish estimates, about 113,000 Soviet prisoners of war were held in the Polish camps in fall 1920, and the deaths of some 47,000 of them cannot be treated as the equivalent of the Katyn massacres of 1940. The Soviet prisoners died not as the result of a documented order by Polish authorities, nor as the result of a documented intent to murder them, but because of inadequate nourishment, lack of heating in winter, bad sanitary conditions, and disease. Contemporary reports made to Soviet authorities on conditions in the prisoner-of-war camps in Poland speak of neglect, but they do not mention any suspicion of murderous Polish intent toward the Soviet prisoners. Conditions in Polish prisoner-of-war camps were no worse than those endured by Poles in Soviet prisoner-of-war camps, of whom some 50 percent failed to return home. Russian and Polish historians now estimate that 16,000–20,000 Soviet prisoners died in Polish camps.[141]

Given the legal and psychological factors affecting the Russian view of Katyn, as well as Russian legal tradition, it is not surprising that the Russian investigation ended without a condemnation of Stalin, the members of his Politburo, the men who carried out the order of death by shooting, and those who produced and maintained the lie of German guilt for almost half a century. This is as unacceptable to most Poles as the Polish claim that the 1940 massacres were a crime of genocide is unacceptable to most Russians. A Polish investigation, announced on 30 November 2004 by the Instytut Pamięci Narodowej [IPN—Institute of National Remembrance], undertaken under pressure from the Katyn Families Association, is unlikely to bring closure, especially since the Russian Main Military Prosecutor's Office denies the IPN access to most of the documents gathered in its own lengthy investigation. Polish President Lech Kaczyński stated in July 2006, "It is not the role of [the] prime minister to lead fights over the past. I want my government and myself to form a group that works for the future. We leave these fights to historians for the time being." It seems, however, that a Polish-Russian reconciliation over the Katyn massacres is still a long way off.[142]

Selected survivors from the three special camps were sent first to Yukhnov camp, just north of Kozelsk, and in late June 1940 to Griazovets camp, just south of the city of Vologda. (See map 4.) They would be joined later by Polish POWs interned in Lithuania and Latvia in 1939 and transferred to NKVD camps in the USSR during summer 1940.

· 85 ·

Soprunenko's Report on the Number of Polish POWs Dispatched to Yukhnov Camp from the Special Camps and the Grounds on Which They Were Sent There*
After 25 May 1940, Moscow

Top Secret
Information on the Prisoners of War Detained
at Yukhnov NKVD Camp

Total sent to Yukhnov camp	395 people[143]
Including:	
a/ On the instruction of the GUGB 5th Department	47 people[144]
b/ At the request of the German Embassy	47 people[145]
c/ At the request of the Lithuanian mission	19 people
d/ Germans	24 people[146]

137 people

---

* Handwritten note on document: "Com. Khudiakova: Preserve. M[akliarsky]."

e/ On instruction from USSR Deputy People's Commissar
of Internal Affairs Comrade Merkulov   91 people[147]
f/ Others[148]   167 people

                                                        _____
                                                        258
                                                        _____

                                     [Total] 395 people

      Head of the USSR NKVD UPV
      GB [State Security] Captain
      P. Soprunenko

The Griazovets camp held surviving Polish military and police men
from Kozelsk, Starobelsk, and Ostashkov camps, most of whom had
been transferred earlier to Yukhnov. On 14 June 1940, as ordered by
Merkulov, 384 POWs from Yukhnov were loaded into five railway
cars at Babynino Station and sent by train no. 1136 on to Griazovets
camp, south of Vologda; nine sick men arrived there later.

· 86 ·

Report on the Number, Ranks, and Professions of Polish POWs in Griazovets Camp
as of 1 July 1940
1 July 1940, Moscow

_____

Top Secret
Report on the Number of Prisoners of War Held
in NKVD Griazovets Camp

	As of 1 July 1940
Total held in camp	394 people[149]
Of these:	
1. Generals	1
2. Colonels	6
3. Police and gendarmerie colonels	2
4. Lt. colonels	16
5. Majors	6
6. Police and gendarmerie majors	2
7. Captains	16
8. Police and gendarmerie captains	2
9. Lieutenants	26
10. 2nd lieutenants	93
11. Police and gendarmerie 2nd lieutenants	2

12. Ensigns	8
13. Cadets	65
14. Sergeants	4
15. Police and gendarmerie sergeants	7
16. Corporals	12
17. Police and gendarmerie corporals	2
18. Police and gendarmerie lance corporals	3
19. Police rank and file	37
20. Platoon leaders	2
21. Prison guards	2
22. Rank-and-file soldiers	11
23. General defense instructors	1
24. [Military] settlers	2
25. Yunaks[150]	7
26. Civil servants	5
27. Train dispatchers	1
28. Millers	1
29. Policemen's sons	3
30. Schoolboys and students	6
31. Traders	1
32. Serviceman's son	1
33. Agronomists	2
34. Refugees	25
35. Engineers	1
36. Those who were in jail	7
37. Those who illegally crossed the frontier	2
38. No profession	1
39. Timber businessman	1
40. Not serving in the army	2

Head of USSR NKVD UPV
GB Captain
(Soprunenko)

Head Department of Administration
Sr. Security Lieutenant
(Makliarsky)

The cover-up began in mid-March 1940, when prisoners in the three special camps were forbidden to write or receive letters. It continued with orders to destroy the correspondence and personal files of the prisoners who had been held in Starobelsk (docs. 87, 88). Nevertheless, thousands of prisoner records were preserved until 1959 (see doc. 110).

· 87 ·

Protocol on the Destruction of POW Correspondence
23 July 1940, Starobelsk

Protocol

On 23 July 1940, we, the signatories [listed] below, the political controller of the NKVD Camp's Special Section, Klok; the head of the NKVD camp's URO [Reception, Records, and Barracks Assignment Section], Sysoev; and the secretary of the NKVD Camp Command, Kuriachy, have on this day, on the basis of UPV NKVD Instruction no. 25/5699, carried out the destruction of the incoming correspondence addressed to the POWs who left the camp:[151]

1. Registered letters   422 pieces
2. Ordinary letters   562   "
3. Registered postcards   148   "
4. Ordinary postcards   3,102 "
5. Telegrams   79   "

All of the [correspondence] listed above was destroyed by burning, about which the present protocol was drawn up.

Political Controller of the NKVD Camp Special Section
Klok

Head of the NKVD Camp 2nd Section
Sysoev

Secretary of the NKVD Camp Command
Kuriachy

In September 1940, Soprunenko repeated the instructions to burn the remaining POW records in Starobelsk camp and gave directives for preserving other records.

· 88 ·

Soprunenko's Instruction to the Head of Starobelsk Camp
and the Head of the Camp OO to Destroy POW Files
10 September 1940, Moscow

No. 25/9050
Top Secret

To the Head of the Starobelsk NKVD Camp
GB Captain Com. Berezhkov

To the Head of the Camp Special Section
GB Sergeant Com. Gaididei

To No. 10/8 of 3 September 1940[152]

The Special Section evidence files of the POWs who left the camp (except those who left for Yukhnov), the data card file, also the alphabetical files with materials on the POWs, should be destroyed by burning.

All the materials on the POWs who left for Yukhnov camp should be sent immediately to the NKVD UPV.

Alphabetical files with materials on the service of the military unit guarding the camp are to be delivered to the archive of the 1st Special Department of UNKVD for Kharkov Oblast.

Alphabetical files with materials on the free, hired contingent,[153] and also on the population surrounding the camp, are active [materials] and are subject to remaining in the camp's Special Section.

A special commission should be organized for the destruction of the materials, made up of the workers of the Special Section, which [commission] is obligated to look carefully through the documents to be destroyed [for all] materials which represent operational interest. These materials are in no circumstances subject to destruction. They should also be sent to the Administration [UPV].

Appropriate protocols are to be written up on the destruction, as well as the transfer of materials to the archive, together with detailed descriptions of the [materials] destroyed.

Report on the implementation.[154]

Head of USSR NKVD UPV
GB Captain (Soprunenko)

Head of the 2nd Department of the USSR NKVD UPV
GB Sr. Lieutenant (Makliarsky)

The vast majority of the Polish military, police, and civilian prisoners selected for survival proved to be just as patriotic, resistant to communist propaganda, and insistent on their rights as their murdered comrades had been. The leader of the "patriotic" group in Griazovets camp was the retired but feisty General Jerzy Wołkowicki. The threat of a hunger strike, combined with a rising fear of Germany and the thought that Polish officers might be needed in the future, probably moved the Soviet leadership to allow the Polish POWs held in Griazovets camp, as well as those held in Kozelsk 2, Suzdal, Rovno, Yukhnov, and the Northern Railway camps, one letter a month by way of a post office box in Moscow. Thus, correspondence broken off in mid-March 1940 was resumed by the survivors in October.

· 89 ·

Special Report to Beria by the UNKVD Head for the Vologda Region,
Pyotr Kondakov, on the Counterrevolutionary Activities
of Some Polish POWs in Griazovets Camp
29 September 1940, Vologda*

No. 7037
Top Secret

To: USSR People's Commissar for Internal Affairs
GB Commissar 1st Rank Comrade Beria

Special Report on the Counterrevolutionary Activities of a Group
of Prisoners of War in the Griazovets NKVD Camp

The prisoner-of-war contingent in Griazovets NKVD camp consists of 384 officers and NCOs of the former Polish Army, officers and rank and file of the former Polish police, as well as a significant number of civilians, among whom we have discovered landowners, military settlers, and agents of the former Polish and Lithuanian intelligence organs.

Recently, the UNKVD has received several reports from the camp which make it clear that a group of POWs made up of former higher and senior

* In the margin: "Taken for control by the Secretariat of the NKVD USSR." In the lower left corner, with the incoming registration number: "Secretariat of the NKVD USSR. 1st Department. No. 75. 29 September 1940." In the top right corner: "Prisoner-of-War Administration, 24 December 1940. Incoming No. 20970."

commanders of the Polish Army, including General Wołkowicki, Colonel Grabicki, Majors Domoń and Lis, military priest Tyczkowski, Naval Captain Ginsbert, and Police Commissioner Bober, are conducting active counterrevolutionary [c-r] activity among the POWs aimed at individuals loyally inclined toward the Soviet Union.[155]

The individuals named above are conducting active c-r agitation among the POWs, propagandizing the idea of restoring a "greater Poland from sea to sea,"[156] and creating nationalistic groups from [among] the young officer cadets and 2nd lieutenants, based on the principle of [uniting] regional countrymen, which they are developing in a nationalist-chauvinist spirit by means of illegal lectures and discussions.

This anti-Soviet influence on the officer cadets and 2nd lieutenants has in several instances provoked open c-r manifestations on their part.

On 20 August of this year, a group of nationalistically minded officer cadets beat up a group of Jewish POWs who had expressed loyal views with respect to the Soviet Union.[157]

The c-r core among the POWs under the leadership of General Wołkowicki has placed itself in active opposition to the mass political work being conducted in the camp. During the period when lectures on the history of the VKP(b)[158] are being conducted at the behest of a significant portion of POWs, they are conducting parallel lectures and discussions of a nationalist-chauvinist character and organizing the singing of c-r nationalist songs.

They are also poisoning [the minds of] individual officer cadets and 2nd lieutenants against the POWs who are participating in mass political work. They threaten the latter that they will settle with them in the "future Poland" or upon their return to German territory. It has been established that similar threats against several POWs have been made by Police Commissioner Bober, who keeps a so-called blacklist of POWs who are loyally inclined toward the Soviet Union.

Out of fear of reprisal, several POWs have stopped attending the lectures on the history of the VKP(b) that are being conducted in the camp.

On 5 September of this year, the UNKVD received a report from the camp that preparations are under way among the POWs to declare a mass hunger strike as a sign of protest against the lack of correspondence with families and relatives.

Through operational and prophylactic measures taken on site, support for the hunger strike among the POWs has been dissipated for the time being.

As has been established, POWs Wołkowicki, Domoń, Lis, and Bober were waiting for a reply to Wołkowicki's statement, addressed to Narkomvnudel [People's Commissariat of Internal Affairs], in which he warned of possible recidivism among the POWs on the grounds of the lack of correspondence with relatives. Wołkowicki's statement was sent to the UPV.[159]

In connection with the lack of reply to this statement, Wołkowicki, together with Domoń, Lis, and Bober, who are connected to him through their c-r activity, began actively preparing for a mass hunger strike among the POWs, which according to the information that has been received, is supposed to be declared during the first few days of October of this year.

Thus it has been established that between 18 and 23 September, Wołkowicki went around to all the POWs in the blocks trying to convince them of the necessity of going to the camp administration every day and raising the issue of correspondence and in this way applying pressure for a positive resolution of this issue.

From the statement made on 23 September of this year by prisoner of war Wołkowicki, it is clear that the creation of a special committee to lead the hunger strike is being prepared. Its task, in addition to leading the hunger strike, will include forming groups to confiscate edible products from POWs and to destroy those products in order to achieve a universal hunger strike.

Simultaneously, Wołkowicki stated that the hunger strike must continue until a positive reply to the issue of correspondence arrives.

The camp administration has in a timely fashion informed the head of the USSR NKVD UPV GB Captain Comrade Soprunenko about the facts set forth here, but so far the camp has not received any specific instructions on these matters.[160]

In order to curtail c-r activity among the POWs in the camp, I think it is necessary to remove from the camp the guiding c-r core in the persons of POWs General Wołkowicki, Colonel Grabicki, Majors Domoń and Lis, the priest Tyczkowski, Captain Ginsbert, and Police Commissioner Bober, about which I request your instructions.[161]

> Head of the NKVD Administration for the Vologda Oblast
> GB Major Kondakov

Beria's order of 26 October 1940 shows that it was customary to reward NKVD workers for carrying out "special tasks," in this case, the execution of the Polish POWs from the three special camps: Kozelsk, Ostashkov, and Starobelsk. Unlike the convoy troops, some of these men were especially trained to shoot prisoners in the back of the skull—the traditional NKVD method of execution—while others participated in support roles. It is ironic that just as these men were being rewarded for shooting the Polish officers and police, Beria and Merkulov were interviewing selected survivors, along with some transferred to Kozelsk 2 and Yukhnov from internment in the Baltic States, to lead a Polish division in the Red Army (doc. 91).

· 90 ·

Beria's Order on Rewards for NKVD Workers for "Clearing Out"
the Prisons and the Three Special Camps
26 October 1940, Moscow

Order of the People's Commissar of Internal Affairs
of the USSR for [the Year] 1940
No. 001365
Moscow
26 October 1940
"On Rewards for NKVD Workers"

For the successful carrying out of special assignments, I order:
the reward of the following workers from the USSR NKVD of the Kalinin, Smolensk, and Kharkov Oblast UNKVDs.[162]

One month's salary:

GB Captain	F. K. Ilin
GB Senior Lieutenant	I. I. Gribov
GB Senior Lieutenant	A. I. Rubanov
GB Senior Lieutenant	T. F. Kupry
GB Lieutenant	V. M. Karavaev
GB Major	V. M. Blokhin
GB Major	A. Ye. Okunev
GB Captain	V. I. Shigalev
GB Captain	A. M. Kalinin
GB Captain	P. A. Yakovlev
GB Senior Lieutenant	I. I. Antonov
GB Senior Lieutenant	I. I. Feldman
GB Senior Lieutenant	I. I. Shigalev
GB Senior Lieutenant	D. E. Semenikhin
GB Lieutenant	A. D. Dmitriev
GB Lieutenant	A. M. Yemelianov
GB Senior Major	[N. I.] Sinegubov
GB Major	[K. S.] Zilberman
GB Captain	I. D. Bezrukov

GB Captain	P. P. Tikhonov
GB Captain	V. P. Zubtsov
Brigadier Commander	[M. S.] Krivenko
Colonel	[A. A.] Rybakov
Colonel	[I. A.] Stepanov
GB Lieutenant	V. P. Pavlov
GB Lieutenant	T. F. Kachin
GB Lieutenant	M. A. Kozokhotsky
GB Lieutenant	A. M. Shevelev
GB 2nd Lieutenant	M. I. Luginin
GB 2nd Lieutenant	M. D. Goriachev
GB 2nd Lieutenant	N. A. Kiselev
GB 2nd Lieutenant	I. S. Barinov
GB 2nd Lieutenant	A. N. Ofitserov
GB Sergeant	I. I. Novoselov
GB Sergeant	K. Ye. Blank
GB Sergeant	R. S. Getselevich
GB Sergeant	N. A. Zubov
GB Sergeant	S. S. Kuznetsov
GB Sergeant	I. A. Stekholshchikov
[No rank given]	A. I. Tsukanov
"	A. A. Karmanov
"	I. P. Smykalov
"	F. I. Doronin
"	N. A. Gvozdovsky

800 rubles:

[No rank given]	I. I. Stelmakh
"	I. Ye. Tikunov
"	T. P. Yakushev
"	A. G. Zaitsev
"	N. M. Seniushkin
"	M. A. Zhila
"	L. A. Tivanenko
"	P. M. Kartsev
"	A. I. Razorenov
"	T. Kh. Babaian
"	I. D. Frolenkov
"	M. M. Solovyev
"	N. K. Kostiuchenko
"	M. P. Grigorev
"	V. A. Belogorlov

"	V. K. Sorokin
"	V. M. Sytin
"	M. F. Ignatev
"	N. I. Sukharev
"	A. S. Aleksandrov
"	V. A. Osipov
"	V. Ye. Skorodumov
"	N. T. Zhuravlev
"	I. I. Krasnovidov
"	P. A. Bogdanov
"	N. A. Galitsyn
"	A. T. Melnik
"	N. V. Melnik
"	I. M. Chuzhaikin
"	M. M. Zhuravlev
"	A. Ye. Zakharov
"	G. N. Tarasov
"	N. P. Zinoviev
"	T. K. Gabrilenkov
"	A. B. Siurin
"	N. A. Mishchenkov
"	A. M. Fadeev
"	P. M. Zorin
"	A. M. Yakovlev
"	P. M. Baranov
"	D. I. Orlov
"	N. I. Golovinkin
"	V. I. Zhiltsov
"	A. V. Yegorov
"	N. V. Loginov
"	M. V. Tsikulin
"	M. D. Lebedev
"	I. P. Mokridin
"	G. K. Levanchiukov
"	V. G. Ivanov
"	A. Ye. Marusev
"	M. A. Baranov
"	I. I. Belov
"	V. K. Chekulaev
"	S. M. Fedoryshko
"	I. A. Gumotudinov
"	G. I. Timoshenko

"   Ye. A. Vigovsky
"   A. G. Deviatilov
"   M. V. Syromiatnikov
"   T. S. Shchepko
"   T. D. Burda
"   S. M. Lazarenko
"   P. G. Prudnikov
"   F. I. Doroginin
"   N. F. Bogdanov
"   V. K. Kostiuchenko
"   G. I. Makarenkov
"   I. I. Komarovsky
"   V. A. Solovyev
"   V. P. Moiseenkov
"   I. B. Medvedev
"   G. F. Karpov
"   I. M. Ivanov
"   D. F. Tikhonov
"   A. A. Moiseenkov
"   G. P. Ziuskin
"   A. S. Kovalev
"   I. M. Silchenkov
"   M. Ye. Davydov
"   A. M. Tochenov

People's Commissar of Internal Affairs USSR
L. Beria

By late October 1940, the Soviet leadership apparently began to envisage the possibility of a war with Germany. Selected Polish officers were brought to Moscow and asked if they would be willing to fight the Germans and organize a Polish division in the Red Army from among the POWs in the USSR.

About the same time, a group of Polish communists and leftists led by Wanda Wasilewska in Lviv celebrated the eighty-fifth anniversary of the death of the Polish national poet Adam Mickiewicz (1798–1855), now hailed as a proto-socialist. The celebration was given wide coverage in the Soviet media. Also, a few exiled Polish communists were sent to the Comintern Party School at Pushkino, near Moscow, for political education. Stalin evidently decided that some Poles could be useful to him.

· 91 ·

Note from Beria to Stalin on the Possible Organization of Military Units
with Polish and Czech Prisoners of War[163]
2 November 1940, Moscow

From Com. Beria
No. 47/13b
Top Secret
TsK VKP (b)

To Comrade Stalin

In implementing your directives regarding Polish and Czech POWs, we
have done the following:

1. In the camps of the NKVD USSR there are at this time 18,297 Polish
POWs. Of this number there are 2 generals,[164] 39 colonels and lt. colonels, 222 majors and captains, 691 lieutenants and 2nd lieutenants, 4,022
noncommissioned officers, and 13,321 rank and file.

Out of 18,297 persons, 11,998 are inhabitants of territories taken by
Germany.[165]

The POWs interned in Lithuania and Latvia and deported to NKVD
USSR camps are estimated to number 3,303 persons.[166]

The vast majority of the remaining POWs, except for leading cadres, are
employed in the construction of a highway and railway line.[167]

Besides the above, 22 officers of the former Polish Army are in the internal prison of the NKVD USSR, having been arrested by the organs of
the NKVD USSR as participants of various anti-Soviet organizations
active on the territories of the western regions of Ukraine and Belorussia.

As a result of the filtration carried out by us (by way of familiarizing ourselves with the evidence and investigation files, as well as direct questioning) a selection was made of 24 former Polish officers: 3 generals, 1 colonel,
8 lt. colonels, 6 majors and captains, 6 lieutenants and 2nd lieutenants.

2. A series of conversations was conducted with all the selected ones, as
a result of which the following was established:

a) All of them have a very hostile attitude toward the Germans and believe a military clash between the USSR and Germany is inevitable in the
future, and express the wish to participate in the inevitable, in their view,
Soviet-German war on the side of the Soviet Union.

b) Some of them express the conviction that the fate of Poland and its rebirth as a national state can be decided only by the Soviet Union, on which

they place their hopes. Others (mostly from among the Poles interned in Lithuania) still hope for the victory of the English, who, in their opinion, will help in the reestablishment of Poland.

c) The majority consider themselves to be free of any obligations regarding the so-called Sikorski government, [but] some state that they can participate in a war with Germany on the side of the USSR only if this will be sanctioned in one form or another by the Sikorski "government."[168] The junior officers declare that they will act in accordance with orders received from any Polish general.

3. Specifically, [we] should take into consideration the stands [taken by] individual persons:

a) General Januszajtis declared that he can take upon himself the command of Polish units if such will be organized on the territory of the Soviet Union to fight Germany, regardless of the Sikorski "government" directives on this issue. However, he considers it appropriate that a special political platform be outlined on the future fate of Poland. Simultaneously with this, as he put it, [there should be] "a softening of the climate" for Poles living in the western regions of Ukraine and Belorussia.

b) General Boruta-Spiechowicz declared that he can take various steps only at the request of the Sikorski "government," which according to him represents the interests of the Polish nation.

c) General Przeździecki made a declaration analogous to that of Boruta-Spiechowicz.[169]

d) Several colonels and lieutenant colonels (Berling, Bukojemski, Gorczyński, Tyszyński) declared that they are putting themselves completely at the disposal of Soviet authorities and that they will with great goodwill undertake the organization and command of any kind of military formations [organized] from the numbers of Polish POWs designated to fight the Germans in the interest of establishing Poland as a national state. They see the future Poland as linked closely with the Soviet Union in one form or another.

4. In order to detect the attitudes of the remaining mass of POWs held in NKVD camps, [we have] sent brigades of operational NKVD USSR workers [who were assigned] appropriate tasks.

As a result of the work carried out, it has been established that the great majority of POWs can be undoubtedly utilized for organizing a Polish military unit.

With this aim, we believe it appropriate to:

While not rejecting the idea of utilizing as commanders of the Polish military unit Generals Januszajtis and Boruta-Spiechowicz, whose names could attract certain circles of former Polish military men, entrust the organization of a division at first to the above-mentioned group of colonels and lt. colonels (information on them is attached),[170] who create the impression of being reasonable people who know military matters, think correctly politically, and are honest.

This group should be given the possibility of reaching an understanding, in a conspiratorial form, with persons of the same mind [who are] in the camps for Polish POWs, and of selecting the cadre composition of the future division.

After selecting the cadres, the future staff and a place for training the division should be organized in one of [the] sovkhozes [state collective farms] in the southeastern part of the USSR. At the same time, with the cooperation of specially appointed workers of the RKKA [Worker-Peasant Red Army] staff a plan will be developed for forming the division, a decision will be made on the type of division (armored, motorized, infantry), and its material-technical supplies will be assured.

At the same time, NKVD organs should carry out appropriate work in the camps for Polish POWs among the soldiers and noncommissioned officers with the aim of recruiting people for the division.

As recruitment proceeds and the recruits are verified, they will be sent in groups to the locale of the divisional staff, where they will be given appropriate training.

The organization of the division and its preparation will be carried out under the direction of the RKKA General Staff.[171] A Special Section [Intelligence] of the NKVD USSR is being organized [together] with the division with the task of carrying out personal background checks of the division cadres.

5. As for the Czech POWs in the NKVD camp, they are estimated to number 577 persons (501 Czechs and 76 Slovaks); of this number [there are]: staff captains and captains—8; junior officers—39; NCOs—176, and 354 rank and file.[172]

In conversations with 13 selected officers it was established that all of them recognize Germany as their age-old enemy and want to fight against it for the restoration of the Czechoslovak state. They consider themselves as pledged to military service in the Czech Army and recognize Benesh [Beneš][173] as their leader, and in case any kind of Czech military units will be organized on the territory of the Soviet Union they will join them on Beneš's order, or at a minimum, on that of their leader, Col. Svoboda, [who is] at present abroad. We have summoned Svoboda to come [here].[174]
Enclosure: pertains to the text[175]

People's Commissar of Internal Affairs of the Soviet Union
L. Beria

A few Polish officers led by Colonel Zygmunt Berling, who had expressed willingness to organize a Polish division in the Red Army, were taken to a dacha in Malakhovka, on the eastern outskirts of Moscow, and told to draw up plans for the division. A May Day outing in Moscow and a film show were organized for them in 1941.

· 92 ·

Gorlinsky and Rodionov to Soprunenko on the 1 May Festivities
for the Berling Group in Malakhovka*
No later than 24 April 1941, Moscow

Top Secret

To the Head of the USSR NKVD UPV
GB Captain Com. Soprunenko

According to the plan approved by People's Commissar of State Security Comrade Merkulov, on 1 and 2 May 1941 for POWs located at the Malakhovka dacha, the following activities will be organized:[176]

1. On the morning of 1 May of this year, the POWs will be moved to Moscow under the escort of a group of operational workers led by department head Comrade Kondratik to be shown the parade on Red Square.[177]

2. On the afternoon of 1 May at the Malakhovka dacha, a banquet will be organized, which the group of operational workers who escorted the POWs to Moscow and back will attend.

3. In the evening, the following moving pictures should be shown:

1 May—*Muzykalnaia Istoria* [A Musical Story].

2 May—*Chapaev* [and] *Tsirk* [The Circus].

In accordance with this, I request that you ensure:

1. the transfer on the morning of 1 May of all the POWs to the group of operational workers led by Comrade Kondratik.

2. a reinforced guard at the Malakhovka dacha during the holidays.

3. the showing of the above-indicated moving pictures.

We are sending money for the moving pictures in the amount of three hundred and seventy-five rubles (375 rubles).

---

* Handwritten across the upper left corner: "Urgent. Com. Polukhin. Give orders concerning security. Com. Lisovsky, secure movie shows on 1 and 2 May. P. Soprun[enko]. 24.04.41. Read. Kosygin. 30 May 1941." In the left margin, middle of the page: "Stamp for incoming mail: NKVD USSR Administration for Prisoner-of-War Affairs, 30 April 1941. No. 5041."

Head of the 3rd Administration NKGB USSR
GB Senior Major Gorlinsky

Head of the 4th Department NKGB
GB Captain Rodionov

The Politburo's confirmation of the SNK [Council of People's Commissars] resolution on forming a Polish division by 1 July 1941 was invalidated by the Sikorski-Maisky agreement of 30 July, which normalized Polish-Soviet relations and included raising a Polish Army in the USSR (doc. 94).

· 93 ·

Excerpt from the Politburo Protocols on the Decision to Create
a Polish Division in the Red Army
4 June 1941, Moscow[178]

Top Secret
No. P33/183
From Special File[179]
Excerpt from the Protocol of the 33rd Session
of the Politburo TsK VKP(b)
To: Com. Timoshenko, Chadaev
Decision of 4 June 1941
[Point] 183—Question of the NKO [People's Commissariat of Defense]

Ratify the following resolution of the SNK USSR:
1. Ratify the resolution proposed by the Commissar of National Defense for establishing within the structure of the Red Army one rifle division made up of persons of Polish nationality and those who know the Polish language.
2. The establishment of the division is to be implemented by complementing by 1 July 1941 the 238th Infantry Division of the Central Asiatic Military Region with Poles and persons knowing the Polish language who are serving in Red Army units.[180]
3. The 238th Infantry Division is to be maintained at [the level of] 10,298 persons.

Secretary, Central Committee

Nazi Germany attacked the USSR on 22 June 1941, which led to a series of new alliances. After the signing of a British-Soviet agreement in London on 12 July 1941, followed by Soviet agreements with the exiled Czechoslovak and Yugoslav governments there, the British government pressed General Sikorski to conclude an agreement with the USSR. The negotiations, mediated by British Foreign Secretary Anthony Eden, were difficult because of the original Polish demand that the Soviet government recognize the prewar border, while Moscow spoke of an "ethnic" Poland. However, Sikorski wanted to raise a large Polish army in the USSR, so he worked out a compromise formula without clear-cut Soviet recognition of the prewar border. This led to a crisis in the Polish government, three of whose leading members resigned in protest (the deputy premier, General Kazimierz Sosnkowski; Foreign Minister August Zaleski; and Justice Minister Marian Seyda). Despite this, and despite the opposition of the president, Władysław Raczkiewicz, on 30 July 1941, Sikorski signed the agreement on behalf of the Polish government and Soviet Ambassador Ivan Maisky signed for the Soviet government.

· 94 ·

Polish-Soviet Agreement on Reestablishing Diplomatic Relations
and Forming a Polish Army in the USSR
30 July 1941, London

Agreement between the Soviet Government and the Polish Government

The Government of the Republic of Poland and the Government of the Union of Soviet Socialist Republics have concluded the present Agreement and decided as follows:

1. The Government of the Union of Soviet Socialist Republics recognizes that the Soviet-German treaties of 1939 relative to territorial changes in Poland have lost their validity.[181] The Government of the Republic of Poland declares that Poland is not bound by any Agreement with any third State directed against the USSR.[182]

2. Diplomatic relations will be restored between the two Governments upon the signature of this Agreement and an exchange of ambassadors will follow immediately.

3. The two Governments mutually undertake to render one another aid and support of all kinds in the present war against Hitlerite Germany.

4. The Government of the Union of Soviet Socialist Republics expresses its consent to the formation on the territory of the Union of Soviet Socialist Republics of a Polish Army under a commander appointed by the Government of the Republic of Poland, in agreement with the Government of the Union of Soviet Socialist Republics. The Polish Army on the territory of the Union of Soviet Socialist Republics will be subordinated in operational matters to the Supreme Command of the USSR on which there will be a representative of the Polish Army. All details as to command, organization, and employment of this force will be settled in a subsequent Agreement.[183]

5. This Agreement will come into force immediately upon its signature and without ratification. The present Agreement is drawn up in two copies, each of them in the Russian and Polish languages. Both texts have equal force.

Secret Protocol

1. Various claims both of public and private nature will be dealt with in the course of further negotiations between the two governments.

2. This protocol enters into force simultaneously with the Agreement of 30 July 1941.

Protocol

1. As soon as diplomatic relations are reestablished the Government of the Union of Soviet Socialist Republics will grant amnesty to all Polish citizens who are at present deprived of their freedom on the territory of the USSR either as prisoners of war or on other adequate grounds.

2. The present Protocol comes into force simultaneously with the Agreement of July 30, 1941.[184]

Władysław Sikorski   I. Maisky

The Polish-Soviet Military Agreement was the legal basis for the recruitment of the Polish Army in the USSR.

· 95 ·

Polish-Soviet Military Agreement
14 August 1941, Moscow

1. The military agreement derives naturally from the political agreement of 30 July 1941.

2. The Polish Army will be organized in the shortest possible time on the territory of the USSR, [wherefore]:

a) it will form part of the armed forces of the sovereign Republic of Poland;

b) the soldiers of this army will take the oath of allegiance to the Republic of Poland;

c) it is designated to take part, with the Armed Forces of the USSR and other Allied states, in the common fight against Germany;

d) after the end of the war, it will return to Poland;

e) during the entire period of common operations, it will be subordinated operationally to the High Command of the USSR. In respect of organization and personnel, it will remain under the authority of the commander in chief of the Polish Armed Forces, who will coordinate the orders and regulations concerning organization and personnel with the High Command of the USSR through the commander of the Polish Army on the territory of the USSR.

3. The commander of the Polish Army on the territory of the USSR will be appointed by the commander in chief of the Polish Armed Forces; the candidate for this appointment [is] to be approved by the Government of the USSR.[185]

4. The Polish Army on the territory of the USSR will consist of units of land forces only. Their strength and number will depend on manpower, equipment, and supplies available.[186]

5. Conscripts and volunteers, having previously served in the Polish Air Force and Navy, will be sent to Great Britain to complement the establishments of the respective Polish services existing there.

6. The formation of Polish units will be carried out in localities indicated by the High Command of the USSR.[187] Officers and other ranks will be called up from among Polish citizens on the territory of the USSR by conscription and voluntary enlistment. Draft boards will be established with the participation of USSR authorities in localities indicated by them.[188]

7. Polish units will be moved to the front only after they are fully ready for action. In principle, they will operate in groups not smaller than divisions and will be used in accordance with the operational plans of the High Command of the USSR.[189]

8. All soldiers of the Polish Army on the territory of the USSR will be subject to Polish military laws and decrees.

Polish military courts will be established in the units for dealing with military offenses and crimes against the establishment, the safety, the routine, or the discipline of the Polish Army.

For crimes against the State, soldiers of the Polish Army on the territory of the USSR will be answerable to the military courts of the USSR.

9. The organization and war equipment of the Polish units will as far as possible correspond to the standards established for the Polish Army in Great Britain.

The colors and insignia of the various services and military ranks will correspond exactly to those established for the Polish Army in Great Britain.

10. The pay, rations, maintenance, and other material problems will be in accordance with regulations of the USSR.

11. The sick and wounded soldiers of the Polish Army will receive treatment in hospitals and sanatoria on an equal basis with the soldiers of the USSR and be entitled to pensions and allowances.

12. Armament, equipment, uniforms, motor transport, etc., will be provided as far as possible by:

a) the Government of the USSR from their own resources[190]

b) the Polish Government from supplies granted on the basis of the Lend-Lease Act[191]

In this case, the Government of the USSR will extend all possible transportation facilities.

13. Expenditures connected with the organization, equipment, and maintenance of the Polish Army on the territory of the USSR will be met from credits provided by the Government of the USSR, to be refunded by the Polish Government after the end of the war.

This problem will be dealt with in a separate financial agreement.[192]

14. Liaison will be established by:

1) a Polish Military Mission attached to the High Command of the USSR.

2) a Soviet Military Mission attached to the Polish High Command in London.

Liaison officers attached to other commands will be appointed by mutual agreement.

15. All matters and details not covered by the agreement will be settled directly between the High Command of the Polish Army on the territory of the USSR and the corresponding authorities of the USSR.

16. This agreement is made in two copies, in the Polish and the Russian languages; both texts are equally valid.[193]

Plenipotentiary of the Polish High Command
[Zygmunt] Szyszko-Bohusz
Brigadier General

Plenipotentiary of the High Command of the USSR
A[leksandr] Vasilevsky
Major General

When released POWs began to arrive at the recruiting centers in Buzuluk, Tatischev, and Totskoe near Kuibyshev [Samara], it became clear that thousands of officers counted on by the commander in chief, General Władysław Anders, were missing, and the search for them began. Polish inquiries met with the assurance that all prisoners had been released. However, point 5 of the Administration for Prisoner-of-War and Internee Affairs (UPVI) report of 3 December 1941 revealed the truth—a truth that would not be admitted publicly until 1990.

The report printed below was prepared for Stalin on the day he was to meet with the Polish premier and commander in chief, General Władysław Sikorski (doc. 97).

· 96 ·

UPVI Report on Polish POWs in NKVD Camps, 1939–1941, with Attachment
3 December 1941, Kuibyshev

Top Secret
Note by Direct Line
For Com. Fedotov
Information on Former POWs of the Polish Army
Who Were Detained in NKVD Camps

1. Total former POWs captured by Red Army units and internees deported from the Baltic States   130,242 people[194]
2. [Those] released from camps and sent to the western oblasts of the UkSSR and BSSR in 1939   42,400 people[195]
3. Those who declared their willingness to leave for German-occupied territory in September and November 1939,

inhabitants of Polish territory taken
by Germany*   42,492 people[196]
4. Invalids [who were] residents of former
   Polish territory taken by Germany or
   individuals of German nationality
   [who were] handed over to the
   Germans in 1940–1941 and also
   those handed over at the request of
   the German Embassy in 1940–1941   562 people[197]
5. Sent to the disposition of the UNKVD in
   April–May 1940 through 1st Special
   [NKVD] Department   15,131 people[198]
6. Sent to formation centers for the Polish
   Army, September–October 1941   25,115 people
7. Those released but not drafted into the
   Polish Army due to illness or refusal
   to serve in it   289 people
8. Individuals of German nationality held
   in Aktiubinsk camp not drafted into
   the Polish Army   263 people
9. Those held in Aktiubinsk camp who were
   rejected by the Polish Army according to
   the documentation of the Special
   Department   2 people
10. Died in the camps during this time   389 people[199]
11. Escaped from the camps during all this time   [200]
12. Losses during the evacuation of Lvov camp   [201]
13. Left the camps for various reasons during
    this time (released after imprisonment, as
    invalids, released on order of the USSR
    NKVD, sent to nursing homes for the
    handicapped, released from the camp,
    and [then] arrested by operations organs)   [no number given]

> Head of the USSR NKVD Administration for Prisoner-of-War
> and Internee Affairs
> GB Captain (Soprunenko)

Began transmission: 9:15. Ended 9:45 [a.m.] Received. Maketov—secret
part.[202]

---

* Written in by hand over crossed-out text: "Handed over to the Germans in the course of
the exchange."

Sources of Information*
Information for point no. 2
　Report of 19 November 1939 (report file for 1939).
　Report of June 1941 (report file no. 45, p. 250).
Information for point no. 3
　See two attached reports of 24 November 1941.
Information for point no. 4
　See information under No. 25/10981 of 14 November 1940 (report file for 1940).
　Sixty [data] cards on those sent to the Germans from November 1940 to May 1941.
Information for point no. 5†
　See three attached reports on Starobelsk, Kozelsk, and Ostashkov camps.
Information for point no. 6
　See attached report.
Information for point no. 7
　See attached report.
Information for point no. 8
　See status memorandum from Aktiubinsk camp (263 people).
Information for point no. 9
　See status report from Aktiubinsk camp (2 people).
Information for point no. 10
　See notes in data book on dead Poles.
Information for point no. 11
　See card file of escaped Polish POWs.
Information for point no. 12
　See report on losses incurred during the evacuation of Lvov camp (see Lvov camp file no. 29, pages 579–593).
Information for point no. 13
　See materials in the alphabetical files.

The Polish premier and commander in chief, General Sikorski, arrived in Moscow on 2 December 1941, after flying to the USSR from London via Cairo and Tehran. He stopped earlier for two days in Kuibyshev, where most Soviet ministries, government offices, and the diplomatic corps had been located since their evacuation from the Soviet capital in October. His goals were to secure the release of thou-

* There are no attachments to the document as published in the Polish and Russian editions.
† Missing from the original document.

sands of Poles still held by the Soviets, especially the officers needed for the army, to improve Soviet provisioning of the Polish troops and their living conditions, and to help the civilian deportees. Stalin was well aware of the missing officers' fate (doc. 96) but could not tell Sikorski the truth. Sikorski's proposals on moving the Polish troops to a warmer climate were justified by the harsh Russian winter, but should be viewed also in the context of his own goal of moving them nearer Iran so they could be armed by the British, who also wanted them there. At the end of October, Churchill had requested Sikorski to secure Stalin's consent for moving the Polish Army to a location near the Iranian border. Indeed, Churchill wished to have some Polish troops stationed in Iran to replace Soviet troops there, or to be sent to the Middle East to supplement British forces. In early November 1941, President Roosevelt also requested of Stalin that Polish troops be moved to Iran. This Anglo-American pressure may explain Stalin's irritation at Sikorski's proposal to move the Polish troops there if they could not be supplied adequately by the Soviets. Stalin's agreement to increase the number of Polish troops to 96,000, along with the necessary food supplies, was due partly to Sikorski's willingness to leave most of them in the USSR, but was probably more an incentive for the Polish leaders to revise the interwar Polish-Soviet frontier in favor of the USSR, which he suggested to Sikorski at the Kremlin banquet the following day. At this time, the Germans were within striking distance of Moscow, but they were thrown back by General Georgy K. Zhukov a few days later.

The conversation between Stalin and Sikorski is given in full, even though there is only some mention of the missing Polish officers, because it is a record of the only substantial dialogue between the two men. It shows Stalin's bargaining technique and his mastery of military detail. It also throws light on the extreme weather conditions and privations endured by Polish troops in the Kuibyshev region at this time. (Polish names are given here with Polish spelling.)

· 97 ·

Conversation of Stalin and Molotov with General Władysław Sikorski,
Polish Premier; General Władysław Anders, Commander of the Polish Army
in the USSR; and Professor Stanisław Kot, Polish Ambassador to the USSR[203]
3 December 1941, Moscow

Top Secret
Record of Conversation between Com. I. V. Stalin and the Chairman of
the Polish Council of Ministers Władysław Sikorski

3 December 1941, at 1800 hours

Com. Stalin receives Sikorski in the presence of Com. V. M. Molotov.

After an exchange of mutual greetings, Sikorski, who arrived accompanied by Polish Ambassador Kot and the commander of Polish forces on USSR territory, General Anders, states that he has never been a supporter of the hostile policy toward the Soviet Union of certain circles in Poland. This gave him a moral right to sign the 30 July 1941 treaty with the USSR.[204] However, Sikorski would not like the slow implementation of the treaty to create difficulties for his [Stalin's] relations with the Poles.[205] He hopes that Com. Stalin will be of help in the implementation of this treaty so that minor shortcomings do not impede the development of Soviet-Polish relations. Sikorski is aware of the difficulties that the Soviet Union has had to endure while four-fifths of all Germany's land forces have been thrown into action against Russia. Sikorski was an advocate for the Soviet Union in London and America. Long ago he composed a memorandum urging the opening of a second front, which Com. Stalin spoke about in his own report of 6 November.[206] However, creating a second front is no easy matter. The creation of a second front must not lead to another Dakar.[207]

Unfortunately, some of the measures that were supposed to be implemented in the USSR in accordance with the Soviet-Polish treaty have yet to be implemented. Many Poles are still in prisons and camps, where they are losing their strength and health instead of serving our common cause. Sikorski and the Polish ambassador cannot produce exact lists of these individuals, but the heads of the concentration camps have these lists in their possession.

Com. Stalin replies that all Poles who were imprisoned have been released under the amnesty. A few of them may have run away somewhere before liberation, to Manchuria, for example.[208] I would like, says Com. Stalin, for Mr. Sikorski to enjoy full confidence that we do not have any intention of detaining even one Pole. We have released all of them, even those who came to the USSR with sabotage assignments from General Sosnkowski.[209]

Com. Molotov says that only those Poles convicted on criminal charges remain imprisoned.

Com. Stalin adds that early in the war we arrested several Poles whom the Germans had smuggled in with radios for purposes of espionage.[210] Indeed, the Polish government is not demanding their release.

Sikorski and Kot reply that the Polish government is not defending such individuals. However, Kot points out, many Polish patriots remain imprisoned.

Sikorski says that the publication of an appeal to Soviet officials and the Soviet population to treat the Poles better would bring great benefit.

Com. Stalin replies that the Soviet population does treat the Poles well.

Sikorski replies that he was witness in Kuibyshev to the sorry plight of one transport of Poles.[211] The population treats the Poles well, but the representatives of the local administration often treat them badly. The Polish government would like to divide the [civilian] Poles in the USSR into two groups. The first group would include those who can and should work. However, these people must work in their own trades. It is bad if a Polish tank specialist is forced to work as a woodcutter. There have been instances when outstanding Polish chemists have been doing physical labor. Many of these individuals could be left where they are settled, while others should be settled in regions with a warmer climate. They could work under the same conditions as Soviet citizens. The second group would include those who cannot work, that is, children, old people, and invalids. They require material assistance. In addition, representatives of the Polish Embassy must have the right to go where Poles have been assembled and render assistance to the Polish population there. The Polish Embassy would also like to have its own representative in Vladivostok to receive transports [of supplies] arriving for Poles from America.[212]

Com. Stalin replies that the amnesty in this country was universal. A few Poles released from the camps may not have been able to leave owing to transportation difficulties. At the present time there are no Poles in prisons, in camps, or in exile except for criminals or those linked with the Germans.

General Anders says that at the present time there are also unliberated Poles in the camps. Individuals who have been released from the camps come to see him all the time and tell him that many Poles remain in the camps.

Com. Molotov notes that if the Poles are coming to see him, then they have been released.

Anders says that the heads of the camps are gradually releasing Poles, and many Poles are still imprisoned. The problem is that releasing the Poles would undermine the work plans of the camp commanders.[213] Therefore, the camp commanders prefer not to release the Poles. Anders hands Com. Stalin a list of Poles who, according to his information, are still in the camps.[214]

Com. Stalin promises to look into this matter once more and to put the matter to rights. As for the question of giving [Soviet] officials instructions to treat the Poles better and the suggestion that Polish specialists be able to work in their own trades and professions, we will do this. We can also give agents of the Polish ambassador the opportunity to carry out the specified work with the Polish population. Com. Stalin directs Sikorski's attention to the difficulties of transportation for the Poles. Right now the Germans have occupied our regions with a more developed railway network. In the eastern regions of the Soviet Union, the railway network is less developed, and this creates difficulties in transporting Poles. Sikorski must realize that it is necessity rather than any ill will that is to blame for these difficulties. Now the situation will be improving gradually, since the evacuation period is over: the evacuation of seventy factories, including aircraft and machine-building plants, is complete.

Com. Molotov adds that at the present time a regulation concerning local representatives of the Polish Embassy is being worked out. This regulation is being coordinated between the Polish Embassy and the Narkomindel [People's Commissariat of Foreign Affairs].[215]

Kot says that those Poles who are being released in the Far East could be settled somewhere in the Altai region and not necessarily be transferred to southern regions.

Com. Stalin says that the region of Alma-Ata and the regions of southern Kazakhstan could be designated for the settlement of Poles.

Anders expresses his wish that the Poles be settled in the Fergana region [Farghona, Uzbekistan].

Com. Stalin explains that Fergana is a region where we import wheat; the land there is planted in cotton. Therefore, we need to stipulate the settlement of Poles in regions that produce ample grain.

Com. Stalin points on the map to those regions where the Poles could be settled.

Sikorski gives his consent to settling the Poles in these regions. Sikorski and Kot say that they want the Poles to help fight Germany, not die in vain in the north.

"We want the same thing," replies Com. Stalin. "We are in favor of friendship with the Poles and a joint struggle against Germany. Enough of all the hostility between the Poles and Russians! History dictates to us the necessity of an alliance of the Slavic nations."

Sikorski goes on to say that it would be desirable to obtain an assistance loan for the Polish population. According to Sikorski, 100 million rubles would fully satisfy the Polish government.

Com. Stalin replies that this can be done.[216]

Com. Stalin asks whether the Poles have any other questions regarding the Polish civilian population in the USSR and, receiving a negative answer, proposes moving on to survey military issues.

Sikorski states that the Poles want to conduct a real rather than a token war against the Germans.

"Where, in the colonies?" asks Com. Stalin.

Sikorski replies that the Polish Army wants to fight on the continent for the liberation of Poland. At the present time, Poles on German-occupied territory are engaged in anti-German sabotage. At the appropriate moment, there will be an uprising in Poland.[217] A million and a half Poles have been deported to Germany. The Polish government is in constant communication with them. These Poles have already created quite a bit of trouble for the Germans, for example, in the metallurgical industry in Westphalia. Moreover, the Poles have facilitated an outbreak of epidemics in Germany by spreading bacteria.[218] Sikorski is reporting this information in complete confidentiality. He has not even told Churchill about the spreading of bacteria, since the English are very sentimental and would not understand this.

Com. Stalin remarks jokingly that if Sikorski tried to tell the English about this, there would be a report about it in the English press the next day.

"Besides," says Sikorski, "we have a corps of our own troops in England."

"How many divisions?" asks Com. Stalin.

"One division, three brigades, and one officers' brigade," replies Sikorski. "There are many Polish officers in England but not enough soldiers. Moreover, we have nineteen air squadrons there."[219]

Com. Stalin asks how many planes there are in a Polish air squadron.

"Twenty-seven planes," replies Sikorski. "Polish pilots have fought well against the Germans, and 20 percent of all the planes knocked out by the English Air Force can be racked up to Polish pilots."[220] Sikorski emphasizes that he is speaking about these affairs as a military man and has no plans for making political use of this.

"When men fight well—that's the best politics," says Comrade Stalin.

Moreover, continues Sikorski, there is one independent Polish brigade in Tobruk.[221] After the liberation of Tobruk it will be transferred to Syria, where it will be motorized and acquire two tank battalions. The Polish government has several battleships in the Atlantic Ocean and the Mediterranean Sea.[222] The Polish government also has military units and large manpower reserves in the USSR. The Poles in the USSR are the sole manpower reserve of the Polish government. If the treaty with the USSR is properly implemented, then the Poles can form eight divisions in the USSR, in addition to supplemental units for corps and divisions. Polish troops in England will compose the vanguard of the English landing force in the event of the formation of a second front in Europe or else will be transferred to the USSR in order, together with the other Polish troops, to participate in the fight against Germany. In that case, Sikorski himself would come to the USSR to lead the Polish troops.

Sikorski expresses his concern over the fact that Polish divisions in the USSR are being formed under very difficult conditions that make it impossible to create a good army. The war could go on for a long time. As it unfolds, the moment nears when the Poles will be able to get a large quantity of military hardware from England and the United States. The English government has assured the Poles that they can get arms and food in England as long as the Polish troops are situated in proximity to English bases.

Anders says that his troops, about 40,000 men, are now in very difficult conditions. So far two divisions have been formed.

"How many artillery battalions do you have?" asks Com. Stalin.

[Anders:] "I have two battalions altogether, with one battery per regiment."

Com. Stalin says that the Poles started the war with the Germans with divisions of 15,000, which included two artillery regiments apiece: one cannon regiment and a howitzer regiment. Such a division proved unwieldy. The howitzers were left behind. [Now] the enemy has no fortifications, so there is less need for the howitzers. The division is lighter. Our military also believe that the division ought to be lighter, so right now our divisions do not have enough artillery. We are reinforcing our divisions with antitank artillery, mortars, and antitank rifles. In this way, the modern division has from 11,600 to 12,000 men.

Anders says he believes that Polish divisions need to be formed on the basis of the same calculation.

Sikorski says that at the present time they have armaments for one division in the USSR. The second division has not been armed. Moreover, the Polish divisions are situated in locations with a very severe climate. Right now it is 33 degrees below zero [Celsius], and the Polish soldiers have to live in tents.[223] Sikorski is worried that they will die without making any contribution to the war against Germany. He has spoken with Churchill about moving the camp somewhere else—for example, Iran—where these divisions could be completed and in four months return to the USSR, possibly accompanied by English troops, and be transferred to a specific sector of the German-Soviet front to fight alongside the Red Army.

Com. Stalin remarks that the army that goes to Iran will never come back.

"Why?" asks Sikorski.

"England has a lot of work to do on the fronts," says Com. Stalin.

"We have work to do here," replies Anders.

Com. Stalin says that later the English will say, "We equipped you; therefore you have to work for us."

Sikorski states that the Polish government disposes of its own army independently. It could return the troops that are transferred to Iran to the USSR and might add to them the brigade now in Tobruk.

Kot adds that the Poles fight better when they are closer to Poland.

"Iran is not close to Poland," says Com. Stalin.

Sikorski states that England today is not what it was when he, Sikorski, saw it in 1940. Now the English have a great number of troops.

Com. Molotov says that as he understands it, the difficulties of forming the units in the USSR make it necessary, in the opinion of the Polish government, to move the Polish troops from the USSR to Iran.

Anders replies in the affirmative and says that they have not received a single building fit for residence, nor lumber to build barracks. There are no stables. The horses are in very bad shape. They [Polish Army] can't build schools.[224] Food is supplied in inadequate quantities.

Sikorski states that he knows Churchill and is confident that he will not make difficulties over the issue of bringing Polish units back to the USSR from Iran. An agreement could be signed to this effect that Churchill, too, would sign.

Com. Stalin points out that we cannot force the Poles to fight. There can be no talk of a treaty. If the Poles don't want to [fight], then we will make do with our own divisions.

Com. Molotov asks what needs to be done in practical terms to improve conditions for the formation of Polish units.

Anders again refers to the cold, to the fact that he is not getting boards for construction, tractors for moving building materials, and so on.

"We aren't going to haggle!" says Com. Stalin. "If the Poles want to fight closer to their own territory, then let them stay with us. If they don't, we can't demand this of them. If it's to be Iran, then let it be Iran. Go ahead! I am sixty-two years old," continues Com. Stalin, "and I have the life experience that tells me that an army is going to fight wherever it is formed."

Sikorski says that they could form the army in Iran under better conditions than in the USSR.

"We won't make difficulties," says Com. Stalin.

Sikorski states that he is not posing this question as an ultimatum. Perhaps there is another region in the USSR where the Polish Army could be formed under better conditions. Unfortunately, it cannot be formed where it is now.

Com. Stalin replies that we do have different climatic zones, but that is not the point. After all, the Poles are not from warm countries either!

Anders replies that in Poland there is never the kind of freezing cold that there is in the USSR. Moreover, the Polish Army includes men from various regions of Poland, including southern regions. At the present time, the Polish Army is simply fighting to survive and not preparing to fight on the fronts.

Sikorski adds that if the Polish Army is not trained, then it will have a hard time fighting at the front. Sikorski says that he was a little stung by Com. Stalin's comment that the Poles don't want to fight.

"I am a bit crude and no diplomat," says Com. Stalin. "I'm putting the question bluntly: Do the Poles want to fight?"

"They do," replies Sikorski.

Com. Stalin points out that probably not all the Poles will go to Iran; some will stay behind.

Com. Molotov asks how the Poles who stay in the USSR will react to the fact that the Polish Army has gone to Iran.

Anders says that the Poles will return from Iran to fight the Germans. He, Anders, is firmly convinced that air and naval operations alone cannot lead to victory over Germany. The bayonet will take Berlin.

Com. Stalin says that the Poles can get armaments more quickly from us than from the English. "I know," says Com. Stalin, "what sea shipments mean."

Anders says that in the USSR the Poles could form an army of 150,000 men, which would mean eight divisions. The pilots would be sent to England to return to the Polish Army in the USSR with the planes. Moreover, there are another eight armored battalions, which at present are felling trees for the camps of the Polish Army.

Com. Stalin reminds the general that the Poles themselves refused to form air and armored units in the USSR.

Anders admits that he did not raise the issue of tanks and aviation during the [negotiations for the] conclusion of the military agreement.[225] He, Anders, by the way, thought it acceptable to shift the Polish armies to the south so that they could get their food via the auto route between Mashad [northeast Iran] and Ashkhabad [Ashgabat, southeast Turkmenistan, on the Iranian-Soviet frontier]. There are many drivers in the Polish Army who could serve in the motor columns.

Com. Stalin says that the Red Army divisions are well dressed and well fed. A large number of men from the south serve in them, but they are not complaining about the climate as the Poles are.

Anders replies that his divisions are not receiving the same [supplies] as Red Army units. They are not getting what they are supposed to. They have absolutely no potatoes, and they are not receiving any vegetables. There are great interruptions in the food supply in general. The soldiers are living in tents and dugouts. The stables are made out of brushwood.

"Do as you wish," says Com. Stalin. "If it's to be Iran, then let it be Iran."

Sikorski says that he did not wish to put the issue so harshly, but would prefer to find a solution in full accord with Com. Stalin.

"I understand," says Com. Stalin. "England needs the Polish troops. England is our ally, so go ahead!"

Sikorski says he is confident that not only Polish but also English divisions would come together from Iran to the USSR. Sikorski is ready to put this question to Churchill. Churchill has assured him that English units are ready to move to a sector of the Russian front. The Polish Army in England is in an independent position. If Sikorski wants to move the Polish troops here from England, he is confident that he could do so without any objections on the part of the English. Only a few Polish airmen in England would remain there, those who are in English units.

Com. Stalin says that he is not against Polish units fighting alongside English troops. Com. Stalin asks what will happen to the Soviet-Polish treaty if the Polish Army goes to Iran? This could not be concealed, and the treaty would collapse.

Anders says that the war against the Germans will continue anyway, so he doesn't see why the treaty should collapse.

"This is a platonic war," says Com. Stalin, and [he] points out that the Polish divisions in the USSR will be able to fight on the front in a month or two. "Right now there are two Polish divisions, a third can be formed, and then we will have a Polish corps."

Anders points out that he has many untrained soldiers.

"But you do have reservists," says Com. Stalin.

"Reservists make up 60 percent of my forces," replies Anders.

"You have 60 percent reservists and you have decided that nothing can be done. You weren't given boards and you think all is lost! We will take Poland and turn it over to you in half a year. We have enough troops, we can manage without you. But what will people say when they find out? And the Polish troops that will be in Iran are going to have to fight wherever the English want."

"Where will they have to fight?" asks Anders.

"Defend Turkey from the Germans," replies Com. Stalin. "Maybe the English will need troops in North Africa, or in half a year Japan will enter [the war] and then the Poles may be sent to Singapore."

"Organize a corps here," continues Com. Stalin, "so that people don't start laughing, and you can shift the rest to Iran. Do you want a place and supplies for seven divisions? If you want to send your troops to Iran, send them, but it would be good for you and for the common cause to form three divisions here. The rest you can send to Iran, if England needs troops. Before long, we ourselves are going to help it out with troops."

Sikorski says that the English are slow to act, but now they are not the same as before. If Com. Stalin can find a place to form Polish divisions in the USSR, then the issue of moving them does not have to be raised, other than transferring Poles to England to reinforce air units [there].

Summoned by Com. Stalin, Major General [Aleksei P.] Panfilov, the General Staff plenipotentiary for forming the Polish Army on the territory of the USSR, enters the study where the conversation is taking place.

Com. Stalin tells him the Poles are complaining that we are not feeding their soldiers, or giving them shoes or clothing, and are keeping them in the cold.

Com. Panfilov replies that the supplying of Polish units is proceeding normally and that recently they were also given stoves.

"Do our troops live any better?" asks Com. Stalin.

Com. Panfilov replies that our troops live no better. If the Polish troops are experiencing shortages in supplies, then General Anders is to blame for not informing Com. Panfilov of this. So far the Polish Army has been given food rations for 30,000, but the army has grown, and after a while they started being given more, but then the supply was cut back to 30,000.[226]

Com. Stalin says that after his conversation with the Polish ambassador the former supplies were restored. The same day he gave instructions to restore the former rate of supply.[227]

Anders points out that the former rate of supply for his troops was not restored.

"Why?" Com. Stalin asks Com. Panfilov.

Com. Panfilov replies that instructions to restore the former number of rations were given by General [Andrei V.] Khrulev.

"They need rations, not instructions," says Com. Stalin.

"Why have the rations been held up?" asks Com. Molotov.

"After all, men live on bread, not instructions!" adds Com. Stalin.

Sikorski says that he did not want to raise the question of taking his troops out of the USSR, but after he saw that their formation was proceeding under such difficult conditions, he raised the question.

Com. Stalin says that he is posing the question once again, honestly and bluntly: If it will be better for the Polish troops in Iran, then let them go to Iran. If the Polish troops want to form up and live in the same conditions as ours, then they can form three to five divisions. Our army has better uniforms and food than the German Army. The Red Army lives better than the German Army does. We can ensure that the Polish Army will have the same conditions as the Red Army.

Anders replies that if he got for his men and horses what they get in the Red Army, he would be quite satisfied.

"You will get that," Com. Stalin says.

Sikorski says a warmer place has to be found and [then] the Polish Army can be formed. His suggestion to move the troops to Iran was prompted only by his desire to get his army ready to fight as quickly as possible.

Com. Stalin says it seemed to him that the whole point was that the English needed troops.

"We want to fight on the continent," Anders declares. "We will stick the bayonet into Berlin."

Com. Stalin says the Russians have been in Berlin twice, and they will be there a third time.[228]

Anders replies that the Poles have never been in Berlin, but they have been at Grunwald.

Com. Stalin reminds him that the Battle of Grunwald took place in the fifteenth century.[229]

Anders confirms this and expresses admiration for Com. Stalin's memory.

Sikorski goes on to say that many Poles have been sent to Uzbekistan to form new units, but the conditions there are difficult.[230]

Com. Stalin instructs Major General Panfilov to find barracks for the Polish troops. This will require closing several schools.

Anders says that the Poles can form eight divisions, plus the corps and auxiliary troops, for a total of 150,000 men.

Com. Stalin asks Anders whether he is not being overly enthusiastic: 150,000 is a very large number. Maybe such a number of Poles want to join the army, but not all of them may want to fight. Maybe some want to join the army just to get fed. They reason thus: "The war will probably be over before we get moved to the front, and in the meantime we will be sure to get fed."

Sikorski says that there may be men like that, but most likely they are Jews.

Com. Stalin says Jews aren't the only ones who can reason like this. As far as Jews are concerned, they are poor fighters.

Anders says he had some Jews who were only in the army to get fed, but they have already run away: 350 of them ran away after [hearing of] an air raid on Kuibyshev, which did not take place.[231]

Com. Stalin asks what armaments Polish troops have been given in the USSR.

Com. Panfilov hands Com. Stalin a list of what Polish troops in the USSR have and have not received. Essentially everything has been provided, Com. Panfilov says. They received more mortars, shells, and grenade throwers than warranted by the size of their military organization. The Poles had no antitank or antiaircraft artillery except for four cannon.

Sikorski asks Com. Stalin about the new locations for the formation of the Polish Army.

Com. Stalin asks whether the Poles would object to forming the army in several locations.

On receiving a negative reply, Com. Stalin points out that Central Asia —Uzbekistan, maybe Turkmenistan, and maybe Transcaucasia—could serve as locations.[232]

Sikorski asks how many divisions can be raised.

Com. Stalin points out that the Red Army does not have corps in it anymore. We have found corps command levels to be a hindrance, so now our divisions are only grouped in armies. Com. Stalin asks whether the Poles want to raise seven divisions. We can equip them just like the Red Army. We will equip them partly on our own and partly they will be [equipped by] the English and the Americans.

Anders says they can raise an army without corps formations.

Sikorski states he will take measures to obtain armaments from America and England.

Com. Stalin remarks that sea transportation is rather difficult, and convoys can be late. Much can happen at sea.

Sikorski says the Poles will form seven divisions. They will transfer their airmen to England. Sikorski asks whether the Soviet Union needs airmen.

Com. Stalin says we are now on a par with the Germans with respect to their air force on our front. In some places we have superiority. Our aircraft are not bad. We are short of tanks.

Sikorski says that a large part of the German Air Force has been shifted to Africa.

"That could be," Com. Stalin replies. "We can tell that the German Air Force is now weaker. Their pilots are bad and their planes somewhat old. The Germans have no fighter planes that can go 580 kilometers an hour or bombers with speeds over 500 kilometers per hour. Their famous Junkers plane can only go 460 kilometers per hour. Moreover, the Germans have very little cannon power on their aircraft."

Sikorski says that he, too, considers the Soviet Air Force very strong.

You cannot compare the air defenses of Moscow and London. Moscow is much better protected than London and the damage in Moscow is minor.

Com. Stalin says that the English are good pilots. They fought well at Murmansk, where they had their fighter planes. "The English pilots are great boys," Com. Stalin says.[233]

Sikorski praises Soviet pilots. They are famous for their skill and courage.

Com. Stalin says he believes the Slavs are the bravest of all European peoples. Besides this, they are quick to learn everything. They are young nations, not yet worn out by life in the slums.

Anders says the Slavs are not like the French.

Com. Stalin says the French are a good people, but their rulers have been bad. The French are a capable people. The Germans have managed to make the Slavs their enemies. The Slavs are going to beat the Germans. This is not what Hitler wanted.

Sikorski says this is also his view.

Sikorski then says he would like to visit the places where Polish troops are forming, also where Poles are concentrated in the USSR, and then fly back to Moscow for a concluding conversation with Com. Stalin.

"I am at your service," replies Com. Stalin.[234]

Sikorski expresses his desire to go on the air tomorrow and broadcast a declaration on behalf of the governments of all the occupied countries. He gave the text of the declaration to Com. Vyshinsky in Kuibyshev.

Com. Stalin replies that he has read the declaration and that it would be very good for Sikorski to read it over the radio.

Sikorski asks for London to be informed of the time of the broadcast so that the declaration can be transmitted from there in other languages.

Com. Stalin says the declaration will be translated in Moscow into twenty-four languages and broadcast from Moscow.[235]

Sikorski hands Com. Stalin a written draft of the Soviet-Polish declaration. Com. Stalin can decide whether or not such a declaration is needed. Sikorski believes this declaration will make a favorable impression on America.

Com. Stalin takes the draft declaration and promises to read it and give his comments tomorrow.[236]

In conclusion, Com. Stalin and Sikorski agree that General Anders and General Panfilov will meet tomorrow to discuss the details of the formation of Polish units.[237]

The conversation took place in the study of Comrade V. M. Molotov in the [building of the] USSR SNK, lasted two hours and thirty minutes, and was conducted in the Polish language. General Anders translated.

Recorded by Podtserob[238]

The background to General Anders's conversation with Stalin in Moscow, 18 March 1942, was a drastic reduction of food rations for the Polish Army. In February and March 1942, Soviet military authorities put increasing pressure on Anders to send the 5th Polish Division, which was almost ready, to the front. He refused, citing the poor physical condition of the men—indeed, many had malaria and typhoid fever—but mainly he refused because both he and General Sikorski wanted the army to fight as a unit. His refusal led to the reduction in food allocations. The reduction also may have been intended to press Sikorski to discuss the postwar Soviet-Polish frontier with Stalin, for at this time the Soviet media consistently gave Polish towns Soviet names, terminology protested by the Polish government. When Anders sent a telegram to Stalin protesting the food reduction, Stalin invited the general to see him in Moscow. At this meeting, Anders suggested that part of the army be transferred to Iran, and Stalin agreed.

The Polish record of the conversation is much longer than Molotov's message to Aleksandr Bogomolov, Soviet ambassador to the Allied governments in London. It contains Anders's question about the missing Polish officers and his plan to fly to London to see General Sikorski. Stalin answered that he did not know the whereabouts of the officers, but said, "We have traces of their stay in Kolyma," which suggests that the known rumors to this effect may have been spread among Polish survivors by the NKVD. Stalin also said, "It may be that they are in camps in territories taken by the Germans and have dispersed there," which was the first time that such a Soviet suggestion was made. He promised to give Anders a plane to fly to Cairo on his way to London, where he was to confer with Sikorski.

· 98 ·

Molotov's Telegram to the Soviet Ambassador in London,
Aleksandr Bogomolov, on Stalin's Conversation with Anders
21 March 1942, Moscow[239]

Outgoing No. 1141
Top Secret
Making of copies prohibited.
Received 1615 hrs., 21 March 1942.
Sent 1930 hrs., 21 March 1942.
Special no. 52
Copy no. 1
Cipher Telegram [to] Soviet Ambassador Bogomolov, London

On 18 March, Com. Stalin, in my presence, received General Anders, who had requested an audience in connection with the decision that as of 21 March the Polish Army in the USSR, numbering about 70,000, would receive food rations for only 40,000.[240] Com. Stalin stated that during the September conference in Moscow, the United States and England undertook the obligation to supply the USSR with 200,000 tons of wheat per month. However, up to the present, only 60,000 tons have been supplied.[241] The cause of this non-implementation of the supply plan is the outbreak of war in the Pacific Ocean.[242] The resulting, unforeseen food deficit forces us, in view of the need to supply combatant troops at the expense of the noncombatants, not only to reduce the number of food rations for the Polish Army but also to limit the formation of some new units for the Red Army.

In the course of the conversation, Com. Stalin agreed to [the following]:

1. Food rations will be supplied for up to the existing number [of men] to the end of March, and from April, rations for 44,000 will be supplied.[243]

2. [Of] the Polish Army, over 44,000 will be transferred to Iran, as proposed by Anders.

3. Of the three Polish divisions formed in the USSR, the USSR will arm two and the English one.

4. If the Polish Army, after forming and arming in Iran, is sent to the Soviet-German front, the USSR will ensure its food supplies.

Com. Stalin emphasized that we are not pressing the Poles to go to the front. The Poles can also come in when the Red Army reaches the frontiers of Poland.

Anders informed [us] that he is flying to London in the first days of April.

I communicate [this to you] for your information.

Molotov
Distributed to: Com. Stalin, Com. Molotov, Com. Vyshinsky. 3 copies.

Pursuant to the Stalin-Anders conversation, part of the Polish Army, together with some civilians, was evacuated to Iran at the end of March and in early April 1942. They went by rail to the port of Krasnovodsk (now Turkmenbashi) and then sailed in cargo ships across the Caspian Sea to the port of Pahlavi, now Bandar-e Anzali, Iran.

· 99 ·

Beria's Note to Stalin on the Polish Army's Evacuation to Iran[244]
4 April 1942, Moscow

Top Secret
No. 583/b
Copy no. 1

To the State Committee on Defense
Com. Stalin

In fulfilling the government directive, the evacuation of some contingents of military servicemen of the Polish Army and [other] Polish citizens was completed on 3 April this year.

42,254 persons were sent from Krasnovodsk to Pahlavi, including 30,099 Polish military [personnel] and 12,155 Polish citizens [civilians].[245]

147 sick persons remained in the hospital in Krasnovodsk.

In the course of the evacuation, there were no disruptions in bringing up railway cars, ships, nor with food and sanitary service.[246]

People's Commissar of Internal Affairs USSR
L. Beria

Distributed to: Com. Stalin, Com. Molotov

At the end of April, General Anders flew to London via Tehran and Cairo, where he met with Churchill and high-level British military officers. In London he met with Sikorski and other members of the Polish government. When he returned to Polish Army headquarters at Yangi-Yul (Tashkent district, Uzbekistan), Anders found rations reduced again, a malaria epidemic, and increased NKVD interference.

Concluding that most of the people would die if they stayed in the USSR, he decided to evacuate the whole army to Iran. He did so despite Sikorski's order to leave part of it in USSR "for reasons of high politics," that is, good Polish-Soviet relations, and to enter Poland together with the Red Army. However, in May–June, when German victories threatened Egypt, Churchill pressed for the transfer of the Polish divisions to the Middle East. Anders telegraphed Stalin on 31 July, thanking him for approving the plan to move the Polish Army to Iran and appealing for renewed conscription in the USSR to supplement its number. There was, however, no further recruitment.

· 100 ·

Telegram from Mikhail Koptelov, Consul General of the USSR in Pahlavi,
to Stalin on the Completion of the Polish Army's Evacuation from the USSR[247]
5 September 1942, Pahlavi, Iran

Cipher Telegram
Top Secret
Making copies prohibited
No. 18105
Special no. 52

[To] Moscow, copy Tehran

The evacuation of Poles from the [Soviet] Union ended on 1 September 1942.

A total of 69, 917 persons arrived at Pahlavi. Among them [were]:
1. military—41,103 persons
2. civilians—28,814 persons

By 4 September 1942, 34,985 persons were transported from Pahlavi [to Tehran], of these:
1. military—25,424 persons
2. civilian—9,561 persons

In the last few days, the departures from Pahlavi were intensified, and on average from 1,300 up to 1,600 persons departed daily. An increase in transportation is expected in order to accelerate the transfer of Poles from Pahlavi. Up to 4 September, 239 persons died of various diseases. The following epidemic diseases were noted: 2 cases of typhus and 29 cases of typhoid fever. People suffer most of all from malaria and colitis.[248]

> 5 September 1941
> Koptelov

Distribution: Stalin, Molotov, Voroshilov, Kaganovich, Mikoyan, Beria, Vyshinsky, Dekanozov, Lozovsky, and Sobolev

In summer 1942, Polish workers employed by the German labor organization Todt (named after its head, Fritz Todt) were working in the Koze Gory [German: Kosogory] area near Smolensk. They heard from local Russians about mass Polish graves in nearby Katyn Forest, found some military items, and placed two wooden crosses there. Lieutenant (later Colonel) Friedrich Ahrens, commander of the 537th Signals Regiment of German Army Group Center (AGC), stationed in the NKVD dacha adjacent to Katyn Forest, allegedly heard of wolf tracks and human bones there, and ordered some digging. A mass grave was discovered, and Ahrens reported this to the AGC headquarters. On 29 March the AGC command ordered the graves to be opened and the number of victims and the circumstances of their deaths to be determined. On 10–11 April a delegation including Polish intellectuals from German Poland visited Katyn and, on their return, radioed a report via the Home Army to the Polish government in London. On 11–12 April the first German report was broadcast from Berlin, but it was the Berlin radio broadcast on 13 April about the discovery of graves containing the corpses of thousands of Polish officers and pointing the finger at the USSR that was picked up by world media.

· 101 ·

Radio Communiqué on the Discovery of Graves of Polish Officers
in the Smolensk Area
13 April 1943, Berlin, 9:15 a.m.[249]

It is reported from Smolensk that the local population has indicated to the German authorities a place in which the Bolsheviks had secretly perpetrated mass executions and where the GPU had murdered 10,000 Polish officers.[250] The German authorities inspected the place called Kosogory, which is a Soviet summer resting place [resort], situated 16 kilometers west of Smolensk, and made the most horrific discovery. A great pit was found, 28 meters long and 16 meters wide, filled with twelve layers of bodies of Polish officers, numbering about 3,000.[251] They were clad in full military uniform, and while some of them had their hands tied, all of them had wounds in the back of their skull caused by pistol shots. The identification of the bodies will not cause great difficulties, because of the mummifying property of the soil and because the Bolsheviks had left on the bodies the identity documents of the victims. It has already been ascertained that among the murdered is General Smorawiński from Lublin. These officers had been previously in Kozielsk [Kozelsk], near Orel,[252] from whence they had been brought in cattle wagons to Smolensk in February and March 1940 and, further on, taken in lorries to Kosogory, where all were murdered by the Bolsheviks.[253]

The discovery of and search for further grave pits is taking place. Under layers dug up already, new layers are found. The total figure of the murdered officers is estimated at 10,000, which would more or less correspond to the entire number of Polish officers taken as POWs by the Bolsheviks. Norwegian press correspondents who arrived to inspect the place, and with their own eyes could ascertain the truth, have reported about the crime to the Oslo newspapers.

The Soviet government promptly denied responsibility and accused the Germans of carrying out the massacre. This was repeated in all official Soviet statements on Katyn until 13 April 1990.

· 102 ·

Communiqué Issued by the Sovinformburo Attacking the German "Fabrications" about the Graves of Polish Officers in Katyn Forest[254]
15 April 1943, Moscow

Vile Fabrications by German-Fascist Murderers

In the past two or three days Goebbels's slanderers have been spreading vile fabrications alleging that Soviet authorities effected a mass shooting of Polish officers in the spring of 1940, in the Smolensk area. In launching this monstrous invention, the German-Fascist scoundrels do not hesitate at the most unscrupulous and base lies in their attempt to cover up crimes which, as has now become evident, were perpetrated by themselves.

The German-Fascist reports on this subject leave no doubt as to the tragic fate of the former Polish POWs who in 1941 were engaged in construction work in areas west of Smolensk and who, along with many Soviet people, residents of the Smolensk region, fell into the hands of the German-Fascist hangmen in the summer of 1941, after the withdrawal of Soviet troops from the Smolensk area.[255]

Beyond doubt Goebbels's slanderers are now trying by lies and calumnies to cover up the bloody crimes of the Hitlerite gangsters. In their clumsily concocted fabrication about the numerous graves which the Germans allegedly discovered near Smolensk, the Hitlerite liars mention the village of Gnezdovaya. But, like the swindlers they are, they are silent about the fact that it was near the village Gnezdovaya that the archaeological excavations of the historic "Gnezdovaya burial place" were made.[256]

Past masters in such affairs, the Hitlerites stoop to the clumsiest forgeries and misrepresentation of facts in spreading slanderous fabrications about some sort of Soviet atrocities allegedly perpetrated in the spring of 1940 and, in this way, try to shake off their own responsibility for the brutal crimes they have committed.

These arrant German-Fascist murders [murderers], whose hands are stained with the blood of hundreds of thousands of innocent victims, who methodically exterminate the populations of countries they have occupied without sparing children, women, or old people, who exterminated many hundreds of thousands of Polish citizens in Poland itself, will deceive no one by their base lies and slander.

The Hitlerite murderers will not escape a just and inevitable retribution for their bloody crimes.

The German radio announcement on the Katyn graves led to outrage in German Poland, whence the accounts of the first Poles to visit the site were radioed by the Home Army Command to the Polish government in London. There was also outrage in the Polish Army in the Middle East, which had come out of the USSR. Its commander, General Anders, demanded that the Polish government obtain an official Soviet explanation of the Katyn graves. When Churchill warned Sikorski on 15 April 1943 against raising the Katyn issue publicly, the general replied that the Polish government was forced to take a stand. The Polish defense minister, General Marian Kukiel, issued a long statement on 16 April detailing all the inquiries that had been made of the Soviet government about the missing officers and stating the Polish government had approached the International Red Cross to investigate the massacre. The formal statement on this matter, designed to balance the Kukiel statement by emphasizing German crimes, was issued by the Polish government the next day, 17 April, when it also made a formal request to the IRC in Geneva.

· 103 ·

Statement of the Polish Government Concerning the Discovery
of the Graves of Polish Officers near Smolensk
17 April 1943, London

No Pole can help but be deeply shocked by the news, now given the
widest publicity by the Germans, of the discovery of the bodies of Polish
officers missing in the USSR in a common grave near Smolensk, and of the
mass execution of which they were victims.

The Polish government has instructed their representatives in Switzerland to request the IRC in Geneva to send a delegation to investigate the
true state of affairs on the spot. It is to be desired that the findings of this
protective institution, which is to be entrusted with the task of clarifying
the matter and of establishing responsibility, should be issued without delay.

At the same time, however, the Polish government, on behalf of the Polish nation, denies to the Germans any right to base on a crime they ascribe
to others, arguments in their own defense. The profoundly hypocritical indignation of German propaganda will not succeed in concealing from the
world the many cruel and reiterated crimes still being perpetrated against
the Polish people.

The Polish government recalls such facts as the removal of Polish officers from prisoner-of-war camps in the Reich and the subsequent shooting
of them for political offenses alleged to have been committed before the
war; mass arrests of reserve officers subsequently deported to concentration camps, to die a slow death—from Kraków and the neighboring district alone, 6,000 were deported in June 1942; the compulsory enlistment
in the German Army of Polish prisoners of war from territories illegally incorporated in the Reich; the forcible conscription of about 200,000 Poles
from the same territories, and the execution of families of those who managed to escape; the massacre of one and a half million people by executions or in concentration camps; the recent imprisonment of 80,000 people of military age, officers and men, and their torture and murder in the
camps of Maydanek and Tremblinka [Treblinka].[257]

It is not to enable the Germans to make impudent claims and pose as the
defenders of Christianity and European civilization that Poland is making
immense sacrifices, fighting, and enduring suffering. The blood of Polish
soldiers and Polish citizens, wherever it is shed, cries for atonement before
the conscience of the free peoples of the world. The Polish government
condemn[s] all the crimes committed against Polish citizens and refuse[s]
the right to make political capital of such sacrifices, to all who are themselves guilty of such crimes.

Stalin had been planning to break off relations with the Polish government for some time before late April 1943. On the eve of the German surrender at Stalingrad (31 January 1943), he told the pro-Soviet Polish communist Wanda Wasilewska that he expected Polish-Soviet relations to break down. She agreed with his view that a new Polish authority should be established in the USSR—which she had advocated for some time—and that a newspaper called *Wolna Polska* [Free Poland] would appear by 1 March. Stalin suggested both the name of the newspaper and the name of the new Polish organization: Związek Patriotów Polskich w ZSSR [ZPP—Union of Polish Patriots in the USSR]. Thus, when the Polish government in London requested the IRC to conduct an investigation of the Katyn massacre and the German Red Cross made the same (formal) request on the same day, Stalin used this as a pretext to break off relations with the Polish government and accused it of collaborating with the Germans. (For the meeting between Polish Ambassador Tadeusz Romer and Molotov on 25 April 1943, see the introduction to Part III.)

· 104 ·

Note from Molotov to Polish Ambassador Tadeusz Romer on the Soviet Government's Decision to Break Off Relations with the Polish Government[258]
25 April 1943, Moscow

Note of the Soviet Government to the Polish Government

Mr. Ambassador,

On behalf of the Government of the Union of Soviet Socialist Republics, I have the honor to notify the Polish Government of the following:

The Soviet Government considers the recent behavior of the Polish Government with regard to the USSR as entirely abnormal, and violating all regulations and standards of relations between two Allied States. The slanderous campaign hostile to the Soviet Union launched by the German Fascists in connection with the murder of the Polish officers, which they themselves committed in the Smolensk area on territory occupied by German troops, was at once taken up by the Polish Government and is being fanned in every way by the Polish official press.

Far from offering a rebuff to the vile Fascist slander of the USSR, the Polish Government did not even find it necessary to address to the Soviet Government any inquiry or request for an explanation on this subject.[259]

Having committed a monstrous crime against the Polish officers, the Hitlerite authorities are now staging a farcical investigation, and for this they have made use of certain Polish pro-Fascist elements whom they themselves selected in occupied Poland, where everything is under Hitler's heel, and where no honest Pole can openly have his say.[260]

For the "investigation," both the Polish Government and the Hitlerite Government invited the IRC, which is compelled, in conditions of a terroristic régime, with its gallows and mass extermination of the peaceful population, to take part in this investigation farce staged by Hitler. Clearly such an "investigation," staged behind the back of the Soviet Government, cannot evoke the confidence of people possessing any degree of honesty.[261]

The fact that the hostile campaign against the Soviet Union commenced simultaneously in the German and Polish press, and was conducted along the same lines, leaves no doubt as to the existence of contact and accord in carrying out this hostile campaign between the enemy of the Allies—Hitler—and the Polish Government.[262]

While the peoples of the Soviet Union, bleeding profusely in a hard struggle against Hitlerite Germany, are straining every effort for the defeat of the common enemy of the Russian and Polish peoples and of all freedom-loving democratic countries, the Polish Government, to please Hitler's tyranny, has dealt a treacherous blow to the Soviet Union.

The Soviet Government is aware that this hostile campaign against the Soviet Union is being undertaken by the Polish Government in order to exert pressure upon the Soviet Government by making use of the slanderous Hitlerite fake for the purpose of wresting from it territorial concessions at the expense of the Soviet Ukraine, Soviet Belorussia, and Soviet Lithuania.[263]

All these circumstances compel the Soviet Government to recognize that the present Government of Poland, having slid on the path of accord with Hitler's Government, has actually discontinued allied relations with the USSR, and has adopted a hostile attitude toward the Soviet Union.

On the strength of the above, the Soviet Government has decided to sever relations with the Polish Government.

By the time the Soviet government broke off relations with the Polish government in London, exhumations were already proceeding at Katyn. Extracts from the report of Kazimierz Skarżyński, general secretary of the Polish Red Cross in the Generalgouvernement (that is, in German-occupied Poland), record the first PRC group visit to Katyn in mid-April and its refusal to serve German propaganda purposes.

· 105a ·

Report by the Secretary of the Polish Red Cross, Kazimierz Skarżyński,
on the PRC Technical Commission's Visit to Smolensk and Katyn,
15–16 April 1943 (Excerpts)[264]
June 1943, Warsaw

The Introductory Period

On 9 April 1943 the president of the Polish Red Cross in the home
country under German occupation, Mr. Wacław Lachert,[265] was informed on the telephone by Dr. Heinrich, the delegate of the German Generalgouvernement to the Polish Red Cross,[266] that he must come at once
to a conference at the Brühl Palace.[267] The president refused, on principle,
to come immediately, saying he could come in an hour's time, but was told
that this would be too late, so the conference contents would be communicated to him. And, indeed, Dr. Heinrich telephoned the same day at
1800 hrs. [6 p.m.] that a decision was made at the conference to send a
delegation to the Smolensk region to see the graves of Polish officers murdered by the Bolshevik authorities; he mentioned that writers, representatives of the Principal Welfare Council,[268] the Municipal Administration,
and others were to participate in the delegation, saying that a place had
been reserved for the PRC president on the plane due to depart for
Smolensk at 8 a.m. the next day. The president refused to take part personally in the delegation, as well as in the name of the other members of
the Presidium of the PRC Executive Board, because of the obvious propaganda character of the whole venture. . . .

At first, the PRC Executive Board, basing itself on the experience of the
nearly four-year-long German occupation and German bestiality, reacted
with great suspicion to all information on Katyn coming from German
sources. . . .

On 12 April the PRC Executive Board received a report from the writer
Ferdynand Goetel, about his visit to Katyn. He said that he had seen the
mass graves and that all indications were that the officers had been murdered in the period March–April 1940. His account, and those of other
members of this first group, disposed of the suspicion that the Germans
had had a hand in the murder.[269] On the morning of 14 April, Dr. [Karl]
Grundman, from the Warsaw District [German] Propaganda Department, came personally to the PRC office and issued an oral invitation for
a five-man PRC delegation to fly to Smolensk at 1300 hrs [1 p.m.] the
same day. At the same time, he indicated that on the same plane, leaving
Kraków in the morning, were the plenipotentiary of the PRC Executive

for the Kraków district, Mr. [Stanisław] Plappert, his deputy Mr. [Adam] Szebesta, and representatives of the clergy nominated by the Prince Metropolitan.[270] The PRC Executive Board decided that it was advisable to send a Technical Commission, free of any propaganda character, to Smolensk and nominated four persons, who were to stay at the site if necessary; also Mr. Skarżyński, secretary and member of the PRC Executive Board. . . .

During [this board] meeting, I dictated [the decision] by telephone to Dr. Grundman for communication to the Kraków [PRC] authorities, with the reservation that I would not serve German propaganda and policy goals.

[On 14 April] at 1300 hours [1 p.m.] I went to the [Warsaw] Okęcie airport with the appointed members of the Technical Commission, Messrs. L. [Ludwik] Rojkiewicz, J. [Jerzy] Wodzinowski, S. [Stefan] Kołodziejski, and Dr. [Hugon] Bartoszewski. We flew off to Smolensk at 1500 hrs. [3 p.m.] . . . The PRC group was joined by Father [Stanisław] Jasiński, sent by the Prince Metropolitan of Kraków—as it turned out, only to bless the corpses—and Dr. [Tadeusz Susz] Pragłowski from Kraków.[271] . . . Aside from these two, there were in the plane Mr. Zenzinger from the Kraków [German] Propaganda Department, who was the official leader of the delegation; three Germans from the Berlin criminal police, allegedly sent to study illegible documents found on the corpses; and three suspicious-looking young Poles in the German service, of whom one was an ordinary film operator.

After arriving in Smolensk on 15 April, I was able to affirm that the care of and direction of work on the officers' graves was in the hands of the local [German Army] propaganda company (Aktivpropagandakompanie), [headed by] Lieutenant Slovenzik. This unit, led by front-line officers (the lieutenant mentioned above and his deputy, 2nd Lieutenant von Arndt), possessed the general characteristics of a military mentality while at the same time having the specific character of the military agency of Mr. Goebbels's office, with a clearly National Socialist [Nazi] attitude. This obliged us to be especially careful in dealing with them. . . .

The next day, 16 April, we arrived at the site at 9 a.m. The Kozie Góry Wood [Russian: Koze Gory] stands a few meters from the road.[272] On the clearing between the graves lay the corpses of our officers that had been exhumed thus far, and large Red Cross flags were spread out above the graves.[273] There was no doubt whatever that we were dealing with a mass execution carried out by an experienced executioner's hand. All the corpses that I saw had an entry wound from a revolver bullet at the base of the skull and an exit wound on the forehead or face. The uniform character of the wounds and the direction of the shots indicate that they were made from small arms at the smallest possible distance from the officers, who were standing up. Some of the corpses had their arms tied behind their backs with strong rope. These were probably men who defended themselves. Polish uniforms, badges, decorations, regimental insignia, overcoats, trousers, and boots were well preserved despite contact with the earth and decomposition. Lower down, deep in the excavated pits, there were more layers of corpses, and one could see skulls, legs, hands, and backs sticking out of the tightly pressed earth. What was striking was the significant percentage of higher ranks (majors, lt. colonels, colonels) among the corpses. I also viewed the corpses of two generals identified as General Smorawiński and General Bohatyrewicz [Bohaterewicz].[274] Generals' insignia and stripes on the trousers confirm their rank. I think that between the older pines, small, self-planted pine trees had grown at the site since the time of the murder, which apparently indicates that the executions must have taken place in spring 1940. It is said that a professional forester affirmed the same age for the small pines from their roots. I did not see the small pines that grew over the graves, for these were already open.[275] As for the number of corpses in the common graves, I had the impression that the 10[,000]–12,000 figure given out by German officers was greatly exaggerated. . . .

In the little hut containing the office, the documents found on the corpses are inspected and sorted. The more interesting ones are exhibited in glass cases. We acquainted ourselves with some of the documents and diaries, all of which break off in the first days of April 1940.[276] After a courteous conversation with Professor Buhtz, a criminologist from Wrocław [Breslau],[277] we left for Smolensk. At the last minute, I was again asked to speak into the [radio] microphone, and I refused again. To the request that I might give at least a private account of my impressions, I replied that I was leaving deeply shaken by what I had seen, and that on this occasion I must express my full respect for the honest and methodical work of the [German] army at the graves. . . .

[Skarżyński left three members of the PRC delegation at Katyn. On the morning of 17 April, on his return to Warsaw, he reported to the PRC Executive Board. At the same meeting, on the basis of his report, the PRC Executive Board decided to declare that it was ready to begin work at Katyń and awaited written permission of the German authorities—given orally by a representative of the Generalgouvernement at a meeting in Kraków on 22 April. After the PRC board meeting on 17 April, Skarżyński had to give a report on his trip that same day to Heinrich and Grundman, but refused their demand that he grant press interviews or write a letter to be published in the press. An extract of the protocol of the PRC board meeting was sent to Heinrich, who had angrily demanded an official report.]

Around noon the same day [17 April], in the office of the director of one of the Warsaw banks, I made an oral report on my trip to the commissioner of civilian warfare, attached to the underground office of the delegate of the Polish government.[278]

[The PRC Executive Board sent a summary report to the IRC in Geneva, which was acknowledged by the IRC president, Max Hubert, on 22 April 1943.][279]

On the basis of Skarżyński's report, a second, larger group, called the PRC Technical Commission, went to Katyn to join the three original members, left there in mid-April, in the work of identifying the exhumed bodies. The second group arrived on 19 April and was joined by new members on 27–28 April, making a total of twelve, though not all were there the whole time. The commission worked until 7 June 1943, the stop date decreed by German authorities three days earlier because of the heat. The other reason was, of course, Soviet air attacks on Smolensk and its vicinity.

· 105b ·

Report of the Polish Red Cross Technical Commission on Its Work
in Katyn, April–June 1943 (Excerpts)[280]
June 1943, Warsaw

The commission, provisionally consisting of three persons, began work on 17 April; the work was divided as follows:
1) Mr. Ludwik Rojkiewicz—examination of documents in the Secretariat of the [German] Field Police.
2) Messrs. Stefan Kołodziejski and [Dr.] Jerzy Wodzinowski—the search for and securing of documents [found] on the corpses in Katyn Wood.

However, on that day work was interrupted by the arrival of a delegation of Polish officers held in German prisoner-of-war camps.[281]

... The work was divided [among the commission members] as follows:

a) one member [to be present] at the exhumation of the corpses

b) two members at the searching of the corpses and removal of documents

c) one member at the verification of the successive number of corpses, [which were] then carried to the new, coterminous grave

d) one member at the new burial of the corpses

e) two to three members at the reading of the documents

f) From 28 April, i.e., from the moment of the arrival of more commission members ... Dr. Wodziński, with the help of laboratory workers from the Kraków Prosektorium [Dissecting Room], carried out detailed inspections of those corpses which could not be identified from documents [found on them].[282]

The further course of the work was as follows:

a) digging up the corpses and bringing them to the surface

b) extracting documents

c) inspection of unidentified corpses by a doctor

d) burial of corpses

Every day, the work lasted from 8 a.m. to 6 p.m., with an hour and a half break for dinner.

The commission affirms that the extraction of the corpses was very difficult because they were tightly pressed together [and] thrown chaotically into the pits. Some had their hands tied behind their backs, some had their coats taken off and thrown over their heads; at the same time, the coat was tied around the neck with a rope and the hands were also tied behind the back, and this rope was tied to the one pulling the coat around the neck. Corpses tied up in this way were found mainly in one special pit filled with subsoil water, from which the commission members themselves extracted forty-six victims. Given the onerous conditions of this work, the German military authorities wanted to fill in this grave.

In just one pit, 600 corpses were found placed face down in equal rows.

The lack of an adequate number of [special] gloves caused great difficulty. . . . The extraction of the corpses was carried out by local inhabitants, rounded up to do the work by the German authorities. The corpses, carried out of the pits on stretchers, were placed sequentially alongside each other, and the procedure for finding documents was for two workers to search each corpse individually in the presence of one PRC Commission member. The workers cut open all the pockets, took out the contents, and handed all the items found to the commission member. Both the documents and [other] objects were placed in envelopes marked with the sequential number, and the same number, engraved on a small metal plate, was attached to the corpse. In order to carry out a more rigorous search for documents, even underwear and boots were cut open. If no documents or memorabilia were found, monograms—if present—were cut out from the clothes or underwear. . . .

[These items were put in envelopes and taken to the German Field Police Office (Secretariat), where the contents were inspected, with PRC members present. Names and contents were written down by a German officer in German, preserving the number if given earlier to the corpse, so the PRC Commission did not give these envelopes new numbers. Corpses that could not be identified were marked "unknown." Some documents were taken by the Germans for translation into German.]

After writing down the contents of each envelope on a sheet of paper, the documents and [other] objects were placed in a new envelope marked with the same number and listing its contents. This was done by the Germans. The inspected, segregated, and numbered envelopes were then placed sequentially in [wooden] chests. . . .[283]

The total number of exhumed corpses was 4,241,[284] and they were re-buried in six new coterminous graves dug near the murder pits. An exception was made for the two generals, who now lie in separate, individual graves. The terrain on both sides of the [new] coterminous graves is low-lying and wet, but the graves themselves are located in an elevated, dry, sandy place. The size and depth of some of the graves is not uniform owing to the features of the terrain and the technical difficulties that arose during the work. The bottoms of the [new] graves are completely dry, and each one, depending on its size and depth, contains several rows of corpses, with several layers in every row. The upper layers were placed at a depth of at least one meter below the terrain, so that after filling in the graves up to at least one meter above the surrounding terrain, the upper layers are covered with two meters of earth. All the [new] graves are flat in shape but have a uniform height and are framed with sod on the sides. A cross of planed wood two and a half meters high was placed on each grave, with a few forest flowers planted at the foot of each. On the surface of each grave, there is a large cross made of sod. The graves were numbered in the [same] sequence as they were filled in, with the aim of retaining the number sequence of the buried corpses. The corpses are placed with their heads to the east, one alongside the other, with the heads a little higher, and the arms folded on the chest. Each layer of corpses so arranged was covered with earth up to 20–30 centimeters high. In graves I, II, III, and IV the corpses were arranged beginning from the right-hand side because they were carried into the graves from the left-hand side. A list of numbers for corpses buried in each grave is attached to this report, as is the layout of the cemetery, which occupies an area of 60 by 36—i.e., 2,160 square meters. . . .[285]

In summing up the above, the commission states that:

1) The corpses taken out of the pits were in a state of decomposition so that [physical] identification was impossible. However, the uniforms were in quite good condition, especially all metal parts, such as rank insignia, medals, eagles, buttons, etc.

2) The cause of death was a shot directed at the base of the skull.

3) From documents found on the corpses, it is evident that the murders took place in the period from the end of March to the beginning of May 1940.[286]

4) The work at Katyn took place under the constant supervision of German authorities, who attached sentries to each group of commission members working there.

5) All the work was done by members of the PRC Technical Commission, German authorities, and inhabitants of adjoining villages, numbering twenty–thirty persons per day. Bolshevik POWs, also sent in the number of fifty per day, were employed solely in digging and then filling in the coterminous graves and in planting the terrain.

6) In general, work conditions were very difficult and nervously exhausting. The decomposing bodies and the air polluted by them created a very difficult atmosphere for the work.

7) The frequent arrival of various delegations, daily visits to the area by significant numbers of [German] military, the dissection of corpses carried out by German doctors and members of visiting delegations, complicated work that was already difficult enough. . . .

From the bullets extracted from the corpses of the officers and from the cartridge cases found in the sand, it can be affirmed that the shots came from small arms of 7.65-mm caliber. They seem to be of German origin. Fearing that the Bolsheviks might utilize this fact, the German authorities did all they could to see to it that no bullet or cartridge case was hidden by the PRC Commission members. This order was naive and its execution impossible. In any case, trusted NKVD officials carrying out the Katyn murder could have had small arms of all kinds of origin.[287]

As of now, the PRC Executive Board has not yet received from Dr. Wodziński the full results of examining the corpses at Katyn.[288] From his report, made after the extraction of the first 1,700 corpses, it is evident that despite the rotting decomposition, which led, owing to the sandy-clay nature of the terrain, to the partial mummification of the upper layers of corpses, and in the deeper layers to the so-called fat-wax transformation, in 98 percent of cases it was possible to ascertain that the shots entered the region of the base of the skull, exiting in the forehead, top of the skull, or face; in 5 percent of cases, there was a repeat shot into the base of the skull, and in 1.5 percent a shot or shots in the neck. It seems very likely that the final figures will not diverge much from the above. Worthy of note will be data on the number of corpses with hands and necks tied with rope, and the number stabbed to death with bayonets.[289]

The PRC Technical Commission's report mentions only in passing that its members exhumed forty-six corpses with their own hands from a water-filled pit. This was a pit that I saw myself when I was in Katyn. It was part of the lower edge of one of the seven large grave pits, which seemed to descend terrace-like down to the low-lying terrain. It was filled with brown, subsoil water, from which parts of corpses stuck out. The Germans promised to supply pumps for the exhumation, but it [the grave] stayed untouched until the last days of work. One day Mr. Wodzinowski ascertained that Russian workers began to fill in the pit. He stopped this work at once and learned from Lieutenant Slovenzik that the [German] Army could not supply the pumps because of constant Soviet air attacks and the permanent fire watch ordered for the whole region, while the workers could not be required to carry out this kind of exhumation. At that moment, five PRC Commission members headed by Mr. Wodzinowski went down into the pit and, in eighteen hours of work, extracted the corpses of forty-six Polish officers from the water.[290]

In dutifully emphasizing this handsome deed of our commission members, I will, in concluding the report on the PRC participation in the exhumation work at Katyn, cite a sentence from the speech by the president of the PRC Main Executive Board at a meeting with the representatives of Polish society in Warsaw, on 14 May 1943:

> The history of Poland is marked by graves
> but there has never been a grave like this . . .

Kazimierz Skarżyński
Warsaw, June 1943

The Red Army liberated Smolensk from the Germans on 25 September 1943. The Soviet Special State Commission that investigated the massacre in January 1944 was named after its chairman, academician Nikolai Burdenko, the chief surgeon of the Red Army and an expert in brain operations. The commission members met first in Moscow and then worked at Katyn on 18–23 January 1944. Medical experts examined 925 corpses, then drafted their report, stating that before the German capture of Smolensk, there were three special camps named "No. 1—ON, No. 2—ON, and No. 3—ON," all of which were located—they said—25 kilometers west of Smolensk. The total number of victims was given as 11,000 and the conclusion was that the Germans had murdered the Polish officers in July–September 1941 (the time was later changed to fall 1941). Among other things, the commission report accused the Germans of "preparing" the graves by removing all documents dated after April 1940.

In fact, a special NKVD group worked on the graves between September 1943 and early January 1944. They prepared the corpses for examination, "finding" some letters and other documents allegedly dated after spring 1940, and "inspired" local Russians to testify as witnesses before the Burdenko Commission, which simply confirmed all the information and conclusions contained in the Merkulov-Kruglov report.

Burdenko allegedly admitted just before his death in 1946 that, as a doctor, he knew the graves were four years old, which would date them to 1940, and that he believed the NKVD had made a great blunder.

· 106 ·

The Burdenko Commission Report (Excerpts)[291]
24 January 1944, Moscow

Statement of the Forensic Medical Appraisal

By order of the Special Commission created to establish and investigate the circumstances surrounding the shooting of Polish prisoner-of-war officers by the German-Fascist aggressors in the Katyn Forest (near the city of Smolensk), an expert forensic medical commission . . . , during the period from 16 to 23 January 1944, conducted an exhumation and forensic medical examination of the corpses of the Polish POWs buried in graves on the territory of Koze Gory in the Katyn Forest, 15 kilometers from the city of Smolensk. The corpses of the Polish POWs had been buried in a common grave measuring approximately 60 × 60 × 3 meters and, in addition, in a separate grave measuring approximately 7 × 6 × 3.5 meters.[292] Exhumed and examined from the graves were 925 corpses.

The exhumation and forensic medical examination of the corpses was performed in order to establish:

a) the identities of the deceased;

b) the causes of death;

c) how long ago they were buried.

For the circumstances of the case, see materials of the Special Commission [not included].

For the objective facts, see the depositions from the forensic medical examinations of the corpses. . . .

Conclusion

The expert forensic medical commission, basing itself on the results of the forensic medical examination of the corpses, has arrived at the following conclusion.

Upon uncovering the graves and extracting the corpses from them, the following was established:

a) among the corpses of Polish POWs there are corpses in civilian dress, but their number compared to the total number of corpses investigated is negligible (2 of 925 extracted corpses), and the corpses were wearing military-style boots;

b) the clothing on the corpses of the POWs attests that they belonged to the officer and partially to the rank-and-file contingent of the Polish Army;[293]

c) the slits in the pockets and boots discovered during examination of the clothing, as well as the pockets turned inside out and torn, show that all the clothing on each corpse (overcoat, pants, and felt boots), as a rule, bears the traces of a search having been performed on the corpses;

d) in some instances, during the examination of the clothing the intact-ness of pockets was noted. In these pockets, as well as in the slit and torn pockets, under the lining of the tunics, in the trouser waistbands, and in the foot bindings and socks, torn out pages were found from newspapers, brochures, prayer books, postal stamps, open and closed letters, receipts, notes, and other documents, as well as valuables (gold bullion, gold dol-lars), pipes, penknives, cigarette papers, handkerchiefs et al.;[294]

e) in some of the documents (even without special research), upon ex-amination, dates were established that pertained to the period from 12 November 1940 to 20 June 1941;[295]

f) the fabric of the clothing, especially of the overcoats, tunics, trousers, and overshirts, was well preserved and was very difficult to tear with the hands;

g) a very small number of the corpses (20 of 925) had their hands tied behind their torsos with white braided cord.[296]

The condition of the clothing on the corpses—specifically, the fact that the tunics, shirts, belts, trousers, and long underwear were buttoned, the boots were on, the scarves and ties were tied around the necks, the braces were fastened, and the shirts were tucked into the trousers—attests that no external examination of the torsos and extremities of the corpses had been made previously.

The state of preservation of the skin coverings on the head and the ab-sence on them, as well as on the coverings of the chest and belly (except for 3 cases out of 925), of any kind of incisions, slits, or other signs of expert activity indicate that no forensic medical examination of the corpses was ever done, judging by the corpses exhumed by the expert forensic medical commission.

External and internal examinations of the 925 corpses provide grounds for asserting the presence of bullet wounds to the head and neck, in four cases combined with injury to the skull with a blunt, hard, heavy object. Moreover, in an insignificant number of cases, injury to the belly was dis-covered that was simultaneous [with injury] to the head wound.

Entry wounds for firearm injuries, as a rule, are singular, more rarely double, and located in the nape area of the head close to the occiput, [that is,] the large occipital opening, or at its edge. In a small number of cases, the bullet entry wounds are found on the rear surface of the neck, corre-sponding to cervical vertebrae 1, 2, and 3.

Exit wounds were usually found in the frontal area, more rarely in the occipital and temporal areas, as well as on the face and neck. In twenty-seven cases, the bullet wounds proved blind (without exit wounds), and at the end of the bullet trajectories, under the soft coverings of the skull, in its bones, in the brain membranes and matter, deformed, weakly deformed, and completely non-deformed cased bullets, the kind used in shooting automatic pistols, primarily 7.65-mm, were found.

The sizes of the entry wounds on the occipital bone permit the conclusion that two calibers of firearms were used in the executions: in the overwhelming majority of cases, smaller than 8-mm, that is, 7.65-mm or less; in a lesser number, larger than 8-mm, that is, 9-mm.

The nature of the fissures in the cranial bones and the discovery in a few cases of powder traces near the entry wound suggest that the shots were fired at point-blank or nearly point-blank range.

The relative positions of the entry and exit wounds show that the shots were fired from behind while the head was bowed forward. In the process, the bullet passed through or close to vitally important sections of the brain, and the destruction of brain tissue was the cause of death.

Injuries to the parietal bones of the cranium made with a blunt, hard, heavy object were concurrent with the bullet wounds to the head but were not in and of themselves the cause of death.

Forensic medical examination of the corpses performed during the period from 16 to 23 January 1944 attests that there were absolutely no corpses in a state of rotting disintegration or destruction.[297] All the 925 corpses are in a state of preservation—in the initial stage of moisture loss by the corpse (which was expressed most often and acutely in the area of the chest and belly, sometimes also in the extremities); that is, the initial stage of *adipocere* [or] an acute degree of adipocere in corpses taken from the bottom of the graves), [or] a combination of dehydration of the corpses' tissues and the formation of adipocere.[298]

Worthy of special attention is the circumstance that the muscles of the torsos and extremities completely preserved their macroscopic structure and almost their usual color; the internal organs of the chest and abdominal cavities retained their configuration; in many cases, sections of the heart muscle showed a clearly distinguishable structure and its normal coloration, and the brain presented the characteristic structural features with a distinctly expressed boundary between gray and white matter. Besides the macroscopic examination of the tissues and organs of the corpses, the expert forensic medical analysis removed the appropriate material for subsequent microscopic and chemical research under laboratory conditions.

The qualities of the soil at the place of their discovery had definite significance in the preservation of the tissues and organs of the corpses.

Upon the opening of the graves and the removal of the corpses and their exposure to the air, they were subjected to the effect of warmth and humidity in the spring–summer period of 1943. This may have caused the acute development in the process of decomposition of the corpses.

However, the degree of desiccation of the corpses and the formation of adipocere in them, the particularly good state of preservation of the muscles and internal organs, as well as of the clothing, give us grounds to assert that the corpses had been in the soil for a brief time.

Comparing the condition of the corpses in the graves on the territory of Koze Gory with the condition of corpses in other places of burial in the city of Smolensk and its closest environs—in Gedeonovka, Magalenshchina, Readovka, camp no. 126, Krasny Bor, etc. (see the report of expert forensic medical analysis dated 22 October 1943)[299]—we can properly say that the burial of the corpses of the Polish POWs on the territory of Koze Gory was carried out approximately two years ago. This finds full confirmation in the discovery in the clothing on the corpses of documents that exclude earlier dates of burial (see point "d" under Article 36 and the list of documents).[300]

On the basis of the data and research results, the expert forensic medical commission:

considers the act of killing by means of execution of POWs and officers and some rank and file of the Polish Army to be an established fact;

asserts that this execution pertains to a period of time approximately two years ago, that is between September and December 1941;

sees in the fact of the discovery by the expert forensic medical commission in the corpses' clothing of valuables and documents with the date 1941 as proof that the German-Fascist authorities who undertook a search of the corpses in the spring-to-summer period of 1943 did not perform it carefully, and the discovered documents attest that the execution was carried out after June 1941;

concludes that in 1943 the Germans dug up an extremely insignificant number of corpses of executed Polish POWs;[301]

notes the full identity between the method of execution of the Polish POWs and the method of execution of peaceful Soviet citizens and Soviet POWs that was widely practiced by the German-Fascist authorities on the temporarily occupied territory of the USSR, including in the cities of Smolensk, Orel, Kharkov, Krasnodar, and Voronezh.

Chief Forensic Medicine Expert of the USSR Narkomzdrav
[People's Commissariat of Health] [and] Director of the State
Scientific Research Institute of Forensic Medicine of the USSR
Narkomzdrav
V. I. Prozorovsky

Professor of Forensic Medicine of the 2nd Moscow State
Medical Institute and Doctor of Medical Sciences
V. M. Smolianinov

Professor of Pathological Anatomy and Doctor of Medical
Sciences
D. N. Vyropaev

Senior Research Associate of the Forensic Medicine Department
of the State Scientific Research Institute of Forensic Medicine of
the USSR Narkomzdrav
Doctor P. S. Semenovsky

Senior Research Associate in the Forensic Chemical Department
of the State Scientific Research Institute of Forensic Medicine of
the USSR Narkomzdrav [and] Senior Lecturer
M. D. Shvaikova

Smolensk, 24 January 1944

Documents Found on the Corpses

In addition to the facts recorded in the certificate of expert forensic
medical analysis, the time of the execution by the Germans of the Polish
officer POWs (fall 1941, and not spring 1940, as the Germans assert) is established also by the documents discovered when the graves were opened,
documents that pertain not only to the second half of 1940 but also to the
spring and summer (March–June) of 1941. [Polish names are given here
with Polish spelling.—AMC]

Of the documents discovered by the forensic medical experts, the following merit special attention:

1. On corpse no. 92:

A letter from Warsaw addressed to the Red Cross at the Central Prisoner-of-War Bureau, 12 Kuibyshev Street, Moscow. The letter is written in
the Russian language. In this letter, Zofia Zygoń asks to be informed of the
place of arrival of her husband Tomasz Zygoń. The letter is dated 12 September 1940. On the envelope there is a German postal stamp—"Warsaw, September 1940"—and a postmark, "Moscow, Post Office, Dispatch Office 9, 28 September 1940," and an instruction in red ink in the
Russian language: "Request to establish the camp and direct for delivery.
15 November 1940" (signature illegible).[302]

2. On corpse no. 4:

A postcard, registered no. 0112, from Tarnopol with the postmark
"Tarnopol, 12 November 1940."

A manuscript text and a faded address.

3. On corpse no. 101:

Receipt no. 10293, dated 19 December 1939, issued by Kozelsk camp upon receipt of a gold watch from Edward Lewandowski. On the reverse of the receipt there is a notation dated 14 March 1941 on the sale of this watch to Glaviuvelirtorg [Main Jewelry Trade Commission].

4. On corpse no. 46:

A receipt (no. illegible), issued on 16 December 1939 by Starobelsk camp upon receipt of a gold watch from Włodzimierz Araszkiewicz. On the reverse of the receipt there is a note dated 25 March 1941 about the watch being sold to Glaviuvelirtorg.

5. On corpse no. 71:

A paper icon depicting Christ, discovered between pages 144 and 145 of a Catholic prayer book. On the reverse of the icon there is an inscription on which there is a legible signature, "Jadwiga," and a date, "4 April 1941."

6. On corpse no. 46:

A receipt dated 6 April 1941, issued by Camp no. 1—ON, on the receipt from Araszkiewicz of money in the amount of 225 rubles.

7. On the same corpse no. 46:

A receipt dated 5 May 1941, issued by Camp no. 1—ON, on the receipt from Araszkiewicz of money in the amount of 102 rubles.

8. On corpse no. 101:

A receipt dated 18 May 1941, issued by Camp no. 1—ON, on the receipt from E. Lewandowski of money in the amount of 175 rubles.

9. On corpse 53:

An unsent postcard in the Polish language addressed to: Irena Kuczyńska, 15 Bagatela, Apt. 47, Warsaw. Dated 20 June 1941. Sender, Stanisław Kuczyński.[303]

General Conclusions

From all the materials at the disposal of the Special Commission, specifically, the testimony above of the hundred witnesses it questioned,[304] the data from the expert forensic medical analysis, and the documents and material proofs taken from the graves in the Katyn Forest, the following conclusions emerge with incontrovertible clarity:

1. The Polish POWs who were in the three camps to the west of Smolensk and engaged in road construction operations before the beginning of the war remained there after the German occupiers invaded Smolensk and until September 1941, inclusively.[305]

2. In the Katyn Forest, in the fall of 1941, the German occupational authorities carried out mass executions of Polish POWs from the above-indicated camps.

3. The mass executions of Polish POWs in the Katyn Forest were carried out by the German military institution, which was concealed under the conventional designation "Headquarters of the 537th Construction Battalion," at the head of which stood Oberleutnant Arnes [Ahrens] and his associates Oberleutnant Reks [Rekst] and Lieutenant Khott [Hodt].[306]

4. In connection with the deterioration of the general military and political situation for Germany by early 1943, the German occupational authorities, for purposes of provocation, undertook several measures intended to ascribe their own evil deeds to organs of Soviet power, calculating that this would sow strife between Russians and Poles.

5. For these purposes:

a) the German-Fascist aggressors, by means of persuasion, bribery, threats, and barbaric tortures, sought "witnesses" from among the Soviet citizens from whom they obtained false testimony on the Polish POWs allegedly having been executed by organs of Soviet power in spring 1940;[307]

b) the German occupational authorities in spring 1943 brought from other places the corpses of Polish POWs whom they had executed and laid them in the graves dug in the Katyn Forest, calculating that this would conceal the traces of their own evil deeds and increase the number of "victims of Bolshevik brutalities" in the Katyn Forest;[308]

c) while preparing for their provocation, the German occupational authorities, for the work of digging up the graves in the Katyn Forest and removing their documents and material proofs that exposed them, employed as many as 500 Russian POWs, who upon completion of this work were executed by the Germans.[309]

6. The facts of the expert forensic medical analysis establish without any doubt:

a) the time of the execution—fall 1941;

b) the use by the German executioners in the execution of the Polish POWs of the same method—a pistol shot to the nape of the neck—that they used in their mass murders of Soviet citizens in other cities, in particular in Oryol [Orel], Voronezh, Krasnodar, and the same in Smolensk.[310]

7. The conclusions from witness testimony and the expert forensic medical analysis on the execution by the Germans of Polish POWs in fall 1941 are wholly confirmed by the material proofs and documents removed from the Katyn graves.

8. In executing the Polish POWs in the Katyn Forest, the German-Fascist aggressors were consistently implementing their own policy of physically destroying the Slavic peoples.

> [Here are repeated the names of the commission members signed above.]
> Smolensk, 24 January 1944

The Soviet delegation to the International Military Tribunal trials of war criminals at Nuremberg charged the Germans with murdering the Polish officers at Katyn. Moscow assumed that the Burdenko Commission report would suffice as proof, because Article 21 of the IMT Charter stated that the tribunal would take note of official government documents and reports of the United Nations, including acts and documents of commissions set up to investigate various crimes. Indeed, Soviet Deputy Prosecutor Yuri Pokrovsky read the Burdenko Commission's "Certificate of Forensic Medical Appraisal" and conclusions at the session of 14 February 1946. This report was presented as USSR Document-054.

The Western prosecutors rejected the Soviet claim that the report was sufficient proof of German guilt. The IMT admitted the request of Hermann Goering's defender, Dr. Otto Stahmer, to call German witnesses for the defense but also the chief Soviet prosecutor's request to admit witnesses for the prosecution. At that point, the Soviet Special Government Commission for Directing the Nuremberg Trials sent instructions to the Soviet prosecutor at Nuremberg, Roman Rudenko.

· 107 ·

Instructions on the "Katyn Matter" Sent by the Special Government
Commission for Directing the Nuremberg Trials to Roman Rudenko,
Chief Soviet Prosecutor at Nuremberg
15 March 1946, Moscow

In connection with the decision of the tribunal of 12 March, a letter should be sent to the tribunal with the following content:

On 12 March, the tribunal approved the petition of the defender of the accused Gering [Goering], Dr. Stahmer, on calling witnesses to refute the accusation that the Germans committed the mass murder of prisoner-of-war Polish officers in the Katyn Forest near Smolensk in September 1941.[311]

The Soviet prosecutor confirmed the accusation mentioned above by presenting the report of the Special Government Commission for Establishing and Investigating the Circumstances of the Shooting of Polish Prisoner-of-War Officers by the German-Fascist Aggressors in Katyn Forest.[312]

According to Art. 21 of the Charter of the IMT, "The Tribunal shall also accept without evidence official government documents and reports of the United Nations, including acts and documents of committees created in various allied countries to investigate war crimes."

The above-mentioned decision of the tribunal [March 12] represents a direct violation of this article of the charter.

By allowing the contention of evidence that is considered incontrovertible under Art. 21, the tribunal exceeds its authority, since the charter represents a mandatory law for the tribunal.

Only the four governments by whose agreement the tribunal's charter was passed are competent to make changes in it.

Allowing the defense the possibility of presenting evidence to repudiate evidence considered indisputable in Art. 21 deprives this article of any meaning. It is obvious that in this case the prosecution will be forced to present other evidence in confirmation of evidence mentioned in Art. 21, whereas the entire intent of this article is that the documents of governmental organs and the United Nations stipulated in it are to be accepted by the tribunal without evidence.

This question has fundamental significance for the entire trial, for the tribunal's decision of 12 March constitutes an extremely dangerous precedent, since it gives the defense an opportunity to prolong the trial indefinitely through attempts to repudiate evidence considered indisputable according to Art. 21.

Regardless of the considerations of principle set out above, which have a fundamental and decisive significance for this question, it is also impossible to pass over in silence the fact that the tribunal considered it possible to call as witnesses such individuals as Arnes, Rekst, Khott[313] et al., who, as is evident from the report presented to the tribunal, are the direct perpetrators of the evil deeds committed by the Germans in Katyn and [who], according to the declaration by the heads of the three governments of 1 November 1943, must be tried for their crimes by a court of the country on whose territory these crimes were committed.[314]

As a consequence of what has been set out above, I believe it essential to insist on the reexamination of the above-mentioned tribunal decision because it directly violates the charter of the IMT.

Rudenko must conduct preliminary discussions with the other prosecutors, stressing the fundamental significance of the procedural violation allowed by the tribunal and the possibility of the defense using the tribunal's decision of 12 March as a precedent, which could seriously affect the entire further course of the trial. It would be best if we could have the letter adduced above sent to the tribunal in the name of the committee of prosecutors.[315] If we cannot get this, it would be desirable to secure the support of at least some of the prosecutors.

If the tribunal still leaves the former decision in force, Rudenko will have to declare to the tribunal that the Soviet prosecution [had] limited itself to the publication of only some of the conclusions from the report of the Special Commission, since this evidence is indisputable according to Art. 21 of the charter.

Inasmuch as the tribunal has a different point of view, the Soviet prosecution will be compelled, on the basis of Art. 24, point "e," of the charter:[316]

1. To request that the tribunal attach to the case the entire decision [report] of the Special Commission and

2. To present, for its part, to the tribunal additional lists of witnesses and experts whose questioning will be essential under the conditions created as a result of the decision taken by the tribunal.

If Lourens[317] asks whom the Soviet prosecution intends to call and when the prosecution will present a list of its witnesses and experts, Rudenko must respond that he is compiling information on the whereabouts of individuals subject to questioning and, upon receipt of such information, will immediately present the list to the tribunal.

Clarify in detail and report the attitudes toward the case of those named in Stahmer's statement: Major General Oberhäuser and First Lieutenant Berg.[318]

Confirm receipt.[319]

After the Allied prosecutors at Nuremberg agreed that each side would present only three witnesses, it was decided in Moscow on 24 May that three witnesses would be presented for the Soviet side, with nominations for two supplementary ones.

· 108 ·

Meeting of the Soviet Special Government Commission
for Directing the Nuremberg Trials
24 May 1946, Moscow

2625v Secret
Protocol no. [not given] of the Meeting of the Commission
for Directing the Nuremberg Trials

Present: Coms. A. Ya. Vyshinsky, S. N. Kruglov, I. G. Goliakov, N. M. Rychkov, G. N. Safonov, L. N. Smirnov, P. I. Bogoyavlensky, L. P. Sheinin, and A. N. Trainin

I. [They] heard:

About the preparation and selection of materials on the case of the German provocation in Katyn.

[They] decided:

1. To charge the commission consisting of Coms. Raikhman (summoner) [authorized to call the others together], Sheinin, and A. N. Trainin with [the task of] familiarizing themselves in a period of five days with all the materials in hand about the German provocation at Katyn and to select those documents, which can be used at the Nuremberg trial to uncover the German provocation at Katyn.

2. That it was appropriate to nominate as witnesses in the Katyn case the following persons:

a) Metropolitan Nikolai

b) Bazilevsky

c) Koleznikov (ROKK)[320]

To charge the commission (par. 1) to nominate two supplementary witnesses.

At the same time, to charge the same commission to secure the summoning of all the witnesses to Moscow and to agree with Coms. Gorshenin and Rudenko regarding the possible date of the witnesses' arrival in Nuremberg.

II. [They] heard:

The draft of Com. Nikitchenko's letter to the members of the IMT about speeding up the conduct of the Nuremberg Trials procedure.[321]

[They] decided:

1. That it was appropriate to send Com. Nikitchenko's letter to the members of the IMT at Nuremberg.

2. To agree to the text of the letter with corrections in par. 3 and 5 [letter not enclosed].

> Chairman of the Meeting
> A. Vyshinsky
>
> Secretary
> M. Gribanov

11 copies

The Madden Committee—so known after its chairman, Ray Madden, a Democratic congressman from Illinois—gathered an enormous amount of information from witnesses in the United States and Europe. It subpoenaed prominent American officials active during the war, trying to prove they had willfully suppressed information on

Katyn. This they denied—but argued that publicizing the Katyn massacre was against the national interest in wartime. The committee issued its final report in December 1952, placing the blame squarely on the Soviet Union and requesting a trial before an international tribunal. The U.S. government, however, declined to press for such a trial because it needed Soviet support to end the Korean War. (For details, see the introduction to Part III.)

· 109 ·

Conclusions of the Congressional Select Committee to Conduct
an Investigation of the Katyn Forest Massacre (Excerpts)[322]
22 December 1952, Washington, D.C.

This Committee unanimously finds, beyond any question of reasonable doubt, that the Soviet NKVD (People's Commissariat of Internal Affairs) committed the mass murders of the Polish officers and intellectual leaders in the Katyn Forest near Smolensk, Russia.

The evidence, testimony, records, and exhibits recorded by this committee in the last nine months, will overwhelmingly show the people of the world that Russia is directly responsible for the Katyn massacre. Throughout our entire proceedings, there has not been a scintilla of proof or even any remote circumstantial evidence presented that could indict any other nation of this international crime.

It is an established fact that approximately 15,000 Polish POWs were interned in three Soviet camps: Kozielsk, Starobielsk [*sic*], and Ostashkov in the winter of 1939–1940. With the exception of 400 prisoners, these men have not been heard from, seen, or found since the spring of 1940. Following the discovery of the graves in 1943, when the Germans occupied this territory, they [the Germans] claimed there were 11,000 Poles buried at Katyn. The Russians recovered the territory from the Germans in September 1943, and likewise they stated that 11,000 Poles were buried in these mass graves.[323]

Evidence heard by this committee repeatedly points to the certainty that only those prisoners interned at Kozielsk were massacred in the Katyn Forest. Testimony of the Polish Red Cross officials definitely established that 4,143 bodies were actually exhumed from the seven mass graves.[324] On the basis of further evidence, we are equally certain that the rest of the 15,000 Polish prisoners—those interned at Starobielsk and Ostashkov— were executed in a similar brutal manner. Those from Starobielsk were disposed of near Kharkov,[325] and those from Ostashkov met a similar fate. Testimony was presented by several witnesses that the Ostashkov prisoners were placed on barges and drowned in the White Sea.[326] Thus the committee believes that there are at least two other "Katyns" in Russia. . . .

This committee unanimously recommends that the House of Representatives approve the committee's findings and adopt a resolution:

1. Requesting the president of the United States to forward the testimony and findings of the committee to the United States delegates at the United Nations.
2. Requesting further that the president of the United States issue instructions to the United States delegates to present the Katyn case to the General Assembly of the United Nations.
3. Requesting that appropriate steps be taken by the General Assembly to seek action before the International World Court of Justice against the Union of Soviet Socialist Republics for committing a crime at Katyn which was in violation of the general principles recognized by civilized nations.
4. Requesting the president of the United States to instruct the United States delegation to seek the establishment of an international commission which would investigate other mass murders and crimes against humanity.[327]

   Ray Madden, Chairman
   Daniel J. Flood
   Thaddeus M. Machrowicz
   George A. Dondero
   Alvin E. O'Konski
   Timothy P. Sheehan

In March 1959 the new head of the KGB, Aleksandr Shelepin, wrote a note for the Soviet Communist Party leader, Nikita Khrushchev, suggesting the destruction of the documents on the Polish prisoners shot in 1940 but the retention of the protocols of the Troika—Merkulov, Kobulov, and Bashtakov—that sentenced them (doc. 47), as well as the documents on the implementation of the sentences.

· 110 ·

Note by Shelepin to Khrushchev, 3 March 1959, Proposing to Destroy the Documents
of the Operation Sanctioned by the Politburo on 5 March 1940[328]
3 March 1959, Moscow

Special File
Top Secret
No. 632-sh[elepin]

To Comrade Khrushchev, N. S.

Since 1940, records and other materials regarding prisoners and interned officers, policemen, gendarmes, [military] settlers, landlords and so
on, and persons from former bourgeois Poland who were shot in that
same year have been kept in the Committee of State Security of the Council of Ministers, USSR. On the basis of the decision by the special Troika of
the NKVD USSR, a total of 21,857 persons were shot; of these, 4,421
[were shot] in the Katyn Forest (Smolensk Oblast), 3,820 in the camp of
Starobelsk, close to Kharkov, 6,311 in the camp of Ostashkov (Kalinin
Oblast), and 7,305 persons were shot in other camps and prisons of western Ukraine and western Belorussia.[329]

The whole operation of liquidating the above-mentioned persons was
carried out on the basis of the decision of the CC CPSU of 5 March 1940.
All of them were sentenced to the highest order of punishment according
to the files started for them as POWs and internees in 1939.

From the time when the above-mentioned operation was carried out,
that is, from 1940, no information has been released to anybody relating
to the case, and all of the 21,857 files have been stored in a sealed location.[330]

All these files are of no operational or historical value to Soviet organs.
It is also highly doubtful whether they could be of any real value to our
Polish friends. On the contrary, any unforeseen incident may lead to revealing the operation, with all the undesirable consequences for our country, especially since, regarding the persons shot in the Katyn Forest, the
official version was confirmed by an investigation carried out on the initiative of the organs of Soviet authorities in 1944, under the name of the
"Special Commission to Establish and Investigate the Shooting of Polish
Prisoner-of-War Officers in Katyn Forest by the German-Fascist Aggressors."

According to the conclusion of that commission, all the Poles liquidated
there are considered to have been killed by the German occupiers.[331] The
materials of the inquiry were extensively covered in the Soviet and foreign

press. The commission's conclusions became firmly established in international public opinion.[332]

On the basis of the above statements, it seems expedient to destroy all the records on the persons shot in 1940 in the above-mentioned operation.

In order to answer possible questions along the lines of the CC CPSU or the Soviet government guidelines, the protocols of the meetings of the NKVD USSR Troika that sentenced these persons to be shot, also the documents on carrying out this decision, could be preserved. The volume of these documents is not large and they could be kept in a special file.

Attached is the draft of the [relevant] decision by the CC CPSU.

> Chairman of the Committee for State Security of the Council of Ministers of USSR
> A. Shelepin
> 3 March 1959

[Enclosure]
Draft
Top Secret
Draft for the Decision by the Presidium of the CC CPSU
of [date left blank] 1959

Empower the State Security Committee of the Council of Ministers, USSR, to destroy all the records on the operation carried out in accordance with the decision of the CC CPSU of 5 March 1940, while preserving the protocols of the meetings of the Troika of the NKVD, USSR.[333]

The Soviet government was impelled to act when interest in Katyn revived in England and the United States in the early 1970s. In January 1971 the reprint of J. K. Zawodny's book *Death in the Forest* (1962) led to reviews in the *Times* of London, which printed correspondence on the topic in January–February, as did the *Daily Telegraph* in March–April.

The declassification of Foreign Office documents for the wartime period in 1972 led to more activity in Britain. The pamphlet *Katyn—Despatches of Sir Owen O'Malley to the British Government* appeared in January, with a foreword by Lord Barnby, chairman of the Katyn Memorial Fund, and an introduction by its honorary secretary, Louis FitzGibbon. (In 1943–1944, Owen O'Malley was the British ambassador to the Polish government-in-exile.) It contained O'Malley's report of 24 May 1943 to Foreign Secretary Anthony Eden, presenting evidence pointing at Russian guilt, as well as a withering critique of the Burdenko Commission report (doc. 106), written for Eden on 11 February 1944. Both were reprinted in FitzGibbon's second book, *The Katyn Cover-Up* (London, 1972). The pamphlet was also published by the Polish-American Congress in Chicago in 1973.

The Soviet government, which protested British media coverage of the Katyn question in 1971–1972, was even more upset in 1973. A fund-raising campaign launched by the KMF in 1972 to build a memorial to the victims of Katyn in London now bore fruit. The Council of the Borough of Kensington-Chelsea offered a location in the long-unused cemetery of St. Luke's Anglican Church, Chelsea, which provoked another Soviet protest.

· 111 ·

Politburo Resolution and Instruction for the Soviet Ambassador in London
Regarding the Projected Katyn Monument (Excerpt)[334]
2 March 1973, Moscow

No. P80/12
Top Secret
To Coms. Brezhnev, Kosygin, Kirilenko, Andropov,
Ponomarev, Katushev, Gromyko
Excerpt from Protocol no. 80 of the Politburo CC CPSU
Session of 2 March 1973
On the Démarche to the English Government in Connection
with the Anti-Soviet Campaign Surrounding the Erection in London
of the So-Called Monument to the Victims of Katyn

1. Ratify the draft of the instruction on this question to the Soviet ambassador in London (attached).

2. Instruct the MID [Ministry of Foreign Affairs] USSR to inform the Polish friends of our declaration to the English government.

Secretary CC

[Enclosure]
On Point 12 of Protocol no. 80.
Secret
London

Soviet Ambassador[335]

Visit the minister of foreign affairs[336] and, based on the [instructions] received, declare the following:

The British government's attention has already been drawn to the fact that attempts are being made in England to fan the anti-Soviet campaign about the long-unmasked fictions of Goebbels's propaganda on the so-called Katyn Question. In the démarche made by the Soviet MID to the British Embassy in Moscow on 13 September 1972 for transmission to the British government, it was emphasized that the construction of a "memorial" to the victims of Katyn, inspired by certain circles, can only provoke justified indignation in the Soviet Union.[337]

However, judging by the materials published in the English press, this "memorial" provocation has not been stopped so far. In particular, there is information that the authorities of the Kensington-Chelsea district of London have apparently agreed to the erection of such a "memorial" on their territory at St. Luke's Church and have already approved the design. What is particularly scandalous—according to reports received—is the character of the inscriptions approved for the aforementioned "memorial." In a coarse manner they distort the historical facts about the real culprits of the Katyn tragedy. In effect, they reproduce the base inventions put about by the Nazis during the Second World War in order to hide the bloody crime of the Gestapo murderers, which is known to the whole world.[338]

The attitude of the English government on this matter stands in clear contradiction to its assurances about [its] efforts to improve relations with the Soviet Union. In Moscow, it is expected that the English government will take appropriate measures to put an end to this campaign, hostile to the Soviet Union, [that is] deployed around the construction of the so-called memorial to the victims of Katyn in London.

Telegraph the implementation [of this instruction].

Soviet pressure, combined with British government reluctance and the intervention of the Consistory Court of the Church of England led to the court's decision in summer 1974 to reject the site offered by the Borough of Kensington-Chelsea in St. Luke's Cemetery, Chelsea. However, a new site was granted by the same borough on property it owned elsewhere, Kensington Cemetery, Gunnersbury Avenue, Hounslow, Middlesex. Furthermore, the Katyn Memorial Committee (a subcommittee of the KMF) signed an agreement on 29 March 1976 with the firm of Gilbert and Turnbull, which was to build the memorial. This news spurred the Politburo to renewed action.

· 112 ·

Politburo Protocol no. 3 on Measures to Counteract Western Propaganda
on the Katyn Question (Excerpt)[339]
5 April 1976, Moscow

No. P3/75
Top Secret
To: The Smolensk Oblast Committee, CPSU
To Coms. Brezhnev, Kosygin, Andropov, Gromyko,
Kirilenko, Ponomarev, Katushev, Smirtiukov
Excerpt from Protocol no. 3 of the Politburo CC CPSU Session
of 5 April 1976
On Countermeasures against Western Propaganda
on the So-Called Katyn Question

1. Agree to [the request of] Polish friends for consultations with the goal
of discussing possible common measures to counteract Western propaganda on the so-called Katyn Question after instructing the Department
of the CC CPSU USSR and the MID USSR to conduct the consultations.[340]

Assume in this case the necessity of closely coordinating the steps [to be
taken] by the USSR and the Polish People's Republic in order to counteract and neutralize antisocialist and anti-Soviet actions and campaigns in
the West in connection with the "Katyn Question."

Consider as inexpedient any official declarations from our side so as to
avoid giving hostile elements cause to use [them] in polemics on this question for anti-Soviet objectives.

2. Instruct the Department of the CC CPSU USSR and MID USSR to
learn the opinions of the Polish friends, expressed in the course of consultations and, in case of necessity, submit appropriate proposals to the CC
CPSU.

3. The MID USSR, in close contact with the diplomatic representatives
of the Polish People's Republic, should firmly resist provocative attempts
to use the so-called Katyn Question to harm Polish-Soviet friendship, being directed in this [resistance] by the decisions of the CC CPSU of 2
March 1973 (No. P80/12).[341]

4. The KGB USSR should, through unofficial channels, make it clear to
persons in government circles of appropriate Western countries that the
renewed use of various anti-Soviet forgeries is seen by the Soviet government as especially intentional provocation aimed at worsening the international situation.

5. Instruct the Smolensk Oblast CPSU Committee and the Oblast Executive Committee to undertake supplementary measures to ensure the proper maintenance of the monument to the Polish officers and the surrounding area.[342]

Secretary CC

Katyn did not attract much Western media attention after September 1976, when a monument was unveiled in London, but it was not forgotten in Poland, where it was openly commemorated by some Poles every year. By 1988, Mikhail Gorbachev's glasnost in the USSR sparked the liberalization of Polish media, which clamored for admission of the truth. At the same time, the Joint Commission of Soviet-Polish Party Historians, which began in 1987 to investigate blank spots in the historiography of Polish-Soviet relations, reached a stalemate. In May 1988 the Polish side produced a devastating critique of the Burdenko Commission report (doc. 106), but the Soviet side could not produce any new documents to support the report. In early February 1989, "Roundtable Talks" began in Warsaw, between the party-government leadership on the one hand and the Solidarity leadership on the other, with the aim of reaching a political agreement. Furthermore, General Wojciech Jaruzelski, first secretary of the United Polish Workers' Party and chairman of the Polish Council of Ministers, also pressed the Soviet government to admit the truth about Katyn. The note printed below shows the first documented suggestion by high-level Soviet officials that the USSR admit the crime was committed by the NKVD.

· 113 ·

Note to the CC CPSU "On the Katyn Question" by Soviet Foreign Minister Eduard Shevardnadze; Valentin Falin, Director of the International Department of the CC CPSU; and Vladimir Kriuchkov, Chairman of the KGB USSR[343]
22 March 1989, Moscow

No. 17-204
Secret
To the CC CPSU
On the Katyn Question

As the critical dates of the year 1939 are approaching, the discussions in Poland on the so-called blank spots in [Polish] relations with the USSR (and Russia) are becoming more and more strident. During recent weeks attention has focused on Katyn. In a series of publications written by authors known for their opposition views, as well as by scholars and publicists close to the Polish leadership, it is stated openly that the Soviet Union is guilty of the deaths of the Polish officers and that they were shot in the spring of 1940.[344]

In the statement by J. Urban, spokesman for the Polish government, this point of view has been, in fact, legalized as the official stand of the authorities, although it is true that the guilt for the Katyn crime is placed on the "Stalinist NKVD" and not the Soviet state.[345]

The tactic of the [Polish] government is understandable—it is trying to reduce the pressure resulting from the nonfulfillment of the promise to throw light on the Katyn question. To some extent, the pressure is directed at us, since for two years already this topic has not moved forward in the Commission of Soviet and Polish Scholars, which was established to find solutions for the "blank spots."

The Soviet part of the commission does not have at its disposal any supplementary materials to support the Burdenko version published in 1944. At the same time, our representatives do not have full powers to discuss the weighty arguments of the Polish side.[346]

Aside from J. Urban's statement, other steps are being considered in Warsaw [by the Polish government], which is forced to give some kind of satisfaction to its own society. In particular, there is the intent to transfer symbolic ashes (urn with soil), from Katyn to the central cemetery in Warsaw and, at the same time, change the inscription on the monument erected there in an appropriate manner.[347]

An analysis of the situation indicates that the more this matter is delayed, the more clearly the Katyn question becomes a stumbling block, not so much for past as for present Soviet-Polish relations. In the pamphlet titled *Katyn,* published under church auspices in 1988, it is stated that Katyn is one of the most horrific crimes in the history of mankind.[348] Other publications suggest that there can be no normal relations between Poland and the USSR as long as the Katyn question is not fully clarified.

The Katyn topic is now being artificially moved up to second place [in public discussion], just after questions connected with the outbreak of World War II and the German attack on Poland. The subtext of this campaign is obvious—it is being suggested to the Poles that the Soviet Union is no better, and perhaps even worse, than the Germany of that time, that it carries no smaller burden of responsibility for the outbreak of the war and the military destruction of the Polish state of that time.

In the Polish People's Republic, the Katyn question may decisively sharpen interest in an explanation of the fate of additional thousands of interned Polish officers, whose trails disappear in the regions of Kharkov and Bologoe—and the longer Katyn remains a question, the greater the actual danger.[349] Thus far, we have not given clear answers to these additional questions put [to us] by the Polish side.

It is clear that we cannot avoid [giving] an explanation to the leadership of the Polish People's Republic and the Polish public of the tragic questions of the past. In this case, time is not our ally. Perhaps it is more advisable to say what really happened and exactly who is guilty, thus effecting closure to the problem. The costs of this kind of action would, in the final reckoning, be less in comparison with the losses [resulting from] present inaction.

The draft of the CC CPSU resolution is attached.[350]

> (E. Shevardnadze)
> (V. Falin)
> (V. Kriuchkov)

The Shevardnadze, Falin, Kriuchkov note of 22 March 1989 (doc. 113) prompted the Politburo to reconsider what official line to take on the Katyn question and to demand suggestions.

· 114 ·

Politburo Protocol no. 152: Instruction by Mikhail S. Gorbachev to the Prosecutor's Office and Other State and Party Agencies to Propose the Future Soviet Line on Katyn (Excerpt)
31 March 1989, Moscow*

No. P152/15
Top Secret
To the Smolensk Oblast Committee:
cc. Coms. Gorbachev, Ryzhkov, Medvedev, Chebrikov, Shevardnadze, Yakovlev, Kriuchkov, Sukharev, Kapto, A. Pavlov,[351] Falin
Excerpt from Protocol no. 152 of the Meeting of the Politburo
of the CC CPSU of 31 March 1989
On the Katyn Question

1. Instruct the Prosecutor's Office of the USSR; the Committee of State Security, USSR; the Ministry of Foreign Affairs; the Departments of State and Law; the International and Ideological [Departments of the CC CPSU], to present within one month a proposal for the future Soviet line on the Katyn question for consideration by the CC CPSU.

* Text in the margin: "To be returned within one month to the CC CPSU (General Department, 1st Sector)."

2. In connection with the request of the Polish side to transfer symbolic ashes from the burial site of Polish officers in Katyn to Warsaw, I, Mikhail S. Gorbachev, grant permission for this [to be done].[352]

Secretary of the CC

· 115 ·

Note on the Katyn Question to the CC CPSU
22 April 1989, Moscow

Secret
To the CC CPSU
On the Katyn Question*

In accordance with the instruction (P152/15 of 31 March 1989),[353] we report:

Acquaintance with the materials we possess on the extermination of 12,000 Polish officers interned in the Soviet Union in 1939[354] gives grounds for the assumption that only a part of this number perished at Katyn. The fate of the rest is thus far unknown. There is information in Polish and Western publications that Polish officers were killed in the regions of Bologoe (Kalinin Oblast)[355] and Dergachi (Kharkov Oblast).

To clarify all the circumstances of what happened, it seems necessary to instruct the Prosecutor's Office of the USSR to conduct a scrupulous investigation in cooperation with the KGB USSR.[356]

Since the question has taken on an extraordinary stridency in Poland and is being used to harm Polish-Soviet relations, it would be expedient to issue a publication on the scrupulous investigation being conducted by competent [Soviet] organs before the arrival of W. Jaruzelski on a working visit to the USSR (27–28 April 1989).

Attached is a draft outline of the decision by the CC CPSU.[357]

A. Sukharev
V. Kriuchkov
A. Aboimov
A. Pavlov[358]
V. Falin
A. Kapto

* Handwritten at the top in the left margin: "*Za* [For (agree)] A. [Aleksandr] Yakovlev." Stamp on top right side: "CC CPSU. 22 April 1989. 09287. To be returned to the General Department, CC CPSU."

In 1988, Natalia Lebedeva, member of the Institute of General History, Soviet Academy of Sciences, obtained access to the Central Archive of the Red Army, where she found the records of the 136th NKVD Convoy Battalion, which escorted the Kozelsk prisoners to Katyn in April–May 1940, and the records of the Main Administration of the NKVD Convoy Troops. She learned that the records of the NKVD UPV were in the Central Special Archive, but access to it was given at that time to Valentina Parsadanova, a specialist on the history of World War II Soviet-Polish relations in the Institute of Slavic and Balkan Studies of the Soviet Academy of Sciences, and member of the Joint Commission of Soviet-Polish Party Historians to look into the blank spots in the historiography of relations between the two nations.

Access to these records (of whose existence he learned from Natalia Lebedeva) was also obtained by Yuri Zoria, docent (associate professor) attached to the Chair of Special Disciplines at the Military Academy of the Soviet Army, whose father, Nikolai Zoria, a Soviet legal counsel at the IMT in Nuremberg, died there in suspicious circumstances on 23 May 1946. Yuri Zoria photocopied hundreds of pages of documents concerning Katyn and passed them on to Yakovlev, who sent them on to the office of President Mikhail Gorbachev. Lebedeva, Parsadanova, and Zoria had articles accepted for publication in June by the time Valentin Falin, director of the International Department of the CC CPSU wrote his note for Gorbachev on 23 February 1990.

· 116 ·

Falin's Note on Katyn for Mikhail Gorbachev[359]
23 February 1990, Moscow

Secret
Additional Information on the Katyn Tragedy

Esteemed Mikhail Sergeevich!

A number of Soviet historians (Yu. N. Zoria, V. S. Parsadanova, N. S. Lebedeva), given access to the collections of the Special Archive and the Central State Archive of the Main Archival Administration of the Council of Ministers of the USSR, also the Central State Archive of the October Revolution, have brought to light hitherto unknown materials of the Main Administration of the NKVD USSR for Prisoner-of-War and Internee Affairs [UPVI], as well as the Administration of NKVD Convoy Troops [GUKV], for the period 1939–1940 that are related to the so-called Katyn Question.[360]

According to these materials, at the beginning of January 1940 there were in the camps of the NKVD USSR Main Administration for Prisoner-of-War and Internee Affairs in Ostashkov, Kalinin Oblast; in Kozelsk, Smolensk Oblast; [and] in Starobelsk, Voroshilovgrad [Luhansk] Oblast approximately 14,000 former Polish citizens. These included officers of the army and navy, police and gendarmerie employees, military and civilian officials, [members of] various types of [intelligence] agencies, as well as military clergy.

None of these persons qualified for release and return to their homeland (NKVD Order no. 00117 of 1939).[361] The question of their fate was considered several times. There are documents with the instructions of Beria and Merkulov to speed up the investigation [and] prepare materials on the former [Polish] employees of penal organs and intelligence organizations for examination by the Special Board of the NKVD USSR.[362]

In April–May 1940 the persons held in all the three camps were transferred in stages to the disposal of various regional NKVD administrations. The lists were drawn up in a centralized manner and a uniform system of numbering was used. Each of these lists contained an average of 100 names, and [they] were sent regularly, sometimes four to five lists per day.[363] The appropriate authorities in Moscow were informed every day of these departures. There were orders to exclude agents-informers and persons of operational interest from those to be sent [out of the camps].[364] In contrast to the general practice of moving prisoners, the camp commanders were instructed to make notes on the departing prisoners only in the camp index card file ("departed according to list number . . . and month"), without sending the data cards to the center.[365]

Before the action began, an order was issued on introducing postal control and the confiscation of all incoming and outgoing correspondence.[366] It was forbidden to give any kind of answer to questions about those held in the camps.[367] All camp workers were warned to keep the places of deportation strictly secret.

After the conclusion of the action, all the "records" of the former internees in the camps were "completed, appropriately processed, and deposited in the archive of the 1st Special Department NKVD." For new contingents arriving in the camps, the instruction was to start "totally new files with regard to the evidence and procedure." Later, the materials of the Kozelsk and Ostashkov camps were sent for preservation to the Main Administration [for Prisoner-of-War and Internee Affairs], but the Starobelsk camp materials were destroyed.[368] The persons detained in the three camps up to April–May 1940 do not figure in later statistical records.

Later, the Kozelsk and Starobelsk camps were used to hold persons of Polish nationality deported from the western regions of Ukraine, Belorussia, and the Baltic region. At the same time, information about the former contingent in these camps was carefully hidden from them. The buildings of Ostashkov camp were consigned in August 1940 to the local history and folklore museum.[369]

In this manner, documents from Soviet archives, even in the absence of orders for the execution by shooting and for burial, allow us to track the fate of the interned Polish officers held in the NKVD camps of Kozelsk, Starobelsk, and Ostashkov. A spot comparison of the lists of names of persons to be sent out of the Kozelsk camp with the identity lists compiled by the Germans in spring 1943 at the time of the exhumations shows numerous coincidences that appear to prove the relationship between the two.

On the basis of newly documented facts, Soviet historians have prepared materials for publication. Some of them have already been approved by editorial boards and accepted for publication. Their appearance is scheduled for June–July [this year].

The appearance of such publications would clearly create a new situation. Our argument—that no materials have been found in the state archives of the USSR uncovering the true underpinnings of the Katyn tragedy—would become unconvincing. The materials uncovered by the scholars will undoubtedly reveal only part of the secrets in comparison with the data on which the Polish side bases its judgments, but this will not allow us to stand by the former versions and avoid putting an end to this question. In view of the approaching fiftieth anniversary of Katyn we should define our position one way or the other.[370]

It seems that the lowest possible costs are connected with the following variant:

To inform W. Jaruzelski that after detailed investigation in the appropriate archives, we did not find explicit proof (orders, directives, etc.) that would allow us to name the exact date and concretely identify those responsible for the Katyn tragedy. At the same time, in the archives of the Main NKVD Administration for Prisoner-of-War and Internee Affairs, also [in the] records of the Administration of NKVD Convoy Troops for 1940, indications have been revealed that undermine the credibility of the "N. Burdenko Report." On the basis of these indications, it is possible to conclude that the extermination of the Polish officers in the Katyn region was the work of the NKVD and personally of Beria and Merkulov.[371]

The question remains as to the time and form of communicating this conclusion to the Polish and Soviet public. Here, the advice of the president of the Polish Republic is required, taking into consideration the necessity of [reaching a] political closure to the problem and, at the same time, avoiding an outburst of emotions.

Please think this over.

Your Falin

Distributed to: Coms. Yakovlev, Shevardnadze, Kriuchkov, Boldin. Please communicate your opinion. M. Gorbachev

In late February the Politburo voted not to allow Russian historians to publish articles based on archival documents about the murder of Polish POW officers and police in spring 1940. However, an interview with Natalia Lebedeva, who gave a survey of the Katyn documents she had found in the archives, was published on 25 March in *Moskovskie Novosti* [Moscow News], and this may have forced the Politburo to reverse its decision not to allow the publication of articles on the subject.[372] At the same time, President Jaruzelski was expected to visit in mid-April, and he had made it clear that he expected an admission of Soviet guilt. In view of all the above, the Politburo decided on 7 April to follow Falin's advice and admit the truth. Thus, at a reception held in the Polish Embassy on 13 April 1990—the forty-seventh anniversary of the German announcement on the Katyn graves—Gorbachev handed Jaruzelski two file boxes containing the NKVD dispatch lists for Kozelsk and Ostashkov and a combined list for Starobelsk. On the same day, the official Soviet news agency, TASS, issued a communiqué admitting the truth and placing the responsibility for the massacres on Beria and Merkulov—without mentioning Stalin.

· 117 ·

TASS Communiqué on Katyn[373]
13 April 1990, Moscow

Statement by TASS

At meetings between representatives of the Soviet and Polish governments and in wide circles of these societies, the question of clarifying the circumstances of the extermination of the Polish officers interned in September 1939 has been raised for a long time. Historians of both countries have conducted careful investigations of the Katyn tragedy, including the search for documents.

Most recently, Soviet archivists and historians have discovered some documents about Polish servicemen held in the NKVD USSR camps of Kozelsk, Ostashkov, and Starobelsk. These documents show that in April–May 1940, out of approximately 15,000 Polish officers held in these three camps,[374] 394 were moved to Griazovets camp,[375] while the majority "were placed at the disposal" of the NKVD administrations in the Smolensk, Voroshilovgrad [Luhansk], and Kalinin Oblasts and do not appear later in any NKVD statistical records.

The archival materials that have been discovered, taken together, permit the conclusion that Beria and Merkulov and their subordinates bear direct responsibility for the evil deeds in Katyn Forest.[376]

The Soviet side, expressing deep regret in connection with the Katyn tragedy, declares that it represents one of the heinous crimes of Stalinism.

Copies of the documents found have been given to the Polish side.[377] The search for archival documents continues.

The Polish government urged President Gorbachev to speed up the criminal investigation into the massacre of Polish officers in spring 1940. The Soviet Prosecutor's Office finally ordered the establishment of a criminal investigation group on 30 August 1990. Investigations had already been initiated by the Kharkov Oblast Prosecutor's Office in March and by the Kalinin Oblast Prosecutor's Office in June of that year, but it was the visit of Polish Foreign Minister Krzysztof Skubiszewski to Moscow in early November 1990 that impelled Gorbachev to issue the decree printed below.[378]

· 118 ·

Decree by President Gorbachev, in Connection with the Visit of Polish Minister of Foreign Affairs Krzysztof Skubiszewski, on Speeding Up the Investigation of the Fate of the Polish Officers Held in the Three Special Camps (Excerpt)
3 November 1990, Moscow

Secret
Decree of the President of the Union of Soviet Republics on the Results of the Visit to the Soviet Union of the Minister of Foreign Affairs of the Polish Republic, K. Skubiszewski.[379]

. . . 8. [I recommend] that the Prosecutor's Office of the USSR speed up the investigation into the fate of the Polish officers held in the Kozelsk, Ostashkov, and Starobelsk camps. [The Prosecutor's Office] should, jointly with the Committee of State Security of the USSR and the Ministry of Internal Affairs of the USSR, secure the search for and utilization of archival materials connected with the repressions regarding the Polish population on the territory of the USSR in 1939 and present the appropriate conclusions.[380]

9. [I recommend] that the Academy of Sciences of the USSR, the Prosecutor's Office of the USSR, the Ministry of Defense, and the Committee of State Security, together with other departments and organizations, conduct investigative work by 1 April 1991 to reveal archival materials relating to the events and facts in the history of bilateral Soviet-Polish relations, which resulted in losses to the Soviet side.[381] In absolutely necessary cases, utilize the material obtained in negotiations with the Polish side on the issue of "blank spots."[382]

> The President of the Union of Soviet Socialist Republics
> M. Gorbachev
> Moscow, The Kremlin
> 3 November 1990

Distributed to: Coms. Gorbachev, Ryzhkov, Kriuchkov, Masliukov, Medvedev, Shevardnadze, Yazov, Sitarianov, Silaev, Kebich, Karamanov, Gubenko, Katushev, V. Pavlov, Yagodin, Marchuk, Geraschchenko, Moskovsky, Shkabardnia*
To be returned

On 14 October 1992 the Russian press published the Politburo decision of 5 March 1940 to shoot the Polish POWs. The document was also delivered to the Russian Constitutional Tribunal as evidence of the criminal nature of the Soviet, now Russian, Communist Party, which opposed President Yeltsin's reforms and which he had de-legalized.

On the same day, the director of Soviet Archives, Professor Rudolf Pikhoia, presented, in President Yeltsin's name, a collection of hitherto secret Katyn documents to Polish President Wałęsa in Warsaw. They contained the infamous resolution of 5 March 1940, documents on the Soviet cover-up of the crime, and some documents from the Soviet Prosecutor General's Office on the Katyn investigation up to 3 September 1991.

Wałęsa thanked Yeltsin in a letter dated 15 October 1992. Its style—

---

* Typewritten at the bottom of page 1: "To be returned to the Presidential Council of the USSR (limit—10 days). No. RP-979." Handwritten at the bottom of page 1: "PS-980 not for distribution." Handwritten at the bottom of the last page: "Results [?] p. 3—see PS-952, 7 February 1991."

especially in paragraphs three and four—indicates that Wałęsa probably dictated it himself.

· 119 ·

Letter from President Lech Wałęsa to President Boris Yeltsin
Thanking Him for the Documents on Katyn
15 October 1992, Warsaw

_____

Highly esteemed Mr. President!

Deeply moved, I wish to thank you in the name of all Poles, and personally in my own, for delivering into my hands the most important documents concerning the monstrous Katyn crime.[383] This was a crime perpetrated against the Polish nation; a crime shrouded in a conspiracy of
silence for almost fifty years; a crime whose consequences we have felt so
painfully and for so long.

Poles have always attached great importance to the Katyn question.
Katyn became a symbol of truth, a test of sincerity between our two na-
tions. The lie about the Katyn Forest served to enslave my fatherland.
That is why we Poles are so sensitive to the name of Katyn.

You have kept your word.[384] Thanks to your courage, the truth hidden
from the world has seen the light of day. This was a difficult decision, in fact
a heroic one. You proved yourself capable of a manly gesture, which many
others were unable to make. I know that even today you have many oppo-
nents. Yesterday, the crime was followed by a lie. Today, the truth, which
you proclaimed to the world, will be followed by trust and honesty. You
have, Mr. President, opened a new page in the relations between our two nations. It is directed to the future, based on mutual understanding, cooperation, and agreement. May this page of dramatic history never be repeated.

I know how difficult is the reform work which you have undertaken. I
wish for your fatherland, and you personally, that it will be crowned with
success, as measured by the expectations and challenges of the time in
which it is our lot to live, and also as measured by the success of future
generations.

I enclose expressions of respect, Lech Wałęsa[385]

Many Poles felt that the Russian government had not done enough
to atone for Soviet crimes against the Polish nation, while Polish historians urged they be given access to the documents on the sentencing
and execution of the prisoners from the three special camps, as well as

on the murder and burial sites of the prisoners executed in NKVD prisons in western Belorussia (Belarus) and western Ukraine in spring
1940. President Yeltsin spoke to these issues in his letter to Wałęsa on
22 May 1995. In so doing, he foreshadowed the attitude that would be
taken by his successor, President Vladimir Putin.

· 120 ·

Letter from President Yeltsin to President Wałęsa on the
Fifty-fifth Anniversary of the Katyn Tragedy
22 May 1995, Moscow

To His Excellency
Mr. L. Wałęsa
President of the Republic of Poland
Esteemed Mr. President,

I know very well the significance that measures connected with the fifty-
fifth anniversary of the Katyn tragedy have in Poland. I fully share your
opinion that this tragic page of our history should finally be closed, while
its memory should be recalled to serve the aim of mutual understanding
between our two countries and the avoidance of elements of distrust and
prejudice.[386]

In this connection, I cannot omit mentioning that solving this complex
task is not aided, as practice shows, by the inflaming of emotions surrounding the Katyn theme in the mass media by certain political circles, by
the escalation of demands presented to the Russian side—from making an
apology to organizing a trial and the payment of compensation.[387] The
stand of democratic Russia regarding the crimes of the Stalinist regime, including Katyn, is well known. It has been expressed more than once over
the past few years, including in my visit to Poland in 1993.[388]

We can well understand the feelings of the Poles. However, totalitarian
terror touched not only their countrymen. In Katyn Forest alone, alongside the remains of Polish officers, there are, according to incomplete data,
about nine thousand victims of political repression, people of various nationalities.[389] There is reliable information about the execution by shooting in that place of over five hundred [Soviet] POWs by the Nazis, who
used [them] in the war years for building secret military objects.[390] Therefore, we consider the Katyn Forest to be a place of remembrance for the
victims of totalitarianism and Nazism, where a memorial should be built
for all the innocent people who lost their lives there. Of course, within the
framework of the memorial, the memory of the Polish officers who per-

ished there should be immortalized in a dignified manner. The Russian side intends to proclaim a competition for the best project [submitted] for the memorial and would appreciate the participation of Polish architects.

We attach great importance to the preparation and carrying out in June this year at Katyn and Mednoe of a ceremony to place memorial signs in places designated for Polish military cemeteries. Appropriate instructions have been given to the authorities of the regions of Smolensk and Tver.[391]

As for the documents that you write of in your letter, the comprehensive measures taken to find them have confirmed their absence in Russian archives, including the archives of the Special Services [KGB]. The questioning in April this year of former workers of the NKVD Archival Services resulted in the conclusion that the above-mentioned materials were destroyed in 1959. This action took place over a period of two weeks by two workers who are no longer among the living. No records of this kind, envisaged in similar cases, have survived.[392]

I would like to assure you, Mr. President, that no one in Russia aims to hide from the Polish side any information regarding the Katyn tragedy. The Main Military Prosecutor's Office, which is conducting an investigation into the Katyn case, has received from the archives of the Federal Security Service about two hundred files and documents, as well as thirty-five volumes of documents concerning the work of the Burdenko Commission.[393] Military prosecutors have had the opportunity to acquaint themselves directly with the archival collections held in the Central Archives of the Federal Security Service and its affiliates; they were able personally to see the necessary files and documents and select those of interest to the investigation.[394]

The Office of the Main Military Prosecutor of the Russian Federation continues to investigate the criminal case of the shooting of Polish citizens in 1940.[395] Part of the materials in this case concern the investigation of the circumstances of the deaths of Polish officers in 1940 in the prisons of western Ukraine and western Belorussia, [which] have been detached and sent to the offices of the prosecutor generals of the now sovereign states—Ukraine and Belarus—for making the appropriate decisions.[396]

I am fully convinced that the steps taken jointly by us will promote the finalization of the Katyn case in all its aspects and, by the same token, the further successful development of relations between our two peoples.[397]

Respectfully,
B. Yeltsin

The speeches of Polish Prime Minister Jerzy Buzek and Russian Deputy Prime Minister Viktor Khristenko at the opening of the Polish and Russian cemeteries at Katyn illustrate the differences in Polish and Russian public opinion on the massacre.

· 121 ·

Speech by Jerzy Buzek, Prime Minister of Poland, at the Ceremonial Opening
of the Polish War Cemetery at Katyn[398]
28 July 2000, Katyn

Esteemed Mr. Deputy Prime Minister of the Russian Federation,[399]
Your Grace, the Cardinal Primate of Poland,[400]
Ladies and Gentlemen, Representatives of the Sejm,[401]
Gentlemen, Officers of the Polish Army gathered here, in Katyn,
Dear, Esteemed Members of Katyn Families, all of whom are family to us,
Ladies and Gentlemen,

There is an image of the Mother of God that is moving in its simplicity of expression. [It is] the sad face of the Savior's Mother, who is pressing to her breast the head of a Polish prisoner of war with a bullet hole through his skull.[402] This [is] the symbol of the victory of love over hate—of hate, which took away the lives of the best sons of our nation, and of love, which will always rise above hate.

"Love demands sacrifice"—these words were the motto of Polish soldiers who fought sixty years ago for the independence of Poland, which they loved.

At Katyn, four and a half thousand soldiers' lives were thrown down on the altar of love for the Fatherland. It is difficult for us to cry for them today because we have no tears left, and our hands, clasped together for so long, are numb.

Ladies and Gentlemen,

Many of us present here today were undoubtedly born in 1940. Seeing the inscription "Katyn 1940," I also recall the year of my birth—when, at this time, in this forest, in this place, our fellow countrymen were thrown into open pits. We belong to the generation of the sons and daughters of these soldiers. Fate decreed that many of us, including myself, did not receive the bad news of the father who would not return home. Still, there is no deeper wound for all Poles than the one which remained unhealed for so long, regardless of whether or not our family members lie in this cemetery.

For Katyn was not only a terrible crime carried out under the majesty of Soviet law; it was also a lie; a lie repeated thousands of times, but one which, for all that, did not cease being a lie. The word "Katyn" will, for whole generations in Poland and in the whole world, signify genocide and a war crime.

Ladies and Gentlemen,

We are here today to say, "We remember, and we will remember." For, as the poet said, "If we forget you—then You, O God, forget us."[403] From here, from this place, I wish to say in the name of the Polish Nation, that we will not rest until we know the names of all the citizens of the [Polish] Republic murdered by Soviet authorities and find their burial sites.[404] We are not doing this out of revenge but out of a feeling for justice.

In our tradition, life has its beginning and its end. Just as we feel joy at the birth of every human being, so every human being must be buried with dignity. Part of this tradition is also the concept of crime and punishment. The Katyn crime must be fully explained. There must also be a full accounting for it.[405]

In this place I pay homage to all the people murdered and tortured to death at Katyn, as well as in the whole territory of the Soviet Union. Our pain is equal to yours.

I am thinking here of the Russians, who are hosting us in their land. I thank you, Russians, and all the other nations that experienced communism, for what you have done to memorialize the past and to settle accounts with it. Without your help and your goodwill we would not be here today; nor would we be at Mednoe and Kharkov.[406]

Ladies and Gentlemen,

I also wish to thank all those, who contributed over the years to uncovering the truth about the crime committed at Katyn, thanks to whom the Polish War Cemetery came to be opened today. Special thanks should go to the Russian Memorial [society], to its Coordinating Committee to Commemorate the Victims of Totalitarianism at Katyn and at Mednoe,[407] and to the authorities of the Smolensk region, especially the governor, as well as the Russian journalists and scholars who uncovered the truth—often despite obstacles [presented] by fate.[408] I also thank the designers and builders of the Polish War Cemetery at Katyn and the Council for the Protection of the Memory of Combat and Martyrdom.[409]

I turn again to the officers and soldiers of the Polish Army. You are the heirs of those who were murdered. Poles have always treated their army with the greatest respect and honor. I am convinced that this legacy passed on to you by your forebears, the officers murdered here, is important for you; a legacy that you will always protect.

I turn now to the Katyn Families. Among you are the widows of those murdered sixty years ago, as well as their closest relatives. I am convinced that none of us can fully understand the enormity of your suffering, the enormity of the misfortune that you had to live with for sixty years. But although these were not our relatives, they are family to us. For this is a fragment of our dramatic, tragic history in the twentieth century.

I would like to thank all of you, members of Katyn Families, for preserving the memory of that crime, from which we can learn.[410]

Ladies and Gentlemen,

Today we have the great chance to make history together without hatred and without lies. When our mutual teacher Jesus Christ was asked how many times a human being should forgive—he answered seventy-seven times. Here at Katyn we should remember these words and learn the difficult art of forgiveness.

I believe that the Polish War Cemetery at Katyn will become for us Poles and for people of other nationalities a place to visit, particularly the young generations. They will come here to see, remember, and forgive. Katyn, Mednoe, Kharkov. Together with Monte Cassino, Powązki, Narvik, Tobruk—our national cemeteries—[they] are part of our national identity, the national identity of Poles.[411]

Here we left our national soul and our tragic national memory. We will draw from here faith, hope, and love.

· 122 ·

Speech by the Deputy Prime Minister of the Russian Federation,
Viktor Khristenko, at the Opening of the Katyn Memorial Complex
28 July 2000, Katyn

Esteemed Mr. Prime Minister of the Polish Republic, Esteemed Polish Guests,

My Fellow Countrymen!

Today we are all witnesses and participants in a historical event—the opening of the Memorial Complex at Katyn dedicated to the memory of Soviet and Polish citizens who were victims of totalitarian repression. I am convinced that it has a special meaning for future Russian-Polish relations and, above all, for their dimension of humanitarian and human relations. Today's ceremony confirms the new character of mutual relations between our states, the higher level of understanding the history that binds together the Russian and Polish peoples and the societies of both countries.

We Russians can well understand the feelings of Poles connected with Katyn [and] the motives that moved the presidents of Russia and Poland in 1992 to judge the crimes of totalitarianism, which brought so much suffering to the peoples of our countries.[412] In fact, it was the peoples of the former Soviet Union who became the first and principal victims of the inhuman Stalinist machine, which broke and mangled millions of human lives.

Indeed, in this earth, four thousand Polish officers rest alongside tens of thousands of our compatriots, and the Katyn Forest will remain in national memory as the symbol of a terrible tragedy that befell our society while also affecting representatives of other states. May their memory live forever!

I fully share the words of the prime minister of the Polish Republic which he spoke recently at the Warsaw ceremony on the occasion of the sixtieth anniversary of the Katyn tragedy, that the concept of Katyn itself should become the "symbol of common memory, of our obligation to jointly surmount a difficult part of our history for the sake of our future, for the sake of strengthening friendly feelings between Poles and Russians, for the sake of building friendly relations between Russia and Poland."[413]

We are gathered here today not only to honor the memory of repressed Russian citizens and Polish military servicemen but also to declare with full responsibility that nothing like this should ever be repeated. The Russian names of the places of Katyn and Mednoe must lose their burden of negative significance in Russian-Polish relations and become the symbols of common mourning and reconciliation. The shadow of the past should in no way darken the present nor, all the more, the future of mutual, two-sided contacts and cooperation between Russia and Poland.

We are obligated to turn over this tragic page of our mutual history and instead strive to banish from Russian-Polish relations the distrust and prejudice remaining from the past.[414] The memory of the Katyn tragedy, the common mourning for those who perished, should not divide but unite our peoples.

I am convinced that this will be so!

List of Documents with Sources

The origin of each document published here is the first source listed for that document. All documents were translated from the Russian unless otherwise stated.

The abbreviation *KD*, followed by volume number and document number, signifies a document published in the Russian series *Katyn: Dokumenty; KDZ*, followed by volume number and document number, signifies a document published in the Polish series *Katyn: Dokumenty Zbrodni*. (For volume titles and publication information, see the abbreviation list at the beginning of the endnotes section; for more information about these series, see Note on the Documents.)

The abbreviation *R* stands for *Rasstrel* [Execution by Shooting], the title of a supplement to *KD1* that contains key documents on the extermination of the Polish prisoners of war in the spring of 1940. *Rasstrel* reproduces facsimiles of fifty-two documents because the editor Natalia Lebedeva had no certainty at the time that further volumes of Katyn documents would be funded. The facsimiles are located at the end of *KD1* and are referred to by their numbers. Most are also printed as documents in *KD2*. Facsimiles of selected documents are likewise printed at the end of *KD2*; their document numbers are given here with page numbers to distinguish them from the documents in *KD1*. Facsimiles of a few documents, considered of particular importance, are reproduced in both Russian volumes. There are also facsimiles of documents in the Polish volumes.

Nearly all the documents came originally from Russian archives. The full names of the archives are given at first mention and also in the list of abbreviations and acronyms at the beginning of this volume; the main archival sources are also listed at the beginning of the endnotes. The names of some archives have changed since the publication of the first Russian volume and the first two Polish volumes of Katyn documents. In 1999, two archives, the Rossiiskii Gosudarstvenny Voenny Arkhiv [RGVA—Russian State Military Archive] and the Tsentr Khranenia Istoriko-Dokumentalnykh Kollektsii [TsKhIDK—Russian Center for Preserving Historical-Documentary Collections] were merged into one: RGVA. The Rossiiskii Tsentr Khranenia i Izuchenia Dokumentov Noveishei Istorii [RTsKhIDNI— Russian Center for the Preservation and Study of Documents of Recent History] was renamed Rossiiskii Gosudarstvenny Arkhiv Sotsialno-Politicheskoi Istorii [RGASPI—Russian State Archive for Social and Political History]. In both cases, the internal reference numbers remained the same. In this volume, the old archive names are given as published, followed by the new archive names in brackets, followed by archival references. The type of document (original or copy, handwritten or typed) is given when the information is available in the *KD* and *KDZ* volumes.

Abbreviations are given with English translation at first mention; the common ones are included in the list of abbreviations and acronyms.

The English translations from the Russian were prepared by Marian Schwartz unless specified otherwise. Where existing English translations were used, most have been modified either to provide a more precise translation or to conform to standard English style.

PART I. PRISONERS OF AN UNDECLARED WAR,
23 AUGUST 1939 – 5 MARCH 1940

1. Non-Aggression Pact between Germany and the Soviet Union, 23 August 1939, Moscow

Arkhiv Vneshnei Politiki Rossiiskoi Federatsii [AVPRF—Foreign Policy Archive of the Russian Federation], f. [*fond*—collection] 3a, d. [*delo*— folder] 243, Germania, *KD1/1*, *KDZ1/1*. Original Russian text, *Dokumenty Vneshnei Politiki [DVP*—Documents on Foreign Policy], vol. XXII, book 1 (Moscow, 1992), no. 484; the English translation given here is by M. Schwartz and A. M. Cienciala. See also the English version of the Russian text in Jane Degras, ed., *Soviet Documents on Foreign Policy, 1917– 1941 [SDFP]*, vol. III: *1933–1941* (London, 1953), pp. 359–360. For an English version of the German text, see *Documents on German Foreign Policy, 1918–1945 [DGFP]*, ser. D, vol. VII (London, Washington, D.C., 1956), no. 228; reprint, Stanisław Biegański et al., eds., *Documents on Polish-Soviet Relations, 1939–1945 [DPSR]*, vol. I (London, 1961), no. 31.

2. Secret Supplementary Protocol to the Non-Aggression Pact between Germany and the Soviet Union, 23 August 1939, Moscow

Arkhiv Prezidenta Rossiiskoi Federatsii [APRF—Archive of the President of the Russian Federation], f. 3, op. [*opis*—collection or inventory within a fond] 64, d. 675a, l. [*list*—page, card] 3–4; *KD1/2*, *KDZ1/2*; *DVP*, vol. XXII, book 1, no. 485; the English translation used here is by M. Schwartz and A. M. Cienciala; for an English translation of the German text, see *SDFP*, vol. III, pp. 360–361; and *DGFP*, ser. D, vol. VII, no. 229; reprint, *DPSR*, vol. I, no. 32.

3. Order no. 005 of the Military Council of the Belorussian Front to the Troops on the Goals of the Red Army's Entry into Western Belorussia, 16 September 1939, Smolensk

Rossiiskii Gosudarstvenny Voenny Arkhiv [RGVA—Russian State Military Archive], f. 35086, op. 1, d. 4, l. 8, printed document; *KD1/5, KDZ1/4.*

4. Soviet Government Note Handed to the Polish Ambassador in the USSR, Wacław Grzybowski, 17 September 1939, Moscow

Russian text, *Izvestia,* 18 September 1939; reprint, *Dokumenty i Materiały do Historii Stosunków Polsko-Radzieckich* [Documents and Materials for the History of Polish-Soviet Relations], vol. VII (Warsaw, 1973), no. 105; *DVP,* vol. XXII, book 2, no. 597; excerpt in *KD1/7,* note 3 (notes to documents in *KD1* are given after p. 392). For the Polish text see Stefania Stanisławska, ed., *Sprawa Polska w Czasie Drugiej Wojny Światowej na Arenie Międzynarodowej* [The Polish Question during World War II in the International Arena] (Warsaw, 1965), no. 44. The English text given here is from *SDFP,* vol. III, p. 374.

5. From the Official Diary of Soviet Deputy People's Commissar of Foreign Affairs Potemkin on a Conversation with Polish Ambassador Grzybowski, 17 September 1939, Moscow

APRF, f. 3, op. 50, d. 410, ll. 35–39, original; *DVP,* vol. XXII, book 2, no. 596; *KD1/7, KDZ1/7.* The English translation from the Russian given here is by A. M. Cienciala.

6. Order of the Commander in Chief of the Polish Army, Marshal Edward Śmigły-Rydz, Regarding the Entry of Soviet Forces into Poland, 17 September 1939, Kuty

Centralne Archiwum Wojskowe [CAW—Central Military Archive], Warsaw, II/1/4, *karta* [card] 245; *KDZ1/6* (typed copy in Polish). The English translation from the Polish given here is by A. M. Cienciala; *KD1/6* (Russian translation from Polish).

7. Politburo Decision on Placing POW Reception Points under NKVD Protection (Excerpt), 18 September 1939, Moscow

APRF, f. 3, op. 50, d. 410, l. 64, typed copy on form used for Politburo session excerpts; *KD1/9, KDZ1/9.*

8. Lavrenty P. Beria's Order no. 0308 on the Organization of the UPV and POW Camps under the NKVD USSR, 19 September 1939, Moscow

Gosudarstvenny Arkhiv Rossiiskoi Federatsii [GARF—State Archive of the Russian Federation], f. 9401, op. 1, d. 532, ll. 432–437, original; *KD1/11, KDZ1/11.* First published in Polish translation in Czesław Grzelak et al., eds., *Agresja Sowiecka na Polskę w Świetle Dokumentów, 17*

Września 1939 [Soviet Aggression against Poland in the Light of Documents, 17 September 1939], vol. 1 (Warsaw, 1994), no. 100.

9. Statute of the NKVD UPV, not before 19 September 1939, Moscow
Tsentr Khranenia Istoriko-Dokumentalnykh Kollektsii [TsKhIDK—Russian Center for Preserving Historical-Documentary Collections, now in RGVA], f. 1/p, op. 1a, d. 1, ll. 55–57, typed copy; *KD1/12, KDZ1/12.*

10. USSR NKVD Instruction to the Osoboe Otdelenia [Special Sections] of POW Camps on Recording Operational Data on the Prisoners, 19 September 1939, Moscow
TsKhIDK [RGVA], f. 1/p, op. 1e, d. 1, ll. 10–13, typed copy; *KD1/13, KDZ1/13.*

11. Report of the USSR Deputy People's Commissar of Defense, Army Commander 1st Rank Grigory Kulik, on the Actions of Red Army Units and Formations in Western Ukraine and the Political and Economic Situation in the Region, 21 September 1939, Stanislavov [Stanisławów]
RGVA, f. 35084, op. 1, d. 7, ll. 4–14, handwritten original; *KD1/16, KDZ1/16.*

12. German-Soviet Treaty on Friendship and the Border between the USSR and Germany, 28 September 1939, Moscow
AVPRF, f. 3a, d. 246, Germania, original; *KD1/25; KDZ1/25; DVP,* vol. XXII, book 2, no. 640; the English translation from the Russian given here is by M. Schwartz and A. M. Cienciala; see also *SDFP,* vol. III, p. 377; for an English translation of the German text, see *DGFP,* ser. D, vol. VIII (London, Washington, D.C., 1957), no. 157; reprint, *DPSR,* vol. I, no. 52.

13a. Secret Supplementary Protocol to the German-Soviet Treaty on Friendship and the Border between the USSR and Germany [Identifying Spheres of Interest and Affirming Agreements], 28 September 1939, Moscow
AVPRF, f. 06, op. 1, l. 8, d. 77, l. 4; Russian text, *DVP,* vol. XXII, book 2, no. 643; *KDZ1/26;* the English translation from the Russian given here is by A. M. Cienciala; see also *SDFP,* vol. III, p. 378; for an English translation of the German text, see *DGFP,* ser. D, vol. VIII, no. 159; reprint, *DPSR,* vol. I, no. 54.

13b. Secret Supplementary Protocol to the German-Soviet Treaty on Friendship and the Border between the USSR and Germany [Establishing Cooperation against Polish Resistance], 28 September 1939, Moscow
APRF, f. 3, op. 64, d. 675a, l. 20, original; *KD1/26; KDZ1/26; DVP,*

vol. XXII, book 2, no. 642; the English translation from the Russian given here is by A. M. Cienciala; see also *SDFP*, vol. III, p. 379; for an English translation of the German text, see *DGFP*, ser. D, vol. VIII, no. 160; reprint, *DPSR*, vol. I, no. 55.

14. Excerpt from a Politburo Protocol: Decision on Prisoners of War, [2–3] October 1939, Moscow
APRF, f. 3, op. 50, d. 410, ll. 148–149, copy on form used for excerpts from Politburo session minutes; *KD1/37*; *KDZ1/37* (includes text regarding sentences of military tribunals). For an English translation with somewhat different wording, printed alongside a photocopy of the Russian text, see Wojciech Materski, ed., *Kremlin versus Poland, 1939–1945: Documents from the Soviet Archives* [English edition by Ryszard Żelichowski] (Warsaw, 1996), no. 1.

15. Politburo Decision on Ratifying Military Tribunal Sentences in Western Ukraine and Western Belorussia, 3 October 1939, Moscow; from Protocol no. 7 (Special no. 7)—Decisions of the Politburo VKP(b) TsK [All Union Central Committee, Communist Party (Bolshevik)], for 4 September–3 October 1939
Rossiiskii Tsentr Khranenia i Izuchenia Dokumentov Noveishei Istorii [RTsKhIDNI—Russian Center for Preserving Documents of Recent History] now the Rossiiskii Gosudarstvenny Arkhiv Sotsialno-Politicheskoi Istorii [RGASPI—Russian State Archive for Social and Political History], f. 17, op. 162, d. 26, l. 21; *KD1/42a, KDZ1/37*.

16. Beria's Directive on Operational-Cheka Work among POWs in NKVD Camps, 8 October 1939, Moscow
TsKhIDK [RGVA], f. 451/p, op. 1, d. 1, ll. 22–27, typed copy; *KD1/46, KDZ1/46*.

17. NKVD UPV Information on the Number of POWs Subject to Release and Those Remaining in the Camps as of 8 October 1939, 8 October 1939, Moscow
TsKhIDK [RGVA], f. 1/p, op. 2a, d. 1, l. 37, typed original; *KD1/49, KDZ1/49*.

18. Beria's Memorandum to Molotov on Sending Home Polish Soldier POWs, Residents of Western Belorussia and Western Ukraine, and Delivering to the German Authorities POWs Who Are Residents of German Poland, 11 October 1939, Moscow
APRF, f. 3, op. 5, d. 615, ll. 47–48, original; *KD1/52, KDZ1/52*, both with facsimiles of the document.

19. Agreement between the NKVD UPV and the Narkomchermet [NKChM—Commissariat of Ferrous Metallurgy] on Utilizing POWs, 14 October 1939, Moscow

TsKhIDK [RGVA], f. 1/p, op. 2e, d. 8, ll. 4–6, typed copy; *KD1/57, KDZ1/57.*

20. Petition by Lieutenant Colonel T. Petrażycki to Starobelsk Camp Commander Aleksandr Berezhkov Regarding POW Correspondence with Families, 15 October 1939, Starobelsk

TsKhIDK [RGVA], f. 1/p, op. 2, d. 1, l. 141, handwritten original in Russian; *KD1/62–64, KDZ1/62* with facsimile.

21. Letter from Polish General Franciszek Sikorski to Army Commander Semyon K. Timoshenko on the Illegal Holding of Polish Lvov [Lwów, Lviv] Defenders in a Camp, 20 October 1939, Starobelsk

TsKhIDK [RGVA], f. 1/p, op. 2v, d. 1, ll. 222–223, typed original; *KD1/69, KDZ1/69.*

22. NKVD UPV Instruction to the Head of Putivl Camp on Detaining POWs with Various Specializations and Backgrounds, 23 October 1939, Moscow

TsKhIDK [RGVA], f. 1/p, op. 2e, d. 6, l. 27, typed copy; *KD1/75, KDZ1/75.*

23. NKVD UPV Report to Beria on the Refusal of Some POWs to Travel to German Poland, 28 October 1939, Moscow

TsKhIDK [RGVA], f. 1/p, op. 2v, d. 4, l. 18, typed original; *KD1/81, KDZ1/81.*

24. Pyotr Soprunenko's Instructions to the Commanders of the POW Camps on Sending [Military] Settlers to Ostashkov Camp, 29 October 1939, Moscow

TsKhIDK [RGVA], f. 1/p, op. 1e, d. 1, l. 112, typed copy; *KD1/84, KDZ1/84.*

25. Petition from POW Physicians and Pharmacists to Marshal Kliment Ye. Voroshilov Regarding Their Illegal Detention, 30 October 1939, Starobelsk

TsKhIDK [RGVA], f. 1/p, op. 2v, d. 1, ll. 176–177, handwritten Russian original with signatures; *KD1/87* with facsimile on p. 174, *KDZ1/87* with facsimile.

26. NKVD UPV Telegram to Vasily Korolev on Sending the UPV Inspector GB Major Vasily Zarubin to Kozelsk Camp, 31 October 1939, Moscow

TsKhIDK [RGVA], f. 1/p, op. 2e, d. 9, l. 34, typed copy; *KD1/90, KDZ1/90.*

27. SNK Resolution on the Admission to the USSR of Polish Military Personnel Interned in Lithuania, 9 November 1939, Moscow
GARF, f. 5446, op. 57, d. 65, ll. 118–119, typed original; *KD1/101, KDZ1/101* with facsimile.

28. NKVD UPV Report on the Number of POWs Sent Away and Held in the Camps, 19 November 1939, Moscow
TsKhIDK [RGVA], f. 1/p, op. 1e, d. 2, l. 223, typed original; *KD1/111* with facsimile, *KDZ1/111* with facsimile.

29. NKVD UPV Proposals to Beria on the Release of Some POWS, after 2 November 1939, Moscow
TsKhIDK [RGVA], f. 3, op. 1, d. 1, ll. 19–21, typed copy; *KD1/121, KDZ1/121.*

30. NKVD UPV Report to Vasily Chernyshov on Conditions in Kozelsk Camp, not before 1 December 1939, Moscow
TsKhIDK [RGVA], f. 1/p, op. 2e, d. 9, ll. 153–159, typed copy; *KD1/124, KDZ1/124.*

31. Politburo Decision to Arrest All Registered Regular Officers of the Former Polish Army, 3 December 1939, Moscow
RTsKhIDNI [RGASPI], f. 17, op. 162, d. 26, l. 119, typed copy from Politburo Decisions of 11 November–9 December 1939; *KD1/126, KDZ1/126.*

32. Report from the Commander of Starobelsk Camp to Semyon Nekhoroshev on the Political and Moral Conditions in the Camp in November 1939, 3 December 1939, Starobelsk
TsKhIDK [RGVA], f. 3, op. 1, d. 3, ll. 57–68, original typed on a Starobelsk camp form; *KD1/127, KDZ1/127.*

33. NKVD Commissar's Order no. 0408 to Organize New Reception and Distribution Centers in the UkSSR, 10 December 1939, Moscow
GARF, f. 9401, op. 1, d. 533, l. 310, typed original; *KD1/137, KDZ1/137,* l. 340.

34. Ivan Serov's Report to Beria on the Arrest of Polish Regular Officers in the Oblasts of Western Ukraine, 14 December 1939, Kiev
Tsentralny Arkhiv Federalnoi Sluzhby Bezopastnosti Rossiiskoi Federatsii [TsA FSB RF—Central Archive of the Federal Security Service of the Russian Federation], f. 3, op. 6, port. [*portfel*—file] 255, ll. 401–402, typed original; *KD1/138, KDZ1/138.*

35. Soprunenko's Instruction Sent by Direct Line to the Head of the UkSSR NKVD Administration of Correctional Labor Colonies, Aleksandr Zverev, on Dispatching Recuperated POW Officers to Various Destinations, 15 December 1939, Moscow

TsKhIDK [RGVA], f. 1/p, op. 2e, d. 18, l. 67, typed copy; *KD1*/140, *KDZ1*/140.

36. Soprunenko's Report on the Number of Polish POW Officers, Police, and Gendarmes, Inhabitants of Western Ukraine, Western Belorussia, and German Poland, Being Held in the NKVD POW Camps, 29 December 1939, Moscow

TsKhIDK [RGVA], f. 1/p, op. 01e, d. 2, l. 282, typed copy; *KD1*/146, *KDZ1*/146.

37. Beria's Instruction to Soprunenko as Head of the USSR NKVD Investigatory Brigade for Ostashkov Camp, 31 December 1939, Moscow

TsKhIDK [RGVA], f. 1/p, op. 1a, d. 1, ll. 220–223, original typed on NKVD USSR letterhead paper; *KD1*/150, *KDZ1*/150 with facsimile of first page of document.

38. Conclusion of the Indictment in the Case of POW Szczepan Olejnik, 6 January 1940, Ostashkov

TsKhIDK [RGVA], f. 1/p, op. 4e, d. 1, l. 163, typed copy; *KD1*/158, *KDZ1*/158 with facsimile.

39. Petition to Soviet Authorities from a Group of Polish POW Colonels to Define Their Status and Observe International Standards for the Treatment of POWs, 7 January 1940, Starobelsk

TsKhIDK [RGVA], f. 3, op. 1, d. 1, ll. 162–164, typed copy; also typed copy with the triangular seal of NKVD USSR UPV, *KD1*/160; *KDZ1*/160 (lists the same archival source but gives pp. 37–39). First published in *Novy Mir* [New World], no. 2 (Moscow, 1991), pp. 213–215.

40. Cipher Telegram from Soprunenko and Stepan Belolipetsky to Beria on the Conclusion of the Investigation and Transfer of POW Cases from Ostashkov Camp to the OSO, 1 February 1940, Ostashkov

TsA FSB RF, f. 3, op. 7, port. 649, l. 334, typed on incoming cipher telegram form, copy; *KD1*/178, facsimile, p. 317; *KDZ1*/178 with facsimile.

41. NKVD UPV Proposals to Beria on Clearing Out Starobelsk and Kozelsk Camps, 20 February 1940, Moscow

TsKhIDK [RGVA], f. 1/p, op. 3a, d. 1, ll. 274–275, typed original; *KD1*/188, *KDZ1*/188 with facsimile.

42. USSR Deputy People's Commissar of Internal Affairs Vsevolod Merkulov's Directive on Transferring to Prisons Certain Categories of Prisoners Detained in Starobelsk, Kozelsk, and Ostashkov Camps, 22 February 1940, Moscow

TsKhIDK [RGVA], f. 1/p, op. 1e, d. 1, l. 230, typed original; *KD1/190, KDZ1/190.*

43. NKVD UPV Report on the Nationality of Polish POW Officers Held in Starobelsk and Kozelsk Camps, 28 February 1940, Moscow

TsKhIDK [RGVA], f. 1/p, op. 01e, d. 3, ll. 98–99, typed copy; *KD1/202, KDZ1/202.*

44. Soprunenko's Report on the Number of Polish Police and Gendarmes Held in NKVD POW Camps, 2 March 1940, Moscow

TsKhIDK [RGVA], f. 1/p, op. 01e, d. 3, l. 110, typed original; *KD1/206, KDZ1/206.*

45. Excerpt from Protocol no. 13, Decisions of the Politburo: Decision on Guarding the State Borders of the UkSSR and BSSR, 2 March 1940, Moscow

RTsKhIDNI [RGASPI], f. 17, op. 162, d. 27, ll. 48–49, typed copy; *KD1/208, KDZ1/208.*

46. Report by Grigory Korytov to the Head of the Special Department of Kalinin Oblast UNKVD, Vasily Pavlov, on the Discussion in the NKVD 1st Special Department about "Clearing Out" the Ostashkov POW Camp, no later than 4 March 1940, Ostashkov

TsA FSB RF, Kollektsia Dokumentov [Documentary Collection], typed copy; *KD1/215, KDZ1/215.*

47. Beria Memorandum to Joseph Stalin Proposing the Execution of the Polish Officers, Gendarmes, Police, Military Settlers, and Others in the Three Special POW Camps, Along with Those Held in the Prisons of the Western Regions of Ukraine and Belorussia, Accepted by the Politburo, 5 March 1940, Moscow

APRF, f. 3, sealed packet no. 1, typed original; *KD1/216* with facsimile, *KDZ1/216* with facsimile. First published in the Russian press on 14 October 1992; *New York Times,* 15 October 1992. For the Russian text with Polish translation, see Wojciech Materski, ed. and trans., *Katyń: Dokumenty Ludobójstwa* (Warsaw, 1992) [henceforth *KDL*]; English version, Wojciech Materski, ed., with an introduction by Janusz Zawodny, *Katyn: Documents of Genocide* (Warsaw, 1993) [henceforth *KDG*], no. 9.

PART II. EXTERMINATION, MARCH–JUNE 1940

48. Soprunenko's Instruction to Korolev at Kozelsk Camp on Transferring POWs to the Smolensk Oblast UNKVD, 7 March 1940, Moscow

TsKhIDK [RGVA], f. 1/p, op. 2e, d. 9, l. 296; typewritten copy; *KDZ2/5*; the English translation from the Polish is by A. M. Cienciala.

49. Beria's Directive to Soprunenko on Compiling Lists of Polish POWs and Family Members, 7 March 1940, Moscow

TsA FSB RF, f. 3, op. 7, port. 13, ll. 46–47, typed copy; *KD1* Supplement, *Rasstrel* (henceforth *R*) 1, facsimile (all *Rasstrel* documents are facsimiles and are given at the end of *KD1* beginning with p. 523); also *KD2/ 3, KDZ2/3*. First published in S. V. Stepashin et al., eds., *Organy Gosudarstvennoi Bezopasnosti SSSR v Velikoi Otechestvennoi Voine: Sbornik Dokumentov* [State Security Organs of the USSR in the Great Fatherland War: Documentary Collection], vol. I (Moscow, 1995), book 1, no. 74, pp. 157–158.

50. Record Form Used for the Families of Prisoners of War, 7 March 1940, Moscow

RGVA, f. 1/p, op. 3a, d. 2, ll. 308–310, typed original; *KD2/4, KDZ2/4*.

51. Record Form for a Polish Prisoner of War, 16 March 1940, Moscow

RGVA, f. 1/p, op. 1e, d. 1, p. 237, typed copy; *KD1, R* 2; also *KD2/8*, and facsimile no. 8, p. 664 (facsimiles in *KD2* are at the end of the volume beginning with p. 663 and have the same numbers as the documents); *KDZ2/17* with facsimile.

52. Beria's Directive to the Commissar of Internal Affairs, Kazakh SSR, GB Senior Major Semyon Burdakov, on the Resettlement in Kazakhstan of Polish POW Families to Be Deported from the Western Oblasts of Ukraine and Belorussia, 20 March 1940, Moscow

TsA FSB RF, f. 3, op. 7, port. 14, ll. 68–70, typed copy; *KD1, R* 3; also *KD2/11, KDZ2/24*.

53. Beria's Order no. 00350 on "Clearing Out" the NKVD Prisons in the Western UkSSR and BSSR, 22 March 1940, Moscow

GARF, f. 9401, op. 1, d. 552, ll. 207–219, typed original; *KD1, R* 4; also *KD2/13, KDZ2/27*.

54. Soprunenko's Instruction to [Aleksandr G.] Berezhkov, Starobelsk Camp, on Sending Information about Polish POWs to the USSR NKVD UPV, 30 March 1940, Moscow

TsA FSB RF, f. 3, op. 7, port. 636, l. 35, handwritten original on NKVD outgoing cipher telegram form; *KD2/18, KDZ2/48* with facsimile.

55. Soprunenko's Directive to Borisovets on Sending Forty-Nine Polish POWs from Ostashkov Camp to the Commander of the Kalinin Oblast UNKVD, 1 April 1940, Moscow

RGVA, f. 1/p, op. 3e, ll. 6–8, typewritten original; *KD1, R* 6; also *KDZ 2/51*.

56. Soprunenko's Directive to the Heads of Ostashkov, Starobelsk, and

Kozelsk Camps on Receiving Lists of Polish POWs from the NKVD UPV, 4 April 1940, Moscow

TsA FSB RF, f. 3, op. 7, port. 636, l. 41, handwritten original on NKVD outgoing cipher telegram form; *KD1, R* 7; also *KDZ2/56*.

57. Soprunenko's Instruction to the Heads of Ostashkov, Starobelsk, and Kozelsk Camps on Sending Agent Record Files to the NKVD UPV, 4 April 1940, Moscow

TsA FSB RF, f. 3, op. 7, port. 636, l. 42, original, handwritten message on NKVD outgoing cipher telegram form; *KD1, R* 8; also *KD2/23*, and facsimile no. 23, p. 666; *KDZ2/57* with facsimile.

58. Beria's Directive to UkSSR and BSSR People's Commissars of Internal Affairs Serov and Tsanava to Arrest NCOs of the Former Polish Army in Western Ukraine and Western Belorussia, 4 April 1940, Moscow

TsA FSB RF, f. 3, op. 7, port. 14, l. 289, typed copy; *KD1, R* 9; also *KD2/22, KDZ2/55*. First published in *Organy,* vol. I, book 1, no. 80, pp. 167–168.

59. Receipt for 343 Polish POWs, 5 April 1940, Kalinin

RGVA, f. 18444, op. 2, d. 278, p. 142, handwritten original on NKVD incoming cipher telegram form; *KD1, R* 10, p. 539; also *KD2/25*, and facsimile no. 25, p. 667; *KDZ2/59* with facsimile.

60. Report from Dmitry Tokarev, UNKVD, Kalinin Oblast, to Merkulov on the Implementation of the First Order, 5 April 1940, Kalinin

TsA FSB RF, f. 3, op. 7, port. 649, l. 808, copy on NKVD incoming cipher telegram form; *KD1, R* 11, and *KD2/26* with facsimile no. 26, p. 668; *KDZ2/60* with facsimile.

61. Solomon Milshtein's Report to Merkulov on the Rail Transport of Polish POWs from Kozelsk to Smolensk for 4 April 1940, 5 April 1940, Moscow

RGVA, f. 1/p, op. 4e, d. 13, l. 49, typed original; *KD1, R* 13, and *KD2/27*; *KDZ2/61* with facsimile.

62. Soprunenko's Instruction to Korolev on Sending Eighty-Nine Polish POWs from Kozelsk Camp to the Head of the Smolensk Oblast UNKVD, 6 April 1940, Moscow

RGVA, f. 1/p, op. 3e, d. 3, ll. 411–416, typed copy; *KD1, R* 14 (Russian spelling of names); *KDZ2/69*, with facsimile of p. 1 (Polish spelling of names).

63. Report by USSR NKVD UPV on the Number of Polish POWs Held in NKVD and Narkomchermet Camps According to Rank or Profession, not earlier than 8 April 1940, Moscow

RGVA, f. 1/p, op. 01e, d. 3, ll. 142–146, typed copy; *KD2/34, KDZ2/77.*

64a. SNK Resolution Confirming the Deportation from Western UkSSR and BSSR of Individuals as Specified in the SNK Decision of 2 March 1940, 10 April 1940, Moscow

GARF, f. 5446, op. 57, d. 68, ll. 123–128, typed original; Beria's cover letter to Molotov and SNK resolution, *KD1, R 12, R 12a;* resolution also in *KD2/36* and facsimile no. 36, pp. 669–670; cover letter, resolution (and instruction) with facsimile of cover letter and p. 1 of resolution, *KDZ2/81.* Draft resolution and instruction sent to SNK on 5 April 1940, first published in *Organy,* vol. I, book 1, no. 81, pp. 168–171.

64b. Instruction on the Deportation of Specified Persons from the Western Oblasts of UkSSR and BSSR, 10 April 1940, Moscow

GARF, f. 5446, op. 57, d. 68, ll. 123–128, original; *KD1, R 17;* also *KD2/ 36* and *KDZ2/81* with facsimiles of Beria's cover letter to Molotov and first page of Instruction. First published in *Organy,* vol. I, book 1, no. 81.

65. Korolev's Report to Soprunenko on the Number of Polish POWs Dispatched from Kozelsk Camp, 11 April 1940, Kozelsk

RGVA, f. 1/p, op. 2, d. 9, l. 326, typed original on Kozelsk camp command form; *KD1, R 19;* also *KD2/37* and *KDZ2/87.*

66. Ivan Khokhlov's Instruction to Zaporozhye Camp Commander L. P. Lebedev to Seek Out Policemen and Officers among Polish POWs, 14 April 1940, Moscow

RGVA, f. 1/p, op. 2e, d. 13, l. 35, typed copy; *KD2/41, KDZ2/96.*

67. Political Report of the USSR NKVD UPV to Merkulov on the Mood of Polish POWs Dispatched from the Three Special Camps, 22 April 1940, Moscow

RGVA, f. 3, op. 1, d. 1, ll. 145–153, typed original; *KD2/53, KDZ2/127.*

68. Khokhlov's Instruction to Camp Heads on Sending the Record Files for Hospitalized Polish POWs to the USSR NKVD UPV, 22 April 1940, Moscow

TsA FSB RF, f. 3, op. 7, port. 636, l. 61, handwritten original on NKVD outgoing cipher telegram form; *KD1, R 26;* also *KD2/52* and *KDZ2/126.*

69. NKVD UPV Directive to the Heads of Ostashkov, Kozelsk, and Starobelsk Camps on Sending Certain Prisoners to Yukhnov Camp, 22 April 1940, Moscow

RGVA, f. 1/p, op. 4e, d. 13, l. 119, typed copy; *KD2/51, KDZ2/124.*

70. Arkady Gertsovsky's Instruction to Khokhlov on Submitting Certain POW Files for Examination, 25 April 1940, Moscow

RGVA, f. 1/p, op. 2e, d. 13, ll. 129–130, handwritten original; *KD2/ 59, KDZ2/137.*

71. Gertsovsky to Khokhlov on Sending Polish POW S. Swianiewicz, Held in Kozelsk Camp, into the Charge of the USSR NKVD, 28 April 1940, Moscow

RGVA, f. 1/p, op. 1e, d. 10, l. 465, typed original on NKVD letterhead form; *KD1, R* 35; also *KD2/65, KDZ2/149.* First published in O. V. Yasnova, ed., *Katynskaia Drama: Kozelsk, Starobelsk, Ostashkov: Sudba Internirovannykh Polskikh Voennosluzhashchykh* [The Katyn Drama: Kozelsk, Starobelsk, Ostashkov: The Fate of the Interned Polish Servicemen] (Moscow, 1991), in the section "Dokumenty" (facsimiles on unnumbered pages following end of text).

72. Summary Report on the Dispatch of Polish POWs from Ostashkov Camp between 6 and 29 April, after 29 April 1940, Moscow

RGVA, f. 1/p, op. 2e, d. 11, l. 143, handwritten original; *KD1, R* 36; also *KD2/66, KDZ2/152* with facsimile.

73. Soprunenko's Report on the Cases against Polish POWs in Ostashkov, Starobelsk, and Kozelsk Camps, 3 May 1940, Moscow

RGVA, f. 1/p, op. 01e, d. 3, l. 173, typewritten copy; *KD1, R* 38; also *KD2/68, KDZ2/155.*

74. Soprunenko's Report on POWs Left in Camps, not earlier than 5 May 1940, Moscow

RGVA, f. 1/p, op. 01e, d. 3, l. 175, typed copy; *KD2/71, KDZ2/163.*

75. Deputy People's Commissar for Internal Affairs Chernyshov's Directive to G. I. Antonov on Transporting Polish POWs from the Krivoy Rog Basin to the Northern Railway Camp, 10 May 1940, Moscow

RGVA, f. 1/p, op. 2e, d. 8, ll. 293–294, typed copy; *KD1, R* 39; also *KD2/73, KDZ2/170.*

76. Korolev's Report on the Number of Orders for Polish POW Death Transports and the Number of Prisoners Dispatched from Kozelsk Camp to Smolensk, Moscow, and Yukhnov According to USSR NKVD UPV Lists, 14 May 1940, Kozelsk

RGVA, f. 1/p, op. 2e, d. 9, ll. 363–364, typewritten original; *KD1, R* 40; also *KD2/79, KDZ2/184* with facsimile.

77. Borisovets's Report on the Dispatch of Polish POWs Sent to Kalinin Oblast UNKVD and the Number Remaining in the Camp, 17 May 1940, Ostashkov

RGVA, f. 1/p, op. 2e, d. 11, l. 395, typed original; *KD1, R* 43 (cover letter); also *KD2/80* (with list of POWS remaining in camp), *KDZ2/193* (cover letter) with facsimile.

78. Berezhkov's Letter to Soprunenko on the Number of Lists Received and the Number of Polish POWs Dispatched from Starobelsk Camp between 5 April and 12 May 1940, with Reports Attached, 18 May 1940, Starobelsk
RGVA, f. 1/p, op. 2e, d. 10, ll. 219–223, typed original; *KD1, R* 44; also *KD2/81, KDZ2/196.*

79. UPV Information on the Implementation of Orders to Send Polish POWs from the Special Camps into the Charge of the UNKVD of the Corresponding Oblasts, not earlier than 19 May 1940, Moscow
RGVA, f. 1/p, op. 01e, d. 3, ll. 203–204, typed copy, unsigned; *KD1, R* 45; also *KDZ2/203* with facsimile.

80. Petition from the Children of Polish POWs to Stalin to Release Their Fathers from Ostashkov Camp, 20 May 1940, Rozovka, Zaporozhye Oblast
RGVA, f. 1/p, op. 4e, d. 1, l. 79, handwritten original in Russian; *KD1, R* 46; also *KD2/85, KDZ2/206* with facsimile.

81. Command Order to the 136th Detached Convoy Battalion on the Successful Execution of the Assignment to "Clear Out" Kozelsk Camp, 21 May 1940, Smolensk
RGVA, f. 38106, op. 1, d. 10, l. 145, typed original; *KD1, R* 47; also *KD2/87, KDZ2/209* with facsimile.

82. Tokarev's Report to Merkulov on Sixty-Four Executions Carried Out, 22 May 1940, Kalinin
TsA FSB RF, f. 3. op. 7, port. 649, l. 1170, typed copy on NKVD incoming cipher telegram form; *KD1, R* 48; also *KD2/88, KDZ2/211* with facsimile.

83. Borisovets's Report to Soprunenko on the Sojourn of Polish POWs in Ostashkov Camp, 25 May 1940, Ostashkov
RGVA, f. 1/p, op. 16, d. 5, ll. 51–55, typed original; *KD2/91, KDZ2/217.*

84. UPV Report on the Number of Polish POWs Dispatched from the Special Camps into the Charge of Three Oblast UNKVDs and to Yukhnov Camp, before 25 May 1940, Moscow
RGVA, f. 1/p, op. 3a, d. 2, l. 273, typed original; *KD1, R* 49; also *KD2/90,* and facsimile no. 90, p. 672; *KDZ2/215* with facsimile.

PART III. KATYN AND ITS ECHOES, 1940 TO THE PRESENT

85. Soprunenko's Report on the Number of Polish POWs Dispatched to Yukhnov Camp from the Special Camps and the Grounds on Which They Were Sent There, after 25 May 1940, Moscow

RGVA, f. 1/p, op. 4e, d. 13, l. 420, typed original; *KD1, R* 50; also *KD2/92*, and facsimile of doc. 92, p. 673; *KDZ2/219*.

86. Report on the Number, Ranks, and Professions of Polish POWs in Griazovets Camp as of 1 July 1940, 1 July 1940, Moscow
RGVA, f. 1/p, op. 1e, d. 3, ll. 194–195, typed copy; *KD2/103, KDZ3/2*.

87. Protocol on the Destruction of POW Correspondence, 23 July 1940, Starobelsk
TsKhIDK [RGVA], f. 1/p, op. 2e, d. 10, l. 268, typed original; *KDZ2/Aneks* [Annex] I/2.

88. Soprunenko's Instruction to the Head of Starobelsk Camp and the Head of the Camp OO to Destroy POW Files, 10 September 1940, Moscow
RGVA, f. 1/p, op. 2e, d. 10, ll. 283–284, typed copy; *KD2/121, KDZ3/43*.

89. Special Report to Beria by the UNKVD Head for the Vologda Region, Pyotr Kondakov, on the Counterrevolutionary Activities of Some Polish POWs in Griazovets Camp, 29 September 1940, Vologda
RGVA, f. 1/p, op. 4b, d. 5, ll. 222–225, typed original on NKVD Vologda Oblast form; *KD2/124, KDZ3/52* with facsimile of p. 1.

90. Beria's Order on Rewards for NKVD Workers for "Clearing Out" the Prisons and the Three Special Camps, 26 October 1940, Moscow
TsA FSB RF, f. 66, op. 1, port. 544, ll. 252–257, typed original; *KD2/128, KDZ2/Aneks* I/6 with facsimiles of first and last pages.

91. Note from Beria to Stalin on the Possible Organization of Military Units with Polish and Czech Prisoners of War, 2 November 1940, Moscow
APRF, f. 3, op. 50, d. 413, ll. 152–153, original on NKVD USSR letterhead paper; *KD2/130, KDZ3/74* (ll. 152–157, including short biographies). First published in Wojciech Materski, trans. and ed., *Z Archiwów Sowieckich* [From the Soviet Archives], vol. 1: *Polscy Jeńcy Wojenni w ZSSR 1939–1941* [Polish Prisoners of War in the USSR, 1939–1941] (Warsaw, 1992), no. 7.

92. Gorlinsky and Rodionov to Soprunenko on the 1 May Festivities for the Berling Group in Malakhovka, no later than 24 April 1941, Moscow
RGVA, f. 1/p, op. 5a, d. 2, l. 191, typed original; *KDZ3/140* with facsimile, translated from the Russian by A. M. Cienciala.

93. Excerpt from the Politburo Protocols on the Decision to Create a Polish Division in the Red Army, 4 June 1941, Moscow
APRF, f. 30, op. 50, d. 283, l. 141, copy; *KD2/153, KDZ3/153* (f. 3). First published in Materski, *Z Archiwów Sowieckich*, vol. 1, no. 8.

94. Polish-Soviet Agreement on Reestablishing Diplomatic Relations and Forming a Polish Army in the USSR, 30 July 1941, London

DVP, vol. XXIV (Moscow, 2000), no. 136; and *KD2/165* (Russian text, minus the Secret Protocol later dropped by the Polish government); Polish text, *KDZ3/189* (minus the Secret Protocol), after *Dziennik Polski* [The Polish Daily] (London), 31 July 1941; the English translation of the official Polish text given here with the Secret Protocol is from *DPSR*, vol. I, no. 106.

95. Polish-Soviet Military Agreement, 14 August 1941, Moscow

DVP, vol. XXIV, no 165 (Russian text); the English translation of the Polish text given here is from *DPSR*, vol. I, no. 112; *KDZ3/198* (Polish translation of *DPSR*, vol. I, no. 112).

96. UPVI Report on Polish POWs in NKVD Camps, 1939–1941, with Attachment, 3 December 1941, Kuibyshev

RGVA, f. 1/p, op. 1e, d. 4, ll. 3–4, handwritten original; *KD2/175* and facsimile no. 175, p. 680; *KDZ3/217* (gives Moscow as place of origin).

97. Conversation of Stalin and Molotov with General Władysław Sikorski, Polish Premier; General Władysław Anders, Commander of the Polish Army in the USSR; and Professor Stanisław Kot, Polish Ambassador to the USSR, 3 December 1941, Moscow

APRF, 048, op. 52a, p. [*papka*—folder] 458, d. 2, ll. 29–49, typed original; *KD2/176, KDZ3/221*. Russian text first published in *Mezhdunarodnaia Zhizn* [International Life], no. 12 (Moscow, 1990), pp. 134–140; for the original Polish record, see Stanisław Kot, *Rozmowy z Kremlem* [Conversations with the Kremlin] (London, 1956), pp. 153–171; and Władysław Anders, *Bez Ostatniego Rozdziału: Wspomnienia z Lat 1939–1946* [Minus the Last Chapter: Memoirs of the Years 1939–1946] (3rd edition, London, 1959), pp. 87–101. (Kot dictated the record to Anders who took part in the conversation and acted as translator.) An English translation of the Polish record is in *DPSR*, vol. I, no. 159; also in the English versions of the Kot and Anders books (see Part III, note 8).

98. Molotov's Telegram to the Soviet Ambassador in London, Aleksandr Bogomolov, on Stalin's Conversation with Anders, 21 March 1942, Moscow

APRF, f. 3, op. 66, d. 63, ll. 132–133, typed copy; *KDZ3/232*. First published in Wojciech Materski, trans. and ed., *Z Archiwów Sowieckich* [From the Soviet Archives], vol. 2: *Armia Polska w ZSSR 1941–1942* [The Polish Army in the USSR, 1941–1942] (Warsaw, 1992), no. 7. An English translation of the Polish record of the Stalin-Anders conversation is in *DPSR*, vol. I, no. 193.

99. Beria's Note to Stalin on the Polish Army's Evacuation to Iran, 4 April 1942, Moscow

APRF, f. 3, op. 66, d. 63, l. 138, original typed on NKVD USSR letterhead paper; *KD2/180*; *KDZ3/236* with facsimile. First published in Materski, *Z Archiwów Sowieckich*, vol. 2, no. 10. The English translation from the Russian given here is by A. M. Cienciala.

100. Telegram from Mikhail Koptelov, Consul General of the USSR in Pahlavi, to Stalin on the Completion of the Polish Army's Evacuation from the USSR, 5 September 1942, Pahlavi, Iran

APRF, f. 3, op. 66, d. 63, l. 159, typed copy; *KDZ3/240*. First published in Materski, *Z Archiwów Sowieckich*, vol. 2, no. 13. The English translation from the Russian given here (with slight stylistic modifications by A. M. Cienciala) is from Materski, *Kremlin versus Poland*, no. 6.

101. Radio Communiqué on the Discovery of Graves of Polish Officers in the Smolensk Area, 13 April 1943, Berlin, 9:15 a.m.

Zbrodnia Katyńska w Świetle Dokumentów [The Katyn Crime in the Light of Documents] (10th edition, London, 1982), p. 85 (Polish translation from German); *KD2/186* (Russian translation from Polish); the English translation from the German given here is from *DPSR*, vol. I, no. 305; see also *The Crime of Katyn: Facts and Documents* (London, 1965), pp. 101–102.

102. Communiqué Issued by the Sovinformburo Attacking the German "Fabrications" about the Graves of Polish Officers in Katyn Forest, 15 April 1943, Moscow

KD2/187, after *Pravda* (Moscow), 16 April 1943; *KDZ4/3*; the English text given here is from *DPSR*, vol. I, no 306, after *Soviet War News* (London), no. 541, 17 April 1943.

103. Statement of the Polish Government Concerning the Discovery of the Graves of Polish Officers near Smolensk, 17 April 1943, London

Polish text in Dariusz Baliszewski and Andrzej Krzysztof Kunert, eds., *Prawdziwa Historia Polaków: Ilustrowane Wypisy Źródłowe, 1939–1945* [The Real History of the Poles: Illustrated Selections from Primary Sources, 1939–1945], vol. 2: *1943–1944* (Warsaw 1999), p. 1016, after *Dziennik Polski* (London), 19 April 1943; *KDZ4/5*. The English translation given here (with slight stylistic modifications by A. M. Cienciala) is from *DPSR*, vol. I, no. 308.

104. Note from Molotov to Polish Ambassador Tadeusz Romer on the Soviet Government's Decision to Break Off Relations with the Polish Government, 25 April 1943, Moscow

KD2/192, after *Vneshnaia Politika Sovestskogo Soiuza w Period Ve-*

likoi Otechestvennoi Voiny [Foreign Policy of the Soviet Union in the Period of the Great Fatherland War], vol. I (Moscow, 1944), pp. 301–303; KDZ4/16; the English text given here is from *DPSR*, vol. I, no. 313; for a Polish translation of the Russian text, see Baliszewski and Kunert, *Prawdziwa Historia*, vol. 2, p. 1045.

105a. Report by the Secretary of the Polish Red Cross, Kazimierz Skarżyński, on the PRC Technical Commission's Visit to Smolensk and Katyn, 15–16 April 1943 (Excerpts), June 1943, Warsaw
    Polish text in Kazimierz Skarżyński, *Katyń* (2nd edition, Paris, 1990), pp. 11–19, translated by A. M. Cienciala.

105b. Report of the Polish Red Cross Technical Commission on Its Work in Katyn, April–June 1943 (Excerpts), June 1943, Warsaw
    For this report, edited by Kazimierz Skarżyński, see his *Katyń*, pp. 39–48; the excerpts here were translated into English by A. M. Cienciala; KD2/199, Russian translation of the report published in Czesław Madajczyk, *Dramat Katyński* (Warsaw, 1989), pp. 150–159. The full Polish text was first published in the weekly *Odrodzenie* [Rebirth], no. 7 (Warsaw, 1989); KDZ4/34. For Skarżyński's testimony before the U.S. Congressional Committee of Inquiry (Madden Committee) see *The Katyn Forest Massacre: Hearings before the Select Committee to Conduct an Investigation of the Facts, Evidence, and Circumstances of the Katyn Massacre*, Eighty-second Congress, 1st and 2nd Sessions, 1951–1952 (Washington, 1952), part 3, pp. 394–415.

106. The Burdenko Commission Report (Excerpts), 24 January 1944, Moscow
    GARF, f. 7445, op. 114, d. 8, ll. 317–348, "Projekt" [Draft], original; KD2/215; final Russian text, *Pravda* (Moscow), 26 January 1944; KDZ4/67; the English text given here is from the *Special Supplement to the Soviet War Weekly* (London, 1944). For a reprint of the full English text, see *Crime of Katyn,* chap. 8.

107. Instructions on the "Katyn Matter" Sent by the Special Government Commission for Directing the Nuremberg Trials to Roman Rudenko, Chief Soviet Prosecutor at Nuremberg, 15 March 1946, Moscow
    GARF, f. 7445, op. 2, d. 391, ll. 61–63, copy; KD2/220; KDZ4/80.

108. Meeting of the Soviet Special Government Commission for Directing the Nuremberg Trials, 24 May 1946, Moscow
    GARF, f. 7445, op. 2, d. 391, ll. 50–51, original; KD2/223.

109. Conclusions of the Congressional Select Committee to Conduct an Investigation of the Katyn Forest Massacre (Excerpts), 22 December 1952, Washington, D.C.

Hearings on the Katyn Massacre. 82nd Congress, House Report no. 2505. Conclusions of the Select Committee (Washington, 1952), pp. 8864, 9240; reprinted in *100th Congress, Congressional Serial Set,* vol. 13875, House Document no. 100–183 (Washington, D.C., 1988), and in *Crime of Katyn,* pp. 291–293; *KD2/226* (excerpts in Russian translation); *KDZ4/92.*

110. Note by Shelepin to Khrushchev, 3 March 1959, Proposing to Destroy the Documents of the Operation Sanctioned by the Politburo on 5 March 1940, 3 March 1959, Moscow
APRF, f. 3, sealed packet no. 1, handwritten original; *KD1, R* 52; also *KD2/227* with facsimile no. 227, pp. 684–685; *KDZ2/*Aneks I/11 with facsimile (following p. 416); *KDZ4/93.* The English translation given here (with slight stylistic modifications by A. M. Cienciala) is from Materski, *KDG,* no. 5.

111. Politburo Resolution and Instruction for the Soviet Ambassador in London Regarding the Projected Katyn Monument, 2 March 1973, Moscow (Excerpt)
APRF, f. 3, op. 78, d. 1617, ll. 100–102, copy on Central Committee letterhead paper; *KD2/230;* the English version given here (with slight stylistic modifications by A. M. Cienciala) is from Materski, *KDG,* nos. 13, 14.

112. Politburo Protocol no. 3 on Measures to Counteract Western Propaganda on the Katyn Question (Excerpt), 5 April 1976, Moscow
APRF, 3, op. 78, d. 1618, ll. 63–68, copy on letterhead paper used for excerpts from the protocols of the Politburo CC CPSU; *KD2/231; KDZ4/* 101. The English version given here (with slight stylistic modifications by A. M. Cienciala) is from Materski, *KDG,* no. 15.

113. Note to the CC CPSU "On the Katyn Question" by Soviet Foreign Minister Eduard Shevardnadze; Valentin Falin, Director of the International Department of the CC CPSU; and Vladimir Kriuchkov, Chairman of the KGB USSR, 22 March 1989, Moscow
APRF, f. 3, copy, *KD2/233; KDZ4/114.* The English translation given here (with slight stylistic modifications by A. M. Cienciala) is from Materski, *KDG,* no. 19.

114. Politburo Protocol no. 152: Instruction by Mikhail S. Gorbachev to the Prosecutor's Office and Other State and Party Agencies to Propose the Future Soviet Line on Katyn (Excerpt), 31 March 1989, Moscow
APRF, f. 3, sealed packet no. 1, *KDZ4/115.* The English translation given here (slightly modified by A. M. Cienciala) is from Materski, *KDG,* no. 20.

115. Note on the Katyn Question to the CC CPSU, 22 April 1989, Moscow
The English translation given here (slightly modified by A. M. Cienciala) from Materski, *KDG*, no. 21; see also *KDZ4/116*.

116. Falin's Note on Katyn for Mikhail Gorbachev, 23 February 1990, Moscow
APRF, f. 3, op. 113, d. 260, ll. 187–190, original; *KD2/234*; *KDZ4/118*. The English translation given here (slightly modified by A. M. Cienciala) is from Materski, *KDG*, no. 23.

117. TASS Communiqué on Katyn, 13 April 1990, Moscow
KD2/235, after *Izvestia*, no. 104, Moscow, 13 April 1990. The TASS communiqué was published with slightly different wording in the world press the next day; see *New York Times* and *Times* (London), 14 April 1990.

118. Decree by President Gorbachev, in Connection with the Visit of Polish Minister of Foreign Affairs Krzysztof Skubiszewski, on Speeding Up the Investigation of the Fate of the Polish Officers Held in the Three Special Camps (Excerpt), 3 November 1990, Moscow
KDZ4/126. The English translation given here (with slight modifications by A. M. Cienciala) is from Materski, *KDG*, no. 24.

119. Letter from President Lech Wałęsa to President Boris Yeltsin Thanking Him for the Documents on Katyn, 15 October 1992, Warsaw
Archiwum Urzędu Prezydenta R. P. [Archive of the Office of the President of the Polish Republic], znak sprawy [reference no.] 87/11, GP 049–206–92, translated by A. M. Cienciala.

120. Letter from President Yeltsin to President Wałęsa on the Fifty-fifth Anniversary of the Katyn Tragedy, 22 May 1995, Moscow
APRF, f. 92, op. 4, d. A 1–1–61–1995, ll. 211–213, copy signed by B. Yeltsin on paper with the letterhead of the president of the Russian Federation; *KD2/236*.

121. Speech by Jerzy Buzek, Prime Minister of Poland, at the Ceremonial Opening of the Polish War Cemetery at Katyn, 28 July 2000, Katyn
Przeszłość i Pamięć [The Past and Memory], no. 3 (Warsaw, 2000), pp. 34–35; *KDZ4/142*. The English translation from the Polish is by A. M. Cienciala; *KD2/238* (Russian translation of the Polish text; the date is erroneously given as 2 September, but the correct date appears in the volume's list of documents).

122. Speech by the Deputy Prime Minister of the Russian Federation, Viktor Khristenko, at the Opening of the Katyn Memorial Complex, 28 July 2000, Katyn

Published according to the shorthand report attached to the video record of V. Khristenko's speech at Katyn on 28 July 2000, *KD2/239; KDZ4/143.*

Appendix of Camp Statistics

TABLE 1   USSR NKVD Camps for Polish Prisoners of War, September 1939–March 1942

A. Distribution Camps

Griazovets camp	7 km from the town of Griazovets, Vologda Oblast, 8 km from the Griazovets Rail Station, in a former monastery.
Kozelshchansk camp	Kozelshchina, Poltava Oblast, 500 m from the Kozelshchina Rail Station.
Oranki camp	Oranki Village, Gorky Oblast, in a former monastery.
Putivl camp	former Safronievsky monastery, 40 km from Putivl, Sumy Oblast, and 12 km from Tiotkino, on the peat bogs.
Vologda camp	near Zaonikeyevo, Vologda Oblast.
Yukhnov camp	Town of Yukhnov, Smolensk Oblast, 32 km from the Babynino Rail Station, 500 m from the village of Shchelkanovo, Yukhnov Rayon.
Yuzha camp	30 km from the town of Yuzha, Smolensk Oblast, at Talitsa.

B. USSR NKVD Special Camps

Kozelsk camp	Kozelsk, Smolensk (Kaluga) Oblast, 8 km from the town of Kozelsk, in the Optina Pustyn monastery.
Ostashkov camp	Ostashkov, Kalinin (Tver) Oblast, Stolbny Island on Lake Seliger.
Starobelsk camp	Starobelsk, Voroshilovgrad (Luhansk) Oblast.

C. Labor Camps

Krivoy Rog camp	Several sections in the Krivoy Rog basin, including Dzherzhinskruda, Oktiabrruda, Lenruda, Nikopol-Marganets, and Glavspetstal mines.
Rovno camp	Town of Rovno, Rovno Oblast; sections of the camp were located all along the highway under construction between Novograd, Volynsky, and Lvov.
Zaporozhye camp	Bolshoe Zaporozhye town, Zaporozhye Oblast, 15 km from the center; deportee settlement no. 9.
Yeleno-Karakuba camp	located in the Stalin Oblast in the deportee settlements of Yelenovka, Karakub, Karakubstroi (Karakuba Construction Plant), and the village of Novo-Troitskoe. In April 1940, the camp was divided into two camps: Yeleno and Karakub.

*Source: KD1/*Prilozhenie [Annex] 5, p. 439; *KDZ1/*Aneks 6, p. 501.

TABLE 2A   Kozelsk Camp, November 1939–March 1940

Ranks and Categories of POWs	1939		1940					
	29 Nov.	31 Dec.	9 Jan.	20 Jan.	4 Feb.	22 Feb.	16 Mar.	1 Apr.
Admirals	1	1	1	1	1	1	1	1
Generals	4	4	4	4	4	4	4	4
Colonels	24	27	27	27	27	27	26	26
Lieutenant Colonels	79	76	76	74	74	73	72	72
Majors	258	240	240	236	235	232	232	232
Captains	653	663	663	652	651	653	647	647
Naval Captains	12	12	12	12	12	12	12	12
Naval Captains 2nd rank	3	3	3	3	3	3	3	3
Naval Captains 1st rank	2	2	2	2	2	2	2	2
Other Officers	3,419	3,439	3,436	3,404	3,437	3,485	3,482	3,480
Military Clergy	7	1	1	1	1	1	1	8
Landowners	4	28	28	6	6	9	9	9
Higher State Officials	43	43	43	33	33	61	61	61
Rank-and-File [Soldiers] Subject to Dispatch	78	173	173	134	134	5	5	5
Refugees	131	54	54	76	82	41	37	37
Totals	4,718	4,766	4,763	4,665	4,702	4,609	4,594	4,599

Source: Tables 2A–D were compiled on the basis of UPV information in RGASPI, f. 1/p, op. 01e, d. 3, pp. 8–37; d. 2, pp. 236–240, 292–295. First published in N. S. Lebedeva, *Katyn: Prestuplenie Protiv Chelovechestva* (Moscow, 1994), pp. 325–328, they are reproduced in the Polish version of that volume, *Katyn: Zbrodnia Przeciwko Ludzkości* (Warsaw, 1998), Aneksy, p. 318; also in *KD1*/Prilozhenia 1–4, pp. 435–439; *KDZ1*/Aneksy 1–4, pp. 481–484.

TABLE 2B Ostashkov Camp, November 1939–March 1940

Ranks and Categories of POWs	1939			1940				
	29 Nov.	31 Dec.	9 Jan.	20 Jan.	4 Feb.	22 Feb.	16 Mar.
Police and Gendarme Officers	199	264	281	281	283	282	288
Police and Gendarme NCOs	603	615	742	740	827	780	775
Police and Gendarme Rank and File	5,016	5,020	4,878	4,932	4,964	5,007	4,924
Prison Workers	104	110	111	111	114	114	189
Intelligence Agents	2	5	6	6	7	8	9
Military Rank and File and NCOs Subject to Dispatch	—	145	140	82	72	72	72
Military Clergy	—	11	11	5	5	5	5
[Military] Settlers	—	27	27	27	35	35	35
Refugees	35	93	89	93	*	*	*
Others	—	1	1	1	71 [67]	64	67 [63]
Total	5,959	6,291	6,286	6,278 [6,185]	6,378 [6,374]	6,371 [6,367]	6,364 [6,360]

Source: See table 2A.
Note: The Polish table in *KDZ11*/Aneks 3 has slightly lower numbers, which are shown in brackets. More refugees were probably included under "Others."
*No data available.

Table 2C Starobelsk Camp, November 1939–March 1940

Ranks and Categories of POWs	1939		1940					
	29 Nov.	31 Dec.	9 Jan.	20 Jan.	4 Feb.	23 Feb.	16 Mar.	1 Apr.*
Generals	8	8	8	8	8	8	8	8
Colonels	57	55	55	55	55	55	55	55
Lieutenant Colonels	130	130	130	127	126	126	126	126
Majors	321	320	320	320	316	315	315	316
Captains	853	854	854	851	847	845	845	843
Other Officers	2,519	2,528	2,528	2,528	2,529	2,528	2,527	2,527
Military Clergy	12	12	12	12	18	9	18	9
Landowners	2	2	2	2	2	2	2	2
Higher State Officials	5	5	5	5	5	5	5	5
Others	— [2]	2	2	2	2 [3]	2	2	2
Totals	3,907 [3,909]	3,916	3,916	3,913 [3,910]	3,910 [3,909]	3,908 [3,895]	3,896 [3,894]	3,893

Source: See table 2A.

Note: The Polish table in KDZ1/Aneks 4 has slightly different numbers, which are listed here in brackets.

* Additional column only in Polish volume.

Table 2D Number of Prisoners of War in USSR NKVD UPV Camps, November 1939–March 1940

Date	Total in UPV camps	Special Camps					Narkomchermet Camps						Rovno
		Total	Starobelsk	Kozelsk	Ostashkov	Yukhnov	Total	Krivoy Rog	Yeleno Karakuba	Nikopol	Zaporozhye		
29 Nov.	39,331	14,948	3,907	4,718	5,959	364	10,172 [10,252]	6,766	1,882	—	1,604		14,211
31 Dec.	38,710	15,087	3,916	4,766	6,291	114	10,326 [10,362]	6,927	1,797	—	1,602		13,297
9 Jan.	38,368	15,079	3,916	4,763	6,286	114	10,326	6,927	1,797	—	1,602		12,963
20 Jan.	38,254	14,971	3,913	4,665	6,278	115	10,320	6,927	1,797	—	1,596		12,963
4 Feb.	38,117	14,990	3,910	4,702	6,378	—	10,287	6,784	1,907	—	1,596		12,840
22 Feb.	38,007	14,888	3,908	4,609	6,371	—	10,279	6,775	1,908	—	1,596		12,840
16 Mar.	37,666	14,854	3,896	4,594	6,364	—	10,170	5,595*	1,890	1,154	1,531		12,642

Source: See table 2A.

Note: The Polish table in *KDZ11*/Aneks 1 has several different numbers, which are listed here in brackets.

*1,154 men were transferred to the new Nikopol camp.

Biographical Sketches

These biographical sketches of selected Polish and Russian officers, officials, and others are based on information in *KD1–2* and *KDZ1–3* as well as biographical dictionaries, biographies, articles, and various sources printed and online. Some specialized information was supplied by Dr. Natalia S. Lebedeva, Institute of General History, Russian Academy of Sciences, Moscow; Professor Wojciech Materski, director of the Institute of Political Studies, Polish Academy of Sciences, Warsaw; and Dr. Vladimir V. Pozniakov, Institute of General History, Russian Academy of Sciences, Moscow.

Aleksandrov, Georgy Fedorovich (1908–1960). Soviet party official. Central Committee [CC] of the Communist Party of the Soviet Union [CPSU] candidate, 1941–1946; head, CC Propaganda and Agitation Department, 1940–1947. Helped organize the Burdenko Commission.

Anders, Władysław (1892–1970). Polish general; born in former Russian Poland. Veteran, Russian Army, 1914–1917; Polish Army, 1918–1925; Polish-Soviet War, 1920. Commander, Cavalry Operational Group, southeastern Poland, September 1939. Wounded, taken prisoner, and imprisoned in Lwów [Lviv], then Moscow, September 1939–August 1941. Commander, Polish Army in the USSR, August 1941–August 1942, then evacuated to Iran. Commander, Polish Army in the Middle East, later the Polish Army 2nd Corps in the British 8th Army, Italy, 1943–1945; took Monte Cassino on 18 May 1944, opening a land route to Rome for the Allied armies. Member, Council of Three (émigré political leaders), London, 1954–1970. Died in London; buried, Polish Military Cemetery, Monte Cassino. Author of memoirs.

Andreev, Andrei Andreevich (1893–1971). Soviet party and government official. Politburo member, 1932–1952; held many posts, including CC secretary and deputy chairman of Sovnarkom [SNK—Council of People's Commissars] USSR.

Andropov, Yuri Vladimirovich (1914–1984). Soviet party official and statesman. Soviet ambassador in Hungary, 1954–1956; supervised crushing of Hungarian revolution, during and after which he supported Hungarian communist leader Janos Kadar. Headed CC CPSU Department of Relations with Communist and Socialist Parties of Socialist Countries, 1957–1967; head, KGB [Committee on State Security], 1967–1982; succeeded Leonid Brezhnev as head of CPSU, November 1982; died in February 1984.

Antonov, G. I. (b. 1902). Soviet security officer. In 1939, GB [State Security] lieutenant and deputy section head, 2nd Special Department NKVD, then instructor in UPV [Administration for Prisoner-of-War Affairs] Political Department. In March–May 1940, led special NKVD brigade to Krivoy Rog camps and organized with A. V. Tishkov the dispatch of Polish POWs to the Sevzheldorlag [Northern Railway camp].

Bashlykov, Ivan Mikhailovich (b. 1906). Soviet security official. Militia 2nd lieutenant, 1939–1940; in Main Administration of the Worker-Peasant Police, 1939; head, UPV Secretariat, from late September 1939; made frequent inspection trips to POW camps.

Bashtakov, Leonid Fokeevich (b. 1900). Soviet security official. GB captain, 1939; major, 1940. Deputy head, end of 1939, and head, 5 March 1940, 1st Special Department [Protection of the Government], NKVD. By Politburo decision of 5 March 1940, appointed member of the Troika assigned to examine cases and decide sentences of Polish POWs in the three special POW camps and those in western Belorussian and western Ukrainian NKVD prisons.

Beck, Józef (1894–1944). Polish foreign minister, December 1932–September 1939. Piłsudski legionnaire and P.O.W. [Polish Military Organization] member in WWI; military intelligence chief, 1920; military attaché in Paris, 1921–1923; army colonel, diploma 1925; head of Piłsudski's cabinet, May 1926–September 1930, then deputy premier. Selected by Piłsudski as undersecretary of state in the Ministry of Foreign Affairs, he succeeded August Zaleski as foreign minister in December 1932. During his tenure, Poland remained an ally of France and Romania while balancing between the USSR and Nazi Germany, having signed nonaggression agreements with each (1932 and 1934, respectively). He accepted a British guarantee of Polish independence on 31 March 1939 and oversaw the signing of a provisional agreement on 6 April 1939 and the conclusion of a Mutual Assistance Treaty with Great Britain on 25 August 1939. To avoid Soviet capture, he crossed with the government and general staff into Romania on the night of 17–18 September 1939 with intent to proceed to France. He was interned in Romania with the rest of the government and died there on 6 June 1944. Wrote a posthumously published account of Polish foreign policy in 1926–1939.

Belolipetsky, Stepan Yefimovich (b. 1905). Soviet security official. GB lieutenant and senior investigator, GUGB [Main Administration for State Security], NKVD Investigation Department, 1939–1940. Beginning on 4 December 1939, led an investigation team to Ostashkov camp to help prepare cases against the POWs for presentation to OSO [NKVD Special Board] by 1 February 1940. Signed indictments of Polish police and prison workers.

Berezhkov, Aleksandr Georgevich (b. 1885). GB captain, 1939–1942; head of Starobelsk camp, 1939–1941; participated in closing down the camp. Head of NKVD camp no. 84 (Sverdlovsk, now Ekaterinburg), 1942–1943.

Beria, Lavrenty Pavlovich (1899–1953). Chief of NKVD [People's Commissariat of Internal Security], 1938–1953, and Stalin's right-hand man in organizing mass repressions of millions of people. On 3 March 1940 he submitted to Stalin the resolution to shoot the Polish POWs, approved by the Politburo on 5 March. He personally examined all principal issues connected with them and, along with Stalin, bears chief responsibility for the execution of Polish officers, police, and other prisoners in spring 1940. Soon after Stalin's death, seen as a threat by Nikita Khrushchev and others in new party leadership, he was arrested, charged with fabricated "anti-state" crimes—all except the real ones—sentenced, and executed, 23 December 1953.

Berling, Zygmunt (1896–1980). Polish general; born in former Austrian Poland. Veteran of Strzeltsy [Riflemen's Association], Polish Legions, 1914–1917; Polish Army, 1918–1939. As lieutenant colonel, arrested by NKVD in Wilno [Vilnius], 1939; survivor, Starobelsk, Yukhnov, and Griazovets camps, 1939–1940. Led a pro-Soviet officer group to work out a force structure for a Polish division in the Red Army, 1940–1941; in Polish Army under Anders in the USSR, 1941–1942, but stayed in the USSR. Promoted to general by Stalin, spring 1943. Commander, Kościuszko Division, then 1st Polish Corps and 1st Polish Army, 1943–1944; member of Polish National Committee of Liberation. Held ministerial posts in Poland, 1953–1957. Author of memoirs.

Birnbaum, Mieczysław (1889–1940). Polish lieutenant, infantry reserves, Warsaw Military District,1939. Journalist, writer, and former intelligence officer. He fought against Ukrainians in Lwów, November 1918, and participated in Polish-Soviet peace negotiations, 1919–1920. Mentioned in NKVD reports as a troublemaker, he was held in Kozelsk camp and shot at Katyn.

Blokhin, V. M. (d. 1955). Soviet security official. One of the NKVD's chief executioners; he personally murdered more than a thousand people. GB major and head, Command Department, AKhU [Administrative-House-keeping Board], NKVD, April–May 1940. Director of operations and chief executioner of Ostashkov POWs in Kalinin/Tver; rewarded by Beria, 26 October 1940, for performing "special tasks." Stripped of his rank, November 1954.

Bober, Jan (b. 1897). Polish police officer. Head, Police Investigation Office, Nowogródek [Belarussian: Novahrudak]. Survivor of Yukhnov and Griazovets camps, 1940–1941; mentioned in NKVD reports as anti-Soviet. Released in fall 1941 and served in Polish Army under Anders in the USSR.

Bohatyrewicz [Bohaterewicz], Bronisław (1870–1940). Polish brigadier general, retired. Born in former Russian Poland; major, Russian infantry, 1914; POW, Germany, 1914–1918. Veteran, Polish-Soviet War; on general staff, Central Lithuania, 1922; retired, 1927. In Kozelsk camp; shot at Katyn; exhumed in 1943.

Boldin, Valery Ivanovich (b. 1935). Soviet party official. Aide to Gorbachev, who was then CC secretary of agriculture, 1981. Head, CC General Department, 1988–1989; reported on secret Katyn file to Gorbachev. Member, Presidential Council, March 1990. Joined failed coup against Gorbachev, August 1991. Author of memoirs.

Borisovets, Pavel Fedorovich (b. 1891). Soviet security officer. NKVD major; head, Ostashkov camp, 1939–1940. Participated in "clearing out" the camp, spring 1940. Deputy head, Griazovets NKVD camp, 1941.

Bór-Komorowski, Tadeusz (1895–1966). Polish general; born in former Austrian Poland. Veteran, Austro-Hungarian Army, WWI, and Polish Army, 1918–1939. Commander, Armia Krajowa [AK—Home Army, i.e., underground army], July 1943–October 1944; led Warsaw Uprising, 1 August–2 October 1944. In German captivity, 5 October 1944–5 May 1945. After World War II, lived in England; died in London. Author of book on Home Army.

Boruta-Spiechowicz, Mieczysław Ludwik (1894–1987). Polish general; born in former Austrian Poland. Veteran, Riflemen's Association, Polish Legions, 1914–1918; commanded operational groups and Army "Kraków," September 1939. Interned in Soviet prisons, 1939–1941. Indicated an interest in fighting Germans together with Soviets and was interviewed by Beria and Merkulov on forming a Polish division in Red Army, October 1940. After release in fall 1941, commanded 5th Infantry Division, Polish Army, under Anders, in the USSR, 1941–1942; in Iran, then Britain, 1942–1945. Returned to Poland, 1945, and in Polish People's Army to 1946. Lived near Szczecin [former Stettin] for eighteen years, then retired to Zakopane. Member, Movement for Defense of Human and Civic Rights, Poland, 1977–1980; supporter of Solidarity movement, 1980–1987.

Brezhnev, Leonid Ilyich (1906–1982). Soviet party leader and statesman. Head of state, 1960–1982, and of CPSU, 1964–1982. Continued cover-up of Katyn massacres. Decided on the Warsaw Pact invasion of Czechoslovakia, August 1968. Sick in the last years of his life; his duties were taken over by Yuri V. Andropov.

Bukojemski, (Nałęcz) Leon (1895–1978). Polish lieutenant colonel. Veteran, Polish Legions, 1914–1917; Polish Army, 1918–1939. Survivor, Starobelsk and Griazovets camps. In Berling group, 1940–1941; in Polish Army under Anders in the USSR, 1941–1942, but stayed in the USSR. Co-organizer with Berling of Kościuszko Division, 1st Polish Army, 1943; in Polish People's Army, 1944–1945.

Bulganin, Nikolai Aleksandrovich (1895–1975). Soviet party official, a close collaborator of Stalin's. Held many high posts under Stalin and Khrushchev; joined failed coup against Khrushchev, 1957, and lost his Presidium CPSU seat in 1958.

Burdakov, Semyon Nikolaevich (b. 1901). Soviet security official. In 1939–1940, as a GB major and commissar, NKVD, Kazakh SSR [Soviet Socialist Republic], he was in charge of resettling in Kazakhstan the deported family members of executed Polish officers, police, and other prisoners.

Burdenko, Nikolai Nilovich (1876–1946). Soviet physician and government official. Pioneer in Soviet neurosurgery; chief surgeon, Red Army, in WWII. In 1944, headed the Special State Commission to prove German guilt for the Katyn massacre. Its report was the standard Soviet version that prevailed until 13 April 1990.

Buzek, Jerzy (b. 1940). Polish politician and statesman. Born in Śmiłowice, Silesia, now in the Czech Republic; professor of chemical engineering. A leader in the Solidarity movement, 1980–1981, and underground opposition, 1981–1989. Helped draw up the economic program of the anticommunist Akcja Wyborcza Solidarność [AWS—Solidarity Election Action], 1997; prime minister, AWS government, 1997–2001; spoke at the opening of Katyn and Mednoe Polish war cemeteries, 28 July and 2 September 2000. Elected to European Parliament, spring 2004.

Chechev, Aleksandr Aleksandrovich (b. 1899). Soviet security officer and official. GB captain. Head, 2nd Section of Main Prisons Office, NKVD USSR, 1939–1941. In charge of transporting Polish prisoners in spring

1940 from west Belorussian NKVD prisons to the Minsk NKVD prison, where they were likely executed. There are indications that at least some of them may be buried at Kuropaty, now within Minsk city boundaries, where mass graves of Stalinist victims were discovered in 1988.

Chekholsky, Danil Lavrentievich (b. 1904). Soviet security official of Polish origin. Political instructor in Kozelsk camp, then controller and translator in Starobelsk camp. Fired for allowing POW correspondence with families after mid-March 1940 and informing relatives that the POWs had left the camp, both actions being in violation of NKVD prohibitions. His fate is unknown.

Chernyshov, Vasily Vasilievich (1896–1952). Soviet security official, commissar. Deputy commissar (from 1946, deputy minister), NKVD USSR, 1937–1952, with rank of lieutenant general. Oversaw GULAG [Main Administration of (Labor) Camps] operations, the special camps, and the Main Prison Administration. A director of operations to "clear out" the three special camps and the prisons of the western oblasts [administrative regions] of Ukrainian SSR and Belorussian SSR, as well as transferring POWs from Narkomchermet [People's Commissariat of Ferrous Metallurgy] camps to Sevzheldorlag and transferring Polish soldiers interned in Lithuania and Latvia to Kozelsk and Yukhnov camps.

Czapski, Józef (1896–1993). Polish artist, painter, and writer; born and raised in Moscow. Veteran, Polish-Soviet War, 1919–1920; captain in reserves. Spent several years as a painter in Paris. Survivor, Starobelsk and Griazovets camps. In Polish Army under Anders in the USSR, 1941–1942, he searched for missing officers. Later, cultural officer, Middle East and Italy. After World War II, settled in Paris and cooperated with the Polish periodical *Kultura* there. Author of memoirs.

Czernicki, Ksawery Stanisław (1882–1940). Polish rear admiral; born in former Russian Vilna [Vilnius, Wilno] Province. Graduated from Kronstadt Naval Engineering School, 1905; lieutenant colonel in Russian Navy, naval shipbuilding, 1917. Veteran, Polish Army, 1920–1925; member, Naval Command, Warsaw, 1925–1926; supervised shipbuilding for Polish Navy in France, 1926–1932; chief of services, Naval Command, 1932–1939; commander, evacuation train of Naval Command, September 1939. Prisoner in Ostashkov and Kozelsk camps; shot at Katyn.

Dekanozov, Vladimir Georgievich (1898–1953). Soviet diplomat, commissar. Beria's comrade-in-arms from 1921. Stalin's emissary to Lithuania, July 1940; later, Soviet ambassador to Germany. Deputy commissar of foreign affairs, 1939–1945. Arrested and executed with Beria, December 1953.

Dmitriev, Aleksandr Dmitrievich. Soviet security official. In 1940, as GB sergeant and, from late March, lieutenant, a member of the 1st Autobase (motor pool), AKhU, NKVD, he was responsible for securing motor transport for the execution of Polish POWs and other Polish prisoners. He was rewarded by Beria, 26 October 1940.

Dmowski, Roman (1864–1939). Polish political writer, ideologue, politician, statesman. Born in Warsaw, former Russian Poland; natural sciences graduate, Russian University, Warsaw. Ideologue and leader of National Democratic movement. Worked for Russo-Polish cooperation in 1906–1916, then for Polish independence as leader of the Polish National Committee in Western Europe. Co-leader of Polish delegation to the Paris Peace Conference and co-signatory for Poland with Ignacy Jan Paderewski of the Versailles Treaty, 28 June 1919. Polish foreign minister, October–December 1923. Opposed Piłsudski during World War I, as well as Polish governments, 1926–1939.

Domoń [Russian misspelling: Domel], Ludwik (b. 1899). Polish major, later lieutenant colonel. Survivor, Starobelsk camp, Kharkov prison, the GULAG, and Griazovets camp. Chief of staff, 6th Infantry Division, Polish Army under Anders in the USSR, 1941–1942, then Polish Army 2nd Corps, Middle East and Italy.

Ewert, Mieczysław Szczęsny (b. 1894). Polish captain, infantry reserves. At headquarters of Polish commander in chief, September 1939. Survivor, Starobelsk camp, Kharkov prison, and the GULAG. In Polish Army under Anders in the USSR, 1941–1942, later Polish Army 2nd Corps, Middle East and Italy.

Falin, Valentin Mihailovich (b. 1926). Soviet party official, diplomat, adviser to Mikhail S. Gorbachev. In October 1988, succeeded Anatoly Dobrynin as head of CC International Department; full CC member, 1989. Recommended admission of Soviet guilt for the Katyn massacres (blaming Beria and Merkulov) and supported Yuri Zoria's archival quest for Katyn documents, 1989–1990. Elected to Soviet Congress of Deputies and Supreme Soviet, 1989.

Fediukov, I. I. Soviet security official. GB major. Head, Gorky Oblast UNKVD [NKVD Administration], 1939–1941. Head of NKVD USSR Construction Site no. 1, October 1939–June 1941.

Fedotov, Pyotr Vasilievich (1898–1963). Soviet security official. Senior major, GB; was deputy head of 2nd Department (Counterintelligence), GUGB, NKVD USSR, September 1939; appointed head, 2nd Administration NKVD, February 1941. Participated in organizing executions of Polish officers, police, and prisoners held in jails; retired from KGB, 1959.

Gaididei, Mikhail Mikhailovich (b. 1898). Soviet security official. GB sergeant. Acting head, then head of OO [Special Section], Starobelsk camp, late April–May 1940; participated in "clearing out" the camp.

Geraschchenko, Victor (b. 1937). Soviet, then Russian official. Chairman, Executive Board, Soviet State Bank, July 1989; director, Credit-Currency Department, International Foundation for Economic and Social Reforms, November 1991.

Gertsovsky, Arkady Yakovlevich (b. 1904). Soviet security official. GB captain and deputy head, 1st Special Department, NKVD USSR, 1940; responsible for drawing up documentation on Polish POWs and dispatch lists for transferring them from the three special camps and prisons to regional UNKVDs (for execution); subsequently in charge of keeping records of the operation; head, Department "A," NKGB [People's Commissariat of State Security] USSR, 1943. Arrested, 1953; convicted in connection with Beria's case, 1954.

Glemp, Józef (b. 1929). Polish churchman. Studied in Gniezno, Poznań, and Rome, 1950–1964; took holy orders, 1956. Bishop, 1979; primate of Poland, 1981; cardinal, 1983.

Goberman, Maks Yefimovich. Soviet security official. GB 2nd lieutenant, 1939; senior inspector, UPV Document Registration Office, late September 1939; later, deputy head, 2nd Department, UPV. Received copies of documents on POWs; participated in "clearing out" the three special camps.

Goetel, Ferdynand (1890–1960). Polish journalist, writer. Visited Katyn, early April 1943, and reported to the Polish Red Cross (PRC) executive on his return. Accused of collaboration with the Germans, he fled Poland and joined the Polish Army 2nd Corps, Italy, where he interviewed Krivozertsev; see his book *Lata Wojny* [War Years] (London, 1956). He lived in Britain, 1946–1960.

Gomułka, Władysław (1905–1983). Polish communist leader; born in former Austrian Poland. District activist of the KPP [Communist Party of Poland], 1926–1938, he served two prison terms. Head of communist PPR [Polish Workers' Party], 1943–1948; charged with nationalist deviation and under house arrest, 1948–1955. As head of the communist PZPR [United Polish Workers' Party], October 1956–December 1970, he presided over a relaxation of the communist system in Poland, but crushed the shipyard workers' revolt in the coastal cities by military force in December 1970, after which he resigned. Author of memoirs; subject of biographies.

Gorbachev, Mikhail Sergeevich (b. 1931). Soviet party official, statesman. Graduated with law degree, Moscow, 1955. Career in Komsomol [communist youth organization], Stavropol, then party 1st secretary there, and CC member, Moscow, 1978, as secretary of agriculture. Secretary general, CPSU, March 1985–December 1991, and last president of the USSR. Best known for his contribution to ending the Cold War and his policies of *perestroika* (economic restructuring) and *glasnost* (open discussion), especially of Stalinist crimes, including the Katyn massacre. Approved TASS communiqué, 13 April 1990, admitting Soviet guilt for Katyn massacre, and handed NKVD dispatch lists for the three special camps to Polish President Wojciech Jaruzelski. Author of memoirs and subject of several biographies.

Gorczyński, Eustachy (b. 1893). Polish colonel; commander, Sapper Reserve Center no. 1, September 1939. Survivor, Starobelsk, Yukhnov, and Griazovets camps. Joined Berling group, then Polish Army under Anders in the USSR; rejoined Berling group in 1942.

Gorlinsky, Nikolai Dmitrievich (1907–1965). Soviet security official. GB captain, deputy commissar, NKVD, Ukrainian SSR, 1938–1940; participated in "clearing out" the prisons in western Ukraine, 1940. Was discharged and stripped of his rank of lieutenant general in 1954.

Grabicki [Russian misspelling: Grobicki], Jerzy (b. 1891). Polish cavalry; colonel, reserves. Survivor, Kozelsk, Yukhnov, and Griazovets camps. Joined Berling group.

Grzybowski, Wacław (1887–1959). Polish diplomat. Ambassador, Prague, 1927–1935; Moscow, 1936–1939; in Western Europe, 1939–1959.

Gusev, Konstantin Mikhailovich (1906–1941). Soviet Air Force lieutenant general. Member, Military Council, Belorussian Front, 1939; air force commander, Far Eastern Front, July 1940. Arrested and shot, 1941; rehabilitated (i.e., declared innocent or cleared of all charges), 1956.

Ivanov, Aleksei Mikhailovich (b. 1916). Soviet security officer. NKVD 2nd lieutenant; company commander in Detached 136th NKVD Convoy Battalion, 1938–1940. In charge of convoying Polish officers from Kozelsk camp to Smolensk and Gnezdovo, April–May 1940.

Januszajtis-Żegota, Marian Józef (1889–1973). Polish general. Born in former Russian Poland. Veteran, Riflemen's Association, Polish Legions; co-organizer of a failed anti-Piłsudski coup, January 1919. Wounded in Polish-Soviet War, 1920. Promoted to brigadier general, 1922, and general, 1924. Governor of Nowogródek [Belarus: Novahrudak] Province, 1926–1929; retired from army, 1929, but served on General Langner's staff during the defense of Lwów against the Germans, September 1939. Organized one of the first Polish anti-Soviet resistance groups in Lwów, 1939, and was arrested there. Having indicated a readiness to fight on the Soviet side against Germany, he was interviewed by Beria and Merkulov in Moscow, October 1940, on forming a Polish division in the Red Army. He was released and transferred to the Polish Military Administration, Britain, August 1941. Died in Crowley, Britain.

Jaruzelski, Wojciech (b. 1923). Polish general and statesman. Born in Kurów, Poland. Deported and in the USSR, 1940–1943; joined 1st Polish Army under Berling, 1943, and fought until war ended in Germany. Chief, general staff of Polish Army, 1965–1968; Polish deputy minister of defense, then minister, 1968–1983. Crushed Solidarity movement by imposing martial law, 13 December 1981. Chairman, Council of Ministers, 1981–1983; 1st secretary, PZPR, 1981–1989; commander, Polish armed forces, 1983–1990; pressed Gorbachev for Soviet admission of truth about Katyn. President, Polish People's Republic, then Polish Republic, 1989–1990. Author of memoirs.

Kachin, Timofei Fedotovich (b. 1902). Soviet security official. GB lieutenant and assistant to head of UNKVD, Kalinin Oblast, Dmitri Tokarev. Received POWs from Ostashkov camp; rewarded by Beria, 26 October 1940.

Kaczyński, Lech (b. 1949). Polish lawyer, politician, minister, president of Poland. Elected senator in June 1989; deputy leader of Solidarity in 1990. Justice minister under Premier J. Buzek; leader of Prawo i Sprawiedliwość [PIS—Law and Justice] party. President of the City of Warsaw, 2002–2005. Elected president of Poland, 23 October 2005. He stated in July 2006 that he would leave disputes over Katyn to historians, at least for the time being. His twin brother, Jarosław, head of PIS, became premier in July 2006.

Kaganovich, Lazar Moiseevich (1893–1991). Soviet official. A close collaborator of Stalin's. Responsible for railways in World War II, including transport for Polish POWs in 1939–1940. As a member of the Politburo, he voted to shoot the Polish POWS, 5 March 1940. Member of collective party leadership, 1953–1957; joined failed coup against Khrushchev and retired in 1957.

Kalinin, Mikhail Ivanovich (1875–1946). Soviet statesman and party functionary. As chairman of Supreme Soviet, he was the nominal president of the USSR in 1938–1946. As a Politburo member, he voted to shoot the Polish POWs, 5 March 1940.

Karamanov, Uzakbey (b. 1937). Soviet official. Deputy minister of construction, Kazakh SSR, 1986; deputy director, Gosbank, Kazakh SSR, 1987–1989; chair, Sovmin [Council of Ministers], Kazakh SSR, July 1989–October 1991.

Katushev, Konstantin Fedorovich (b. 1927). Soviet official. CC secretary, 1968–1977; Soviet ambassador to Cuba, 1982. Chairman, State Committee for Foreign Economic Affairs, 1985–1988; minister of internal economic affairs, 1988.

Kebich, Vyacheslav (b. 1936). Soviet, then Belarussian economist. Deputy chair, Sovmin, Belarussian SSR, 1985–1990; chairman, April 1990; chairman, Sovmin, Republic of Belarus, September 1990.

Khlomov, Mikhail D. (1905–1945). Soviet official. Signed documents as head of Chancellery, Sovnarkom, USSR, 1939–1940.

Khodas, Nikolai Vasilievich. Soviet official. Commissar, Ostashkov camp, April 1940; commander, Griazovets camp, May–August 1941.

Khokhlov, Ivan Ivanovich. Soviet security officer; worked in security organs, 1918–1953. GB lieutenant and deputy head, operational work, UPV, 1939–1940. Directed the "clearing out" of the three special camps. Substituted in Moscow for absent Pyotr Soprunenko, 14–28 April 1940; signed POW dispatch lists sent to the three special camps.

Kholichev, Dmitry Karlovich (1908–1951). Soviet security official. In 1939, a GB lieutenant and senior commissioner, GEU [Main Economic Administration], NKVD. Traveled to Ostashkov camp as a member of the investigation brigade led by Soprunenko and participated in "clearing out" the camp.

Khristenko, Viktor Borisevich (b. 1957). Russian statesman. Deputy finance minister, 1997–1998; secretary of state, 1st deputy minister of finance, April–September 1998; 1st deputy prime minister, May 1999–February 2004; made a speech at the opening of the Polish War Cemetery at Katyn, 28 July 2000. Appointed acting prime minister by Russian President Vladimir Putin, February 2004.

Khrulev, Andrei Vasilevich (1892–1962). Soviet brigadier general; deputy commissar of defense, USSR; and chief, Red Army Rear [Quartermaster] Services, August 1940. In charge of supplying the Polish Army under Anders in the USSR, 1941–1942.

Khrushchev, Nikita Sergeevich (1894–1971). Soviet party leader and statesman. Rose in party ranks under Stalin. 1st secretary, UkSSR 1938–1941; political officer and lieutenant general in Red Army, 1941–1944; head of party and chairman of the Council of Ministers, UkSSR, 1944–1949. Organized arrest of Beria, 1952, and overthrew Malenkov, 1955. Leader of CPSU and USSR, 1955–1964. Famous for condemning (some) Stalinist crimes and the cult of personality at the Twentieth Party Congress, February 1956. He accepted Gomułka as the new Polish party leader but crushed the Hungarian revolution by force in fall 1956; he sanctioned the building of the Berlin Wall in 1961; and he placed nuclear missiles in Cuba in 1962. Overthrown by Leonid Brezhnev's group in October 1964, he retired. Author of memoirs and subject of biographies.

Khudiakova, T. N. Soviet security official. Worked in NKVD Personnel Department. Assistant inspector, UPV, 1939. In charge of Kozelsk camp archives, 1939–1940.

Kirilenko, Andrei Pavlovich (1906–1990). Soviet official. As CC and Politburo member, 1957–1982, he supported first Khrushchev, then Brezhnev. As a member of the CC Secretariat, he oversaw the party organization and Soviet industry, 1964–1982.

Kirov, Sergei M. (1886–1934). Soviet party leader. Head, Leningrad Party Organization, 1926–1934. Widely considered Stalin's heir apparent, he was assassinated in his office building in Leningrad, either on Stalin's orders or with his assent, in December 1934. Stalin used his death as a pretext to purge the CPSU of old Bolsheviks, the most prominent of whom appeared in staged public trials. Polish POWs were shown a propaganda film of Kirov's life.

Kirshin, Mikhail Mikhailovich (b. 1902). Soviet security officer. NKVD battalion commissar, 1939; major, 1943. Commissar, Starobelsk camp, 1939–1940; participated in "clearing out" the camp.

Kiselev, N. A. Soviet security official, investigator. As a GB 2nd lieutenant, he was a member of the Belolipetsky Brigade sent to Ostashkov camp in December 1939; there he participated in preparing POW dossiers for the OSO. Rewarded by Beria, 26 October 1940.

Kobulov, Bakhcho [Bogdan] Zakharovich (1904–1953). Soviet security official. One of Beria's closest Georgian comrades. Deputy commissar, NKVD; GB commissar 3rd rank; and head, GEU, NKVD, and its investigative unit, 1938–1941. Member of Troika appointed by Politburo, 5 March 1940, to draw up sentences, examine the cases, and decide the sentences of Polish officers and police from the three special camps. Colonel general and deputy commissar, GB USSR, 1941–1945. Executed together with Beria, December 1953.

Kondakov, Pyotr Pavlovich (1902–1970). Soviet security official. GB major; head, UNKVD, Vologda Oblast, September 1939–February 1941. He held several high administrative NKVD and ministerial posts in 1941–1961.

Korboński, Stefan (1901–1989). Polish politician, resistance leader. Served in Polish military organizations and army, 1917–1921, and was a regional Peasant Party leader, 1930–1939. Under the German occupation of Poland, he was the co-founder of the underground Political Council, 1939; head of Civilian Resistance, 1941–1945; and last delegate of the Polish government in Warsaw. He escaped from Poland in 1947 and settled in the United States. Author of books on the Polish resistance. Received Medal of Freedom from President Ronald Reagan.

Korolev, Vasily Nikolaevich (b. 1902). Soviet security official. GB 1st lieutenant, March 1940; head, Kozelsk camp, 1939–1941; deputy head of several GULAG camps, 1941–1944.

Korytov, Grigory Vasilevich (b. 1900). Soviet security official. As GB 1st lieutenant, he was head of OO, Ostashkov camp; he ratified POW cases for handing over to OSO and signed off on cases sent to the OSO in Moscow, early 1940. Reported on Moscow conference of February 1940 regarding sentencing of Ostashkov prisoners and participated in "clearing out" the camps.

Kosygin, Mikhail Grigorievich (b. 1901). Soviet security official. Senior inspector, 1st Department, UPV, late September 1939. Made several trips to POW camps.

Kot, Stanisław (1885–1975). Polish historian, Peasant Party politician, government official. Opposed Piłsudski and successor governments, 1926–1939. Close aide and adviser to General Władysław Sikorski, 1939–1943; Polish ambassador, USSR, 1941–1942; minister in Near East and minister of information, London, 1943–1944. Returned to Poland, 1945; Polish ambassador in Rome, 1945–1947, then émigré in England. Author of historical studies and editor of documents on his embassy in the USSR. Died in London.

Kovalev, Mikhail Prokofevich (1897–1967). Soviet military officer. Army commander 2nd rank, 1939; colonel general, 1943. Commanded forces of Kiev Military District, December 1937–1939; of Belorussian Military District, April–September 1939; of Belorussian Front, September 1939. Commander of 15th Army in Soviet-Finnish War, 1939–1940, and of Kharkov Military District, May 1940.

Kriuchkov, Vladimir Aleksandrovich (b. 1924). Soviet security official, lawyer, diplomat. Succeeded Chebrikov as KGB chairman, 1988. Politburo member, September 1989–July 1990, and member of Gorbachev's Presidential Council, March 1990. Opposed giving access to state archives to Russian historians and participated in failed coup against Gorbachev, August 1991.

Krivenko, Mikhail Spiridonovich (1904–1954). NKVD officer. Brigade commander, chief of staff, USSR NKVD Convoy Troops, 1938–1941. Responsible for convoys and guarding POWS transported by rail from Ostashkov camp to Kalinin/Tver, April–May 1940; rewarded by Beria, 26 October 1940.

Krivozertsev, Ivan (pseudonym: Mikhail Loboda; 1915–1947). An inhabitant of Gnezdovo who testified before the German and International Medical Commissions in 1943 as a witness to Soviet responsibility for the Katyn massacre. Lengthy interviews were conducted with him in Italy by Polish writers Ferdynand Goetel and Józef Mackiewicz. He accompanied the Polish Army 2nd Corps to Britain after the war and lived in a Polish camp there. His death in 1947 was ruled a suicide, but he was likely murdered by an NKVD agent. His testimony was posthumously entered in the U.S. Congressional (Madden Committee) Hearings on Katyn, 1951–1952.

Kruglov, Sergei Nikiforovich (1907–1977). NKVD official. A deputy commissar, NKVD, USSR, 1939; oversaw cadres, including the UPV and the POW camps. Co-author with Merkulov of a report on the Katyn massacre for the Burdenko Commission, before it began its work at Katyn in January 1944. Dismissed from post as minister of internal affairs with rank of colonel general, 1956.

Kuczyński-Iskander Bej, Stanisław (b. 1907). A Polish cavalry captain of Tatar descent taken prisoner by the Red Army in late September 1939; his records were faked by the NKVD. The Burdenko Commission claimed to have found at Katyn a signed but unsent postcard to his wife, dated Kozelsk, 20 June 1941. Russian records show, however, that he was held at Starobelsk and was taken out of the camp in December 1939. He was allegedly taken to Moscow, but was most likely transferred to the NKVD jail in Kharkov. He is listed in the Polish War Cemetery book for Kharkov as shot there.

Kukiel, Marian (1885–1973). Polish general, politician, historian; born in former Austrian Poland. Veteran, Polish Legions and Polish-Soviet War, 1919–1920. Opposed Piłsudski, 1926–1935. Professor at Jagiellonian University and curator at Czartoryski Museum, Kraków, 1926–1939. Joined the Sikorski government in France, then England. As Polish minister of defense, he issued a communiqué on 16 April 1943 detailing Polish inquiries of Soviet authorities on the fate of the POWs in 1941–1942. Director of the General Sikorski Historical Institute (now the Polish Institute and Sikorski Museum), London, 1946–1972. Author of several works on Polish military history and a biography of General Władysław Sikorski.

Kulik, Grigory Ivanovich (1890–1950). Deputy commissar of defense, USSR, and chief, Main Artillery Directorate, 1939–1940. Wrote a report in late September 1939 on Red Army actions and the situation in Western Ukraine. Marshal and hero of the Soviet Union, 1940. He mismanaged the re-equipment of the Red Army; was demoted and was then dismissed for incompetence by Marshal Zhukov after the Battle of

Kursk (July 1943); worked in the reserves. Retired and presumably imprisoned in 1946, he was shot in 1950, but was rehabilitated with his rank of marshal restored in 1957.

Kupry, Timofei Fedorovich. Soviet security official. GB 2nd lieutenant, 1940; promoted to lieutenant, March 1940. Commandant, AKhU, UN-KVD, Kharkov Oblast, 1940–1941. According to the deposition by a witness (Syromiatnikov), he personally executed Polish officers from Starobelsk camp in Kharkov prison. He was rewarded by Beria, 26 October 1940.

Kuznetsov, A. S. (b. 1899). Soviet security official. GB lieutenant colonel, 1943; colonel 1953. Head, 1st Department, NKVD USSR, 1943–1953. Responsible until 1943 for storing files of Polish POWs shot in spring 1940.

Kwaśniewski, Aleksander (b. 1954). Polish politician and statesman; born in Białogard, northwestern Poland. Minister of youth and sports, 1981–1989. Cofounder of the Sojusz Lewicy Demokratycznej [SLD—Democratic Left Alliance], 1989, which was viewed by many Poles as successor to the PZPR. Member of Seym (lower house of Polish Parliament), 1991. Led SLD to victory in 1993; narrowly defeated Lech Wałęsa in presidential election in 1995; reelected president in 2000; spoke at the opening of the Polish Military Cemetery in Kharkov, June 2000. During his tenure, Poland joined the European Union in 2003. He actively participated in negotiations leading to a peaceful resolution of the Ukrainian Orange Revolution crisis in November–December 2004.

Kwolek, Stanisław Józef (1901–1940). Polish lieutenant, reserves; engineer. Veteran, Silesian uprisings, 1920–1921. Worked in Lwów regional administration. Fought in defense of city, September 1939. Organized patriotic celebration in Starobelsk camp, 11 November 1939; was transferred to Kharkov jail and sentenced to forced labor. Died in a GULAG camp in Komi Autonomous Soviet Socialist Republic [ASSR].

Lachert, Wacław (1872–1951). Polish industrial manager. President, Executive Board, Polish Red Cross (PRC) under German occupation, 1939–1945; sanctioned sending first PRC delegation, then the PRC Technical Commission, to Katyn, spring–summer 1943.

Langner, Władysław Aleksander (1896–1972). Polish general; born in former Austrian Poland. Veteran, Polish Legions, 1914–1917; Austro-Hungarian Army, 1917–1918; fought in Polish-Soviet War. Commander, defense of Lwów against Germans; surrendered to Red Army, 22 September 1939; pleaded in Moscow for release of his soldiers. Escaped to Romania, then France. In Polish Army in Britain, 1940–1945. Died in Newcastle-on-Tyne, England.

Lebedev, L. P. (b. 1903). Soviet security official. Section head, 11th Department, GUGB, UNKVD, Moscow Oblast, 1939; GB lieutenant, head of Zaporozhye mining camp, 1940. In charge of transferring POWs from the mining camp to Sevzheldorlag, May 1940.

Lewandowska, Janina Antonina (1908–1940). Polish pilot; daughter of General Józef Dowbór-Muśnicki (1867–1937). Cadet ensign or 2nd lieutenant, air force reserves. Trained in Poznań as a radio telegrapher, pilot, and parachutist. The only known female military prisoner in any of the three special camps. Held in Ostashkov camp, then Kozelsk. Exhumed at Katyn, 1943.

Lis, Józef (b. 1897). Polish major, artillery. Survivor, Starobelsk, Yukhnov, and Griazovets camps. Briefly in Berling group, then Polish Army under Anders in the USSR and the Middle East; later, in Polish Army 2nd Corps in Italy.

Łopianowski, Narcyz (1898–1984). Polish captain, cavalry. Served in Podlasie Cavalry Brigade, September 1939. Survivor, Griazovets camp. Briefly in Berling group (as a spy), then Polish Army under Anders, later in Britain. Parachuted into Poland, 1944; fought in Warsaw Uprising. After World War II, lived in western Europe. Author of memoirs.

Mackiewicz, Józef (1902–1985). Polish journalist, writer, Katyn expert. A passionate anticommunist, he contributed to the Wilno Polish-language newspaper *Goniec Codzienny* [Daily Courier], published under German control after July 1941. He visited Katyn in May 1943, where he first met Krivozertsev, and published a report in the paper—both with the assent of the local Polish underground authorities. Accused by communists of collaboration with the Germans, he fled Poland and joined the Polish Army 2nd Corps in Italy, where he conducted a long interview with Krivozertsev. He accepted the commission offered by journalist Zdzisław Stahl of the Office of Studies of the Polish Army 2nd Corps to write a book on the Katyn massacre titled *Zbrodnia Katyńska* [The Crime of Katyn]; it was first published in London in 1948. His authorship was never acknowledged, mainly because of the widely known charge that he collaborated with the Germans, so the book is generally attributed to Zdzisław Stahl. The fifth edition was translated into English as *The Crime of Katyn* (London, 1965). Mackiewicz wrote another book on Katyn, which was published in eight languages, the first in German translation as *Katyn: Ungesühntes Verbrechen* [Katyn: An Unexpiated Crime] (Zürich, 1949; reprinted in Frankfurt am Main, 1983). The slightly enlarged English version is titled *The Katyn Wood Murders* (London, 1951). After living a few years in Britain, he settled in the German Federal Republic in 1954. The Polish-language original of his German book on Katyn, as well as his published articles on the subject, were published in Poland in 1997.

Maisky [real name: Liakhovetsky], Ivan Mikhailovich (1884–1975). Soviet diplomat and minister. As Soviet ambassador to Britain, 1932–1943, he signed the Soviet-Polish Agreement, London, 30 July 1941. Deputy commissar, minister of foreign affairs, 1943–1946. Author of censored memoirs on his embassy to Britain.

Makliarsky, Ivan Borisovich. Soviet security official. GB 1st lieutenant, 1939; head, UPV Registration Department, September 1939. Participated in preparing and implementing the "clearing out" of the three special camps.

Malenkov, Georgy Maksimilianovich (1902–1988). Soviet official, party and state leader. CC CPSU member, 1939; full Politburo member, 1946. After Stalin's death, chairman, Sovmin, and a secretary of the CC CPSU. Overthrown by Khrushchev, February 1955; joined failed coup against him, 1957; was exiled to Kazakhstan, where he managed a power station, but later returned and lived for many years as a pensioner in Moscow.

Marchuk, Gury Ivanovich (b. 1925). Soviet academician. Mathematician and expert on nuclear reactors. CC member, 1981–1991; supporter of Gorbachev. Elected president, Soviet Academy of Sciences, 1986–1991.

Maslennikov, Ivan Ivanovich (1900–1954). Soviet security official. Army general and hero of the USSR, 1945. As a deputy commissar NKVD USSR in 1939, he oversaw border, convoy, and interior troops. Commander, armies and fronts in World War II. Candidate member of CC CPSU, 1939–1954.

Medvedev, Vadim Andreevich (b. 1929). Soviet academic and party official. Head of CPSU Academy of Social Sciences, 1978–1983. Elected a member of the CC CPSU at the Twenty-seventh Party Congress; a secretary of the CC, March 1986; and member of Politburo, 1989, the year he was also elected to Parliament. Not reelected to Politburo, he became a member of the Presidential Council, 1990.

Mekhlis, Lev Zakharovich (1889–1953). Soviet party official. A political commissar during the Russian Civil War, he later worked in Stalin's Secretariat and edited *Pravda,* 1930–1937. Deputy commissar of defense, 1937–1945; State Control commissar; and chief of Red Army Main Political Administration, 1940–1941. A member of military councils in World War II, he was minister of State Control, 1945–1949.

Merkulov, Vsevolod Nikolaevich (1895–1953). Soviet security official. Closest aide and friend of Beria's from 1922; responsible for mass repressions and inhumane methods of interrogation. Member of Troika appointed by Politburo, 5 March 1940, to examine the cases and decide sentences of Polish officers and police from the three special camps and of prisoners in western oblasts of UkSSR and BSSR. In charge of the entire operation of "clearing out" the camps and prisons in April–May 1940. Arrested with Beria in summer 1953 and executed in December 1953. Named together with Beria in the TASS communiqué of 13 April 1990 as responsible for murdering the Polish POWs in 1940.

Mikołajczyk, Stanisław (1885–1966). Statesman and Peasant Party leader. Deputy premier of exile government, 1941–1943; premier, 1943–1944. Tried but failed to reach agreement with Stalin on the Polish-Soviet border. Accepted Yalta agreements on Poland, spring 1945; second deputy premier and agriculture minister in the new Polish government formed in Moscow, June. Lost rigged elections, 1947; escaped from Poland when his life was threatened; politically active in the United States, 1947–1966; author of memoirs.

Mikoyan, Anastas Ivanovich (1893–1978). Soviet official, commissar, minister. Close associate of Stalin, then Khrushchev and Brezhnev. Negotiated German-Soviet trade agreements of 1936 and 1939. As Politburo member, signed resolution to shoot Polish POWs, 5 March 1940. Deputy chairman, then premier, Council of People's Commissars/Ministers, 1937–1955, and first deputy chairman, 1955–1964. Retired, 1968.

Milshtein, Solomon Rafalovich (1899–1955). Soviet party official. Friend and close collaborator of Beria's. As GB commissar 3rd rank and head of GTU [Main Transport Administration], NKVD, 1940, he took an active part in executions of Polish POWs by providing and reporting on trains used to transport them to places of execution. In 1954, he was tried and sentenced in connection with Beria's case; was presumably shot in 1955.

Minkiewicz-Odrowąż, Henryk (1880–1940). Polish general. Born in former Russian Poland, he studied medicine and the fine arts in Kraków. Veteran, Polish Legions and Polish-Soviet War; organizer and commander, Korpus Ochrony Pogranicza [KOP—Frontier Protection Corps], 1924–1929; retired 1934. Arrested at his home and held at Kozelsk camp; shot at Katyn.

Mironov, Vasily Dmitrievich. Soviet security official. Worked in 5th Department, GUGB. Participated in executions of Polish officers, April–May 1940. Worked with Zarubin in Soviet intelligence in the United States, 1941–1944. Recalled to the USSR in 1944, arrested, and placed in a camp. He is reported to have told some fellow prisoners what he knew about Katyn. Shot, 28 July 1945.

Mościcki, Ignacy (1867–1946). Polish chemist; president of Poland. Inventor of a nitrogen acid production process, he worked in Switzerland, then at the Polytechnic in Lwów. He was a member of the P.O.W. in World War I and a loyal supporter of Józef Piłsudsk who selected him to be president of Poland in 1926; he was president until 1939. Interned in Romania, September 1939; he was allowed to leave for Switzerland (he held dual Polish and Swiss citizenship), where he died. Author of autobiography.

Mostovoi, Pavel (b. 1931). Soviet official; supporter of Gorbachev. Director, State Committee for Material-Technical Supplies, 1978–1989; deputy chair, Sovmin, July 1989–December 1990.

Murashov, Nikolai Matveevich (1907–1942). Soviet security officer. GB 1st lieutenant and chief of staff, 236th NKVD Convoy Battalion, 1940. Commanded convoys guarding Polish POWs from Ostashkov to Kalinin/Tver. Disappeared without a trace, May 1942.

Nekhoroshev, Semyon Vasilevich (b. 1899). Soviet security official. Regimental commissar; head, Political Department; and commissar, UPV, 1939–1941. Led an operational brigade to Starobelsk camp, January 1940; participated in "clearing out" the three special camps. Retired in 1952 with the rank of colonel from the MVD Contacts with Abroad Department, Moscow Military District.

Paderewski, Ignacy Jan (1860–1941). Famous Polish pianist and statesman. He made several concert tours of the United States beginning in 1891; worked for Polish independence there during World War I and is credited with influencing President Woodrow Wilson to support an independent Poland. Premier and foreign minister of Poland, January–December 1919, he was also the chief Polish delegate at the Paris Peace Conference, 1919, and co-signer with Roman Dmowski of the Versailles Treaty for Poland. He opposed Piłsudski's governments, 1926–1935, and those of his successors; supported the new Polish government headed by General Władysław Sikorski, established in France on 30 September 1939. He died in New York, 29 June 1941, while on a visit to the United States. Buried at Arlington National Cemetery, his remains were returned to Poland at President Lech Wałęsa's request and reinterred in a crypt of St. John's Cathedral, Warsaw, in July 1992.

Panfilov, Aleksei P. (b. 1898). Soviet major general, tank forces; head of GRU [Main Military Intelligence Administration of the RKKA/Red Army; short name: Razvedka]. Member of Red Army General Staff, and of the Gosudarstvenny Komitet Oborony [GKO—State Defense Committee], 1941. In charge of matters concerning the Polish Army under Anders in the USSR, 1941–1942.

Pavlov, Valentin Sergeevich (b. 1937). Soviet official. Supporter of Gorbachev. 1st deputy finance minister, January–August 1986; chair, State Committee on Prices, 1986–1989. In July 1988, as chair of the State Foreign Tourism Committee, proposed visits to Katyn by victims' families.

Pavlov, Vasily Pavlovich (b. 1910). In 1939–1940 he was a GB captain, head of the Special Department of the Kalinin Military District and of the UNKVD in the Kalinin region. He actively participated in liquidating the Ostashkov POW camp.

Petrażycki, Tadeusz (1885–1940). Polish officer, lawyer. Colonel, retired. Born in Ukraine; law graduate of Kharkov University; veteran, Polish Army, 1918–1921. Judicial assessor and judge, Polish Supreme Military Court, 1931–1935; senator, 1935–1939; member, Polish Red Cross Executive Board. While a prisoner in Starobelsk camp, he petitioned Soviet authorities for POW rights; listed in Polish records as shot in Kharkov.

Pikhoia, Rudolf Germanovich. Archivist, historian. Director general, ROSARKHIV [Russian Archives], 1992–1995. Deputy chair, beginning in 1995, of the editorial board of the series *Rossiia: XX vek* [Russia: The 20th Century], which includes *Katyn: Plenniki Neobiavlennoi Voiny* [Katyn: Prisoners of an Undeclared War] (1997). On behalf of President Boris Yeltsin, conveyed Russian Katyn documents to Polish President Lech Wałęsa, October 1992.

Piłsudski, Jozef (1867–1935). Polish Socialist leader and revolutionary, writer, military leader, statesman. Born in former Russian Vilna Province (Polish, Wilno, now Vilnius, capital of Lithuania). A Polish Socialist Party (PPS) leader, 1892–1914; commander of Polish Legions fighting alongside the Central Powers against Russia, 1914–1917; refused further cooperation in July 1917 and was imprisoned in Germany, 1917–1918. Head of Polish state, November 1918–December 1922. As commander in chief, led Polish and Ukrainian troops to Kiev, May 1920; was pushed back to gates of Warsaw by the Red Army, but defeated it in mid-August 1920. Resigned from all posts in 1923; seized power, May 1926. Presided over authoritarian governments, directed military affairs, and guided foreign policy until his death in May 1935.

Podtserob, Boris Fedorovich (1910–1983). Worked in the People's Commissariat of Foreign Affairs, 1937–1949; secretary general of ministry, 1952–1953, later deputy minister and ambassador to Turkey and Austria. As Molotov's personal secretary, he recorded the Stalin-Sikorski conversation of 3 December 1941.

Polukhin, Iosif Mikhailovich. Soviet security official. Major and deputy head of UPV, 1939–1941, responsible for finances, housekeeping, and security in the three special camps. Headed investigation brigade in Kozelsk camp, January 1940.

Pomaznev, Mikhail Trofimovich (1911–1987). Soviet official. Secretary, Ekonomsoviet [Economic Council], attached to Sovnarkom, 1939.

Ponomarenko, Panteleimon Kondratevich (1902–1984). Soviet party official and lieutenant general, 1943. Served in Red Army, 1918; held various army and party posts to 1938. 1st secretary, CC Belorussian Bolshevik Party, 1938–1941. In September 1939, as member of the Military Council, Belorussian Front, signed the order justifying invasion of eastern Poland. Head, general staff of partisan movement in World War II. Chair, Belorussian Council of Ministers, 1944–1948; and secretary CC Belorussian Communist Party, 1948–1952. After fall of his patron, Malenkov, he was given several diplomatic assignments, 1956–1964.

Ponomarev, Boris Nikolaevich (1905–1990). Soviet party official. Worked in the Comintern [Communist International] central office and was deputy director of the Marx-Engels-Lenin Institute. Deputy director, CC CPSU Foreign Policy Department, 1947; member, CC International Relations Department, 1955–1985; member, CC, 1986–1989.

Potemkin, Vladimir Petrovich (1874–1946). Soviet economist and diplomat. As deputy commissar for foreign affairs, 1937–1940, presented Soviet note to Polish ambassador, Moscow, 17 September 1939. Member of Burdenko Commission; commissar of education, 1940–1946.

Przeździecki, Wacław (1883–1964). Polish brigadier general. Born in former Russian Poland; veteran, Russian Army, World War I, then 1st Polish Corps, Russia; fought in Polish-Soviet War, 1919–1920. Army group commander, September 1939; interned in Lithuania, 1939–1940, then USSR. Interviewed by Beria and Merkulov, October 1940, about organizing a Polish division in the Red Army. Joined the Polish Army under Anders in the USSR; later, in the Polish Army 2nd Corps, Middle East and Italy, 1942–1945. Settled in England after World War II. Died in Penley, Wales.

Putin, Vladimir Vladimirovich (b. 1952). President of Russia. Born in Leningrad, he graduated with a law degree there, 1975. As a KGB intelligence officer, he spent several years in East Germany; resigned, 1991. Served in St. Petersburg administration, then brought into the Kremlin by President Boris Yeltsin, who appointed him head of intelligence services in 1998, premier in 1999, and acting president, December 1999. Elected president in 2000; reelected in 2004. Presided over the closing of the formal Russian investigation of Katyn, 2004–2005.

Raczkiewicz, Władysław (1885–1947). Polish minister, provincial governor, and interwar Senate speaker. President of Polish government in exile, October 1939–July 1945, he never recognized the inclusion of former eastern Poland in the USSR.

Raczyński, Edward (1891–1993). Polish diplomat, minister. Polish representative, League of Nations, 1932–1934; ambassador to Britain, 1934–1945; acting foreign minister, 1940–1943. Prominent émigré politician in London, 1954–1972; president of Polish government-in-exile, London, 1979–1986. Author of memoirs.

Raikhman, Leonid Fedorovich (d. 1991). Soviet security officer. GB major and deputy head, 2nd Department (Counterintelligence), GUGB, NKVD USSR, 1939–1941. Carried out a "cleanup" (arrests, executions) in western oblasts, UkSSR, fall 1939–spring 1940. Supervised special NKVD detail preparing evidence at Katyn for Burdenko Commission, fall 1943–early 1944. Prepared some materials for the International Military Tribunal on the "Katyn Affair," Nuremberg, 1946. Arrested and imprisoned in 1951 as alleged member of a "Zionist" conspiracy, he was released in 1956.

Rodionov, [first name unknown]. Soviet security officer. GB 1st lieutenant and section head, 2nd Department, GEU, NKVD, USSR, 1939. Together with Nekhoroshev, supervised POW investigations at Starobelsk camp in early 1940.

Romer, Tadeusz (1894–1978). Polish diplomat, minister. Secretary, Polish National Committee, Paris, 1917–1919; ambassador in Lisbon, 1933–1937; Tokyo, 1937–1941; Moscow, 1942–1943. Foreign minister, Polish government, London, 1943–1944. Settled in Montreal, Canada, in 1948.

Rowecki, Stefan (1895–1944). Polish general. Born in former Russian Poland; veteran, Polish Legions and Polish-Soviet War; brigade commander, September 1939. Active in Polish military resistance in occupied Poland from fall 1939; he persuaded several different groups to unite in the AK under his leadership in 1942. Arrested by Gestapo, Warsaw, 30 June 1943, and sent to Sachsenhausen concentration camp. He rejected German proposals to organize a Polish battalion to fight the USSR. He was shot after the outbreak of the Warsaw Uprising (1 August 1944).

Różański, Konrad (1892–1940) and **Wojciech** (1920–1940), father and son. Polish officers. Konrad was a lawyer and a 2nd lieutenant in the reserves. Wojciech was a cadet. Both were mentioned as troublemakers in an NKVD report, 22 April 1940. Both were in Kozelsk camp, and both were shot at Katyn.

Rushailo, Vladimir (b. 1953). Russian politician. Interior minister, 1999–2001; spoke at opening of Polish War Cemetery at Mednoe, 2 September 2000. Executive secretary of Commonwealth of Independent States, 2004.

Rybakov, Aleksei Aleksandrovich (b. 1901). Soviet security officer. Chief of staff, 15th Brigade, NKVD Convoy Troops, April 1939–March 1940; colonel, head, Operations Department, GUKV [Main Administration of Convoy Troops], NKVD, March 1940–November 1941. Responsible for guarding and transporting Polish POWs from Starobelsk to Kharkov, spring 1940.

Ryzhkov, Nikolai Ivanovich (b. 1929). Soviet, then Russian economist; an architect of Gorbachev's perestroika. CC CPSU member, 1982; head, CC Economic Department, 1985; Politburo member, September 1985; chair, Sovmin; member, Presidential Council, March–December 1990.

Safonov, Grigori Nikolaevich (1904–1972). Lawyer, Soviet deputy prosecutor general, 1946–1948; prosecutor general, 1948–1953.

Safonov, Pyotr Sergeevich. Soviet security officer. GB captain. Deputy chief of GULAG, 1939. As head of UNKVD, Kharkov Oblast, he was in charge of executions in Kharkov prison of POWs from Starobelsk camp and prisoners transferred from prisons in western oblasts of UkSSR in April–May 1940.

Sapieha, Adam Stefan (1867–1951). Polish churchman, prince. Archbishop Metropolitan of Kraków, 1925–1951. Under German occupation, sheltered endangered clergy, including Karol Wojtyła (elected pope in 1978); cardinal, 1946.

Saski, Edward Józef (1882–1940). Polish colonel, retired. Born in Riga; law graduate, Odessa University, 1911. Veteran, Russian Army, 1914–1917, then 1st Polish Corps, Russia; in Polish Army, 1919–1934. Judicial assessor; member, Military Judiciary Corps; and judge on Polish Supreme Military Tribunal, 1929. Service in 1939 unknown. Presented demands on behalf of fellow officer POWs in Starobelsk camp. Listed as shot in Kharkov.

Serov, Ivan Aleksandrovich (1905–1990). Soviet security commissar and general. GB commissar 3rd rank, NKVD, UkSSR, 1939; deputy commissar NKVD, USSR, 1941. Directed mass repressions and deportations from western oblasts of UkSSR, 1939–1941. Directed "clearing out" of prisons there and presumably transfer of prisoners from NKVD jails in western Ukraine to those in central Ukraine, including Kharkov and Kherson, spring 1940. Organized the kidnapping of sixteen Polish underground leaders and their transportation to Moscow, March 1945, where they were tried in June 1945. Chair, KGB, with rank of army general, 1954–1958. Stripped of his title, "Hero of the Soviet Union," and demoted to major general, 12 March 1963.

Shelepin, Aleksandr Nikolaevich (1918–1994). Soviet official. As head of KGB, 1958–1961, proposed destruction of Polish POW files in 1959. Was deposed in Russian Katyn investigation, December 1992.

Shevardnadze, Eduard Amvrosevich (b. 1928). Soviet official, minister, head of state. Member, Soviet CC, 1958–1961; candidate member, Politburo, 1978. Supported Gorbachev for secretary general of the Communist Party, 1985. As Soviet foreign minister, 1985–1990, contributed to ending the Cold War. President of Georgia, 10 March 1992–23 November 2003.

Shkabardnia, Mikhail (b. 1930). Soviet official. Chief, Chancellery, Sovmin, USSR, 1980–1989.

Shtemenko, Sergei Matveevich (1907–1976). Soviet general. Army major, 1939; general, 1968. Signed Kulik report on situation in Western Ukraine, 21 September 1939. Chief of general staff and minister of armed forces, 1948; chief and deputy chief, armed forces, 1962–1968. Author of memoirs.

Sikorski, Franciszek Józef (1889–1940). Polish brigadier general, retired, 1933; engineer. Born in former Austrian Poland; veteran, Polish Legions and Polish-Soviet War. In September 1939, with General Langner, led defense of Lwów against the Germans. Wrote to Marshal Semyon Timoshenko on behalf of fellow officer POWs. In Starobelsk camp; listed as shot in Kharkov.

Sikorski, Władysław Eugeniusz (1881–1943). Polish general, statesman. Born on the border of former Russian and former Austrian Poland. Commander, 5th Polish Army defending Warsaw, August 1920; chief, general staff, 1921–1922; premier, 1922–1923; war minister, 1924–1925; in opposition, 1926–1939. Prime minister of new Polish government, 30 September 1939–4 July 1943; commander in chief, Polish armed forces, November 1939–July 1943. Signed Polish-Soviet agreement with Ivan Maisky, London, 30 July 1941, restoring relations between the two countries, releasing Polish prisoners, and forming a Polish Army in the USSR; had long conversation with Stalin and Molotov, Moscow, 3 December 1941. Died in plane crash off Gibraltar, 4 July 1943.

Silaev, Ivan Stepanovich (b. 1930). Soviet, Russian official and minister. Deputy prime minister, USSR, 1985–1990; chair, Committee for Operational Direction of the National Economy, USSR, and prime minister, 1990–1991; Russian representative to European Union, 1991–1994.

Sinegubov, N. I. Soviet security official. GB senior major, 1939–1940. Appointed by Politburo decision as head and, simultaneously, deputy head, Investigative Department, GTU, September 1939. Among those in charge of executing Polish POWs from Ostashkov camp in Kalinin/Tver, spring 1940, he was rewarded by Beria, 26 October 1940.

Sitarianov, Stepan Aramaisovich (b. 1930). Soviet, Russian economist, academician. Deputy prime minister, USSR, 1989–1990. Director, Institute of International Economic Studies, Russian Academy of Sciences, 1989–1990.

Skarżyński, Kazimierz (1887–1962). Polish industrialist and secretary general, Executive Board of the Polish Red Cross, 1940–1945. He reported on his visit to Katyn, April 1943; edited the PRC Technical Commission report, June 1943; and gave a copy to the British Embassy, Warsaw, March 1946. Accused of collaboration with the Germans, he escaped from Poland and settled in Canada; testified before Madden Committee, 1952.

Skubiszewski, Krzysztof (b. 1926). Polish professor, judge, international arbitrator, minister, author. Professor of international law, Adam Mickiewicz University, Poznań; Polish foreign minister, 1989–1992.

Śmigły-Rydz [alternative: Rydz Śmigły], Edward (1886–1941). Polish officer and artist. Born in former Russian Poland, he was a close collaborator of Piłsudski's, as a Legionnaire officer, 1914–1917; commander of P.O.W., 1914–1918; and commander of an army in the Polish-Soviet War, 1920. Inspector general of the army, 1921–1935; marshal, November 1936; army inspector general; commander in chief, September 1939. Interned in Romania, he escaped via Hungary to Poland to join the underground military resistance there, but was rejected. He lived under an assumed name in Warsaw and died of heart disease. Buried in the military section of Old Powązki Cemetery as Adam Zawisza, schoolteacher. Author of reflections, published posthumously in Paris, 1962, on whether Poland could have avoided war in 1939.

Smirnov, Sergei Petrovich (b. 1898). Soviet security official. As deputy head of 1st Special Department, NKVD, UkSSR, 1989–1990, responsible for drawing up reports on and list of Polish prisoners held in Ukrainian NKVD jails as a basis for their execution.

Smorawiński, Mieczysław Makary (1893–1940). Polish brigadier general. Born in former Russian Poland, he studied chemistry at Lwów Polytechnic, 1912–1914. Veteran, Polish Legions and Polish-Soviet War; commander, Lublin Military District, 1934–1939. Began to organize a command at Kowel [Kovel] in mid-September 1939. Acting on Marshal Śmigły-Rydz's order not to fight the Soviets, he gave his troops the choice of either surrendering or making their way to Hungary and thence to France. He negotiated the surrender of the town of Włodzimierz-Wołyński [Volodymyr-Volynskyi] with Red Army authorities, allowing the disarmed Polish troops to march under Soviet escort to the Bug River. They were, however, stopped immediately, escorted back to the town, placed in jail, and later moved to POW camps. General Smorawiński opted to go to Hungary but was caught, placed in the special camp in Kozelsk, and shot at Katyn.

Solski, Adam Teofil (1895–1940). Polish major; author of diary for the years 1939–1940. Born in former Austrian Poland; veteran, Polish Legions and Polish-Soviet War; served in Personnel Office, War Ministry. Mobilized to reserve center, 14th Infantry Division, September 1939. Held in Kozelsk camp and shot at Katyn. Diary found and restored in 1943; published in 1989.

Soprunenko, Pyotr Karpovich (1908–1992). Soviet security official. Worked as assistant in NKVD Secretariat in 1938 and won Beria's confidence. As head of UPV, September 1939–early 1944, oversaw all POW matters. Supervised "clearing out" the three special camps until mid-April 1940, when he was replaced in Moscow by Khokhlov, and again in May. Was deposed as a witness to the Katyn massacre in October 1990.

Sosnkowski, Kazimierz (1885–1969). Polish general. Born in Warsaw, former Russian Poland. Completed high school, Warsaw and St. Petersburg; studied at Lwów Polytechnic. Closest cooperator with Piłsudski, 1905–1918; Legionnaire, 1914–1916; arrested and imprisoned in Germany with Piłsudski, 1917–1918. Deputy minister of war, March–April 1920; organizer and commander of Reserve Army, May–August 1920; minister of war, 1925–1926. Commander, Southern Front, September 1939; escaped and joined Sikorski government in France. In charge of underground resistance, September 1939–30 June 1940. Vice president, Polish government in London, 1940–1941; resigned from government in protest over the lack of Soviet recognition of the 1921 Polish-Soviet frontier in Sikorski-Maisky agreement of 30 July 1941. Vice president of Poland, July 1943, and commander in chief, Polish Armed Forces West, July 1943–30 September 1944; he was dismissed after openly accusing the British government of not fulfilling its obligations as an ally of Poland. After World War II, lived in England, then settled in Canada; his remains were reinterred in St. John's Cathedral, Warsaw, 1992. Author of studies and memoirs.

Stalin, Joseph [Iosif Vissarionovich Dzhugashvili] (1879–1953). Soviet leader. Born in Georgia, he was a member of Vladimir I. Lenin's Bolshevik faction of the Russian Social Democratic Party, 1903–1917; he was general secretary of the CPSU, 1922, and built up his power as a party bureaucrat, 1922–1928. As Soviet leader, 1928–1953, he carried out forced collectivization of peasant farms at the cost of millions of lives. He also carried out forced industrialization. He implemented wholesale purges of the CPSU, 1935–1938, decimated the Red Army officer corps, and presided over an enormous expansion of the GULAG. He opted for Hitler in 1939, when the USSR concluded a Non-Aggression Pact and Secret Protocol with Germany, 23 August 1939, followed by a Border and Friendship Treaty with Germany, 28 September 1939. He approved and perhaps initiated the Politburo approval of Beria's resolution of 5 March 1940 to shoot Polish POWs in the three special NKVD camps and in NKVD prisons in western Belorussia and Ukraine. He led the USSR to final victory over Germany and established Soviet domination over most of Eastern Europe, 1944–1945. Denounced by Khrushchev in February 1956 for the "cult of personality" and unjust sentencing of many party members, his massive crimes were uncovered in the Gorbachev era. Many Russians, however, still see him as a great leader who defeated Hitler and made the USSR a world power.

Steinberg, Baruch (1897–1940). Head rabbi, Polish Army, 1936. Born in Tarnopol region, former Russian Poland (later Poland, now Ukraine), into a rabbinical family. Volunteered for service in a riflemen's company organized by P.O.W., 1918, and served in Polish Army in Polish-Soviet War, 1919–1920. Later, he continued his studies of eastern languages in Kraków and Lwów. Awarded Polish military decorations; from 1928, head rabbi in Polish Military Districts I and II. Deputy head rabbi, Polish Army, 1930; rank of major, 1934. Head rabbi, 1936; also senior rabbi in Warsaw Military District. Held in Starobelsk camp. Survivor accounts report his emphasis on the unity of all Poles, regardless of religion. He was taken prisoner in September 1939 and taken out of Starobelsk camp on 24 December; his name appears on an NKVD Kozelsk camp list in April 1940. He is listed as shot at Katyn.

Stelmakh, I. I. Soviet security officer. GB lieutenant, 1940. As commandant of internal prisons in the Smolensk region, he participated in executing the Polish officers from Kozelsk camp. Rewarded by Beria, 26 October 1940.

Stepanov, Ivan Alekseevich (b. 1890). Soviet security officer. Colonel and deputy head, Operations Department, GUKV [Main Administration of Convoy Troops], NKVD, 1940–1947. In Kozelsk camp, in charge of transporting Polish POWs to Smolensk and Gnezdovo, March–May 1940. Rewarded by Beria, 26 October 1940.

Sukharev, Aleksandr Yakovlevich (b. 1923). Soviet law official. First deputy minister of justice, 1970–1984; minister, 1984–1988; prosecutor general, 1988–1990.

Swianiewicz, Stanisław (1899–1997). Polish economist, Katyn survivor. Born and raised in Russia to 1918. Veteran, Polish-Soviet War, 1919–1920. Specialist on Nazi and Soviet economies, Stefan Batory University, Wilno, late 1930s. In Kozelsk camp, 1939–1940; survived because NKVD wanted him for interrogation. Held in NKVD prisons, 1940–1941; sentenced to eight years for "espionage" and sent to northern labor camp complex, Komi ASSR. When released, he joined the Polish Army under Anders in the USSR, spring 1942. After World War II, he was a university professor in Halifax, Canada; he published a book on forced labor in the Soviet economy in 1985. Died in London. Author of Katyn memoirs.

Syromiatnikov, Mitrofan Vasilievich (b. 1908). Soviet security officer, Kharkov. As militia lieutenant in the Kharkov Oblast UNKVD, participated in executions of Polish officers from Starobelsk camp in NKVD prison, Kharkov, spring 1940; rewarded by Beria, 26 October 1940. Was deposed during Soviet, then Russian Katyn investigation in 1990–1992 as a witness to the massacre of Polish POW officers in Kharkov, spring 1940.

Sysoev, Vasily Nikonovich (b. 1908). Soviet security official. Militia sergeant and senior inspector, URO [Reception, Records, and Barracks Assignment Section], Yukhnov camp, winter 1939–1940. Acting head, 2nd Section (URO), Starobelsk camp, early March 1940; participated in "clearing out" the camp.

Tatarenko, [first name not known]. Soviet security officer. Commander, 2nd Company, Detached 136th NKVD Convoy Battalion, 1940; in charge of operational group "clearing out" Kozelsk camp. Rewarded by battalion commander, 21 May 1940.

Tikhonov, P. P. Soviet security officer. GB captain and deputy head, UNKVD Administration, Kharkov region, 1940. Participated in execution of Polish Starobelsk POWs in NKVD prison in Kharkov; rewarded by Beria, 26 October 1940.

Timoshenko, Semyon Konstaninovich (1895–1970). Soviet general. Commanded Ukrainian Front, September 1939; accepted surrender of Polish Army units under General Władysław Langner in Lwów. Led Soviet offensive in Finland, 1939–1940; defense commissar, 1940–1941, then deputy commissar, also commander of fronts in German-Soviet War, 1941–1945. Postwar commander of South Ural and Belorussian Military Districts; inspector general, 1960–1961.

Tishkov, Arseny Vasilevich (b. 1909). Soviet security official. GB lieutenant and head, 1st Special Department, UPV, 1939–1940. In charge of operation to expose Polish POW officers and police in Narkomchermet camps, and transferring them to the three special camps, April–June 1940; also transferred 8,000 POWs from Narkomchermet camps to Sevzheldorlag.

Tiulenev, Ivan Vladimirovich (1892–1978). Soviet general. Army commander 2nd rank, 1939; general, 1940. Commander, Kamenets-Podolsk (Southern) Army Group (12th Army) of Ukrainian Front, September 1939. Commander of war fronts in 1941–1945.

Tokarev, Dmitry Stepanovich (1902–1993). Soviet security official. As GB colonel and head of UNKVD, Kalinin Oblast, spring 1940, oversaw shooting of Polish POWs from Ostashkov camp in NKVD prison, Kalinin/Tver. Was deposed in March 1991 by Soviet Katyn investigators as witness to 1940 executions.

Trainin, Aron Naumovich. Soviet law professor; member of Soviet Academy of Sciences. Academic consultant in Soviet delegation at the International Military Tribunal, Nuremberg, 1946.

Tsanava, Lavrenty Fomich [real surname: Dzhanzhgava] (1900–1955). Soviet security official. GB senior major, 1939; commissar, NKVD, BSSR, 1938–1941. One of Beria's most trusted henchmen, he participated in organizing mass executions and torture of Soviet citizens. In charge of "clearing out" prisons in western Belorussia, April–May 1940. Commissar, then minister, of Belorussian State Security, 1943–1951, and deputy minister, 1951–1952. Dismissed from his post, February 1952; arrested, April 1953; died in prison.

Ulrikh, Vasilii Vasilevich (1889–1951). Soviet lawyer, official. As chair of the Military Board, Supreme Court, USSR, 1926–1948, participated in Stalin purges, 1935–1938, and allegedly "verified" Polish Starobelsk POWs for execution in NKVD Kharkov prison, spring 1940 (Syromiatnikov deposition). Conducted the rigged trial of sixteen kidnapped Polish underground leaders in Moscow, June 1945. Head of Soviet delegation at the International Military Tribunal, Nuremberg, 1946.

Vorobyev, Nikolai Alekseevich. Soviet security official. Senior political instructor, 1926–1948. Member, Political Section, 1st Department, GUGB, 1939. Deputy head, Political Department, UPV, late September 1939. Made trips to POW camps with Nekhoroshev.

Voroshilov, Kliment Yefremovich (1881–1969). Soviet marshal. Close associate of Stalin's. Deputy chairman, then chairman, Soviet Defense Council, 1940–1941. Marshal of the Soviet Union, 1940. As Politburo member, signed the decision to shoot Polish prisoners of war, 5 March 1940. Held high political appointments, 1945–1953; chairman, Presidium of Supreme Soviet, 1953–1960; member of Politburo/Presidium of CC CPSU, 1926–1960. Stripped of all his posts by Khrushchev in 1961.

Vyshinsky, Andrei Yanuarevich (1883–1955). Soviet lawyer, minister. Chief prosecutor at the Stalinist purge trials, 1936–1938. CC member, 1939–1955. As deputy foreign commissar, then deputy foreign minister, 1940–1949, was in charge of government commissions to guide the Soviet delegation at the International Military Tribunal, Nuremberg, 1946.

Wałęsa, Lech (b. 1943). Leader of Polish Solidarity movement and president of Poland. An electrician at the Gdańsk shipyards in August 1980–December 1981, he led the Solidarity movement, the first mass workers', then national movement in the Soviet bloc. It demanded free trade unions, human and religious rights, and self-government for state enterprises, demands taken up nationally for all types of associations. As leader of the Gdańsk Solidarity movement, he signed an agreement with the government in the Gdańsk shipyards, 31 August 1980 (a similar agreement was signed in Szczecin on 30 August); later he headed the movement as a whole. Crushed by martial law in December 1981, the movement survived underground to negotiate a series of agreements with the government-party leadership in spring 1989. Wałęsa, interned from December 1981 to November 1982, received the Nobel Peace Prize for leading the peaceful Solidarity movement. Elected president of Poland, December 1990. Corresponded with President Yeltsin of Russia on Katyn. Lost election for second term in office to Aleksander Kwaśniewski, December 1995, and lost another reelection bid to Kwaśniewski in 2005. Today, Solidarity is not a party but a Polish labor union, one of many. Wałęsa resigned from Solidarity in early 2006 because he disagreed with the new leadership. Author of autobiography.

Wasilewska, Wanda (1905–1964). Polish left-wing socialist, writer, political activist. Member of the prewar left-wing Polish Socialist Party (PPS). Led group of Polish communists and left-wing socialists in Lwów, 1939–1941. A secret Ukrainian Communist Party member, she was elected to the West Ukrainian national assembly, then to the Supreme Soviet. Her third husband was the Ukrainian writer Oleksandr Korneichuk [Kornijchuk]. She was head of the ZPP [Union of Polish Patriots in the USSR], 1943–1946, and deputy chair, Polish Committee of National Liberation, July–December 1944. After World War II, lived in Kiev. Author of posthumously published memoirs recorded on tape in her lifetime.

Wołkowicki, Jerzy (1883–1983). Polish general. Born in former Russian Poland. Russian naval lieutenant; awarded St. George's Cross for bravery at the Battle of Tsushima, 1905. In the Polish Army under Haller in France, 1918–1919; fought in Polish-Soviet War. Held various posts in

Polish Army and retired, August 1938; recalled to active service, September 1939. Survivor, Kozelsk and Griazovets camps; noted in NKVD reports as a troublemaker. He may have survived because he was known as a hero to many Russians from the popular historical novel *Tsushima,* by Soviet writer Aleksei Ivanovich-Novikov Priboi (1st English translation, New York, 1937). Wołkowicki was in the Polish Army under Anders in the USSR and the Middle East. After World War II, settled in England. Died in London.

Yakovlev, Aleksandr Nikolaevich (1923–2005). Soviet official. One of the chief architects of Gorbachev's perestroika and glasnost policies, he is best known for investigating and rehabilitating victims of Stalinism. A prominent supporter of Gorbachev's policies as a CC, then Politburo member, he supported collecting and publicizing documents on the German-Soviet Non-Aggression Pact and the Katyn massacres. As a member of the Presidential Council, he did not seek reelection to the CC and left the Politburo in July 1990. Wrote articles and a book titled *A Century of Violence in Soviet Russia* (English edition, New Haven, Conn., 2003) vigorously condemning Russia's Soviet past.

Yeltsin, Boris Nikolaevich (1931–2007). Soviet party politician, president of the Russian Federation. Born into a peasant family in Butka village, Sverdlovsk [Yekaterinburg] region; obtained a degree in engineering and pursued a party career in Sverdlovsk. Member of the CC CPSU, 1981; 1st secretary of the Moscow party committee, late 1985. Broke with Gorbachev and resigned from the party in October 1987. Won election as a delegate to Congress of Deputies, March 1989; elected to Supreme Soviet in 1990; and was the first democratically elected president of the Russian Republic of the USSR. Mobilized support to stop attempted coup against Gorbachev, August 1991; took over power from him and finalized the dissolution of the USSR in late December 1991. In October 1992, allowed the publication of the 5 March 1940 Politburo resolution to shoot Polish POWS and gave copies of this and other Katyn documents to Polish President Lech Wałęsa. Elected president of the Russian Federation, 1996. Appointed Premier Vladimir Putin as acting president, 31 December 1999. Author of memoirs and subject of biographies.

Yurasov, Ivan Alekseevich (b. 1890). Soviet security official. Until 1939, served in the GUKV; commissar, Ostashkov camp, September 1939–July 1940; participated in "clearing out" the camp.

Zaleski, August (1883–1972). Polish diplomat, statesman. Born in former Russian Poland (Warsaw). Worked for Polish independence in England during World War I. Polish foreign minister, 1926–1932; again,

1939–1941 (Sikorski government). Resigned in protest over lack of Soviet recognition of the 1921 Polish-Soviet frontier in the Sikorski-Maisky agreement, 31 July 1941. President of exiled Polish government, London, 1947–1972.

Zarubin, Vasily Mikhailovich (1894–1972). Soviet security official. GB major and senior operative, 5th Department (Intelligence), Main Directorate, GUGB, 1939–1940. Headed team of operatives in Kozelsk camp to investigate prisoners and recruit agents, late October 1939, and played an active part in "clearing out" the camp, spring 1940. Sent as "resident" GUGB officer to United States, end of 1941, with personal instructions from Stalin. Retired with rank of major general, 1948, after which he held several low-ranking jobs courtesy of the KGB.

Zhdanov, Andrei Aleksandrovich (1896–1948). Soviet party official. Close associate of Stalin's; party leader in Leningrad, 1932–1944; led city's defense against German siege, 1941–1943. Organized "socialist realism" in the arts. Played a prominent role in establishing the Communist Information Bureau [Cominform], 1947.

Zhukov, Georgy Sergeevich. Soviet security officer. GB major, 1940; deputy head of Military Intelligence under General Panfilov; also deputy head of 1st Special Department, 2nd Administration, NKVD. Liaison officer with high command, Polish Army under Anders in the USSR, 1941–1942. Subsequently, as GB commissar 3rd rank and Sovnarkom plenipotentiary, he was in charge of foreign formations on Soviet territory. Liaison officer with communist-led Polish Kościuszko Division under General Berling, spring–summer 1943. Allegedly drafted first official Soviet denial of responsibility for the Katyn massacre, 15 April 1943.

Glossary of Organizations and Political Parties

Belorussky Natsionalny Komitet [Belorussian National Committee]. Organized by the Belorussian political leader Vyacheslav Adamowicz, Sr., the committee established itself as the Belorussian government in October 1920, with General Stanislav Bulak-Balakhovitch [Polish: Bułak-Bałachowicz] (1883–1943) as head of state. It coordinated activities of Belorussian organizations in Poland and illegal activities in the Soviet Belorussian Republic. *See* Zeleny Dub.

Biskupa Kubina [Bishop Teodor Kubina's Organization]. Bishop Kubina (1880–1951), who headed the Częstochowa diocese, was linked to the small Catholic Narodowe Stronnictwo Pracy [National Labor Party] and exerted influence on the academic youth association Odrodzenie [Rebirth].

Bratstvo Russkoi Pravdy [BRP—Brotherhood of Russian Truth]. Russian émigré organization with branches in several countries. The NKVD accused it of establishing insurrectionary and terrorist organizations in the USSR.

Instytut Pamięci Narodowej—Komisja Ścigania Zbrodni Przeciwko Narodowi Polskiemu [IPN—Institute of National Remembrance—Commission for Prosecuting Crimes against the Polish Nation]. Founded on the basis of the law of 18 December 1998, the IPN collects and controls access to documents of state security organizations drawn up between 22 July 1944 and 31 December 1989; it also conducts prosecutions of Nazi and communist crimes and directs educational activities. The institute accepts documents from various state archives as well as organizations and individuals.

Komissia dlia Rossii [Commission for Russia]. Polish branch of an organization established in 1924 and connected with the Vatican. Its goal was the union of the Roman Catholic and Orthodox Churches in combating communism and the USSR. It trained cadres for work in eastern Poland.

Komitet Pomoshchi Russkim Emigrantom [Aid Committee for Russian Émigrés]. Self-help organization with headquarters in Warsaw and branches in most Polish towns.

Komitet Zashchity Krestow [Polish: Komitet Obrony Krzyżów—Committee for the Defense of Crosses]. According to the NKVD, this was a Catholic organization established by the Jedzierski (Jezierski?) brothers from Mohylew [Mogilev] to work among Catholics living in the USSR.

Komunistyczna Partia Polski [KPP—Polish Communist Party]. Formed in December 1918 out of the left wings of the SKPiL [Social Democracy of the Kingdom of Poland and Lithuania] and PPS-Lewica [Polish Socialist Party, Left]. Its name was originally Komunistyczna Partia Robotnicza Polski [Communist Workers' Party of Poland], but it assumed the name Komunistyczna Partia Polski in 1925. It was dissolved by Stalin in 1938, who had already ordered the shooting of its leading members who had sought asylum in the USSR. The official justification for the dissolution was infiltration by Polish police, but the real reason was the Trotskyite sympathies of its members. It was officially rehabilitated in February 1956, a few days before Khruschchev's famous speech at the Twentieth Congress of the CPSU, when Khruschchev admitted the rigging of the 1935–1938 purge trials and condemned the Stalin personality cult.

Korpus Ochrony Pogranicza [KOP—(Polish) Frontier Protection Corps]. A special military formation under the Ministry of War, established in August 1924 to defend Poland's eastern borders. In case of war with the USSR, KOP was to cooperate with special infantry and cavalry regiments as cover for the deployment of Polish military formations.

Legion Mladykh [Polish: Legion Młodych—Legion of Youth]. An association established in February 1930 to support pro-government university students and young intelligentsia as a counter to the National Democratic Union of Polish Democratic Youth.

National Democrats [Endeks]. Members of the nationalist party created in 1897 by Zygmunt Balicki (1856–1918) and Roman Dmowski (1864–1939) to fight for Poland's independence. Under different names, it was the major right-wing political movement in interwar Poland.

Natsionalny Trudvoi Soiuz Novogo Pokolenia [NTSNP—National Labor Union of the New Generation]. A Russian émigré organization for young people outside Russia, established in the early 1920s, with headquarters in Belgrade and branches in most countries; the Polish branch was established in 1930.

Orhanizatsiia Ukrainskykh Natsionalistiv [OUN—Organization of Ukrainian Nationalists]. A Ukrainian nationalist organization active in former southeastern Poland, it was established in Vienna in 1929 and had its headquarters in Berlin. OUN carried out a series of terrorist actions in Poland, including attacks on Polish landlords and officials in summer 1930, which provoked a Polish military "pacification," and the assassination of Tadeusz Hołówko, head of the Eastern Department of the Ministry of Foreign Affairs, in 1931.

Osadniki [Polish: Osadnicy—Military Settlers]. Selected veterans of the Polish-Soviet War of 1919–1920 who were given farmland in eastern Poland in order to strengthen the Polish element there. Viewed by Soviet authorities as a "socially dangerous element," they and their families were deported from former eastern Poland in 1940.

Pilsudchiki [Polish: Piłsudczycy—Piłsudskiites]. Supporters of Józef Piłsudski (1867–1935), Polish soldier and statesman.

Polska Organizacja Wojskowa [P.O.W. (Russian: POV)—Polish Military Organization]. Semisecret underground organization established by Józef Piłsudski that recruited and trained military personnel for the future Polish Army under German occupation, 1914–1917. Active from 1917 to 1919, it included units in Russia and Ukraine. Although it was dissolved in 1921, Soviet authorities claimed that it continued to exist; party and non-party members were charged with belonging to it in the Stalin purges of 1935–1938, and membership was a crime against the USSR.

Polska Partia Robotnicza [PPR—Polish Workers' Party]. Established in Moscow, fall 1941, the first leaders were parachuted into the Warsaw region at the end of December 1941. Its goal was to draw away support from the underground parties supporting the Polish government in London. After the death of the first two leaders, Władysław Gomułka became the leader, without Moscow's prior consent, in 1943. It never enjoyed majority support in Poland and was replaced by the PZPR [United Polish Workers' Party] in December 1948.

Polska Partia Socjalistyczna [PPS—Polish Socialist Party]. Founded in Paris on 21 November 1892 and in Warsaw in 1893, the PPS fought for Polish independence and participated in the first Polish governments. It supported the Piłsudski coup d'état in May 1926 but soon turned against him. Party representatives were in the Polish government-in-exile and in the leadership of underground civilian resistance in occupied Poland during World War II.

Polska Zjednoczona Partia Robotnicza [PZPR—United Polish Workers' Party]. Established in December 1948 from the union of the PPR [Polish Workers' Party] and the left wing of PPS [Polish Socialist Party], it was the ruling party in Poland until June 1989, when it lost the elections to the Solidarity bloc.

Prawo i Sprawiedliwość [PIS—Law and Justice]. Right-wing political party established in 2001 by the twin brothers Jarosław and Lech Kaczyński. Under President Lech Kaczyński, elected in October 2005, it has pursued the goal of uncovering all public officials who cooperated in the past with communist security services. Jarosław became head of the party in fall 2005 and premier in July 2006.

Rossiiskii Obshchevoiskovoi Soiuz [ROVS—Russian All-Military Union]. Russian emigré organization with headquarters in Paris. In 1930 a branch was established in Wilno, Poland.

Savinkovtsy [Savinkovites]. Russian émigrés led by Boris V. Savinkov (1879–1925), who supported Piłsudski's federal plans, 1919–1920. Savinkov returned to Russia, was caught, and died in prison.

Sionisty [Zionists]. Members of the Jewish Socialist Party, Poalei Sion, established around 1900. They worked for adoption of a socialist program in Poland, as well as for an independent Jewish state in Palestine. Split in 1918–1920, it lost its radical left wing. Members were active in Poland among Jewish workers.

Soiuz Advokatov [Polish: Związek Adwokatów Polskich—Polish Attorneys' Union]. A professional organization accused by the NKVD of having contacts with the 2nd Department, Polish General Staff (Military Intelligence), and of infiltrating the Polish communist movement.

Soiuz Byvshykh Voennykh [Union of Former Military Men]. Mainly veterans of General Bulak-Balakhovitch's Belorussian People's Volunteer Army, which existed in 1919–1922 and fought on the Polish side against the Red Army in 1919–1920. Bulak-Balakhovitch fought in defense of Warsaw, September 1939, and participated in Polish armed resistance against the Germans. He died in a Gestapo roundup in Warsaw in 1943.

Soiuz Ofitserov [Polish: Związek Oficerów Rezerwy R.P.—Officers' Union of the Republic of Poland]. Established in 1922, it had about 26,000 members in 1939. There was also a Union of Retired Officers with 4,000 members in 1939.

Soiuz Povstantsev Volyni [Union of Volhynia Insurgents]. Veterans of anti-Bolshevik units in the Russian Civil War who fought on the Polish side in 1920. The NKVD accused the union of combating the communist movement in the marshland Polesie region of eastern Poland.

Soiuz Russkoi Molodzezhi [Union of Russian Youth]. Émigré self-help organization active in the USSR and Lithuania. The NKVD accused it of receiving subsidies from Polish military intelligence.

Soiuz Unter-ofitserov [Polish: Związek Podoficerów Rezerwy—Noncommissioned Reserve Officers' Union]. Established in western Poland in 1922, it became a national union in 1926. A patriotic and self-help organization, it had about 55,000 members in 1939.

Sojusz Lewicy Demokratycznej [SLD—Democratic Left Alliance]. A party based on democratic socialist traditions, formed in Poland in 1999. One of its founders, Leszek Miller (b. 1946), a former PZPR [United Polish Workers' Party] official, was premier in 2001–2005, when Aleksander Kwaśniewski, an SLD member, was president.

Streltsy [Polish: Strzelcy—Związek Strzelecki—Riflemen's Association]. A national socioeducational youth organization founded in December 1919 whose rank and file were mainly young workers and peasants. In independent Poland, it was subject to the Ministry of War. The association conducted sporting and paramilitary activities and was politically linked to the Piłsudskiites.

Ukrainskoe Natsionalno-Demokraticheskoe Obiedinenie [UNDO—Ukrainian National-Democratic Union]. A Ukrainian nationalist organization with liberal tendencies, established in Lwów in July 1925. UNDO was active mainly in former southeastern Poland and Volhynia (now both in western Ukraine).

Zeleny Dub [Green Oak]. A peasant party organized in fall 1918 by the Belorussian political leader Vyacheslav Adamowicz, Sr. Active during and immediately after the Polish-Soviet War of 1919–1920 with the aim of creating an independent Belorussia, Zeleny Dub established a partisan movement supporting the Belorussian People's Volunteer Army, led by General Bulak-Balakhovitch.

Maps and Aerial Photographs

For context and discussion see the introductions to Parts I, II, and III.

Map 1. Eastern Europe, 1938, 1942, 1945, and 1999

(From Timothy Snyder, *The Reconstruction of Nations: Poland, Ukraine, Lithuania, Belarus, 1569–1999* [New Haven: Yale University Press, 2003], pp. xiv–xv. Copyright 2003 Yale University. Reprinted with permission from the publisher.)

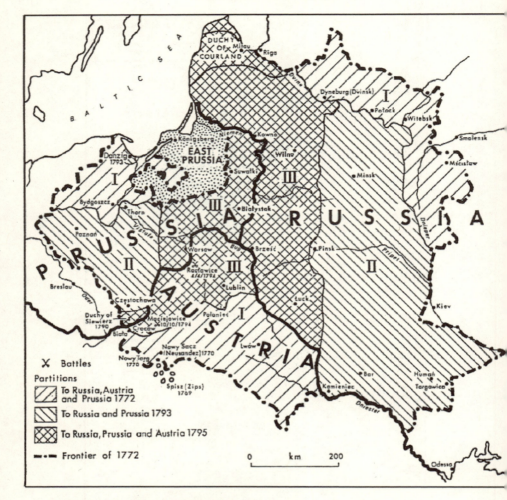

Map 2. The Partitions of Poland, 1773–1795

(From Norman Davies, *God's Playground: A History of Poland*, vol. I: *The Origins to 1795* [Oxford: Oxford University Press, 1981; New York: Columbia University Press, 1982], p. 512. Copyright 1981 and 1982 Norman Davies. Reprinted with permission from Oxford University Press and Columbia University Press.)

Map 3. Poland under German and Soviet Occupation, 1939–1941

(From Tadeusz Piotrowski, *Poland's Holocaust: Ethnic Strife, Collaboration with the Occupying Forces and Genocide in the Second Republic, 1918–1947* [Jefferson, N.C.: Mc-Farland, 1998], p. 8. Reprinted with permission from Eliza McClennen, Cartographer.)

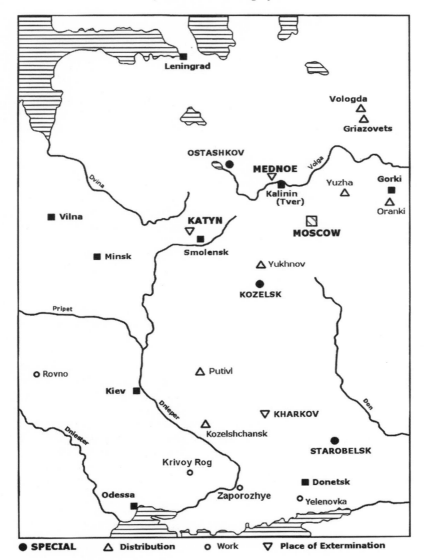

Map 4. NKVD Special Camps for Polish Prisoners of War and the Sites of the Prisoners' Execution

(Computer graphic by Judith Olsak-Glass based on sketch maps in *KDZ1*, p. 502; and *KDZ2*, following p. 515.)

Map 5. The Katyn-Gnezdovo Area, Russia, 1959

1. Site of the eight mass graves created by the Soviets in 1940 to conceal the murdered Polish officers from Kozelsk camp. The site is near the center of the Katyn Forest, between the Smolensk-Vitebsk Highway and the Dnieper [Dnepr] River. The road leading through the forest and past the site was removed in this 1959 map by American cartographers, although it is evident in aerial images, as well as in German and Soviet-era maps. The villages of Katyn-Uspenskoe and Katyn-Pokrovskoe are approximately 6.2 kilometers west of the map area.

2. Site of the dacha where the NKVD officers stayed, just above the loop of the Dnieper River.

3. The farm of Parfemon Kiselev, the only witness who claimed to have heard gunshots. The farm is just over 1,000 meters east of the mass burial site.

4. The Dnieper River, which sometimes, as it changes course, erodes ancient burial mounds and, in a few instances, as here, has exposed small burial pits apparently from the early Soviet era.

5. Site of the railway siding, 1,500 meters northwest of Gnezdovo Station, where the Kozelsk prisoners were detrained, according to the witness Ivan Krivozertsev as related to the Polish journalist Józef Mackiewicz. Near the siding are NKVD structures, possibly used for executions.

6. Ancient burial mounds dating from the time of the Slavonic tribes (tenth century) and the subsequent Viking occupation. The Soviets, in *Soviet War News* (17 April 1943), stated that the Germans "remain silent" about their discovery of Polish mass graves near the archaeological excavations of the historic Gnezdovo burials. An estimated 3,000 mounds still exist today; 2,000 or more may have been eroded away over the centuries by the meandering Dnieper River.

7. A forested area where a dozen or more official Soviet dachas are evident in stereomicroscopic analysis of German Luftwaffe photographs from 1942. The long structures are storage buildings, also evident in the 1942 photographs. Even before the Russian Revolution, Gnezdovo and the area as far as Borok Station, near the two Katyn villages, were known for their scenic beauty and contained many country retreats for the Smolensk elite. Katyn Forest itself was owned, before the revolution, by two Polish noble families, the Lednickis and Koźlinskis.

8. Gnezdovo Station. Stanisław Swianiewicz testified that he was detrained near the square by the station and witnessed NKVD vehicles taking Polish prisoners away from the train.

9. Glushchenki village, where, according to Józef Mackiewicz and Kazimierz Skarżyński, the German Field Police exhibited items found in the Katyn graves for viewing by invited journalists and other visitors in spring–summer 1943.

(Penisnar, Sheet 4827 I, Series N701, Edition I AMS. March 1959. Army Map Service Corps of Engineers. Cartographic Branch, National Archives Records Administration, College Park, Md. Annotations by Wacław Godziemba-Maliszewski.)

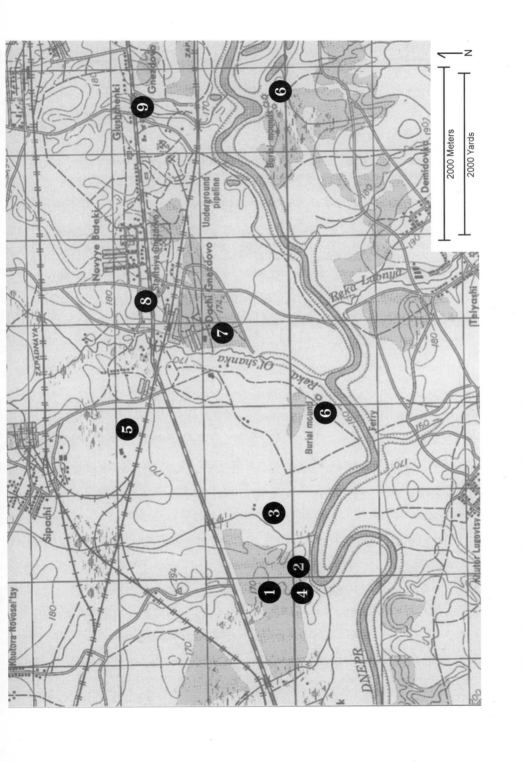

Khutora Novosel'tsy

Sipachi

ZAPADNAYA

Novyye Bateki

Glushchenki

Gnezdovo

ZAP.

180

180

170

Stantsiya Gnezdovo

180

Dachi Gnezdovo
174

Underground
pipeline

Burial mounds

Demidovka 190?

190

180

170

Reka Ol'shanka

Reka Lyonya

180

Burial mound
190

Ferry

170

160

DNEPR

160

Khutor Lugovtsy

Telyashi

170

194

170

170

170

① 1
② 2
③ 3
④ 4
⑤ 5
⑥ 6
⑦ 7
⑧ 8
⑨ 9
⑥ 6

N

2000 Meters

2000 Yards

Katyn Forest, Russia, 1942

1. Intersection of the Smolensk-Vitebsk Highway and the Katyn Forest road, which leads past the Kozelsk officers' mass graves and ends at the Dnieper River.
2. The farm of the Russian witness Parfemon Kiselev.
3. Site of burial pits 1–7. Number 8 is southwest, below the later Polish War Cemetery and in the forest.
4. The modern Polish War Cemetery where the remains of the Polish officers are interred. Stereomicroscopic analysis of the image reveals ground marks here, confirmed by the Germans to indicate mass graves from the 1930s containing victims of the Stalin Terror.
5. Site of the NKVD dacha. Stereomicroscopic analysis shows that there were three buildings in the clearing, one of which was the NKVD garage. The dacha is gone, destroyed in 1944; the garage was still present in 1989. The site now has an official Russian rest home; another residence has been built nearby. Many small roads are evident on the surrounding land, but the former use of the area is unknown. It was off limits to Polish forensic experts during the exhumations of the 1990s.
6. The Dnieper River at high water. To the left of the bend are crop marks within vestigial fields, perhaps indicating land use by prehistoric Slavonic tribes. An ancient burial mound may be there, too.

(Luftwaffe image from 2 September 1942. Flight GX 1562 F2077, frame 104. National Archives Records Administration, Record Group 373, College Park, Md. Annotations by Wacław Godziemba-Maliszewski.)

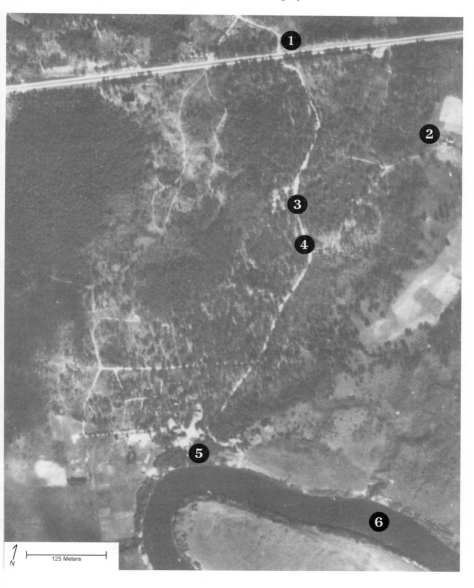

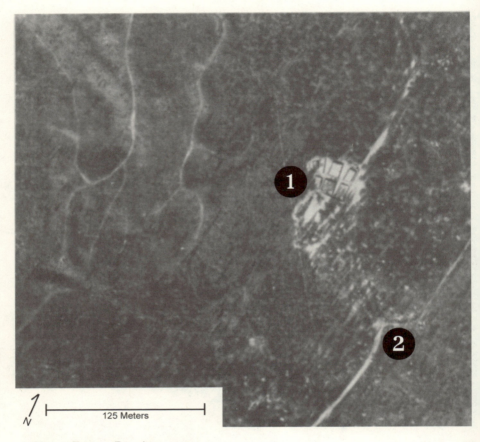

Katyn Forest, Russia, 1943

1. The Polish Red Cross Cemetery, created after the German and International Medical Commissions exhumations and later destroyed by the Soviets. Six rectangular mounds mark the graves of reburied officers. To the upper left of the clearing are two smaller mounds that contain the remains of Generals Mieczysław Smorawiński and Bronisław Bohatyrewicz. The present Polish War Cemetery is in the same clearing.

2. Site of the present Russian Memorial Cemetery for Soviet victims murdered and buried in Katyn Forest in the 1920s and 1930s.

(Luftwaffe image from 13 October 1943. Flight GX 4344 F 4076 43 SD, frame 76. National Archives Records Administration, Record Group 373, College Park, Md. Annotations by Wacław Godziemba-Maliszewski.)

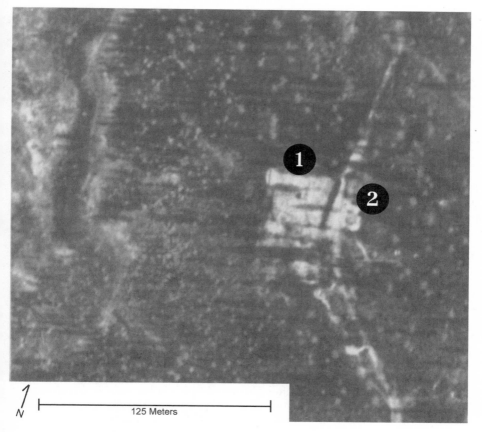

125 Meters

Katyn Forest, Russia, 1944

1. A Soviet DOK-class bulldozer in operation near the center of the clearing, visible in more detail under a stereomicroscope. The photograph was taken in April 1944, indicating that Soviets were destroying material evidence well after the Burdenko Commission exhumations in January. The back of the bulldozer can be seen, as can the treads. (The shadows in the image fall to the left.) Exhaust is rising from the stackpipe. Striations within the excavation indicate many passes by the bulldozer.

2. An escarpment near the western side of the road indicating, by the long black shadow, a very deep excavation at the site of the Polish Red Cross Cemetery. This supports the contention that the cemetery was largely emptied. Polish authorities have testimony (unverified) from a woman who claimed to have seen trainloads of earth, in which bones and uniform parts were commingled, leave the Smolensk region in the spring of 1944. In the 1990s, Polish forensic experts conducted spot exhumations and dug test holes, finding a few dozen skeletal remains deep down or near the borders of the former cemetery; some uniform fragments and other material evidence were also found.

(Luftwaffe image from 28 April 1944. Flight GX 3707 B, frame 40. National Archives Records Administration, Record Group 373, College Park, Md. Annotations by Wacław Godziemba-Maliszewski.)

Map 6. Kharkov [Kharkiv] Wooded Park, Ukraine, 1962

1. Site of Piatikhatki village (Pyatikhatka on map), where the Starobelsk victims were buried in mass graves, according to the former NKVD officer Mitrofan Syromiatnikov. Syromiatnikov worked at the Kharkov jail and gave his testimony in June 1990. Several high-rise apartment buildings stand at the site now.

2. Site of the mass graves of Polish officers and other victims exhumed in the 1990s. The area is in the VIth Quarter of the Kharkov Wooded Park, entered by the Chyornaia Doroga, the "Black Road." An NKVD building dating back at least to the early 1940s still stands nearby.

3. The Belgorod-Kharkov Highway. The Cheka fenced off the forested area east and west of this highway in the late 1920s. The NKVD kept the forest a restricted area.

4. Site of Sokolniki settlement, surrounded by Soviet military installations in 1941. Evident in the Luftwaffe reconnaissance image from 24 September, made before the Germans occupied the territory, are several earth marks indicative of mass graves. The *Soviet War News* (London) of 23 December 1943 reported that "the forest park near the Sokolniki settlement on the outskirts of Kharkov is densely covered with graves containing the victims of German-Fascists."

5. Site of a compound with high fences and guard towers, according to the Luftwaffe image of 24 September 1941. Several groups of military buildings were in the vicinity.

6. Site of a bean-shaped clearing in the forest with two large rectangular ground marks and six pits, apparently burial sites, which are evident in the Luftwaffe reconnaissance imagery of 24 September 1941. A radio tower is in the clearing now. In 1991, Polish prosecutor Zbigniew Mielecki asked Russian and Ukrainian authorities if the Polish forensic team could explore the site, but permission was denied. The remains of some victims from Starobelsk and elsewhere, possibly Kiev, may be buried here.

7. Site of a large rectangular clearing in the forest containing eighteen or more pits with NKVD buildings nearby, all visible in the Luftwaffe reconnaissance imagery of 24 September 1941. The site remains unexplored, as do several other forested areas west and east of the Belgorod-Kharkov Highway. Buried there may be people executed during and after the Revolution, the Red Terror of 1920–1921, and the purges and Stalin Terror of the 1930s, as well as casualties of the four battles of Kharkov and citizens executed as collaborators during and after World War II.

(Kharkov North Sheet 5518 III, Series N701. Edition 1. First printing, December 1962. Army Map Service, Corps of Engineers. Cartographic Branch, National Archives Records Administration, College Park, Md. In point 4, the 24 September 1941 Luftwaffe image is from Flight TUGX 1282 460 SK, frame 55, National Archives Records Administration, Record Group 373, College Park, Md. Annotations by Wacław Godziemba-Maliszewski.)

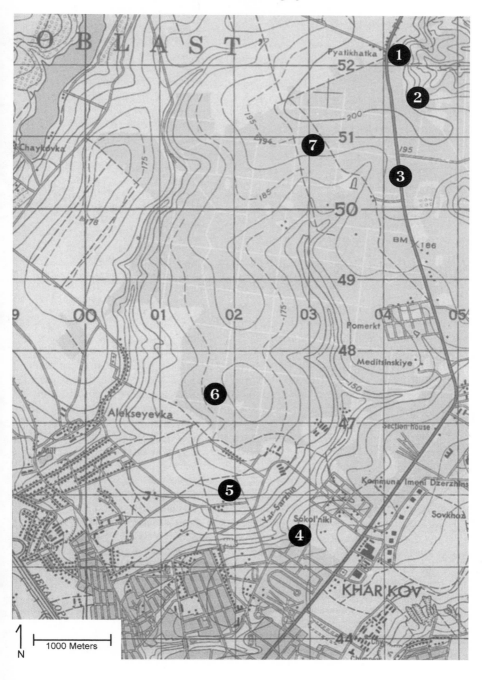

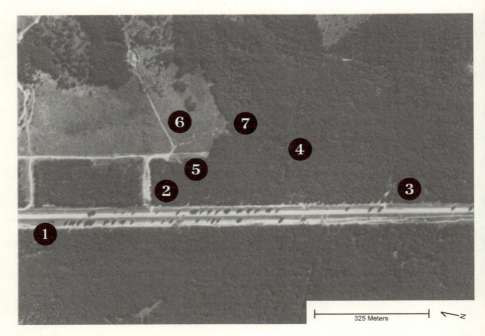

Kharkov, Ukraine, 1943

1. The Belgorod–Kharkov Highway, bordering the Kharkov Wooded Park. About 900 meters to the north is Piatikhatki village, the site of mass graves exhumed in 1991–1995.
2. A closed gate, blocking the former main entry to the Black Road, now disused.
3. A small entry to the Black Road, partially obscured by the forest tree canopy. This is now the entry to the war cemetery. A monument to Soviet victims is immediately beyond the entry; the Polish monument is deeper in the forest, near number 4 on the photograph. Other footpaths lead into the forest from the Belgorod–Kharkov Highway. Although most of the Starobelsk prisoners were executed at the NKVD prison in Kharkov, there are reports that some were shot in the forest.
4. Site of the mass graves of Starobelsk officers. Stereomicroscopic study reveals disturbances in the earth, including a horseshoe-shaped spot on the Black Road. The Polish forensic team was limited to a fenced area, where they uncovered fifteen mass graves. Some graves clearly extended beyond the fence, but permission to continue excavating was denied. It is possible that the first prisoners buried here were not from the Starobelsk camp but were Polish civilian internees transported to the Kharkov prison from the prison in Kiev.
5. A path leading into the forest. At the edge of the forest are marks in the earth indicating the presence of mass graves. The Polish forensic team was not allowed to explore this area in the 1990s.
6. A large open space that was completely forested in the earliest aerial imagery of 1941. Several artillery redoubts in semicircular shapes, as well as several machine-gun positions, are evident in a stereomicroscopic analysis of this image. The area was deforested for military purposes before the second Battle of Kharkov in 1942.
7. An NKVD building in the shadow of the forest canopy, still present today.

(Luftwaffe aerial image of 15 August 1943. Flight GX 3943 F1184 SK, frame 160. National Archives Records Administration, Record Group 373, College Park, Md. Annotations by Wacław Godziemba-Maliszewski.)

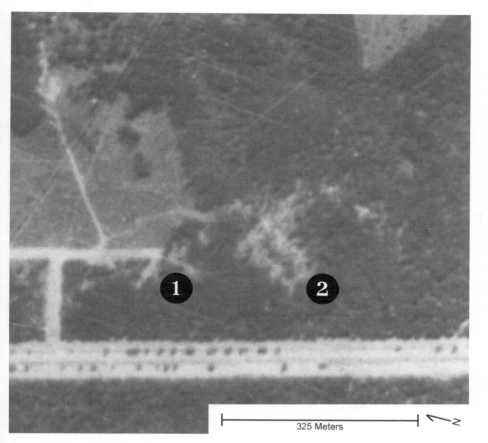

Kharkov, Ukraine, 1944

1. Deforestation in the immediate vicinity of the mass graves of the Starobelsk officers. Evidence suggests that some of the grave pits may be reburials. Luftwaffe aerial photographs of Katyn, taken in 1944 and looking much like this one, show Soviet excavations made after the German occupation, so maybe the Soviets excavated here, too. In the early 1990s layering of the earth in some graves at Kharkov was found to be inconsistent with undisturbed burials. (Similar ambiguous layering was evident when mass graves were exhumed at Kurapaty, Belarus, in 1988.) According to Polish authorities, there are also reports of Polish bodies in uniform being blown from the earth during a battle in 1942 and of Polish military buttons being found by local children in the 1980s.
2. Two large trenches in the shape of rabbit ears and, nearby, several smaller pits and a long irregular-shaped mark in the earth, also evident in 1941 imagery. In the 1990s, Polish forensic teams were not allowed to explore this area, which is north of the fenced area they worked in. The 30 July 1991 statement by the former NKVD officer Mitrofan Syromiatnikov that he and other staff had "dug a pit large enough for a truck to drive into," a pit that took six men ten days to dig, may relate to this area. The pit may also contain the remains of additional prisoners from Starobelsk or from any of several Ukrainian NKVD prisons transported to Kharkov for execution.

(Luftwaffe aerial image of 8 June 1944. Flight GX 536 F 173 SK, frame 319. National Archives Records Administration, Record Group 373, College Park, Md. Annotations by Wacław Godziemba-Maliszewski.)

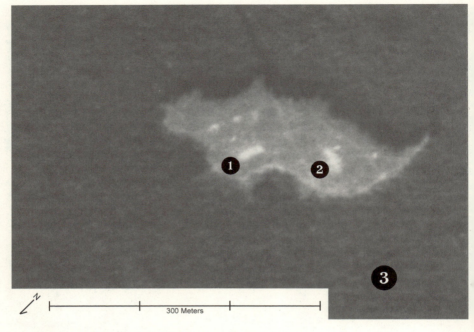

300 Meters

Kharkov and Sokolniki, Ukraine, 1941

Shown is the forest clearing in Map 6 at point 6. The clearing, which is approximately 300 meters long, is located 2 kilometers northwest of the Sokolniki suburb of Kharkov, just above the ravine of Sarzhin Yar and beyond the military installations and separate fenced compound with guard towers. This aerial photograph, taken on 24 September 1941, before the German occupation of Kharkov, reveals several earth and shadow marks suggestive of mass graves. Unlike similar areas north and west of the Belgorod–Kharkov Highway, the area shown here was probably the site of concealed graves dating from 1940; the former areas, where the edges of the clearings show more plant reclamation of the land, are apparently NKVD burials from the Stalin Terror of the 1930s or from even earlier Cheka executions. In 1991, Polish authorities were not allowed to explore soils surrounding the site, now occupied by a radio transmission tower.

The dark upper edge of the clearing is the shadow line of the trees (the shadows fall toward the viewer). The white pathlike line near the lower edge is a seasonal rivulet, here dry.

1. A long, rectangular mark in the earth approximately 33 meters long by 11 meters wide (indicating, in forensic taphonomy, a smaller burial site within the larger disturbance). The image was taken at the end of a hot summer, so the browned new-growth grass is surrounded by still-green old-growth grass and other groundcover vegetation. The sharpness of the shape suggests a 1940 burial site. Above it are at least four circular pits (A).
2. Another large rectangular mark in the earth, this one approximately 31 meters long by 15 meters wide. At least two circular pits are evident nearby (B).
3. A crossline of the forest divisions. From the 1920s the forest was fenced off, first by the Cheka, and later it was maintained by the NKVD as a restricted area where entry was forbidden.

(Luftwaffe aerial image of 24 September 1941. Flight TUGX 1282 460 SK, frame 055. National Archives Records Administration, Record Group 373, College Park, Md. Annotations by Wacław Godziemba-Maliszewski.)

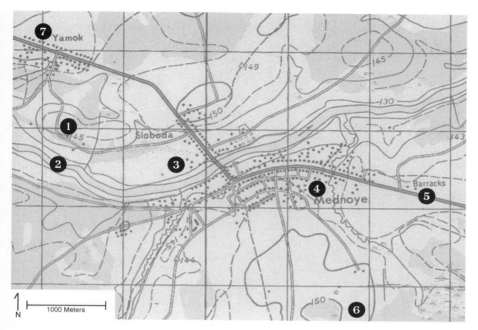

Map 7. The Mednoe-Yamok Area, Russia, 1963

1. Area where mass graves of the Ostashkov prisoners dating to 1940 were excavated in the 1990s. Also shown are several NKVD buildings. Although GB Captain Tokarev described how the prisoners were shot one by one in the cellar of the NKVD jail in Kalinin/Tver, it is possible that some were shot at Mednoe at the edge of a burial pit. According to Prosecutor Yablokov, Tokarev called this "a more stupid procedure" than the one he heard mentioned regarding Smolensk (see introduction to Part II).

2. The Tvertsa River. German aerial imagery from 1942 shows Soviet barracks and military installations below the river.

3. Area of Polish mass graves, which may have been traversed by tanks in a Soviet-German battle here in October 1941, when Soviet forces were collected in and around the forested area with the concealed graves. It is impossible to assess the extent of battle damage to the grave site in this area. Luftwaffe reconnaissance imagery dated 10 June 1942 reveals Soviet artillery and machine-gun positions in the area, as well as antitank defense positions just above the present settlement of Sloboda. According to postwar German sources, the battle took place on 17–19 October 1941. The Wehrmacht Panzer-Lehrbrigade 900 captured the Tvertsa Bridge at Mednoe but, overpowered by Soviet forces, retreated to Kalinin.

4. The village of Mednoe (Mednoye on the map), which had expanded to several times its prewar size when this map was drawn.

5. The Kalinin (now Tver) Highway.

6. Area of mass graves with dog-bone shapes and smaller irregular pits visible in a Luftwaffe aerial photograph dated 22 August 1942 (see second photograph below).

7. Yamok village, greatly expanded from its prewar size. The site of the Polish mass graves is closer to Yamok than to Mednoe, but because Mednoe was the chief administrative village, the site is named after it.

(*Mednoye:* N701 Sheet 5431 IV, Edition I, first printing, November 1963. Army Map Service Corps of Engineers, National Archives Records Administration, Cartographic Branch, College Park, Md. The aerial imagery mentioned in point 2 is a Luftwaffe image of 22 August 1942, Flight GX 1594 F18565, frame 52, National Archives Records Administration, Record Group 373, College Park, Md. Annotations by Wacław Godziemba-Maliszewski.)

The Mednoe-Yamok area, Russia, 1942

The shadows fall to the left.

1. Area where mass graves of Ostashkov victims were dug up in the 1990s. Massive soil scarring is evident beyond the area exhumed by Polish forensic specialists. To what extent some of this scarring was caused by the Battle of Mednoe Bridge between Soviet and German tanks on 17–19 October 1941 cannot be ascertained. Twenty-three mass graves have been identified, but not enough to account for the total number of known victims (6,314).

2. Dark shapes within a larger rectangular area of browned groundcover, possibly indicating prehistoric crop fields, or early peat gathering, a known activity in the Mednoe area.

3. An NKVD building and, above it, a field cleared recently, before the photograph was taken. At least two other NKVD buildings are evident in the forest west and south of the mass grave area (point 1). Since German imagery from 1941 has not been located yet, it is not known exactly when the field was cleared.

4. A much larger NKVD building, on the same scale as the dacha used by the NKVD at Katyn.

5. A berm, open only on the northern side: possibly the remnant of an ancient fortification.

6. The Tvertsa River, below which, out of the picture frame, are the Soviet military installations.

(*Mednoe* Russia. Luftwaffe aerial image of 12 June 1942, Flight GX 943 F835 SK, frame 082. National Archives Records Administration, Record Group 373, College Park, Md. Annotations by Wacław Godziemba-Maliszewski.)

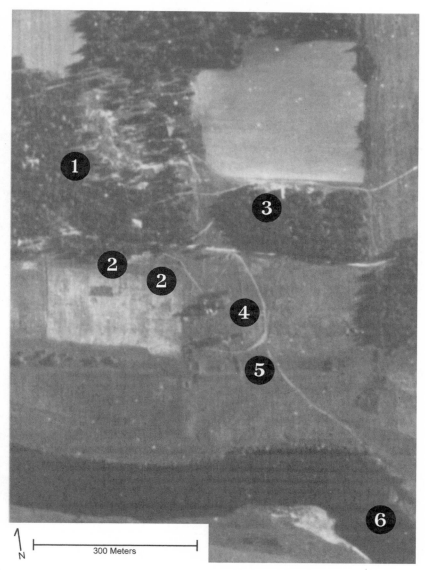

N

300 Meters

Mednoe, Russia, 1942

In Mednoe, which includes the villages of Yamok, Sloboda, and Novaya Mermeriny, there are several possible mass graves, likely created by the Kalinin (now Tver) NKVD before and during World War II. Although Tokarev testified that some of the Ostashkov prisoners were shot in Kalinin jail, this Luftwaffe photograph of 22 August 1942 may indicate that some were shot at this suspected burial site. The photograph may possibly relate to Prosecutor Anatoly Yablokov's statement to Tokarev that "a mistake" was made at Mednoe. Alternatively, it may show an additional location used by the same NKVD excavation and burial personnel.

The present annotator sent this photograph, along with other materials, to Nikolai Danilov of the Odessa section of the Russian Memorial society. In an official reply, dated 15 September 1995, Danilov said that he had given the photograph to representatives from the Tver section of the Memorial society, who presented the evidence to Russian authorities in 1994. According to Danilov, the Russians quickly placed a cordon around the area and forbade entry by representatives of the Memorial society. The area was also off limits to the Polish exhumation teams of the 1990s.

1. A symmetrical group of dog-bone-shaped marks in the earth, bordered to the west and south by other irregular marks (see Map 7, point 6). A bulldozer makes repeated passes when excavating a trench. At each end of a pass, the soil is turned away to left and right, creating wider scars of earth, readily seen from the air. Tokarev testified that a backhoe, often with a bulldozer attachment, was employed at Mednoe to create mass burial pits for the Ostashkov prisoners. The present annotator showed this image and others to the Polish archaeologist Professor Kazimierez Godłowski of the Jagiellonian University of Kraków, who did not believe that the marks indicated land use by a premodern culture. The widened dog-bone-like ends of the trenches suggest that they are not peat excavations, either. The Russian response to being shown the photograph also suggests the probability of a mass burial pit complex. The dog-bone shapes are sharper in detail than the irregular shapes, suggesting that the trenches were dug later and were made using a different technique. They may date from 1940; the other, irregular shapes, with more advanced plant growth along the edges, may date from the 1930s.

2. A dirt road leading due north to Mednoe village, approximately 2 kilometers distant. The road forks to the south, leading to another possible area of concealed graves.

(*Mednoe* Russia. Luftwaffe aerial image, 22 August 1942. Flight GX 1594 F 1855, frame 053. National Archives Records Administration, Record Group 373, College Park, Md. Annotations by Wacław Godziemba-Maliszewski.)

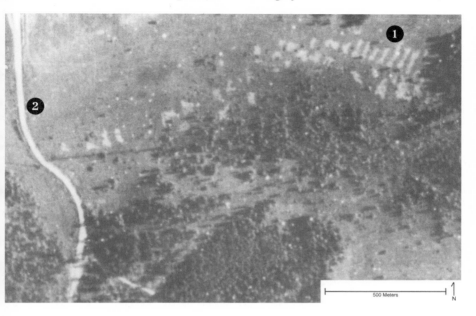

Notes

ABBREVIATIONS OF MAIN SOURCES

In this volume documents come primarily from the following sources.

AVPRF   Arkhiv Vneshnei Politiki Rossiiskoi Federatsii [Foreign Policy Archive of the Russian Federation], Moscow

DGFP   *Documents on German Foreign Policy, 1918–1945*, ser. D, 1937–1945 (London, Washington, D.C., 1949–1964)

DPSR   Stanisław Biegański et al., eds., *Documents on Polish-Soviet Relations, 1939–1945* (London, 1961–1967)

DVP   *Dokumenty Vneshnei Politiki* [Documents on Foreign Policy], vols. XXII–XXIV (Moscow, 1992, 1998, 2000)

GARF   Gosudarstvenny Arkhiv Rossiiskoi Federatsii [State Archive of the Russian Federation]

KD1   Natalia S. Lebedeva and Wojciech Materski et al., eds., *Katyn: Plenniki Neobiavlennoi Voiny* [Katyn: Prisoners of an Undeclared War] (Moscow, 1997), vol. 1 in the series *Rossiia, XX Vek: Dokumenty* [Russia, the Twentieth Century: Documents]

KD2   Natalia S. Lebedeva and Wojciech Materski et al., eds., *Katyn: Mart 1940 g.–Sentiabr 2000 g.: Dokumenty* [Katyn: March 1940–September 2000: Documents] (Moscow, 2001)

KDG   Wojciech Materski, ed., *Katyń: Documents of Genocide* [English edition of *KDL* by Ryszard Żelichowski], trans. Jan Kolbowski and Mark Canning (Warsaw, 1993)

KDL   *Katyń: Dokumenty Ludobójstwa* [Katyn: Documents of Genocide], trans. and ed. Wojciech Materski (Warsaw, 1992)

KDZ1   Natalia S. Lebedeva and Wojciech Materski et al., eds., *Katyń: Dokumenty Zbrodni* [Katyn: Documents of a Crime], vol. 1: *Jeńcy Nie Wypowiedzianej Wojny* [The Prisoners of an Undeclared War] (Warsaw, 1995)

KDZ2   Natalia S. Lebedeva and Wojciech Materski et al., eds., *Katyń: Dokumenty Zbrodni* [Katyn: Documents of a Crime], vol. 2: *Zagłada,*

Marzec–Czerwiec 1940 [Extermination, March–June 1940] (Warsaw, 1998)

KDZ3   Natalia S. Lebedeva and Wojciech Materski et al., eds., *Katyń: Dokumenty Zbrodni* [Katyn: Documents of a Crime], vol. 3: *Losy Ocalałych, Lipiec 1940–Marzec 1943* [The Fate of the Survivors, July 1940–March 1943] (Warsaw, 2001)

KDZ4   Natalia S. Lebedeva and Wojciech Materski et al., eds., *Katyń: Dokumenty Zbrodni* [Katyn: Documents of a Crime], vol. 4: *Echa Katynia, Kwiecień 1943–Marzec 2005* [Echoes of Katyn, April 1943–March 2005] (Warsaw, 2006)

R   Natalia S. Lebedeva and Wojciech Materski et al., eds., *Katyn: Mart 1940 g.–Sentiabr 2000 g. Rasstrel, Sudby Zhivykh, Ekho Katyni: Dokumenty* [Katyn: March 1940–September 2000. Execution by Shooting, the Fate of the Survivors, the Echoes of Katyn: Documents] (Moscow, 2001), a supplement to *KD1*

SDFP   Jane Degras, ed., *Soviet Documents on Foreign Policy, 1917–1941,* 3 vols. (London, 1951–1953)

PART I. PRISONERS OF AN UNDECLARED WAR

1. For a concise history of the Commonwealth, 1385–1795, focusing on Lithuania, see Timothy Snyder, *The Reconstruction of Nations: Poland, Ukraine, Lithuania, Belarus, 1569–1999* (New Haven, 2003), pp. 17–26; for a detailed history, see Daniel Stone, *The Polish-Lithuanian State, 1386–1795* (Seattle, 2001); see also Norman Davies, *God's Playground: A History of Poland* (New York, 1982; rev. edition, 2005), vol. I, part II.

2. For a brief account of Polish-Russian relations during the "Time of Troubles," see Stone, *Polish-Lithuanian State,* pp. 140–142. Ivan Susanin was the peasant who allegedly saved the tsar's life and his name was Glinka's personal choice for the title, but Tsar Nicholas I changed the title to "A Life for the Tsar"; for discussion see Halina Goldberg, "Appropriating Poland: Glinka, Polish Dance and Russian National Identity," in David L. Rensel and Bożena Shallcross, eds., *Polish Encounters, Russian Identity* (Bloomington, Ind., 2005), pp. 74–88. For a Polish historian's account of the Polish occupation of Moscow in Russian national memory, see Janusz Tazbir, "Historia Rzeczpospolitej nad Moskwą Panowania" [The History of the Commonwealth's Rule over Moscow], *Polityka,* no. 3 (2487), (Warsaw, 22 January 2005), pp. 78–81. For a brief history of Russo-Polish relations from the Polish point of view, see Andrzej Nowak, "Russo-Polish Historical Confrontation," *Sarmatian Review,* 17, no. 1 (January 1997), pp. 432–442.

3. For a brief account of the decline and partitions of Poland, see Piotr S. Wandycz, *The Lands of Partitioned Poland, 1795–1918* (Seattle, 1974), chap. 1. For more detail, see Jerzy Lukowski, *The Partitions of Poland, 1772, 1793, 1795* (London, 1999).

4. Stanislaus Blejwas, *Realism in Polish Politics: Warsaw Positivism and Survival in Nineteenth Century Poland* (Boulder, Colo., 1984).

5. For Polish lands during the partition period and World War I, see Wandycz, *Lands of Partitioned Poland;* and Davies, *God's Playground,* vol. II, chaps. 1–17.

On the 1905–1907 revolution, see Robert Blobaum, *Rewolucja: Russian Poland, 1904–1907* (Ithaca, N.Y., 1995). For nineteenth-century Russian images of the Poles in political literature, see John Radziejowski, "The Image of the Pole in Russian Publicistic Writings (1864–1918)," *Acta Poloniae Historica*, vol. 66 (Warsaw, 1992), pp. 114–139; Andrzej Walicki, "The Slavophile Thinkers and the Polish Question in 1863," and Mason de Courten, "Vladimir Solovev's Views on the Polish Question," both in Rensel and Shallcross, *Polish Encounters*, pp. 89–99, 110–121. For Dostoevsky on Poles, see Nina Perlina, "Dostoevsky and His Polish Fellow Prisoners from the House of the Dead," in Rensel and Shallcross, *Polish Encounters*, pp. 100–109. On Russian rejection of Polish claims to the borderlands and even to the Polish core, see Leonid Gorizontov, "The Geopolitical Dimension of Russian-Polish Confrontation," in Rensel and Shallcross, *Polish Encounters*, p. 141.

6. Józef Piłsudski, "Jak Stałem się Socjalistą" [How I Became a Socialist], in Wacław Jędrzejewicz, ed., *Wybór Pism* [Selected Writings] (New York, 1944), p. 5 (translated by A. M. Cienciala). For a positive, popular biography of Piłsudski, see Wacław Jędrzejewicz, *Piłsudski: A Life for Poland* (New York, 1982); for a highly critical, scholarly work, see Andrzej Garlicki, *Józef Piłsudski, 1867–1935,* trans. and ed. John Coutovidis (London, 1995).

7. The only English-language study of Dmowski to date is Alvin M. Fountain, *Roman Dmowski: Party, Tactics, Ideology, 1896–1907* (New York, 1989); for the best Polish biography, see Roman Wapiński, *Roman Dmowski* (Lublin, 1988). For the late nineteenth-century rise of the ethnocentric brand of Polish nationalism typified by the National Democrats, see Brian Porter, *When Nationalism Learned to Hate: Imagining Modern Politics in Nineteenth Century Poland* (Oxford, 2000).

8. Great Poland was the former Grand Duchy of Posen [Poznań]. For Polish questions at the Paris Peace Conference, also the Polish-Lithuanian dispute over Wilno (now Vilnius) and the Polish-Ukrainian fighting over East Galicia (now part of western Ukraine), see Anna M. Cienciala and Titus Komarnicki, *From Versailles to Locarno: Keys to Polish Foreign Policy, 1919–1925* (Lawrence, Kans., 1984). For a detailed, chronological study of all Polish issues, see Kay Lundgreen-Nielsen, *The Polish Problem at the Paris Peace Conference: A Study of the Great Powers and the Poles, 1918–1919* (Odense, 1979).

9. On Piłsudski's federal plans, see K. M. [Kamil Marian] Dziewanowski, *Joseph Piłsudski: A European Federalist, 1918–1922* (Stanford, Calif., 1969); for a recent, detailed study of Piłsudski's eastern policy, see Andrzej Nowak, *Polska i Trzy Rosje: Studium Polityki Wschodniej Józefa Piłsudskiego do Kwietnia 1920 Roku* [Poland and the Three Russias: A Study of Józef Piłsudski's Eastern Policy to April 1920] (Kraków, 2001).

10. See Michael Palij, *The Ukrainian-Polish Alliance, 1918–1921: An Aspect of the Ukrainian Revolution* (Edmonton, 1995). For the views of post-Soviet Ukrainian historians, see Władysław Werstiuk, "Ukraińskie Aspekty Wojny Polsko-Radzieckiej 1920 r. Kilka Uwag z Punktu Widzenia Postradzieckiej Historiografii Ukraińskiej" [Ukrainian Aspects of the Polish-Soviet War of 1920: A Few Comments from the Point of View of Post-Soviet Ukrainian Historiography], in Anna M. Cienciala and Piotr Wandycz, eds., *Wojna Polsko-Bolszewicka 1919–1920 w Ocenach Historyków* [The Polish-Bolshevik War, 1919–1920, as Evaluated by Historians] (Warsaw, 2003), pp. 31–40.

11. On the question of East Galicia and Poland's eastern frontier in 1919–1921, see Cienciala and Komarnicki, *From Versailles to Locarno,* chap. 6, with references to other works there; and Lundgreen-Nielsen, *Polish Problem,* sections on territorial and frontier problems in each chronological chapter. For the Curzon Line and the ethnic structure of eastern Poland, see Cienciala and Komarnicki, *From Versailles to Locarno,* map on p. 185. For the Curzon Line with variants A and B and the farthest Soviet advance into Poland, on August 1920, see Paul Robert Magocsi, *Historical Atlas of Central Europe* (rev. edition, Seattle, Wash., 2002), map 38. For the Russian text of Lenin's speech on 22 September 1920, see *Istoricheskii Arkhiv* [Historical Archive] (Moscow 1992), no. 1, pp. 14–29; for translated extracts, see Richard Pipes, *Russia under the Bolshevik Regime* (New York, 1993), pp. 180–183.

12. For English-language works on the war, see Norman Davies, *White Eagle, Red Star: The Polish-Soviet War, 1919–1920* (London, 1972); and Adam Zamoyski, *The Battle for the Marchlands* (Boulder, Colo., 1988). For Piłsudski's and Tukhachevsky's analyses of the Battle of the Vistula, see Józef Piłsudski, *Year 1920 and Its Climax: Battle of Warsaw during the Polish-Soviet War, 1919–1920* (London, 1972). On the diplomatic aspect of the war, see Piotr S. Wandycz, *Soviet-Polish Relations, 1917–1921* (Cambridge, Mass. 1969). For different historical perspectives, see Cienciala and Wandycz, *Wojna Polsko-Bolszewicka.* For a recent account of the war by a Russian historian, see Mikhail I. Meltiukhov, *Sovetsko-Polskiie Voiny: Voenno-Politicheskoe Protivostoianie 1918–1939* [Soviet-Polish Wars: Military-Political Confrontations 1918–1939] (Moscow, 2001), pp. 14–106; and the expanded version, Meltiukhov, *Sovetsko-Polskiie Voiny: Bely Orel Protiv Krasnoi Zvezdy* [Soviet-Polish Wars: White Eagle against Red Star] (Moscow, 2004), pp. 17–172.

13. On the Polish victory, see Davies, *White Eagle, Red Star,* chap. 5. On the diplomatic battles over Western recognition of Poland's new eastern frontier, see Cienciala and Komarnicki, *From Versailles to Locarno,* pp. 212–221. On Poles reading Red Army codes in 1919 and 1920, see Grzegorz Nowak's summary of his book in "Szyfrołamacze" [Code Breakers], *Polityka,* no. 32 (Warsaw, 2005), pp. 68–70.

14. Zamoyski, *Battle for the Marchlands,* chap. 11.

15. For the Polish texts of the Polish-Romanian alliance and military convention, signed on 3 March 1921, see Tadeusz Jędruszczak and Maria Nowak-Kiełbikowa, eds., *Dokumenty z Dziejów Polskiej Polityki Zagranicznej, 1918–1939* [Documents on the History of Polish Foreign Policy, 1918–1939], vol. 1: *1918–1932* (Warsaw, 1989), nos. 32, 33. For the "Poland-Romania" Soviet war plans, see Bruce Menning, "Soviet Railroads and War Planning, 1927–1939," paper read at the Annual Convention of the American Association for the Advancement of Slavic Studies (Boston, November 1996).

16. For a recent study, see Yuri Dyakov and Tatyana Bushuyeva, *The Red Army and the Wehrmacht* (Amherst, N.Y., 1995).

17. On the Soviet-Polish negotiations for the Non-Aggression Pact of 1932, see Oleg Ken, *Collective Security or Isolation? Soviet Foreign Policy and Poland, 1930–1935* (St. Petersburg, Russia, 1996), chap. 1. For a detailed study, see Ken,

Moskva i Pakt o Nenapadenii s Polshei (1930–1932 gg.) [Moscow and the Non-Aggression Pact with Poland (1930–1931)] (St. Petersburg, 2002). For the Polish text of the pact and protocols, see Jędruszczak and Nowak-Kiełbikowa, *Dokumenty z Dziejów,* vol. I, no. 106, pp. 487–489; for the English text, see Stanisław Biegański et al., eds., *Documents on Polish-Soviet Relations, 1939–1945* (henceforth *DPSR*), vol. I, *1939–1942* (London, 1961), no. 6.

18. For the Polish text of the Polish-German Declaration of Non-Aggression, see Tadeusz Jędruszczak and Maria Nowak-Kiełbikowa, eds., *Dokumenty z Dziejów Polskiej Polityki Zagranicznej, 1918–1939,* vol. II: *1933–1939* (Warsaw, 1996), no. 8; for the English text, see *Documents on German Foreign Policy, 1918–1945* (henceforth *DGFP*), ser. D, vol. II (London, Washington, D.C., 1959), no. 219.

19. For the Polish texts of the Polish-Soviet extension agreement and the protocol on Lithuania, see Jędruszczak and Nowak-Kiełbikowa, *Dokumenty z Dziejów,* vol. II, nos. 22, 23; for the English text, see *DPSR,* vol. I, no. 10. On Soviet intelligence reports regarding the Polish-German agreement, see Ye. M. Primakov, ed., *Ocherki Istorii Rossiiskoi Vneshnei Razvedki* [Sketches from the History of Russian Foreign Intelligence], vol. III (Moscow, 1997), p. 288. On Soviet war plans, 1935–1939, see Menning, "Soviet Railroads." For sketches of the November 1938 Soviet war plans, see David M. Glantz, *Stumbling Colossus: The Red Army on the Eve of World War* (Lawrence, Kans., 1998), pp. 85–86. On the arrest and imprisonment of Soviet citizens of Polish nationality in 1937–1938, see N. V. Petrov and A. B. Roginskii, "Polskaia Operatsiia NKVD 1937–1938 gg." [The NKVD Polish Operation, 1937–1938], in Aleksandr Gurianov, ed., *Repressii Protiv Poliakov i Polskikh Grazhdan. Istoricheskie Sborniki "Memoriala." Vypusk 1* [Repressions of Poles and Polish Citizens: Historical Collections of "Memorial." Issue no. 1] (Moscow, 1997), pp. 22–43; Stanisław Ciesielski, Wojciech Materski, and Andrzej Paczkowski, *Represje Sowieckie wobec Polaków i Obywateli Polskich* [Soviet Repression of Poles and Polish Citizens] (Warsaw, 2000), p. 5. On the deportations of ethnically Polish villagers from Soviet Ukraine and mass arrests of Soviet urban Poles during the Stalin Terror, see Kate Brown, *A Biography of No Place: From Ethnic Borderland to Soviet Heartland* (Cambridge, Mass., 2003).

20. For Piłsudski's statement to the French ambassador on Poles not going into Ukraine, see Jules Laroche, *Une Ambassade à Varsovie, 1926–1935* [An Embassy in Warsaw, 1926–1935] (Paris, 1953), p. 194. On French-Polish relations in the period 1926–1936, see Piotr S. Wandycz, *The Twilight of French Eastern Alliances, 1926–1936: French-Czechoslovak-Polish Relations from Locarno to the Remilitarization of the Rhineland* (Princeton, N.J., 1988).

21. For studies of interwar Polish foreign policy by postcommunist Polish historians, see Piotr Łossowski, ed., *Historia Dyplomacji Polskiej* [The History of Polish Diplomacy], vol. IV: *1918–1939* (Warsaw, 1995). For a critical survey of standard Soviet and Western interpretations, see Anna M. Cienciala, "Polish Foreign Policy, 1926–1939: 'Equilibrium': Stereotype and Reality," *Polish Review,* 20, no. 1 (New York, 1975), pp. 42–57.

22. See Wandycz, *Twilight,* chap. 11.

23. The Biddle report of 19 June 1938 is in *Poland and the Coming of the*

Second World War: The Diplomatic Papers of A. J. Drexel Biddle, Jr., the United States Ambassador to Poland 1937–1939, ed. Philip V. Cannistraro, Edward D. Wynot, Jr., and Theodore P. Kovaleff (Columbus, Ohio, 1977), pp. 208–227, esp. pp. 208–209. See also Cienciala, "Polish Foreign Policy, 1926–1939."

24. On the Soviet leadership not intending to fight for Czechoslovakia, see Igor Lukes, "Stalin and Czechoslovakia in 1938–39: An Autopsy of a Myth," in Igor Lukes and Erik Goldstein, *The Munich Crisis, 1938: Prelude to World War II* (London, 1999), pp. 14–37; and Bruce Menning, "The Munich Crisis in Light of Soviet Planning and Military Readiness," paper read at the Southern Conference of Slavic Studies (Wilmington, N.C., Spring 2000). For another view, see Hugh Ragsdale, "Soviet Military Preparations and Policy in the Munich Crisis: New Evidence," *Jahrbücher für Geschichte Osteuropas,* 47 (1999), pp. 211–226; and Ragsdale, *The Soviets, the Munich Crisis, and the Coming of World War II* (Cambridge, England, 2004). According to Russian sources, the Red Army General Staff had no plan for giving military aid to Czechoslovakia in 1938; see S. Z. Slutch, "Polsha w Politike Sovetskogo Soiuza, 1938–1939," [Poland in Soviet Policy, 1938–1939], in Eugeniusz Duraczyński and A. N. Sakharov, eds., *Sovetsko-Polskie Otnosheniia v Politicheskikh Usloviakh Evropy 30-kh Godov XX Stoletia* [Soviet-Polish Relations in the European Political Conditions of the 1930s] (Moscow, 2001), pp. 161 and 184 n. 27.

25. See Anna M. Cienciala, "The Polish Government's Policy on the Polish-Soviet Frontier in World War II as Viewed by American, British, and Canadian Historians," *Polish Review,* 46, no. 1 (2001), pp. 3–36 (corrections: vol. 46, no. 2, p. 254).

26. See Piotr S. Wandycz, *France and Her Eastern Allies, 1919–1925: French-Czechoslovak-Polish Relations from the Paris Peace Conference to Locarno* (Minneapolis, 1962), chap. 8. For Polish texts of the political alliance and military convention, see Jędruszczak and Nowak-Kiełbikowa, *Dokumenty z Dziejów,* vol. I, nos. 29, 30; for the French text of the military convention, see Kazimiera Mazurowa, "Przymierze Polsko-Francuskie z Roku 1921" [The Polish-French Alliance of 1921], in *Najnowsze Dzieje Polski: Materiały i Studia z Dziejów 1914–1939* [Recent History of Poland: Materials and Studies on the History of 1914–1939], vol. 11 (Warsaw, 1967), pp. 212–214.

27. For two very different interpretations of who was to blame for the German-Soviet Non-Aggression Pact, see Michael Jabara Carley, *1939: The Alliance That Never Was and the Coming of World War II* (Chicago, 1999); and Anna M. Cienciala, "The Nazi-Soviet Pact of August 23, 1939: When Did Stalin Decide to Align with Hitler, and Was Poland the Culprit?" in M. B. B. Biskupski, ed., *Ideology, Politics and Diplomacy in East Central Europe* (Rochester, N. Y., 2003), pp. 147–226. On Polish reactions to the Soviet-German pact and on Poland in Soviet strategic plans in 1939, see Marek Kornat, *Polska 1939 Roku wobec Paktu Ribbentrop-Mołotow* [Poland in 1939: Facing the Ribbentrop-Molotov Pact] (Warsaw, 2002), chap. 6.

28. See the account of the German-Soviet negotiations by the first secretary at the German Embassy in Moscow, Hans von Herwarth, with S. Frederick Starr, *Against Two Evils* (New York, 1981), p. 165. Herwarth, an anti-Nazi, German

diplomat, leaked information on Nazi proposals and the contents of the German-Soviet Pact to his tennis partner, Charles Bohlen of the U.S. Embassy in Moscow.

29. Donald C. Watt, "Francis Herbert King: A Soviet Source in the Foreign Office," *Intelligence and National Security,* 3, no. 4 (1988), pp. 62–82; Watt, "An Intelligence Surprise," *Intelligence and National Security,* 4, no. 3 (1989); list of warnings, pp. 533–553. See also Nigel West and Oleg Tsarev, *The Crown Jewels: The British Secrets at the Heart of the KGB Archives* (New Haven, 1999), pp. 281–286.

30. For the Supreme Soviet's condemnation of the Secret Protocol of 23 August 1939, see *Pravda,* 28 December 1989; and a brief excerpt in *The Current Digest of the Soviet Press,* 42, no. 109 (1990), 11.1. At the Munich Conference of 28–29 September 1938, British and French leaders signed an agreement with the German and Italian leaders to hand over the Czech Sudetenland to Germany. Soviet historians described the Munich agreement as an anti-Soviet alliance, which is what President Putin probably had in mind by calling it the "Munich Conspiracy" when he also mentioned the German-Soviet Non-Aggression Pact of 23 August 1939; see the text of the Putin interview with Radio Slovensko and Slovak Television Channel STV, 22 February 2005, at the Russian presidential website: http://www. kremlin.ru/eng/speeches/2005/02/22/2038_type82916_84445.shtml. The interview took place in Bratislava just before Putin's meeting with President George W. Bush.

31. On the last Ribbentrop-Lipski meeting of 31 August 1939, see Wacław Jędrzejewicz, ed., *Diplomat in Berlin, 1933–1939: Papers and Memoirs of Józef Lipski, Ambassador of Poland* (New York, 1968), p. 610. On Western policy toward Poland in 1939, see Anna M. Cienciala, "Poland in British and French Policy in 1939: Determination to Fight or Avoid War?," *Polish Review,* 34, no. 3 (1989), pp. 199–226, reprinted with some abbreviations in Patrick Finney, ed., *The Origins of the Second World War* (London, 1997), pp. 413–433.

32. On the British and French General Staffs' agreement regarding Poland, see Cienciala, "Poland in British and French Policy in 1939."

33. For the delivery of Śmigły-Rydz's orders in besieged Warsaw, see Alfred Michael Peszke, *The Polish Underground Army, the Western Allies, and the Failure of Strategic Unity in World War II* (Jefferson, N.C., 2005), p. 21. On the German-Polish War, see Robert M. Kenney, *The German Campaign in Poland, 1939* (Washington, D.C., 1956); for a broader study incorporating Polish materials, see Steven Zaloga and Victor Madej, *The Polish Campaign, 1939* (New York, 1985); see also Steven Zaloga, *Poland, 1939: The Birth of Blitzkrieg* (Oxford, 2002).

34. On Richard Sorge's message, see Jonathan Haslam, *The Soviet Union and the Threat from the East* (Pittsburgh, 1992), p. 131; on Soviet-Japanese negotiations, see ibid., pp. 135–137. On the fighting, see Alvin J. Coox, *Nomonhan: Japan against Russia, 1939,* vol. 2 (Stanford, Calif., 1985).

35. See Natalia S. Lebedeva and Wojciech Materski et al., eds., *Katyn: Plenniki Neobiavlennoi Voiny* [Katyn: Prisoners of an Undeclared War] (henceforth *KD1*), in the series *Rossiia, XX Vek: Dokumenty* [Russia, the Twentieth Century: Documents] (Moscow, 1997), vol. 1, docs. 3–4; Lebedeva and Materski et al., eds., *Katyń: Dokumenty Zbrodni* [Katyn: Documents of a Crime] vol. 1: *Jeńcy Nie*

Wypowiedzianej Wojny [The Prisoners of an Undeclared War] (henceforth *KDZ1*) (Warsaw, 1995), doc. 3, and Supplement, nos. 1, 2, pp. 543–547. (For more on these sources and their mode of citation, see Note on the Documents.)

36. Schulenburg to Ribbentrop on the agreed text of the Soviet note of 17 September 1939, *DGFP*, ser. D, vol. VIII (London, Washington, D.C., 1957), no. 80.

37. For the reactions of Western communist parties, see Kevin McDermott and Jeremy Agnew, *The Comintern: A History of International Communism from Lenin to Stalin* (New York, 1997), pp. 192–197. For the reaction of a young German communist in the USSR, see Wolfgang Leonhard, *Betrayal: The Hitler-Stalin Pact of 1939* (New York, 1982), chap. 2. For NKVD reports of critical remarks by Soviet citizens on German-Soviet collusion in the destruction of Poland, see Sarah Davies, *Popular Opinion in Stalin's Russia: Terror, Propaganda, and Dissent, 1934–1941* (Cambridge, England, 1997), pp. 98–99.

38. For Wacław Grzybowski's account of his meeting with Vladimir Potemkin, see the ambassador's final report of 6 November 1939 on his tenure in Moscow, 1936–1939, in *DPSR*, vol. I, no. 69 (English translation). For the Soviet note to ambassadors and envoys in Moscow, see *Dokumenty Vneshnei Politiki* [Documents on Foreign Policy] (henceforth *DVP*), vol. XXII, book 2 (Moscow, 1992), no. 598. For extracts from Molotov's radio broadcast of 17 September 1939, see *DPSR*, vol. I, no. 46; and Jane Degras, ed., *Soviet Documents on Foreign Policy, 1917–1941* (henceforth *SDFP*), vol. III: *1933–1941* (London, 1953), pp. 375–376. For the German-Soviet communiqué of 18 September 1939, see *DVP*, vol. XXII, book 2, no. 600.

39. For the Polish government protest against the Soviet invasion, see *DPSR*, vol. I, no. 45.

40. See Anna M. Cienciala, "Jak Doszło do Internowania Rządu R. P. w Rumunii we Wrześniu 1939" [How the Polish Government Came to Be Interned in Romania in September 1939], *Niepodległość* [Independence], 22 (New York, 1989), pp. 18–65.

41. See *KD1/14*; *KDZ1/14*.

42. Vsevolod Vishnevsky's diary, 11 November 1939, cited in Krzysztof Jasiewicz, *Zagłada Polskich Kresów: Ziemiaństwo Polskie na Kresach Północno-Wschodnich Rzeczypospolitej pod Okupacją Sowiecką 1939–1941* [Extermination in the Polish Borderlands: The Polish Landed Gentry in Northeastern Poland under Soviet Rule in 1939–41] (Warsaw, 1998), p. 155.

43. On the fighting in eastern Poland, see Ryszard Szawłowski, "The Polish-Soviet War of 1939," in Keith Sword, ed., *The Soviet Takeover of the Polish Eastern Provinces, 1939–1941* (New York, 1991), pp. 20–43. For a brief account, see Zaloga, *Poland, 1939*, pp. 78–84. For a documented Polish study, see Czesław Grzelak, *Dziennik Sowieckiej Agresji, Wrzesień 1939* [The Diary of Soviet Aggression, September 1939] (Warsaw, 1994). For a recent Russian study, see Meltiukhov, *Sovetsko-Polskiie Voiny* (2001), pp. 303–350; (2004), pp. 463–492.

44. On the murdered KOP officers, see *BBC Monitoring Service* (United Kingdom), 8 November 2002. For estimates of the number of Polish citizens killed in eastern Poland in 1939–1941, see Sławomir Kalbarczyk, "Zbrodnie Sowieckie na Obywatelach Polskich w Okresie Wrzesień 1939–Sierpień 1941" [Soviet Crimes

against Polish Citizens in the Period September 1939–August 1941], in *Pamięć i Sprawiedliwość* [Memory and Justice], no. 33 (Warsaw, 1996), p. 33.

45. For adjusted numbers of Poles, Ukrainians, and other nationalities in all of Poland in 1931, see Jerzy Tomaszewski, *Rzeczpospolita Wielu Narodów* [The Multinational Republic] (Warsaw, 1985), p. 35; these numbers are reproduced in Tadeusz Piotrowski, *Poland's Holocaust* (Jefferson, N.C., 1998), p. 294. For estimated numbers and percentages of Poles, Ukrainians, Jews, and Belorussians in Soviet eastern Poland in 1939–1941, see Piotrowski, *Poland's Holocaust*, table 1, p. 14. For slightly different figures and percentages, see *Concise Statistical Yearbook of Poland, September 1939–June 1941* (Polish Ministry of Information, London, December 1941), table 16, p. 9.

46. For the number of publications in interwar Poland not in the Polish language, see Jan T. Gross, *Revolution from Abroad: The Soviet Conquest of Poland's Western Ukraine and Western Belorussia* (Princeton, N.J., 1988), pp. 7–8.

47. On Ukrainians in interwar Poland, see Paul Robert Magocsi, *A History of Ukraine* (Toronto, 1996; reprint: Seattle, 1998), chap. 44; for a Polish perspective, see Stanisław Skrzypek, *The Problem of Eastern Galicia* (London, 1948), part 2. On Stalin's forced collectivization, see Robert Conquest, *The Harvest of Sorrow* (2nd edition, London, 1992); and Sheila Fitzpatrick, *Stalin's Peasants: Resistance and Survival in the Russian Village after Collectivization* (Oxford, 1994). On Soviet Jews, see Solo W. Baron, *The Russian Jew under the Tsars and Soviets* (2nd edition, New York, 1987).

48. On the Jewish population of eastern Poland at this time, see Norman Davies and Antony Polonsky, eds., *Jews in Eastern Poland and the USSR, 1939–1946* (New York, 1991); and Ben-Cion Pinchuk, *Shtetl Jews under Soviet Rule: Eastern Poland on the Eve of the Holocaust* (Oxford, 1991).

49. The NKVD figures for Białystok Province in 1940 show that the majority of agents and informants were Poles. Some government, militia, and party positions, however, were held by Jews; see Krzysztof Jasiewicz, "Research Still Needed on the Neighbors," in William Brand, ed., *Thou Shalt Not Kill: Poles on Jedwabne* (Warsaw, 2001), pp. 128–138. On Polish resentment of Jewish cooperation with Soviet authorities, and the participation of some Poles in the German-supervised massacre of Jews in Jewabne and other towns in this region in July 1941, see Anna M. Cienciala, "The Jedwabne Massacre: Update and Review," *Polish Review*, 48, no. 1 (2003), pp. 49–72 (corrections are in "Corrigenda," 48, no. 4).

50. The NKVD reports are cited in Grzegorz Motyka, "Białorusini i Ukraińcy wobec Władzy Komunistycznej na Kresach Wschodnich R. P. w Latach 1939–1941" [Belorussian and Ukrainian Attitudes toward Communist Rule in the Eastern Borderlands of the Polish Republic in 1939–1941], in Tomasz Strzembosz, ed., *Studia z Dziejów Okupacji Sowieckiej, 1939–1941* [Studies in the History of the Soviet Occupation, 1939–1941] (Warsaw, 1997), pp. 49–60.

51. Gross, *Revolution from Abroad*, chaps. 4–6; Sword, *Soviet Takeover of the Polish Eastern Provinces*, chaps. 9–14. For studies based on NKVD figures, see Gurianov, *Repressii Protiv Poliakov*, pp. 1–96. See also Ciesielski, Materski, and Paczkowski, *Represje Sowieckie*, pp. 11–13 and p. 26 (table, section II), which uses some of the same NKVD statistics. The NKVD statistics are also used by Na-

talia Lebedeva in "The Deportation of the Polish Population to the USSR, 1939–41," *Journal of Communist Studies and Transition Politics,* 16, nos. 1–2 (2000), pp. 29–45.

52. On the destruction of the Polish landed gentry in northeastern Poland in 1939–1941, see Jasiewicz, *Zagłada Polskich Kresów.* On deportees, see Lebedeva, "Deportation of the Polish Population"; Aleksandr Gurianov, "Mashtaby Deportatsii v Glub SSSR v Mae–Iunie 1941" [The Dimensions of the Deportations into the Soviet Interior in May–June 1941], in Gurianov, *Repressii Protiv Poliakov,* pp. 137–175.

53. For examples of Soviet literary attacks on Poland and the Poles in the fall of 1939, see Ewa M. Thompson, *Imperial Knowledge: Russian Literature and Colonialism* (Westport, Conn., 2000), after p. 168.

54. For the Russian text of the directive of 16 September 1939, extract 226, see Michał Gnatowski, *W Radzieckich Okowach* [In Soviet Irons] (Łomża, 1997), pp. 195–197.

55. See General Władysław Anders, *Bez Ostatniego Rozdziału: Wspomnienia z Lat 1939–1946* [Minus the Last Chapter: Memoirs of the Years 1939–1946] (3rd edition, London, 1959), pp. 25, 29 ff.; the English version is Anders, *An Army in Exile: The Story of the Second Corps* (Nashville, Tenn., 1981), pp. 17–41.

56. On Wanda Wasilewska's activity in western Ukraine in 1939–1941, see Eleonora Syzdek, *Działalność Wandy Wasilewskiej w Latach Drugiej Wojny Światowej* [The Activity of Wanda Wasilewska in the Years of the Second World War] (Warsaw, 1981), chap. 2. For Soviet policies on Polish literature at that time, see studies by Bogdan Czaykowski and Mieczysław Inglot in Sword, *Soviet Takeover,* chaps. 7–8.

57. Ambassador Schulenburg's report to the German Foreign Ministry, 25 September 1939, *DGFP,* ser. D, vol. VIII, no. 131.

58. On the Soviet-style elections of 22 October 1939, see Gross, *Revolution from Abroad,* chap. 2. On Nikita Khrushchev's activity in western Ukraine in 1939–1941, and the propaganda film titled *Liberation* made by his protégé Oleksandr Dovzhenko, see William Taubman, *Khrushchev: The Man and His Era* (New York, 2003), pp. 135–137. After the inclusion of Western Belorussia and Western Ukraine in the Soviet republics, the official terminology for these former Polish territories was "western oblasts" [administrative regions] of the Belorussian and Ukrainian Republics; the previous terminology—"Western Ukraine" and "Western Belorussia"—appeared mainly in newspapers, but with a geographical rather than a political-administrative connotation. (Information from Professor Wojciech Materski.)

59. The Polish word *Pan,* like the Russian word *Gospodin,* originally meant a lord as distinguished from a peasant, but by the late nineteenth century both were the equivalent of "Mr." On Bolshevik propaganda during the Polish-Soviet War of 1919–1920, see Tadeusz Teslar, *Propaganda Bolszewicka podczas Wojny Polsko-Rosyjskiej 1920 Roku* (Warsaw, 1990).

60. See M. B. B. Biskupski, "The Military Elite of the Polish Second Republic, 1918–1945: A Historiographical Review," *War and Society,* 4, no. 2 (University of New South Wales, October 1996), p. 59 and n. 4.

61. Account of a Polish reserve officer, Dr. Mieczysław Srokowski, cited in Tadeusz Pieńkowski, *Droga Polskich Żołnierzy do Katynia, Miednoje, Piaticha-tek i . . . ?* [The Polish Soldiers' Road to Katyn, Mednoe, Piatikhatki, and . . . ?] (Warsaw, 2001), p. 51.

62. For such a leaflet in Polish, with Timoshenko's name printed at the bottom, see *The Crime of Katyn: Facts and Documents* (London, 1965; translation of the 3rd Polish edition), facing p. 17; the English translation is on p. 12. The Polish edition is *Zbrodnia Katyńska w Świetle Dokumentów* [The Katyn Crime in the Light of Documents] (1st edition, London, 1948; 13th edition, 1989). The first edition was written—without attribution—by Józef Mackiewicz; see Biographical Sketches. The Polish text of the leaflet is also in Dariusz Baliszewski and Andrzej Krzysztof Kunert, eds., *Prawdziwa Historia Polaków. Ilustrowane Wypisy Źródłowe, 1939–1945* [The Real History of the Poles: Illustrated Selections from Primary Sources, 1939–1945], vol. 1: *1939–1942* (Warsaw, 1999), p. 72.

63. See *KDZ1*, p. 18. Lebedeva cites 240,000–250,000, of whom 10,000 were officers; see *KD1*, p. 15. See also John Erickson, "The Soviet March into Poland, September 1939," in Sword, *Soviet Takeover*, p. 22. According to recently published Russian military statistics, in late September 1939 the Soviets held 457,700 Polish POWs, and the Germans held 420,000; see Meltiukhov, *Sovetsko-Polskie Voiny* (2001), table 30, p. 404; (2004), table 33, p. 597. In October 1939, however, Molotov claimed the capture of 230,000 Polish soldiers, and on the first anniversary of the invasion, on 17 September 1940, the Red Army paper *Krasnaia Zvezda* [Red Star], gave the total number of rank-and-file soldiers plus officers who were prisoners as 190,589; see Keith Sword, *Deportation and Exile: Poles in the Soviet Union, 1939–48* (New York, 1994), p. 2. The lower figures probably indicate the prior release of thousands of rank-and-file soldiers. On these provisional camps, their names and dates, see Jan. T. Gross, "Polish POW Camps in the Soviet-Occupied Western Ukraine," in Sword, *Soviet Takeover*, pp. 44–56.

64. The UPV [Administration for Prisoner-of-War Affairs] report on military ranks gives information, dated around 28 February 1940, on the numbers and ranks of Polish POW officers, police, and gendarmes; see *KD1/201; KDZ1/201.*

65. The classic work on the GULAG is Aleksandr Solzhenitsyn, *Gulag Archipelago, 1918–1956: An Experiment in Literary Investigation,* trans. Thomas P. Whitney, 2 vols. (New York, 1974–1978); see also Anne Applebaum's Pulitzer Prize–winning study based on published sources, Russian archives, and personal interviews with survivors, *Gulag: A History* (New York, 2003); see also Oleg V. Khlevniuk, *The History of the Gulag: From Collectivization to the Great Terror,* trans. Vadim A. Staklo, with editorial assistance and commentary by David J. Norlander and with a foreword by Robert Conquest (New Haven, 2004).

66. For a list of the camps, see Appendix, table 1; for locations, see Maps and Aerial Photographs, map 4. The special camps [*osoboe lageria*] were strict-regime camps established to hold political prisoners and individuals classified as socially dangerous elements.

67. For biographical information on selected NKVD personnel, other Russian officials and officers, and selected Poles mentioned in the documents, see Biographical Sketches.

68. For Beria's directive of 15 September 1939, see S. V. Stepashin et al., eds., *Organy Gosudarstvennoi Bezopasnosti SSSR v Velikoi Otechestvennoi Voine: Sbornik Dokumentov* [State Security Organs of the USSR in the Great Fatherland War: Documentary Collection], 3 vols. in 6 books (Moscow, 1995–2003), vol. 1, book 1, no. 33, point 6, p. 80.

69. German-Soviet negotiations led to the transfer of 42,492 Polish rank-and-file soldiers to the Germans between 24 October and 23 November 1939 (doc. 96). Several hundred Czech military who refused to accept the German annexation of the Czech lands in mid-March 1939 crossed into Poland. Many left for France, but the rest formed a Czechoslovak Legion led by General Lev Prchala. They fought as a unit of the Polish Army in September 1939 and were taken prisoner by the Red Army. On Polish officers' statements to *politruks* [political instructors], see the memoirs of Stanisław Swianiewicz, *W Cieniu Katynia* [In the Shadow of Katyn] (Paris, 1976), p. 93; the English version, translated and edited by his son, Witold Swianiewicz, is *In the Shadow of Katyn: "Stalin's Terror"* (self-published; distributor, Bunker to Bunker Books, Calgary, Alberta, Canada, 2003), p. 61.

70. See *KD1/79*, 103; *KDZ1/79*, 103.

71. On the Poles interned in Lithuania, see Andrzej Bogusławski, *W Znak Pogoni: Internowanie Polaków na Litwie, IX 1939–VII 1940* [Under the Sign of the Chase: The Internment of Poles in Lithuania, September 1939–July 1940] (Toruń, 2004). "Chase" refers to the coat of arms of the Grand Duchy of Lithuania.

72. Simon Schochet, "Polish-Jewish Officers Who Were Killed in Katyn: An Ongoing Investigation in Light of Documents Recently Released by the USSR," in Lucjan Dobroszycki and Jeffrey S. Gurock, eds., *The Holocaust in the Soviet Union: Studies and Sources on the Destruction of the Jews in the Nazi-Occupied Territories of the USSR, 1941–1945* (Armonk, N.Y., 1993), pp. 237–247; see also Simon Schochet, "Reflections on Soviet Documents Relating to Polish Prisoners of War Taken in September 1939," in Antony Polonsky, ed., *Polin: Studies in Polish Jewry,* vol. 13: *Focusing on the Holocaust and Its Aftermath* (Oxford, 2000), pp. 73–77. Most of the Jewish officers in the Polish Army were physicians; for the memoirs of a Kozelsk survivor, see Solomon W. Slowes, *The Road to Katyn: A Soldier's Story,* ed. Władysław Bartoszewski, trans. Naftali Greenwood (Oxford, 1992).

73. For accounts of travel to the camp and camp life, see *Crime of Katyn,* chaps. 1, 2. Pieńkowski, *Droga,* chaps. 3, 4; and Jan A. Stepek, ed., *Pamiętniki Znalezione w Katyniu* [Diaries Found at Katyn] (2nd edition, Paris, Warsaw, 1990).

74. See photographs of Kozelsk camp in Jędrzej Tucholski, *Mord w Katyniu* [Murder in Katyn] (Warsaw, 1991), plates 86–95; see NKVD sketch maps of the camp in *KD1*, p. 127; *KDZ1*, p. 143. For a detailed map of the Kozelsk region, see American Map Service Series N701, sheet 5426 II "Kozelsk," 1963, in the bilingual Polish-English work by Wacław Godziemba-Maliszewski, "Interpretacja Zdjęć Lotniczych Katynia w Świetle Dokumentów i Zeznań Świadków / Katyn:

An Interpretation of Aerial Photographs Considered with Facts and Documents," *Fotointerpretacja w Geografii: Problemy Telegeoinformacji* [Photo Interpretation in Geography: Problems in Teleogeographic Information], no. 25 (Warsaw, 1995), p. 23. For a rare photograph of the Kozelsk monastery, see Slowes, *Road to Katyn,* facing p. 126. For a prisoner's drawing of crowded bunks inside a Kozelsk barrack, see *Crime of Katyn,* facing p. 32. For the Kozelsk Optina Pustyn today, see *The Kozelsky Region Study Museum with a Literary Section "Optina Pustyn,"* http://kaluga.amr-museum.ru/filial/filial_8/e_index.html. A. M. Cienciala would like to thank Professor Eve Levin for information on the importance of this monastery complex in nineteenth-century Russia.

75. For POW numbers, see Appendix, table 2A. The four generals in Kozelsk camp were Bronisław Bohatyrewicz [alternate spelling: Bohaterewicz], Henryk Minkiewicz-Odrowąż, Mieczysław Smorawiński, and Jerzy Wołkowicki. Rear Admiral Ksawery Czernicki, also in the camp, held the army rank of general. Only Wołkowicki survived.

76. For the civilian professions of reserve officers in Kozelsk, see *Crime of Katyn,* p. 18. For a photograph of Janina Lewandowska, listed as a 2nd Lieutenant Reserve, see Tucholski, *Mord,* plate 116; the same photograph is in Janina Snitko-Rzeszut, ed., *Katyń: Księga Cmentarna Polskiego Cmentarza Wojennego* [Katyn: The Cemetery Book of the Polish War Cemetery] (Warsaw, 2000), p. 343.

77. A photograph and sketch plan of Ostashkov camp are in Tucholski, *Mord,* plates 189–190. A camp map is in *KD1,* p. 126; *KDZ1,* p. 141.

78. The military settlers were veterans of the Polish-Soviet War of 1919–1920 who received small parcels of land in eastern Poland in the years 1919–1923 to strengthen the Polish element there; see doc. 11, point 1. For the number of prisoners held in Ostashkov camp in 1939–1940, see Appendix, table 2B.

79. A. M. Cienciala would like to thank Professor Eve Levin for information on the Starobelsk monastery. See photographs of Starobelsk camp in Tucholski, *Mord,* plates 290–293.

80. For the civilian professions of Starobelsk reserve officers, see *Crime of Katyn,* pp. 21–22; for the number of prisoners held in Starobelsk in April 1940, see Appendix, table 2C.

81. Report on Starobelsk by Senior NKVD UPV Inspector Captain I. S. Bunakov, 3 October 1939, in *KD1/43; KDZ1/43;* his second report, dated no earlier than 13 October 1939, in *KDZ1/56;* and the report by UPV head Soprunenko and UPV Commissar Semyon Nekhoroshev on the situation in the POW camps, written no earlier than 15 November 1939, in *KD1/109; KDZ1/109.* See also Swianiewicz, *W Cieniu Katynia,* chap. 3; Swianiewicz, *In the Shadow of Katyn,* chap. 3; Stepek, *Pamiętniki.*

82. Józef Czapski, *Wspomnienia Starobielskie* [Starobelsk Memories] (first published by the Department of Culture and Press, Polish 2nd Corps, Middle East, 1944; reprint, Rome, 1945), excerpted in *Crime of Katyn,* pp. 34–38. See also Bronisław Młynarski, *W Niewoli Sowieckiej* [In Soviet Captivity] (London, 1974).

83. Józef Rychalski, "Ostashkov," in *Crime of Katyn,* pp. 39–44; Józef Chle-

bowicz, "Wspomnienia z Ostaszkowa" [Ostashkov Memories], *Zeszyty Historyczne* [Historical Notebooks], no. 84 (Paris, 1988), pp. 121–140.

84. *Crime of Katyn,* pp. 37–38. Kowalski might have fought in the 1863–1864 uprising against Russia and then been deported to Stolbny, where he worked to earn his keep.

85. Młynarski, *W Niewoli Sowieckiej,* cited in Pieńkowski, *Droga,* pp. 77–78; for 150 rubles per month, see Beria directive of 3 October 1939 on the treatment of POWs in Starobelsk camp, point 6, *KD1/40; KDZ1/40.*

86. "Regulations for the Treatment of Prisoners of War," 19 September 1939 (Project), probably drawn up by Beria and accepted by the Economic Committee of the Council of People's Commissars, USSR; see *KD1/15; KDZ1/15,* points 14a and 16.

87. Młynarski, *W Niewoli Sowieckiej,* p. 201 (trans. A. M. Cienciala).

88. Swianiewicz, *W Cieniu Katynia,* p. 99; Swianiewicz, *In the Shadow of Katyn,* p. 66.

89. For the names of clergymen killed, e.g., Jan Potocki, with dates of death or when last seen, and the two survivors out of forty-five, see Pieńkowski, *Droga,* appendix 3, tables I, II, pp. 183–190; for the five others, see ibid., table III, p. 191.

90. Czapski, *Wspomnienia Starobielskie,* pp. 30–31.

91. Ibid.; *Crime of Katyn,* p. 38; Pieńkowski, *Droga,* p. 88.

92. Domoń and Ewert are listed in Biographical Sketches. On the arrest and death of Kwolek, see *KD1/127,* n. 4; *KDZ1/127,* n. 4. On 22 May 1989 the Investigation Department of the Kharkov Regional KGB Administration declared that each of the three convictions lacked evidence that the officers had been guilty of "anti-Soviet activity"; see Pieńkowski, *Droga,* pp. 88–89.

93. Swianiewicz, *W Cieniu Katynia,* p. 101; Swianiewicz, *In the Shadow of Katyn,* p. 67.

94. For the Ostashkov musical group, see *Crime of Katyn,* p. 44; for the prisoners' song, see Pieńkowski, *Droga,* pp. 101–102 (trans. A. M. Cienciala).

95. Czapski, *Wspomnienia Starobielskie,* p. 38.

96. Zygmunt Berling, *Wspomnienia* [Memoirs], vol. I: *Z Łagrów do Andersa* [From the Camps to Anders] (Warsaw, 1990), chap. 5.

97. See Swianiewicz, "Kombrig Zarubin" in *Zbrodnia Katyńska,* pp. 27–28, excerpted in *Crime of Katyn,* p. 23; and Biographical Sketches, s.v. Zarubin.

98. Swianiewicz correctly described Zarubin's task as collecting intelligence on the prisoners; see Swianiewicz, *W Cieniu Katynia,* p. 97; Swianiewicz, *In the Shadow of Katyn,* p. 64.

99. Soprunenko to Berezhkov, 26 February 1940, in *KD1/196; KDZ1/196.*

100. Makliarsky to Korolev, 27 February 1940, in *KD1/198; KDZ1/198.* For the supplementary questionnaire, see *KD1/157; KDZ1/157.*

101. For the Russian text of the German-Soviet Friendship Treaty of 24 April 1926, also known as the Treaty of Berlin, see *Dokumenty Vneshnei Politiki SSSR* [Documents on the Foreign Policy of the USSR], vol. IX (Moscow, 1964), no. 141; for the German text and exchange of notes, see *Akten zur Deutschen Auswärtigen Politik, 1918–1945* [Documents on German Foreign Policy, 1918–1945], ser. B, vol. II, part 1 (Göttingen, 1967), no. 168.

102. In the original Soviet project of the pact, dated 19 August 1939, the proposed duration was five years; see *DVP*, vol. XXII, book 1, no. 474, article 4, p. 618.

103. The postscript to the Soviet project stated that the pact was valid only with the simultaneous signature of a special protocol specifying the interests of the two parties in the realm of foreign policy, and that the protocol was an organic part of the pact; see *DVP*, vol. XXII, book 1, no. 474, p. 619.

104. See doc. 1.

105. The secret protocol had more than a dozen maps of Poland and the Baltic States attached to it, showing the spheres of influence of both parties. On 23 September 1939, *Pravda* published a map of the Soviet-German demarcation line on Polish territory; it ran along the Vistula River, even dividing Warsaw, and included the Pisa River in the north, as added by Molotov and German Ambassador Schulenburg on 28 August; see *DVP*, vol. XXII, book 1, no. 507. (See Maps and Aerial Photographs, map 3.)

106. Before the treaty of 28 September 1939, both governments agreed that there would be no rump Polish state; see doc. 12.

107. On Polish policy and the minorities in prewar eastern Poland, see the introduction and notes 45–48.

108. "White terror" refers to anticommunist terror.

109. The new Soviet government's Declaration of the Rights of the Nations of Russia of 2 November (15 November, old Russian dating style) 1917 recognized the right of all nations conquered by tsarist Russia to self-determination and independence. On 29 August 1918 the Council of People's Commissars issued a decree annulling all imperial Russian treaties with Germany and Austria; Article 3 annulled the treaties partitioning Poland (1772, 1793, 1795) as contrary to the undeniable right of the Polish nation to independence; see *SDFP*, vol. I: *1917–1924* (London, 1952), p. 98; *DPSR*, vol. I, no. 1.

110. Reference to the Polish frontier established by the Treaty of Riga of 18 March 1921, after the Polish victory in the Polish-Soviet War in 1920; see *DPSR*, vol. I, no. 3.

111. Poles were depicted as "lords," or aristocrats, just as they were presented in Soviet propaganda during the Polish-Soviet War of 1919–1920. "Second imperialist war" was the Soviet label for World War II until the German attack on the USSR on 22 June 1941.

112. There were numerous attacks on Polish authorities in eastern Poland, including the military and the police, although most occurred in what is now western Belarus. The strongest attack, in Grodno, was put down by Polish forces who defended the town against the Red Army for three days. The town of Skidel was taken by rebels but retaken by Polish forces. Some attacks were led by local communists, others by Soviet military units parachuted into the region.

113. See docs. 1 and 2.

114. This was the ideological justification for the Soviet attack; see also docs. 4 and 5. Soviet historians referred to the Soviet entry into eastern Poland as the "war of liberation."

115. By this time, the Germans had taken most of western Poland, but Warsaw

was still resisting a German siege, and Polish armies were fighting the Germans in central and southeastern Poland; see Zaloga and Madej, *Polish Campaign,* pp. 131–138.

116. The Polish government was then stationed at Kuty, the high command in Kolomija [Kołomyja]; both cities were on the Polish side of the Polish-Romanian frontier; see doc. 6.

117. These are references to the Treaty of Riga of March 1921, which established the Polish-Soviet frontier after the war of 1919–1920; the Polish-Soviet Non-Aggression Pact of July 1932, extended in May 1934 until 31 December 1945; and the Polish-Soviet Trade Agreement of February 1939; see *DPSR,* vol. I, nos. 3, 6, 10, 16. The USSR and Poland had also signed an International Convention for the Definition of Aggression in London on 3 July 1933, which defined any attack or support of attack on another state as aggression; see *DPSR,* vol. I, no. 7.

118. For this justification, see doc. 3.

119. See doc. 4 above. In this account of his conversation with the Polish ambassador, Potemkin used the present tense to emphasize some of the statements made by Grzybowski.

120. At this time, the Polish Army still retained about 50 percent of its initial strength, and a major battle was proceeding on the Bzura River, in central Poland. The Polish government and General Staff were stationed on a segment of the Polish frontier with Romania.

121. In fact, Ambassador Nikolai Sharonov left most of the embassy staff in Warsaw while he accompanied the Polish government in its retreat eastward, departing for Moscow on 11 September. According to the report of Kostin Bolshakov, commissar in the Soviet Embassy in Warsaw, dated 19 October 1939, Sharonov had told the embassy staff to stay put; he said the Germans would take Warsaw in two to three days, and they would be safe; see Arkhiv Vneshnei Politiki Rossiiskoi Federatsii [Foreign Policy Archive of the Russian Federation], Moscow (henceforth AVPRF), f. 06, d. 145, p. 14.

122. Contact was established through the Polish Embassy in Bucharest, courtesy of the Soviet government.

123. At this time the Red Army was drawing near to Kremenets; Grzybowski did not know his government's location.

124. England and France entered the war with Germany on 3 September but did not give any effective aid to Poland by attacking the Germans in the west, as the French had committed to do in May 1939, or by bombing western Germany, as the British had undertaken to do.

125. This was the intent of the Polish commander in chief's order of 17 September; see doc. 6.

126. For Grzybowski's report on this conversation, see the English translation of his "Final Report to the Minister of Foreign Affairs [August Zaleski]," Paris, 6 November 1939, in *Polish White Book* (London, New York, n.d.), no. 184, pp. 211–212, reprinted in *DPSR,* vol. I, no. 68, pp. 87–88.

127. For Śmigły-Rydz (alternative spelling: Rydz-Śmigły), see Biographical Sketches.

128. The order—reconstructed from a copy, with missing words added in

brackets—was issued on 17 September, probably around 2200 hours, or just before Śmigły-Rydz crossed the frontier into Romania with the Polish General Staff and government; see *KD1/6*, n. 1; *KDZ1/6*, n. 1. Owing to breakdowns or lack of radio communications, the order did not reach all Polish Army units.

129. Modlin (Russian, Georgevsk), a fortress town at the confluence of the Wisła and Narew Rivers, defended itself for sixteen days, 13–29 September. Warsaw withstood ground and air attacks from 7 to 27 September; see Zaloga and Madej, *Polish Campaign,* pp. 138–141. It is not widely known that Major Edmund Galinat arrived by plane in besieged Warsaw on 26 September with two orders for the city's military command from Marshal Śmigły-Rydz: one, for the city to surrender in order to avoid further loss of life and property, and the other, for an underground military organization to be established; see Peszke, *Polish Underground Army,* p. 21.

130. Soviet military and NKVD commanders had orders to prevent Polish troops from crossing the border into Romania; see *KD1/14*; *KDZ1/14*. However, about 35,000 reached France and joined the new Polish army there; see Steven J. Zaloga and Richard Hook, *The Polish Army, 1939–45,* Men-at-Arms Series, no. 117 (London, 1982; New York, 1996), p. 14.

131. Beria had asked for Molotov's consent to this resolution the day before; see *KD1/8*; *KDZ1/8*.

132. The Regulations for the Treatment of Prisoners of War were approved by the Economic Council of the People's Commissars' Council on 19 September; see *KD1/15*; *KDZ1/15*. They dealt with various categories of prisoners taken during military action in September 1939, including civilians accompanying the army, as well as other nationals taken prisoner and held in the USSR. Some of the regulations on prisoner rights, e.g., military pay and correspondence, were not observed in practice. For the UPV statute, see doc. 9.

133. The UPV staff were approved by Beria the same day, according to an appendix to this order. There were fifty-six people on the staff, including the chief and three of his deputies; a secretariat with twelve office workers; a Political Department consisting of eight people, headed by the commissar of the UPV; the 1st Department (Administration), with eight staff members; the 2nd Department (Records and Registration), with ten staff members; the 3rd Department (Supplies), with eight people; and the 4th Department (Medical), with six staff members; see *KD1/11*, n. 3; *KDZ1/11*, n. 3. More departments were added later.

134. The staff schedule for the POW camps was also approved by Beria in an appendix to this order. It provided for 134 payroll positions per camp, with 10,000 POWs in each. Aside from the commissar, the camp commandant, his deputy and an assistant, three command orderlies, and twelve clerical workers, the following units were listed: Special Section (Intelligence), with nine staff members; Political (seven); Records and Registration (thirteen); Supplies (nineteen); Financial (five); and Medical (seven). In addition, the following were organized: a Fire Unit (nine) and an Internal Security Unit (forty-six), *KD1/11*, n. 4, p. 398; *KDZ1/ 11*, n. 5, pp. 82–83.

135. Cheka is the abbreviation for Cherezvychainaia Komissia po Borbe s Kontrrevoliutsii i Sabotazhem [Extraordinary Commission for Fighting Counter-

revolution and Sabotage], first name of the Soviet political police, 1917–1922. The word "chekist" was often used later for NKVD personnel. The Osoby Otdel [OO—Special Department] of the NKVD USSR was headed by State Security Major 1st Rank Viktor Bochkov, whose deputies were Nikolai Osetrov, also chief of the Investigative Unit, and Aleksandr Belianov. They supervised the POW camps on a regular basis. Regional NKVD departments served as local organs of the Special Department of the NKVD USSR, which was also the Special Department of the Main Administration of State Security (OO GUGB), headed by Vsevolod Merkulov. The commanders of these special UNKVD departments served simultaneously as heads of Special Departments of military districts, which supervised POW investigations. As a rule, the Special Sections in the camps (also OO—Osoboe Otdelenie) were staffed by those who had served in Special Departments of oblast UNKVDs (NKVD Administrations). They also supervised the everyday activities of the camp Special Section personnel, the *osobisty;* see *KD1/11*, n. 5; *KDZ1/11*, n. 6.

136. See doc. 16.

137. In reality, camp commanders were paid 3,500 rubles per month. By comparison, the secretary general of the Comintern, Georgy Dimitrov, and secretaries of the Executive Committee of the Comintern each received 2,300 rubles per month; see *KD1/11*, n. 7; *KDZ1/11*, n. 8.

138. Many regular staff members in the camps received 700 to 1,000 rubles per month; *KD1/11*, n. 7; *KDZ1/11*, n. 8.

139. The Department of Correctional Labor Colonies' camps were for minors, but some were used to hold POWs.

140. The UPV was mentioned in many documents under different names. The confusion continued until mid-September 1939, when the official name was finally fixed as the NKVD Administration for Prisoner-of-War Affairs (NKVD UPV). In July 1940, when Polish military internees were transferred from Lithuania to POW camps in the USSR, its name was changed to the Administration for Prisoner-of-War and Internee Affairs (UPVI). During the war, it was renamed the Main Administration for Prisoner-of-War and Internee Affairs (GUPVI), but UPV remained in general use. The administration was liquidated in 1953, after POW repatriation had been officially completed; see *KD1/11*, n. 2; *KDZ1/11*, n. 2. A new Polish-Soviet repatriation agreement was signed in late 1956, but most of these repatriates had been arrested in 1944–1945.

141. These allowances were not paid except to the survivors, who received money in August 1941.

142. See *KD1/15*; *KDZ1/15*. Also see note 132 above. Some rank-and-file prisoners were assigned to forced labor in Soviet industries; see doc. 14, point 2.

143. The personal questionnaire (*oprosny list*) was filled out by the camp's URO (Reception, Records, and Barracks Assignment Section) personnel upon the POW's arrival at the camp. It indicated the prisoner's family name, first name, and patronymic; date and place of birth; last address before entering military service; social origin (class); nationality; citizenship; profession or specialization; political party affiliation; general education; latest rank or post held; matriculation number (military registration number); unit name and branch of service when taken pris-

oner; marital status; information on wounds or injuries; occupation or jobs held before military service. On the first page were noted the name of the camp, the case number (corresponding to the number entered in the registration book), and the date of arrival at the camp; the prisoner's photograph was attached. At the bottom of the first page was the signature of the interrogator and the interrogation date. On the reverse side, the camp staff member filling out the questionnaire indicated the prisoner's physical characteristics and results of the physical examination. Space was also provided on the reverse side for entering current information on the prisoner, such as date of transfer (departure from the camp); violations of camp discipline and disciplinary measures taken; and criminal proceedings, plus various special notations; see *KD1/13*, n. 1; *KDZ1/13*, n. 1.

144. Cards with the information provided in the questionnaires were filed in alphabetical order in the camp's card registers. If a prisoner was transferred, his card was immediately forwarded to UPV; see *KD1/13*, n. 2; *KDZ1/13*, n. 2. For this type of record, see doc. 51.

145. There was a file folder for each POW. On the cover was the name of the camp, the date of his arrival, the case number; the family name, first name, and patronymic; and when and why the file was discontinued. The file contained the questionnaire, various other documents, and fingerprints, with a table of contents attached at the end; see *KD1/13*, n. 3; *KDZ1/13*, n. 3.

146. For the organizations listed in this document, see Glossary of Organizations and Political Parties.

147. The contents of this order are unknown.

148. The contents of this order are unknown.

149. Prisoners arrested in the camp.

150. The Polish commander in chief's order (doc. 6) did not reach most of the KOP units because of faulty radio communication. The regular Polish forces in Lwów surrendered to the Red Army rather than the Germans (doc. 21). Several battles were fought in Podlachia [Polesie] and Volhynia [Wołyń]; the town of Grodno resisted for three days.

151. The Osadniki [Osadnicy] were military settlers selected from among Polish veterans of the Polish-Soviet War of 1919–1920. They were given land in Polish eastern territories gained in 1920—today's western Ukraine and western Belarus—to strengthen the Polish element there and had agricultural, defense, and sometimes administrative obligations. They numbered about 9,000 in 1930; see Janina Stobniak-Smogorzewska, *Kresowe Osadnictwo Wojskowe 1920–1945* [Eastern Military Settlement, 1920–1945] (Warsaw, 2003). In fall 1939, most of those taken prisoner when serving in the Polish Army or KOP were placed in Ostashkov POW camp (doc. 24), while others were deported along with their families on 10 February 1940 (see note 224).

152. The Gruntovoi Uchastok [Dirt-Road Sector] was an administrative, financial, and technical unit of the Military Road Service for the repair and guarding of strategically important dirt roads. Its other function was to organize POW transportation along such roads; see *KD1/16*, n. 2; *KDZ1/16*, n. 3.

153. The enthusiastic greetings offered the Red Army were sometimes organized by its political officers or agents sent ahead of the military units, especially in

predominantly Polish areas, but there was a spontaneous welcome by Ukrainians and Belorussians, peasants and young, urban Jews, many of whom had communist sympathies. The intelligentsia (educated people) were mostly ethnic Poles but included assimilated Jews. Most of the merchants were Orthodox Jews.

154. The Polish government successfully evacuated the gold reserves of the National Bank to Romania, then France, and later Britain, but part of the paper money was seized by the Soviets.

155. These authorities were the local soviets [councils] and militia set up by Soviet authorities; both included many criminal elements.

156. These items were in short supply because of the war, and Red Army soldiers bought up what was left.

157. Peasants were encouraged to loot landowners' estates by Soviet agitators who accompanied the Red Army. "Land reform," i.e., distribution of confiscated land, was implemented almost immediately, but very soon peasants were burdened with high delivery quotas; Soviet authorities later used failure to meet them to force the peasants into collective farms.

158. In this part of prewar Poland, there were Polish schools, Ukrainian schools—of which primary schools were the most numerous—and mixed Polish-Ukrainian schools; see *Concise Statistical Yearbook of Poland, 1938* (Warsaw, 1938), table 7, p. 310.

159. Most of the Jewish population of prewar Poland spoke and wrote Yiddish; boys learned Hebrew in Yeshivas to study the Torah.

160. There were some Ukrainian attacks on Poles. For a balanced view of Polish-Ukrainian relations, see Magocsi, *History of Ukraine*, pp. 583–598 (includes tables and a map). For a Polish specialist's view, see Skrzypek, *The Problem of Eastern Galicia*, pp. 44–59 (includes tables and maps).

161. See doc. 13a. For facsimiles of the Russian and German maps signed by Stalin and Ribbentrop, see *KD1*, pp. 98–99; *KDZ1*, pp. 110–111. For the Russian Secret Supplementary Protocol of 4 October 1939, detailing the course of the boundary, see *DVP*, vol. XXII, book 2, no. 657; for the German text in English translation, see *DGFP*, ser. D, vol. VIII, no. 193, reprint in *DPSR*, vol. I, no. 59.

162. The treaty was ratified in Berlin on 14 December 1939; see *DVP*, vol. XXII, book 2, no. 862. The Soviet-German Frontier Delimitation Commission finished its work on 27 February 1940; see *DVP*, vol. XXIII, book 1 (Moscow, 1998), no. 66.

163. See doc. 2.

164. This was the Marijampol region, for which Molotov proposed in August 1940 that the USSR pay Germany $3,860,000 in gold. Hitler agreed—and the Germans used the money to purchase raw materials they needed to attack the USSR in Operation Barbarossa on 22 June 1941; see the discussion and documents in Sławomir Dębski, *Między Berlinem a Moskwą: Stosunki Niemiecko-Sowieckie 1939–1941* [Between Berlin and Moscow: German-Soviet Relations, 1939–1941] (Warsaw, 2003), pp. 247–248. For maps signed by Stalin and Ribbentrop, see *KD1/25*; *KDZ1/25*.

165. According to Professor Wojciech Materski, a German-Soviet training center for security forces was established in Zakopane, Poland, in December 1939,

but no documents on this cooperation have been found to date; see *KDZ1*, p. 18. According to another Polish historian, cooperation against Polish independence movements began with a meeting of NKVD and SS officers in Lviv [Lwów] in October 1939, followed by meetings in Zakopane in December 1939 and Kraków in March 1940; see Piotr Kołakowski, *NKWD i GRU na Ziemiach Polskich, 1939–1945* [The NKVD and GRU on Polish Territories, 1939–1945] (Warsaw, 2002), pp. 66–67.

166. Another confidential protocol signed on 28 September concerned the transfer of German nationals and persons of German origin to the German sphere of interest, and of persons of Ukrainian or Belorussian origin to the Soviet sphere; see *DVP*, vol. XXII, book 2, no. 641; *DGFP*, ser. D, vol. VIII, no. 158, reprint in *DPSR*, vol. I, no. 53.

167. First printed in *Z Archiwów Sowieckich* [From the Soviet Archives], vol. 1: *Polscy Jeńcy Wojenni w ZSSR 1939–1941* [Polish Prisoners of War in the USSR, 1939–1941], trans. and ed. Wojciech Materski (Warsaw, 1992), no. 1. The Politburo decision concerning the POWs was made on 3 October, as is clear from Beria's letter to Stalin of that day, with stamps of approval for the solution he proposed. Politburo protocols were not always recorded on the day of the meeting; the discussion on the POWs was included in the minutes of the day before; *KD1/* 37, n. 1; *KDZ1/37*, n. 1.

168. For the Beria and Mekhlis note to Stalin of 2 October on POWs, see *KD1/* 36; *KDZ1/36*; for data on Mekhlis and other Politburo members, see Biographical Sketches.

169. For work on this site, see Beria's Order no. 0315, 25 September 1939, *KD1/24*; *KDZ1/24*. The place-names in the document are Russian, with former Polish names in brackets; the present Ukrainian names are: Novohrad-Volynskyy, Korets, Lviv.

170. On Czechs in the Polish Army, see note 69. Beria informed Molotov on 29 October 1939 that all the Czechs had made the appropriate statements; 553 had expressed the wish to proceed to France through Romania, 82 the wish to stay in Romania, and the rest the wish to stay in USSR. But Romanian authorities refused to issue visas, and the departure of the Czechs was postponed until summer 1940; see *KD1/37*, n. 2, p. 404; *KDZ1/37*, n. 3. The Czechs who left eventually made their way to France, then Britain. Those who stayed behind later formed the nucleus of the Czech Brigade, then Army Corps, in the Red Army led by Colonel, later General, Ludvik Svoboda; see *KD1/177*, n. 1; *KDZ1/177*, n. 1; also Natalia S. Lebedeva and Wojciech Materski et al., eds., *Katyn: Mart 1940 g.–Sentiabr 2000 g.: Dokumenty* [Katyn: March 1940–September 2000: Documents] (henceforth, *KD2*) (Moscow, 2001), doc. 101; Lebedeva and Materski et al., eds., *Katyń: Dokumenty Zbrodni* [Katyn: Documents of a Crime], vol. 2: *Zagłada, Marzec–Czerwiec 1940* [Extermination, March–June 1940] (henceforth, *KDZ2*) (Warsaw, 1998), docs. 240 and 242, n. 1. For the Czechoslovak government's efforts on the prisoners' behalf and their travel routes, see *Československo-Sovétské Vztahy w Diplomatických Jednànich 1939–1945* [Czechoslovak-Soviet Relations in Diplomatic Negotiations], vol. I (Prague, 1998), no. 24, n. 2.

171. In November 1939, Kozelsk became a camp for Polish officers after the

transfer of rank-and-file soldiers originating from German Poland to the Germans; the natives of Western Ukraine and Western Belorussia were released to their homes.

172. This document indicates that Deputy People's Commissar for Internal Affairs Merkulov in Lviv and the head of the NKVD Spetsotdel [Special Department], Viktor Bochkov, in Minsk, did not always send Polish prisoners of war to the POW camps. Some were handed over for trial to military tribunals, which had the right to sentence them to death; see *KD1/42a,* n. 1; *KDZ1/37,* n. 1. The Polish edition has a distribution list: Kalinin, Voroshilov, Ulrikh, Mekhlis, Beria, Goliakov, Pankratev (the last two are underlined in the document); see *KDZ1,* p. 133. Ivan T. Goliakov was chair of the Soviet Supreme Court; Mikhail I. Pankratev was head of the Prosecutor's Office; ibid. For Ulrikh, see Biographical Sketches.

173. See doc. 8.

174. Polish, Okręgowe Dowództwo Korpusu.

175. On Bishop Teodor Kubina, see Glossary, s.v. Biskupa Kubina. Bishop Kubina's organization was probably a Polish student group; on all these parties and organizations mentioned here, see *KD1/46,* notes, and *KDZ1/46,* notes. For the most important, see Glossary of Organizations and Political Parties.

176. These parties were dissolved by the Comintern in 1938 on the charge of Polish police penetration. They were rehabilitated in 1956.

177. For the one extant record of such an investigation, see doc. 38.

178. Survivors reported efforts to recruit them for intelligence work on German troop movements and other military matters in German Poland, or to report on their comrades in the camp, or on Poles elsewhere. Thus, the NKVD asked the pro-Soviet Colonel (later General) Zygmunt Berling to undertake such a mission in Vilnius, but he refused; see his memoirs, *Wspomnienia,* vol. I, p. 44.

179. On 9 October, Soprunenko sent this information to Beria, proposing to place soldiers subject to exchange in the Kozelsk, Putivl, Yuzha, Oranki, and Yukhnov camps. Soprunenko also proposed placing 3,500 officers in Kozelshchansk camp because Starobelsk's capacity was 7,500; see *KD1/49,* n. 1; *KDZ1/49,* n. 1.

180. On Czech prisoners, see note 170.

181. On the work site, see note 169.

182. Extracts were sent to Beria and Molotov. "Protocol 8/61," handwritten on the document, refers to the minutes of the Politburo meeting of 13 October 1939, which ratified Beria's proposals as a Politburo decision. The protocol is also mentioned in the footnote; see notes to *KD1/52,* p. 144.

183. See doc. 14.

184. Beria's proposal was approved by the Politburo on 13 October 1939; see *KD1/53; KDZ1/53;* it was first published in Materski, *Polscy Jeńcy Wojenni,* no. 2. On 16 October the armed forces of the Kiev and Belorussian military districts received the People's State Defense Commissar's Directive no. 34280, signed by Kliment Voroshilov, which read: "You are allowed to receive POWs that the German Command is offering to us as natives of Western Belorussia and Western Ukraine." However, "intelligence and counterintelligence officers, gendarmes, prison guards, and policemen identified in the reception process are to be

handed over to the NKVD organs for placement in the camps"; see *KD1/52*, note, p. 409; *KDZ1/52*, n. 2.

185. This document is dated according to the later agreement of 7 February 1940, point 10, which mentioned the protocol of 14 October 1939; see *KD1/182*; *KDZ1/182*.

186. Prisoners sent to Narkomchermet were rank-and-file soldiers. A preliminary draft of this document was titled "On the Labor Conditions of 13,700 POWs." It differed from the later version in the number of men placed in specific POW locations, but the principle of their division was the same in both versions; see *KD1/57*, note, p. 409; *KDZ1/57*, n. 1.

187. This meant payment for food out of wages.

188. Narkomchermet enterprises did not create appropriate living and working conditions for the POWs, which became a constant source of friction between that institution and the NKVD UPV.

189. The right of POWs to exchange correspondence was specified by the Geneva Conventions. Furthermore, according to point 16 of Beria's Regulations on the Treatment of Prisoners of War of 19 September 1939, prisoners had the right to write and receive letters and parcels, but the Poles were not allowed to do so until the end of November or early December 1939; see *KD1/15*; *KDZ1/15*. Petrażycki's request was sent to Soprunenko on 16 October and registered at the UPV on 17 October. Petrażycki was shot in the NKVD prison in Kharkov in spring 1940 (see Biographical Sketches).

190. Letter first published in *Novy Mir*, 2 (Moscow, 1991), pp. 211–212. On F. Sikorski, see Biographical Sketches.

191. No record has been found thus far of the conversation between General Langner and Army Commander Timoshenko. On Langner and Timoshenko, see Biographical Sketches.

192. Polish forces in Lwów resisted German attacks on 12–22 September, after which the Germans retreated and the city was surrounded by Red Army troops.

193. Reference to Śmigły-Rydz order of 17 September 1939; see doc. 6.

194. The Capitulation Act, signed by Polish officers and Soviet officers representing Timoshenko, guaranteed freedom to all defenders of the city, as well as the possibility of leaving the country. These guarantees were violated immediately after the Polish military laid down their arms when 2,000 officers were sent to Starobelsk camp. For the Polish text of the Capitulation Act, see Z. S. Siemaszko, *W Sowieckim Osaczeniu: 1939–1943* [In the Soviet Trap: 1939–1943] (London, 1991), appendix 5, pp. 340–341, cited in *KDZ1*, p. 204, n. 4.

195. Langner was allowed to travel to Moscow, where he pleaded for the release of his men and, apparently, was promised this would be done.

196. Sikorski was persistent. On 22 November, Soprunenko forwarded to Beria another letter of his, this time addressed to Molotov. Soprunenko wrote that this was the third request by the general, who had the support of a group of officers in the camp. He suggested that Sikorski be transferred to another camp and kept in isolation; see *KD1/69*, n. 4, p. 411; *KDZ1/69*, n. 5. However, Sikorski remained in Starobelsk. He was shot in Kharkov in spring 1940.

197. Order no. 14028, received by direct (telephone) line on 20 October, stated

that refugees from Western Ukraine and Western Belorussia should be sent to the camps with the POW echelons and on the same principles. Refugees from Polish territory occupied by Germany were to be held in the camp pending further orders. People with professions mentioned in doc. 22 and other specialists who had been drafted as officers were to be held in the camps; see *KD1/75*, n. 1, p. 412; *KDZ1/ 75*, n. 1. For Beria's Order no. 001177 on prisoners of war, dated 3 October 1939 and approved that day by the Politburo, see doc. 14. The princes were Jan Lubomirski and Edmund Ferdynand Radziwiłł.

198. On 11 October Beria had proposed an exchange of POWs with Germany; see doc. 18. A Soviet-German conversation on a mutual agreement in this matter took place in Moscow, 15 October 1939; see *DVP*, vol. XXII, book 2, part 1, no. 687. The Germans showed interest in the Polish officers as late as 21 September 1940; *DVP*, vol. XXIII, book 1, no. 393.

199. Soprunenko's instructions to Kozelsk camp, dated 4 November, show what kind of orders he had received from the NKVD head, Beria: "Having studied the statements by POWs forwarded to us concerning their refusal to return to their homes [on territory annexed by Germany], the Administration for Prisoner-of-War Affairs concludes that their motives are unconvincing. You must explain to them clearly that they should return to their permanent places of residence and send them home"; see *KD1/81*, n. 1; *KDZ1/81*, n. 2.

200. On the military settlers, see notes 151 and 224.

201. The first Geneva Convention, "For the Amelioration of the Condition of Sick Armed Forces in the Field," was signed by representatives of sixteen countries in Geneva on August 1864. It mandated respect for the neutrality of civilians and medical personnel, as well as hospital ships marked with a red cross. This was reaffirmed in the Geneva Convention on the treatment of POWs, dated 27 July 1929, which was not signed by the USSR, although the Soviet government claimed to respect it.

202. For UPV instructions on detaining certain categories of POWs, see doc. 22.

203. On the same day, a similar appeal was addressed by the same group to Beria. These letters were forwarded to him together with a report by the Special Operations Group in Starobelsk, consisting of Boris Trofimov, M. E. Yefimov, and Yegorov, who wrote: "In case a favorable resolution is reached with regard to the issue raised by the POWs, please advise whether we should recruit agents from among these POWs." It is not known whether this message reached Beria, but on 1 December, Soprunenko informed the camp's commandant and Chief of Special Operations Yefimov, "The issue of the physicians-officers will be resolved simultaneously with the rest of the POWs on the same terms"; *KD1/87*, n. 1, p. 414; *KDZ1/87*, unnumbered note, p. 228. See also the UPV instruction to Berezhkov of 10 November 1939 that UPV directives, not the Geneva Conventions, were to guide his work, in *KD1/103*; *KDZ1/103*.

204. For Zarubin's biography, see Biographical Sketches. For Swianiewicz's comments on Zarubin, see the introduction to Part I.

205. First published in Materski, *Polscy Jeńcy Wojenni*, no. 4, this resolution is identical to the one adapted by the Politburo on the same day, "On the Entry into

the USSR of Former Polish Military Interned in Lithuania"; see *KD1/101*, n. 1, p. 416; *KDZ1/101*, n. 2.

206. "Selection" probably meant selection for intelligence activities and recruitment of agents. Shortly thereafter, a resolution was passed not only to accept prisoners but also to transfer to Lithuania the POW rank-and-file and junior officers of the Polish Army who were natives of Vilnius [Wilno] and other former Polish territories annexed to Lithuania; see *KD1/101*, n. 2, p. 416; *KDZ1/101*, n. 1.

207. More Polish military would be transferred from Lithuania to the USSR in 1940.

208. These are the numbers for the three special camps. See also Appendix, tables 2A, 2B, 2C, and 2D, "Totals" for 29 November 1939.

209. For slightly different numbers in the special camps and labor camps in late November 1939, see Appendix, table 2D. For Rovno camp, see note 211.

210. See docs. 18 and 28.

211. Construction Site no. 1 was the highway from Novograd-Volynsky to Lvov, which included the POW camp in Rovno [Równe]; see *KD1/24*; *KDZ1/24*. The camp contained 23,163 men employed in six sections of the road-building project; see the UPV 2nd Department report of 19 October 1939 on the employment of POWs in the Rovno camp, *KD1/67*; *KDZ1/67*.

212. See doc. 19; Appendix, table 2D, last column on right.

213. On 1 and 2 November 1939, the Supreme Soviet granted the petitions by the National Assemblies of Western Ukraine and Western Belorussia for union with the respective Soviet republics. Soprunenko clearly assumed that this meant automatic Soviet citizenship. The Presidium of the Supreme Soviet formalized the matter by a decree of 29 November conferring Soviet citizenship on the inhabitants; see *DPSR*, vol. I, nos. 67, 68, 71.

214. The number of officers given here is slightly higher than in doc. 28, and it may include police officers. Soprunenko had requested Beria on 17 November to allow him to go to Kozelsk, Starobelsk, and Ostashkov to investigate the situation in each camp, and apparently this report was written after the trip. Although Soprunenko's suggestions were not approved, his requests may have inspired Beria to initiate investigations of the entire contingent in the Ostashkov camp, for which purpose Belolipetsky's brigade was sent there on 4 December; see doc. 40; *KD1/121*, n. 1, p. 419; *KDZ1/121*, n. 4.

215. The numbers for 1 December are slightly different in other reports; see also Appendix, table 2A, column 1, "Total."

216. This was Prince Jan Lubomirski (b. 1913), 2nd Lieutenant Infantry Reserve; he survived; see *KD2/30*; *KDZ2/71*.

217. For prisoners' diary accounts of living conditions in the camps, see Stepek, *Pamiętniki*. For Polish forensic experts' work on the diaries in Kraków in 1943–1944 and their later history, see the introduction to Part III.

218. Many officers tore off their insignia on capture, assuming that rank-and-file soldiers would be released. Many were recognized and placed in the special camps.

219. Cards were banned in the USSR at this time as a "capitalist game."

220. Ensign Bazyli Zacharski served in an armored unit of the Polish Army; see Tucholski, *Mord,* p. 253.

221. Artur Ożóg (1890–1940), major, retired; Kozelsk camp, was shot at Katyn. Eugeniusz Ożóg (1890–1940), major, retired; a prisoner in Starobelsk, was shot in Kharkov, spring 1940.

222. For the report on Zacharski's death, see *KD1*/133; *KDZ1*/133. There was also an emergency political report by the commander and commissar of Kozelsk camp, dated 2 December 1939; see *KD1*/124, n. 1; *KDZ1*/124, n. 3.

223. On work with the staff and support personnel aimed at "raising their political level," see *KD1*/124, n. 2.

224. From Minutes no. 9 (Special no. 9), Decisions of the VKP(b) TsK Politburo for 11 November–9 December 1939. This order was carried out on 10 December; see doc. 34. On 4 December the Politburo passed another resolution on the "NKVD issue." It approved the deportation of all Osadniki (Polish military settlers) and their families living at the time in western Ukraine and western Belorussia; see *KDZ1*/126, n. 1, p. 297. On the settlers, see note 151. On their fate, see survivors' accounts in Teresa Jeśmanowa, ed., *Stalin's Ethnic Cleansing in Eastern Poland: Tales of the Deported, 1940–1946* (London, 2000); also Tadeusz Piotrowski, ed., *Polish Deportees of World War II* (Jefferson, N.C., 2004).

225. This is a more detailed report on camp conditions than the one on Kozelsk (doc. 30). The best description of conditions and moods in Starobelsk camp from the Polish side is the short memoir by a survivor, the artist Józef Czapski: *Wspomnienia Starobielskie.*

226. Molotov speech on Soviet foreign policy, 31 October 1939, extracted in Degras, *SDFP,* vol. III, pp. 388–400.

227. Molotov speech of 6 November 1939, *Pravda* (Moscow), 7 November 1939.

228. The 5th (Extraordinary) Session of the Supreme Soviet USSR took place on 31 October–2 November 1939. The Supreme Soviet accepted the request of the Western Belorussian and Western Ukrainian assemblies for union with the respective Soviet republics.

229. Elders: the specific name for senior officers elected by POWs in each camp bloc to represent them to camp authorities.

230. In late November or early December 1939, the prisoners were finally permitted to receive letters from relatives and could write them one postcard a month. On the likely reason for this permission, see the discussion about Litauer in the introduction to Part II.

231. For Molotov's speech on Poland and Soviet foreign relations at the 5th (Extraordinary) Session of the Supreme Soviet, 31 October 1939, see Degras, *SDFP,* vol. III, pp. 388–400. In the speech Molotov called Poland "this ugly offspring of the Versailles Treaty"; p. 388.

232. For Molotov's speech of 29 November 1939 on the Soviet invasion of Finland, see Degras, *SDFP,* vol. III, pp. 403–405.

233. For the English text of the Stalin Constitution of December 1936, as amended through 17 June 1950, see James H. Meisel and Edward S. Kozera, eds.,

Materials for the Study of the Soviet System (Ann Arbor, Mich., 1950), no. 107. For Stalin's report on the draft constitution at the 8th USSR Congress of Soviets, 25 November 1939, see no. 106.

234. On Kirov, see Biographical Sketches.

235. *Komsomolsk* (1938), a film made by the Soviet director Sergei Gerasimov, glorified the building of this industrial port city on the Amur River, Khabarovsk Region, in 1932, as an example of "Great Socialist Construction." It was allegedly built by Komsomol [Young Communists' League] volunteers. In reality, much of the work was done by GULAG prisoners, as was the case with all such construction projects. In the 1960s, nuclear submarines began to be built in Komsomolsk.

236. On Ewert, Domoń, and Kwolek, see Biographical Sketches.

237. No such inspection ever took place.

238. Shepetovka (western Ukraine) was a distribution camp from which prisoners were sent to other camps.

239. For the Politburo decision of 3 December to arrest Polish officers in western Ukraine, see doc. 31. The arrests were carried out on the same day that Chernyshov sent Beria's order, 10 December; see doc. 34.

240. "Displacement" [*dyslokatsia*] apparently meant moving the people in these centers and colonies elsewhere, for the NKVD intended to use some of these places as camps for the Polish POWs. Before the order of late December 1937, minors had been sent to the same labor camps as adults.

241. This document was first published in Stepashin et al., *Organy*, vol. I, book 1, no. 62; see also docs. 31 and 33 above. On Serov, then deputy head of the NKVD and head of the NKVD in Ukraine, see Biographical Sketches.

242. The 3,878 officers were taken prisoner in Lwów in September 1939; see doc. 21. The vast majority of the high-ranking officers were held in Starobelsk; the highest ranks lived in separate quarters in town; hence, Starobelsk camp was sometimes referred to in the plural, as "camps."

243. Sick and wounded Polish officers were in the care of the UITK, which had its own hospitals and rest centers.

244. Soprunenko used the word "*plenienia*" [capture] regarding German soldiers and officers wounded and taken prisoner by the Poles in the former eastern Poland. They were taken over by the Red Army and cared for in Soviet-run hospitals. The German Embassy in Moscow asked for their return on 28 October and again on 18 December 1939; see *DVP*, vol. XXII, book 2, nos. 737, 869.

245. Compare this figure with the figure for the officer contingent in doc. 28. Numbers of POWs in NKVD reports often varied because POWs arrived and departed or were miscounted.

246. On 31 December 1939, Beria also issued orders on sending special NKVD officers to Starobelsk and Kozelsk. They were to help organize evidence gathering and ensure that a high level of information was obtained from the prisoners' questionnaires, but there was no mention of preparing cases against the prisoners; see *KD1*/151 and n. 1; *KDZ1*/151 and n. 1.

247. For the indictment of a Polish policeman from Ostashkov camp, see doc. 38. For the conclusion of work in Ostashkov camp, see doc. 40.

248. A special investigation brigade had been sent to Ostashkov camp on 4 December 1939; see *KD1/130*; *KDZ1/130*. Soprunenko was to speed up the work there.

249. This point was also in Beria's instruction of 8 October 1939; see doc. 16.

250. See doc. 16.

251. This was either the personal questionnaire that prisoners filled out on arrival in the camp (see doc. 10) or a new document of the same kind.

252. Soprunenko remained in Ostashkov until 1 February 1940, when he and Stepan Belolipetsky telegraphed Beria that the investigation of the policemen's cases had been completed; see doc. 40. During this time, the acting UPV head in Moscow was Soprunenko's deputy, Ivan Khokhlov. Half a century later, Soprunenko claimed that his task in Ostashkov was only to find housing and good working conditions for the investigators; that he took no part in the investigation, knew nothing about its results, and was not required to report on it; see Protocol of Soprunenko Interrogation, 25 October 1990, Moscow, *KDZ2/Aneks II/1*, p. 425 (Polish translation from Russian).

253. Olejnik's file, no. 649, contains all the basic personal data and documents on the case. According to this information, Olejnik's father was a restaurant owner; the prisoner's party affiliation was not established; he was married; he had no children; he was held in Ostashkov camp. Olejnik was taken prisoner on 25 September 1939 in the town of Borshchevo [Polish, Borszczów; Ukrainian, Borshchiv] and had served as a policeman there since 1936. Also attached to the file was the relevant excerpt from the lists of relatives of all POWs with their addresses; these lists were used to facilitate the relatives' future deportation. Olejnik was number 77 on NKVD Ostashkov dispatch list no. 033/2 dated 16 April 1940; see Tucholski, *Mord*, p. 840; see also *KD1/158*, n. 1; *KDZ1/158*, n. 1.

254. Article 58, Paragraph 13, of the RSFSR Penal Code read: "Any act or active struggle against the working class or the revolutionary movement of which any person was guilty while in a responsible or a secret post (i.e. as agent) under the czarist regime or with any counter-revolutionary government during the period of the civil war entails the measures of social defense prescribed in Art. 58 (2) of the present code." The "supreme measure of social defense" was death by shooting, or confiscation of property, deprivation of citizenship, and banishment from USSR, or, if there were extenuating circumstances, confiscation of property and three years' imprisonment; see *The Penal Code of the Russian Socialist Federal Soviet Republic* [English text of the 1926 Code (with Amendments up to 1 December 1932) with three Appendices], Foreign Office, July 1934 (London, 1934), pp. 22, 25. The full text of Article 58, though in somewhat different wording, is in Robert Conquest, *The Great Terror: Stalin's Purges of the Thirties* (London, 1968), appendix G.

255. First published in *Novy Mir,* 2 (1991), pp. 213–215.

256. The British Embassy in Moscow was theoretically looking after Polish interests and citizens in the USSR, for Britain, an ally of Poland, was not at war with the USSR. However, as Sir R. Stafford Cripps (British ambassador in Moscow, 1940–1942) told General Sikorski in June 1941, the "Bolsheviks" had refused all conversations with British representatives on assistance to Poles in Russia. They

had even arrested six Poles, former officials of the British legation in Tallinn (Estonia), who had British passports, when they tried to leave the country; see *DPSR*, vol. I, no. 85, p. 107.

257. The prisoners were in touch with relatives in the former eastern Poland—now part of the USSR—but wished to contact relatives living elsewhere, especially in German Poland.

258. Correspondence with families—restricted to writing one letter or postcard per month—was granted in late November–early December 1939. The goal may have been to encourage Sikorski to recognize the Soviet annexation of the former eastern Poland in exchange for releasing the Polish POWs (see discussion at end of introduction to Part II).

259. The prisoners had to haul wood and water for the kitchen.

260. Generals and their orderlies, eighteen persons in all, were held in buildings on Volodarskaia Street in town; colonels and lieutenant colonels, ninety-six persons in all, were held at 32 Kirov Street, while General F. Sikorski and his staff were held at 19 Lenin Street (information provided by Professor Materski).

261. This letter was apparently delivered by Colonel Edward Saski. On 2 February 1940 the UPV executive sent Beria a report regarding a "Declaration" delivered by Saski in the name of a group of lieutenant colonels. Saski listed demands similar to those in the Declaration. Khokhlov and Vorobyev asked Beria for instructions, but no reply has been found; see *KD1/160*, n. 2; *KDZ1/160*, n. 2. On Saski, shot in Kharkov, see Biographical Sketches.

262. For the tasks of the investigation, see doc. 37.

263. According to NKVD figures for 4 February 1940, the police and gendarmes at Ostashkov numbered 6,378 (Russian version), 6,374 (Polish version), but on 22 February, there were 6,371 (Russian), 6,367 (Polish); cf. Appendix, table 2B, "Totals," column 6, and Appendix, table 2D, column 6.

264. This indicates that the document could be taken out by selected officials but had to be returned.

265. First published in Stepashin et al., *Organy*, vol. I, book 1, no. 71. Soprunenko's suggestions for releasing the categories of prisoners were not followed. However, Beria issued a directive concerning some categories of prisoners listed in Soprunenko, par. 3; see doc. 42.

266. In the interrogation of Soprunenko, carried out on 25 October 1990 by officers of the Soviet Main Military Prosecutor's Office, the former head of the UPV claimed that he had made this recommendation "from the noblest of motives." He said that some 800 men were envisaged from two camps (the total of those mentioned in points 1 and 2); see *KDZ2/Aneks II/1*, p. 426.

267. The P.O.W. and Strzelcy were not political parties but associations; see Glossary.

268. The 2nd Department was the Intelligence Department.

269. The directive was connected with plans to clear out the camps, but it left the military and policemen in place. More detailed instructions were issued by Beria and communicated to camp commandants on 23 February 1940; see the following note.

270. For the UPV instruction of 23 February 1940 to POW camp commandants

on carrying out the Beria directive as set out in this document, see *KD1/194; KDZ1/194.*

271. The same number is given in the NKVD report for 23 February 1940, but it includes a few persons from other categories than officers; see Appendix, table 2C, column 7. Column 7 includes an error in addition, for its actual total is 3,907, not 3,908.

272. According to another count for Kozelsk, the total on 22 February was 4,609, but this included nonmilitary prisoners; see Appendix, table 2A, column 7.

273. Georgians fought against the Bolsheviks for an independent homeland in 1919–1921. Later some served as contract officers in the Polish Army.

274. In a report of 2 March 1940, Soprunenko listed the military officers held in NKVD camps by rank as follows: 1 admiral, 12 generals, 82 colonels, 201 lieutenant colonels, 551 majors, 1,498 captains, 17 naval captains, and 6,014 lieutenants, 2nd lieutenants, and ensigns; see *KD1/207; KDZ1/207;* facsimiles in *KD1*, p. 376; *KDZ1*, p. 459. According to another UPV report, also dated around 28 February 1940, out of a total number of 8,442 army officers held in the camps at that time, 2,336 were regulars; the majority, 5,456, were reserve officers with professional careers in civilian life, and 650 were retired. There were also 19 naval officers, of whom 11 were regulars; see *KD1/201, KDZ1/201.*

275. This number seems too low. On the basis of first names of known victims, it is estimated that Jewish officers probably accounted for about 10 percent of all officer prisoners, most of them in the army's medical services; see Schochet, "Polish-Jewish Officers Who Were Killed in Katyn." For the memoirs of a Jewish physician who was held in Kozelsk and survived, see Slowes, *Road to Katyn.*

276. The numbers fluctuated in different reports. For slightly different Ostashkov figures for 22 February and 16 March 1940, see Appendix, tables 2B and 2D.

277. Extract from Protocol no. 13, Decisions of the Politburo, 13 February–17 March 1940. Natalia Lebedeva believes that the decision to shoot the officers and police was made on 28 February; the documents show that it was approved by the Politburo on 5 March; see doc. 47. For a discussion of the timing and motives of the decision, see the introduction to Part II.

278. Nikita S. Khrushchev was then 1st Secretary of Ukraine and member of the Soviet Politburo.

279. This order led to the second wave of deportation of people resident in these border regions as well as the families of the "repressed"—i.e., of those in the NKVD prisons of western Belorussia and western Ukraine. (The first ones to be deported, on 10 February 1940, were military settlers and their families; see note 224.) Estimates of the total number of Polish citizens deported in 1940–1941 vary. For the numbers of deportees in each of the three deportations according to NKVD figures, see Lebedeva, "Deportation of the Polish Population," pp. 29–45; Ciesielski, Materski, and Paczkowski, *Represje Sowieckie,* pp. 13–17.

280. This suggests that they would be either deported to labor camps or shot.

281. The regulation for the removal of refugees from the border area also applied to most members of the former Polish Communist Party who had fled from the Germans. However, refugees from German Poland who had been convicted of illegally trying to enter or leave the USSR—a crime according to Soviet law—were

ordered by Beria to be deported to the Sevvostlag [Northeastern labor camps, Vladivostok]; see *KD1/204; KDZ1/204.*

282. A German-Soviet agreement regarding population exchanges was signed on 15 November 1939; see *DVP*, vol. XXII, book 2, no. 787; additional protocol, no. 788. The Gestapo set up an office in Lviv to process Polish refugee applications to return home to German Poland but rejected most Jewish applicants. Soviet authorities deported not only the Jewish refugees but also some 90,000 Jews resident in the former eastern Poland, probably those classified as "socially dangerous elements." Thousands of others fled ahead of the German Army in summer 1941. It seems that most of the deported Jews survived.

283. On G. V. Korytov and V. P. Pavlov, see Biographical Sketches.

284. Korytov's sentence in the penultimate paragraph, beginning "But it is rumored that in March . . . ," may indicate that he wrote the letter at the end of February.

285. These were rank-and-file policemen, residents of Polish territory, then in Germany.

286. The mention of travel for at least a month is explained in a subsequent paragraph where Korytov speaks of 600 cases of Ostashkov camp prisoners sentenced to several years (of hard labor) in Kamchatka. It is clear that these sentences were changed to death by shooting, as per Beria's proposal approved by the Politburo on 5 March 1940; see doc. 47.

287. The NKVD officials at the conference apparently expected this kind of sentence for most of the Polish police and gendarmes held in Ostashkov.

288. The Red Army held only about 1,000 Finnish POWs. Stalin probably knew at this time that the Finnish government was ready for peace negotiations; see the introduction to Part II.

289. This is a reference to Beria's directive of 23 February, see *KD1/194; KDZ1/194,* summarized in Merkulov's directive of 22 February 1940 (doc. 42).

290. The date "5.III.40" is written in by hand. *KD1/216* gives the date as "earlier than 5 March 1940," but *KDZ1/216* gives "5 March 1940" (facsimile of document in both). Natalia Lebedeva sees Beria's request for lists of prisoners, resulting in the reports on the nationality of Polish POW officers in the Starobelsk and Kozelsk camps (28 February 1940, doc. 43) and the number of Polish police and gendarmes held in NKVD POW camps (2 March 1940, doc. 44), as preparation for his resolution to have them shot. She therefore dates the Politburo approval of the resolution earlier than 5 March 1940; see N. S. [Natalia Sergeevna] Lebedeva, "Proces Podejmo-wania Decyzji Katyńskiej" [The Decision-Making Process on Katyn], in Krzysztof Jasiewicz, ed., *Europa Nie Prowincjonalna / Non-Provincial Europe* (Warsaw, 2000), p. 1169. The date of 5 March 1940 is generally accepted, however, because the resolution was summarized in an extract from Protocol no. 13 of the Politburo sessions dated 5 March 1940; *KD1/217; KDZ1/217.*

291. For NKVD interrogations of Polish officers and civilians arrested for underground resistance to Soviet authorities in eastern Poland (then, and since 1944, western Belorussia/Belarus and western Ukraine), see the bilingual Polish-Russian documentary publication *Polskie Podziemie na Terenach Zachodniej Ukrainy i Zachodniej Białorusi w Latach 1939–1941 / Polskoe Podpolie na Territorii Za-*

padnoi Ukrainy i Zapadnoi Belorussii 1939–1941 gg. [The Polish Underground in the Territories of Western Ukraine and Western Belorussia, 1939–1941], 3 vols., ed. Wiktor Komogorow et al. (Warsaw and Moscow, 2001–2004). Volume 2 contains the interrogations and sometimes also personal depositions by several high-ranking Polish officers, including Generals Władysław Anders, Marian Januszajtis-Żegota, and Mieczysław Boruta-Spiechowicz; the first became the commander of the Polish Army, USSR, 1941–1942 (doc. 95), later the Polish 2nd Corps, and the last two were interrogated by Beria and Merkulov in late October 1940 for participation in creating a Polish division in the Red Army (doc. 91). There is also a Polish-Ukrainian publication on the Polish underground in eastern Poland in 1939–1941, but it contains a different set of documents: *Polskie Podziemie, 1939–1941/Polske Pidpillia, 1939–1941*, 3 vols., ed. Zuzanna Gajowniczek, Grzegorz Jakubowski et al. (Warsaw and Kiev, 1998–2004). The NKVD quickly infiltrated the resistance groups and liquidated all of them by spring 1941.

292. It seems that these prisoners were selected by the NKVD for execution at the same time as the POWs. Nonpolitical refugees and illegal border-crossers were deported to the Northeastern labor camps (doc. 45).

293. According to a note dated 9 March 1959, written by Aleksandr Shelepin, then head of the KGB, for Nikita Khrushchev, head of the CPSU, 7,306 people were shot in the prisons of western Ukraine and western Belorussia (doc. 110).

294. On Kobulov and Bashtakov, see Biographical Sketches. The text in sections I–III was the one used in the Politburo resolution of 5 March 1940, point 144, "The Question of NKVD USSR"; see *KD1/217*; *KDZ1/217*. Point 144 figured in the 5 March 1940 Politburo agenda along with the following items: the construction industry; binocular production; the [Ivan F.] Tevosian Commission (orders for military goods from Germany); the Supreme Court of the USSR; the construction of a new sarcophagus for Lenin; and the contracting of suppliers for military shipyards; see *Katyń: Dokumenty Ludobójstwa* (henceforth *KDL*), trans. and ed. Wojciech Materski (Warsaw, 1992), no. 8; or Wojciech Materski, ed., *Katyń: Documents of Genocide* (henceforth *KDG*) [English edition of *KDL* by Ryszard Żelichowski], trans. Jan Kolbowski and Mark Canning (Warsaw, 1993), no. 3.

PART II. EXTERMINATION

1. On the deportations from eastern Poland, see Part I, note 279. On Poles in Kazakhstan in 1940–1946, see Stanisław Ciesielski, *Polacy w Kazachstanie w Latach 1940–1946* (Wrocław, 1997). On the experiences of Polish women, see Katherine R. Jolluck, *Exile and Identity: Polish Women in the Soviet Union during World War II* (Pittsburgh, Pa., 2002).

2. Dispatch lists and departures from Kozelsk and Ostashkov are in camp commanders' reports; for a reconstructed table of Starobelsk train departures from Voroshilovgrad and Valooiki Stations to Kharkov, see Natalia S. Lebedeva and Wojciech Materski et al., eds., *Katyń: Dokumenty Zbrodni* [Katyn: Docu-

ments of a Crime], vol. 2: *Zagłada, Marzec–Czerwiec 1940* [Extermination, March–June 1940] (henceforth *KDZ2*) (Warsaw, 1998), Supplement 1.

3. On the last prisoner transport from Kozelsk, to Babynino Station, see the memoirs of a survivor, Father Z. Peszkowski, *Wspomnienia Jeńca z Kozielska* [Memoirs of a Kozelsk Prisoner of War] (2nd edition, Wrocław, 1992), pp. 23–24, cited in Wojciech Materski, "Katyń—Motywy i Przebieg Zbrodni: Pytania i Wątpliwości" [Katyn—The Motives and Course of the Crime: Questions and Doubts], in Marek Tarczyński, ed., *Zbrodnia Katyńska po 60 Latach: Polityka, Nauka, Moralność* [The Katyn Crime 60 Years Later: Politics, Learning, Morality], Zeszyty Katyńskie [Katyn Notebooks], no. 12 (Warsaw, 2000), p. 39. On the processing and selection for life decisions see Natalia S. Lebedeva and Wojciech Materski et al., eds., *Katyn: Mart 1940 g.–Sentiabr 2000 g.: Dokumenty* [Katyn: March 1940–September 2000: Documents] (Moscow, 2001) (henceforth *KD2*) (Moscow, 2001), pp. 25–26, 89–90, 102–103, 129, 172–173, 280–281. A. M. Cienciala would like to thank Dr. Vladimir Pozniakov of the Institute of General History, Russian Academy of Sciences, the leading expert on Razvedka in World War II, for information that there is no evidence of Soviet intelligence warnings of the impending German attacks on Belgium, Holland, and France.

4. Ambassador Schulenburg explained that he had wanted to give Molotov documents sent by the German government on the night of 9–10 May, but the plane had been delayed in Königsberg [Kaliningrad], and since Molotov had already heard the news, the ambassador did not insist on being received immediately by the commissar; see *Dokumenty Vneshnei Politiki* [Documents on Foreign Policy] (henceforth *DVP*), vol. XXIII, book 1 (Moscow, 1998), no. 145, p. 258; Molotov remark, p. 259.

5. *Facts and Documents Concerning Polish Prisoners of War Captured by the USSR during the 1939 Campaign* (London, February 1946; for private circulation only), p. 107. This work was compiled for the Polish government-in-exile by Professors Marian Sukiennicki, Marian Heitzman, and others on the basis of survivors' interviews and written accounts. A copy was handed to the British government in March 1946; see the introduction to Part III. A. M. Cienciala would like to thank Dr. Maciej Siekierski, curator, East European Collection, Hoover Institution on War, Revolution and Peace, Stanford, Calif., for making his personal copy of this rare work available to her.

6. For verified names, brief biographical information, and number of prisoners killed at Katyn, Kharkov, and Kalinin/Tver, see Maria Skrzyńska-Pławińska, ed., *Indeks Represjonowanych* [Index of the Repressed], vols. I–III (Warsaw, 1995–1997). Volume I is on the victims murdered at Katyn; volume II, on those murdered at Kharkov; and volume III, on those murdered at Kalinin/Tver.

7. Interrogation of Dmitry Tokarev by the military prosecutor Lieutenant Colonel Anatoly Yablokov at Vladimir-Volynsky [Polish, Włodzimierz-Wołyński; Ukrainian, Volodymir-Volynskij], 20 March 1991, Investigation Materials in the Case of the Katyn Crime, *KDZ2*/Aneks II, "Zeznania Oprawców" [Depositions by the Torturers], no. 2, pp. 432–472 (Polish translation from Russian, reprint). For Tokarev quotation on executions, see *KDZ2*, p. 440; on Smolensk, p. 467; on M. Romm, pp. 469, 472. For Gertsovsky to Khokhlov, 27 April 1940, regarding

Stanisław Swianiewicz and Michał Romm, see *KD2/64*; *KDZ2/145*. Tokarev's claim that three of the executioners went mad and committed suicide, *KDZ2*, p. 453, is contradicted in Materski, "Katyń—Motywy," p. 37. Tokarev's account is summarized in *KD2*, pp. 35–36; for a summary as given to the American author David Remnick by Colonel Aleksandr Tretecky, senior military prosecutor in the Soviet Main Military Prosecutor's Office, who participated in these interrogations, see David Remnick, *Lenin's Tomb: The Last Days of the Soviet Empire* (New York, 1993), pp. 3–7. Tretecky told Remnick he had operated the video camera during the interview, but Yablokov does not mention his presence. For Yablokov's personal account of the interrogation, see I. S. Yazhborovskaia, A. Yu. Yablokov, and V. S. Parsadanova, *Katynskii Sindrom v Sovetsko-Polskikh i Rossiisko-Polskikh Otnosheniakh* [The Katyn Syndrome in Soviet-Polish and Russian-Polish Relations] (Moscow, 2001), pp. 355–358; and the version written for the Polish reader, Inessa Jażborowska, Anatolij Jabłokow, and Jurij Zoria, *Katyń: Zbrodnia Chroniona Tajemnicą Państwową* [Katyn: The Crime Protected as a State Secret] (Warsaw, 1998), pp. 266–271. For an aerial photographic interpretation of Mednoe, indicating burial sites outside the officially permitted exhumation area in 1991, see Wacław Godziemba-Maliszewski's map in Frank Fox, *God's Eye: Aerial Photography and the Katyń Forest Massacre* (West Chester, Pa., 1999), plate 4 and explanatory note in "Illustrations."

8. The reconstructed table showing prisoner-of-war railway transports sent 5 April–4 May 1940 from Voroshilovgrad and Valooiki Stations to the NKVD Administration of the Kharkov Oblast is in *KDZ2*, Supplement 1.

9. Skrzyńska-Pławińska, *Indeks Represjonowanych*, vol. II.

10. The first interrogation of M. Syromiatnikov, 20 June 1990, *KDZ2*, pp. 472–476.

11. The second interrogation of Syromiatnikov, 10 April 1991, *KDZ2*, pp. 476–479; third interrogation, 15 May 1991, *KDZ2*, pp. 479–481.

12. Fourth interrogation of Syromiatnikov, 30 July 1991, *KDZ2*, pp. 481–497.

13. For the second interrogation, see note 11 above; on Kupry taking the money, see *KDZ2*, p. 498; on the local supervisors, see *KDZ2*, p. 479; for the fifth interrogation, 6 March 1992, see *KDZ2*, pp. 497–500. A. M. Cienciala wishes to thank Professor Maia Kipp for the translation of Kupry's "alyo." The first and second exhumations conducted in Kharkov in 1991 and 1994 showed that some of the officers had been shot with rifle bullets, indicating that they were not shot in the Kharkov NKVD prison. Such bullet casings were also found in some of the burial pits in 1994, indicating that the victims had been shot on site; see the Katyn expert Jędrzej Tucholski's "Diariusz Ekshumacji w Charkowie i Miednoje" [Diary of Exhumations in Kharkov and Mednoe], in Marek Tarczyński, ed., *Zbrodnia Katyńska: Droga do Prawdy* [The Crime of Katyn: The Road to Truth], Zeszyty Katyńskie [Katyn Notebooks], no. 2 (Warsaw, 1992), pp. 198, 202, 204; and the account by the journalist Jerzy Morawski, *Ślad Kuli* [The Trace of the Bullet] (Warsaw and London, 1992), which has photographs of Syromiatnikov; see also the archaeologist Andrzej Kola's "Archeologiczne Badania Sondażowe i Pomiary Geodezyjne Przeprowadzone w 1994 Roku w Charkowie" [Archeological Probes and Geodesic Measurements Made in Kharkov in 1994], in *Katyń, Miednoje,*

Charków—Ziemia Oskarża [Katyn, Mednoe, Kharkov—The Earth Accuses] (Warsaw, 1996), p. 127.

14. *Facts and Documents,* p. 46; Cf. *The Crime of Katyn: Facts and Documents* (henceforth *Crime of Katyn*) (London, 1965), p. 54. This is the translation of the third edition of *Zbrodnia Katyńska,* whose first edition appeared in London in 1948. The author and compiler of the first edition was the journalist and writer Józef Mackiewicz; see Biographical Sketches.

15. Stanisław Swianiewicz, *W Cieniu Katynia* (Paris, 1976), p. 110; the English version, translated and edited by his son, Witold Swianiewicz, is *In the Shadow of Katyn: "Stalin's Terror"* (self-published; distributor, Bunker to Bunker Books, Calgary, Alberta, Canada, 2003), p. 76. Swianiewicz first gave his testimony of what he saw at Gnezdovo Station as "Mr. B" (to protect relatives and friends in communist Poland) in *The Katyn Forest Massacre: Hearings Before the Select Committee to Conduct an Investigation of the Facts, Evidence, and Circumstances of the Katyn Massacre* (henceforth *Hearings*), Eighty-Second Congress, 1st and 2nd Sessions, 1951–1952 (Washington, 1952), part 4, pp. 605–606. For a map of the Katyn-Gnezdovo region, see Maps and Aerial Photographs, map 5.

16. Solski diary, 29 September 1939–9 April 1940, in Jan A. Stepek, ed., *Pamiętniki Znalezione w Katyniu* [Diaries Found at Katyn], foreword by Janusz K. Zawodny (2nd expanded edition, Paris and Warsaw, 1990), pp. 94–105, endnotes p. 105; see also *KDZ2,* p. 22 (trans. A. M. Cienciala). The ellipses denote a part of the entry that could not be restored by Polish experts who worked on the diaries in Kraków (see the story of the diaries in the introduction to Part III). An extract of Solski's diary was produced in English as Exhibit 28A in *Hearings,* part 4, pp. 733–734. For an English translation of an extract covering Solski's travel from Kozelsk through Smolensk, see *Crime of Katyn,* pp. 189–190.

17. For the diary by an unknown officer, see Stepek, *Pamiętniki Znalezione,* p. 63, cited in *KDZ2,* p. 22. For an aerial photographic study of the Katyn-Gnezdovo area, see, in Maps and Aerial Photographs, map 5 and the accompanying photographs.

18. For Krivozertsev's testimony, cited after his death, see *Hearings,* part 4, pp. 429–452, 840–842; see also note 22 below.

19. On the theory that the prisoners were shot elsewhere, see Michał Synoradzki, Jacek Grodecki, and Victoria Plewak, "Katyń: Modus Operandi," *Arkadia,* nos. 9–10 (Mikołów, June 2001), p. 8; for an abbreviated version, see "Katyn: Technika Zbrodni" [Katyn: Technique of a Crime], *Gazeta Wyborcza* [The Election Gazette], 48 [4298] (Warsaw, 2003), pp. 10–11. The Polish journalist Józef [Joseph] Mackiewicz, who visited Katyn at the time, inspected the garage near the dacha with the German forensic medicine expert Professor Gerhard Buhtz and found no trace of any bullets there; see Joseph Mackiewicz, *The Katyn Wood Murders* (London, 1951), p. 154. On the indications that the Kozelsk victims could have been shot in the area of the Gnezdovo Station, see Wacław Godziemba-Maliszewski, "Interpretacja Zdjęć Lotniczych Katynia w Świetle Dokumentów i Zeznań Świadków / Katyn: An Interpretation of Aerial Photographs Considered with Facts and Documents," *Fotointerpretacja w Geografii: Problemy Telegeoinfor-*

macji [Photo Interpretation in Geography: Problems in Teleogeographic Information], no. 25 (Warsaw, 1995), photographs and notes, pp. 45–49, and conclusion, p. 107, points 3–6; Godziemba-Maliszewski, "Katyn: Where Were the Victims Shot?" unpublished work, revision of September 2005, made available to A. M. Cienciala by the author.

20. Yazhborovskaia, Yablokov, and Parsadanova, *Katynskii Sindrom,* pp. 351–352, 378 n. 73. The authors cite from the Katyn case files of the Soviet Main Military Prosecutor's Office, to which they had access as experts. For an account of a similar method used in executing foreign communists in Stalin's purges, see Aleksandr Milchakov's remarks in Remnick, *Lenin's Tomb,* pp. 138–139. Zakirov, who conducted his own private Katyn investigation, feared for his life and sought refuge in Poland in 2001; see Jerzy Pomianowski, *Na Wschód od Zachodu: Jak Być z Rosją* [To the East of the West: How to Live with Russia] (Warsaw, 2004), p. 293 (this is a reprint of an article published in 2003).

21. The others were Kuzma Godunov (real name: Godezov), Matthew Zakharev, and Grigory Silvestrov; see the German official publication, cited in *Crime of Katyn,* p. 115. For the 1943 commissions and their reports, see the introduction to Part III.

22. For Krivozertsev's account to Mackiewicz, see Mackiewicz, *Katyn Wood Murders,* chap. 15; see also *Crime of Katyn,* chap. 11; for the original Polish text of Mackiewicz's German version, which was the first to be published (*Katyn. Ungesuchtes Verbrechen* [Zurich, 1949]), see Józef Mackiewicz, *Katyń: Zbrodnia bez Sądu i Kary* [Katyn: A Crime without Trial and Punishment], comp. and ed. Jacek Trznadel (Warsaw, 1997), pp. 145–158. For Ferdynand Goetel's account of what Krivozertsev told him, see *Hearings,* part 4, p. 842. It was thought unlikely that Polish officers from Kozelsk traveled along the road to Katyn in mid-March, as per Krivozertsev, for NKVD records show that the "clearing out" of the camps began in early April. However, a separate group of Kozelsk prisoners were sent out on 8 March, so they were probably seen on the road by Krivozertsev on 14 March. The Polish texts of Krivozertsev's depositions—one to the Germans and five in the West—are given in Jacek Trznadel, "Rosyjscy Świadkowie Katynia (1943–1946–1991)" [The Russian Witnesses to Katyn, 1943–1946–1991], in Tarczyński, *Zbrodnia Katyńska: Droga do Prawdy,* pp. 96–111; on the separate Kozelsk group sent out on 8 March, see p. 110.

23. See Józef Mackiewicz, "Tajemnicza Śmierć Iwana Kriwoziercowa, Głównego Świadka Zbrodni Katyńskiej" [The Mysterious Death of Ivan Krivozertsev, the Chief Witness of the Katyn Crime], *Wiadomości* [News], nos. 15–16 (London, 1952), reprinted in Aleksandra Kwiatkowska-Viatteau, ed., *Katyń: Wybór Publicystyki 1943–1988 i "Lista Katyńska"* [Katyn: Selected Publications, 1943–1988, and the "Katyn List"] (London, 1988), pp. 122–127. The "Katyn List," compiled by Adam Moszyński, was published in London in 1949. It contained the names of the victims known at the time. The Mackiewicz article is also reprinted in Mackiewicz, *Katyń,* pp. 366–372.

24. Anatoly Marchenko, *My Testimony* (London, 1969), p. 157; Światosław Karawański, "Łagrowe Echa Katynia" [Gulag Echoes of Katyn], *Orzeł Biały* [White Eagle], 185 (London, January 1980), reprinted in Kwiatkowska-Viatteau,

Katyń: Wybór Publicystyki, pp. 156–157. The story was also published in other Polish émigré papers and periodicals at the time.

25. On Andreev's file, see Yazhborovskaia, Yablokov, and Parsadanova, *Katyn-skii Sindrom,* pp. 341–342; Jażborowska, Jabłokow, and Zoria, *Katyń: Zbrodnia Chroniona,* pp. 244–247. On the NKVD intimidation of witnesses who appeared before the Burdenko Commission, see the introduction to Part III. The witnesses who met a sudden death were (S.) Andreev, Godezov (real name: Godunov), Krivozertsev, Magishev, Medzhidov, Otroshchenko, Silvestrov, Zhigulev, and others; see *Katynskii Sindrom,* p. 353.

26. Cited in *KD2,* pp. 38–39; *KDZ2,* p. 24. Gribov and Gvozdovsky were mentioned by Zakirov; see text and note 20 above. The execution site in Smolensk might have been a slaughterhouse there; see Godziemba-Maliszewski, "Katyn: Where Were the Victims Shot?"

27. See Zuzanna Gajowniczek, ed., *Ukraiński Ślad Katynia* [The Ukrainian Trail of Katyn] (Warsaw, 1995); the identifications were made by Gajowniczek. This publication, made possible by the cooperation of the Ukrainian and Polish Security Services, contains thirty-four lists of victims. The lists were sent with a cover letter dated 25 November 1940 by GB 1st Lieutenant Feodor A. Tsvetukhin to the head of the NKVD 1st Special Department, Moscow, GB Major Leonid F. Bashtakov. Tsvetukhin, head of the 1st Special Department, Ukraine, 1939–1940, wrote that he was enclosing 3,435 files in five sacks (p. xxii). The list numbers are from the same series as those for the three special camps that Gorbachev gave to General Jaruzelski in Moscow on 13 April 1990, when the Soviet news agency TASS admitted Soviet guilt for the Katyn massacre (doc. 117).

28. On counting the prisoners and making lists of same, see N. S. [Natalia Sergeevna] Lebedeva, "Proces Podejmowania Decyzji Katyńskiej" [The Decision-Making Process on Katyn], in Krzysztof Jasiewicz, ed., *Europa Nie Prowincjon-alna / Non-Provincial Europe* (Warsaw, 2000), p. 1169. The texts are in Polish with English summaries.

29. N. S. Lebedeva, "The Deportation of the Polish Population to the USSR, 1939–41," *Journal of Communist Studies and Transition Politics,* 16, nos. 1–2 (March–June 2000), p. 37; Lebedeva, "Proces Podejmowania Decyzji," *Europa,* pp. 1169, 1371–1372.

30. Some 250,000 Soviet Poles were deported from Western Ukraine and Western Belorussia in 1935–1938. On these deportations and the arrests of urban Poles in 1937–1938, see studies by V. N. Khaustov, N. V. Petrov, and A. B. Roginskii, in Aleksandr Gurianov, ed., *Repressii Protiv Poliakov i Polskikh Grazhdan. Is-toricheskie Sborniki "Memoriala." Vypusk 1* [Repressions of Poles and Polish Citizens. Historical Collections of "Memorial." Issue no. 1] (Moscow, 1997), pp. 10–43; the brief account in Stanisław Ciesielski, Wojciech Materski, and Andrzej Paczkowski, *Represje Sowieckie wobec Polaków i Obywateli Polskich* [Soviet Repression of Poles and Polish Citizens] (Warsaw, 2000), pp. 3–5; and the survey in Andrzej Paczkowski, "Poland, the 'Enemy Nation,'" in Stéphane Courtois et al., eds., *The Black Book of Communism: Crimes, Terror, Repression,* trans. Jonathan Murphy and Mark Kramer (Cambridge, England, 1999), pp. 364–367. For vivid accounts of the deportations of Soviet Poles from Ukraine to Kazakhstan in the

early 1930s, also the arrests of Soviet Poles in the cities, based on NKVD documents and interviews with surviving deportees, see Kate Brown, *A Biography of No Place: From Ethnic Borderland to Soviet Heartland* (Cambridge, Mass., 2004); see also Timothy Snyder, *Sketches from a Secret War* (New Haven, 2005), chap. 6.

31. Around 139,000 members of military settler families were deported on 10 February 1940. These were mostly women and children, with only 33,000 men above the age of eighteen. By the time of their release in August 1941, according to NKVD records 131,938 were still alive; see Lebedeva, "The Deportation," pp. 35–38. Many, however, died on the way to Polish Army centers in Uzbekistan, and still more perished in a typhoid epidemic there; for the accounts of survivors, see Teresa Jeśmanowa, ed., *Stalin's Ethnic Cleansing in Eastern Poland: Tales of the Deported, 1940–1946* (London, 2000); Tadeusz Piotrowski, ed., *The Polish Deportees of World War II: Recollections of Removal to the Soviet Union and Dispersal Throughout the World* (Jefferson, N.C., 2004). For a fascinating personal memoir, see Wesley Adamczyk, *When God Looked the Other Way: An Odyssey of War, Exile, and Redemption* (Chicago, 2004).

32. Beria's order is cited in the directive of Mikhail Krivenko, chief of the NKVD Convoy Troops Administration, to the commissars of Convoy Troops in Kiev, Minsk, Kuibyshev (Samara), and Novosibirsk, 2 March 1940; see Natalia S. Lebedeva and Wojciech Materski et al., eds., *Katyn: Plenniki Neobiavlennoi Voiny* [Katyn: Prisoners of an Undeclared War], in *Rossiia, XX Vek: Dokumenty* [Russia, the Twentieth Century: Documents] (henceforth *KD1*) (Moscow, 1997), vol. 1, doc. 204; Lebedeva and Materski et al., eds., *Katyń: Dokumenty Zbrodni* [Katyn: Documents of a Crime], vol. 1: *Jeńcy Nie Wypowiedzianej Wojny* [The Prisoners of an Undeclared War] (henceforth *KDZ1*) (Warsaw, 1995), doc. 204.

33. Lebedeva, "The Deportation," p. 40. The third and fourth waves of deportations took place in April and May–June 1941; pp. 41–42.

34. For Polish estimates totaling 1,450,000 deportees, see Tadeusz Piotrowski, *Poland's Holocaust* (Jefferson, N.C., 1998), table 1, p. 14. For NKVD figures for deportee distribution and totals, see Lebedeva, "The Deportation," pp. 41–47; Ciesielski, Materski, and Paczkowski, *Represje Sowieckie*, pp. 13–16; A. E. Gurianov, "Sowieckie Represje wobec Polaków i Obywateli Polskich w Latach 1939–1956 w Świetle Danych Sowieckich" [Soviet Repressions of Poles and Polish Citizens in the Years 1939–1956 in the Light of Soviet Data], in Jasiewicz, *Europa*, table, p. 973. In April 1943 the Polish Embassy in the USSR reported that there were 271,000 Polish citizens in the country, of whom 106,602 were Jewish; the report listed them all according to their places of residence; reprint in Dariusz Baliszewski and Andrzej Krzysztof Kunert, *Prawdziwa Historia Polaków: Ilustrowane Wypisy Źródłowe, 1939–1945* [The Real History of the Poles: Illustrated Selections from Primary Sources, 1939–1945], vol. 2: *1943–1944* (Warsaw, 1999), no. 983, pp. 1060–1061.

35. Wojciech Materski notes that about 6,000 persons were in these prisons in early March 1940, so Beria must have included several thousand more Poles intended for arrest in April as part of the passportization action planned for that month; see Materski, "Katyń—Motywy," pp. 35–36. It is known that 7,300 of those held in prisons were shot; see doc. 110.

36. Summary of Beria resolution, extract from Politburo Protocol no. 13, 1940, *KD1/217; KDZ1/217; KD2/1; KDZ2/1.* Troikas had been used during the Stalin Terror to issue summary sentences on opponents and suspects on the spot, but were abolished in November 1938; see Amy Knight, *Beria: Stalin's First Lieutenant* (Princeton, N.J., 1993), pp. 89–90; Jacques Rossi, *The Gulag Handbook: An Encyclopedia Dictionary of Soviet Penitentiary Institutions and Terms Related to the Forced Labor Camps,* translated from the Russian by William A. Burhans (New York, 1989), p. 453.

37. Orders to Kozelsk, Ostashkov, and Starobelsk commanders to come immediately to Moscow, 13 March 1940, see *KD2/5–6; KDZ2/9–12.*

38. *New York Times,* 15 October 1992, cited in Knight, *Beria,* p. 104.

39. See J. K. (Janusz Kazimierz) Zawodny, *Death in the Forest: The Story of the Katyn Forest Massacre* (Notre Dame, Ind., 1962), p. 127 and n. 1.

40. Norman Davies, *God's Playground: A History of Poland,* vol. II (New York, 1982), p. 452. Davies does not emphasize class in the revised version of vol. II (New York, 2005), p. 335, where he writes that 20,000 Polish officers were executed in spring 1940. He probably had in mind the approximate total for the POWs shot in the three special camps as well as in the prisons of western Ukraine and western Belorussia.

41. For Lebedeva on POW attitudes and Stalin in 1920, see *KD1,* pp. 36–37.

42. Materski, "Katyń—Motywy," pp. 28–33; *KDZ2,* p. 26. The German "A-B Aktion" exterminated some 3,500 Polish social and political activists and intellectuals in German Poland in the spring and summer of 1940; see Piotrowski, *Poland's Holocaust,* chap. 2.

43. Yazhborovskaia, Yablokov, and Parsadanova, *Katynskii Sindrom,* p. 113; Jażborowska, Jabłokow, and Zoria, *Katyń: Zbrodnia Chroniona,* p. 214.

44. For a detailed account of Franco-British military plans to cut off Scandinavian iron ore supplies for Germany and send military help to Finland in 1939–1940, see Llewellyn Woodward, *British Foreign Policy in the Second World War,* vol. 1 (London, 1970), chaps. 1–4; for Tanner to French minister, 28 February, see p. 91. For Molotov's telegram of 6 March 1940 to Aleksandra Kollontai, Soviet minister in Stockholm, on the Swedish communication to him that day of Finland's desire for peace negotiations, see *DVP,* vol. XXIII, book 2, part 2, p. 771. For the English text of the peace treaty between the USSR and Finland dated 12 March 1940, see Jane Degras, ed., *Soviet Documents on Foreign Policy, 1917–1941* (henceforth *SDFP*), vol. III: *1933–1941* (London, 1953), pp. 421–423.

45. On the Soviet intelligence mission in Finland, headed by Boris Rybkin, at the time of secret Soviet-Finnish talks in 1938, see E. M. Primakov, ed., *Ocherki Istorii Rossiiskoi Vneshnei Razvedki* [Sketches from the History of Russian Foreign Intelligence], vol. III (Moscow, 1997), pp. 296–309.

46. For the theses of October 1939, see Marian Kukiel, *Generał Sikorski: Żołnierz i Mąż Stanu Polski Walczącej* [General Sikorski: Soldier and Statesman of Fighting Poland] (London, 1970), pp. 99–100.

47. For Sikorski's statements as reported by Stefan Litauer to the Foreign Office on 25 November 1939, and Sikorski's own views, see Anna M. Cienciala, "The Question of the Polish-Soviet Frontier in 1939–1940: The Litauer Memorandum and Sikorski's Proposals for Re-establishing Polish-Soviet Relations," *Polish Re-*

view, 33, no. 3 (1988), pp. 295–324; for Litauer's report to the Foreign Office, see ibid., p. 303.

48. Protocol of Pyotr Soprunenko's Interrogation by Lieutenant Colonel Aleksandr Tretecky, a military prosecutor of the Administration Department, Soviet Main Military Prosecutor's Office, then in charge of the Katyn case, with the participation of the head of the above office, Colonel Nikolai Anisimov. First interrogation, 25 October 1990, Moscow, *KDZ2*/Aneks II/1 (reprint of a Polish translation from the Russian), pp. 423–431; Soprunenko statement on the officers and the Soviet aim of an agreement with the Polish government, p. 425.

49. Berling wrote that at this meeting with Beria and Merkulov he was accompanied by Colonel Eustachy Gorczyński; see Zygmunt Berling, *Wspomnienia* [Memoirs], vol. I: *Z Łagrów do Andersa* [From the Camps to Anders] (Warsaw, 1990), p. 95; for another account of this conversation, see *Crime of Katyn,* pp. 96–97.

50. Starszyński was probably August Starzeński. As of 20 April 1940, some of these prisoners were held in Smolensk jail; for biographical data on these prisoners, see *KDZ2*/5, p. 51.

51. This was Merkulov's directive summarizing Beria's instruction on the transfer of certain categories of nonmilitary prisoners from the camps to prisons; see doc. 42.

52. This was the more detailed UPV instruction to camp commanders on the prisoner transfer; see *KD1*/194, *KDZ1*/194.

53. On 7 March 1940, Soprunenko and Nekhoroshev instructed the commanders of the three special camps to draw up these lists. Soprunenko also requested Beria's deputy, Chernyshov, to send appropriate UPV NKVD workers to carry out special tasks in the Kozelsk, Ostashkov, and Starobelsk camps; see *KD2*/3, n. 2; *KDZ2*/3, n. 2. For the officials sent, see *KD2*/4, n. 2; *KDZ2*/4, n. 2.

54. For the record form listing family information, see doc. 50. The families were to be deported.

55. The inclusion in the lists of prisoners' families of those living in German Poland may indicate that the lists were to be checked for persons sought by the German government. For the deportations of POW families, see docs. 52, 64a, and 64b.

56. The five-day deadline may have been connected with plans to hold a conference with camp commanders in Moscow. Such a conference took place there on 15 March.

57. A questionnaire for more detailed family information was enclosed with Beria's directive of 7 March 1940 to the commissars of internal affairs for Ukraine and Belorussia, I. A. Serov and L. F. Tsanava; see *KD2*/2.

58. This instruction indicates that separate lists were made for POW families living in German Poland.

59. Militia [GB] 2nd Lieutenant I. M. Bashlykov, who signed the attestation, was head of the Secretariat, 1st Special Department NKVD.

60. The documentation on Troika decisions is unavailable to this day, but death sentences might have been approved in a wholesale manner on the basis of Article 58, Paragraph 13, of the Soviet Criminal Code, as in the case of policeman Olejnik; see doc. 38.

61. First published in S. V. Stepashin et al., eds., *Organy Gosudarstvennoi Be-zopasnostii SSSR v Velikoi Otechestvennoi Voine: Sbornik Dokumentov* [State Security Organs in the Great Fatherland War: Documentary Collection], 3 vols. in 6 books (Moscow, 1995–2003), vol. I, book 1, no. 78, pp. 165–166.

62. *KD2/11; KDZ1/24*; Natalia S. Lebedeva and Wojciech Materski et al., eds., *Katyn: Mart 1940 g.–Sentiabr 2000 g. Rasstrel, Sudby Zhivykh, Ekho Katyni: Dokumenty* [Katyn: March 1940–September 2000. Execution by Shooting, the Fate of the Survivors, the Echoes of Katyn: Documents] (Moscow, 2001) (supplement to *KD1*, henceforth *KD1, R*), facsimile no. 3, pp. 526–527, gives 76,000–100,000 people.

63. Prostitutes were prohibited in the USSR, and Polish ones could be working for the enemy.

64. The contents of NKVD USSR Order no. 001223–39 are unknown.

65. Internal passports were required for all Soviet residents, but the deportee passports restricted movement to the district of settlement.

66. More than these 3,000 prisoners are known to have been murdered in Ukraine. The death lists for 3,435 were delivered on 25 November 1940 by GB 1st Lieutenant Feodor Tsvetukhin, head of the 1st Special Department, NKVD in Ukraine, to Major Leonid Bashtakov, head of the 1st Special Department, NKVD; see Gajowniczek, *Ukraiński Ślad,* p. xxii; *KDZ2/Aneks/I/7*. Of these, 2,000 have been identified; see Gajowniczek, *Ukraiński Ślad,* p. xxii. In May 1994 the lists were given by General Andrei Khomich, deputy chief of the Ukrainian Security Service, to the Polish deputy prosecutor general, Stefan Śnieżko; see Gajowniczek, *Ukraiński Ślad,* p. x.

67. This was to make room for the prisoners to be transferred from western Ukraine.

68. *KDZ2/27*, p. 84, incorrectly lists Vilna [Wilno, Vilnius] prison. Vileika [Wilejka], located southwest of Smarhon [Smorgonie] on the Vilia [Polish, Wilia; Lithuanian, Neris] River, was the regional administrative center, and prisoners from the whole region were brought there.

69. No trace has been found thus far of the 3,000 persons transferred to Minsk prison and presumably shot there. Republic of Belarus authorities have refused Polish requests for access to archival documents and permission to search for the remains.

70. See also Beria's directive of 21 March to Lazar Kaganovich, commissar of communications, on the transport of the prisoners to their destinations; *KD2/12; KDZ2/26*.

71. The head of the NKVD USSR Secretariat, GB Major Stepan S. Mamulov, ordered the immediate transmission of Beria's order over high-frequency wires to Serov in Kiev, and Tsanava in Minsk; see *KD2/13*, n. 1; *KDZ2/27*, n. 4.

72. The information meant here was the Kobulov form (doc. 51). A similar instruction was sent to Korolev, Kozelsk camp, where the higher-ranking officers were sent out in the first transports, mainly on the basis of the 6 April 1940 list; these transports left Kozelsk on 7 April; see *KD2/18*, n. 1; *KDZ2/48*, n. 1. In February, Soprunenko had proposed that people without compromising materials against them should be freed to go home; see doc. 41.

73. This, like the other NKVD Russian-language dispatch lists, was first pub-

lished in Jędrzej Tucholski, *Mord w Katyniu* [Murder in Katyn] (Warsaw, 1991), pp. 721–722. (Original errors in these lists are corrected in *KD2* and *KDZ2*.) There are ticks between the number and the name for nos. 5, 6, 7, 12, 13, 14, and no. 11 is circled. The document published in the current volume gives the Polish spelling of the names. On the same day, 1 April, Soprunenko sent Berezhkov another list of 100 prisoners to be sent to Kalinin; see *KD2/19; KDZ2/49*. For details on the Ostashkov death lists, see *KD2/19*, n. 1; *KDZ2/51*, p. 116 n.

74. In Kozelsk camp, Reserve Politruk [political instructor] Sirotkin was delegated to receive the death lists, but the first lists were delivered personally by Colonel Ivan Stepanov, sent to Kozelsk to direct the prisoners' departures and their conveyance to places of execution. Death lists for Ostashkov camp were delivered by UPV NKVD USSR Inspector Andrei Frolov, who was ordered there and brought some lists with him. Bukhterev (first name unknown), security commander for Ostashkov camp, was also delegated for this purpose; see *KDZ2/56*, n. 1. The original death lists sent to Starobelsk camp have not been found, but on 13 April 1990, Soviet President Mikhail Gorbachev gave Polish President Wojciech Jaruzelski a photocopy of a combined list of 4,031 Starobelsk victims, along with copies of all the lists for Kozelsk and Ostashkov camps. All are printed in their original form in Tucholski, *Mord,* pp. 593–987.

75. Statement by N. S. Lebedeva to A. M. Cienciala in early December 2000.

76. The leaders of these organizations in the cities were generally army officers, but elsewhere some leaders were NCOs. For interrogations of members of the Polish underground resistance movements in western Ukraine, which were quickly penetrated and crushed by the NKVD, see the bilingual Polish-Russian volumes of documents on the Polish underground in western Ukraine and western Belorussia: *Polskie Podziemie na Terenach Zachodniej Ukrainy i Zachodniej Białorusi w Latach 1939–1941 / Polskoe Podpolie na Territorii Zapadnoi Ukrainy i Zapadnoi Belorussii 1939–1941 gg.* [The Polish Underground in the Territories of Western Ukraine and Western Belorussia, 1939–1941], 3 vols., ed. Wiktor Komogorow et al. (Warsaw and Moscow, 2001–2004). See also the Polish-Ukrainian series: *Polskie Podziemie 1939–1941 / Polske Pidpilia 1939–1941* [The Polish Underground in 1939–1941], 3 vols., ed. Zuzanna Gajowniczek, Petro Kulakowski et al. (Warsaw and Kiev, 1998–2004).

77. Passportization was carried out on the basis of the Politburo decision of 29 November 1939, which granted Soviet citizenship to the inhabitants of these districts. The personal data on the passport application forms were used to track down Polish NCOs. On 30 December 1939 the Sovnarkom [Council of People's Commissars] issued Decree no. 2130/622s on implementing passportization in these regions. Those denied passports were also denied work and were "resettled" elsewhere in the USSR; see *KD2/22*, n. 2; *KDZ2/55*, p. 124 n.

78. On 4 April 1940, Convoy no. 236 of the NKVD USSR Convoy Troops transported these prisoners to Kalinin and delivered them the next day to GB Lieutenant Timofei Kachin of the UPV NKVD USSR, Kalinin Oblast.

79. This means the 343 prisoners, received 5 April, were executed the same day; see doc. 59.

80. According to some of Milshtein's reports, the railway cars were unloaded in

Smolensk, not Gnezdovo, which indicates that those prisoners may have been shot in the NKVD jail in Smolensk. For other Milshtein reports sent that day and later, see *KD2/27*, n. 1; *KDZ2/61*, n. 1.

81. First published in Russian as NKVD death list no. 015/2, in Tucholski, *Mord,* pp. 622–626, and reprinted in *KD1, R* 14. The document is typed on an NKVD USSR form and dated according to the last death list, no. 014 of 6 April 1940 (see also doc. 76, where list no. 015/2 is included with two other lists in column 2). The names are given here in Polish.

82. The prisoners named in this document were sent out of the camp on 8 April. The list included the four generals held in Kozelsk: Bronisław Bohatyrewicz [alternate spelling: Bohaterewicz], Henryk Minkiewicz-Odrowąż, and Mieczysław Smorawiński (nos. 6, 7, 68). However, the fourth, General Jerzy Wołkowicki (no. 8), was spared because he and a few other officers were of interest to the 5th Section (Intelligence) of GUGB [Main Administration for State Security] NKVD; see *KD2/17, 28; KDZ2/63*. For a key factor in Wołkowicki's survival, see Biographical Sketches.

83. Name unknown; he was one of several valets serving Ignacy Mościcki, president of Poland from 1926 to 1939.

84. "Other officers" included the only woman prisoner in Kozelsk camp, Polish Air Force Lieutenant (sometimes listed as Cadet Ensign) Janina Lewandowska. Her remains were found in the Katyn exhumations of April–June 1943.

85. Construction Site no. 1. was the road from Rovno to Lvov.

86. This figure is for 1 April, so it does not include the transports sent from the camps between 1 and 8 April; see *KD2/34*, n. 1; *KDZ2/77*, n. 2.

87. The Yeleno-Karakuba labor camp was the basis for establishing two independent camps, the Yelenovsk and Karakuba camps see *KD2/34*, n. 3.

88. The Krivoy Rog labor camp was the basis for establishing the Oktiabrruda, Dzherzhinskruda, Leninruda, and Nikopol-Marganets camps; see *KD2/34*, n. 3.

89. First printed in *Organy,* vol. I, book 1, no. 81. Beria had sent a cover letter with the draft resolution to Molotov on 5 April; see the facsimile in *KD1, R* 12, p. 541; *KDZ2/81*, p. 162.

90. For the SNK resolution of 2 March 1940, see doc. 45.

91. Most of these were Jews; see Part I, note 282.

92. Beria had already so instructed the Kazakh SSR commissar of internal affairs on 20 March 1940; see doc. 52.

93. See docs. 45 and 64a.

94. The deportation took place on 13 April 1940; see Lebedeva, "The Deportation," p. 41. Some exceptions were made. Merkulov wrote to Serov on 6 April 1940 instructing him to suspend, until receipt of a special decree, the deportation of the wives and children of eight Polish officers of special interest to the NKVD; they survived; see *KD2/29; KDZ2/66*.

95. On refugees rejected by the Germans, most of whom were Jewish, see Part I, note 282. Many of these refugees were deported in June 1940.

96. According to deportees' memoirs, the feeding was irregular at best, a fact also confirmed by NKVD reports on some of the transports.

97. On 29 December 1939 the SNK had approved the NKVD instruction on the

procedure for "resettling" Polish military settler families from the western oblasts of the Ukrainian and Belorussian Soviet Republics, that is, former eastern Poland. The instruction gave detailed directives on what the families could take with them and specified that they were to be sent to Narkomles logging operations in Kirov, Perm, Vologda, Arkhangelsk, Ivanovo, Novosibirsk, Sverdlovsk, and Omsk Oblasts, the Krasnoyarsk and Altai Krais [Territories], and the Komi ASSR [Autonomous Soviet Socialist Republic]. There they were to be formed into settlements of 100–500 families each. Supplementary regulations described how the settlements were to be administered by the NKVD; Gosudarstvenny Arkhiv Rossiiskoi Federatsii [State Archive of the Russian Federation] (henceforth GARF), f. R-5446, op.57, d. 65, p. 165. A. M. Cienciala wishes to thank Professor Lebedeva for providing this document. On this deportation, see Part I, notes 224 and 279.

98. On 9 April 1940, Soprunenko sent a directive to the commanders of the three special camps instructing them to report in cipher the number of prisoners sent out at the departure of every transport according to the lists; see *KD2/35*; *KDZ2/80*. This directive was rigorously carried out to the end of the operation.

99. The file contains over ten analogous reports sent to the UPV from 11 April to the end of the whole operation in mid-May; see *KD2/37*, n. 1; *KDZ2/87*, n. 1 (date error in Polish edition: note gives 19 instead of 9 April).

100. This meant the document was to be circulated only in the camp Special Section; see *KDZ2/96*, n. 8.

101. Camp commander Lebedev replied on 23 April that he had known of these directives for several months. The prisoners had been interrogated several times, and again after receiving the instruction of 14 April, but no evidence of army officers or policemen had been found. The search would continue; see *KD2/41*, n. 1; *KDZ2/96*, p. 185 n.

102. This meant that no prisoners were left in the town where some had been quartered.

103. For the 14 April report on the moods of prisoners being dispatched from Starobelsk, see *KD2/40*; *KDZ2/95*. It noted some "subversive" activity, such as spreading rumors that the prisoners would be sent to Siberia or Karelia; patriotic slogans on the rebirth of a great Poland; less willingness to work in the camp since prisoners were leaving; and an attack on a guard.

104. Polish-Jewish engineers, physicians, and other highly trained specialists could suffer social discrimination but not "national oppression" in prewar Poland, where they were much needed and respected. Petitions of this kind were generally rejected (see doc. 23), but these were granted, for they were death lists from Starobelsk; see *KD2/53*, nn. 2–4; *KDZ2/127*, nn. 2–4.

105. Maxime Weygand (1867–1965), French general; commander in chief of the French Armed Forces in France and Syria in May 1940.

106. Mieczysław Birnbaum, a journalist and former Polish intelligence officer, probably deduced this from Molotov's speech of 29 March 1940, broadcast by Soviet radio, on the Soviet war with Finland. Molotov mentioned suspicious activity in Syria—the creation of colonial armies under General Weygand, perhaps for purposes hostile to the Soviet Union; see Degras, *SDFP*, vol. III, p. 447. For French

proposals to seize Baku, see Woodward, *British Foreign Policy,* vol. I, pp. 78, 101, 104, 110–112, 454, 523.

107. While most Kozelsk prisoners were sent through Smolensk to Gnezdovo, the station for Katyn, there are indications that some were shot in the NKVD prison in Smolensk.

108. The commissar for Kozelsk camp, Senior Politruk Mikhail Alekseev, reported on 17 April that there was a two-day delay in sending prisoners out of the camp, which caused anxiety among the prisoners, but that the dispatch was resumed on 17 April. The departures were delayed because of a delay by the UPV in sending the lists to Kozelsk camp; see *KDZ2/114* and n. 2.

109. For a Kozelsk survivor's report on the situation in the camp at this time, see the memoirs of Professor Stanisław Swianiewicz (1899–1997). He writes of mandatory inoculations for all POWs against typhoid fever and cholera. He witnessed the receipt by camp officials of orders telephoned from Moscow regarding the makeup of the transports to leave the camp; see Swianiewicz, *W Cieniu Katynia,* pp. 105–106; Swianiewicz, *In the Shadow of Katyn,* pp. 70–71. Such telephone instructions most likely concerned changes in the dispatch lists.

110. The NKVD had already been transferring hospitalized prisoners to the special camps; see *KDZ2/101.*

111. The enclosed list contained the names of 26 men from Kozelsk, 7 from Ostashkov, and 15 from Starobelsk, with a cover letter from Gerstsovsky to Khokhlov on sending them to Yukhnov camp; see *KDZ2/124,* note. On the same day, a UPV directive was sent to the head of Yukhnov camp stating that 64 men would be sent to him from Starobelsk, 107 from Kozelsk, and 29 from Ostashkov. He was told to prepare for their arrival; see *KDZ2/125.* Surviving POWs from Kozelsk camp were sent to Yukhnov on 22–26 April, and those from Starobelsk, on 27 April; see *KDZ2/125,* n. 2; on the list of 273 names compiled by the NKVD 1st Special Department to be sent to Yukhnov camp, see *KD2/51,* n. 1.

112. All the persons listed in the document figured earlier on the lists of the 5th Department, that is, the Inostranny Otdel [INO—Foreign Intelligence Department] of GUGB NKVD USSR and, in accordance with its directive, were included in the records' control; see *KD2/59,* n. 1; *KDZ2/137,* n. 1. The personal files of those excluded from the control data were transferred to the Troika (doc. 47), which decided on their life or death. On the INO, see Knight, *KGB,* p. 278.

113. Teodorowicz survived. All the rest were shot.

114. *KD2/65* gives the date of 18 April (p. 131), but the correct date, 28 April, is in the list of documents (p. 598). The document was first published in O. V. Yasnova, ed., *Katynskaia Drama: Kozelsk, Starobelsk, Ostashkov: Sudba Internirovanykh Polskikh Voennosluzhashchykh* [The Katyn Drama: Kozelsk, Starobelsk, Ostashkov: The Fate of the Interned Polish Servicemen] (Moscow, 1991), ninth (unnumbered) document at end of book.

115. Gertsovsky had already sent a letter to Khokhlov on 27 April saying that according to a directive from Merkulov, the dispatch of Swianiewicz (from Kozelsk) and Michał Romm (from Ostashkov) was to be held back; see *KD2/64; KDZ2/145.* Swianiewicz describes this event in his memoirs, *W Cieniu Katynia / In the Shadow of Katyn.* The 2nd Department of GUGB was the Sekretny

Politichesky Otdel [SPO—Secret Political Department], responsible for political surveillance of the Communist Party, the intelligentsia, and religious and other groups; see Knight, *KGB,* p. 279.

116. The same echelon number is listed for 12 and 13 April. This might be an accounting or typographical error.

117. As of 16 March 1940, before the death transports to Kalinin/Tver began, there were 6,364 POWs in Ostashkov camp; see Appendix, table 2D. For other figures, see doc. 73.

118. Stanislav Redens, NKVD chief for the Moscow region in 1936–1938, who fell together with NKVD chief Nikolai Yezhov, "confessed" that he had managed to arrest and convict up to 3,000 persons a month using the "album method." This meant that forms with the victims' biographies and case summaries were sewn together in batches of 100 into albums. The judges decided up to 1,000 cases in a few hours, and the decisions were sent on to Yezhov. He signed the last page of each set automatically, without further ado, as long as the names were Polish; see Kate Brown, *A Biography of No Place* (Cambridge, Mass., 2004), p. 159.

119. This is more than the total cited in another report, probably filed earlier, which gave the number of cases completed as 14,846; see *KD2/68,* n. 1. *KDZ2/155,* n. 1, cites a different document, giving 14, 904.

120. *KD2/70; KDZ2/160.*

121. This text fills in the gaps left in *KD1, R* 39, facsimile, pp. 578–579. G. I. Antonov [first name unknown], the head of the central NKVD apparatus in the Krivoy Rog labor camp complex, was the co-organizer with Arseny V. Tishkov, head of the UPV 1st Special Department, of the dispatch of POWs to the Northern Railway camp. On 14 May 1940, Beria signed Order no. 0192, directing that prisoner labor build the North Pechora-Vorkuta Railway Line to increase coal transport from the Vorkuta region; 4,506 prisoners were sent there in May. On 9 June 1940, Chernyshov issued an order for restructuring the camps of the Krivoy Rog Basin in connection with sending 8,000 POWs to the Northern Railway camps. For both orders, see *KDZ2/170,* n. 1. For a list of 4,105 Polish citizens who worked as GULAG prisoners in the Vorkuta region from September 1939 to January 1944, see Agnieszka Knyt, ed., *Indeks Represjonowanych* [Index of the Repressed], vol. X, part I: *Więźniowie Łagrów w Rejonie Workuty* [Labor Camp Prisoners in the Vorkuta Region] (Warsaw, 1999).

122. For this order, see Soprunenko to Antonov, 9 May 1940, *KD2/72* and *KDZ2/169.*

123. The file also contains the names of prisoners not sent to the NKVD in Smolensk or to Yukhnov camp. On 12 May 1940 the remaining six prisoners were sent to Yukhnov camp, thus completing the action of "clearing out" Kozelsk camp. (*KDZ2/184,* p. 295 n., erroneously gives the last death transport date as 20 May.) Yukhnov, also known as Pavlishchev Bor (name of a sanatorium), was a transitory camp; some prisoners sent there from the three camps were executed, but most were sent later to Griazovets camp and survived.

124. The verified Polish number of Kozelsk officers buried at Katyn is 4,410; see Skrzyńska-Pławińska, *Indeks Represjonowanych,* vol. I. However, this number is probably too low.

125. The verified Polish number is 6,314; see Skrzyńska-Pławińska, *Indeks Represjonowanych,* vol. III. For a table showing dates and the number of prisoners dispatched from Ostashkov to Kalinin from 24 April to 13 May 1940, see *KD2/78; KDZ2/182.*

126. The enclosure listed the names of nineteen prisoners not sent out of the camp for various reasons; see *KD2/80,* pp. 148–151; *KDZ2/194.* Another report, also dated 17 May, listed the names of sixteen prisoners who had died in the camp; see *KDZ2/195.*

127. Berezhkov received orders to send 3,891 persons to the Kharkov Oblast UNKVD and 80 to Yukhnov. However, six orders for Kharkov were issued by mistake, so the total sent to Kharkov Oblast came to 3,885; see *KD2/81,* n. 1. The last death transport left Starobelsk for Kharkov on 12 May 1940. The verified Polish number of officers murdered in Kharkov is 3,739; see Skrzyńska-Pławińska, *Indeks Represjonowanych,* vol. II. For the ranks of prisoners sent to their death between 5 and 9 April, see *KD1, R 21,* pp. 558–560; *KD2/40; KDZ2/95.* The serial dispatch lists sent to Starobelsk were probably destroyed along with other documentation on the Polish prisoners held in that camp in 1939–1940, see doc. 110. For the reconstructed railway transport of prisoners from Starobelsk to Kharkov, covering the period 4 April–5 May 1940, see *KDZ2/Supplement 1* (following the index of place-names at the end of the book).

128. Barbiulek was not registered in Starobelsk; the name may be misspelled. Krzyżanowski (preceding paragraph) may be Edmund, not Edward; see *KDZ2/196,* notes.

129. Most of the prisoners sent to Yukhnov camp survived.

130. Doc. 77, dated 17 May, gives 6,229 dispatched.

131. Doc. 76, dated 14 May, gives a total of 4,620 on lists received.

132. The cover letter to doc. 78 gives lists received for 3,891 people. The difference in figures may be due to the camp administration's inability to send all the prisoners on the lists for technical or other reasons; see also note 127.

133. For the families of Polish POWs shot in April–May 1940 who were deported to northeastern Kazakhstan, see docs. 49, 52, 64a, 64b, and notes. For help in finding POW husbands and fathers many turned to Soviet institutions and leaders, including Stalin; see *KD2/85,* n. 1. For a letter to Stalin from the children of 2nd Lieutenant Eugeniusz Mikucki, see *KD2/93* and *KDZ2/221.*

134. Probably the son of policeman Jan Denyszyn from the Grodno region.

135. Probably the son of policeman Antoni Jędrzejczyk, prewar location unknown.

136. Not identified.

137. Probably the daughter of policeman Tadeusz Kowalewski from Marcinkowce; see identifications in *KDZ2/206.*

138. The 136th Detached Battalion of NKVD USSR Convoy Troops, quartered in Smolensk, was part of the 15th Brigade. The battalion guarded Kozelsk camp and participated in convoying the POWs from Kozelsk to their place of execution. The battalion commander, Major Terenty Mezhov, stayed in Kozelsk camp from 19 March to mid-May 1940. When he went to Kozelsk camp, he was accompanied by the dispatcher, several officers, and a full complement of rank-and-file sol-

diers; see *KD2/87*, n. 1; *KDZ2/209*, p. 338 n. On 26 October 1940, Beria issued an order listing rewards for NKVD workers involved in "clearing out" the camps, including those who did the killing; these rewards were much higher than those for this convoy battalion; see doc. 90.

139. On 21 May, Kachin received 294 prisoners from Convoy Commander Murashov, and they were shot that day. On 22 May, Soprunenko issued a directive to the camp heads to put the prisoner card files in exemplary order within seven days, noting information on those killed, putting the files in alphabetical order, and sending them by courier to UPV; see *KD2/88*, n. 1; *KDZ2/212*. Ostashkov did not get this directive on 22 May because prisoners were sent out that day for execution. Korolev sent 4,901 data cards, model 2, in alphabetical order to UPV on 1 June; see *KDZ2/212* and p. 340 n.

140. "White," a term from the Russian Civil War (1918–1922), was applied to all anticommunist forces fighting the Bolsheviks, including the Polish Army in the Polish-Soviet War (1919–1920).

141. Evidently, the author identified the Polish prisoners as Western counter-revolutionaries.

142. According to verified Polish figures, the total was 6,314; see Skrzyńska-Pławińska, *Indeks Represjonowanych,* vol. III.

143. This terminology was probably applied in NKVD circles to Polish policemen and gendarmes.

144. One may wonder how the commander managed to work out the value of prisoner labor and prisoner upkeep if the Housekeeping Department was incapable of keeping accounts, as stated here.

145. Not printed, see *KDZ2/217*, n. 1.

146. For the breakdown of prisoners sent to Yukhnov camp, see doc. 85.

147. In the information given by the NKVD UPV on 3 December 1941, the total number of POWs held in the three special camps, whose files went through the 1st Special Department of the NKVD USSR, is given as 15,131 (doc. 96, point 5). This is more than the number of prisoners in the three special camps as of 16 March 1940 (Appendix, table 2D, column 2), and more than the number in UPV information given on 25 May 1940. However, the death transports included additional prisoners from Rovno camp, the Narkomchermet camps, hospitals, etc., so the number 15,131 may be close to the truth; see *KDZ2/215*, n. 1, pp. 344, 346. For Shelepin's figures of 9 March 1959, see doc. 110. For verified Polish numbers of those killed from each camp, see the notes to docs. 76–78.

148. The "others" were those not included in the categories listed for extermination in the Politburo decision of 5 March 1940 (see doc. 47). The figure of 395 survivors out of the 14,857 prisoners held in the three special camps, the survivors being those sent to Yukhnov camp, is generally accepted by Russian and Polish historians, although 400–440 is thought possible.

PART III. KATYN AND ITS ECHOES

1. For Soprunenko's 22 July 1940 report to Chernyshov on Polish police, military men, and civilians formerly interned in Lithuania, then held in Kozelsk 2 and

Yukhnov, see Natalia S. Lebedeva and Wojciech Materski et al., eds., *Katyn: Mart 1940 g.–Sentiabr 2000 g.: Dokumenty* [Katyn: March 1940–September 2000: Documents] (henceforth, *KD2*) (Moscow, 2001), doc. 106 (misdated as 2 July); Lebedeva and Materski et al., eds., *Katyń: Dokumenty Zbrodni* [Katyn: Documents of a Crime], vol. 3: *Losy Ocalałych, Lipiec 1940–Marzec 1943* [The Fate of the Survivors, July 1940–March 1943] (henceforth *KDZ3*) (Warsaw, 2001), doc. 12. Ultimately, Griazovets held 1,673 Polish prisoners; 1,967 were placed in Suzdal, and some were sent to Yuzha camp; see Ewa Rybarska, ed., *Indeks Represjonowanych* [Index of the Repressed], vol. V: *Jeńcy w Griazowcu i Suzdalu* [Prisoners in Griazovets and Suzdal] (Warsaw, 1998). On the French, British, and Belgian military prisoners who escaped from German captivity to the USSR only to be interned there, see *KD2*/151, n. 3; *KDZ3*/149, n. 3.

2. See Tadeusz Pieńkowski, "Działalnia NKWD w Związku Sowieckim po Czerwcu 1940 wobec Polskich Żołnierzy Internowanych po 17 Września 1939 r." [NKVD Activity in the USSR after June 1940 Regarding the Polish Military Interned after 17 September 1939], in *Studia z Dziejów Rosji i Europy Środkowo-Wschodniej* [Studies on the History of Russia and East Central Europe], vol. 39 (Warsaw, 2004), pp. 263–281. Major Olędzki is mentioned in *KDZ3*, pp. 115, 158, 189–190. Mr. Pieńkowski, a noted Polish Katyn expert, believes that many of the 5,600 prisoners moved to Kozelsk 2 after 17 June 1940 may have met the same fate as Olędzki, and that this issue is still to be resolved (e-mail letter from T. Pieńkowski to A. M. Cienciala, 3 May 2006). On Leon Kozłowski, see Maciej Kozłowski, *Sprawa Premiera Leona Kozłowskiego: Zdrajca czy Ofiara* [The Case of Premier Leon Kozłowski: Traitor or Victim?] (Warsaw, 2005), pp. 94–98. Leon Kozłowski left the Polish Army in the USSR without permission and crossed the front line aiming to rejoin his family in German Poland, but was taken by German authorities to Berlin, where he died in an air raid in 1944. He was condemned by a Polish court-martial as a traitor and was viewed as such by Polish public opinion, but his nephew claims that he did not commit treason. Maciej Kozłowski obtained his uncle's file as the relative of a politically repressed person.

3. Zygmunt Berling, *Wspomnienia* [Memoirs], vol. I: *Z Łagrów do Andersa* [From the Camps to Anders] (Warsaw, 1990), p. 95; Narcyz Łopianowski, *Rozmowy z NKWD, 1940–1941* [Conversations with the NKVD, 1940–1941], ed. Andrzej Krzysztof Kunert (Warsaw, 1990), pp. 6–7.

4. Józef Czapski, *Wspomnienia Starobielskie* [Starobelsk Memories] (first published by the Department of Culture and Press, Polish 2nd Corps, Middle East, 1944; reprint, Rome, 1945), pp. 60–61; *Zbrodnia Katyńska w Świetle Dokumentów* [The Katyn Crime in the Light of Documents] (10th edition, London, 1982), pp. 80–82; *The Crime of Katyn: Facts and Documents* (London, 1965; translation of the 3rd Polish edition), pp. 96–97. See doc. 98 and note 239.

5. See Anna M. Cienciala, "General Sikorski and the Conclusion of the Polish-Soviet Agreement of 30 July 1941: A Reassessment," *Polish Review*, 41, no. 4 (1996), pp. 401–434. For documents on the negotiations, see Eugeniusz Duraczyński, *Układ Sikorski-Majski: Wybór Dokumentów* [The Sikorski-Maisky Agreement: Selected Documents] (Warsaw, 1990).

6. See Władysław Anders, *Bez Ostatniego Rozdziału: Wspomnienia z Lat*

1939–1946 [Minus the Last Chapter: Memoirs of the Years 1939–1946] (3rd edition, revised and corrected, London, 1959), p. 54; English version, *An Army in Exile: The Story of the Second Corps* (Nashville, Tenn., 1981), p. 45.

7. For Polish inquiries about the missing officers, see Anders, *Bez Ostatniego Rozdziału*, pp. 55–140; Anders, *An Army in Exile*, chaps. 5–12; also Józef Czapski, *The Inhuman Land* (London, 1951), chaps. 8–10; *Zbrodnia Katyńska*, chap. 4; *Crime of Katyn*, chap. 4; J. K. Zawodny, *Death in the Forest: The Story of the Katyn Forest Massacre* (Notre Dame, Ind., 1962), chap. 1. For a list of Polish inquiries, see the communiqué by General Marian Kukiel, London, 16 April 1943, in Stanisław Biegański et al., eds., *Documents on Polish-Soviet Relations, 1939–1945* (henceforth *DPSR*), vol. I: *1939–1942* (London, 1961), no. 306; and the Russian translation in *KD2/188*. For Ambassador Stanisław Kot's conversations with Soviet statesmen, see Natalia S. Lebedeva, "Stalin, Sikorskii, Anders i Drugie," *Mezhdunarodnaia Zhizn*, no. 1 (Moscow, 1991), pp. 128–133; for an English translation, see "Stalin, Sikorski et al.," *International Affairs*, no. 1 (Moscow, 1991), pp. 121–126; see also *KDZ3*, pp. 571–573; and *Dokumenty Vneshnei Politiki* [Documents on Foreign Policy] (henceforth *DVP*), vol. XXIV (Moscow, 2000), nos. 246, 255, 282, 283, 292, 297. For Kot's record of his conversations, see Stanisław Kot, *Listy z Rosji do Generała Sikorskiego* [Letters to General Sikorski from Russia] (London, 1956); and Kot, *Rozmowy z Kremlem* [Conversations with the Kremlin] (London, 1959); for an English translation of these two volumes, see Stanisław Kot, *Conversations with the Kremlin and Dispatches from Russia*, trans. and arranged by H. C. Stevens (London, 1963).

8. For the Russian text of the Sikorski-Stalin conversation on 3 December 1941, see *KD2/176*; for the Polish record, see Anders, *Bez Ostatniego Rozdziału*, pp. 87–101; for an English summary, see Anders, *An Army in Exile*, pp. 84–88; for an English translation of the full Polish record, see *DPSR*, vol. I, no. 159. For the resolution by the Committee for State Defense, USSR, 25 December 1941, see *KD2/177*; *KDZ3/223*, text and facsimile, pp. 511–513.

9. "Note of a Conversation between General Sikorski and Stalin during Dinner at the Kremlin, Lieutenant General Anders Taking Part," 4 December 1941, in Anders, *Bez Ostatniego Rozdziału*, pp. 101–102; for an English translation, see *DPSR*, vol. I, no. 160. No Russian record of this conversation has surfaced thus far.

10. *DVP*, vol. XXIV, no. 310; for an English translation from the Polish, see *DPSR*, vol. I, no. 161.

11. On the Curzon Line, see the introduction to Part I. On Stalin's proposal to Eden, see "First Meeting, 16 December 1941, 7 p.m.," in Oleg A. Rzheshevsky, ed., *War and Diplomacy: The Making of the Grand Alliance*, translated from the Russian by T. Sorokina (Amsterdam, 1996), no. 4, p. 17.

12. "Confidential. Additional Protocol to the Treaty," in Rzheshevsky, *War and Diplomacy*, no. 5.

13. Ibid.

14. "Notes on a Conversation between General Sikorski and Mr. Churchill at Chequers on the Problem of Polish-Soviet Relations and of Stalin's Expansionist Aims," London, 31 January 1942 (original Polish text), in Marek Kazimierz

Kamiński and Jacek Tebinka, eds., *Na Najwyższym Szczeblu: Spotkania Premierów Rzeczypospolitej Polskiej i Wielkiej Brytanii podczas II Wojny Światowej* [On the Highest Level: The Meetings of the Prime Ministers of Great Britain and the Polish Republic during World War II] (Warsaw, 1999), no. 10; for an English translation, see *DPSR*, vol. I, no. 179. For the English translation of the Polish record of the Sikorski–Stafford Cripps conversation, 26 January 1942, see *DPSR*, vol. I, no. 176. On the Litauer report of November 1939, see the introduction to Part I.

15. Sikorski-Eden conversation, 3 March 1942, in Anthony Polonsky, ed., *The Great Powers and the Polish Question, 1941–1945* (London, 1976), no. 33 (the spelling of place-names is as in the document). Sikorski read seemingly moderate ideas on Lwów into Stalin's statements to him at the banquet on 4 December 1941; see also note 12 above on the Soviet confidential protocol to the treaty in Eden-Stalin conversations.

16. Soviet note, 23 January 1942, protesting Polish Foreign Minister Edward Raczyński's interview in the 11 January 1942 *Sunday Times*, in *DPSR*, vol. I, no. 175; for the Russian text, see *Dokumenty i Materiały do Historii Stosunków Polsko-Radzieckich* [Documents and Materials for the History of Polish-Soviet Relations], vol. VII (Warsaw, 1973), no. 190. (There is a parallel Russian edition with the same title.) For Sikorski's statement to Bogomolov, see Marian Kukiel, *Generał Sikorski: Żołnierz i Mąż Stanu Polski Walczącej* [General Sikorski: Soldier and Statesman of Fighting Poland] (London, 1970), p. 192.

17. For Anders's account of Soviet food reductions for the Polish Army in Uzbekistan and the first evacuation, see his memoirs, *Bez Ostatniego Rozdziału*, esp. pp. 107–112; Anders, *An Army in Exile*, chap. 10, esp. pp. 96–98. For Molotov's record of his conversation with Churchill in London, 10 June 1942, see Rzheshevsky, *War and Diplomacy*, no. 118; on evacuating Poles from the USSR, see pp. 295–296. For the Molotov-Sikorski conversation in London of 10 June 1942, see Rzheshevsky, no. 117. Sikorski planned to pay another visit to Moscow to see Stalin, but died in a plane crash off Gibraltar on 4 July 1943.

18. For a Comintern agent's report on anti-Soviet attitudes in the Polish Army in late March 1942, see *KDZ3/234*. Anders's telegram to Stalin, 31 July 1942, is in Wojciech Materski, trans. and ed., *Armia Polska w ZSSR 1941–1942* [The Polish Army in the USSR, 1941–1942] (Warsaw, 1992), no. 12 (Russian facsimile with Polish translation). For Anders's account of his decision to move the rest of the army to Iran, including his record of his conversation with Stalin of 18 March 1942, see Anders, *Bez Ostatniego Rozdziału*, pp. 125–135; Anders, *An Army in Exile*, chap. 11.

19. For an excellent survey of Polish-Soviet relations in 1941–1943, based on published and archival Polish and Russian sources, see chaps. 4 and 5 by Wojciech Materski, in Waldemar Michowicz, ed., *Historia Dyplomacji Polskiej* [History of Polish Diplomacy], vol. V: *1939–1945* (Warsaw, 1999), pp. 211–396. For an English-language survey, see Jan Karski, *The Great Powers and Poland, 1919–1945: From Versailles to Yalta* (Lanham, Md., 1985), chap. 26.

20. Stalin's telegram to Molotov, 24 May 1942, in Rzheshevsky, *War and Diplomacy*, no. 38, p. 122, pt. 1.

21. See Natalia S. Lebedeva, "The Comintern and Poland in 1939–1943," *International Affairs*, no. 8 (Moscow, 1993), pp. 83–94.

22. Note from the People's Commissariat of Foreign Affairs to the Polish Embassy in the USSR, Kuibyshev, 16 January 1943, *Dokumenty i Materiały*, vol.VII, no. 232 (Russian text); *KDZ3/244* (Polish text); *DPSR*, vol. I, no. 285 (English text). This step followed Beria's note to Stalin of 15 January 1943 on the necessity of giving Soviet citizenship to Polish citizens in the USSR and the Politburo decision of the same day; see *KD2/184, 185; KDZ3/242, 243*.

23. For the estimates by the Polish Embassy in Kuibyshev of the total and regional numbers of Polish citizens in the USSR in April 1943, see Dariusz Baliszewski and Andrzej Krzysztof Kunert, eds., *Prawdziwa Historia Polaków: Ilustrowane Wypisy Źródłowe, 1939–1945* [The Real History of the Poles: Illustrated Selections from Primary Sources, 1939–1945], vol. 2: *1943–1944* (Warsaw, 1999), pp. 1060–1061, 1062 (map). For Beria's count, see note 22.

24. Tomas Venclova, *Aleksander Wat: Life and Art of an Iconoclast* (New Haven, 1996), pp. 147–157; for Wat's Polish-language memoirs, tape-recorded in his conversations with the Polish poet Czesław Miłosz, see Aleksander Wat, *Mój Wiek: Pamiętnik Mówiony* [My Century: An Oral Memoir] (London, 1977); and the English version, Wat, *My Century: The Odyssey of a Polish Intellectual*, ed. and trans. Richard Lourie, foreword by Czesław Miłosz (Berkeley, Calif., 1988).

25. On the Wasilewska-Stalin conversation and agreements, see Feliks Tych et al., eds., "Wspomnienia Wandy Wasilewskiej" [The Memoirs of Wanda Wasilewska], in *Archiwum Ruchu Robotniczego* [The Archive of the Workers' Movement], vol. VII (Warsaw, 1982), p. 383; more in Anna M. Cienciala, "The Activities of Polish Communists as a Source for Stalin's Policy towards Poland in the Second World War," *International History Review*, VII, no. 1 (February 1985), pp. 129–145.

26. The name of the actual execution site varies according to the language used: Kosogory (German); Koze Gory (Russian); Kozie Góry (Polish). On the choice of Katyn rather than Gnezdovo, see Rudolph-Christoph von Gersdorff, *Soldat im Untergang* [A Soldier in Defeat] (Frankfurt am Main, 1977), pp. 140–141. Von Gersdorff participated in several failed attempts to assassinate Hitler. A couple of other German military men claimed to have "discovered" Katyn; for a discussion of who first learned of the Katyn graves and when, see Adam Basak, *Historia Pewnej Mistyfikacji: Zbrodnia Katyńska przed Trybunałem Norymberskim* [The History of a Certain Mystification: The Katyn Crime before the Nuremberg Tribunal] (Wrocław, 1995), p. 37.

27. Czesław Madajczyk, *Dramat Katyński* [The Katyn Drama] (Warsaw, 1989), pp. 35–36. Madajczyk's narrative is reprinted in Russian translation in O. V. Yasnova, ed., *Katynskaia Drama* (Moscow, 1991), pp. 14–104. Yasnova's book has articles by the Russian historians of Katyn: Valentina Parsadanova, Natalia Lebedeva, Yuri Zoria, and some others, as well as selected Russian documents to which Madajczyk did not have access in 1989.

28. *The Goebbels Diaries, 1942–1943*, ed. and trans. Louis P. Lochner (New York, 1948; reprint, Westport, Conn., 1970), p. 318.

29. On Edmund Seyfried's report and his later sentencing and imprisonment in

communist Poland, also the sentences of two workers who visited Katyn, see Stanisław M. Jankowski, "Pod Specjalnym Nadzorem, przy Drzwiach Zamkniętych: Wyroki Sądowe w PRL za Ujawnienie Prawdy o Zbrodni Katyńskiej" [Under Special Surveillance, with Doors Closed: Sentences in People's Poland for Revealing the Truth about Katyn], in Marek Tarczyński, ed., *Zbrodnia Katyńska: Polskie Śledztwo* [The Crime of Katyn: The Polish Investigation], Zeszyty Katyńskie, no. 20 (Warsaw, 2005), pp. 95–135. On the first Polish delegation's accounts not leaving any doubt about the authenticity of the massacre, see *Armia Krajowa w Dokumentach, 1939–1945* [The Home Army in Documents, 1939–1945], vol. II (London, 1973), no. 416, 14 April 1943; a more detailed report is in no. 425, 21 April 1943. A report on the visit appeared in the German-controlled *Nowy Kurjer Warzawski* [New Warsaw Courier], 14 April 1943, see Baliszewski and Kunert, *Prawdziwa Historia*, vol. 2, p. 1007; see also F. Goetel's articles published in *Wiadomości Literackie* [Literary News] (London, 1949), reprinted in Aleksandra Kwiatkowska-Viatteau, ed., *Katyń: Wybór Publicystyki 1943–1988 i "Lista Katyńska"* [Katyn: Selected Publications, 1943–1988, and the "Katyn List"] (London, 1988), pp. 93–106.

30. For the German broadcast of 11 April 1943 and the Kościuszko Radio broadcast of 12 April 1943, see Baliszewski and Kunert, *Prawdziwa Historia*, vol. 2, p. 1005.

31. The radio report cited in Baliszewski and Kunert, *Prawdziwa Historia*, vol. 2, p. 1006, was on a press conference in the German Foreign Ministry, broadcast on 13 April 1943; it is different from the official radio communiqué of that day (doc. 101).

32. Anders's telegram to the Polish minister of defense, London, 15 April 1943, is in *Zbrodnia Katyńska*, pp. 86–87; and, in English, in *Crime of Katyn*, p. 103.

33. *DPSR*, vol. I, note to no. 307, p. 609; Kukiel, *Generał Sikorski*, p. 224. The decisions of 15 April were confirmed by the Council of Ministers two days later; see *Protokoły z Posiedzeń Rady Ministrów Rzeczypospolitej Polskiej* [Protocols of the Meetings of the Council of Ministers of the Polish Republic], vol. V: *Wrzesień 1942–Lipiec 1943* [September 1942–July 1943], ed. Marian Zgórniak and Wojciech Rojek with the assistance of Andzej Suchcitz (Kraków, 2001), doc. 168.

34. For Polish (Raczyński) and British (Churchill) memoranda on the Churchill-Sikorski conversation of 15 April 1943, see Kamiński and Tebinka, *Na Najwyższym Szczeblu*, no. 16, pp. 83–96. For a study of the attitudes of the British government and public opinion on Katyn in 1943, see P. M. H. Bell, *John Bull and the Bear: British Public Opinion, Foreign Policy and the Soviet Union, 1941–1945* (London, 1990), chap. 4. For a historical survey and documents, see [British] Foreign and Commonwealth Office, *Katyn: British Reactions to the Katyn Massacre, 1943–2003* (London, 2003) (henceforth *Katyn: British Reactions*).

35. For the communiqué by the Polish minister of defense, London, 16 April 1942, see *DPSR*, vol. I, no. 307; for a Russian translation, see *KD2*/188. The official Polish request to the IRC was made on 17 April; see below. For Polish inquiries to Soviet authorities about the prisoners, see note 7.

36. *Die Tagebücher von Joseph Goebbels* [The Joseph Goebbels Diaries], ed.

Elke Frölich et al., Part II: *Diktate von 1941–1945* [Dictations for 1941–1945], vol. 8, ed. Harmut Mehringer (Munich, 1993), p. 116.

37. For the cipher telegram from Major Szczęsny Choynacki, Bern, 19 April 1943, to the Presidium of the Council of Ministers, received in London, 20 April 1943, see *Armia Krajowa*, vol. II, no. 420. On the first German request of 15 April, see Zawodny, *Death in the Forest*, p. 33.

38. See Tadeusz Żeńczykowski, *Dwa Komitety, 1920–1944: Polska w Planach Lenina i Stalina* [Two Committees, 1920–1944: Poland in the Plans of Lenin and Stalin] (Paris, 1983), p. 57. This account is not confirmed by other sources.

39. "Polskie Sotrudniki Gitlera" [Hitler's Polish Collaborators], *Pravda*, 19 April 1943; see *KD2/189.*

40. The Russian word *prervats* can mean either "interrupt" or "break off"; see Stalin to Churchill, 21 April 1943, in *Stalin's Correspondence with Churchill, Attlee, Roosevelt and Truman, 1941–45* (New York, 1958), vol. I, no. 150, reprinted in Polonsky, *The Great Powers*, no. 51. An almost identical letter went from Stalin to Roosevelt.

41. For the Polish text of Sikorski's conversation with Eden of 24 April 1943, see *Protokoły z Posiedzeń Rady Ministrów*, vol. V, 27 April 1943, no. 170A. For an English translation, see *Documents on Polish-Soviet Relations* (henceforth *DPSR*), vol. II (London, 1967), Supplement 15, pp. 696–702; the Eden quotation is on p. 698. A Polish summary is in Edward Raczyński, *W Sojuszniczym Londynie: Dziennik Ambasadora Edwarda Raczyńskiego, 1939–1945* [In Allied London: The Diary of Ambassador Edward Raczynski] (2nd edition, London, 1974), p. 173; English version, Raczyński, *In Allied London* (London, 1962), p. 142.

42. For Aleksander Mniszek's record of the Molotov-Romer conversation and a facsimile of Romer's Polish-language note of 26 April 1943 to Molotov, see Baliszewski and Kunert, *Prawdziwa Historia*, vol. 2, pp. 1045–1048; for an English translation, see *DPSR*, vol. I, no. 316. For Romer's account of his mission as ambassador to the Soviet Union, see "Moja Misja Jako Ambasadora R. P. w Związku Sowieckim," in *Zeszyty Historyczne* [Historical Notebooks], vol. 30 (Paris, 1974), pp. 138–165, where he mentions the Soviet charges and his reply.

43. For Dimitrov to Finder, 27 April 1943, see *KD2/194*; for the Wasilewska speech of 28 April 1943, see *Dokumenty i Materiały*, vol. VII, no. 247; for the Polish government communiqué of 30 April 1943, see *DPSR*, vol. I, no. 321.

44. For Stalin's response, see *KD2/196* (Russian text); and *DPSR*, vol. II, no. 2 (English text).

45. For the Vyshinsky speech, see *DPSR*, vol. II, no. 7 (English text); and Baliszewski and Kunert, *Prawdziwa Historia*, vol. 2, pp. 1100–1107 (Polish text).

46. *KD2/196.*

47. On the connection between the dissolution of the Comintern and the Churchill-Roosevelt meeting, also the transfer of Comintern departments to the CC CPSU, see N. S. [Natalia Sergeevna] Lebedeva and M. M. Narinsky, eds., *Komintern i Vtoraia Mirovaia Voina* [The Comintern and the Second World War], part II: *Posle 22 Iunia 1941 r.* [After 22 June 1941] (Moscow, 1998), pp. 68–69. See also *The Diary of Georgi Dimitrov, 1933–1939*, ed. Ivo Banac (New Haven,

2003), pp. xxxvii, 217–280; *Biuletyn Informacyjny* statement of 3 June 1943, in Baliszewski and Kunert, *Prawdziwa Historia*, vol. 2, p. 1157.

48. Michał Synoradzki, Jacek Grodecki, and Wiktoria Plewak, "Katyń: Modus Operandi," *Arkadia*, 9–10 (Mikołów, June 2001); an abbreviated version was published as "Katyń: Technika Zbrodni" [Katyn: Technique of a Crime], *Gazeta Wyborcza* [Election Newspaper], 48 (Warsaw, 2003), pp. 20–21. For a discussion of the ways in which the prisoners of war may have been murdered in Katyn Forest, see the introduction to Part II.

49. The PRC Technical Commission reported 4,423 bodies exhumed; the Germans reported 4,413; the verified number of Katyn victims is 4,410 (see Part II, note 124). For a summary of the work of Dr. Robel and his staff, see Zawodny, *Death in the Forest*, pp. 59–60. For more detail, see Andrzej Rybicki, "Archiwum Robla" [Robel's Archive], in Adam Roliński and Andrzej Rybicki, eds., *Kłamstwo Katyńskie: Katalog Wystawy, 8 Kwietnia–15 Maja 2000* [The Katyn Lie: Exhibition Catalog, 8 April–15 May 2000] (Kraków, 2000), pp. 89–98; on the 2,333 names identified later, see p. 91; see also Stanisław M. Jankowski, *Czterdziestu co Godzinę* [Forty per Hour], ed. Marek Tarczyński, Zeszyty Katyńskie, no. 14 (Warsaw, [2000]), pp. 26–36. On the diaries, see the foreword by J. K. Zawodny to twenty diary texts found at Katyn, in Jan A. Stepek, ed., *Pamiętniki Znalezione w Katyniu* [Diaries Found at Katyn] (2nd expanded edition, Paris and Warsaw, 1990), pp. 7–8.

50. See Werner Beck's deposition, which can be read in *The Katyn Forest Massacre. Hearings before the Select Committee to Conduct an Investigation of the Facts, Evidence, and Circumstances of the Katyn Forest Massacre* (henceforth *Hearings*), Eighty-second Congress, 1st and 2nd sessions, 1951–1952 (Washington, D.C., 1952), part 5, p. 1517; summarized in Zawodny, *Death in the Forest*, pp. 61–64. For Mikołajczyk to Zawodny on the chest surviving at Radebeul and later in American hands, see Janusz K. Zawodny, *Katyń* (Lublin and Paris, 1989), doc. 8, p. 272; on the chest that disappeared in Kraków, see Zawodny's foreword to Stepek, *Pamiętniki Znalezione w Katyniu*, pp. 7–8.

51. Jankowski, *Czterdziestu*, pp. 26–27; Roliński and Rybicki, *Kłamstwo*, pp. 94–95.

52. Roliński and Rybicki, *Kłamstwo*, p. 95.

53. See Stanisław M. Jankowski and Adam Roliński, eds., *Inwentarz Dokumentów Katyńskich Przechowywanych w Archiwum Kurii Metropolitalnej w Krakowie* [Inventory of Katyn Documents Preserved in the Archive of the Metropolitan Curia at Kraków] (Kraków, 2002), pp. 23–29; for photographs of Dr. Robel, his assistant Jan Cholewiński, the secretary, Irma Fortner, and the Friedbergs, see the photograph section after p. 16; for a photograph of the whole staff, see Roliński and Rybicki, *Kłamstwo*, p. 92. The Metropolitan Curia, in this case, included the office and staff of Prince Adam Stefan Sapieha (1867–1951), the archbishop of the Kraków diocese, who became a cardinal in 1946.

54. Burdenko to Molotov, 22 September 1943, KD2/201 (date error; the correct date is 2 September); G. Aleksandrov to A. Shcherbakov, 22 September 1943, KD2/202; Burdenko to Molotov, 27 September 1943, Russian State Archive of

Social and Political History (henceforth RGASPI), f. 82 [Molotov Collection], op. 3, d. 1048, p. 63 (original). A. M. Cienciala would like to thank Natalia Lebedeva for making a photocopy of Burdenko's letter of 27 September 1943 to Molotov available to her. The letter has now been published in Polish translation: Natalia S. Lebedeva and Wojciech Materski et al., eds., *Katyń: Dokumenty Zbrodni* [Katyn: Documents of a Crime], vol. 4: *Echa Katynia, Kwiecień 1943–Marzec 2005* [Echoes of Katyn, April 1943–March 2005] (henceforth *KDZ4*) (Warsaw, 2006). Smirnov, a physician, became a member of the Burdenko Commission. Trainin was a law professor.

55. For the resolution to establish the Burdenko Commission, dated 12 January 1944, see *KD2/205*; in fact, the commission was created by a Politburo decision the next day. On the enclosure [*prilozhenie*] to the draft [*proekt*] of 12 January 1944, Molotov crossed out the names of Wanda Wasilewska, head of the executive board of the ZPP [Union of Polish Patriots], and one of its members, the left-wing social-ist—later communist—Bolesław Drobner; see "P[rotokol] 42/271 of 13 1 [January] 44 g. [1944]" with copies to Vyshinsky, Molotov, Beria, and [Jacob J.] Chadaev (administrator of the Sovnarkom office), in RGASPI, f. 17, op. 163, pp. 157–159 (original) *KDZ4/40*. For the official Politburo decision of 13 January 1944, see De-cision no. 42 of 13 January 1944, short entry, also in RGASPI, f. 17, op. 163, p. 67; full text, p. 244. A. M. Cienciala would like to thank Natalia Lebedeva for making Xeroxes of both these documents available to her. On the NKVD preparation of documents and witnesses, see *KD2*, pp. 430–432. On the investigation of the Katyn crime and the depositions of surviving witnesses in the early 1990s, see also I. S. Yazhborovskaia, A. Yu. Yablokov, and V. S. Parsadanova, *Katynskii Sindrom v Sovetsko-Polskikh i Rossiisko-Polskikh Otnosheniakh* [The Katyn Syndrome in Soviet-Polish and Russian-Polish Relations] (Moscow, 2001), p. 339 ff.

56. Burdenko Commission Protocol no. 1, *KD2/206*. On the Merkulov-Kruglov report, see *KD2*, pp. 430–432. The other members of the special state commission were the people's commissar of education, V. P. Potemkin; the chair of the All Slavic Committee, A. S. Gundurov; and the chair of the Executive Committee of the Red Cross and Red Half Moon Society, S. A. Kolesnikov. On Burdenko's ad-mission to Boris Olshansky, Jr., see Zawodny, *Death in the Forest*, pp. 158 and 167 n. 57. Burdenko's daughter-in-law told Yuri Zoria that when Burdenko was very sick, he admitted that the NKVD had falsified documents, including the dates of the Katyn crime; see Inessa Jażborowska, Anatolij Jabłokow, and Jurij Zoria, *Katyń: Zbrodnia Chroniona Tajemnicą Państwową* [Katyn: The Crime Protected as a State Secret] (Warsaw, 1998), p. 299. This is a more popular, Polish version of the later Russian work by Inessa S. Yazhborovskaia, Anatolii Yu. Yablokov, Valentina S. Parsadanova, titled *Katynskii Sindrom*.

57. English translation, "Report of the International Medical Commission," *Crime of Katyn*, chap. 7, pp. 126–130; see also Zawodny, *Death in the Forest*, pp. 17–18.

58. Reprinted in *Hearings*, part 3, pp. 228–309; and *Crime of Katyn*, pp. 139–171; for an analysis, see pp. 269–270; for a summary, see Zawodny, *Death in the Forest*, chap. 4. For the Russian text of the "project" (draft) of the Burdenko Com-mission report, 24 January 1944, with notes, see *KD2/215*.

59. For Article 6 of the IMT Charter and the powers of the tribunal, see "The Judgment: The Charter Provisions," in William C. Frey and Lisa A. Spar, co-directors, *The Avalon Project at Yale Law School*, http://www.yale.edu/lawweb/avalon/imt/proc/judprov.htm (modification dated 4 April 2007).

60. Rudenko had directed the rigged June 1945 Moscow trial of sixteen Polish underground leaders seized by the NKVD in Warsaw; see Andrzej Chmielarz and Andrzej Krzysztof Kunert, eds., *Proces Szesnastu: Dokumenty NKWD* [The Trial of the Sixteen: NKVD Documents], translated from Russian into Polish by Kazimierz Stembrowicz and Fryderyk Zbiniewicz (Warsaw, 1995).

61. The commission members included A. Ya. Vyshinsky, chair; Soviet Prosecutor General K. P. Gorshenin; chair, Supreme Tribunal, USSR, I. T. Golyakov; Deputy People's Commissar for Security B. Z. Kobulov; Deputy People's Commissar for Internal Affairs S. N. Kruglov; D. I. Kydryatsev; and A. N. Trainin. According to a Politburo decision of 6 September, V. S. Abakumov, head of Counterintelligence ("Smersh'"), was an additional member. This and subsequent information on the Nuremberg Trials is based on N. S. Lebedeva, "The USSR and the Nuremberg Trial," *International Affairs*, 42, no. 5–6 (Moscow, 1996), pp. 233–254.

62. See *Avalon Project*.

63. On Rudenko's demand and the deal with Nikitchenko, see Telford Taylor, *The Anatomy of the Nuremberg Trials: A Personal Memoir* (New York, 1992), p. 466 ff. General Taylor was a member of the U.S. delegation; see also *KD2*, p. 438; and Lebedeva, "The USSR and the Nuremberg Trial," p. 246 ff.

64. *KD2/222–224*.

65. See a summary account in Lebedeva, "The USSR and the Nuremberg Trial," p. 251; see also Zawodny, *Death in the Forest*, chap. 5. The transcript of the hearings on 1–2 July 1946 is in *International Military Tribunal*, vol. XVII: *Proceedings 6/25/1946–7/8/1946* (Nuremberg, 1947), pp. 274–374; and *Nuremberg War Crimes Trial Online* (Aristarchus Knowledge Industries, Seattle, Wash.).

66. Ambassador O'Malley's letters to Foreign Secretary Eden on Katyn in May 1943 and on the Burdenko Commission Report in February 1944 were first published in January 1972, in a pamphlet titled *Katyn—Despatches of Sir Owen O'Malley to the British Government* (London, 1972), with a preface by Lord Barnby, a supporter of the Polish cause, and an introduction by the American journalist Louis FitzGibbon. FitzGibbon also published them in his three books, *The Katyn Cover-Up* (London, 1972), *Unpitied and Unknown* (London, 1975), and *The Katyn Massacre* (London, 1977). See also the British publications listed in the next note.

67. For Cadogan's comment of May 1943, see FitzGibbon, *Unpitied and Unknown*, pp. 58–59. On British government reactions to Katyn in 1943, see Bell, *John Bull and the Bear*, pp. 109–127. See also Rohan D'Olier Butler, "The Katyn Massacre and Reactions of the Foreign Office. Memorandum by the Historical Adviser [10 April 1973]," in *Katyn: British Reactions*.

68. On this work, see Zawodny, *Death in the Forest*, p. xiv; and the introduction to Part II.

69. Anders, *Bez Ostatniego Rozdziału*, pp. 374–375; Anders, *An Army in Exile*, p. 297.

70. Fragment of the Skarżyński interrogation, 2 July 1945, in Madajczyk, *Dramat Katyński*, pp. 160–164. For the interrogation records of writers and critics, see Stanisław M. Jankowski and Ryszard Kotarba, *Literaci a Sprawa Katyńska—1945* [Literary People and the Katyn Case—1945] (Kraków, 2003), pp. 135–241. For the sentences meted out in People's Poland to participants in Polish delegations to Katyn in 1943, see Jankowski, "Pod Specjalnym Nadzorem," pp. 95–135.

71. Leszek Martini, probably a relative of Roman Martini, published a short note to the effect that Roman had found an NKVD document in Minsk proving Soviet guilt and had appended the document, allegedly a report from the Minsk Oblast NKVD to the Main NKVD Administration in Moscow, dated 10 June 1942; reprinted in *Tygodnik Powszechny* [The Common Weekly], no. 27 (Kraków, 1989); for the English translation, see Zawodny, *Death in the Forest*, pp. 114–115; and FitzGibbon, *Unpitied and Unknown*, pp. 440–41. It is now considered a forgery; see below. On the seduction theory, see Ferdynand Goetel, "Zachód i Katyń" [The West and Katyn], *Wiadomości* [News], 27 (London, 1951), cited in Kwiatkowska-Viatteau, *Katyń: Wybór Publicystyki*, p. 108.

72. On the two young "communists" and their names, see Zawodny, *Death in the Forest*, p. 172; Zawodny, *Katyń*, p. 141. On Słapianka and Wróblewski and the latter's escape, sentencing, and execution, see Józef Bratko, *Dlaczego Zginąłeś Prokuratorze?* [Prosecutor, Why Did You Perish?] (Kraków, 1998); a summary is in Jankowski and Kotarba, *Literaci*, p. 69 n. 282.

73. The Martini report was shown to be a fake in a series of articles published in the Polish-language press in Britain by the Polish writer Józef Mackiewicz between 1949 and 1975. Of these, the most important was titled "Tajemnica Archiwum Mińskiego NKWD" [The Secret of the Minsk NKVD Archive], published in the London weekly *Wiadomości* [News], no. 35 (London, 1975); see Józef Mackiewicz, *Katyń: Zbrodnia bez Sądu i Kary* [Katyn: A Crime without Trial and Punishment], comp. and ed. Jacek Trznadel, Zeszyty Katyńskie, no. 7 (Warsaw, 1997), pp. 421–433. A. M. Cienciala would like to thank Mr. Ludomir Garczyński-Gąssowski of Stockholm for drawing her attention to this article.

74. Lebedeva, "The USSR and the Nuremberg Trial," p. 249. The text of the Secret Protocol was also published in the *Manchester Guardian* on 30 May 1946. For photographs of Nikolai Zoria and a facsimile of Seidl's 20 May 1946 request to include the Secret Protocol of 23 August 1939 and the Friendship and Frontier Treaty of 28 September 1939 in the Hess case documents, see Jażborowska, Jabłokow, and Zoria, *Katyń: Zbrodnia Chroniona*, photograph section after p. 256; see also photographs of Nikolai Zoria and his son Yuri in Yazhborovskaia, Yablokov, and Parsadanova, *Katynskii Sindrom*, photograph section after p. 160; this section also has the map, signed by Stalin and Ribbentrop, dividing Poland as per the treaty of 28 September 1939.

75. Jażborowska, Jabłokow, and Zoria, *Katyń: Zbrodnia Chroniona*, p. 146.

76. The author of the articles in *Nowy Świat*, Ignacy Morawski, printed documents supplied by the editors of *Zbrodnia Katyńska* [Crime of Katyn], also published in 1948. A. M. Cienciala would like to thank Dr. Iwona Korga, director of the Józef Piłsudski Institute of America, New York, for the loan of the *Nowy Świat* newspaper microfilm. On Katyn in American foreign policy and public opinion, see Crister S. Garrett and Stephen A. Garrett, "Death and Politics: The Katyn For-

est Massacre and American Foreign Policy," *East European Quarterly*, 20, no. 4 (January 1987), pp. 429–446.

77. Robert Szymczak, "A Matter of Honor: Polonia and the Congressional Investigation of the Katyn Forest Massacre," *Polish American Studies*, 41, no. 1 (1984), p. 41.

78. Szymczak, "A Matter of Honor," p. 41. Epstein accepted as true the alleged Martini dossier as published in Stockholm, but Mackiewicz soon published an article showing that it was a fake; see Mackiewicz, *Katyn*, pp. 319–324.

79. *The Congressional Record*, 81st Congress, vol. 95, part 15 (1949), p. A4356, cited in Szymczak, "A Matter of Honor," p. 42.

80. Szymczak, "A Matter of Honor," p. 43.

81. Szymczak, "A Matter of Honor," p. 45.

82. Szymczak, "A Matter of Honor," p. 47.

83. Szymczak, "A Matter of Honor," p. 48. The committee members were Ray J. Madden (D-Ind.), Daniel J. Flood (D-Pa.), Foster Furcolo (D-Mass.), Thaddeus Machrowicz (D-Mich.), George A. Dondero (R-Mich.), Alvin E. O'Konski (R-Wis.), Timothy P. Sheehan (R-Ill.). Madden was chair; Roman Pucinski, a young Chicago lawyer, later a Democratic congressman, was appointed as investigator (see the obituary in *Nowy Dziennik* [New Daily] (New York), 5–6 October 2002). John J. Mitchell was named chief counsel and Barbara Brooke as secretary; see Szymczak, "A Matter of Honor," pp. 52–53.

84. There are differing accounts of what Franklin D. Roosevelt said to Rozmarek during his October 1944 visit to Chicago, but it seems that he promised to work for an "independent Poland"; see Karski, *The Great Powers and Poland*, p. 561; and Edward J. Rozek, *Allied Wartime Diplomacy: A Pattern in Poland* (New York, 1958; reprint, Boulder, Colo., 1989), p. 324 n. 178.

85. For a brief survey of the Polish Question and the policies of the Great Powers during World War II, see Anna M. Cienciala, "The View from Poland," in Arnold A. Offner and Theodore A. Wilson, eds., *Victory in Europe, 1945: From World War to Cold War* (Lawrence, Kans., 2000), pp. 47–76. (N.B. On p. 59, the bottom lines of the text state that at Tehran "Stalin's demand that Königsberg, East Prussia, go to the USSR had not been granted." In fact, it was.)

86. *KD2/225* and n. 1.

87. For the press campaign, see the Polish Party paper *Trybuna Ludu* [People's Tribune] of 1 March 1952, cited in Zawodny, *Katyń*, p. 142; and the article in the Czechoslovak Party paper *Rudé Právo* [Red Law] (Prague), 5 March 1952. A. M. Cienciala would like to thank Professor Igor Lukes, Boston University, for a photocopy of the latter. Also, a book titled *Prawda o Katyniu* [The Truth about Katyn] (Warsaw, 1952), written by a certain Bolesław Wójcicki (probably a pseudonym), touted the Moscow line, attacked the United States, and included photographs of alleged American war crimes in Korea; see Zawodny, *Death in the Forest*, pp. 173–175.

88. Cited in Szymczak, "A Matter of Honor," pp. 58–59. "Soviet's" is in the original text.

89. On Colonel Van Vliet's missing May 1945 report and his testimony before the congressional committee, see Zawodny, *Death in the Forest*, pp. 179–80; and *Hearings*, part 7, p. 2294. Van Vliet's second report, dictated later, was published

in fall 1950; see also the record of Zawodny's interview with Van Vliet in December 1988 (in Polish), in Zawodny, *Katyń*, no. 4, pp. 184–195. On Van Vliet, Szymanski, and Earle, see Garrett and Garrett, "Death and Politics," pp. 438–439 (Szymanski is misspelled as Syzmanski); and Zawodny, *Death in the Forest*, pp. 178–183. On U.S. government wartime censorship of information on Katyn in a Polish-language radio station see Zawodny, *Death in the Forest*, pp. 183–184.

90. Szymczak, "A Matter of Honor," p. 63.

91. Allen Paul, *Katyn: Stalin's Massacre and the Seeds of Polish Resurrection* (Annapolis, Md., 1991).

92. Sergei N. Khrushchev, *Nikita Khrushchev and the Creation of a Superpower* (University Park, Pa., 2000), pp. 165–166. It is worth noting Serov's statement that the Katyn massacre was carried out by "Belorussian Chekists" (the NKVD), which confirms Ivan Krivozertsev's statement that the executioners came from Minsk (see the introduction to Part II).

93. On Khrushchev's alleged Katyn proposal and Gomułka's refusal, see P. Kostikov and B. Roliński, *Widziane z Kremla: Moskwa-Warszawa: Gra o Polskę* [Seen from the Kremlin: Moscow-Warsaw: The Play for Poland] (Warsaw, 1992), p. 58; for a summary, see Yazhborovskaia, Yablokov, and Parsadanova, *Katynskii Sindrom*, pp. 203–204. The Polish journalist Bohdan Roliński recorded his friend Pyotr Kuzmich Kostikov's oral memoirs in Moscow in 1992. Kostikov, educated as a historian, worked in the Polish Section of the Central Committee's Department of Relations with Socialist Countries, 1968–1981, and was its head for many years.

94. On Shelepin's statements in 1992, see notes 328–333. It is known that the files of the Starobelsk prisoners were destroyed in 1940 (docs. 87, 88), but perhaps copies of some were kept in Moscow. On the different number of these files given in NKVD documents, see Bolesław Woszczyński, "Dokumentacja Katyńska: Stan—Potrzeby—Możliwości Uzupełnienia" [The Katyn Documentation: Present Status—Needs—Possibilities of Completing It], in Marek Tarczyński, ed., *Zbrodnia Katyńska po 60 Latach: Polityka, Nauka, Moralność* [The Katyn Crime 60 Years Later: Politics, Learning, Morality], Zeszyty Katyńskie, no. 12 (Warsaw, 2000), p. 5.

95. *KD2/227*, n. 2.

96. For the Russian text, see N. S. Lebedeva "60 Lat Fałszowania i Zatajania Historii Zbrodni Katyńskiej" [60 Years of Falsifying and Concealing the History of the Katyn Crime], in Tarczyński, *Zbrodnia Katyńska po 60 Latach*, p. 113. For the original monuments and inscriptions, see Zawodny, *Katyń*, following p. 142 and photograph facing p. 144; for the Polish inscription seen in 1976, see Zdzisław Jagodziński, "Łże Pomnik Katyński" [The Katyn Memorial Lies], *Tydzień Polski* [Polish Week], 19 (London, 1976), reprinted in Kwiatkowska-Viatteau, *Katyń: Wybór Publicystyki*, p. 144.

97. Bob Woodward and Carl Bernstein, *The Final Days* (New York, 1976), p. 227. A. M. Cienciala wishes to thank Professor Igor Lukes of Boston University for drawing this to her attention. A photograph in *Memoirs: Mikhail Gorbachev* (New York, 1996), in the photo gallery after p. 386, also confuses Katyn with the Belorussian village of Khatyn.

98. For the Politburo resolution of 15 April 1971, see *KD2/228*. The film title came from a Churchill comment on a Foreign Office report on Katyn in 1943. For

a similar comment by Churchill to Eden, 30 January 1944, see Martin Gilbert, *Winston S. Churchill*, vol. VII: *Road to Victory, 1941–1945* (Boston, 1986), p. 665.

99. Lord Hankey, House of Lords Debate on Katyn, 1971, cited in Butler, "The Katyn Massacre . . . Memorandum," par. 64, in *Katyn: British Reactions*. Hankey referred to the different execution dates on the documents as given by the IMC in April 1943 and the Burdenko Commission in January 1944.

100. The chairman of the Katyn Memorial Fund was Lord Barnby; the deputy chairmen were Lord St. Oswald and members of Parliament Airey Neave and Toby Jessel, with Louis FitzGibbon as honorary secretary. Another prominent member was George Brown, a former foreign secretary. The patrons were Lords Salisbury and Arran; Sir Roy Bucher, chairman of the Anglo-Polish Association; Sir John Sinclair; and Winston Churchill, grandson of Winston S. Churchill. More members joined the KMF later. The Polish contingent included Major Eugeniusz Lubomirski and Dr. Stefan Zamoyski; see Stanisław Grocholski, ed., *O Prawdę i Sprawiedliwość* [For Truth and Justice] (London, 1977), p. 31. A. M. Cienciala would like to thank a prominent British historian of Poland, Adam Zamoyski, for information on some of the KMF members, who included his father, Dr. Stefan Zamoyski.

101. For the Politburo resolution of 8 September 1972 on the protest to the British ambassador, Moscow, see *KD2/229*; Sir John Killick's report, 13 September 1972, in *Katyn: British Reactions*, p. ix and note 21. For the comment on the KMF monument project, see *Katyn: British Reactions*, pp. ix–x.

102. *Katyn: British Reactions*, p. x.

103. On the proposal to place the Katyn memorial in St. Luke's Cemetery, Chelsea, and the hearing before the Church of England Diocesan Consistory Court, see FitzGibbon, *Unpitied and Unknown*, chap. 6.

104. Statement by the Kensington-Chelsea Borough Council on direct Soviet pressure, cited in John Ezard, "Storm over the Katyn Memorial," *The Guardian* (London), 26 September 1976.

105. Shinwell, born into a Jewish family in Warsaw, was British minister for defense in 1950–1951 and helped organize the Katyn debate in the House of Lords in 1971. For a description of the ceremony and the quotation from Shinwell, see *The Guardian*, 26 September 1976. For more details and photographs, also Polish translations from the British press, see Grocholski, *O Prawdę i Sprawiedliwość*.

106. On the arrest and trial of the four Confederation of Independent Poland leaders, Leszek Moczulski, Tadeusz Stański, Romuald Szeremietiew, and Tadeusz Jańdziszak, see Tadeusz Stański, "Pierwszy Proces Polityczny a Sprawa Katyńska" [The First Political Trial and the Katyn Question], in Stefan Melak and Wacław Karłowicz, eds., *W 60 Rocznicę Ujawnienia Zbrodni Katyńskiej* [On the 60th Anniversary of the Disclosure of the Katyn Crime] (Warsaw, 2003), pp. 41–46; for photographs of the Katyn crosses put up at Old Powązki Cemetery and Katyn Committee activists, see the photograph section at the end of the text.

107. See Jaruzelski's foreword to Jarema Maciszewski, *Wydrzeć Prawdę* [To Tear Out the Truth] (Warsaw, 1992), pp. 8–10. It should be noted that prominent non-party members of the Rada Konsultacyjna [Consultative Council] had urged Jaruzelski to make an official approach on Katyn to the highest Soviet authorities. (After proclaiming martial law on 13 December 1981, Jaruzelski had established the council as a body to be in contact with Polish public opinion.) These non-party

members, especially the lawyer Władysław Siła-Nowicki, proposed setting up a Polish-Soviet historical commission with access to Soviet archives to study the Katyn massacre; see Robert Jarocki, *Opowieść o Aleksandrze Gieysztorze* [The Story of Alexander Gieysztor] (Warsaw, 2001), p. 269. Gieysztor, an internationally known Polish medievalist, a moving spirit for the restoration of the Royal Castle, Warsaw, and then its resident director, was also a prominent non-party member of the Consultative Council.

108. See Anatoly Chernayev, *My Six Years with Gorbachev*, trans. and ed. Robert D. English and Elizabeth Tucker (University Park, Pa., 1993), pp. 129–130. Viktor M. Chebrikov was a Politburo member and deputy head of the KGB; Anatoli Lukianov was a Politburo member and first vice president of the Supreme Soviet; for V. Boldin, see Biographical Sketches. The historian Jarema Maciszewski headed the Polish group in the Joint Commission of Soviet-Polish Party Historians, and Gorbachev mentions its establishment on Jaruzelski's initiative; see *Memoirs: Mikhail Gorbachev*, p. 480. On the Soviet group of party historians and their dependence on Politburo guidance, see Jażborowska, Jabłokow, and Zoria, *Katyń: Zbrodnia Chroniona*, chaps. 2, 4, and the photograph section after p. 256; see also Yazhborovskaia, Yablokov, and Parsadanova, *Katynskii Sindrom*, after p. 160.

109. Politburo decision, 5 May 1988, *KD2/232*. Here, the Politburo changed the Burdenko Commission's claim that the Nazis had murdered the Soviet POWs who had worked on building military objects for them in the Smolensk area into the claim that they had murdered the POWs who dug up and exhumed the corpses of Polish officers at Katyn. There is no evidence to substantiate this claim.

110. *BBC Summary of World Broadcasts*, SU/0166 A2/1 (1 June 1988), A: International Affairs; 2: Eastern Europe.

111. Maciszewski, *Wydrzeć Prawdę*, p. 97; the author gives the Polish side of the story, while the chairman of the Soviet group, Professor Georgy Lukich Smirnov, gives his in *Uroki Minuvshevo* [Lessons of the Past] (Moscow, 1997). For another account of the Soviet group and its problems, see Yazhborovskaia, Yablokov, and Parsadanova, *Katynskii Sindrom*, chap. 4; also Jażborowska, Jabłokow, and Zoria, *Katyń: Zbrodnia Chroniona*, chap. 2. Yazhborovskaia was a member of the Soviet group.

112. British Embassy, Warsaw, to EED (East European Department), Foreign and Commonwealth Office, 10 March 1989, in *Katyn: British Reactions*, pp. xxiii–xxiv and n. 96.

113. *Polityka*, 33/1685 (1989), pp. 13–14. For the full text of the Polish historians' expert assessment of the Burdenko Commission report, see Jarema Maciszewski, comp. and ed., *Zbrodnia Katyńska: Z Prac Polskiej Części Wspólnej Komisji Partyjnych Historyków Polski i ZSRR* [The Crime of Katyn: From the Work of the Polish Part of the Joint Commission of Soviet-Polish Party Historians] (Warsaw, 1990; offset); see the Russian text in Yasnova, *Katynskaia Drama*, pp. 179–201.

114. For reports on these events from the British Embassies in Warsaw and Moscow, see *Katyn: British Reactions*, p. xxiv and nn. 95–98.

115. Jack F. Matlock, Jr., *Autopsy of an Empire* (New York, 1995), pp. 285–286. The author misdates the article on Katyn that he cites from *Moscow News* with evidence pointing clearly to Stalin's guilt, dating it in 1989; it was published

on 25 March 1990; see Lebedeva interview, note 119. Zbigniew Brzezinski added a footnote to the account of his trip to Katyn in 1989 in an e-mail of 7 May 2007 directed to Yale University Press: "When I arrived in Smolensk, the local party secretary greeted me ceremoniously (having been instructed to do so by the Kremlin) and presented me with a wreath which I could then lay at the foot of the monument to the victims in Katyn. During the drive from Smolensk to Katyn I noticed that the wreath had an inscription on it to the effect that it was in honor of 'Polish victims of Hitlerite fascism.' I then removed that ribbon and attached to the wreath a simple sheet of paper on which I wrote in large capital letters, "In memory of the Polish officers murdered by Stalin and the NKVD." The party secretary was absolutely appalled when he noticed what I had done, but he could not object. Moreover, my remarks to Moscow's television about the need for Russian-Polish reconciliation somewhat mollified him, and by the evening it became clear that the official permission for me to visit Katyn was part of a carefully orchestrated effort, undertaken by the Kremlin, to prepare the Russian public for the eventual revelation of Soviet responsibility."

116. Natalia [S.] Lebedeva, *Katyn: Prestuplenie Protiv Chelovechestva* [Katyn: A Crime against Humanity] (Moscow, 1994; 2nd edition, 1996), pp. 3–8; or the Polish translation, Natalia Lebiediewa, *Katyń: Zbrodnia Przeciw Ludzkości*, trans. Kazimierz Bidakowski (Warsaw, 1998), pp. 15–20. Abarinov says that Lukin's letter, addressed to Minister of Internal Affairs Aleksandr Vlasov was forwarded to him (Abarinov), and that Lukin, a resident of Kalinin/Tver, had appealed to Vlasov to help historians clear up the Katyn issue; see Vladimir Abarinov, *The Murderers of Katyn*, with a foreword and chronology by Iwo Cyprian Pogonowski (New York, 1993), p. 19. This is a translation of the Russian original, *Katynskii Labirint* [Katyn Labyrinth] (Moscow, 1991).

117. Yuri Zoria told his research story in Jażborowska, Jabłokow, and Zoria, *Katyń: Zbrodnia Chroniona*, chap. 3; for Aleksandr Yakovlev's information, see his foreword to Natalia S. Lebedeva and Wojciech Materski et al., eds., *Katyn: Plenniki Neobiavlennoi Voiny* [Katyn: Prisoners of an Undeclared War] (henceforth *KD1*), in the series *Rossiia, XX Vek: Dokumenty* [Russia, the Twentieth Century: Documents] (Moscow, 1997), p. 6; on Lebedeva's archival research, see her *Katyn: Prestuplenie*, p. 7, or her *Katyń: Zbrodnia Przeciw*, p. 19. Articles on Katyn by Parsadanova and Zoria appeared in May–June 1990 in *Novaia i Noveishaia Istoriia* [Modern and Recent History] and the *Voenno-Istoricheskii Zhurnal* [Military History Journal], respectively.

118. Jaruzelski's statement is in the preface he wrote for Maciszewski, *Wydrzeć Prawdę*, p. 12. See also the Yeltsin letter to Jarulzelski, p. 152f.

119. Lebedeva claims that her interview forced the Politburo to reconsider its decision; see *KD2/234*, p. 580, note 1. On the "explosion" and her departure for London, see Lebedeva, "60 Lat Fałszowania," p. 120. On the Kharkov Prosecutor's Office opening a criminal investigation of the mass graves on 22 March 1990, see Yazhborovskaia, Yablokov, and Parsadanova, *Katynskii Sindrom*, p. 306.

120. See the photograph of President Gorbachev handing two file boxes with NKVD lists of victims from the three camps to President Jaruzelski on 13 April 1990 in *New York Times*, 14 April 1990; also in Yazhborovskaia, Yablokov, and Parsadanova, *Katinskii Sindrom*, photo gallery after p. 160.

121. Trubin to Gorbachev, 17 May 1991, in *Katyń: Dokumenty Ludobójstwa* (henceforth *KDL*), trans. and ed. Wojciech Materski (Warsaw, 1992), no. 40; or see the English edition, Wojciech Materski, ed., *Katyń: Documents of Genocide* (henceforth *KDG*) [English edition of *KDL* by Ryszard Żelichowski], trans. Jan Kolbowski and Mark Canning (Warsaw, 1993), no. 26. For the Soprunenko and Tokarev depositions, see the introduction to Part II.

122. Aleksandr N. Yakovlev, *KD1*, p. 6; Yakovlev interview, in Michael Dobbs, *Down with Big Brother: The Fall of the Soviet Empire* (New York, 1996), pp. 447–448.

123. *Memoirs: Mikhail Gorbachev*, p. 481.

124. Valery I. Boldin, *Krushenie Pedestalu: Shtrikhi k Portretu M. S. Gorbachova* [The Crumbling of the Pedestal: Sketches for a Portrait of M. S. Gorbachev] (Moscow, 1995), pp. 257–258. In the English-language version, *Ten Years That Shook the World: The Gorbachev Era as Witnessed by His Chief of Staff*, trans. Evelyn Rossiter (New York, 1994), Boldin does not mention Katyn.

125. *Memoirs: Mikhail Gorbachev*, p. 481. For the record of Boldin's opening of the Katyn file on 18 April 1989, see Dmitri Volkogonov, *Autopsy for an Empire*, trans. and ed. Harold Shukman (New York, 1998), p. 528.

126. Volkogonov, *Autopsy for an Empire*, p. 528. According to another source, Volkogonov, together with other commission members, "discovered" "Secret Packet no. 1" with the Katyn documents on 24 September 1992 and reported this to Yeltsin, who decided to send copies to Wałęsa, the Constitutional Tribunal, and the Prosecutor General's Office and to publish it for the general public to see; see "Sekrety Paketa No. 1" [Secrets of Packet No. 1], an interview with the Director of the Presidential Archive, A. V. Korotkov, in *Novoe Vremia* [New Times], no. 39 (1994), p. 38, cited in Jażborowska, Jabłokow, and Zoria, *Katyń: Zbrodnia Chroniona*, p. 309.

127. Wałęsa to Yeltsin, 13 January 1992, Archiwum Urzędu Prezydenta R. P. [Archive of the President of the Polish Republic], sygnatura [reference no.] 87/11, t. 4, pp. 26–27; *KDZ4*/130. A. M. Cienciala would like to thank Professor Materski for making a copy of the letter available to her, and Dr. Daria Nałęcz, former director of the Head Office of State Archives in Poland.

128. Celestine Bohlen, "Russian Files Show Stalin Ordered Massacre of 20,000 Poles in 1940," *New York Times*, 16 October 1992, pp. A 5–6; for Gorbachev's denial, see p. 1; see also Andrew Nagorski, "At Last, a Victory for the Truth: Moscow Admits to an Infamous Massacre," *Newsweek*, 26 October 1992, p. 41. For the text of the ITAR-TASS Agency report of 14 October 1992 and Gorbachev's comment, see Vera Toltz, "The Katyn Documents and the CPSU Hearings," *Radio Free Europe/Radio Liberty Research Reports*, vol. 1, no. 44 (Munich, 1992), pp. 27–35.

129. Wałęsa to Yeltsin, 28 October 1992, Archiwum Urzędu Prezydenta R. P., sygn. 87/11, GP 049–206–92; A. M. Cienciala is grateful to Professor Materski for a copy of the letter and to Dr. Daria Nałęcz for the location, reference number, and permission to cite it.

130. For a personal account of the unveiling of the Polish cemetery in the wooded park near Piatikhatki, near Kharkov, see Maria Pawulska-Rasiej, "Cmen-

tarz w Charkowie," *Przegląd Polski* [Polish Review] (New York), 6 October 2000, pp. 8–9. The author's father, Captain Stanisław Pawulski, a prisoner of war in Starobelsk, was shot in the NKVD Kharkov jail in spring 1940. For the stories of this family and two others, see Paul, *Katyn: Stalin's Massacre*. For a report on the Mednoe ceremony, see "Stalin's Polish Victims Mourned," *BBC News*, 3 September 2002, http://news.bbc.co.uk/2/hi/europe/908253.stm. For Kwaśniewski's message to the participants of the Mednoe ceremony and Buzek's speech of 2 September 2002, see *KD2/240*, and n. 2; for Rushailo's speech at Mednoe 2 September, see *KD2/241*; *KDZ4/141, 144*.

131. Memorial statement on cataloguing 800 Stalinist execution sites and Polish remains, *Nowy Dziennik* [New Daily] (New York), 17–18 June 2006. For more on the Memorial society see note 407. On the first reports on the Polish exhumations at Bykovnia [Bykownia] and Professor Wojciech Materski's view that Poles named in the Ukrainian list might be buried there, see reports and interview with Materski in *Gazeta Wyborcza* (Warsaw), 8 August 2006. For an account of previous Ukrainian exhumations at the site and comments on Polish remains, see the interview with the Ukrainian military prosecutor Andrij Amons, who conducted an investigation there in the 1990s, in *Gazeta Wyborcza*, 14 August 2006.

132. For the statement by Polish President Aleksander Kwaśniewski, then visiting Moscow, on the discontinuation of the Katyn investigation by the Russian Military Prosecutor's Office, see *Nowy Dziennik*, 29 September 2004. For the statement by Aleksandr Savenkov, 11 March 2005, on closing the Katyn investigation, see *Gazeta Wyborcza*, 11 March 2005. For comments on the Russian military prosecutor's statement, see *Gazeta Wyborcza*, 3 March 2006; *Nowy Dziennik*, 4–5 March 2006.

133. The two other commission members were Professor Boris N. Topornin and Dr. Lev V. Belayev. On Yablokov's motion of 13 June 1994, see Yazhborovskaia, Yablokov, and Parsadanova, *Katynskii Sindrom*, p. 400; Jażborowska, Jabłokow, and Zoria, *Katyń: Zbrodnia Chroniona*, pp. 329–330. For the report of the Russian Commission of Experts, 2 August 1993, see *Katynskii Sindrom*, pp. 446–494 (Russian text); Jażborowska, Jabłokow, and Zoria, *Katyń: Zbrodnia Chroniona*, pp. 358–422 (Polish text).

134. For a photograph of Yeltsin laying a wreath at the Katyn monument, Warsaw, see the photograph section in *Katynskii Sindrom*. For a 1994 interview with Yazhborovskaia and Parsadanova, see "Zakoncheno Li Katynskoe Delo?" [Has the Katyn Case Been Concluded?], in *Novoe Vremia* [New Times], 39 (Moscow, 1994), p. 38.

135. For the Polish text of the press conference during President Putin's visit to Poland, 16 January 2002, see the Polish press of 17 January and the internet site for the President of Poland, www.prezydent.pl.

136. Jażborowska, Jabłokow, and Zoria, *Katyń: Zbrodnia Chroniona*, p. 334.

137. Ibid., p. 335; Yazhborovskaia, Yablokov, and Parsadanova, *Katynskii Sindrom*, pp. 423–424.

138. For works claiming that the Burdenko Commission report is true and the published documents on Russian guilt are fakes, see Iuri Mukhin, *Katynskii Detektiv* [Katyn Detective] (Moscow, 1995); and Mukhin, *Antirossiiskaia Podlost:*

Nauchno-Istoricheskii Analiz [An Anti-Russian Dirty Trick: A Scientific-Historical Analysis] (Moscow, 2003). A demonstration in support of the Burdenko Commission report by a group calling itself The Army of the People's Will took place at Ostankino (television studios), Moscow, on 13 April 2006, the anniversary of both the German announcement of 1943 and the TASS communiqué of 1990; see the Polish-language report at http://rawelin.com/forum/viewtopic.php?t=559. A. M. Cienciala would like to thank Mr. Wacław Godziemba-Maliszewski for sending her this report.

139. On reconciling the names of Polish officers shot at Katyn on the German and Russian lists, see Aleksandr Pamiatnykh, "O Identyfikacji Nazwisk Polskich Oficerów Rozstrzelanych w Katyniu" [On the Identification of the Last Names of Polish Officers Shot at Katyn], in Tarczyński, *Zbrodnia Katyńska: Polskie Śledztwo*, pp. 136–149. On the alleged Polish murder of Soviet prisoners of war, 1920, see Irina Mikhutina, "Ne 20 Tysiachy, a Gorazdo Bolshe" [Not Twenty Thousand, But Much More], *Pravda*, 2 June 1994.

140. See Mikhail I. Meltiukhov, "Sovetsko-Polskaia Voina" [The Soviet-Polish War], in B. Lozovskii, comp., *Blitzkrig v Evrope 1939–1941: Polsha* [Blitzkrieg in Europe, 1939–1941: Poland] (Moscow, 2003), p. 375.

141. For the deaths of Soviet POWs according to Polish records, see Zbigniew Karpus, *Jeńcy i Internowani Rosyjscy i Ukraińscy w Polsce w Latach 1918–1924* [Russian and Ukrainian Prisoners of War and Internees in Poland in the Years 1918–1924] (Toruń, 1991), pp. 50, 92–93, and 108. For reports on the bad living conditions of Soviet POWs in Polish camps in 1920, see *Polsko-Sovietskaia Voina 1919–1920: (Ranee ne Opublikowannye Dokumenty i Materiały)* [The Polish-Soviet War, 1919–1920: (Documents and Materials Not Published Earlier)], ed. I. I. Kostiushko and M. N. Chernykh, with the participation of V. N. Savchenko (Moscow, 1994), part II, nos. 160, 184, 189, 210, 218. According to Polish records, out of 51,351 Polish POWs held in Soviet Russia, only 26,440 returned home; see Stanisław Alexandrowicz, Zbigniew Karpus, and Waldemar Rezmer, eds., *Zwycięzcy za Drutami: Jeńcy Polscy w Niewoli (1919–1920): Dokumenty i Materiały* [The Victors Behind Barbed Wire: Polish Prisoners in Captivity (1919–1920): Documents and Materials] (Toruń, 1995), p. viii. For recent Polish and Russian estimates, which are close, see Vladimir P. Kozlov and Daria Nałęcz, eds., *Krasnoarmeetsy w Polskim Plenu v 1919–1921. Sbornik Dokumentov i Materialov* [Red Army Men in Polish Captivity, 1919–1921. Collected Documents and Materials] (Moscow, 2004).

142. Under pressure from the Katyn Families Association, Professor Leon Kieres, then head of the IPN, announced on 30 November 2004 that the institute would launch its own investigation of the 1940 massacres of Polish POWs; see the interview with Kieres in *Rzeczpospolita* [The Republic] (Warsaw), 12 December 2004. The head of the Russian Main Military Prosecutor's Office, however, said in his statement of 11 March 2005 on the closing of the Russian investigation that of the 183 volumes of collected material, 116 fell under the secrecy clause; 67 volumes were open to the public, but his office would not agree to the making of verified copies; see *Gazeta Wyborcza*, 11 March 2005. For an overview of the Polish investigation as of 2005, see the account of the Polish prosecutor, Małgorzata

Kuźniar-Plota, "Informacja o Stanie Śledztwa w Sprawie Zbrodni Katyńskiej" [Information on the Status of the Investigation of the Katyn Crime], in Tarczyński, *Zbrodnia Katyńska: Polskie Śledztwo*, pp. 48–57. For the statement by President Lech Kaczyński, see *EUobserver* (Brussels), 20 July 2006. A. M. Cienciala would like to thank Mr. Wacław Godziemba-Maliszewski for making this item available to her.

143. See doc. 84; and Part II, note 148.

144. The 5th Department of GUGB [Main State Security Administration] was Intelligence.

145. The German Embassy in Moscow interceded for some Poles from German Poland, also for Poles whose release was requested by Italian dignitaries, for example, the artist Józef Czapski. In early August 2005, the Polish press reported the existence of a special collection in the German Foreign Ministry archives titled "Polish Prisoners of War, 1939–1941." It contains letters from POW relatives to the ministry appealing for action to secure their release on the basis of German descent or profession and German-Soviet correspondence on this subject; see Wojciech Czuchnowski, "Nieznane Akta Katyńskie Znaleziono w Niemczech" [Unknown Katyn Documents Found in Germany], *Gazeta Wyborcza*, 2 August 2005.

146. These were ethnic Germans, citizens of prewar Poland.

147. These were likely informers or potential informers.

148. "Others" meant those not included in the POW categories listed in the Politburo decision of 5 March 1940: rank-and-file soldiers, NCOs, cadets, members of semi-military youth organizations, and civilians. Quite a few of them were agents and informers; see *KD2/92*, n. 1.

149. See Lebedeva and Materski et al., eds., *Katyń: Dokumenty Zbrodni* [Katyn: Documents of a Crime], vol. 2: *Zagłada, Marzec–Czerwiec 1940* [Extermination, March–June 1940] (henceforth, *KDZ2*) (Warsaw, 1998), Aneks [Annex] I/1, n. 1. In August ten prisoners were sent to Moscow and later handed over to the Germans. In early September the camp held 386 prisoners, of whom 306 were Poles, with Jews, Belorussians, Germans, Russians, and Lithuanians making up the rest; see *KD2/103*, n. 1; *KDZ3/2*, p. 55 n.

150. Yunaks were those in the paramilitary youth service.

151. See Soprunenko and Makliarsky's directive to the Starobelsk commander, Berezhkov, 13 June 1940, *KD2/99*, and 15 June, *KDZ2/237*. The protocol of 19 June recorded the destruction of incoming and outgoing POW correspondence for Starobelsk, as well as 105 POW photographs, and the washing out of the emulsion on 4,398 photographic plates; see *KD2/99*, n. 1; *KDZ2/241*. Presumably, the correspondence destroyed on 23 July had arrived after 19 June.

152. On 3 September 1940, Berezhkov had sent an inquiry (No. 10/8) to the NKVD UPV asking what to do with materials left in the Starobelsk camp's Special Section after the dispatch of the POWs. He stated that these materials contained 4,031 personal POW files, "operational service" special files on the "contingent" and the guard unit, the card file on the prisoners, and many other materials. Handwritten note by Soprunenko: "Com. Makliarsky! Issue an urgent order that everything concerning the prisoners of war is to be burned. Call a commission." See *KD2/121*, n. 1; *KDZ3/43*, n. 1.

153. These were free Soviet workers hired to work in the camp.

154. The dead prisoners' documentation was burned on 25 October 1940; see *KDZ3/69.*

155. For biographical data on Bober, Domoń, and Lis, see Biographical Sketches.

156. The notion of a Poland stretching from the Baltic to the Black Sea—as Poland-Lithuania did in 1569 (see Maps and Aerial Photographs, map 1)—was very popular among nationalistic young Poles in the prewar period. It was particularly offensive to Russians and Ukrainians, and Soviet propaganda attributed it to the Polish government-in-exile, which did not support it.

157. For a report on this incident, see *KD2/112; KDZ3/25.*

158. Stalin's *Short Course on the History of the Communist Party of the Soviet Union* (Russian edition, Moscow, 1938; English edition, New York, 1939) was the textbook for these lectures.

159. For Wołkowicki's letter of 6 September 1940, requesting that prisoners be allowed to write and receive letters, see *KD2/118; KDZ3/40.* In another letter of 26 September 1940, Wołkowicki requested warm winter clothes for the prisoners and a monthly cash allowance for personal purchases. Above all, he said, prisoners worried about their families, so the NKVD should issue instructions on aid for them and inform the POWS that this was done; see *KD2/122; KDZ3/49,* facsimile, p. 148.

160. Soprunenko wrote Merkulov on 28 September 1940 proposing one letter a month for prisoners in Griazovets, Kozelsk, Suzdal, Rovno, Yukhnov, and the Northern Railway camps. He also suggested concealing the location of the camps by using a Moscow post office box address and having the correspondence go through the UPV; see *KD2/123.* Merkulov must have agreed, for Soprunenko sent a telegram the same day to Vasily Volkov, commandant of Griazovets camp, saying that the prisoner correspondence issue had been settled and that he would send instructions by mail, see *KD2/123,* n. 1; *KDZ3/51.*

161. In mid-October, Merkulov wrote Kondakov that the proposed removal of some officers from the camp was inexpedient and that Major Lis had been sent to Moscow. At the same time, Volkov—who succeeded Khodos as camp commander—was instructed to take measures to prevent counterrevolutionary activity among the prisoners; see *KD2/124,* n. 1; *KDZ3/64.*

162. It is very likely that other NKVD personnel also received rewards, for this list includes practically none of the following: UPV workers in the three special camps; the UNKVD commanders of the three regions, Smolensk, Kharkov, and Kalinin; workers of the central NKVD apparatus present in these camps, e.g., Zarubin; and even such key figures in "clearing out" the camps as Soprunenko, Khokhlov, and Gertsovsky; see *KD2/128,* n. 1; *KDZ2/Aneks I/6,* n. 1. Some names were given without initials, which are here supplied in brackets.

163. The Russian text with Polish translation was first published in *Z Archiwów Sowieckich* [From the Soviet Archives], vol. I: *Polscy Jeńcy Wojenni w ZSSR 1939–1941* [Polish Prisoners of War in the USSR, 1939–1941], trans. and ed. Wojciech Materski (Warsaw, 1992), no. 7. Point 2 was missing here, as in the photocopy then available to the Polish editor.

164. At this time, there was only one general in Griazovets camp, Jerzy Wołkowicki. General Wacław Przeździecki, one of the officers held at the Lu-

bianka prison, Moscow, as described by Beria in this letter, was later sent to Gria-zovets. The two other generals mentioned in Beria's report, Marian Żegota-Januszajtis and Mieczysław Boruta-Spiechowicz, had been arrested in Lviv.

165. The number 18,297 is probably an accounting error; the correct number was higher. Some of these men had been interned in Lithuania and Latvia (see note 166 below). On 12 October 1940, Soprunenko reported a total of 24,804 Polish military POWs, of whom 1,098 were rank-and-file troops—see *KDZ3/57*—so the total given by Beria on 2 November was 6,507 less than Soprunenko's figure.

166. On 6 July 1940, Beria signed Directive no. 00806 on the transfer of Polish military men and police from internment in Lithuania to NKVD camps in the USSR; and on 15 August 1940 he signed Directive no. 001011 on transferring those from Latvia to NKVD camps in the USSR; see *KD2/104, 109; KDZ3/3, 21.* The officers and police transferred from Lithuania and Latvia were held in Kozelsk 2—see *KD2/142; KDZ3/127*—and Yukhnov. Many policemen were transferred later to the Ponoi labor camp in the Murmansk region to build an aero-drome. A total of almost 4,000 Polish POWs worked there for six months in ex-tremely difficult conditions; see *KD2/142,* n. 1.

167. This is a reference to NKVD Construction Site no. 1, Rovno camp, and the Sevzheldorlag [Northern Railway camp].

168. This is a reference to the Polish government-in-exile, London, with Gen-eral Władysław Sikorski as premier and commander in chief, although it was then not recognized by the USSR.

169. Polish spelling of names as in *KDZ3/74.* For biographical data on these generals, see Biographical Sketches.

170. For the attachment on members of the Berling group, see *KDZ3/74.* For biographical data on this group of officers, see Biographical Sketches.

171. See doc. 93.

172. On Czech and Slovak POWs, formerly in the Czechoslovak Legion at-tached to the Polish Army in 1939, their capture, and their later release, see Part I, doc. 14 and note 170.

173. Edvard Beneš (1884–1948); foreign minister, 1918–35; president of Czechoslovakia, 1935–1938; president of the Czechoslovak Committee, the gov-ernment-in-exile in France and then Britain, 1939–1945; president of Czechoslo-vakia, 1945–1948.

174. For General Ludvik Svoboda, see note 172.

175. This is the biographical information on members of the group in favor of close cooperation with the USSR, see *KDZ3/74.*

176. These officers had been taken from Griazovets camp to the Lubianka prison, Moscow, in October–November 1940; see *KD2/130,* n. 12. After interro-gation there (doc. 91), selected officers were taken to an isolated villa in Mala-khovka, a village with dachas for government and other officials on the eastern outskirts of Moscow. In spring 1941 the group consisted of twelve officers, led by Lieutenant Colonel Zygmunt Berling; see Stanisław Jaczyński, *Zygmunt Berling: Między Sławą a Potępieniem* [Zygmunt Berling: Between Fame and Condemna-tion] (Warsaw, 1993), pp. 92–95. For Berling's account of conversations with Be-ria and Merkulov and of the Malakhovka period generally, see Berling, *Wspom-nienia,* vol. I, chaps. 9–12. For a critical view of the Malakhovka group and

conversations at this time with high-level NKVD officers, see Łopianowski, *Rozmowy z NKWD*. The author joined the group on the orders of his superior, General Przeździecki, to report on them.

177. According to Captain Kazimierz Rosen-Zawadzki, who was with the group in Moscow that day, they were placed near the reviewing stand for the parade in Red Square so that they could see the German ambassador but could not be seen by him (A. M. Cienciala, typed notes of conversation with Rosen-Zawadzki, Warsaw, 16 June 1980). Berling confirms seeing Ambassador Schulenburg at the parade, in Berling, *Wspomnienia*, vol. I, p. 98.

178. First printed in Materski, *Polscy Jeńcy Wojenni*, no. 8.

179. These special files were of two kinds: the first contained all the resolutions made on a certain date and was accessible to a fairly wide circle of party officials; the second, which contained decisions of special importance falling into the areas of competence of the Commissariats of Internal Affairs, Foreign Affairs, Justice, Defense, and Armaments, was accessible to a much smaller number of party officials. This document belongs to the second category; see Materski, *Polscy Jeńcy Wojenni*, p. 104, n. 1.

180. An undetermined number of former Polish citizens—including perhaps as many as 200,000 Poles—were conscripted into the Red Army from western Belorussia and western Ukraine in 1939–1941.

181. This was Sikorski's compromise formula between the original Polish demand for Soviet recognition of the prewar Polish-Soviet frontier and the Soviet stand on an "ethnic Poland"—that is, recognition of the Soviet annexation of the former eastern Poland. On the negotiations, see Cienciala, "General Sikorski," pp. 401–434; and Duraczyński, *Układ Sikorski-Majski*.

182. This was an oblique reference to the British note to the Polish government of 30 July 1941, with an assurance of the nonrecognition of territorial changes in Poland since August 1939. For Maisky's protest, see Polonsky, *The Great Powers*, no. 18. On the same day, Foreign Secretary Anthony Eden stated in the House of Commons that the British note did not involve any guarantee of frontiers in Eastern Europe; see *DPSR*, vol. I, no. 108.

183. See doc. 95; and notes 185–193.

184. "Amnesty" was a face-saving term for the Soviet government's consent to release the Polish prisoners. The Politburo decided on 12 August 1941 to free all Polish military prisoners and deported citizens; see *KD2/169*; *KDZ3/197*. This document was first published in Materski, *Polscy Jeńcy Wojenni*, no. 9. The Presidium of the Supreme Soviet decreed on 12 August 1941 that all Polish citizens held on Soviet territory as POWs or on some other sufficient basis should be granted amnesty; see *KD2/168*, *KDZ3/196*. The Russian text does not include the secret protocol as in the Polish text.

185. Almost immediately after the Sikorski-Maisky agreement, the two governments agreed that the commander would be General Władysław Anders, who was freed from Lubianka prison on 4 August 1941; see Anders, *Bez Ostatniego Rozdziału*, pp. 52–54; Anders, *An Army in Exile*, pp. 44–45.

186. The Soviet side at first wanted just one Polish division; see the report on the session of 16 August 1941 in *Russkii Arkhiv. 14. Velikaia Otechestvennaia. 3 (1). SSSR i Polsha: 1941–1945* [The Russian Archive. 14. The Great Fatherland

[War]. 3 (1). The USSR and Poland: 1941–1945] (Moscow, 1994), chap. 1, no. 7; *DVP*, vol. XXIV (Moscow, 2000), no. 165; and the Polish record, *Dokumenty i Materiały*, vol. VII, no. 140; *DPSR*, vol. I, no. 113 (English translation). Three days later it was agreed that the Polish Army should consist of two divisions; see Russian text no. 2, 19 August 1941, *SSSR i Polsha*, chap. I, no. 8; and an English translation of the Polish text in *DPSR*, vol. I, no. 114. According to Protocol no. 2, NKVD Major and Red Army General Georgy S. Zhukov (not to be confused with General, later Marshal, Georgy K. Zhukov) handed General Anders a list of 1,658 Polish Army officers held in Soviet camps. On 3 November 1941 the Soviet State Defense Committee resolved that the Polish Army on Soviet territory should number 30,000 men; see *KD2/173*; *KDZ3/211*; the document was first published in English in Wojciech Materski, *Kremlin versus Poland, 1939–1945: Documents from the Soviet Archives*, English edition by Ryszard Żelichowski (Warsaw, 1996), no. 4, pp. 27–28. The number of men was increased to 96,000 after Sikorski's conversation with Stalin on 3 December 1941 (doc. 97).

187. Polish military units were formed at first in the Kuibyshev (Samara) region, central Russia.

188. Joint Polish-Soviet military draft boards were set up to interview recruits and volunteers in the camps holding Polish military personnel. However, thousands of Poles traveled to the recruiting centers on their own, a movement the NKVD tried to check, because labor was in short supply, by offering volunteers wages and accommodations to stay put. The NKVD also diverted civilians to work on collective and state farms in Kazakhstan and Uzbekistan, where many died from malnutrition and disease.

189. Later, both Anders and Sikorski insisted that the Polish Army not be sent to the front in divisions but as a unit, whereas the Soviet authorities insisted on divisions being sent as soon as they were ready.

190. The British supplied uniforms and some arms from their bases in Iran.

191. The Lend-Lease Act was passed by the U.S. Congress on 15 March 1941 for Britain. It was extended to the USSR in November of that year, and then to the Polish and other Allied governments.

192. The Soviet State Defense Committee resolution of 3 November 1941 on the Polish Army on Soviet territory included an interest-free loan of 65,000,000 rubles to the Polish government for expenditures related to the army until 1 January 1942; the 39,300,000 rubles spent on the Polish Army since 1 November 1941 was to be covered by the loan. The Polish government was to repay the loan within ten years of the end of the war; see *KD2/173*; *KDZ3/211*, first published in Materski, *Polscy Jeńcy Wojenni*, no. 12; and Materski, *Kremlin versus Poland*, no. 3. The resolution was followed by a Polish-Soviet agreement signed in Kuibyshev on 31 December 1941 for a loan of 100,000,000 rubles to assist Polish citizens in the USSR and another agreement signed there on 22 January 1942 for a loan of 300,000,000 rubles for expenditures on the formation and maintenance of the Polish Army in the USSR; see an English translation of the Polish texts in *DPSR*, vol. I, appendixes 6, 7, pp. 554–557.

193. The Russian text is in *DVP*, vol. XXIV, no. 165; the English text is in *DPSR*, vol. I, no. 112.

194. In July 1941 the Polish government-in-exile estimated the number of Pol-

ish prisoners taken by the Red Army in September 1939 to total 191,000 privates and about 9,000 officers; see "Conversation between General Sikorski and Ambassador Maisky, London, 5 July 1941," *Dokumenty i Materiały*, vol. VII, no. 129 (Russian record); *DPSR*, vol. I, no. 91 (English record by Alexander Cadogan). Polish historians now estimate the number of prisoners taken by the Red Army in 17–30 September 1939 to total 240,000–250,000 including about 10,000 army officers; see Lebedeva and Materski et al., eds., *Katyń: Dokumenty Zbrodni* [Katyn: Documents of a Crime], vol. 1: *Jeńcy Nie Wypowiedzianej Wojny* [The Prisoners of an Undeclared War] (henceforth *KDZ1*) (Warsaw, 1995), p. 18.

195. Some of these soldiers were conscripted as (new) Soviet citizens into the Red Army, while others were put to work on road construction in the new western regions of the USSR.

196. These prisoners, mostly rank and file, were transferred according to a German-Soviet exchange agreement.

197. Some German Embassy (Moscow) requests for German nationals held as Polish POWs are recorded in *DVP*, vol. XXIII, books 1 and 2 (Moscow, 1998); see *KDZ3/62*, p. 179 n.; *KDZ3/219*.

198. These were the prisoners from the three special camps murdered by the NKVD in spring 1940. According to Beria's resolution to shoot them, approved by the Politburo on 5 March 1940, they totaled 14,736 (doc. 47), but according to Aleksandr Shelepin's note to Khrushchev of 3 March 1959, they totaled 14,552 (doc. 110). The UPV report of 3 December 1941, part 5, gives the highest number of victims. The number generally accepted by historians is 14,552.

199. For the names of the thirty deceased officers, see *KDZ3/220*.

200. The printed version gives "683 men," but another version gives 1,082; *KD2/175*, p. 385, n. a; cf. *KDZ2/217*, p. 415.

201. The printed version gives 1,834; *KD2/175*, p. 425, n. a; same figure in *KDZ2/217*, p. 415.

202. This subheading is in *KD2/175*, p. 385, but not in *KDZ3/217*.

203. For published texts of this conversation, see note 8. For Sikorski's account to British Ambassador Sir Stafford Cripps, see Cripps's report, written in Moscow on 6 December 1941, in Polonsky, *The Great Powers*, no. 30. For Sikorski's account in his letter to Churchill of 17 December 1941, see *DPSR*, vol. I, no. 165.

204. See doc. 94.

205. The English translation of the Polish record reads: "I would not want that a slow realization of the agreement weaken the policy of approach and friendly coexistence between our two nations"; see *DPSR*, vol. I, no. 159, p. 232, lines 1–2.

206. In a memorandum on the Eastern Front dated 20 July 1941, Sikorski wrote that a speedy Russian defeat would deprive the Allies of the benefits of Russia tying down considerable German forces in a Russo-German war. Therefore, he advised aid to Russia by a direct Allied attack on the Germans "now"; see Roman Wapiński, *Władysław Sikorski* (Warsaw, 1978), p. 301. For Stalin's speech at the Moscow Soviet on 6 November 1941, see *DVP*, vol. XXIV, no. 271.

207. The leader of the Free French Forces, General Charles de Gaulle, persuaded the British to launch an Anglo-French expedition to take the port city of Dakar, Senegal. However, on arriving there on 22 September 1941, it met with

strong resistance by French forces loyal to Marshal Philippe Pétain and withdrew three days later.

208. Manchuria, part of northern China plus part of Inner Mongolia, had been a puppet state under Japanese occupation since 1932; its Japanese name was Manchukuo.

209. General Kazimierz Sosnkowski was the minister in the Polish government-in-exile in charge of the resistance in Poland, but he resigned to protest the lack of Soviet recognition of the prewar Polish-Soviet frontier in the Sikorski-Maisky agreement of 30 July 1941. By "sabotage assignments" Stalin probably had in mind the Polish underground in western Ukraine in 1939–1941, which was infiltrated and then destroyed by the NKVD; see the bilingual Polish-Russian documentary collection on the Polish underground there, in *Polskie Podziemie na Terenach Zachodniej Ukrainy i Zachodniej Białorusi w Latach 1939–1941 / Polskoe Podpolie na Territorii Zapadnoi Ukrainy i Zapadnoi Belorussii 1939–1941 gg.* [The Polish Underground in the Territories of Western Ukraine and Western Belorussia, 1939–1941], 3 vols., ed. Wiktor Komogorow et al. (Warsaw and Moscow, 2001–2004). There also is a Polish-Ukrainian publication on the Polish underground: *Polskie Podziemie 1939–1941 / Polske Pidpillia 1939–1941*, 3 vols., ed. Zuzanna Gajowniczek, Grzegorz Jakubowski et al. (Warsaw and Kiev, 1998–2004).

210. These Poles are unknown. The possession of radio transmitters without a permit was a crime under Soviet criminal law. People caught with them were charged with espionage.

211. Sikorski was referring to Polish military personnel and civilians freed from the camps who often traveled in unheated railway cattle cars without food to recruitment centers and to the Polish Embassy in Kuibyshev (Samara). Some arrived frozen to death, and many were starving.

212. Aid packages for Poles interned in the USSR, sent by Polish-American relief organizations to the Polish Embassy, Kuibyshev, and the Polish Red Cross in USSR, were shipped to the far eastern Russian port city of Vladivostok. After the Japanese attack on Pearl Harbor, these supplies were sent mostly through Britain to Arkhangelsk and Murmansk. For a list of various supplies (in kilograms) received between 5 December 1941 and 1 November 1942, see Beria's note to Stalin, 15 January 1943, on Polish citizens in the USSR, in *KD2/184*; *KDZ3/242*.

213. This applied particularly to Soviet forest-clearing camps. Mikhail Saltykov, deputy commissar for the Soviet Forest Industry, wrote Vasily Chernyshov on 24 September 1941 requesting that he speed up the delivery of 80,000 POWs to work in forest clearing; see *KDZ3/205*.

214. According to the Polish record, Sikorski handed Stalin a list of 4,000 officers still held in prisons and labor camps. He said the list was incomplete because it was made from memory; see Anders, *Bez Ostatniego Rozdziału*, p. 89; Anders, *An Army in Exile*, p. 85; and *DPSR*, vol. I, no. 159, p. 233.

215. See "Rules Regulating the Scope of Activities of Delegates of the Polish Embassy Drawn Up in Consultation with Representatives of the Commissariat of Foreign Affairs, Kuibyshev, 23 December 1941," *Dokumenty i Materiały*, vol. VII, no. 178 (Russian text); *DPSR*, vol. I, no. 166 (English translation of Polish text). The Polish Embassy was allowed to name about 120 delegates to find and help Poles in various parts of the USSR.

216. On this and other Polish-Soviet financial agreements, see note 192.

217. The Armia Krajowa in German Poland was to stage an uprising when the Germans were retreating. In the meantime, it conducted sabotage and limited armed actions; see the account of General Tadeusz Bór-Komorowski, AK commander in chief, 1943–1944, in his *Secret Army* (New York, 1950); and, in Polish, his *Armia Podziemna* (London, 1950; 5th edition, 1985); see also the book by the head of civilian resistance and the last government delegate in Poland, Stefan Korboński: *The Polish Underground: A Guide to the Underground, 1939–1945*, trans. Marta Erdman (New York, 1978).

218. Poles were deported to forced labor in Germany. Poles had worked in Westphalia and the Ruhr since the second half of the nineteenth century. A doctor in the resistance in German Poland produced typhoid bacteria, but it is not known whether they led to any epidemic outbreaks in Germany.

219. By the officers' brigade, Sikorski probably meant the detached Polish Parachute Brigade formed to support the planned uprising against the Germans; see *KDZ3/221*, n. 3.

220. Polish pilots contributed significantly to the British victory over the Germans in the Battle of Britain; see Lynne Olson and Stanley Cloud, *A Question of Honor: The Kościuszko Squadron: Forgotten Heroes of World War II* (New York, 2003); and Adam Zamoyski, *The Forgotten Few: The Polish Air Force in the Second World War* (New York, 1995).

221. The Polish Carpathian Brigade, formed in Syria in 1939 from soldiers escaping west through the Balkans, was initially part of the French Army. After the fall of France, it served with the British Army. In September 1941 it was shipped from Egypt to Tobruk. The battle for Tobruk was in its first phase during Sikorski's visit to Moscow; see Steven J. Zaloga and Richard Hook, *The Polish Army, 1939–45*, Men-at-Arms Series, no. 117 (London, 1982; New York, 1996), p. 18.

222. See Michael Alfred Peszke, *Poland's Navy, 1918–1945* (New York, 1999).

223. Thirty-three degrees below zero Celsius equals minus 25 degrees Fahrenheit. The Polish Army headquarters were located in Buzuluk, about 150 miles southeast of Kuibyshev. The other areas of concentration were in nearby Tatishchev and Totskoe.

224. Schools are not mentioned in the Polish record, but it is known that Anders wanted to build officers' training schools, and they were established. After leaving the USSR in summer–fall 1942, Anders also set up schools for the children of military families in Iran and, later, in the Middle East.

225. For the Polish-Soviet Military Agreement of 14 August 1941, see doc. 95 and its notes.

226. See the SNK resolution "On the Polish Army on the USSR Territory," 3 November 1941, setting the number at 30,000 men; see *KD2/173*; *KDZ3/211*, first published in Materski, *Polscy Jeńcy Wojenni*, no. 12, pp. 95–96; Materski, *Kremlin versus Poland*, no. 3, pp. 27–28. For Panfilov to Anders, 6 November 1941, on limiting the Polish Army to 30,000 men, see *SSSR i Polsha*, chap. I, no. 20, pp. 46–47; and *DPSR*, vol. I, no. 140, pp. 197–198 (English translation).

227. In the Stalin-Kot conversation of 14 November 1941, Stalin mentioned Soviet difficulties and shortages but said the situation should improve in three

months. He also said he had no objection to even seven Polish divisions, provided the Poles themselves supplied the arms and the food for them; see *DVP*, vol. XXIV, no. 282, p. 423 (Russian); *KDZ3/212* (Polish translation); Kot, *Listy z Rosji*, no. 49, pp. 169–180 (Polish record); Kot, *Conversations with the Kremlin*, no. B13, pp. 106–116; and *DPSR*, vol. I, no. 149 (English translation of Polish record).

228. The Russians burned down Berlin in 1760 and passed through it in 1813.

229. On 15 July 1410 the Polish-Lithuanian armies defeated the Teutonic Knights at the Battle of Grunwald (German, Tannenberg).

230. The NKVD was forcibly assigning many Poles released from labor camps in northern Russia to state and collective farms in Uzbekistan.

231. The English translation of the Polish record has Anders saying: "Two hundred Jews deserted from Buzuluk [Polish Army headquarters at this time] upon hearing the false report on the bombing of Kuibyshev"; see *DPSR*, vol. I, p. 241; see also Kot, *Conversations with the Kremlin*, p. 153. Many Jews deserted the Polish Army when it was stationed in Palestine to fight for a Jewish homeland, but those who remained fought bravely in the Anders-led Polish 2nd Corps in Italy.

232. The Polish Army headquarters was moved in January–February 1942 to Yangi Yul, near Tashkent, Uzbekistan, near the Iranian border. Many Poles suffered from malnutrition and disease; many died of malaria or typhoid fever.

233. The quotation marks were supplied by A. M. Cienciala. An English fighter squadron was stationed at Murmansk to protect supply ships coming from Britain against German attacks.

234. In a conversation between Stalin and Sikorski at the banquet held the next day, 4 December 1941, Stalin proposed that they settle the frontier question by themselves, before the peace conference. Sikorski said the 1939 frontier could not be questioned, but asked to return to the problem later, a proposal Stalin welcomed; see *DPSR*, vol. I, no. 160, pp. 244–245; Anders, *Bez Ostatniego Rozdziału*, p. 102; Anders, *An Army in Exile*, p. 89. Sikorski, however, did not fly back to the Soviet capital after his visit to the Polish troops. He did not meet with Stalin again.

235. For the Polish text of Sikorski's radio speech to the Polish people from Moscow on 4 December 1941, see *Dokumenty i Materiały*, vol. VII, no. 170; an excerpt in English translation is in *DPSR*, vol. I, no. 162.

236. This was the Polish-Soviet Declaration of Friendship and Mutual Assistance, signed in Moscow by Sikorski and Stalin on 4 December 1941; for the Polish text, see *Dokumenty i Materiały*, vol. VII, no. 169; for an English translation, see *DPSR*, vol. I, no. 161; for the Russian text, see *DVP*, vol. XXIV, no. 310, p. 479.

237. See Protocol no. 8 of the Joint [Soviet-Polish] Commission for the Formation of the Polish Army on the Territory of the USSR. It assumed the formation of six to seven Polish infantry divisions, of which four would be formed in the Uzbek, Kazakh, Kirghiz, and Turkmen Soviet Republics; see *SSSR i Polsha*, chap. I, no. 22, pp. 51–52. On 25 December 1941 the State Defense Committee resolved that the Polish Army in the USSR would number 96,000 men; see *KD2/177*; *KDZ3/223*, first published in Materski, *Armia Polska*, no. 3. The next day, 26 December

1941, the commander of the Red Army's Rear Services, General Andrei Khrulev, issued a directive on supplying the 96,000-man Polish Army; see *SSSR i Polsha*, chap. I, no. 26, pp. 56–58.

238. Boris Podtserob (1910–1983) worked at this time in the central apparatus of the People's Commissariat of Foreign Affairs; see *KD2/176*, n. 6.

239. The Russian text and Polish translation were first published in Materski, *Armia Polska*, no. 7; the English translation of the Russian text is by A. M. Cienciala. For the Polish record of Anders's conversation with Stalin in Moscow on 18 March 1941, made by Anders's chief of staff, General Leopold Okulicki, see Anders, *Bez Ostatniego Rozdziału*, pp. 112–122; *DPSR*, vol. I, no. 193 (English translation); Anders, *An Army in Exile*, pp. 99–100 (summary).

240. Anders claims the rations had been reduced to 26,000, but according to General Panfilov's report of a conversation with Anders in Moscow on 16 March 1942, Anders said the Polish Army was receiving rations for 30,000, a figure also given in Stalin's telegram to Anders as cited in Anders's memoirs; see *Armia Polska*, no. 6; *KDZ3/231*. The text of Stalin's telegram has not been found.

241. At the Moscow conference on aid for the USSR at the end of September 1941, W. Averell Harriman had agreed for the United States and Lord Beaverbrook for Britain that the Soviet Union would receive specified armaments. Furthermore, it was to receive 200,000 tons of wheat and 20,000 tons of sugar per month, to be sent through Arkhangelsk, Vladivostok, and the Persian Gulf; see *Foreign Relations of the United States, 1941*, vol. 1 (Washington, D.C., 1958), pp. 841–846.

242. There were earlier shortages in shipping, and the outbreak of war in the Pacific severely disrupted supplies for the USSR. Food rations for the Poles, however, had been cut back before Japan entered the war by attacking Pearl Harbor on 7 December 1941; see the Stalin-Panfilov exchange of 3 December in doc. 97 and note 226.

243. Panfilov confirmed Stalin's decision and discussed the evacuation with Anders on 19 March 1942; see *SSSR i Polsha*, chap. I, no. 37.

244. *KD2/180* has the wrong date (14 March). The Russian text and Polish translation were first published in Materski, *Armia Polska*, no. 10; the English translation from the Russian is by A. M. Cienciala. Beria's note covers the first stage of the evacuation.

245. The first stage of the evacuation was probably completed on 5 April, the departure date of the last transport. It included three incompletely formed divisions, made up largely of men in poor physical condition whose chances of survival were much greater outside the USSR, as well as men designated for air and sea service in the west; see *KDZ3/236*, p. 542 n. For Russian documents on the evacuation, see *SSSR i Polsha*, chap. I, no. 35 ff; for Polish documents in English translation, see *DPSR*, vol. I, nos. 198–201; see also Anders's account, in Anders, *Bez Ostatniego Rozdziału*, pp. 122–125; and Anders, *An Army in Exile*, pp. 101–102. For a British officer's reports on the arrival and care of the Polish evacuees at Bandar-e Pahlavi (now Bandar-e Anzali), Iran, see Irena Beaupré-Stankiewicz et al., eds., *Isfahan: City of Polish Children* (Hove, Sussex, England, 1989), pp. 69–90; for other individual accounts, see chaps. 1–6.

246. Some of those ready to leave were left behind because they could not reach

the trains or were too sick to go on board the ships. Contrary to Beria's report, many sick people died either in Krasnovodsk or on the ships for lack of basic sanitation and medication.

247. For Anders to Stalin on 31 July 1941, see *KDZ3/239*. Koptelov's report to Stalin on 7 September 1942 was first published in Materski, *Armia Polska*, no. 13; an English translation is in Materski, *Kremlin versus Poland*, no. 6. Stalin had agreed to the evacuation under considerable British pressure. For Anders's account of his trip to London, his return to the USSR, his decision to evacuate all the troops and civilians, and the second evacuation, see Anders, *Bez Ostatniego Rodziału*, pp. 125–140; Anders, *An Army in Exile*, pp. 103–115. See also British Colonel Alexander Ross's "Report on Polish Refugees in Persia: April 1942–December 1943," in Beaupré-Stankiewicz et al., *Isfahan*, pp. 80–90, with a table of ships and number of passengers per ship.

248. Many people died of these diseases; many others also died when they ate food too rich for their stomachs, used to minimal intake for two years; see Beaupré-Stankiewicz et al., *Isfahan*, pp. 61–68.

249. For a Polish translation, see *Zbrodnia Katyńska*, p.85; for an English translation, see *Crime of Katyn*, pp. 101–102, and *DPSR*, vol. I, no. 305. For an earlier broadcast on the same day of a conference on the Katyn graves in the German Foreign Ministry, see Baliszewski and Kunert, *Prawdziwa Historia*, vol. 2, p. 1006 (Polish translation).

250. The Germans used the 10,000 figure because this was the number of missing officers cited by Polish authorities. The GPU [State Political Administration] was the name of the Soviet Security Police in 1922–23; it was named OGPU from November 1923 to July 1934, then GUGB NKVD. NKVD is the name generally used for the war period; see Amy W. Knight, *The KGB: Police and Politics in the Soviet Union* (Boston, 1988), p. 315.

251. This was the largest grave, shaped like an *L*; see the PRC report, doc. 105b. It probably held about 600 bodies.

252. Kozelsk is located north of Orel. On Smorawiński, see Biographical Sketches.

253. Most of the Kozelsk officers were transported in prison railway cars through Smolensk to Gnezdovo between early April and mid-May 1940, but some were shot in Smolensk. "Goat Hills," so named after the hilly landscape of the burial site, had been used for executions by the Cheka and its successors, perhaps as far back as the Russian Civil War of 1918–1922.

254. The Polish text appears in Stefania Stanisławska, ed., *Sprawa Polska w Czasie Drugiej Wojny Światowej na Arenie Międzynarodowej* [The Polish Question during World War II in the International Arena] (Warsaw, 1965), part II, no. 69; Baliszewski and Kunert, *Prawdziwa Historia*, vol. 2, pp. 1010–1011.

255. According to the Polish record of the Stalin-Anders conversation of 18 March 1942, Stalin suggested that the prisoners might have dispersed in territories taken by the Germans; see note 239 (doc. 98).

256. The spelling is as in the *DPSR*, vol. I, no 306. The reference was to the well-known Gnezdovo "Kurhan" burial mounds. The name of the village was Gnezdovo, and the use of "Gnezdova" and "Gnezdovaya" was due to writing the text in a hurry. According to a statement made in March 1989 to the Russian journal-

ist Vladimir Abarinov by General Leonid Fedorovich Raikhman, head of the 2nd Department (Counterintelligence) in GUGB NKVD in 1939–1941, the author of the Soviet communiqué was NKVD Major Georgy S. Zhukov, then head of the Central and East European Section in the 2nd Department, who was the first to recall the historical graves at Gnezdovo; see Abarinov, *Katynskii Labirint*, p. 97; and, in an English translation, Abarinov, *The Murderers of Katyn*, pp. 156, 174–175. Zhukov was the liaison officer between the NKVD and General Anders in 1941–1942 and then with the commander of the Kościuszko Division, General Berling (promoted in rank by Stalin), in 1943. (See Biographical Sketches.)

257. In citing the German massacre of 1,500,000 people, Sikorski was referring to both ethnic Poles and Jewish Poles. In April 1943, Majdanek and Treblinka were mainly death camps for Jews, but they also held some Polish military prisoners. The spelling "Tremblinka," used in the document, was most likely designed to help with pronunciation; see the Polish text in Baliszewski and Kunert, *Prawdziwa Historia*, vol. 2, p. 1016.

258. The English text given here is in *DPSR*, vol. I, no. 315. The Russian text ends with the words "Please accept, Mr. Ambassador, the assurances of my highest respect." Molotov presented the note personally to Polish Ambassador Romer, who refused to accept it because he could not agree with the charges against his government, but the note was delivered in an envelope to his hotel.

259. For a list of the numerous Polish inquiries about the missing prisoners addressed to Soviet authorities, see the Polish minister of defense communiqué, London, 16 April 1940, *DPSR*, vol. I, no. 307; Russian translation, *KD2/188*. For the Polish official statement of 17 April, see doc. 103. The Soviet reply was a violent attack on the Polish government in *Pravda* on 19 April, titled "Polish Collaborators of Hitler"; see *KD2/189*.

260. This is a reference to the official German investigation and the Poles allowed by the Germans to visit Katyn in the first half of April; for more, see doc. 105a and the introduction to Part III.

261. The German occupation of Poland was much more brutal than that of Czechoslovakia. The IRC was not compelled to act. On 23 April it announced that it could not undertake the investigation (Soviet consent was lacking). On the next day, British Foreign Secretary Anthony Eden told Sikorski that Stalin would not break off relations if the Polish government withdrew its appeal to the IRC and declared that the Katyn affair was "an invention of German propaganda." Sikorski said he would not push the appeal but could not blame the Germans. On 4 May the Polish government declared that the appeal to the IRC had lapsed.

262. There was no such cooperation between the Polish and German governments in this or any other matter. For the Soviet press campaign against the Polish government, see Ewa Rosowska, *Otnoshenia Polshi i SSSR v 1939–1945 Godakh i Sovetskaia Pressa* [Soviet-Polish Relations in the Years 1939–1945 and the Soviet Press] (Candidate of Historical Sciences dissertation, Moscow State University, Moscow, 1993), chap. 3, section 3, part 2, esp. pp. 123–146. A. M. Cienciala would like to thank Dr. Rosowska, a co-editor of the Polish Katyn volumes, for giving her a copy of her dissertation.

263. This is a reference to the Polish government's official stance on the inviolability of the prewar Polish-Soviet frontier.

264. Excerpts from the report by Skarżyński on his visit to Katyn, written in June 1943 and sent to the Polish government-in-exile, London, as well as the report of the PRC Technical Commission, written in June 1943, appeared in Polish émigré publications from 1948 onward, in the Polish underground press in 1988, and officially in the paper *Odrodzenie* [Rebirth], no. 7, 18 February 1989; excerpts of the PRC report appear in Russian translation in *KD2/199*. A slightly different text given by Skarżyński's widow to Janusz Kazimierz Zawodny is printed in Zawodny, *Katyń*, pp. 196–204, as are the PRC Technical Commission report and papers, pp. 205–248. For English translations of Skarżyński's report and the PRC Technical Commission report, see *Hearings* (Madden Committee), exhibit 7, pp. 397 ff. The translation here, from Kazimierz Skarżyński, *Katyń* (2nd edition, Paris, 1990), is by A. M. Cienciala.

265. For Wacław Lachert, see Biographical Sketches.

266. The German occupation authorities in the Generalgouvernement allowed the PRC to function as an officially recognized institution.

267. The Brühl Palace was the wartime residence of the governor of Warsaw, the Nazi lawyer Ludwig Fischer (1904–1947). He was condemned to death in 1946 by the IMT for ordering mass executions of Poles and Jews; the sentence was carried out in Poland in 1947.

268. Rada Główna Opiekuńcza [RGO—The Principal Welfare Council] looked after needy Poles under German occupation in World War I. The Germans allowed Adam Feliks Ronikier (1891–1952), a prewar supporter of Polish cooperation with Germany, to reactivate and head the RGO in German Poland from 1940 to 1943.

269. Ferdynand Goetel, a well-known writer (see Biographical Sketches), went to Katyn with the permission of Polish underground authorities and reported on his visit to them. He testified before the U.S. Congressional (Madden) Committee on the Katyn Forest Murders; see also his account, in several articles in the London émigré paper *Wiadomości* [News] in 1949, reprinted in Kwiatkowska-Viatteau, *Katyń: Wybór Publicystyki*, pp. 93–106. On the Goetel group, see Madajczyk, *Dramat Katyński*, pp. 36–37. The commander of the Polish Home Army, General Stefan Rowecki, radioed General Sikorski on 14 April that the Polish delegates' accounts of their visit to Katyn left no doubt that mass murder had been committed there. He also reported public outrage; see *Armia Krajowa*, vol. II, no. 416, pp. 491–492.

270. Prince Adam Stefan Sapieha, head of the Roman Catholic Church in Poland; see Biographical Sketches.

271. Canon Stanisław Jasiński was head of the Catholic charitable organization Caritas; Dr. Pragłowski was a colleague of Dr. Marian Wodziński from the Institute of Forensic Medicine, Kraków; see Madajczyk, *Dramat Katyński*, p. 40.

272. The road runs between Vitebsk and Smolensk (see Maps and Aerial Photographs, map 5).

273. The flags were to protect the site from Soviet planes, which were bombing nearby Smolensk and vicinity.

274. For Generals Mieczysław Smorawiński and Bronisław Bohatyrewicz (sometimes spelled Bohaterewicz), see Biographical Sketches. It seems that the body of General Henryk Minkiewicz-Odrowąż, who was also held in Kozelsk and assumed shot at Katyn, was not identified during the spring 1943 exhumations.

275. It was established by counting the tree rings that these pines were three years old and had been transplanted onto the graves from a previous location.

276. For details on the exhumations and the Katyn diaries, see the introduction to Part III.

277. Professor Gerhardt Buhtz was in charge of the exhumations. For a photograph of Buhtz with Lieutenants Vos and Slovenzik (misspelled Sloventczyk), see FitzGibbon, *Unpitied and Unknown*, p. 243.

278. The head of civilian—as opposed to military—resistance at this time was Stefan Korboński (see Biographical Sketches). The Home Army commander in chief, General Stefan Rowecki, sent this report to Polish authorities in London on 22 April 1943; see *Armia Krajowa*, vol. II, no. 425.

279. For the original French text of the PRC letter of 20 April 1943 to the IRC, Geneva, see Baliszewski and Kunert, *Prawdziwa Historia*, vol. 2, p. 1025; for the Polish translation, see p. 1026. For the IRC communiqué of 23 April 1943 on the Polish and German requests for an investigation and its replies, see *DPSR*, vol. I, no. 311 (in French). The Soviet government did not give its consent, and the Polish government withdrew its request on 4 May 1943, so the IRC investigation did not take place.

280. The full English text of the PRC Technical Commission report is in *Hearings*, part 3, 13 and 14 March 1952, exhibit 8, pp. 404–410; the Russian translation of Polish extracts is in Madajczyk, *Dramat Katyński*, pp. 150–160; *KD2/*199. This translation from the Polish is by A. M. Cienciala, with page references to Skarżyński, *Katyń*. The commission had twelve members. The report contains a table of their names with the dates of their departure for and return from Katyn; see Skarżyński, *Katyń*, p. 23.

281. The names of the six officers in this delegation are listed in Skarżyński, *Katyń*, pp. 39–40; see also Madajczyk, *Dramat Katyński*, p. 150; *KD2/199* (names, p. 480). The PRC had refused a German invitation to visit Polish prisoners held in German POW camps to inform them about the Katyn graves, so the Germans invited some Polish POW officers as well as a few other Allied POW officers to Katyn and flew them there.

282. Dr. Marian Wodziński, who worked at Katyn for five weeks, also wrote a report, "Pięć Tygodni na Miejscu Zbrodni" [Five Weeks at the Site of the Crime], dated London, September 1947; see *Zbrodnia Katyńska*, pp. 157–188; *Crime of Katyn*, pp. 191–228 (English version).

283. Some accounts list fourteen, others nine such chests. They were sent to the Institute of Forensic Medicine, Kraków, where the contents of the envelopes were cleaned and catalogued; for details, see the introduction to Part III.

284. Skarżyński, *Katyń*, p. 45, par. 2. With the two named generals, the total number of corpses exhumed, as reported by the PRC Technical Commission, was 4,243; see *Hearings*, part 3, exhibit 8, p. 409. Aleksandr Shelepin's letter to Khrushchev of 9 March 1959 gave a higher number: 4,421 (doc. 110). The Germans reported 4,143 exhumed; see "Final Report of the German Police Dated June 10, 1943," in *Crime of Katyn*, p. 117. The number of Katyn victims verified by Polish scholars on the basis of Soviet, Polish, and German sources is 4,410; see *Indeks Represjonowanych* [Index of the Repressed], vol. I: *Rozstrzelani w Katyniu*

[Those Shot at Katyn], ed. Maria Skrzyńska-Pławińska (Warsaw, 1995). Shelepin's higher number, accepted by Polish scholars, probably included victims from places besides Kozelsk.

285. The list of corpse numbers is not reproduced in Skarżyński, *Katyń*. The PRC Technical Commission reported that its members were present when lists of items were made for numbers 03901 to 04243, but the Germans took some items away and the PRC commissioners did not know if they were returned. The identification of corpse numbers 1 to 112 and 01 to 0420 was made by the Germans before the arrival of the PRC Commission; see Skarżyński, *Katyń*, p. 44; *Hearings*, part 3, p. 408 (English text). The cemetery plan is not reproduced in the Skarżyński book, but is included in the Wodziński report. However, even the written description differs greatly from a view of the cemetery as it existed in 1998 (*KDZ2*, third unnumbered sketch map after p. 515), for after the liberation of Smolensk by the Red Army, most of the bodies were removed by the NKVD in the period September 1943–January 1944, prior to the arrival of the Burdenko Commission (see the introduction to Part III).

286. The Kozelsk prisoners were murdered between early April and mid-May 1940; see the introduction to Part II and docs. 56, 57, 61, 62, 65 and notes.

287. These bullets, stamped "Geco 7.65D," made by the German firm of Gustaw Genschaw (Durlach, Germany), were exported to Poland and the USSR in the 1920s and 1930s.

288. For Dr. Marian Wodziński's report, see note 282. For the reports of Dr. W. Beck, Dr. G. Buhtz, Lieutenant Voss, and others, see the German publication *Amtliches Material zum Massenmord von Katyn* [Official Material on the Massacre of Katyn] (Berlin, 1943). The report of the International Medical Commission (IMC) organized by the Germans, the Wodziński report, and testimony given later by other witnesses are summarized in *Crime of Katyn*, chaps. VI, VII.

289. It is now estimated that about 20 percent of the officers had their hands tied behind their backs with a double rope or barbed wire; they were found in one grave; see *KDZ2*, p. 23, n. 54; and the introduction to Part II. Some corpses also bore the marks of bayonet wounds, made by a square, Soviet-type bayonet. On stab wounds and broken jaws, see the Buhtz report, summary, points 7, 8, in *Zbrodnia Katyńska*, p. 112; *Crime of Katyn*, p. 124.

290. This was the pit, mentioned in the first part of the report, in which the corpses were tied up, as described in note 289.

291. *KD2/215* gives the full report dated 24 January 1944, Moscow. The English version was first published in *VOKS Bulletin*, no. 1 (Moscow, 1944). The version published here is taken from the Special Supplement to the *Soviet War Weekly*, 3 February 1944 (London), which, with the original wording but with slight changes in punctuation, was reprinted in *Hearings*, part 3, pp. 228–309. The part titled "Forensic Medical Appraisal" was submitted in German translation as Document USSR-054 by Soviet Deputy Prosecutor Yuri Pokrovsky at the IMT, Nuremberg, on 14 February 1946; see *Trial of the Major War Criminals before the International Military Tribunal*, vol. VII (Nuremberg, 1947), pp. 425–428; also note 311 below.

292. The PRC Technical Commission had reported eight original graves in

spring 1943, the number of corpses exhumed as 4,243 (the number verified later was 4,410), and their reburial in six new graves, with separate graves for two generals (doc. 105b and notes 280–290). German aerial photographs of the area made in early 1944 showed signs of a large-scale moving of soil; see Wacław Godziemba-Maliszewski, "Interpretacja Zdjęć Lotniczych Katynia w Świetle Dokumentów i Zeznań Świadków / Katyn: An Interpretation of Aerial Photographs Considered with Facts and Documents," *Fotointerpretacja w Geografii: Problemy Telegeoinformacji* [Photo Interpretation in Geography: Problems in Teleogeographic Information], no. 25 (Warsaw, 1995). See also, in Maps and Aerial Photographs, the photographs accompanying map 5. It is not surprising that Polish-Russian exhumation experts working at Katyn in 1994 found the grave sites to be very different from those reported by the PRC Technical Commission, nor that they found no human remains; see Andrzej Kola and Andrzej Przewoźnik, eds., *Katyń, Miednoje, Charków—Ziemia Oskarża* [Katyn, Mednoe, Kharkov—The Earth Accuses] (Warsaw, 1996), pp. 50–52.

293. In spring 1940, Kozelsk was an officer camp. Moreover, foreign correspondents brought to Katyn by the Soviet authorities in January 1944 noted that most of the exhumed bodies on display wore winter clothes, which was inconsistent with the original Soviet claim that they had been murdered by the Germans in summer–early fall 1941; see *Crime of Katyn*, p. 255. Therefore, the Soviet report changed the dates of execution from July-September to September-December 1941. For the names of American journalists brought to Katyn in January 1944, see the interview with Clarence Cassidy, an American jurist who visited Katyn in January 1944, in *Hearings*, part 2, pp. 201–219.

294. These were presumably corpses not searched in spring–summer 1943 or corpses brought in from other burial sites.

295. On these items and their alleged owners, see notes 302 and 303.

296. Cord like this, used to tie hands behind the back, was also reported by German and other investigators in spring 1943, who stated that it was Soviet made.

297. This statement, like most other descriptions of corpses, is also to be found in the reports of the German commission, the IMC, and the PRC Technical Commission in 1943. However, these reports also noted that in the largest pit the lower layers of corpses were stuck together.

298. Adipocere is "a fatty or waxy substance produced in decomposing corpses exposed to moisture"; see *Webster's New World Dictionary of American English* (3rd college edition, New York, 1991), p. 16. The Hungarian forensic expert Dr. Ferenc Orsos, a member of the IMC, claimed that the date of the massacre had to be 1940 because the degree of adipocere in the skulls indicated a three-year period of decomposition. For a photograph of Dr. Orsos, see the photo gallery in FitzGibbon, *Unpitied and Unknown*. Orsos escaped to the West and testified later before the Madden Commission (doc. 109).

299. These locations were presumably the burial sites of Soviet citizens murdered by the Germans.

300. It is not known what Article 36 refers to; for the list of documents, see "Documents Found on the Corpses" at the end of this report.

301. On the number of corpses exhumed in 1943, see note 292.

302. Tomasz Zygoń (1897–1940), an NCO reservist, figures in none of the published Polish registers of dead, surviving, and missing POWs but appears as No. 81/1147 on Ukrainian death list no. 57/1, sent by NKVD Lieutenant Feodor A. Tsvetukhin with other lists to the head of the NKVD 1st Special Department, Moscow, the Troika member Leonid F. Bashtakov, on 25 November 1940; see Zuzanna Gajowniczek, ed., *Ukraiński Ślad Katynia* [The Ukrainian Trail of Katyn] (Warsaw, 1995), p. 130 (biographical information) and photograph no. 63.

303. Edward Lewandowski, Włodzimierz Araszkiewicz, and Stanisław Kuczyński were on the dispatch lists for Ostashkov and were shot in Kalinin/Tver in spring 1940. Stanisław Kuczyński-Iskander Bej, who allegedly signed the unsent postcard to his wife, was never at Kozelsk camp. See Biographical Sketches.

304. The testimony of several Russian witnesses printed in the Burdenko Commission report is not included here.

305. American POWs brought to Katyn by the Germans—for example, Colonel John H. Van Vliet—noticed that the officers' boots were in good condition, so their owners could not have worked on road construction. On Van Vliet, see the introduction to Part III.

306. These three officers were named by the Soviet prosecutor at Nuremberg as the perpetrators of the Katyn massacre; however, they served in the 537th Signals Battalion, not the 537th Construction Battalion; see the introduction to Part III.

307. The PRC Technical Commission reported that no duress was used on the Soviet witnesses by the Germans. It is true that some of the same witnesses who testified to Soviet guilt in spring 1943 testified to German guilt when questioned by the Soviet Special Commission in January 1944, but they did so to avoid punishment for treason. One of the witnesses, Ivan Krivozertsev, escaped to the British occupation zone in western Germany. He made a deposition there and another detailed deposition at the headquarters of the 2nd Polish Army Corps in Ancona, Italy; see the introduction to Part II.

308. There is no evidence of such German activity, but the NKVD did what they accused the Germans of doing; see the introduction to Part III.

309. There is no evidence that the Germans executed these Soviet prisoners. According to the PRC Technical Commission report, local Russians and 50—not 500—Soviet prisoners were employed to exhume and rebury the corpses.

310. The Germans sometimes used this method, but they generally executed groups of people using rifles or machine guns.

311. Goering's defender originally asked the IMT for permission to call six witnesses, including the officers mentioned in USSR Document-054.

312. See the Burdenko Commission report, doc. 106.

313. These are the misspelled names of the German officers mentioned in USSR Document-054. The correct spellings are Ahrens, Reks, and Hodt.

314. This is a reference to the Declaration on Nazi Responsibility of 30 October 1943, signed by Roosevelt, Churchill, and Stalin; see N. S. Lebedeva, *Podgotovka Niurnbergskogo Protsessa* [Preparations for the Nuremberg Trials] (Moscow, 1975), pp. 22–24; *KD2/220*, p. 553, n. 5.

315. Rudenko sent this letter to the tribunal on 18 March 1946; see *KD2/221*.

316. According to Article 24, point "e," of the IMT Charter, witnesses to the crime were to be questioned, then witnesses for the defense, after which the prosecutor or defense was to present evidence to refute evidence presented by the other side, insofar as the tribunal deemed it acceptable; see *KD2/220*, p. 553, n. 7.

317. The presiding British judge was Sir Geoffrey Lawrence.

318. Major General Eugen Oberhäuser was the chief of communications for the German AGC, whose units occupied the Smolensk area, including the Katyn Forest, in July 1941–September 1943. He was called by Stahmer to testify for the defense (*KD2/220*, p. 553, n. 9), as was Colonel Ahrens. Both also testified before the U.S. Congressional (Madden) Committee on Katyn. First Lieutenant Berg did not testify at Nuremberg.

319. The American, British, and French chief prosecutors declined to support the Soviet proposal and stood by their decision of 12 March.

320. Metropolitan Nikolai, head of the Russian Orthodox Church, was also a member of the Burdenko Commission (doc. 106). Only Boris Bazilevsky testified at Nuremberg. He was an astronomy professor, had been deputy mayor of Smolensk under the German occupation, and agreed to cooperate with the NKVD as a witness. ROKK is apparently an abbreviation of Rossiiskoe Obschestvo Krasnogo Kresta [Russian Red Cross Society]; *KD2*, p. 557, n. v.–v.

321. Yona T. Nikitchenko (1895–1967) was the Soviet member of the IMT at Nuremberg; see *KD2/223*, p. 558, n. 3.

322. The Russian translation given in *KD2/226* omits paragraph 2 of the resolution in the original English text, as well as points 1 and 2. The committee conclusions, originally printed in *Hearings on the Katyn Massacre, 82nd Congress, House Report no. 2505. Conclusions of the Select Committee* (Washington, D.C., 1952), pp. 8864, 9240, were reprinted in *Crime of Katyn*, pp. 291–293, and in *100th Congress, Congressional Serial Set*, vol. 13875, House Document no. 100–183 (Washington, D.C., 1988).

323. The Germans originally claimed there were 10,000 bodies at Katyn but soon reduced the number to about 4,000.

324. The total given by the Germans was 4,143; the PRC total was 4,243; the verified Polish total is 4,410; see note 284.

325. In 1991 the NKVD officer Syromiatnikov described the executions of Starobelsk prisoners in the NKVD jail at Kharkov and their burial site; see the introduction to Part II; Biographical Sketches.

326. This was widely believed by Polish prisoners who survived, but lacks documentary confirmation. The Ostashkov victims were shot in the cellars of the NKVD jail in Kalinin/Tver and buried at Mednoe; see the Tokarev deposition, in the introduction to Part II.

327. These recommendations were later supplemented as follows: "If the United Nations cannot act, then the President of the United States should seek the assistance of an International Commission of nations other than Germany and Russia to sit as a Jury, hear the facts of the Katyn Forest Massacre, weigh the evidence, record its findings, and make such recommendations as it determines are required by justice"; *Hearings*, p. 9240, Amendment "b." The U.S. president did not take the action requested.

328. Shelepin's note was first published with a Polish translation in Materski, *KDL*, no. 10, and with an English translation in *KDG*, no. 5. In December 1992, Shelepin deposed, as a witness in the Russian Katyn investigation, that he was told some documents should be destroyed because space was needed, and he only signed a document prepared for him. He also claimed that the lack of Khrushchev's written decision on this matter was because some proposals were sanctioned orally only and that such proposals were typed with only one copy; see Jażborowska , Jabłokow, and Zoria, *Katyń: Zbrodnia Chroniona*, p. 321.

329. Shelepin's total of 21,857 is accepted by Polish historians. The number of Katyn victims as verified by Polish experts is 4,410 (doc. 105b; note 284). The verified number of Starobelsk victims is 3,739; see Maria Skrzyńska-Pławińska, ed., *Indeks Represjonowanych* [Index of the Repressed] (Warsaw, 1995–1997), vol. II. The verified number of Ostashkov victims is 6,314; see Skrzyńska-Pławińska, *Indeks Represjonowanych*, vol. III. Of the 7,300 Poles shot in the western USSR in spring 1940, those shot in Ukraine numbered 3,435, of whom 2,000 have been identified; see Gajowniczek, *Ukraiński Ślad Katynia*. (Those shot in Belarus are assumed to total 3,865 of the 7,300 shot in the western USSR.) The total as verified by Polish scholars is 21,763, slightly lower than the Shelepin total, although the latter is generally accepted. There is no documentation so far on those shot in what is today western Belarus.

330. The Starobelsk prisoners' personal files were burned in July 1940 (doc. 88), so the Soviet official preparing the data for Shelepin's note may have used the 21,857 number from a document at hand without checking all previous information; or perhaps copies of some of the destroyed Starobelsk POW files were stored with others in the sealed location. See Biographical Sketches, s.v. Kuznetsov.

331. See Burdenko Commission report, doc. 106.

332. Shelepin disregarded the conclusions of the Madden Committee of December 1952 (doc. 109); in any case, they did not have a significant impact on Western opinion.

333. Natalia Lebedeva believes that Khrushchev ordered all three categories of documents to be destroyed. Wojciech Materski, however, thinks the protocols may still exist, because there is no record of their destruction and because so many other documents on the prisoners have survived in Russian archives. On the destruction of all the documents, see *KD2/227*, n. 2; for Wojciech Materski on the possible survival of the Troika protocols, see *KDZ2/Aneks I/11*, n. 2.

334. These two Russian texts were first published with Polish translations in Materski, *KDL*, nos. 19 and 20; English translations in *KDG*, nos. 13 and 14; the Russian texts with Polish translations are also in Jacek Snopkiewicz and Andrzej Zakrzewski, eds., *Dokumenty Katynia: Decyzja* [Katyn Documents: The Decision] (Warsaw, 1992), pp. 62–63. This instruction followed the suggestions to the Central Committee by Deputy Foreign Minister Vasily Kuznetsov in a note dated 27 February 1973; see *KD2/230*, pp. 570–571, n. 1.

335. The Soviet ambassador in London was Mikhail Smirnovsky.

336. The British foreign secretary in the Conservative government of the time was Sir Alec Douglas-Home.

337. For the circular on this topic sent to members of the Politburo on 7 Sep-

tember 1972, see Materski, *KDG*, no. 11 (English translation). The instruction, Politburo resolution, and text of 8 September 1972, in *KD2/229*, were first published in Materski, *KDL*, nos. 19, 20. "Certain circles" is a reference to the members of the KMF and their supporters.

338. The inscription on the projected monument gave the date of the massacre as 1940 and affirmed Soviet guilt.

339. This document was first published in Materski, *KDL*, no. 22; a Polish translation also appears in Snopkiewicz and Zakrzewski, *Dokumenty Katynia: Decyzja*, pp. 66–68.

340. The Central Committee department involved was the Department of Contacts with Fraternal Communist Parties.

341. See doc. 111.

342. This was the monument erected at Katyn in memory of the Polish officers after the Burdenko Commission investigation in January 1944 and renovated in 1969. The inscription, in Russian and Polish, stated that the officers were murdered by the German-Fascist occupiers in the fall of 1941; for photographs, see Zawodny, *Katyń*, facing p. 144.

343. This document was first published with a Polish translation in Materski, *KDL*, no. 32; also in Snopkiewicz and Zakrzewski, *Dokumenty Katynia: Decyzja*, pp. 100–104.

344. The PRC report of June 1943 (docs. 105a, 105b) was published in the Polish periodical *Odrodzenie* [Rebirth] on 16 February 1989 and in the highly respected weekly *Polityka* two days later.

345. Jerzy Urban (b. 1933), at that time the Polish government spokesman, stated at a press conference on 7 March 1989 that in the opinion of the Polish historians on the Joint Commission of Soviet-Polish Party Historians, everything pointed to the NKVD's responsibility for the massacre. This was reported by Polish media on 7–8 March 1989.

346. The Joint Commission of Soviet-Polish Party Historians was established with the agreement of Gorbachev and Jaruzelski in May 1987. On 6 March 1989, Falin reported to the CC on the stalemate reached by the joint commission and noted the publication of the PRC Technical Commission report in Poland. He favored the Polish government's idea of giving some satisfaction to the Polish public by relocating symbolic Katyn ashes to Warsaw; see Materski, *KDL*, no. 32; *KDG*, no. 18. But this idea was abandoned. For the Polish historians' critique of the Burdenko Commission report and an account of their work on the joint commission, see Maciszewski, *Zbrodnia Katyńska*; Yasnova, *Katynskaia Drama*, pp. 179–201 (Russian trans.). For an account of the commission's work from the Russian side, see Yazhborovskaia, Yablokov, and Parsadanova, *Katynskii Sindrom*, chap. 4; also Jażborowska, Jabłokow, and Zoria, *Katyń: Zbrodnia Chroniona*, chap. 2.

347. The monument envisaged was at Katyn. There was no monument in Warsaw.

348. This publication has not been identified. For a bibliography of publications on Katyn from 1943 through mid-1993, see Maria Harz, *Bibliografia Zbrodni Katyńskiej: Materiały z Lat 1943–1993* (Warsaw, 1993).

349. Many Poles, and evidently also the authors of this note, believed the Os-

tashkov prisoners had been sent through Bologoe to Arkhangelsk and were then towed out to sea in barges, which were sunk with the men on board; see FitzGibbon, *Unpitied and Unknown*, p. 437. It seems this was a rumor spread by the NKVD among Poles in the USSR in 1941–1942, for it is not confirmed by any documents.

350. It is not printed.

351. This was not A. but V. S. Pavlov, Soviet finance minister, 1989–1991.

352. Members of the Council for the Protection of the Memory of Combat and Martyrdom visited Katyn on 5 April. At a ceremony attended by Prelate Zdzisław Król, Polish military personnel, members of the Katyn Families Association, and newspaper correspondents, the delegates gathered some earth from the cemetery and brought it to Warsaw. The next day the earth was placed in urns with the name "Katyn" in the Warsaw Garrison Church. See Polish press accounts for 6–7 April 1989.

353. See doc. 114.

354. Polish historians now accept 15,000 as an approximate figure for those murdered from the three special camps: about 5,000 were ordinary policemen; about 7,300 were shot in NKVD prisons; see *KDZ1*, p. 18. For verified numbers of victims from the three special camps, see note 329 above.

355. See note 349.

356. This is the first mention of such an investigation.

357. The draft decision proposed that an investigation be carried out and a report be made around 1 August 1989; see Materski, *KDL*, no. 34; *KDG*, no. 22.

358. This should be V. S. Pavlov; see note 351.

359. The document was first published in Materski, *KDL*, no. 35. It is date-stamped 23 February 1990, but according to a handwritten note under Falin's signature, the date was 22 February 1990; see facsimile in Materski, *KDL*.

360. The Special Archive and the Central State Archive were one and the same archive, which held the collection of the Administration for Prisoner-of-War and Internee Affairs [UPV, UPVI]. It is now the Russian State Military Archive [RGVA]; see Note on Archives, *KD2/234*, bottom of p. 578.

361. The correct order number was 001177. For Beria's order of 3 October 1939, see *KD1/38*; *KDZ1/38*. This order followed the Politburo decision of the same day, see doc. 14; for its implementation, see doc. 22.

362. See docs. 37, 40, 41, and 42.

363. For the Russian-language dispatch lists for Kozelsk and Ostashkov and a combined list for Starobelsk, see Tucholski, *Mord w Katyniu* [Murder at Katyn] (Warsaw, 1991), pp. 593–987.

364. See doc. 57.

365. For example, Soprunenko's instruction to camp commanders of 11 April 1940; see *KDZ2/65*, n. 1.

366. This document has not been found. However, on 13 June 1940, Soprunenko and Merkulov wrote Commander Berezhkov at Starobelsk that twenty "open documents" had been seized, having been sent out of the camp in June, although all correspondence by POWs was forbidden on 16 March 1940; therefore, Berezhkov was ordered to conduct an inquiry; see *KD2/97*; *KDZ2/234*. The last

letters received by relatives of the prisoners in the three camps were dated early March 1940. For IRC inquiries to German authorities in mid to late March 1940 on whether the camps still existed and the replies that as far as the Germans knew, they did, see *Documents on German Foreign Policy,* ser. D, vol. VIII (Washington, D.C., 1957), no. 676 and notes.

367. Only one NKVD official is known to have broken this rule. Danil Chekholsky [Daniel Czecholski], who was of Polish origin, worked in Starobelsk as a translator and censor. He wrote the prisoners' wives that their husbands had left the camp. This led to the inquiry ordered by Soprunenko and Merkulov on 13 June; see note 366. On 19 June, Chekholsky signed the protocol on the destruction of incoming and outgoing prisoner correspondence, as well as photographs, negatives, and photographic plates; see *KDZ2/241.* He was dismissed on 23 June, and his fate is unknown; see *KD2,* p. 25; *KDZ2,* p. 20, n. 42. Another batch of prisoner correspondence was destroyed on 23 July 1940; see doc. 87. For the procedure on dealing with incoming correspondence and parcels for prisoners formerly in the three special camps, as well as for the survivors in Griazovets camp, see Soprunenko's proposal to Kobulov, 13 August 1940, in *KDZ2/Aneks I/3,* p. 401.

368. See docs. 87, 88. It is doubtful that all the Starobelsk POW records were destroyed. According to a note by the deputy head of the NKVD 1st Special Department dated 4 August 1943, 21,353 "archives" [files?] of former Polish POWs were preserved. On 30 August, 21,365 "documents on Polish affairs, 1940," were transferred from the 1st Special Department of the NKVD to Department "A," NKGB; see *KD2/200; KDZ4/36;* also Biographical Sketches, s.v. Kuznetsov. Shelepin's note to Khrushchev of 3 March 1959 proposed the destruction of 21,857 files (doc. 110 above), which was the sum total of the figures he gave for the POWs from the three camps and in NKVD prisons in western Ukraine and western Belarus who had been shot. No explanation has been found thus far for the different numbers of POW files in the NKVD notes of 4 and 30 August 1943 and the Shelepin note of 3 March 1959.

369. The deportations from former eastern Poland took place in 1940–1941; see docs. 45, 64a, and 64b; Part I, notes 277–282; Part II, notes 89–97. The Ostashkov buildings were historical monastic buildings before the Soviet government closed down monasteries and convents in the 1920s and used them as prisons or for storage, which was also the case in Kozelsk and Starobelsk.

370. The fiftieth anniversary of the Katyn-Mednoe-Starobelsk massacres was in spring 1990.

371. General Jaruzelski, who pressed for Soviet admission of the truth on Katyn, writes that he was informed before his visit to Moscow in mid-April that documents regarding the massacre had been found; see Maciszewski, *Wydrzeć Prawdę,* p. 12; and the introduction to Part III.

372. On the Politburo decision to forbid the publication of articles by Parsadanova, Zoria, and Lebedeva and its reversal, see *KD2/234,* n. 1.

373. TASS [Telegraphic Agency of the Soviet Union] was the official Soviet news agency, and 13 April is the date of the communiqué's publication in *Izvestia.*

374. The verified total is 14,463; see note 329.

375. The surviving prisoners were moved first to Yukhnov, and later to Griazovets camp; see Maps and Aerial Photographs, map 4.

376. See Falin's note to Gorbachev (doc. 116).

377. See photograph taken at the Polish Embassy, Moscow, 13 April 1990, of Gorbachev handing Jaruzelski two file boxes with copies of the NKVD dispatch lists for prisoners from Kozelsk, Ostashkov, and Starobelsk camps to their deaths in spring 1940, *New York Times*, 14 April 1990.

378. The document was first published in Materski, *KDL*, no. 36; it appears in English translation in *KDG*, no. 24. Points 1–7 of Gorbachev's decree contained instructions to several Soviet ministries to work out agreements on various aspects of Soviet-Polish relations other than Katyn, on the basis of concerns expressed by the Polish foreign minister to Gorbachev.

379. Krzysztof Skubiszewski (b. 1926), professor of International Law at the Adam Mickiewicz University, Poznań, was foreign minister in the first, predominantly noncommunist Polish government formed by the prominent Solidarity leader Tadeusz Mazowiecki in September 1989.

380. The dates should be 1939–1941. The search for documents by various government agencies had been ineffective thus far, mainly owing to obstruction by Kriuchkov, head of the KGB.

381. Gorbachev might have had in mind Soviet counterclaims to possible Polish claims for compensation. Some Polish historians believe that his instruction encouraged Russian historians to find Polish "crimes" to balance Katyn. Whatever the case may be, a series of articles and a book were published in 1994 claiming that tens of thousands in the Soviet military, taken prisoner in 1920, had suffered a "Polish Katyn." Despite Polish rebuttals, this charge has continued to be made occasionally in Soviet media, including other publications, ever since.

382. See doc. 113.

383. These documents were first published in Materski, *KDL*; a shorter selection appeared in English translation in *KDG*.

384. It seems that during Wałęsa's state visit to Moscow in May 1992, Yeltsin promised to release the secret Katyn documents at some future date.

385. A. M. Cienciala would like to thank Professor Wojciech Materski for making a copy of this letter available to her. She would also like to thank Dr. Daria Nałęcz, former director of the Head Office of State Archives in Poland, for supplying the archival location and reference numbers and for permission to publish an English translation of Wałęsa's letter to Yeltsin.

386. This is a reference to sentiments expressed by Wałęsa in his letter to Yeltsin of 15 October 1992 (doc. 119).

387. These demands, made chiefly by the Katyn Families Association, appeared from time to time in various Polish media. Although consecutive Polish governments raised the demands in bilateral negotiations, they did not press them, to avoid harming Polish-Russian relations.

388. Yeltsin paid a state visit to Poland in August 1993. At this time, he laid a wreath at the Katyn monument in the military sector of Old Powązki Cemetery, Warsaw.

389. Local Russians told the German Commission of Inquiry in spring 1943 that the Koze Gory area had been known as a place of execution since 1918; see *Crime of Katyn*, p. 115. Presumably, most of the victims were Soviet citizens shot there in the Stalin purges of 1935–1938.

390. It is not known what Nazi "secret military objects"—if any—were built by Soviet POWs in the Katyn region; however, the Burdenko Commission report (doc. 106) cited a "witness" who saw the Nazis shoot the 500 Soviet POWs who had been forced to dig up the bodies of the Polish officers, but the PRC report mentioned 50 Soviet POWs. There is no evidence that they or other Soviet POWs were shot by the Germans at Katyn.

391. The cornerstone for the Katyn Polish and Russian memorial complex was laid on 4 June 1995. Cornerstones were also laid that summer at Kharkov and Mednoe. The cemetery at Katyn was opened with the unveiling of the Polish and Russian monuments on 28 July 2000 (doc. 122). The Polish and Ukrainian cemeteries at Kharkov were opened on 17 June 2000, and the Polish and Russian at Mednoe on 2 September.

392. Wałęsa's letter to Yeltsin on this question was unavailable to A. M. Cienciala, the American editor, but evidently Wałęsa asked for the records of the Troika decisions and their implementation. Shelepin had suggested to Khrushchev in March 1959 that the prisoners' personal files be destroyed but that the abovementioned records be kept. It seems, however, that Khrushchev also ordered them to be destroyed; see *KD2/236*, p. 583, n. 4; see also doc. 110 and notes 328–333.

393. For the Burdenko Commission report, see doc. 106.

394. Polish historians were able to acquire the interrogation protocols for Soprunenko, Tokarev, and Syromiatnikov; Soprunenko is cited in the introductions to Part I and II, Tokarev and Syromiatnikov in the introduction to Part II. For an account of the Katyn investigation by the Russian Main Military Prosecutor's Office, see Yazhborovskaia, Yablokov, and Parsadanova, *Katynskii Sindrom*, chaps. 5 and 6; for the conclusions and recommendations of the Commission of Experts of the Main Military Prosecutor's Office, 2 August 1993, see pp. 446–494; see also Jażborowska, Jabłokow, and Zoria, *Katyń: Zbrodnia Chroniona*, chaps. 4, 5, and Aneks, pp. 358–422.

395. Prosecutor Yablokov's concluding proposal of a verdict of guilty was rejected. On the Russian investigation, see the introduction to Part III.

396. On 5 May 1994, the deputy chief of the Ukrainian Security Service, General Andrei Khomich, gave the Polish deputy prosecutor general Stefan Śnieżko a document listing 3,435 names of Polish prisoners executed in the NKVD prisons of Ukraine in spring 1940. The lists were published with identifications of 2,000 of the victims in Gajowniczek, *Ukraiński Ślad Katynia*. The government of the Belarus Republic claims that no evidence of the crime has been found on its territory; it has refused permission for archaeological investigation.

397. The Russian Military Prosecutor's Office made it known unofficially in September 2004 that the Katyn investigation was closed. The official closing was announced in March 2005. Meanwhile, a Polish investigation began on 30 November 2004; see the introduction to Part III.

398. For the Polish text see *KDZ4/142*; a Russian translation appears in *KD2/238*.

399. For Polish Prime Minister Jerzy Buzek and Russian Deputy Prime Minister Viktor Khristenko, see Biographical Sketches.

400. Cardinal Józef Glemp (b. 1929) was the Roman Catholic Primate of Poland.

401. The Sejm is the lower house of the Polish Parliament.

402. Buzek refers to the image known as the *Matka Boska Katyńska* [Katyn Mother of God].

403. The quotation is from the Polish national poet, Adam Mickiewicz (1798–1855). The precise wording is: "Jeśli zapomnę o nich, Ty Boże na niebie, zapomnij o mnie" [If I forget about them, then You, God in Heaven, forget about me]; see Adam Mickiewicz, *Dzieła* [Works], vol. 3 (Warsaw, 1995), p. 144 (translation by A. M. Cienciala). A. M. Cienciala would like to thank Professor Halina Filipowicz of the University of Wisconsin, Madison, for providing the reference.

404. Buzek was referring to the prisoners shot in the jails of what is today western Belarus in spring 1940 and elsewhere in the USSR in 1939–1941. Many names and burial sites are unknown to this day. The names of the prisoners shot in the jails of western Ukraine at that time are known, but not the dates of executions and burial sites.

405. This is a reference to the Russian investigation of the 1940 massacres.

406. The two other Polish war cemeteries opened in 2000.

407. Memorial is the Russian organization that worked to uncover and publicize Stalinist crimes, including the executions at Katyn and Mednoe. It also published the work edited by A. Yu. Daniel, L. S. Eremina, T. I. Kasatkina, M. M. Koralov, and N. G. Okhot, *Istoricheskiie Sborniki "Memoriala," Repressii Protiv Poliakov i Polskikh Grazhdan* [Historical Collections of "Memorial," Repression of Poles and Polish Citizens] (Moscow, 1997). The name is short for the International Volunteer Public Organization "Memorial Historical, Educational, Human Rights and Charitable Society."

408. This is a reference to the journalist Vladimir Abarinov and the historians Natalia Lebedeva, Valentina Parsadanova, and Yuri Zoria and to the obstacles they met in their search for the truth about Katyn.

409. The Rada Ochrony Pamięci Walk i Męczeństwa [Council for the Protection of the Memory of Combat and Martyrdom], at the Polish Academy of Sciences, was involved in financing the construction of the Polish cemeteries. It also subsidized the publication of the second Russian volume of Katyn documents (*KD2*), thanks especially to its general secretary, Andrzej Przewoźnik; see *KD2*, p. 10.

410. The Katyn Families Association has a central organization as well as regional ones. Members lobby the Polish government to press the Russian government for an official apology for the crime and compensation for the victims' families. They pressed the Institute of National Remembrance (IPN) to open an investigation, which it did on 30 November 2004. Above all, they work to preserve the memory of Katyn.

411. Monte Cassino has a Polish war cemetery for those who perished in taking it from the Germans in May 1944, as well as for those who died later and wished to be buried there, including General Anders. Powązki is the name commonly used for the main cemetery in Warsaw, located in the district of Powązki; it has a mili-

tary section as well as a section for famous Polish artists, scholars, statesmen, writers, and others. The Polish war cemeteries at Narvik, Norway, and Tobruk, North Africa, hold the bodies of Polish military men who died in those battles.

412. This is a reference to President Yeltsin's publication and condemnation of the Soviet Politburo decision of 5 March 1940 to shoot the Polish POWs and to President Wałęsa's letter of thanks, 15 October 1992 (doc. 119).

413. Khristenko was citing a fragment of Buzek's televised speech to his fellow citizens on the sixtieth anniversary of the Katyn crime; see *KD2/239*, p. 588, n. 1.

414. This is a reference to a phrase in Wałęsa's letter to Yeltsin of 15 October 1992 (doc. 119).

Illustration Credits

Figures are numbered in the order in which they appear in the gallery.

Figs. 1–13. *Amtliches Material zum Massenmord von Katyn* [Official Material on the Mass Murder at Katyn]. Berlin, 1943, no. 4, top of p. 277; no. 4, bottom of page p. 277; no. 3, p. 276; no. 36, p. 309; no. 11, p. 284; no. 22, p. 295; no. 27, p. 300; no. 17, p. 290; no. 18, p. 291; no. 34, p. 307; no. 33, p. 306; no. 20, p. 293; no. 45, p. 318. Identifications in fig. 12 were provided by the Katyn expert Tadeusz Pieńkowski, in Warsaw, and by Kazimierz Skarżyński's daughter, Maria Skarżyńska, in Calgary, Canada.

Fig. 14. From the collection of Wacław Godziemba-Maliszewski.

Fig. 15. Composite photograph made for Anna M. Cienciala in June 2000 by Colonel Zdzisław Sawicki, then director of the Katyn Museum / Museum of the Polish Army, Warsaw. The individual photographs were not labeled with the officers' names.

Fig. 16. Courtesy of Dr. Simon Schochet, New York, N.Y.

Figs. 17–18. Courtesy of Tadeusz Pieńkowski, Warsaw. Photographs by Dr. Janina Gellert, Warsaw.

Figs. 19–22, 24–27. Katyn Museum / Museum of the Polish Army, Warsaw. Tadeusz Pieńkowski made the identifications in figs. 22, 26, 27.

Fig. 23. Courtesy of Tadeusz Pieńkowski. Photograph by Tadeusz Pieńkowski.

Index

Page numbers followed by *n* indicate footnotes. Page numbers followed by *n* plus a number indicate endnotes. Page numbers followed by *t* indicate tables. To look up specific information directly and for further information, see Abbreviations and Acronyms, Biographical Sketches, and Glossary of Organizations and Political Parties.

Cold War, 235, 236, 237

collectivization, 22, 23, 121, 172

Comintern (Communist International), 213, 214, 218, 275, 462n137; dissolution of, 221

Commission for the Rehabilitation of the Victims of Political Repression, 135–136

communism, 8, 14, 18, 221, 262; Jews associated with, 23, 77; and Poland, 24, 145, 213–215, 217, 218, 220, 221, 225–226, 233, 236, 275, 309; Polish collapse of, 245, 247, 248; and Polish POWs, 34, 89–94, 178; and post-Soviet Russia, 256; and U.S. anticommunists, 214, 236, 237, 239

Communist Party of the Soviet Union, 115, 221, 239; Central Committee (*see* TsK); and Katyn files, 255–256. *See also* Politburo; Russian Communist Party

Communist Youth League (Komsomol), 90, 471n235

Congress, U.S., Katyn investigation by. *See* Madden Committee

Congress Poland (1815–1839), 8–9

Convoy Troops (NKVD), 48–49, 117, 123–124, 180–181; and camp external security, 201; and NKVD prison "clearing out," 155; records of, 341–345; rewards to, 199–200, 341; UPV directives to, 250–251

Council for the Protection of the Memory of Combat and Martyrdom, xvii, 239, 351, 535n409

counterrevolutionary crimes, 21, 23–24, 25, 37, 142, 143; and camp security, 201–202; deportations for, 24, 114; interrogations about, 35–39; Katyn witness accounts seen as, 134–135; numbers of Soviet citizens shot for, 147; Operational-Cheka Work directive on, 64–67; Polish officers linked with, 23, 25, 27, 140, 147, 269–271; posthumous exonerations for (1989), 34; as POW execution rationale, 118–120, 138, 140, 142, 161, 262; reported POW instances of, 33–34, 94–95, 269–271; Soviet Criminal Code on, 37, 105, 135, 262; targeted groups, 65–66

Crime of Katyn, The (Mackiewicz), 242, 398

crimes against humanity, 232, 242; definition of, 229; Stalin and Politburo charged with, 260; and statute of limitations, 261

Criminal Code of the Russian Federal Republic, 260, 261–262

Criminal Code of the Russian Soviet Federal Socialist Republic (Soviet Union), 37, 105, 260, 262, 472n254

Cripps, Sir Stafford, 211, 472n256

Curzon, George (Lord Curzon), 8

Curzon Line, 8–10, 210–211

Czapski, Józef, 31, 35, 209, 388, 510n145

Czechoslovakia, 13, 15, 27, 281; minorities in, 22; POWs from, 27, 63, 112, 113, 278; proposed Polish federation with, 212

Czechoslovak Legion, 456n69

Czernicki, Ksawery, 185, 388, 457n75

Czerwiecki (Polish lieutenant), 176

Danzig (Gdańsk), 9, 15, 16, 412

Davies, Norman, 142

Death in the Forest (Zawodny), 242, 333

Declaration of Friendship and Mutual Assistance (1941), 210

Declaration of Nazi Responsibility (1943), 527n14

Dekanozov, Vladimir, 47, 230, 305, 388

Denyszyn, Iwan, 198

deportations, 4, 121, 152–154, 170–175, 214; Beria directive on, 152–154; numbers of Polish citizen, 138, 139; SNK resolution on, 170–175; as Soviet policy, 23, 24, 113–115, 138–139, 343, 474n279. *See also* families, POW

Dimitrov, Georgy M., 214, 218, 220, 462n137

Dmitriev, Aleksandr, 51, 272, 389

Dmowski, Roman, 5–6, 7, 389, 416, 447n7

Dnieper (Dnepr) River, 131, 132, 179; map, 427

Dniestr (Dnestr) River, 57; map, 427

Dobbs, Michael, 254

Domoń (Domel), Ludwik, 33, 34, 94–95, 270, 271, 389

Dom Otdykha Imenii Maxima Gorkogo (Gorky Rest Home), 29, 50

Dondero, George A., 235, 331

Donovan, William, 236

Dostoevsky, Fyodor, 5, 29

Douglas-Home, Sir Alec, 529n336

Dovudstvo Okrengovo Korpusnove, 65, 466n174

Dresden, 224, 225

Dulles, Allan, 236

Mniszek, Aleksander, 219–220
Moczulski, Leszek, 505*n*106
Modzielak, Edward, 176
Mokrzhitsky, S. M., 133
Molotov, Vyacheslav: Bogomolov telegram from, 301, 302–303; and break in Polish relations, 219–220, 309–310; and British relations, 213; and German invasions of Europe, 123; and German-Soviet Friendship and Border Treaty, 24, 59–60, 61, 62; and German-Soviet Non-Aggression Pact, 14, 40, 41, 246; and Katyn massacre denial, 226; and missing Polish officers, 209; and Nuremberg Trials prosecution, 230; and Polish Army reconstitution, 213, 289–290, 303, 305; and Polish POW executions resolution, 120*n*, 140; and Polish POW families' deportations, 171–172; Polish POW petitions to, 203; and Polish POW policies, 70–71, 79–80, 90, 92, 93; Sikorski meeting with, 289–290; and Soviet invasion of Poland, 18, 24, 43–45, 46, 47–48
Mongolia, 17, 291
Monte Cassino, 213, 535*n*411
Morawski (POW "provocateur"), 149
Mościcki, Ignacy, 167, 401
Moscow: evacuation from (1941), 209, 287; May Day events in, 79–80; NKVD prison in, 207; numbers of prisoners sent to, 191, 192; Polish occupation of (seventeenth-century), 3; radio broadcasts, 246–247, 248; Sikorski-Stalin meetings in, 287–300, 301
Moscow-Kiev Railway, 50, 162–163
Moshkov, A., 255
Moskovskie Novosti (newspaper), 252, 344
Mostovoi, Pavel, 346, 401
Münch, Henryk, 225
Munich agreement (1938), 13, 15, 27
Murashov, Nikolai, 401
Muscovy, Duchy of, 3
Mussolini, Benito, 16

Nagan pistol, 125, 127
Narkomchermet (People's Commissariat of Ferrous Metallurgy), 26, 30, 36, 139, 172; NKVD POW labor agreement, 71–73, 81–83; POW numbers, 81, 169–170
Narkomfin (People's Commissariat of Finance), 80, 172
Narkomindel (People's Commissariat of

Foreign Affairs), 80*n*, 197, 291. *See also* Molotov, Vyacheslav
Narkomles (People's Commissariat of Forests), 172, 488*n*97
Narkomtorg (People's Commissariat of Trade), 172
Narkomvnudel. *See* NKVD
Narodowa Demokracja policy, 6
Neave, Airey, 242
Nekhoroshev, Semyon, 38, 49, 69*n*, 401; and camp "clearing out," 110, 148–149, 150; and camp conditions, 31, 83–99; report on mood of dispatched POWs, 176–182
Nikitchenko, Yona, 231, 329
Nikolai, Metropolitan, 227, 329
Nikopol-Marganets labor camp, 72, 169, 189, 378*t*
Nil Hermitage, 30
Nikopol-Marganets Trust, 72
Nixon, Richard, 241
NKID (People's Commissariat of Foreign Affairs). *See* Narkomindel
NKO (Narodny Komissariat Oborony), 280
NKPS (Narodny Komissariat Putei Soobshcheniia), 58, 171–172
NKVD (Narodny Komissariat Vnutrennikh Del), 21, 58; archives of, 249, 255, 342, 343, 349; and Burdenko Commission, 135, 227–228; counterrevolutionary roundups by, 23, 33–34; deportations of POW families by, 113–115, 138, 139; doctoring of Katyn massacre evidence by, 227, 228–229, 233, 318–325; execution documentation by, 122; execution method of, 122, 125, 133, 271; GULAG camps of, 26, 34, 81–83, 115–117, 188–190; indictment file of POW policemen, 104–106; interrogations/investigations by, 35–39, 102–106, 110–111; Katyn files of, 255–256, 341–344, 349; Katyn massacre by, 121–137, 143, 148–149, 216, 240, 247–253, 330–331, 338, 343; Katyn resort, 131–132, 215, 305; lists of rewarded workers, 136, 199–200, 207–208, 272–275; and Polish Army in USSR, 303; POW administration, 1, 25–35, 48–54, 80, 101–102, 342; POW categorization by, 75–77; POW dispatch lists, 252, 342; POW document destruction by, 267–268; and POW informers, 206; and POW numbers released vs.

BOOKS IN THE ANNALS OF COMMUNISM SERIES